Simulation
With GPSS
And GPSS V

SIMULATION WITH GPSS AND GPSS V

P. A. BOBILLIER

IBM Switzerland
and
Professor of Management Science
Swiss Federal Institute of Technology, Lausanne

B. C. KAHAN

IBM European Systems Research Institute
International Education Centre
La Hulpe, Belgium

A. R. PROBST

IBM Switzerland
and
Professor of Computer Science
University of Lausanne

Prentice-Hall, Inc., *Englewood Cliffs, New Jersey*

Library of Congress Cataloging in Publication Data

Bobillier, P   A   1930–
   Simulation with GPSS and GPSS V.

   Bibliography: p.
   Includes index.
     1. Digital computer simulation. 2. GPSS
(Computer program language) I. Kahan, Basil
Charles, joint author. II. Probst, A.R.,
1937– joint author. III. Title.
QA76.9.C65B6   001.4'24   75–40316
ISBN 0–13–810549–9

10 9 8 7 6 5

Printed in the United States of America

PRENTICE-HALL INTERNATIONAL, INC., *London*
PRENTICE-HALL OF AUSTRALIA PTY. LIMITED, *Sydney*
PRENTICE-HALL OF CANADA, LTD., *Toronto*
PRENTICE-HALL OF INDIA PRIVATE LIMITED, *New Delhi*
PRENTICE-HALL OF JAPAN, INC., *Tokyo*
PRENTICE-HALL OF SOUTHEAST ASIA PTE. LTD., *Singapore*

Contents

Preface . . . . *xv*

Historical Introduction *1*

1. Basic Ideas in Simulation 4

　1.1 Definitions 4

　　　1.1.1 System *4*
　　　1.1.2 Subsystem 5
　　　1.1.3 Model. 5
　　　1.1.4 Simulation 6

　1.2 Types of Model 6

　　　1.2.1 Examples of Physical Models. 6
　　　1.2.2 Examples of Abstract Models 7
　　　1.2.3 Using the Model 7
　　　1.2.4 Deterministic and Stochastic Processes *8*
　　　1.2.5 Historical and Artificial Data 10

　1.3 Value of Models *10*

　1.4 Summary of the Basic Concepts of Simulation *11*

　1.5 Limitations and Problems of Simulation Models *14*

　1.6 Simulation Languages *16*

2. First Steps in Model Building *18*

2.1   Problem 1—The Doctor's Telephone *18*

    2.1.1   The System *18*

    2.1.2   The Model.......................... *18*

2.2   Problem 2—Barbershop *20*

    2.2.1   The System *20*

    2.2.2   The Model.......................... *20*

2.3   Manual Simulation of the Barbershop *22*

2.4   Simulation Concepts Used in the Model *24*

2.5   Presentation of the Model *25*

2.6   Structure of the Model *30*

3. Organization of a Simulation Study *31*

3.1   Problem Formulation *31*

3.2   Choice of Method *33*

3.3   Variables to be Included in the Model *33*

3.4   Collection and Analysis of System Data *34*

3.5   Defining the Structure of the Model *35*

3.6   Documentation: Programming the Model *36*

3.7   Validation of the Model *38*

3.8   Simulation *39*

3.9   Analysis and Critique of Results *41*

3.10 Summary *41*

4. Basic Concepts of GPSS *43*

4.1   Model Representation *43*

4.2   Logical Level *43*

4.3   GPSS Implementation Level *45*

4.4   GPSS Permanent Entities *46*

4.5   GPSS Temporary Entities *48*

4.6   GPSS Events *48*

4.7 Blocks *49*

    4.7.1   Dynamic Operations *49*

    4.7.2   Explicit Handling of Attributes *50*

    4.7.3   Delays to Transactions *50*

    4.7.4   Transaction-Flow Modification 50

    4.7.5   Synchronization of Transactions and
              Interactions between Transactions 51

    4.7.6   Accumulation and Production of Results 51

  4.8   Model Development 52

  4.9   Submitting the Program for Computer Simulation 52

  4.10 Conclusion 53

5. Basic Modeling Concepts as Implemented in GPSS 54

  5.1   Discrete Event Simulation 54

  5.2   Static Aspect 55

    5.2.1   The Static Structure 55

    5.2.2   Permanent and Temporary Entities 55

  5.3   Dynamic Aspect 56

    5.3.1   The Dynamic Structure 56

    5.3.2   Time Division and Ordering of Events.................... 56

    5.3.3   Control Program Requirements.......................... 58

    5.3.4   Clock Mechanism 58

  5.4   The GPSS Control Program 58

    5.4.1   Control of the Flow of Transactions 59

    5.4.2   Progress of a Transaction 60

    5.4.3   Sequencing of Transactions 60

    5.4.4   Possible States of a Transaction 60

  5.5   Coding and Operation of Two Simple GPSS Models 61

    5.5.1   The Barbershop Problem 61

    5.5.2   Statistical Functions in GPSS 62

    5.5.3   A Simple Queueing Model.............................. 64

    5.5.4   Detailed Trace of the Simulation 64

    5.5.5   Computation of Statistics 68

6. A GPSS Subset 70

  6.1   Control Statements 70

  6.2   Block-Definition Statements 75

    6.2.1   Transaction-Oriented Blocks 75

    6.2.2   Equipment-Oriented Blocks 80

    6.2.3   Transaction-Flow Modification 85

    6.2.4   Storage and Retrieval of Information 90

6.3   Entity-Definition Statements 92
    6.3.1   Storage-Definition Statement 92
    6.3.2   Variable-Definition Statement 93
    6.3.3   Function-Definition Statement 94
    6.3.4   Save-Matrix Definition Statement 97
    6.3.5   Save and Matrix Initialization 97

6.4   Attributes 98
    6.4.1   Standard Numerical Attributes 98
    6.4.2   Computational Entities 100
    6.4.3   Standard Logical Attributes 101

6.5   Indirect Addressing 101

6.6   Programming Examples 103
    6.6.1   SMALL Manufacturing and Delivery Company 103
    6.6.2   Traffic Lights 107
    6.6.3   Machine Repair 113
    6.6.4   Teleprocessing System 117
    6.6.5   Four-Disk System 129

6.7   Conclusion 133

7. **The Complete GPSS Language** 134

7.1   Control Statements 134
    7.1.1   Initialization of the Random-Number Generators 134
    7.1.2   Reallocation of Entities 135
    7.1.3   Saving and Reading-In Models 136
    7.1.4   Batching GPSS Jobs 138
    7.1.5   Rewinding Job Tapes 138
    7.1.6   Output Editor 138
    7.1.7   GPSS V Additional Statements 138

7.2   Block-Definition Statements 139
    7.2.1   Transaction-Oriented Blocks 139
    7.2.2   Equipment-Oriented Blocks 147
    7.2.3   Transaction-Flow Modification 156
    7.2.4   User Chains 168
    7.2.5   Group Entity 174
    7.2.6   Accumulation and Printing of Information 179
    7.2.7   Special Blocks 186
    7.2.8   Facility and Storage Availability and Unavailability 187

7.3   Entity-Definition Statements *190*

     7.3.1   Boolean Variable-Definition Statement *191*

     7.3.2   Function-Definition Statements *192*

     7.3.3   Statistical Tables *193*

7.4   Attributes *193*

     7.4.1   Standard Numerical Attributes *194*

     7.4.2   Computational Entities *195*

     7.4.3   Standard Logical Attributes *195*

     7.4.4   Additional Attributes in GPSS V *197*

7.5   Assembly Control Statements *198*

     7.5.1   The Equivalence Statement *198*

     7.5.2   The Macro Facility *199*

7.6   Programming Examples *201*

     7.6.1   Assembly Line *201*

     7.6.2   Inventory Control *204*

     7.6.3   Simple Factory Model............................... *207*

7.7   A Re-examination of the GPSS Control Program *214*

8.   Special Features and Debugging *220*

8.1   Report Program *220*

     8.1.1   List of Statements Available with REPORT *221*

     8.1.2   Statements Format *222*

     8.1.3   Graphic Output *229*

8.2   HELP Block *232*

     8.2.1   The Basic GPSS V HELP Block—Assembler Language *236*

     8.2.2   GPSS V HELP Routines—Fortran and PL/I *236*

     8.2.3   HELPC Block and Statistical Evaluation of
            Simulation Results *240*

8.3   Debugging GPSS programs *245*

     8.3.1   Divide Programs into Modules *246*

     8.3.2   Use the Diagnostics *246*

     8.3.3   Check the Generated Distributions *250*

     8.3.4   Anticipate Results *250*

     8.3.5   Make Short Runs................................... *250*

     8.3.6   Glance at the Results *251*

     8.3.7   Use the Status Printout *253*

     8.3.8   Use the PRINT Block *253*

     8.3.9   Use the SAVEVALUE Block *254*

8.3.10 Use the TRACE Feature *256*

8.3.11 Conclusion *257*

9. Simulation of an Automatic Warehouse *259*

9.1 The System *259*

    9.1.1 Introduction *259*

    9.1.2 Description of the Warehouse *259*

    9.1.3 Warehouse Operations *260*

9.2 The Problem *263*

    9.2.1 Problem Description *263*

    9.2.2 Numerical Data *263*

9.3 The GPSS Model *264*

    9.3.1 Correspondence Between System Elements
        and GPSS Entities *264*

    9.3.2 Parameters and Save Locations *265*

    9.3.3 Functions and Variables *266*

    9.3.4 Numerical Values *267*

    9.3.5 Flowchart and Program *268*

9.4 Experiments and Results *278*

    9.4.1 Choice of Zone Allocation *278*

    9.4.2 Cranes *288*

    9.4.3 Results *289*

9.5 Conclusions *290*

10. Simulation of a Subway Transportation System *292*

10.1 The System *292*

    10.1.1 Introduction *292*

    10.1.2 Description of the Subway *293*

    10.1.3 Train Movements.................................*293*

    10.1.4 Passenger Entry and Exit *294*

10.2 The Problem *294*

    10.2.1 Problem Description *294*

    10.2.2 Numerical Data *295*

10.3 The GPSS Model *298*

    10.3.1 Correspondence Between System Elements
        and GPSS Entities *298*

    10.3.2 Parameters and Save Locations *299*
    10.3.3 Variables and Functions *301*
    10.3.4 Statistical Tables *303*
    10.3.5 Numerical Values. *303*
    10.3.6 Flowchart and Program *304*

10.4 Experiments and Results *321*
    10.4.1 Three Trains Running in Each Direction *321*
    10.4.2 Four Trains Running in Each Direction *322*
    10.4.3 Further Experiments *322*

10.5 Alternative Modeling Strategies *325*
    10.5.1 Passenger Representation *325*
    10.5.2 Passenger Generation *326*
    10.5.3 Station Operations *326*
    10.5.4 Program Debugging *326*

10.6 Conclusions *327*

11. Simulation of a Job Shop *328*

11.1 Introduction: Job Shop Scheduling *328*

11.2 The System *329*

11.3 Model Requirements *330*

11.4 Numerical Characteristics *330*

11.5 The GPSS Model *332*
    11.5.1 Correspondence Between System Elements
            and GPSS Entities *332*
    11.5.2 Model Overview *332*
    11.5.3 Program Description *340*

11.6 Experiments and Results *346*

11.7 Conclusions *349*

12. Simulation of a Teleprocessing System *351*

12.1 The System *351*
    12.1.1 Introduction *351*
    12.1.2 System Description *352*

12.2 The Problem *354*
    12.2.1 Problem Description *354*
    12.2.2 The Transactions *354*

12.2.3   Numerical Data *355*

12.2.4   Application Programs *357*

12.2.5   Other Considerations *357*

12.3   The GPSS Model *357*

12.3.1   Correspondence Between System Elements
and GPSS Entities *357*

12.3.2   Parameters, Matrices, and Savevalues *361*

12.3.3   Functions and Variables *362*

12.3.4   Tables Available for Output *364*

12.3.5   Program Description *364*

12.4   Experiments and Results *380*

12.4.1   Analyzing the Results of the Model *380*

12.4.2   Simulation Runs: Condensed Results *380*

12.5   Conclusions *382*

13.   **General Appraisal of GPSS** *384*

13.1   The Case for GPSS *384*

13.2   Practical Modeling and Programming Hints *386*

13.2.1   General Rules *386*

13.2.2   Various Ways To Look at GPSS Blocks *388*

13.3   Classical Errors *391*

13.4   Program Efficiency *398*

13.5   When To Use GPSS *400*

14.   **Planning Simulation Experiments** *402*

14.1   Simulation and Statistical Tools *402*

14.2   Input Data Analysis *403*

14.3   Statistical Reliability *404*

14.4   Comparisons of System Responses *410*

14.5   Conclusion *410*

15.   **The Future of Simulation
and Simulation Languages** *413*

15.1   Programming, Debugging, and Validation *414*

15.2   Production Runs of the Simulation Model *415*

Appendices *417*

A Operating-System Control Cards for GPSS *419*

A.1 GPSS Data Sets Required to Execute GPSS *419*

A.2 Procedure to Execute GPSS *420*

B Summary of GPSS Components

BLOCK STATEMENTS
CONTROL AND ENTITY-DEFINITION STATEMENTS,
AND STANDARD NUMERICAL ATTRIBUTES *423*

C GPSS V: Extensions to GPSS/360 .... *453*

C.1 New Features *453*

C.2 New Instructions (Blocks) and Extensions of Previous
     Instructions *454*

C.3 Additional SNAs *454*

D Generation of Random Numbers and Random Variates *456*

D.1 Generation of Random Numbers *456*

     D.1.1 The Mid-Square Technique *457*
     D.1.2 The Mid-Point Technique *458*
     D.1.3 The Congruential Method *458*

D.2 Generation of Random Variates *460*

E Summary of Current Simulation Languages *465*

E.1 Event-Oriented Approach: SIMSCRIPT II *466*

     E.1.1 Static Structure *466*
     E.1.2 The Dynamic Structure of the Model *467*
     E.1.3 The Timing Routine *468*
     E.1.4 Miscellaneous Features *468*

E.2 Process-Oriented Approach: SIMPL/I *468*

     E.2.1 The Process Concept *469*
     E.2.2 Process-Handling *471*
     E.2.3 The Timing Routine *472*
     E.2.4 The Entity Attribute *473*
     E.2.5 List-Handling *473*

E.2.6   Output 474
E.2.7   SIMPL/I Library 475

E.3   Another Process-Oriented Approach: SIMULA 67 475

E.3.1   Algorithmic Capability, Input/Output, and
        String Handling 476
E.3.2   Manipulation of Classes, Prototypes, and Objects 476
E.3.3   Behavior of Objects and Interactions between Objects 477
E.3.4   Manipulation of Sets of Objects 479
E.3.5   Simulation-Oriented Features 479
E.3.6   Miscellaneous Features 481

Index 483

Preface

For several years, we have been involved with simulation, both as practitioners and instructors. During this time we have delivered courses to audiences with widely varying backgrounds, including university students, IBM systems engineers, and practising engineers with no specialized experience of data processing. We were concerned that the current literature did not seem to include a suitable text for our needs.

As a direct consequence of our experience, we decided to produce a comprehensive text book that would introduce the subject of simulation from first principles, demonstrate the techniques, show the need for simulation languages, discuss statistical implications, and present one simulation language with completely programmed examples taken from various areas. The General Purpose Simulation System, GPSS, was chosen as the base language both for its block-diagramming structure, which is relatively simple for the nonprogrammer to understand, and because it is widely used.

We selected the GPSS V version for our book because it is essentially a superset of all other implementations of GPSS/360. Therefore, previous versions of the language are compatible with GPSS V, and programs written for GPSS/360 will run under GPSS V. Instructions peculiar to GPSS V are indicated clearly in the text and the differences between it and other versions of the language are summarized in Appendix C. Appendix B gives all instructions, control statements, and entity definitions available in GPSS V. Thus the reader can also use this book to study other versions of the language.

We emphasize that our purpose is not to replace the programming manuals published by IBM. A user who requires specific details of a particular version of the simulator should consult the appropriate GPSS user's manual, which will provide a complete description of the language and the simulator. There, answers will be found to questions that are not even considered in the present book. Nevertheless, we believe that our book will serve a specific purpose: the subject is developed logically to make it easy to follow and several topics are covered that have not, to our knowledge, been presented previously in a single text.

We present GPSS concepts by stages, giving, first, a simple idea and later introducing more detailed and systematic explanations related to the topics previously discussed. Although this involves some repetition, it has the advantage of avoiding repeated cross references.

We hope that we have managed to make our book suitable for readers with widely differing skills. We have tried to keep the introductory chapters completely basic, for the benefit of the reader with no previous knowledge of the subject. Later we introduce a basic GPSS subset, common to all levels of GPSS/360, explain the use of the instructions, and describe several models in detail. This is followed by considerations of the full GPSS V language, with more comprehensive programmed examples. The following four chapters are devoted to case studies on automatic warehousing, subway transportation, job shop scheduling, and teleprocessing. Later chapters discuss statistical aspects of simulation and interpretation of results. We also discuss the requirements for simulation languages, the value of GPSS as a programming language, and devote Appendices D and E, respectively, to the generation of random numbers and outlines of some other simulation languages.

As far as possible we have made each chapter self-contained so that the reader can study the subject in a modular way.

The material contained in our book is based on teaching and practical experience gained by solving real problems. We should like to acknowledge the assistance which we have received from the students of IBM's ESRI (European Systems Research Institute), from the lecturers and students of EPFL (Ecole Polytechnique Fédérale, Lausanne), and from the ITEP (Institut de Technique des Transports), who attended our courses on simulation and GPSS, contributed to the courses, and were engaged in study projects. In particular, we wish to thank I. Amihud, J. Ph. Berney, Y. Etgar, J. Greyfie de Bellecombe, R. Guette, H. Ney, G. Vinet, U. Waehli, and U. Wiedemar.

Our special thanks go to Erika Bosshard, who typed the original manuscript with great patience, sometimes under great pressure, but always with a smile. We would also like to recognize the valuable comments made, during the revision phase, by our colleague Klaus Rittmann.

Finally, we want to thank the management of IBM. Without their support, we would not have been able to write this book. Part of the contents is based on notes developed for courses given at the IBM European Systems Research Institute, and we appreciate IBM's agreement to the publication of this material.

P. A. BOBILLIER

B. C. KAHAN

A. R. PROBST

Historical Introduction

The General Purpose System Simulator, GPSS, was developed by Geoffrey Gordon and presented in two papers in 1961 and 1962 [E.1] and [G.1].* The first release of the GPSS language, often called the "Gordon Simulator," was implemented on the IBM 704, 709, and 7090 computers [G.2].

The language was designed to be used by analysts who were not specialists in computer programming. The use of flowcharts to describe a system was well-known, so GPSS was structured as a block-oriented language. This philosophy allowed the analyst to submit a model to the computer in the form of a network of blocks, connected in the same order as a sequence of events. A set of 25 specific block types was defined, each representing a basic system action and each associated with a time to perform that action. Blocks could be used repeatedly; the interpretation of the action represented by a block operation was the responsibility of the analyst and the time for performing the action was also specified by the analyst.

General units of traffic in the system, such as people, vehicles, messages, or goods, were represented by *transactions*, which were defined to model the dynamic components of a system. The transactions moved through the block diagram under the control of the blocks and were created and destroyed as required.

The fundamental concepts of block-diagram structure and transactions have been retained throughout the evolution of GPSS.

---

*Numbers and/or letters within brackets refer to the reference lists that appear at the ends of chapters. The first number and/or letter indicates the chapter, the second the number of the reference itself. "G" (for "general") references will be found at the end of the "Historical Introduction"; other alphabetic references appear at the ends of the appendixes, which follow Chapter 15.

A second version, GPSS II [G.3] and [G.4], was a more powerful language that followed the same philosophy as the original release.

For GPSS III [G.5] and [G.6], however, a major change in design was made. Time delays were eliminated from the blocks and a single block, ADVANCE, was used to model all passages of time. Consequently, the whole block structure was redefined and system actions were represented by three blocks, which specified start of action, delay, and end of action, respectively. These new blocks tended to be less complicated than their equivalents in the original versions. The characteristics of this release, which is simpler to use and more powerful than the original, are described in [G.7]. Many other improvements were made, including better branching control, more complete diagnostic messages, and the introduction of user chains. User chains gave the analyst more control over the behavior of individual transactions and could also be used to increase the speed of simulation. The basic structure of the language has remained unaltered since GPSS III and all further releases are upward-compatible. This obviates the need for reprogramming models when changing to a later version of the language.

In 1967, GPSS/360 was announced [G.8], [G.9], and [G.10], and the name was changed to General Purpose Simulation System. This version had many new features, including: matrices, for storing one- or two-dimensional arrays, preempting on priority, and groups, which allowed the user to address and manipulate all transactions with given characteristics. The random-number capabilities were extended to give eight independent random-number generators, and Boolean variables were introduced. To simplify the coding, components of the model could be identified by name, the number of parameters that could be associated with a transaction was increased, macros could be defined to represent lines of common code by a single statement, and HELP routines could be used to interface with Assembler language if more powerful computing instructions were required. An output editor was supplied so that the user could present results in the most convenient form, including, for example, graphical output of tables as histograms.

Two additional releases have since been made, a second version of GPSS/360 and GPSS V [G.11] and [G.12]. As the features of GPSS V are discussed at length in this book, at this point we shall only outline the improvements to the language. These changes were directed mainly to simplifying the routine tasks of modeling and to relaxing restrictions on the size of models. A run timer can be set to limit the total computer execution time used. When run time expires before the end of simulation, output is produced and the simulation run is terminated. The HELP block has been extended so that the analyst has a simple interface to the power of FORTRAN or PL/I. Free-form coding reduces the labor of program preparation. New types of parameters and arrays give more flexible data handling within the model, and the number of parameters that can be associated with each transaction has been increased significantly.

Since its inception, GPSS has maintained the objective of catering for the analyst. The only major change in language structure increased its power and simplified its use but retained the fundamental block-diagramming concept. All other features have been incorporated into the language either to reduce modeling effort without complicating the coding or to increase the scope and detail of models. In sum, GPSS is particularly well-suited for modeling traffic and queueing systems, situations in which it is necessary to study the interactions of a dynamic situation in detail.

General References

G.1. G. GORDON, "A General Purpose Systems Simulator," *IBM Systems Journal*, Vol. 1, No. 1, 1962.

G.2. *General Purpose Systems Simulator: Program Library*, Ref. 7090-CS-05X, International Business Machines Corporation.

G.3. R. EFRON and G. GORDON, "A General Purpose Digital Simulator and Examples of Its Application: Part I, Description of the Simulator," *IBM Systems Journal*, Vol. 3, No. 1, 1964.

G.4. *General Purpose Systems Simulator II: Reference Material*, International Business Machines Corporation.

G.5. *General Purpose Systems Simulator: Program Library*, Refs. 7090-CS-15X and 7040-CS-14X, International Business Machines Corporation.

G.6. *General Purpose Systems Simulator III: User's Manual*, H20-0163, International Business Machines Corporation.

G.7. H. HERSCOVITCH and T. SCHNEIDER, "GPSS III—An Expanded General Purpose Simulator," *IBM Systems Journal*, Vol. 4, No. 3, 1965.

G.8. R. L. GOULD, "GPSS/360—An Improved General Purpose Simulator," *IBM Systems Journal*, Vol. 8, No. 1, 1969.

G.9. *General Purpose Simulation System/360: Introductory User's Manual*, GH20-0304, International Business Machines Corporation.

G.10. *General Purpose Simulation System/360: User's Manual*, GH20-0326, International Business Machines Corporation.

G.11. *General Purpose Simulation System V: Introductory User's Manual*, SH20-0866, International Business Machines Corporation.

G.12. *General Purpose Simulation System V: User's Manual*, SH20-0851, International Business Machines Corporation.

G.13. *GPSS V-OS-Operations Manual*, SH20-0867, International Business Machines Corporation.

1 Basic Ideas in Simulation

In business, industry, and government today, large-scale, complex projects are the rule rather than the exception. To minimize the high cost of such projects, planning and implementation must be as streamlined as possible. Preliminary studies to assess the suitability of plans *before* they are adopted are thus vital to efficient and economical execution of all projects of any size. One technique of running such pilot studies, which yields results quickly and at relatively low cost, is based on *modeling* and is known as *simulation*.

One begins by studying the salient features of the project. This process, which involves a measure of abstraction, is known as modeling. A model is not necessarily a replica; it consists of a description that may be physical, verbal, or abstract in form, together with a set of operating rules. Further, because the model is dynamic, its response to input can be used to study the behavior of the project or system from which it was developed.

The process of running a model is called simulation. Basically simulation involves the design and playing of a game of strategy. The concept is not new: practical simulation in the form of army maneuvers has been used for centuries as an aid in military training; unfortunately, it is costly in time and man power. By comparison, simulation by computer is quick and inexpensive. When the model is sufficiently flexible, it can be used to evaluate and compare many different operating strategies.

1.1 Definitions

1.1.1 System

A *system* consists of a set of parts organized functionally to form a connected whole.

4

For example, a dockyard consists of many parts or components such as wharves, cranes, railheads, road transport, ships, cargoes, and passengers. Thus a dockyard system is composed of all the men and materials necessary for its construction and use.

1.1.2 Subsystem

A *subsystem* is a component of the total system which can be treated either as a part of the total system or as an independent system.

For example, the wharves in the dockyard mentioned above can be studied independently of the dockyard or as a part of the whole dockyard. In practice, every system is a subsystem of the universe—the terms "system" and "subsystem" depend on the scope of the situation described.

In this book the term "system" will be applied to the whole situation being studied for the duration of such studies. Thus systems generally change dynamically with time. The behavior of the total system depends on the internal relationships among the subsystems and also on the external relationships that connect the system to the environment, that is, the universe outside the system.

1.1.3 Model

A *model* is a representation of a system. A basic requirement for any model is that it should describe the system in sufficient detail for the behavior of the model to provide valid predictions of the behavior of the system. More generally, the characteristics of the model must correspond to some characteristics of the system being modeled.

Figure 1.1 shows the concept of a model. The shape has been idealized to show that the model is usually a simplification of real life. Parameters specifying characteristics or attributes of both system and model appear in each case. Input to and

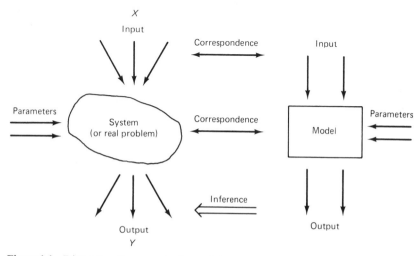

Figure 1.1   Diagrammatic concept of a model.

output from the real system have been formalized in the model and correspondence between input to both system and model have been identified. However, the two outputs do not necessarily have the same correspondence. As both the system and the model can be considered as functions that transform input to output, the output from a suitable model might be used to infer the output from the system that it represents.

1.1.4 Simulation

Simulation is the technique of constructing and running a model of a real system in order to study the behavior of that system, without disrupting the environment of the real system. It is usually described as an art, or a soft science, because the useful results of the study depend upon the skill of the modeling team. At the present state of the art, there is no scientific theory to guarantee the validity of a simulation process before the experiment is performed. Instead, the suitability of a model is judged by the correspondence of results from the model with known results obtained by observations of systems comparable with the system under examination. However, when the aim is to study a new system, simulation provides a means of generating artificial history that can be used to identify problem areas.

In any simulation study some subsystems may follow a well-known behavior pattern or lend themselves to direct mathematical analysis. Such systems should not be simulated, but their contribution to the total system must be included in the model. Thus the model used for simulation may often seem quite different from the actual system.

1.2 Types of Model

Models can be classified in many ways, but most are either physical or abstract. Physical models include globes, wind tunnels, flight simulators, and planetaria. Abstract models include chemical formulae, circuit diagrams, flow charts, mathematical equations, and budgets.

1.2.1 Examples of physical models

Flight simulator

Use: to train aircrew in flight operations, with particular emphasis on emergency procedures.

Physical system: airborne aircraft.

Model: land-based replica of aircraft flight deck, possibly with devices to change attitude and orientation.

Advantages: disaster conditions can be simulated in safety, which may be the only feasible way to give such training; saves operating costs of a training aircraft.

Disadvantage: lack of realism and therefore less stress than would be expected in the real situation; more stress can be induced by increasing the speed at which the clocks run.

Flight plan

Use: preparation for a trip.

Physical system: airspace, aircraft, aircrew, and meteorological conditions.

Model: small-scale, two-dimensional model of a portion of the earth's surface; weather forecast.

Advantages: gives time and position objectives, which help the aircrew to complete the trip successfully.

1.2.2 Examples of abstract models

Budget

Use: to plan finances.

Physical system: bank balance, loans, cash received, payments made over a period of time.

Model: a statement of expected cash movements.

Advantage: ability to compare actual and expected cash movements at all times and thus modify financial policy as necessary.

Chemical formula

Use: to predict resources required to obtain specified quantities of a product.

Physical system: chemical plant, ingredients, energy sources.

Model: idealized equations of chemical reaction.

Advantages: estimates of requirements of ingredients and resources.

Disadvantages: output from bulk processes may be radically different from that estimated by equations formulated at a molecular level.

This book is devoted to the consideration of abstract models of real systems. The characteristics or attributes of the system are therefore represented by variables and parameters. Because models formulated in this abstract manner can be stored in, and manipulated by, a computer, this type of model can be expressed as a computer program. Apart from illustrating the modeling process with some elementary examples of manual simulation, we shall concentrate on computerized simulation.

1.2.3 Using the model

Mathematical analysis. When the interrelations among all the components of the model are known and defined mathematically, its response to given inputs can be calculated. If such calculations are possible, mathematical analysis is the technique that should be used.

Simulation. When it is not possible to express the interrelations in a convenient mathematical form because the system is too complex or because responses are subject to random variation, it is necessary to formulate operating rules and to study behavior by simulation.

1.2.4   Deterministic and stochastic processes

A process is defined as *deterministic* if for every value of the input the output can be determined in some reproducible fashion.

For example, if the equation $y = x + 4$ is considered as a process, then whenever the input x is equal to 3, the output y equals 7. The formula is true for all values of x.

By contrast, a *stochastic* process is random. When sufficient observations have been made, it may be possible to find the statistical distribution that governs the behavior of the system.

For example, how many people will be sitting in the next car that you see? The number will probably lie in the range 0 to 6; it is not possible to be more definite. The only reason that the range can be estimated at all is because observation of numerous cars has given us a good idea of their average size.

The system to be studied can be either deterministic or stochastic; the models of these systems can also be either deterministic or stochastic. Thus four combinations are possible:

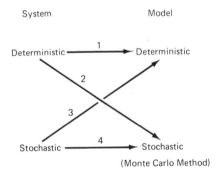

1. Both the system and the model are deterministic—for example, the mathematical equations of motion of a missile. The set of equations that constitute the model can be solved analytically to predict system behavior.
2. The model is stochastic, but the problem is deterministic. We consider the evaluation of a definite integral by means of a stochastic process.

Estimate the area under the curve $f(x, y) = 0$ for the range $0 \leq x \leq 1$ (Figure 1.2). The Monte Carlo method states that if there is an equal likelihood of selecting any point in the unit square shown in Figure 1.2 and if sufficient points are selected at random, then the required area is given by:

$$A = \lim_{N \to \infty} \frac{n}{N}$$

where

$$N = \text{total number of points}$$

$$n = \text{number of points lying in the required area}$$

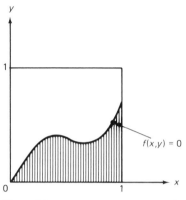

Figure 1.2

To perform this experiment it is necessary to generate random-number pairs in the range (0, 1) such that all points in the unit square occur with equal probability. Then $f(x, y)$ is calculated for each number pair to test whether the point "hits" the target under the curve $f(x, y) = 0$, and the ratio n/N is computed.

Although the method would not usually be applied in this primitive manner, the example illustrates the basic concept of the Monte Carlo technique.

3. The problem is stochastic, but the model is deterministic—for example, the generation of random numbers by computer. The feasibility of this process was assumed in (2) above.

Remark: A computer program is deterministic because output can be calculated. However, sequences of numbers which appear random to the user can be produced by computer programs that use algorithms based on the theory of numbers. These "pseudo-random" number sequences are discussed in Appendix D. An apparent paradox exists, because anyone who knows the algorithm could predict every number in advance, which contradicts the concept of randomness. Nevertheless, most users find that pseudo-random number sequences are valuable simulation aids.

4. Both the system and the model are stochastic. Simulation is normally used in this case.

Some examples, with an indication of the random problem variables, are given in Table 1.1. This short list could be greatly extended. Most real-life problems are naturally stochastic and cannot be fully described by an analytical model. Many studies in operations research aim to find an optimum strategy, such as minimizing operating costs or maximizing throughput or profit. Simulation does not usually optimize, but it can be used to select the most suitable strategy from several alternatives.

Table 1.1

Problem (System)	Random Variables
Inventory	Demand, lead time
Job shop	Process time, time between failures
Replacement problems	Life time, breakdowns
Real-time systems	Traffic (for instance, messages from terminals on computer systems)
Traffic	Arrivals and speed of vehicles, reaction times
Business and war games	Decisions of participants, parameters that describe economic factors, etc.

The technique of simulation is now applied in all the areas listed in Table 1.1 and will certainly be further developed in the future. For additional information on the areas in which simulation is practicable, consult references [1.1] to [1.6], and proceedings of subsequent conferences on simulation.

1.2.5 Historical and artificial data

When records of an existing system are available, it is possible to create a file of historical data for running a simulation model. For example, an inventory model can be run with last year's demand data. By modifying strategies it is possible to determine which strategy would have been best for last year's operation. Extrapolation of the results can then be used to decide how to operate in the future.

An alternative approach is to use the Monte Carlo method. The system is analyzed to determine the statistical properties of the data; artificial samples of input are then generated by using pseudo-random numbers. Such input can be kept on file to ensure that other strategies will use the same input as that for the historical data file just mentioned.

In both the above cases the data are artificial insofar as they consist of information that is not derived from the current system operation. One very important factor is the sensitivity of the model to changes in the input data. Whether the data source is historical or artificial, the modeler should check the output to see if responses vary widely with relatively small changes in input.

1.3 Value of Models

The most important function of simulation is prediction. The objective of experimenting with models is to answer the question: "What would happen if. . . ?"

One advantage of simulation models is that there is no limit to their complexity. When a complicated system defies mathematical analysis or when the inclusion of random variables with nonstandard distributions makes a statistical formula difficult to find, a simulation model may still be constructed.

In addition, the structure of a simulation model gives access to all the variables within the model. Therefore, during model building, some relations may be discovered among internal variables. Such relations should always be validated and any extension beyond the domain studied during simulation must be justified. Such discoveries increase the analyst's understanding of the problem and aid in the development of more realistic models.

Simulation is also applicable to the design of a new system, such as an automatic warehouse, considered in Chapter 9. The model can be used to predict system performance under varying conditions and with different equipment, by using a number of operating disciplines before a firm decision to purchase equipment is made. During the life of the system, simulation can be used to test possible modifications, without interfering with normal operation of the installation. Such development studies will use the actual data from the system operation instead of the predicted data of the initial design studies. Simulation thus becomes a dynamic part of the total system design.

The technique of simulation can also be used as a training aid in business and management. A management game is a model that simulates the behavior of an economic system in which the "players" have to live. As in real life, the players make decisions regarding the operation of the business, usually for the next quarter. The model simulates the behavior of the economic system, given the decisions of the players; based on the results, the players can make the decisions for the next quarter, and so on. The time necessary to make a decision for the next quarter depends on the degree of realism (and therefore complexity) of the game; it is usually of the order of 1 to 2 hours. This is an excellent way of training decision makers. Different strategies can be compared, and in particular the effect of disastrous decision errors can be studied in detail with no loss to the real system. As a final example of modeling, we mention war games, which simulate the operation of the armed forces in battle. The opponents (players) make decisions on strategy as they would in practice. The model then predicts the consequences of those decisions, which changes the military situation, and the cycle continues. The advantages of such studies are that costly maneuvers can be planned effectively to reduce costs and man power needed for the training program.

1.4 Summary of the Basic Concepts of Simulation

When developing a model for use in a simulation experiment, divide the system under study into a number of interconnected subsystems. Each subsystem, in turn, is composed of interconnected elements, each with its own dynamic behavior.

The relations among subsystems must be defined first and then the dynamic behavior of the system. Total system behavior depends on behavior of the subsystems and the environment in which the system exists. Figure 1.3 summarizes the process by which the analyst builds up a logical structure for a simulation experiment, starting with the basic components of the system from which the final model is constructed.

The steps that are followed during a simulation experiment are shown in block-

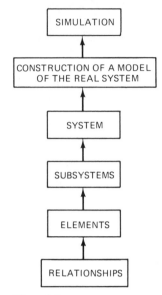

Figure 1.3

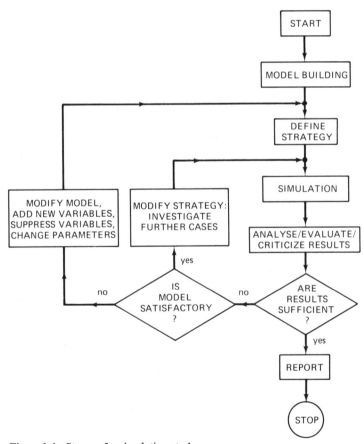

Figure 1.4 Stages of a simulation study.

diagram form in Figure 1.4. First, simulation is an iterative process. A simulation experiment gives the value of the parameters during and at the end of simulation. Analysis of the output will suggest modifications to the strategy, such as changes in priority or sequencing rules. Thus, step by step, we gain more knowledge about the system and its performance until there is sufficient information to make final recommendations about the system to be implemented.

Second, as noted previously, simulation is not normally used to find the optimum solution of a problem. The simulation specialist defines alternatives and chooses the one that gives the best performance. It does not follow, however, that this solution is the optimum for the system.

In contrast with simulation, a mathematical programming technique, such as linear programming, yields a unique, optimum solution, if one exists. (The drawback with such a technique, however, is that it is static for each set of input data.) It would thus appear that simulation is less powerful than mathematical programming or other mathematical methods. This conclusion is not justified, however, because the two methods are not comparable. Simulation is an excellent technique when other methods fail.

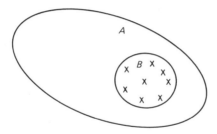

Figure 1.5

The skill of the practitioner is more important in simulation than in other methods. This fact is illustrated in Figure 1.5, where we assume that A is the set of all possible solutions satisfying the constraints of the problem and B is the subset of cases that are to be studied by simulation. When simulation is complete, we choose the most suitable solution from the subset B and make recommendations. Selection of the cases to be simulated is thus most important. They should always be chosen to give a high probability of being in the neighborhood of the true optimum. Because this selection is always very difficult, avoid planning for too many sequential simulation runs in advance. It is much better to analyze the results of one case carefully before deciding on the next run; after each run, knowledge of the problem will increase and therefore the probability of identifying cases closer to the optimum.

The importance of selecting the cases to be simulated shows why some people say that simulation is an art. We would add: the art of defining the subset B properly. It is more an art than a science because no general theory has yet been found to guide this selection. Moreover, for economic reasons, the subset B has to be small, which does not simplify the problem.

1.5   Limitations and Problems of Simulation Models

The principal difficulty of simulation lies in its use. Any problem that can be solved simply and satisfactorily by an analytical technique should be solved analytically. Simulation should be used only when other methods cannot provide a suitable solution. Further, describe *parts* of the problem analytically whenever possible.

Following are some of the difficulties inherent in simulation. They are significant and should be kept in mind before and during a simulation study.

Simulation may not give the optimum solution of a problem. The analyst must consider the relative merits of the cases simulated and choose the most promising model. The degree of success of the study depends on the quality of the selection of the cases to be examined. One should have a thorough knowledge of the problem in order to identify the cases of potential importance.

The accuracy of simulation results is somewhat unpredictable, even for well-defined models. This is because we manipulate random variables and we experiment only with limited samples. The results depend on the input data's accuracy, which is also limited for practical reasons. Increasing the accuracy (or reducing the confidence intervals of the results) usually requires more machine time and increases costs.

The validation of complicated models, especially of systems in the planning stage, can be very difficult. If the programming is consistent with the rules of the simulation language, then *errors*, due to invalid data or incorrect logic, unfortunately do not usually prevent the model from working and thereby producing spurious results. This is disturbing for the obvious reason that an elaborate model is of no use if it cannot be trusted.

Simulation can be very expensive in use of computer time. For important studies one should always try to reduce the machine time, for example by applying variance-reduction techniques (see Chapter 14). Unfortunately, such methods normally increase the complexity of the model.

The apparent simplicity and realism of simulation models and of the method itself are dangerous, especially for the uninformed. When facing a new and difficult problem, one is tempted to use simulation because of the immediate correspondence that can be established between the problem and the model. The dangers are twofold. First, the naïve approach consists of defining a one-to-one correspondence so that the model represents the system as exactly as possible. The aim of the experienced analyst should always be to reproduce the structure of the system rather than its form. This obviously requires a measure of abstraction of the system to produce an efficient model. However, demonstrating a one-to-one correspondence may be a vital factor in selling the simulation concept to management.

Second, the simplifying assumptions that have to be made when building a model should never be forgotten, otherwise, one may have too much confidence in the results and try to extrapolate properties of the model found by the simulation experiments and apply them to a domain outside the cases studied. This type of error occurs quite often when one attempts to answer questions relating to cases not covered by the model and for which the necessary modifications would take too long to implement. In brief, one should remain conscious of these limitations and strongly resist generalization without additional simulation experiments.

To illustrate these pitfalls, suppose that a model is built to study the response time of a computer system and that we obtain the results represented in Figure 1.6. The results indicate a linear relation between response time and load. This linear relation is valid in the range (a, b). It would be extremely dangerous to extend it outside that range, especially to values of the load greater than b.

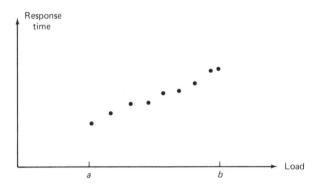

Figure 1.6

At the start of a simulation experiment, the model is usually inactive. One must take suitable action to initialize the model, or to reach equilibrium (if we are interested in steady-state information), before starting to gather statistical data. The chosen language should possess a feature for this purpose; otherwise, a lengthy programming effort may be necessary.

Results of simulation experiments are almost always autocorrelated; the analyst must therefore plan simulation experiments carefully and spend some time on the analysis and appraisal of the results. Two approaches may be taken: the experiments may be planned so as to eliminate the autocorrelation effects, or the latter may be used to advantage by a suitable method. An example of autocorrelated data is the waiting time of transactions in a simple queueing system: single queue, single server, with exponentially distributed arrival and service times. The behavior of a transaction will obviously be influenced by the preceding transaction. If a transaction is delayed for a long time, the following transaction will have to wait for a long time. This effect will persist until the queue becomes empty. It is only when all queues are empty that transaction behavior is independent of past history.

This enumeration of potential problems inherent in the use of simulation should not dismay the reader. We merely wish to place simulation, as one of the operations research methods, in its proper perspective. In addition, we want to stress that despite these difficulties, simulation is the only way to tackle many problems that would otherwise remain unsolved. It is also a means of discovering many unsuspected properties of the systems that we study with this method, and it therefore helps us to improve our understanding of these problems.

1.6 Simulation Languages

There are two distinct stages in any computerized simulation study: first, *systems analysis*—to define the simulation model; and, second, *computer programming*—to code the model for data processing.

Throughout this book it will be seen that, although simulation can be applied to many diverse systems, there are fundamental components or *entities* common to many models. Each entity has certain characteristics or *attributes* that can be used by the analyst to describe details of its function in the model. By defining a suitable set of such modeling entities the effort of coding can be drastically reduced. The totality of modeling elements forms a simulation programming language of which GPSS V is an example. Additional examples of simulation languages are given in Appendix E.

To be effective a simulation language must handle the following functions, with minimum effort on the part of the user:

Time: simulation is dynamic; the modeler therefore needs to examine the behavior of the system with time. A mechanism must be provided for the modeler to introduce delays into the model and to record simulated time.

Events: the model will deal with continuous time of a real system, but for the sake of economy of instructions the model will change only when there is a significant change in the state of the system. For example, the act of drinking a glass of water is dynamic, but it can be defined as a quasi-static state of the system. The state changes when drinking starts and when drinking stops—that is, because a new event has entered the system. The modeling language must handle all events in a logical order. In other words, the numerous events that take place during any simulation must be sequenced correctly, subject to priority conditions if any, and must also handle congestion that may alter the scheduling scheme originally planned.

Random variables: the simulation language should provide efficient random-number generation techniques for running stochastic models on the computer.

Accumulation and printing of statistics: the simulator should collect some statistics automatically and should provide simple procedures for the analyst to specify and gather data of specific importance to the current model. A standard output should be supplied when the run terminates, either on normal completion of simulation or on recognizing an error condition, and the analyst must have options to modify order and content. It is also desirable to be able to record statistics at intervals during the run to study the dynamic behavior of the system.

Language: the language must be capable of describing the status of the model at any time. This means that permanent and temporary entities must be defined in a simple manner. The selection of components depends on the language used. The components of GPSS V are reviewed briefly in Chapter 4.

Control of simulation: to permit dynamic change of status, commands must be available to control internal and external components of the model.

Ease of operation: this requirement includes many features: error checking and debugging facilities, program readability, model initialization and stability tests, the ability to make several runs sequentially, ease of modification either during or between runs, possibility of building useful models from a basic subset of instructions, and, finally, modularity of instructions and model structure.

The above characteristics should be true of any simulation language if it is to handle the purely administrative functions of modeling and allow the analyst to concentrate on the fundamental tasks of creating a valid abstraction from the proposed system. If the analyst had to perform the clerical tasks listed, the effort required would exceed that necessary for the actual simulation, and the objective of the study would be defeated.

References

1.1. "Applications of Simulation Languages," Special Issue, *IEEE Transactions on Systems Science and Cybernetics*, Vol. SSC-4, No. 4, 1968.

1.2. *Proceedings of the Second Conference on Applications of Simulation, New York, 1968*, Association for Computing Machinery, New York, 1969.

1.3. *Proceedings of the Third Conference on Applications of Simulation, Los Angeles, 1969*, Association for Computing Machinery, New York, 1969.

1.4. *Proceedings of the Fourth Conference on Applications of Simulation, New York, 1970*, Association for Computing Machinery, New York, 1970.

1.5. *Proceedings of the 1972 Summer Computer Simulation Conference, San Diego, Calif.*, Simulation Councils, LaJolla, Calif., 1972.

1.6. K. W. Gohring, N. D. Swain, and R. L. Sawder, eds., *Fifth Annual Conference on Simulation* (Progress in Simulation, Vol. 2), Gordon and Breach, New York, 1972.

2 First Steps in Model Building

In this chapter we consider two very simple systems and show, in an elementary manner, how each may be modeled. We shall note the similarities and differences of each system and thus identify some of the modeling entities required for computerized simulation. Finally, we will follow the behavior of the second model through a manual simulation.

2.1 Problem 1: The Doctor's Telephone

2.1.1 The system

A doctor's receptionist has a telephone which, for the purposes of this study, is used only for receiving telephone calls. Patients ring up throughout the day to ask the doctor to visit or to make an appointment. If the telephone is busy, the patient waits for a short time and then dials again. The process is repeated until a reply is obtained.

Model the system to determine how many times a patient has to dial before being connected, the average time that a patient waits from first dialing attempt until the end of the conversation, and the utilization of the telephone.

2.1.2 The model

This simple system is clearly described by the block diagram shown in Figure 2.1. Several assumptions have been made:

18

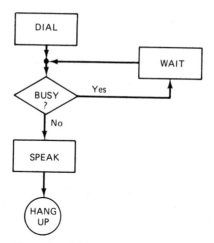

Figure 2.1 Flow chart of a doctor's telephone system.

1. Dialing, response time, and disconnect time are included in either speaking time or waiting time.
2. There is a means for representing time delays. This allows new calls to enter the system with a specified interarrival time distribution and also accounts for waiting and speaking times.
3. There is a method of representing the telephone and recording its status as busy or free.
4. There is a method of representing a patient who is trying to call the receptionist.
5. There is no priority in the model. A patient who has made several unsuccessful attempts to call has no precedence.

A simulation programming language should supply:

1. A definition of the telephone and its status.
2. A means for implementing time delays.
3. The creation and destruction of telephone calls.
4. A means of gathering statistics.
5. Branching control on the telephone status, busy or free.

The modeler must specify:

1. The time distribution of calls entering the system.
2. The time delays for speaking or waiting to redial.
3. The statistics to be gathered.
4. The length of time to be simulated.

2.2 Problem 2: The Barbershop

2.2.1 The system

A barber can serve only one customer at a time. Customers enter the shop and wait for service if the barber is busy. Customers are served in arrival order. The waiting room can accommodate all waiting customers. Model the system so that statistics on the level of service to customers and the utilization of the barber can be found.

2.2.2 The model

The block WAIT shown in Figure 2.2 contains a list of customers in arrival order. This is consulted when the barber finishes serving the current customer. If customers are waiting, the barber stays busy. It is assumed that there is no policy of planned appointments in the shop.

The two systems, the doctor's telephone and the barbershop, may be compared as shown in Table 2.1. There is only one logical *difference* between this system and the first example: customers are served in arrival order in the second system.

Figure 2.2 Flow chart of barbershop operation.

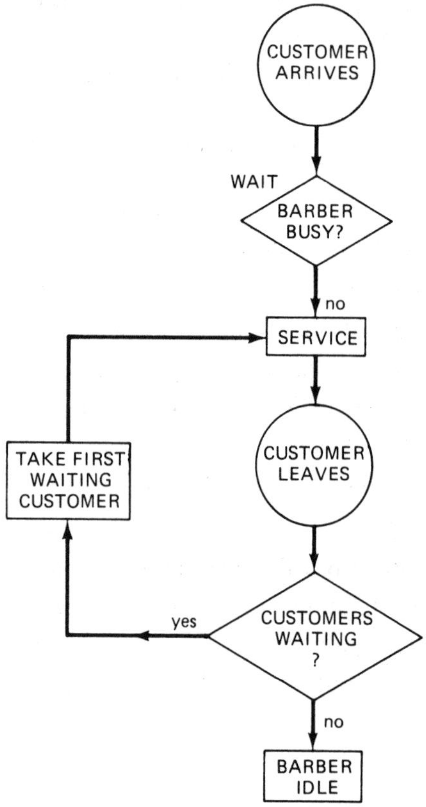

Table 2.1

Problem 1	Problem 2
Telephone	Barber
Telephone call (patient)	Customer
Speaking time	Service time
End call	Leave shop

The barbershop model contains two distinct types of element, as shown in Figure 2.3.

1. *Constant* or *permanent:* These elements remain throughout the period of simulation. The barbershop and barber are present throughout simulation. These elements can therefore be considered as part of the environment and thus as permanent. The barber is a "facility," an entity that can serve only one customer at a time. The barbershop is also a waiting room; it provides the "queue," where customers wait.

2. *Temporary* or *transient:* These elements enter and leave the model during simulation. Customers arrive at random and leave when served. The only constraint is that they can appear only during the time when the barbershop is open. Such elements, called "transactions," are dynamic in character.

It has already been stated that simulation involves the definition and playing of a game of strategy. The following rules apply to the barbershop simulation:

1. Transactions move as far as possible, at any point in time. A customer enters the shop and is served immediately if the barber is free. He then waits for

Figure 2.3 Barbershop.

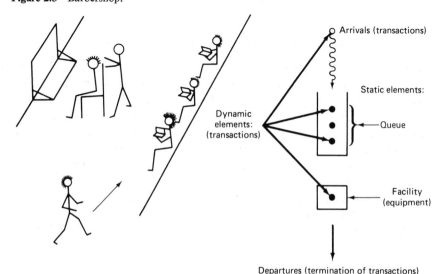

service to be completed. If the barber is busy, the customer waits for service. In both cases the transaction has to wait before moving farther through the model.

2. The barber (facility) can accept one transaction if he is free and will refuse a transaction if he is busy. The facility remains busy throughout the whole period of service. When service is completed, the facility is released and the first waiting transaction, if any, will seize it.

3. Customers queue and are served in arrival order—first come, first served. This is called a first in–first out, or FIFO, queueing discipline.

2.3 Manual Simulation of the Barbershop

To simulate this system, details of the arrival and service time distributions are required. Suppose that information has been gathered about the random variables t_a (interarrival times) and t_s (service times). These are summarized as probability functions in Table 2.2, which defines the two random variables completely. For the sake of simplicity, we have chosen very elementary distributions, but there is no difficulty in using more complicated relationships. The distributions are artificial because all times are expressed in multiples of 5 minutes. Thus time is discontinuous in this model: the clock can only record 5 minute intervals. This simplifying assumption should be justified. In all discrete-event simulation models, the time is advanced by finite steps; it is therefore important to choose a time unit small enough to ensure that nothing critical can occur during a fraction of that time unit.

Table 2.2

Interarrival Time t_a	Probability	Service Time t_s	Probability
5	$\frac{1}{6}$	30	$\frac{1}{6}$
10	$\frac{2}{6}$	20	$\frac{1}{6}$
20	$\frac{3}{6}$	15	$\frac{4}{6}$

We need a device to generate random values for t_a and t_s with the defined probabilities. Since, in this example, all probabilities are given in sixths, let us consider throwing a die. There are six outcomes of throwing a die: 1, 2, 3, 4, 5, and 6, each assumed to be equally likely. We must therefore establish a correspondence between these scores and the values of t_a and t_s to be generated. One possible way is shown in Table 2.3. The probability of obtaining the value 20 for t_a is the same as the probability of scoring 4, 5, or 6 with the die. If the die is unbiased, this probability is $\frac{3}{6}$, which corresponds to the data of the problem.

For the actual simulation it is convenient to devise a worksheet to record the progress of each customer through the barbershop; see Table 2.4. If the shop opens at 8:00, then the simulation starts at 8:00. To bring the first customer into the system,

Table 2.3

	Arrivals				Service		
Die Score	Probability	t_a		Die Score	Probability	t_s	
1	$\frac{1}{6}$	5		1	$\frac{1}{6}$	30	
2	$\frac{1}{6}$	10		2	$\frac{1}{6}$	20	
3	$\frac{1}{6}$	10		3	$\frac{1}{6}$	15	
4	$\frac{1}{6}$	20		4	$\frac{1}{6}$	15	
5	$\frac{1}{6}$	20		5	$\frac{1}{6}$	15	
6	$\frac{1}{6}$	20		6	$\frac{1}{6}$	15	

Table 2.4

Customer Number	Random Number	t_a	Arrival Time	Start Service	Waiting Time	Random Number	t_s	End of Service	Idle Time
1	5	20	8:20	8:20	—	4	15	8:35	20
2	1	5	8:25	8:35	10	1	30	9:05	—
3	4	20	8:45	9:05	20	1	30	9:35	—
4	5	20	9:05	9:35	30	3	15	9:50	—
5	6	20	9:25	9:50	25	5	15	10:05	—

we throw the die and score 5. This implies an interarrival time of 20 minutes; so the customer reaches the shop at 8:20, which means that the barber is idle for 20 minutes. There is no waiting time for this first customer.

The die is then thrown to obtain customer service time using the service-time distribution. The score is 4: therefore, the service time is 15 minutes, and we calculate the end of service time as 8:35. We must also generate the second customer by throwing the die and interpreting the score, using the arrival-time distribution. The score is 1: therefore, the second customer arrives 5 minutes after the first at 8:25, and we see that he must wait 10 minutes for service. Additional customers are introduced and service times calculated in the same way.

Note that it is convenient to work with interarrival times so that a new customer is generated as soon as a customer enters the shop. This overcomes the difficulty, particularly awkward with large models, of having to generate all the transactions for a simulation run before any processing takes place. In our simple example, it is unrealistic because customers cannot arrive simultaneously. The validity of this assumption must be considered when the model is formulated.

Suppose that the simulation ends after 10 customers have been served. From the completed worksheet we can compute statistics of the barbershop operation. These statistics include total idle time for the barber, average waiting time for customers, and average queue length. The worksheet for all 10 customers, including an entry for queue lengths, is given in Table 2.5. The information on the worksheet emphasizes the concept of discrete time. The model can change state only at intervals that are

Table 2.5

Customer Number	Random Number	t_a	Arrival Time	Start Service	Queue Length at Arrival Time	Waiting Time	Random Number	t_s	End of Service	Idle Time
1	5	20	8:20	8:20	0	—	4	15	8:35	20
2	1	5	8:25	8:35	1	10	1	30	9:05	—
3	4	20	8:45	9:05	1	20	1	30	9:35	—
4	5	20	9:05	9:35	1	30	3	15	9:50	—
5	6	20	9:25	9:50	2	25	5	15	10:05	—
6	4	20	9:45	10:05	2	20	4	15	10:20	—
7	6	20	10:05	10:20	1	15	3	15	10:35	—
8	5	20	10:25	10:35	1	10	6	15	10:50	—
9	5	20	10:45	10:50	1	5	5	15	11:05	—
10	4	20	11:05	11:05	0	—	3	15	11:20	—

multiples of 5 minutes. Events such as customer arrival and start and end of service cause a change of state of the model. Therefore, this is an example of discrete-event simulation.

The passage of time is modeled by a simulated clock which can work in one of two modes:

Fixed increment or *variable increment*.

A fixed-increment clock is updated at every time interval and the model examined to see whether an event has occurred.

A variable-increment clock is updated to the time when the next event is due to occur. The organization of the timing routine is more complicated than for the fixed-increment technique but has the advantage that the simulation considers only those times that are relevant to the model. Therefore, it is often more efficient than the fixed-increment timing technique. Most computer simulators, including all versions of GPSS, use the variable clock technique, so we shall not consider the fixed-increment method in further detail.

2.4 Simulation Concepts Used in the Model

In the simple barbershop problem we have introduced several fundamental concepts common to all models. Basic, routine tasks of modeling which should be performed automatically in any computer simulation programming language include:

Clock or timing mechanism: because our models are dynamic, a clock is needed to represent the simulated time. Updating the clock is a tedious task which should be handled automatically by a control program built into the simulator.

Sequencing mechanism: every time that the state of the model changes, an event is said to occur. For each event the appropriate operations must be executed and the time of the next event computed and stored. For instance, in the example, events are of two kinds: (a) *arrival of a customer*, and (b) *end of service*.

Events scheduled for different times are ordered in sequence. If several events are due to occur simultaneously, additional rules are required to handle them. If no action is taken, the simultaneous events will occur in the same order as they were defined, although the simulated clock time will remain constant. This gives the analyst no control over the logic and could lead to inaccurate results.

Stochastic functions: to build stochastic models we must be able to generate random variates, that is, sample values of random variables. As most simulation models are stochastic, it is necessary to be able to introduce random variables into the model in a simple way, using statistical functions as in our example. See Appendix D for a discussion of random-number generating techniques.

Collection of statistics: during simulation the accumulation of statistics about the performance of the system is a vital but largely clerical task. Any simulation program should provide such capabilities automatically. In addition, there should be a simple method to collect any additional statistical data not part of the normal output.

2.5 Presentation of the Model

When we introduced the barbershop problem in Section 2.2, we outlined the logic by a rudimentary flowchart and then examined and logged a small sample of customers on a worksheet.

In the case of more complicated systems the model must be defined in complete detail so that there are no ambiguities. We suggest that it is always advisable to draw a block diagram of the system so as to present the logic graphically. This shows the interactions more clearly than is possible with a verbal description.

Before producing the block diagram we list the variables used in the model:

t = arrival time of the customer

t_a = interarrival time to the next customer

t_s = service time

t_e = end of service time for the customer

N = number of customers served

T_w = cumulative waiting time for customers

T_i = cumulative idle time for the barber

N_{max} = total number of customers to be served

The variables $t, t_a, t_s,$ and t_e take a specific value for each customer in the system; values $N, T_w,$ and T_i describe observations on the whole system.

It is obvious that t_a and t_s, the interarrival time of a customer and his service time, are input to the system and not subject to the organization of the barbershop. They are *exogenous*, or external, variables. However, the variable t_e, end of service time, does depend on the order in which customers are served and therefore is an *endogenous*, or internal, variable of the system. Variables T_w and T_i accumulate information about customer waiting time for service and barber idle time, respectively. In fact T_i can also be considered as barber waiting time for customers.

To illustrate the process of producing the block diagram we show first a simplified form of logic in Figure 2.4, which describes customers entering the barbershop and being served. At this initial stage we have not included the accumulation of statistics

Figure 2.4 Barbershop block diagram without handling of the queue.

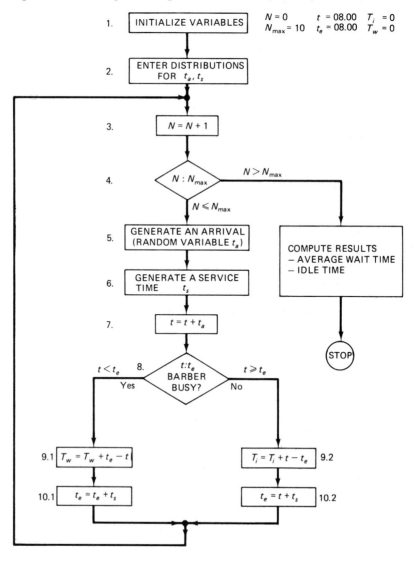

about queues. This is the normal procedure—first to specify the basic structure of the model. It is always possible to make refinements later.

The variables t and t_e are initialized to 8:00 hours, and N, the number of customers served, is set to zero. The counters T_i and T_w are also set to zero. Distributions for t_a and t_s are specified and N_{max}, the total number of customers to be served, is chosen.

Blocks 1 and 2 show this initialization. Blocks 3 and 4 control the customers entering the loop, which describes the processing of one customer. The current variable N, together with the decision at block 8, makes the loop suitable for all customers entering the shop. Block 5 determines the time between successive customers and block 6 specifies the service time for the next customer. Block 7 adds the time interval, t_a, to the arrival time of the previous customer to compute the time of arrival of the next customer. At block 8 this time of arrival, t, is compared with t_e, the time when the barber will become free. If the barber is busy when the customer enters the shop, control passes to block 9.1 and the customer waiting time is accumulated in T_w. If the barber has to wait for a customer, control passes to block 9.2 and idle time is accumulated in T_i. The time t_e, when this customer's service ends, is also calculated.

When the test at block 4 shows that N_{max} customers have been served, control passes to an output block to compute statistics of waiting and idle times.

This model describes a system in which every potential customer enters the shop and waits until he is served. In practice, the number of customers queueing for service should be considered, because the size of the shop will limit the number of people who can wait. Further, customers may decide to leave the shop immediately if the queue is too long, or the barber may refuse to accept more customers if too many people are waiting. Thus a more realistic model includes logic to gather queueing statistics.

The block diagrams of Figures 2.5 and 2.6 incorporate queueing in the basic model without using it to control the response of the model. In both examples customers join a queue as they enter the shop. The difference lies in testing the queue and whether the barber is busy. As before, the total number of customers is limited to N_{max}.

In the first case (Figure 2.5), the logic is similar to the simpler model of Figure 2.4 until the customer enters the queue. If the queue length is unity, we test for barber idle and follow the previous logic to accumulate idle time and calculate the time that service ends. At the end of service, the queue size is reduced by unity. If the barber is busy, the next customer is generated. If the queue length exceeds unity, the last arrival time is compared with the end-of-service time of the current customer. If the customer arrives before end of service, another customer is generated to determine if the next event is a new arrival or end of service. If service ends before customer arrival, the first waiting customer is taken from the queue and his arrival and service times, t' and t_s, respectively, are used to increment the total waiting time and compute a new end of service time, t_e. The queue contents are reduced by unity and a new customer is generated.

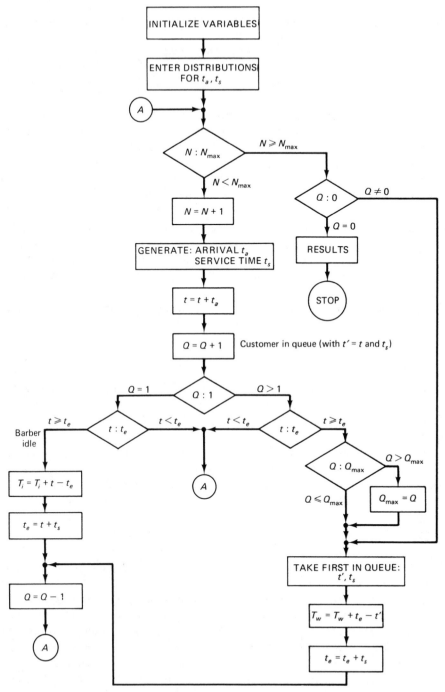

Figure 2.5 Barbershop block diagram with queue handling (first approach).

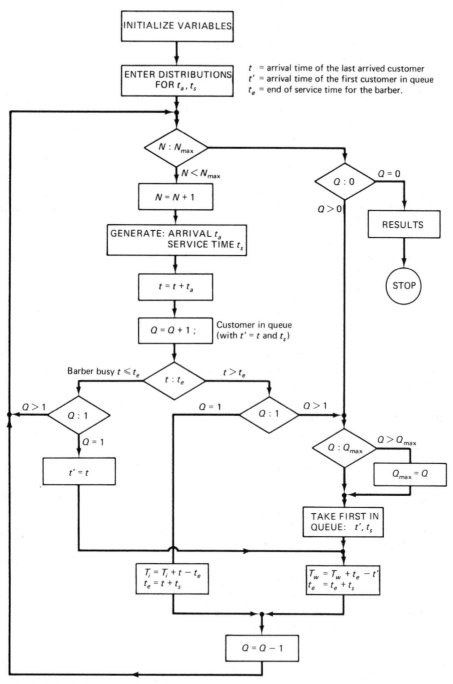

t = arrival time of the last arrived customer
t' = arrival time of the first customer in queue
t_e = end of service time for the barber.

Figure 2.6 Barbershop block diagram with queue handling (second approach).

The main difference in the logic of the second case (Figure 2.6) is that the first test is whether the new customer arrives before or after the end of service. After this test the queue contents are tested and appropriate action is taken.

In each block diagram the logic flow is determined by queue length and the busy or idle state of the barber. Both of these must be examined, but the order of testing is immaterial. This phenomenon is quite common when modeling complex systems. It explains why many apparently different models of a system can be formulated.

2.6 Structure of the Model

A simulation model is specified by its *static description* and its *dynamic behavior*.

The static description consists of all the information required to describe the model completely at a given time. This requires the definition of all components or entities in the model. The entities can be either permanent or temporary. Permanent entities exist throughout the period of simulation: for example, the barber and the shop in the previous example. Temporary entities can be created and destroyed during the simulation: for example, the customers are created when arriving at the barbershop and destroyed when service ends.

The dynamic behavior of a model is described by the succession of states which the model assumes as time varies. It is specified by rules governing the events that are scheduled to occur. An event can be the arrival of an object in the model, the movement of an object from one place to another, the modification of an attribute of an object, and so on. There are two types of event: exogenous, scheduled and caused from outside the model, and endogenous, taking place internally as a consequence of interactions among the variables of the model. The conditions for events to occur are called the *decision rules* of the model. These rules should be exhaustive and consistent; that is, every condition that can occur in the model must be handled logically and unambiguously.

The examples given in this chapter show that the ability to formulate a model is the fundamental requirement of simulation. The labor involved in the manual simulation of a very simple system shows that the method must be automated to make simulation an effective tool for the appraisal of complex projects. It is evident that the procedures outlined in the two examples can be programmed for a digital computer. It has also been shown that many aspects of simulation, such as the accumulation of statistics, timing, queueing, and logical control, are common to all simulation problems. Therefore, specialized simulation programming languages have been developed to simplify the task of formulating and running models. Such languages perform all the routine functions of simulation automatically and allow the operations research worker to concentrate on the basic task of producing a valid model.

3 Organization of a Simulation Study

All simulation studies pass through several phases before completion. In this chapter, we discuss points of planning, design, and implementation which apply to all simulation studies, regardless of the system being modeled. These considerations comprise an "aide-mémoire" for the simulation specialist.

3.1 Problem Formulation

Before attempting to solve a problem, define the system in detail and determine the form of solution required. Although this directive may seem self-evident, it is fundamental to any successful simulation project. An ill-conceived model wastes manpower and computer resources and the task of reformulation wastes time and may delay the project. We stress that time is a resource that must not be wasted by sloppy thinking. If simulation is to be an effective planning tool, it must provide adequate information quickly.

In practice, proper definition of the modeling project will require several detailed discussions between the analyst and management. Such effort is never wasted: it reduces the likelihood of having to redefine the project later. In addition, the analyst should check with management from time to time to confirm that the objectives of the study and the modeling requirements have not altered. Such discussions are a requirement of most operational research studies.

It is vital to define the limits or boundaries of the model clearly. Decide what must be included and what can be ignored. Those aspects of the system excluded from the model must be considered as exogenous, and provision must be made to include their effect, if required, in the external environment as it interfaces with the model.

The importance of selecting boundaries is illustrated by the following actual case. The problem was to design an on-line banking system, consisting of a central computer, with terminals to be installed at the counters. The major requirement, as in all such studies, was for minimum response time, subject to an economical configuration. Particular questions posed included whether separate terminals were needed at each window or whether two adjacent clerks could share a terminal, and whether control units could be shared. The extent of the model had to be decided and two proposals were made:

1. Simulate only the computer system and terminals, or
2. Simulate the whole system, including the banking hall and the customers.

Opinions were divided, until the banking operation was examined in more detail. It was found that the majority of customers were regular users who knew the clerks. A typical transaction would begin with an exchange of greetings, followed by a short conversation. The opening remarks took up to 1 minute, which had to be included in the calculation of total customer transaction time. This simple study of banking habits demonstrated the enormous difference between practical times, over which no control was possible, and the computer response, which had to be minimized. It was obviously ridiculous to increase total systems cost to save a fraction of a second when customer processing time was of the order of 1 or 2 minutes. The problem was reformulated to reflect these findings and the recommendation resulting from the simulation study was accepted unanimously.

When the scope of the model has been decided, it is necessary to specify initial conditions to start the simulation and to determine how conditions at the boundary vary with time. In the case of the banking model, the door could be considered as the limit of the model. The boundary conditions would specify customer arrivals as a function of time, which would include the status of the door implicitly, by terminating arrivals for those times when the bank is closed.

The initial status of the model requires careful specification. Most simulations start with an empty system; this is sometimes referred to as a *cold start*. As units of traffic, temporary entities, enter the model according to interarrival functions, which are defined by the user, the system gradually warms up. Statistics obtained during this initial period of simulation do not provide an adequate guide to normal operation of the system because the model is not subject to all the interactions present in a busy system. Determination of the time when the model has reached a steady state comparable with busy system operation is not easy. In most cases the analyst will have to make several preliminary trials. During this phase it is advisable to store the model in the form that it reached at the end of a given run. Then, when the analysis of accumulated results shows that the simulation run was too short, it is easy to continue from the point where it was stopped, instead of starting again from the beginning. This requires the ability to reload the program in the same form as it was stored at the end of the previous run, and then restarting.

Problem definition also includes a statement of results required and the form in which such results should be presented. For example, a queueing problem could yield information about the average waiting time in the queues or the average length of the queues. A different requirement, which is more difficult to meet, is to find the standard deviation of the variables or to produce their distribution in tabular form. One might also wish to obtain global results accumulated over the whole time of simulation or intermediate results, known as snapshots, to determine the dynamic response of the model.

Remember also that because it is usually easier to delete portions of a program than to add new portions, always plan the model in a flexible manner so as to make modifications easy to implement.

3.2 Choice of Method

After having defined the problem in suitable detail, we must analyze it and select the type of mathematical tools appropriate to its study. If a mathematical method is available, it should normally be used, but if no analytical tool can be found, we can use simulation. However, the decision should not be made before all the appropriate, existing, operations research tools have been found unsuitable. Simulation is often a popular tool with management because the clearly demonstrable logic of a block diagram can be followed, whereas a sophisticated mathematical technique may be incomprehensible to the layman. This is not a justifiable reason for using the simulation approach and should be resisted, particularly if the analytical solution is quick and cheap.

3.3 Variables to be Included in the Model

Prior to the actual formulation of the model the analyst must decide which variables or parameters of the real system should be included and which ones can be neglected. The choice is not easy. Look at the problem as a whole and try to rank variables and constraints according to importance. During the preliminary discussions with management (Section 3.1), the analyst should obtain opinions of system specialists to confirm this ranking. Do not reject any variable from the model until it is established that there are no cases where its presence is important to the study. A decision to omit a vital variable can cause serious reprogramming problems when the mistake is discovered; the decision to suppress a superfluous variable later in the study involves much less effort. The optimal selection of variables depends largely on in-depth knowledge of the mechanics of the system, experience, and intuition. The analyst must avoid oversimplification, which can result in a trivial model, and overspecification, which can lead to inefficiency and intractability.

Variables may be classified in several ways. For example, one may distinguish between endogenous variables and exogenous variables. As noted previously, the latter are variables that can be considered as input to the model; they reflect the external behavior of the model. The endogenous variables are internal to the model. In the barbershop model of Chapter 2, the interarrival times and the service times were exogenous variables; the customer waiting time and the barber's idle time were endogenous variables.

Variables may also be classified as either quantitative or qualitative. Qualitative variables are generally subjective variables, such as preference. They are difficult to quantify, and in such cases it is best to get as much specific information as possible from the people involved with the problem. Such questions as "Under certain conditions, what would be the preference between alternatives A and B?" are posed to several people and a resulting function constructed. Curves that plot the utility attached to money under risk (or the risk aversion) are established in the same way when simulating decision-making situations (consult [3.1], for example).

A final distinction may be made between directly measurable variables and indirectly measurable ones. The difference is obvious, but it should be noted that, in a model, all variables are measurable. This is an advantage of simulation over direct experimentation. Any variable of the model can be displayed and may therefore be considered as a response of the model during simulation.

3.4   Collection and Analysis of System Data

Data collection is very time-consuming and costly, consequently due care must be taken to organize surveys efficiently. Most discrete simulation models are stochastic, so we have to introduce random variables into our simulation experiments. This means that either the probability density or the cumulative distribution function must be available in mathematical or tabular form. Many data must be accumulated so that the problem is not trivial. Experience shows that for complex problems data collection can take months, or even years. See, for example, J. G. Taylor, J. A. Navarro, and R. H. Cohen, "Simulation Applied to a Court System" [1.1].

During data collection all available classical statistical tools may be required to transform recorded data into a form suitable for the simulation study. The techniques may include regression analysis, confidence interval estimation, analysis of time series, and analysis of variance. The quality of data must be checked thoroughly because it will affect the validity of the simulation output. Statistical tests should be used to screen the data and identify flaws in the survey procedure.

To remove the possibility of unconscious bias in the statistical surveys, try to ensure that the observers are not subjectively involved. Asking an employee to report on his own performance is unlikely to yield an unbiased observation. It is also very important to be tactful when gathering statistics of other people's performance at work; otherwise, the objective of the survey may be misconstrued and resistance to the observers will result in the collection of inaccurate data. Explain why the survey is being made, how the data will be used, and invite the employees to suggest how the survey can be organized so that it will not disrupt normal working. Unnecessary secrecy will breed distrust and a fear of redundancies. Sometimes, the problem must

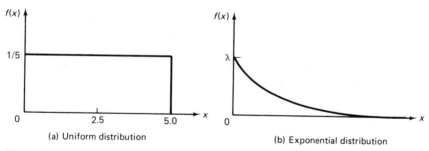

Figure 3.1

be studied using existing data. In such cases, there is no chance of organizing a new measuring campaign, and this is where intuition or experience is necessary.

For example, suppose that in a teleprocessing problem we are told that the average time between arriving requests is 2.5 seconds. If this is the only information available, we have to make further assumptions about the distribution of the random variable that describes the interarrival times, and we could choose any distribution. Two possible assumptions are:

Uniform distribution: we assume that interarrival times are equally distributed over the range 0 to 5 seconds. We would then have the probability function of Figure 3.1(a).

Poisson distribution: gives exponential interarrival times [see Figure 3.1(b)]. This assumption might be made because we have prior knowledge of similar problems and have observed Poisson distributions in several situations, such as customers at banks, vehicles at given points, telephone calls in networks, and orders for factories.

If there is no obvious choice of distribution, it is advisable to make two simulation runs to see whether the actual form of the distribution is critical to the response of the model. This type of situation emphasizes the dynamic character of any modeling effort; we are unable to specify the final form of the model until a pilot model is working. It is well known in queueing theory that the exponential case is more critical than the uniform distribution. When the output is very sensitive to the type of distribution, it is vital to request more accurate information; this may necessitate a new survey.

The saying "Garbage in–Garbage out," or GIGO, is not unique to simulation but it emphasizes the point that meaningful results can be expected only when the input is valid. The time spent validating the input data is necessary and justifiable.

3.5 Defining the Structure of a Model

Several features of a model contribute to its structure. First in importance are, of course, all the components, or entities, and their attributes. These entities are logically connected by mathematical or statistical relationships, which are an intrinsic part of the model. As noted earlier, such relationships are sometimes called decision rules, because they define the conditions under which the model changes its status. Changes of status are produced by events which, as we have previously seen, can be either exogenous or endogenous. In addition, relationships between elements of the model can be time-dependent or time-independent. In the simple barbershop model (Chapter 2), the arrival and service times are examples of time-independent variables. If arrival rates were to vary during the day, the variables would be time-dependent. Although time-dependent variables can easily be introduced into a simulation model, they may complicate mathematical analysis sufficiently to make a theoretical treatment extremely difficult.

Great care must be taken when designing and building the model; in particular, it should be as flexible as possible so that later modifications and extensions can be made with ease. All possible variations should be taken into account from the start. Even if not programmed, their possible inclusion in the model should be planned and necessary entry points provided. Adding to a piece of code where the linkage had been foreseen is much simpler than making additions to a closed program. In the latter case, side effects of unplanned modification are extremely difficult to anticipate.

3.6 Documentation: Programming the Model

Once the model is developed, it is time to write the computer program. Although the form of model will probably depend, to some extent, on the features of the simulation language used, the basic design of the model should be produced before programming starts. With a suitable language the programming should be a mainly clerical task of defining model components in a suitable form for the computer.

We believe it essential to prepare a good flowchart or block diagram of the model. This is a basic piece of documentation which aids programming and explains the model graphically for people who may wish to use it later. The time used in detailed analysis to produce the flowchart is well spent; most of the problems of logic will have been resolved before coding begins.

The model is coded using a *programming language*. The choice must be made between a general-purpose language and a specialized simulation language. The advantages of specialized simulation languages were discussed earlier. For a further illustration of the question the reader is referred to [3.2], where, in Chapter 10, a comparison is made between the use of Fortran and of GPSS for the simulation of a computer system. With GPSS/360, programming and debugging time was 15 per cent of that required with Fortran. The corresponding machine time used for compiling and simulation was 32 per cent. Such results are not atypical.

One argument sometimes made against simulation languages, however, especially by experienced programmers, is that they lack flexibility. Clearly a high-level language with very powerful commands allows the user to modify the model extensively with few instructions. But if one needs a language with the ability to make highly selective and detailed modifications to a model, a high-level language may not be sufficiently flexible. On the whole, however, we believe that such arguments tend to be academic rather than practical and that the most important requirement today is overall efficiency. The saving of manpower and reduction of total project time usually justify the use of a simulation language. The use of a language tailored to the general requirements of simulation also simplifies the task of documentation. The historical argument of increased computer running time is no longer economically acceptable as computers become faster and cheaper and the cost of skilled professional analysts continues to rise.

Error checking and debugging are two other important factors which affect the choice of simulation language. The availability of good error-checking features can significantly reduce the total time needed for developing a simulation model. In GPSS, for example, excellent diagnostics at the source language level, at compile time, and during the simulation allow the user to debug programs quickly. Such tools do not exist generally in high-level languages, a further burden on the programmer. During the debugging phase, it is necessary to decide when the model works satisfactorily; this is the verification phase. Debugging any computer program is a complicated and tedious process even when the problem is deterministic. Debugging a simulation program is much more difficult, especially when programming stochastic models. The verification of such models should be planned systematically so that the probability that it will run correctly is high.

In particular, we believe it extremely important to anticipate the order of magnitude of the results before they are produced by the computer. To illustrate the point, suppose that our program simulates a simple queueing system and that, after a few debugging runs, we believe that it operates correctly. As we submit the first case to be explored, we want to know the average waiting time of the transactions in a specific queue. The result is 152.6. Is this result valid? Being human, we are going to try to convince ourselves that this result is plausible. However, if we make a crude estimate of the order of magnitude of the result before making the simulation run we will have a means to appraise the output. Suppose that the calculation indicates that the result should lie in the range 200 to 300. When we get the result 152.6, we are forced to explain the discrepancy. Either we made an error in our evaluation of the range or our program does not operate correctly. Following this approach guarantees a higher chance of finding errors in programs. Our experience in teaching simulation has confirmed this conclusion.

The dynamic nature of simulation models is one of the reasons why they are difficult to debug. Whenever exceptional conditions are observed, it is necessary to have details of the system status to account for the behavior of the model. All simulation languages should include easily programmed features to print system status and other model statistics on demand. If execution is terminated because of a severe error, such output should be supplied automatically.

To identify obscure errors it may sometimes be necessary to trace the operation of a model step-by-step through each event and print relevant details whenever the status changes. This tracing facility must be provided by the simulation language because it would be impracticable for the user to implement it. However, a trace feature should be used with caution because it requires considerable computer time and can produce a vast quantity of output, most of which is unnecessary. A good tracing feature can be started and stopped anywhere in the program and at any time during the execution, so that this detailed study can be limited to suspect portions of the code.

Generation of random data or random variates in stochastic models should be automatic. This presupposes the availability of at least one random-number generator. An important factor in the choice of simulation language is the ease of specifying statistical distributions.

Finally, the production of the output report also depends on the features available in the language chosen. Some have no features at all and others automatically produce a complete report and also give the user options to suppress data, modify the layout, produce special tables, and plot results in graphical form. An interesting article on this subject was published in 1966 by P. J. Kiviat [3.3].

3.7 Validation of the Model

Verification of the model involves checking that the written program performs as expected. Validation requires proof that the model accurately represents the system to be simulated. This is a very difficult problem from the philosophical point of view. If we say that the model is correct or valid, it should mean that we are confident that it is a true representation of the real problem; but it is obvious that (1) we can never be absolutely certain, and (2) no model, however sophisticated, can be the true representation of the real world. As usual in such intractable situations, we must seek a compromise. We try to obtain the highest level of confidence possible, consistent with the resources available for validation.

Although we cannot define general rules for model validation, the following points should always be considered:

Statistical analysis of the output variables: the variables we observe are random. The properties of the samples we obtain from replicated simulation runs, with constant input and different random-number sequences, give valuable information. If we observe large variances, we will tend to have less confidence in the results and possibly in the model than if all results are fairly consistent and the variances small.

Simplifying the model: a complicated model is difficult to handle; therefore, attempt to simplify or reduce the size of the model. For example, replace the random variables by constants or known functions in order to produce a model that can either be analyzed mathematically or be bracketed between two cases that can be solved analytically. Although this approach tends to be more theoretical than practical because in models of real systems such a procedure is often impossible, the technique can help to produce crude bounds that the analyst can use to estimate the stability of observations.

Simulation of known situations: when the model is developed to simulate an existing system, it is always possible to simulate a known past situation. In this case, actual observations are available and the simulation results can be compared with them. They should be reasonably consistent. If the results do not agree, the model should be modified.

Submodel validation: test every subset of the whole model which can be tested independently. Even in nonexistent systems, parts of the model will consist of known entities that should be tested separately. This reduces the danger of aggregating invalid elements.

Sensitivity analysis: change the input variables slightly and observe the behavior of the output variables. By such experiments we determine the effect of components on total-system response. Some variables will have little effect on the behavior of the model and others may appear to be critical. The latter should be investigated carefully because they could indicate inherent instability in the model. If small variations in the input produce wildly fluctuating output, we must refer back to the real system. If the observations cannot be explained logically, the variance of the output variables should be computed for use as a guide.

Mathematical analysis: we have stressed the point that simulation should never be used alone. Every opportunity to analyze parts of the model mathematically should be taken. Very often it is necessary to make simplifying assumptions in order to compute values of internal or external variables. These calculations will be compared with the results of the simulation. The depth of the theoretical analysis will be decided dynamically, depending on the information gathered during model building and testing. Validation cannot be considered as a one-step procedure; it is a progressive activity in which every stage is planned according to the level of validation reached and degree of confidence we have in the model.

From these remarks it is obvious that validation of a complicated stochastic model is a major task. In simulation projects, it is quite normal to find that the resources required for planning, building, and validating the model exceed the cost of the computer time used in production simulation runs.

3.8 Simulation

When we are reasonably confident that the model is a valid representation of the real system and that the computer program will execute successfully, simulation runs can begin. Each computer run is a statistical experiment that is time-consuming, for two reasons. First, there is a wait for computer output, and, second, there is the time required to analyze that output. We have already stated that time is a fundamental resource that may be limited by the schedule for the overall project; it is thus vital to plan the simulation experiments to obtain information efficiently.

The objective of the study is, of course, to understand and predict the behavior of a real system, particularly the variation in response when modifications are made either to the input or to the decision rules. The simulation results are then used to optimize system performance. The requirements of optimization depend on the system being modeled and are usually intended to improve some aspect of overall performance. For example, when examining different queueing disciplines, the objective may be to reduce total queueing time, to minimize the total number of servers, or to find the best compromise between both objectives (in most cases an improvement in one aspect of operation will cause deterioration in others). When trying to select the optimum red–green phases for traffic lights, the objective may be to minimize average waiting time for all vehicles; the solution could make some vehicles wait for a much longer time than if the objective were different.

In general, there are numerous parameters in the model, each of which may take a range of values. To examine all combinations of all parameters is prohibitive because of the number of cases involved. Suppose, for instance, that we have 3 factors, each of which can take 10 values. Simulations of all 1000 cases would require 1000 computer runs and 1000 analyses. A more efficient approach would be to select from the 1000 cases the sample runs with the highest probability of producing the optimum situation. All the information available about the problem, intuition, and common sense are required to make this selection. We must remember that we can obtain the predicted response of the system only for those cases that we simulate. An intelligent selection will improve the chances of finding the true optimum. During production runs always allow time for appraisal and analysis so that future runs are planned to make the best use of computing resources. For example, preliminary studies may indicate that the optimum value of a parameter lies in the range 10 to 80. There is a great temptation to perform a series of simulation experiments with the parameter indexed at small intervals, say 1 or 5, throughout the range. This is a sure way to waste computer time and generate superfluous information. With a little extra thought it should be possible to define the range more accurately and thus concentrate on a few experiments where the values should be close to optimum. To do this we use all the information at our disposal, particularly that obtained from the most recent runs. Thus planning further simulation runs is a dynamic process.

For every experiment it is necessary to define the length of time to be simulated. This is important because too short a run will lead to uncertain results and too long a run would waste computer time. This is another optimization problem. When seeking this optimum we should always save the model in its current state at the end of a run. This allows us to resume simulation from the state reached. Determination of the length of simulation depends on factors such as type of results sought, confidence interval requirements, and stability of the model.

It is possible to include tests in a simulation program so that the run will end when a specified condition occurs. In practice, this technique is seldom used, except to terminate execution when a logical error is detected. The reason is that most models are complex, so that many conditions should be tested simultaneously. In general, the extra programming effort and the additional computer running time cannot be justified.

Most simulation models have no built-in optimizing procedures. There are two major reasons for this. First, the output from a run of a stochastic model is just one statistical sample; because other runs would yield different results, many runs would have to be made to find the response distribution. Attempts to reduce computer time by making a sequence of runs starting each new run from where the last one ended are unsatisfactory because the output would be highly autocorrelated. Second, optimization is a compromise involving many parameters of the system. As in the case of programmed termination the effort required to implement optimization is not justifiable.

3.9 Analysis and Critique of Results

Since the technique of simulation involves such subjective approaches as abstraction, intuition, and projection, results must be thoroughly analyzed and justified before a report can be submitted to management. The problems involved in this analysis are delineated in Chapter 8 of reference [3.2]. We present here the two primary objectives of the analysis of simulation results: (1) to decide if the information obtained from the simulation experiments is sufficient, and (2) to reduce, summarize, and present the data as a decision-making aid for management.

Under point (1) we might want to explore new alternatives, such as changes in the model structure and/or parameter values to gauge their effect. We might want to investigate apparently important cases in greater depth, either because there is insufficient information or because the confidence intervals are too large. (We discuss the determination of confidence intervals in Chapter 14.)

3.10 Summary

The steps described in the previous sections are summarized as a block diagram in Figure 3.2, which is similar to Figure 1.4. The details have been discussed at length for the simulation specialist. We have saved two vital points for this final section because they may be overlooked.

The first point is communication with management. After a long, complicated study the analyst knows the problem so well that he believes it to be simple. He is sometimes unable to realize that others cannot follow his presentation. However, if you do not convince management that your recommendations are sound, your whole modeling project will have failed. To circumvent such an unhappy result, examine your entire report in detail: Does it describe the problem and technique clearly and adequately? Is it free from unnecessary jargon? Are the results pertinent and understandable? Are your recommendations precise and feasible? When you are satisfied that the report is perfect, show it to a colleague who is unacquainted with the problem —preferably not a simulation specialist—and ask for his candid opinion. You will not like his answer, but, as you redraft your presentation, console yourself with the thought that it has a much better chance of being accepted.

The second point is that if your findings are approved, the study has just begun. A good model should be maintained as a practical tool for decision makers throughout

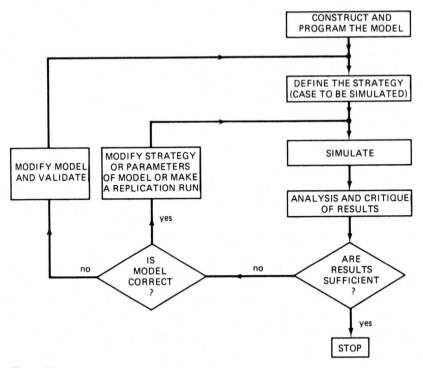

Figure 3.2

the life of the system. This is when the value of the initial planning for future extensions and modifications and the effort spent on good documentation really becomes apparent.

References

3.1. D. LINDLEY, *Making Decisions*, Wiley–Interscience, New York, 1971.

3.2. J. R. EMSHOFF and R. L. SISSON, *Design and Use of Computer Simulation Models*, Macmillan, New York, 1970.

3.3. P. J. KIVIAT, *Simulation Language Report Generators*, Rand Corporation, Santa Monica, Calif., 1966.

4 Basic Concepts of GPSS

GPSS has evolved steadily over several years and now contains features not contemplated in its early releases. This fact alone is an indication of the flexibility and durability of the language. Although earlier models are certainly useful, their scope is, of course, somewhat limited. Most simulation models do not use all of the capabilities of GPSS V, therefore useful simulation can be accomplished with a subset of GPSS V instructions.

The instructions of GPSS are called *blocks* because they are associated with the blocks of the flowchart of the model. An entity referenced in a block operation is identified either by a reference number or a *label*, which is the name that the programmer assigns to that entity.

4.1 Model Representation

See Figure 4.1.

4.2 Logical Level

The elements or entities with their attributes define the static structure of the model, which is the complete status at any given time. We can consider these entities as being created when required by the program. In fact GPSS implements such creation by activating the entity from a predefined collection of elements available to the programmer.

Permanent entities are created by GPSS when first referenced in the program. For example, when GPSS encounters a block SEIZE X, where X is either a label or

43

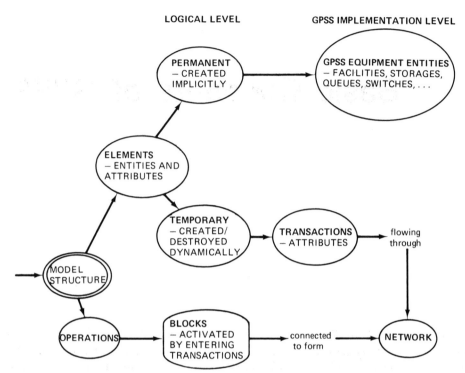

Figure 4.1 In earlier chapters we saw that a simulation model consists of an assemblage of basic elements with a set of operating rules. This figure shows the connection between this model structure and the block diagramming philosophy and terminology of the GPSS language.

a reference number, a corresponding FACILITY is created automatically if the referenced entity does not exist. When the program is submitted to the computer, there is an assembly phase, during which the code is checked for obvious errors and transformed into a suitable form for execution, and permanent entities are created implicitly.

Temporary entities are created when required by the simulation during program execution. These entities, called transactions, are created by the blocks GENERATE, SPLIT, and JOBTAPE. The movement of transactions through the network of blocks is controlled by the operations of the blocks used. The operations of blocks define the dynamic behavior of the model.

Some attributes are automatically defined and updated by the GPSS simulator, whereas others can be specified and controlled by the user. All the statistical attributes of permanent entities are collected automatically, which releases the user from much tedious programming effort. GPSS also allows the user to gather additional statistics about permanent entities if required. This fundamental flexibility ensures that some statistics are always supplied and that there are extensive capabilities to amplify the level of detail.

EXAMPLES OF ATTRIBUTES:

(1)   Permanent entity: STORAGE

This entity provides a service that can handle several transactions simultaneously. A storage is typified by its capacity, a user-defined attribute. GPSS defines and computes such statistical attributes as current contents, remaining available capacity, average utilization, maximum contents, and average time that each transaction used storage. The values of these attributes can be referenced by the user to control the logic of the simulation program.

(2)   Temporary entity: TRANSACTION

Transaction attributes assigned by GPSS include internal number, MARK or creation time, block departure time (BDT), current block number, next block address (NBA), and several indicators. The attributes are used to control movement of the transaction efficiently and to provide the user with information about transaction statistics. The user can specify further attributes such as priority, parameters, and membership of a group. Note that, although these attributes are present in the model, some of them are internal to GPSS and cannot be referenced by the user during program execution. However, they can be displayed, together with all the other information, in the status printout, to help the user to understand the model status and to ease the task of program debugging. The status printout is a list of all the temporary entities and their attributes, which gives a complete description of the model status at the time produced. It is supplied automatically when an execution error causes an abnormal end of job, to help the user to identify the error and make appropriate corrections.

4.3 GPSS Implementation Level

A GPSS program consists of blocks logically interconnected to form a network. Every block performs a given function on permanent or temporary entities. Blocks are the instructions of the GPSS language. The activation of a block and the execution of a GPSS instruction (or of an event) are caused by the arrival of a transaction at the block. An exception is the first transaction, created by the GENERATE block (or by a JOBTAPE). In this particular case GPSS has to create a transaction before anything can move through the model. This creation constitutes the first exogenous event to be scheduled and must take place at the proper time. Subsequently, all blocks operate in the standard way by executing the appropriate function whenever activated by a transaction. The movement of transactions from one block to the next is controlled and executed automatically by the simulator. The user needs no deep knowledge of this aspect of the simulation unless he needs to modify the standard processing. When a transaction enters a TERMINATE block, it is destroyed and references to it are removed from the model.

As previously mentioned, the status of the model is modified by events. As transactions move from one block to the next, attributes of either permanent or temporary entities may be changed. As such changes can involve calculations, the simulator must include computational features. GPSS includes these capabilities in the block operations to avoid the necessity of calling computational subroutines. For example, reference to a permanent entity can be made by using a specific number or by using the value of a variable, which might be a complicated expression. The variable must be defined in the program, but its value is computed automatically during simulation when the entity is referenced by the arrival of a transaction at a block. Practically all blocks can use such computational expressions. The language supplies VARIABLEs, FUNCTIONs, and random-number generators (RNs) as computational entities. A variable may be arithmetic (fixed or floating point) or a Boolean expression.

FUNCTIONs can be discrete or continuous and may have numeric or attribute arguments. They provide a simple method for including experimental and statistical data in the model. By using inverse cumulative distribution functions the analyst can also specify random variates.

Many values calculated during the course of simulation apply only to a particular transaction; these are stored with the transaction in a transaction parameter. Other information may be system-wide and would be stored in a word of storage called a *savevalue* to be available for all transactions. To illustrate this point, consider the number of hours worked in a factory: if a workman is represented by a transaction, his total working hours would be accumulated in a transaction parameter; but total hours worked in the factory would be stored in a savevalue. The purpose of the two attributes is similar but their scope is different.

Savevalue contents are modified by a SAVEVALUE block. To avoid possible confusion between the attribute and the block we shall adopt the convention of referring to savevalue attributes as "saves." (Some books use the term "savex" because the GPSS symbol for a savevalue is X.) In many models it is necessary to consider sequences or arrays of saves. To simplify the task of referencing elements of storage in such cases, matrix saves allow the user to specify arrays of up to two dimensions. These arrays actually allow three levels of indexing: row, column, and array number.

4.4   GPSS Permanent Entities

In this section we list and briefly describe the permanent entities of the language. Blocks available only in GPSS V are noted. Although the list appears to be short, the user will find that it is sufficiently powerful to model very complex systems. The GATE blocks mentioned test the status of certain entities and can be used either to block or to branch transactions.

FACILITY	An entity that can accept only one transaction at a time; it can be used to model single server components of a system.
Examples:	Gasoline pump at a service station; machine tool producing single items; bank cashier; and telephone handset.
Associated blocks:	SEIZE, RELEASE, PREEMPT, RETURN, and GATE; GPSS V also has FAVAIL and FUNAVAIL.

STORAGE	An entity that will accommodate several transactions; a storage is characterized by its capacity, which is user-defined.
Examples:	Parking lot or marshaling yard; buffer storage in a computer; capacity of a hotel or theater; shelves in a supermarket.
Associated blocks:	ENTER, LEAVE, and GATE; GPSS V also has SAVAIL and SUNAVAIL.
LOGIC SWITCH	An indicator that can be set (on), reset (off), or inverted (flip-flop).
Examples:	Traffic signal; railway points for train routing; starting and stopping subsystem operations.
Associated blocks:	LOGIC and GATE.
QUEUE	A statistics-gathering entity that can accept any number of transactions. It is used to record the time that a transaction waits for a service or condition. The transaction can be physically delayed, as at the checkout of a supermarket, or it may proceed through the model, as in the case of waiting for a library book to become available.
Examples:	Customers waiting for service in a bank; jobs waiting for computer processing; standby flight list—transaction not delayed.
Associated blocks:	QUEUE and DEPART.
USER CHAIN	An entity that can accept any number of transactions that are inactivated when linked to the chain. This is a very powerful GPSS feature which has many uses. First, it can speed up program execution by accepting delayed (queueing) transactions, which are not processed again until unlinked. Second, it can be used to reorganize the queue regardless of the time when linked. It provides the user with a tool to override the normal GPSS sequence of operations to model special conditions.
Examples:	Any queue involving a physical delay.
Associated blocks:	LINK and UNLINK.
GROUP	A set entity whose members, which can be either transactions or numerical values, are identified by a common attribute. Members of the group can be manipulated singly or as sets.
Examples:	Vacant versus occupied hotel rooms; salesmen in a region.
Associated blocks:	JOIN, REMOVE, EXAMINE, SCAN, and ALTER.

4.5 GPSS Temporary Entities

Transactions, the units of traffic previously mentioned, are the temporary entities of GPSS. They are created by GENERATE blocks and destroyed by TERMINATE blocks. After generation, a transaction enters the next sequential block and then moves through the network of blocks, in zero simulated time, until delayed by one of the following conditions:

1. Time delay imposed by an ADVANCE block (for instance, service time in a facility).
2. Entry into the next block refused (for example, logical condition not met).
3. Deactivation of the transaction (linkage to a user chain).
4. Destruction of the transaction (TERMINATE block).

Transactions can be SPLIT to form an *assembly set* and subsequently gathered, assembled, or matched. This feature is very useful for modeling a system in which a process divides into a number of simultaneous suboperations which must be kept in phase.

The permanent and temporary entities discussed in this chapter, together with the blocks, events, and other system features, depend on computer storage. At this stage the reader does not need to know the mechanism by which they are made available. They are activated automatically by GPSS from a collection of entities specified in the program job-control cards. The user can alter the maximum number of entities in a particular model by means of a REALLOCATE card.

4.6 GPSS Events

When transactions move through the block diagram, the system state alters. This change of state is an event. Thus events are implicitly part of the dynamic function of transactions. To control the logical sequence of simulation GPSS arranges transactions in chains that are ordered lists. Several different types of chain are available to model a variety of situations but the following two, which are automatically defined and maintained, are part of every GPSS program:

1. The current-events chain.
2. The future-events chain.

Transactions in the current-events chain are ready to move as soon as the condition that has stopped them is removed. The future-events chain contains transactions that are due to move at some future time. The transaction attribute used for this purpose is block departure time (BDT). This is the time when the transaction is scheduled to move if not prevented by a logical condition.

If the current clock time is C1, the chains will contain:

1. Current-events chain: transactions with $BDT \leq C1$.
2. Future-events chain: transactions with $BDT > C1$.

Other transaction attributes containing information to define the event include current block location of the transaction, next block address (NBA), and priority.

During simulation, events must be executed chronologically, so the chains are maintained in ascending order of BDT. The future-events chain is organized in this manner. The current-events chain performs an additional task when different transaction priorities are used. As transactions join the current-events chain, those with highest priority are placed ahead of lower-priority transactions. Within any priority class the order is by ascending BDT.

To execute events the current-events chain is scanned to determine whether a transaction can move. If so, it moves as far as possible until stopped by one of the conditions specified in Section 4.5. If the transaction is unable to move, the scan continues. When a transaction moves, it may alter the status of the model and allow previously stopped transactions to continue. Therefore, when model status alters, GPSS restarts scanning the current-events chain. This process continues, at the specified clock time, until either the current-events chain is empty or no remaining member can move. At this stage the clock is updated to the next event and all transactions with that BDT are transferred from the future-events chain to the current-events chain.

4.7 GPSS Blocks

When activated by a transaction, most GPSS blocks perform several tasks on the entities of the model. Each block is a small subroutine or macro instruction. In this section we list the blocks under six headings and briefly comment on their use in modeling.

4.7.1 Dynamic operations

Creation and destruction of transactions. This topic was previously mentioned in Section 4.5. The GENERATE/TERMINATE instructions are complementary and the JOBTAPE provides the means to introduce a predefined transaction stream into the model. The SPLIT/ASSEMBLE pair are also complementary. SPLIT forms an assembly set of the master transaction and a specified number of twins. ASSEMBLE collects transactions of the same assembly set and destroys all but the first one arriving at the ASSEMBLE block.

Modification of permanent entity status. SEIZE/RELEASE and PREEMPT/RETURN are complementary pairs for use with facilities. Seized facilities can be preempted, and preempted facilities can also be preempted on priority. Both these instructions also test status to verify that the operation can be performed before allowing entry to the transaction.

ENTER/LEAVE is a complementary pair for use with storages. The ENTER block can also refuse a transaction if storage is full.

QUEUE/DEPART are for use with queue entities. They never refuse entry to transactions.

JOIN/REMOVE are a complementary pair used to modify the membership of a group.

4.7.2   Explicit handling of attributes

Transaction attributes: MARK, PRIORITY, ASSIGN.   The creation time of a transaction is recorded in the mark attribute. Whenever a transaction enters a MARK block, the current clock time replaces the existing mark time. Transaction priority can be set at creation time and may be modified at any time during simulation by the PRIORITY block. ASSIGN is used to change the values of transaction parameters.

Logic switch status: LOGIC S, LOGIC R, LOGIC I.   The status of the logic switch introduced in Section 4.4 can be modified by the above instructions.

System attributes: SAVEVALUE/MSAVEVALUE.   These entities were introduced at the end of Section 4.3. Although saves and matrix saves are system-wide, their contents can be modified only when a transaction enters a SAVEVALUE or MSAVEVALUE block.

4.7.3   Delays to transactions

Planned delays.   The ADVANCE block is used to delay a transaction for a specified time. It can be used to simulate service time or process time and never refuses entry to a transaction. On entry to an ADVANCE block the time is evaluated and added to current clock time to compute block departure time, and the transaction is placed on the future-events chain.

Delays caused by model interactions.   GATE blocks, which test entity status, and TEST blocks, which test arithmetic or logical condition, can operate in refusal mode to delay a transaction until specific conditions exist. SEIZE, PREEMPT, and ENTER blocks can also delay transactions. Some forms of the TRANSFER block can also make transactions wait.

4.7.4   Transaction-flow modification

Transactions normally move in sequence from one block to the next. It is often necessary to change this order when the model offers a choice of strategies or for programming convenience.

The TRANSFER block offers several alternative methods of branching control, including:

Unconditional: a standard branch instruction.

Statistical: a two-way branch sending a randomized proportion of transactions to each location.

BOTH: tries to branch to locations 1 and 2 in that order and delays the transaction if neither branch can be made.

ALL: generalization of BOTH to more than two alternatives.

SBR: branch to a GPSS subroutine.

FN: branch on a function value.

P: branch on a parameter value.

GATE and TEST blocks can also specify an address to which transactions are routed if the condition tested is not met.

LOOP is used to send transactions several times through a sequence of blocks. The loop counter, contained in a transaction parameter of the looping transaction, is decreased by unity at each loop. When reduced to zero, the looping sequence terminates.

The LINK block tries to send a transaction to a specified address. If the transfer is not possible, the transaction is linked to a specified user chain. It is also possible to specify unconditional linkage.

When the current transaction enters an UNLINK block, an attempt is made to reactivate and remove one or more transactions from the user chain.

The following blocks can also include branching on condition: SPLIT, PREEMPT, SELECT, REMOVE, EXAMINE, SCAN, ALTER, and, in GPSS V, FUNAVAIL and SUNAVAIL.

4.7.5 Synchronization of transactions and interactions between transactions

Of same assembly set: MATCH, GATHER, ASSEMBLE. MATCH makes a transaction wait until another transaction of the same assembly set reaches the conjugate MATCH block. This feature is valuable when simulating parallel processes.

GATHER has a similar function but keeps all transactions waiting at the same block until a specified number arrive.

When matching or gathering conditions are met, the transactions proceed through the block network.

ASSEMBLE is similar to GATHER, but all transactions arriving after the first are destroyed. Care must be taken to ensure that this first transaction is the one required.

Independent of each other: UNLINK, SCAN, ALTER. UNLINK has been defined briefly above.

SCAN and ALTER search a group for one or several members with a given property; in addition, ALTER may modify one of their attributes.

4.7.6 Accumulation and production of results

GPSS collects statistical information automatically whenever a transaction enters a block. These data are supplied at run termination.

Every block has two associated counters:

N, total number of transactions which entered the block; and

W, number of transactions currently in the block.

The standard printout has been briefly summarized in Section 4.2. The programmer can request further information to analyze the model in greater depth or to assist in correction of errors.

TABULATE is used to create statistical tables, or histograms, additional to those supplied automatically. The user specifies details in a TABLE card.

PRINT is used to produce specific output during the simulation or as a diagnostic device.

TRACE is supplied for diagnostic purposes only. When turned on, the simulator traces every transaction through every block and supplies details of system status. This feature should be used with care because it slows execution drastically and produces enormous output. To make tracing more economical a complementary block, UNTRACE, is supplied so that the user can restrict observations to the segments of code which are suspect.

4.8 Model Development

Before coding begins, the correspondence between the problem parameters and GPSS entities should be defined. Allowance must be made for possible increases in the size of system to be modeled. Select a realistic time unit—the largest that would separate events effectively within the real system. For example, a time unit of 15 minutes may be suitable for berthing ships; 1 second may be adequate for telephone calls; but control storage of a computer could require a time unit of less than 1 microsecond.

In most models the analyst will use symbolic names for some of the entities to make the program more readable. In more complicated problems the user may find it necessary to identify the entity by the value of another attribute; this is called *indirect addressing*. A program using both symbolic names and indirect addressing to refer to the same entity requires careful planning to avoid possible confusion when the model is extended.

We also stress the need for adequate documentation. Before coding begins, this will consist of a block diagram and a detailed description of the system, with assumptions and abstractions. Comments should be used liberally throughout the program coding so that other users can follow the logic easily.

4.9 Submitting the Program for Computer Simulation

The GPSS simulation program is usually submitted directly to the computer as a deck of punched cards or remotely from a terminal. The GPSS compiler transforms symbolic names into equivalent numeric references and checks the code for errors. The simulation program executes if the code contains no serious errors and the user has requested a run.

At the end of simulation, output is supplied and GPSS then reads the next statements. These could be CLEAR or RESET, which would signify a further simulation run, possibly with changes of input parameters, or END, which terminates the GPSS program.

4.10   Conclusion

This chapter has given an overview of GPSS to acquaint the reader with the concepts and structure of the language. It is important to understand the value of the services provided automatically in terms of programming effort and hence project time saved. In the next chapter we consider how these features are applied through two examples of manual simulation.

5 Basic Modeling Concepts as Implemented in GPSS

In this chapter we restate the basic modeling concepts of Chapter 2 and show how they are realized in a GPSS model. We consider two simple models, discuss manual simulation of the associated systems, and thus demonstrate further requirements of a computer simulation language.

5.1 Discrete-Event Simulation

In previous chapters we showed that simulation models can be described statically by their state at a given time and dynamically by their changes with time. This dual aspect is a direct consequence of handling time discretely so that the system is represented by a sequence of images produced when significant events occur. Such treatment is not unique to simulation studies; it is used in many scientific and industrial processes. For example, a television program or a motion picture is a sequence of "stills" projected in quick succession to produce a "moving picture." Time-division multiplexing is used to transmit many telephone conversations simultaneously on the same line. Of course, the receiver only hears a sample of the actual transmission, but careful choice of the sampling interval gives the impression of continuous speech. Finally the process of discrete-time sampling is sometimes used to make a dynamic process appear static; this occurs when a strobe lamp is adjusted so that a rotating machine part appears stationary.

These examples show that discrete-event processes are accepted by the human senses provided a suitable sampling interval is chosen. In a similar way, simulation can give the analyst a dynamic impression of system behavior if the model is adequate.

To ensure the validity of the discrete-event abstraction it is necessary to consider model structure in detail and to understand how it will be interpreted in the simulation program [5.1].

5.2 Static Aspect

5.2.1 The static structure

To define the time-dependent framework the analyst must be able to identify and represent:

1. The components, or entities, of the system, together with their characteristics, or attributes.
2. The classes, or sets, to which the different entities belong. During simulation the members of a set may change; it must therefore be possible to change the membership and characteristics of a set.
3. The relationships between entities. In the very simple barbershop problem the components are the barber and the customers. Attributes of customers include the sort of service required, such as shave or haircut, and the associated service time. A relationship between the barber and a customer is given by specifying that the barber can handle only one customer at a time. This connection is made in GPSS by a transaction (customer) seizing a facility (the barber).

5.2.2 Permanent and temporary entities

In the real world all objects are temporary. However, in a simulation model it is important to distinguish between objects which are present throughout the simulation and those which exist for just a part of the simulation. The first type can be treated as permanent and the others as temporary entities. This distinction is an important factor in simulation language design because it affects the main storage requirements and cross-referencing techniques.

In Chapter 4 we briefly reviewed the permanent entities of GPSS, such as storages and facilities, and transactions, which are the temporary entities of the language. All these entities have attributes, called Standard Numerical Attributes, or SNAs for short. Some attributes describing entity status may be handled automatically by the simulator and others may be set and modified by the user.

Permanent entities are activated from the entity pool by the first reference in a block which implies its existence. For example, the block SEIZE BARB implies the existence of a facility called BARB and activates the facility. When a transaction enters this block, the attribute describing the facility status is changed from NU (not in use) to U (in use).

5.3 Dynamic Aspect

5.3.1 The dynamic structure

A real system changes its state continuously with time. A simulation model must reflect this behavior. In discrete-event simulation the model maintains a given quasi-static state until the occurrence of an event changes the state.

Difficulties of organizing computer simulation arise because:

1. Many events and thus many changes of state can occur at the same simulated time, and

2. The computer handles events sequentially.

Thus, in discrete-event simulation, the computer must serialize parallel processes. By considering time as discrete, the system is examined only when an event occurs. During the intervening periods the system is considered to be in a quasi-static state. It is important to appreciate the difference between a dormant system and a simulation model that assumes an apparently static state for a finite period. In the first case, nothing happens in the system during the specified time, but in the second no new event of importance to the model occurs, even though the system is not dormant. For example, a model of a telephone call involves two events which specify the status of the telephone facility—first, a connection event when the distant party answers and, second, a disconnection event when the call ends. For the purposes of simulation the system is in a static state throughout the conversation because the telephone and the speakers are busy during that time. The dynamics enter when the call ends, the telephone becomes free, and the speakers can pursue other activities.

5.3.2 Time division and ordering of events

The organization required for discrete-event simulation can be exemplified by a graphical representation of a run of a simple model. Figure 5.1 is a pictorial form of the worksheet of the barbershop problem which highlights these requirements.

1. Time is organized on the horizontal axis in discrete 5-minute steps. Although the barber does not open until 8:00 the time origin has been set at 7:40; this allows an extension of the basic model to handle customers waiting outside the shop for the barber to arrive.

2. The time during which each customer is in the shop is represented by a rectangle that consists of a shaded portion (waiting time) and a blank portion (service time). Three events, arrival, start of service, and end of service, are defined for each customer and the associated event numbers are in ascending order. If a customer arrives when the barber is free, the first two events are modeled to occur simultaneously, but they must be handled in logical order: a customer cannot sit in the barber's chair until he has entered the shop.

3. Events must be processed in the proper sequence but they are not necessarily defined in that sequence. This is because a sequence of events may have to wait for a specific state before it can be defined. The several cases shown in

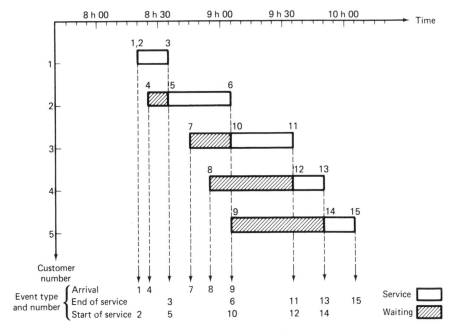

Figure 5.1 Discrete time division in the barbershop problem.

the graph depend partially on the logic of the model. Whenever a customer service starts, the end-of-service event is created immediately, but the start of the next customer's service cannot be scheduled until the current customer actually leaves. Thus, at 9:05, events occur for three customers: event 6, end of service for customer 2; event 9, arrival of customer 5, defined externally; and event 10, start of service for customer 3, undefined until event 6 has occurred but modeled to be simultaneous with event 6. The simulation program must ensure that the FIFO queueing discipline is maintained: customer 5 is not allowed to sit in the chair before customer 3, even though it has just been vacated and event 9 was defined before event 10. If arrival events are defined independently, as shown in the diagram, it is seen that events 7 and 8 both occur before event 6. Even if arrival times are modeled internally using an interarrival time distribution, the end-of-service event for customer 2 would still be defined before the arrival event for customer 4 but would occur after customer 4 arrived.

4. Whenever an event occurs, the state of the system is altered. The diagram shows how customers change status from waiting for service to being served, how the barber changes status from idle to busy, and so on. Therefore, the simulation program must handle changes in system numerical attributes, SNAs, as well as time and sequencing of events, so that the status of the system can be referenced at all times. This consideration is most important when handling conditional events—that is, events that cannot be specified until certain conditions are met.

The problems of organization shown in this example occur in most simulation studies and can be solved by creating a list or chain of events. The main activity of the simulation process is the creation and scanning of the events, which is the function of a control program.

5.3.3 Control program requirements

A simulation control program can be organized in many different ways, but the following requirements are basic:

1. Find the next scheduled event.
2. Determine whether the event can occur.
3. Process the event.

To perform these tasks any control program has two central functions:

1. Create and update an event list.
2. Scan the list of all potential events for the next most imminent event.

These functions imply that either the whole list must be scanned for the next event or that some sorting must take place when events are added to the list. The list is usually ordered by scheduled event time, but this may be modified by priority considerations.

5.3.4 Clock mechanism

To provide correct sequencing of events the passage of time is modeled by a simulated clock. As mentioned previously, this device can be either fixed increment or variable increment. Most simulation languages in current use increment the clock to the time of the next scheduled event, which requires more sophisticated programming but uses the computer more efficiently. A good discussion of possible time-flow mechanisms is given in reference [5.2].

In simulation it is important to note that time can be mentioned in three contexts [5.3]:

Real time: the time scale of the system being modeled.

Simulated time: the represention of real time within the model recorded by the simulated clock.

Computer time: the actual processing time taken by a computer to perform a simulation run. This time depends on the complexity of the model and the power of the computer.

The flowchart of Figure 5.2 summarizes the basic operations of simulation. The initialization phase is used to enter data that define the environment of the model and external event structure.

5.4 The GPSS Control Program

In this section we present the rationale of the GPSS control program in outline and amplify the introduction given in Section 4.6.

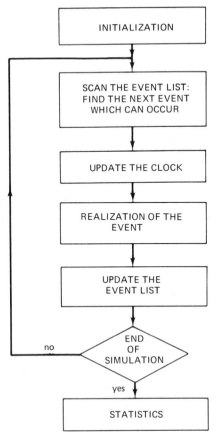

Figure 5.2 Summary of the basic operations.

5.4.1 Control of the flow of transactions

The concept of transactions moving through a block diagram may seem to suggest that GPSS is not directly concerned with events. However, the flow of transactions is controlled by event chains under the control of an event-updated simulation clock; GPSS can thus be regarded as an event-driven simulator.

GPSS specifies several types of list from which transactions can be referenced. Two such lists which are present in every GPSS model are the current-events chain and the future-events chain. The GPSS control program references two transaction attributes to manipulate the members of these chains:

Block departure time, BDT: the simulated clock time when the next event for that transaction is scheduled to occur. This is the time when the transaction is theoretically due to be handled by the GPSS control program. Transactions with BDT$\leq$C1 (current clock time) are in the current-events chain; note that scheduled departure time can be prior to current time because a condition may exist which prevents the transaction from moving. When BDT>C1, the transaction is on the future-events chain.

Next block address, NBA: the location of the next block to which the transaction proceeds when directed by the GPSS control program.

5.4.2   Progress of a transaction

We have previously mentioned that the control program moves transactions through the block diagram, executing blocks in logical sequence in zero simulated time until stopped by a time delay, a status condition, termination, or deactivation in a user chain. In fact, transactions only appear to move in this manner. Every transaction is activated from a transaction pool, which is a predefined area of storage. The apparent movement of transactions through the block diagram is handled by the GPSS control program, which updates the next block address (NBA attribute) according to the decision rules of the model.

5.4.3   Sequencing of transactions

The future-events chain contains transactions with block departure time greater than the current clock time. When the future event is defined, the transaction is placed on the chain in ascending order of BDT. As shown previously, events are not necessarily created in order of occurrence, so the organization of the chain entails some sorting.

Transactions enter the current-events chain when block departure time equals current clock time. They may be transferred from the future-events chain or can enter the current-events chain directly. In the current-events chain transactions are sorted in priority order by ascending BDT within priority class. By using two chains in this manner the GPSS control program effectively sorts transactions first in–first out within priority class, using just two passes for each transaction.

A transaction being handled by the control program remains on the current-events chain until it cannot move farther through the block diagram. At this point it may be placed on another type of chain, to be discussed later in Chapter 7. The ADVANCE block removes the transaction from the current-events chain and places it on the future-events chain. A simple status condition could leave it on the current-events chain. A LINK block would place the transaction on a user chain, and MATCH or GATHER would place it on a matching chain.

5.4.4   Possible states of a transaction

Transactions can exist in any one of four possible states:

Active: a transaction is active when it is being directed by the control program.

Suspended: transactions are in suspended state when on the future- or current-events chain. This means that a suspended transaction is waiting to be instructed by the control program. A transaction in these chains may also be interrupted by a higher-priority transaction requiring the same facility.

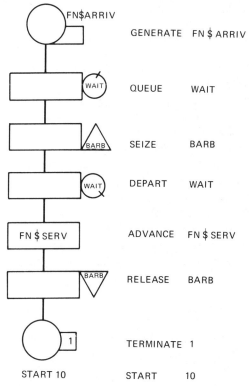

		GENERATE	FN $ ARRIV
		QUEUE	WAIT
		SEIZE	BARB
		DEPART	WAIT
		ADVANCE	FN $ SERV
		RELEASE	BARB
		TERMINATE	1

START 10   START   10

Figure 5.3 Barbershop block diagram and the program.

Passive: the transaction is on a user chain. It can be reactivated only by another transaction passing through an UNLINK block. This is controlled by the simulation programmer.

Terminated: the transaction has been destroyed by a TERMINATE or ASSEMBLE block.

5.5 Coding and Operation of Two Simple GPSS Models

In this section we illustrate the operations of GPSS described in Chapter 4 and the previous sections of Chapter 5 with two simple models. This should consolidate the reader's knowledge of GPSS terminology and demonstrate how GPSS works internally.

5.5.1 The barbershop problem

Consider the problem of Chapter 2. The barbershop system is modeled by:

Transactions, which represent the customers,

A facility called BARB, which represents the barber,

A queue called WAIT, which represents the waiting room.

The model is very simple; see Figure 5.3, which shows the block diagram and the program. The statistical functions specifying interarrival distribution and service times are described below.

61

The START instruction is a control statement which performs two tasks: it starts simulation and stops the run when a specified number of transactions have been terminated. This instruction can also be used to control output.

The following summary describes the model in GPSS terminology. Transactions (customers) are created by the GENERATE block, with interarrival time specified by a statistical function. They enter a queue and wait to seize the facility BARB. When a transaction is able to seize the barber, the transaction leaves the queue, a service time is computed, and the transaction spends this time in the ADVANCE block. Then it releases the barber and terminates. When 10 customers have been processed, the simulation stops and the results are printed.

During the simulation GPSS performs many housekeeping tasks automatically. These include keeping track of interactions between transactions and blocks, sequencing of events, updating the simulated clock, and the accumulation and printing of statistics.

5.5.2 Statistical functions in GPSS

There are two random variables in the barbershop model:

ARRIV   interarrival times

SERV   service times

which are defined by their statistical distributions. Later we will show how samples of a random variable are generated by inverting the cumulative distribution function, which is represented graphically in Figure 5.4.

The argument of both functions is RN2 (random number 2), which produces a uniformly distributed random number between 0 and 1 every time it is referenced. This property means that function ARRIV will yield the values

5 in $\frac{1}{3}$ of the cases

10 in $\frac{1}{3}$ of the cases

20 in $\frac{1}{3}$ of the cases

These values are the same as those specified in the definition of the problem. The type of the function and number of points is specified in the function definition statement. In this example both functions are discrete with three points: D3.

The GPSS card images which specify the two functions are given below. It is usual to insert such definitions before the actual program blocks shown in Figure 5.3.

*INTERARRIVAL FUNCTION ARRIV

  ARRIV   FUNCTION   RN2,D3   The function name is ARRIV; the
.333,5/.667,10/1.,20   argument is RN2, type is discrete
                                      with three points.

*SERVICE TIME FUNCTION SERV

  SERV   FUNCTION   RN2,D3   The function name is SERV, etc.
.167,30/.333,20/1.,15

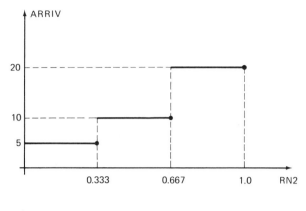

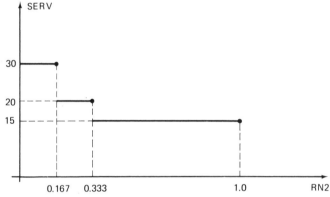

Figure 5.4

A simulation run of this model would stop when 10 customers have terminated, and the following statistical information would be produced:

Clock time at the end of the simulation.

For all blocks:	Number of transactions that entered the block.
	Number of transactions remaining at the block.
For the facility BARB:	Number of transactions processed.
	Average time spent by transactions in the facility.
	Average utilization of the facility.
	Number of the transaction, if any, currently using the facility.
For the queue WAIT:	Number of entries, number of transactions that did not wait.
	Average length; maximum and current length.
	Average time spent by transactions and average time excluding those transactions which did not wait.

If more information is required, such as a detailed table or a histogram of the times spent in the queue, the analyst can specify the requirements by means of a QTABLE card.

5.5.3 Simple queueing model

To illustrate how GPSS works internally the following model has constant interarrival times and constant service times. The reader is advised to follow the logic step-by-step using a worksheet (see Figure 5.6) to record the state of the clock time C1, the current-events chain, and the future-events chain. To minimize this task only the transaction number and its BDT are recorded.

The system. Four transactions enter the system at intervals of 3 time units, starting at time unit 1. They try to seize facility MACH for 4 time units and then try to enter storage BUFFE (with capacity 2) before releasing MACH. After 9 time units in BUFFE, they leave storage and terminate. In this model the number of transactions must be limited because it has been devised to cause catastrophic congestion.

The following GPSS instructions model the system:

```
BUFFE     STORAGE       2
          GENERATE      3,,1,4
          QUEUE         WAIT
          SEIZE         MACH
          DEPART        WAIT
          ADVANCE       4
          ENTER         BUFFE
          RELEASE       MACH
          ADVANCE       9
          LEAVE         BUFFE
          TERMINATE     1
          START         4
```

The behavior of the model related to this coding is shown in Figure 5.5. It has the following characteristics:

Arrivals of transactions opposite the GENERATE block.

Time in queue WAIT opposite the QUEUE block.

Time in facility MACH opposite the first ADVANCE block.

Time in storage BUFFE opposite the second ADVANCE block.

Terminations opposite the TERMINATE block.

5.5.4 Detailed trace of the simulation

For brevity the following standard GPSS acronyms are used in this paragraph:

XAC   for transaction.

FUT   for future-events chain.

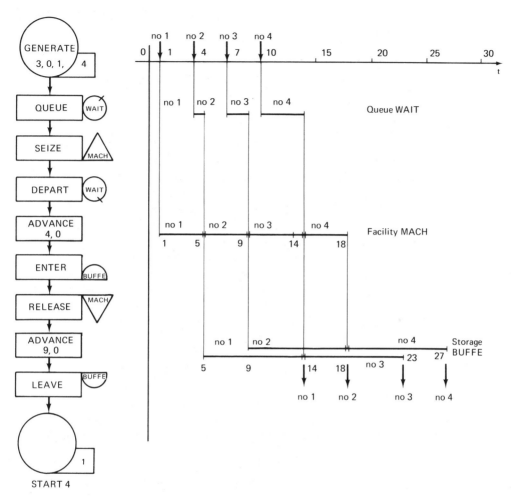

Figure 5.5 Graphical behavior of the queue, facility, and buffer.

CUR   for current-events chain.

C1   for clock time.

BDT   for block departure time.

When the program is executed, the first step is to generate the first XAC for every GENERATE block. Here we have an offset of 1; therefore, one XAC (number 1) is put in FUT with BDT=1.

When simulation starts, C1 is set to 1, the smallest value of FUT, XAC1 is moved from FUT to CUR, and GPSS begins scanning CUR. It finds XAC1 and moves it from the GENERATE to the QUEUE block. When XAC1 leaves the GENERATE block, the generation time of the next XAC is computed as 1+3=4 and XAC2 is put in FUT with BDT=4. XAC1 then moves, in turn, to the SEIZE block and to

ADVANCE, where the new BDT is computed to give the advance time, $(C1+4)=5$. Now $5>C1$, so XAC1 is put in FUT with BDT=5.

CUR is now empty, so C1 is updated to 4, the smallest value of FUT, and XAC2 is moved from FUT to CUR. The GPSS scan finds XAC2 and moves it from the GENERATE into the QUEUE block. Then XAC3 is scheduled for time 7 $(C1+3)$ and put in FUT. XAC2 cannot seize MACH, which is busy, so its BDT is unchanged at 4 and it therefore stays in CUR. GPSS records the fact that XAC2 waits for a change of status of MACH, and XAC2 is temporarily inactivated.

The scan has finished for time 4, so C1 is updated to 5 (the lowest time in FUT) and XAC1 moves back to CUR. The scan finds XAC2 inactive, then examines XAC1, and moves it from the ADVANCE to the ENTER block, then to RELEASE MACH (which reactivates XAC2) and to ADVANCE 9, where a new BDT of $(C1+9)=14$ is computed, and XAC1 is again put in FUT. The scan restarts, finds XAC2 active, and moves it to the SEIZE, DEPART, and ADVANCE blocks. The advance time (4) is added to C1, which gives a BDT of 9, and XAC2 is attached to FUT.

Now that we have examined the operation of the current-events chain, it is meaningful to comment on the scanning mechanism. When a transaction has been moved as far as possible, GPSS must decide whether the scan for the current clock time is complete. To do this the *status flag* of CUR, which is set whenever the status of the model is changed, is examined. If the flag is set, the scan is reinitialized from the top of CUR. If the flag is reset (off), the scan continues with the next transaction on the chain. At the end of the scan, when no more transactions can move, the clock is updated to the first time on FUT, and the status flag is reset.

CUR is again empty, so C1 is updated to 7, XAC3 moves to CUR, and the scan restarts. XAC3 is moved from the GENERATE block, and XAC4, the next transaction, is scheduled for time 10 and put on FUT with a BDT of 10. XAC3 moves to the QUEUE block, where it waits because MACH is seized by XAC2. It remains in CUR because its BDT is 7. C1 is updated to 9, XAC2 moves from FUT to CUR, and the scan begins, finds XAC3 inactive, moves XAC2 in turn to the ENTER block (which accepts it because the storage is not full), the RELEASE block, and the ADVANCE block. The advance time (9) is added to C1, which gives XAC2 a BDT of 18. XAC2 is then put in FUT. The status of the model has changed, so the scan restarts. XAC3 moves from the QUEUE to the SEIZE, DEPART, and ADVANCE blocks. A new BDT of 13 is computed and XAC3 is put on FUT. C1 then changes to 10 and XAC4 moves from FUT to CUR. It leaves the GENERATE block but remains in the QUEUE block in an inactive state because facility MACH has been seized by XAC3. Therefore, XAC4 remains in CUR.

C1 is updated to 13, XAC3 moves to CUR, and the scan begins, finds XAC4 inactive, and tries to move XAC3 from the ADVANCE block to the ENTER block but does not succeed because storage BUFFE is full. XAC3 is made inactive and remains in CUR. No status change has occurred, so the scan is finished.

The status of the model at this stage is given by Figure 5.6. Clock time is 13, CUR contains XAC4 with BDT=10 and XAC3 with BDT=13. FUT contains XAC1 with BDT=14 and XAC2 with BDT=18.

| | Current-Events Chain | | Future-Events Chain | |
C1	Number	BDT	Number	BDT
~~1~~	~~1~~	~~1~~	~~1~~	~~1~~
~~4~~	~~2~~	~~4~~	~~2~~	~~4~~
~~5~~	~~1~~	~~5~~	~~1~~	~~5~~
~~7~~	~~3~~	~~7~~	~~3~~	~~7~~
~~9~~	~~2~~	~~9~~	1	14
~~10~~	4	10	~~2~~	~~9~~
13	3	13	~~4~~	~~10~~
			2	18
			~~3~~	~~13~~

Figure 5.6

C1 is updated to 14, XAC1 is moved to CUR, and the scan begins. XAC4 and XAC3 are inactive. XAC1 is moved to the LEAVE block, changes the status of the model, and terminates. The A-operand of the TERMINATE block is subtracted from the termination count, which is specified by the A-operand of the START statement. This count is therefore reduced to 3.

The status switch is now set, so the scan restarts from the top of CUR, finds XAC4 inactive and XAC3 reactivated by the change of status of storage BUFFE. XAC3 is moved, in turn, to the ENTER and RELEASE blocks. This makes XAC4 active and changes the status of the model. XAC3 proceeds to the ADVANCE block, where the new BDT of 23 is computed and is then put on FUT. The scan begins again, finds XAC4, which is moved to the SEIZE, DEPART, and ADVANCE blocks. XAC4 is put on FUT with a BDT of 18.

C1 is updated to 18 and we now have two simultaneous events: XAC2 and XAC4 both have BDT=18 and are moved from FUT to CUR.

In this model, the response would be unaltered if XAC4 appeared before XAC2. However, in some situations the sequencing of simultaneous events could be critical. An example of this type is discussed in Section 6.6.2. XAC2 is moved from the ADVANCE block to the LEAVE and TERMINATE blocks, which reduces the termination count to 2. XAC4 then moves from the ADVANCE to the ENTER, RELEASE, and ADVANCE blocks. Its BDT is set to 27 and XAC4 is put on FUT.

C1 is updated to 23, and XAC3 moves to CUR, leaves the ADVANCE block, and passes through the LEAVE and TERMINATE blocks. The termination count is reduced to 1.

C1 is updated to 27, and XAC4 moves from FUT to CUR. The status of the model at this point is given by Figure 5.7, where the clock time is 27, CUR contains XAC4 with BDT=27, and FUT is empty.

The scan finds XAC4 and moves it to the LEAVE and TERMINATE blocks. The termination count is reduced to zero and the simulation ends. The end of simulation invokes printing of the standard output report.

Remark: When XAC1 terminated, it was returned to the transaction pool. When a new transaction is generated, GPSS always selects the first unused member of the

C1	Current-Events Chain Number	BDT	Future-Events Chain Number	BDT
~~1~~	~~1~~	~~1~~	~~1~~	~~1~~
~~4~~	~~2~~	~~4~~	~~2~~	~~4~~
~~5~~	~~1~~	~~5~~	~~1~~	~~5~~
~~7~~	~~3~~	~~7~~	~~3~~	~~7~~
~~9~~	~~2~~	~~9~~	~~1~~	~~14~~
~~10~~	~~4~~	~~10~~	~~2~~	~~9~~
~~13~~	~~3~~	~~13~~	~~4~~	~~10~~
~~14~~	~~1~~	~~14~~	~~2~~	~~18~~
~~18~~	~~2~~	~~18~~	~~3~~	~~13~~
~~23~~	~~4~~	~~18~~	~~3~~	~~23~~
27	~~3~~	~~23~~	~~4~~	~~18~~
	4	27	~~4~~	~~27~~

Figure 5.7

pool. Thus XAC1 could be used many times during simulation to perform different modeling tasks.

5.5.5 Computation of statistics

Statistics of the behavior of permanent entities, such as facilities, storages, and queues, are recorded automatically by GPSS. The logic of the example in Section 5.5.4 is used to illustrate the statistical techniques.

Facility. *Total utilization* is the sum of times during which the facility is in the SEIZED state. In the example, this was $4 + 4 + 5 + 4 = 17$. *Facility utilization* is the ratio of total utilization and total time simulated, in this case $\frac{17}{27} = 0.629$, or 62.9 per cent. *Average time per transaction* is total utilization divided by number of seizing transactions, which gives $\frac{17}{4} = 4.25$.

Storage. *Total utilization* is computed by summing the product of the storage contents by the time interval during which this content does not change. It can also be interpreted as the sum of the times spent by all transactions in the storage. In the example this total is 36. *Average contents* is equal to this total divided by the total simulated time, which gives $\frac{36}{27} = 1.333$. *Average utilization* is equal to the average contents divided by the storage capacity: $1.333/2 = 0.666$.

Queue. *Average contents* and *average time per transaction* are computed in the same way as for storages. Thus average contents is $\frac{7}{27} = 0.259$ and average time per transaction is $\frac{7}{4} = 1.75$.

$average time per transaction is computed by dividing the total waiting time by the number of transactions which spent time in the queue: $\frac{7}{3} = 2.333$. This average excludes those transactions which passed through the queue without being delayed. The number is printed, as well as the percentage of the total number of transactions it represents.

Maximum queue length is the maximum contents of the queue during the simulation run—in this example, 2.

Remark: It is useful to have two average waiting times, those including and those excluding zero entries. This is important information for every queueing system. Two queues with the same total average waiting time but different percentages of zero entries will have different effects on system behavior.

References

5.1. P. J. KIVIAT, *Digital Computer Simulation: Computer Programming Languages,* RM/5883-PR, Rand Corporation, Santa Monica, Calif., 1969.

5.2. R. E. NANCE, "On Time Flow Mechanisms for Discrete System Simulation," *Management Science,* Vol. 18, No. 1, 1971.

5.3. O. J. DAHL, "Discrete Simulation Languages," Lectures delivered at the NATO Summer School, Villars-de-Lans, 1966.

6 A GPSS Subset

One of the advantages of GPSS is that it can be used effectively even if only a subset of instructions is known. To speed the learning process, we have defined a workable subset, simple enough to be learned quickly and sufficiently complete to solve practical problems.

This subset consists of

  5 control statements

18 block-definition statements

  5 entity-definition statements

and makes use of 19 standard numerical, computational, and logical attributes.

The proposed subset is arbitrary. One could select several different subsets to perform the same function. To show the connection between the subset and the full language, Table 6.1 contains all the control, block-definition, and entity-definition statements, as well as the GPSS attributes. These are divided to show those instructions which are in the subset and those not part of the subset.

6.1 Control Statements

Request for simulation.

SIMULATE

requests a simulation run after the assembly.

In GPSS V, optional A and B fields are available:

SIMULATE   A,B

Operation:

The run terminates automatically after the time specified by field-A and subsequent action is specified by field-B.

Table 6.1 GPSS Subset and Full Language

Description	Subset	Full Language
Control Statements		
Request for simulation	SIMULATE (with timer in GPSS V)	
Control of run	START	
End of job	END	
Clearance of model	CLEAR	
Clearance of accumulated statistics	RESET	
Initialization of random-number generators		RMULT
Reallocation of entities		REALLOCATE
Saving the model, reading in again		SAVE/READ
GPSS job card		JOB
Jobtape rewinding		REWIND
Printing of nonstandard output		REPORT
Extra statements in GPSS V		AUXILIARY, LOAD
Block-Definition Statements		
Transaction-Oriented Blocks		
Creation and destruction of transactions	GENERATE/ TERMINATE	SPLIT/ASSEMBLE, JOBTAPE
Time delay	ADVANCE	
Access to or handling of attributes	ASSIGN, PRIORITY	MARK, INDEX
Synchronization of transactions		MATCH, GATHER, ASSEMBLE
Equipment-Oriented Blocks		
Facility	SEIZE/RELEASE PREEMPT/RETURN	PREEMPT in priority mode
Storage	ENTER/LEAVE	
Queue	QUEUE/DEPART	
Switches		LOGIC
Counting, Selecting of permanent entities		COUNT, SELECT
Transaction-Flow Modification		
Transfer	TRANSFER (unconditional, BOTH, statistical, SIM)	TRANSFER (ALL, PICK, FN, P, SBR)
Testing	GATE, TEST	GATE on switch and match
Loop		LOOP
Buffer		BUFFER, PRIORITY BUFFER
User chain		LINK/UNLINK

Table 6.1 (continued)

Description	Subset	Full Language
Storage and retrieval of information	SAVEVALUE/ MSAVEVALUE	
Group entity		JOIN/REMOVE, EXAMINE, SCAN, ALTER
Accumulation and printing of information		TABULATE, PRINT, TRACE/ UNTRACE, WRITE
Special blocks		CHANGE, EXECUTE, HELP
Additional blocks in GPSS V		
Availability/unavailability of facilities and storages		FAVAIL/FUNAVAIL SAVAIL/SUNAVAIL

Entity-Definition Statements		
Storage capacity	STORAGE	
Variable	VARIABLE/FVARIABLE	BVARIABLE
Function	FUNCTION (C, D, L types)	FUNCTION (E, M, S types)
Save matrix definition	MATRIX	
Save and matrix initialization	INITIAL	
Statistical table		TABLE/QTABLE

Attributes		
Standard numerical attributes		
System		
clock time	C1	AC1 (in GPSS V)
random-number generators	RNj	
terminations to go		TG1 (in GPSS V)
Block	Nj/Wj	
Transaction	Pj/M1/PR	MPj
Additional attributes in GPSS V	PFj/PHj/PBj/PLj	MPjPx
Facility	Fj	FRj/FCj/FTj
Storage	Sj/Rj	SRj/SCj/SAj/SMj/STj
Queue	Qj	QCj/QAj/QMj/QZj/QTj/QXj
Save locations and matrices	Xj/XHj/MXj(k,ℓ)/ MHj(k,ℓ)	
Additional attributes in GPSS V	XBj/MBj(k,ℓ) XLj/MLj(k,ℓ)	
Group		Gj
User chain		CHj/CAj/CMj/CCj/CTj
Table		TCj/TBj/TDj
Computational entities		
Variable	Vj	BVj
Function	FNj	FNj
Random number	RNj	
Standard logical attributes		
Transaction		Mj/NMj
Facility	Uj/NUj	FUj/FNUj/FIj/FNIj/Ij/NIj
Storage		SEj/SNEj/SFj/SNFj
Switch		LRj/LSj
Additional attributes in GPSS V		FVj/FNVj SVj/SNVj

Operands:

A: The maximum computer execution time in minutes.
B: Indicates action at termination: SAVE will save the model as it is; REPLY
     allows the user to decide at termination time.

EXAMPLE:

                    SIMULATE   5,SAVE

would print the results after 5 minutes have elapsed and save the model (on the
device specified in the DRDSAVEO OS DD card; see Appendix A).

Control of run.

                    START   A,B,C,D

Operation:

This statement instructs GPSS that the simulation run must occur and contains the
information necessary to terminate the run.

Operands:

A: The run termination count.
B: The print-suppression field. If NP, no statistics are printed at the end of the
     run.
C: A snap interval count for intermediate printout of statistical results.
D: The status printout signal. A 1 indicates that each standard printout must
     include the status printout (current- or future-events chains, etc.).

The A-field (run termination count) is a counter which is decremented when a
transaction enters a TERMINATE block with a nonzero A-field. The number subtracted is given by the A-field. When the counter is reduced to zero or less, simulation
ends and the results are printed. The same procedure applies to the C-field used to
produce intermediate statistical printout; but when reduced to zero, it is reinitialized
to control printing of the next snap results.

EXAMPLES:

     (1)   NORM   TERMINATE   1
                        .
                        .
                        .
              FAIL   TERMINATE
                        START   1000,,500

          In this run we require 1000 transactions to go through the NORM block before
          simulation ends. Transactions that enter the FAIL block are ignored. We
          also request an intermediate printout, after processing 500 transactions.

     (2)   NORM   TERMINATE   1
                        .
                        .
                        .
              FAIL   TERMINATE   1
                        START   1000,,,1

We require 1000 transactions to go through either the NORM or FAIL blocks with no intermediate printout. The status printout is to be included in the results at the end of the simulation run.

(3)   NORM   TERMINATE   1
                     .
                     .
                     .

          FAIL   TERMINATE
                     .
                     .
                     .

          ERROR   TERMINATE   1000
                    START   1000

We require 1000 to go through the NORM block. However, if one transaction reaches the ERROR block, 1000 is subtracted from the run termination count and therefore stops the simulation. The standard results would be printed. This is an easy way to stop a simulation run whenever one specific situation is encountered.

(4)   NORM   TERMINATE
                     .
                     .
                     .

          FAIL   TERMINATE
          *   DEFINE AN AUXILIARY CLOCK
                    GENERATE   3600
                    TERMINATE   1
                    START   2

In this program, we do not count the transactions processed. We have an "auxiliary clock" which generates one transaction every 3600 units of time. If the time unit is 1 second, we would get one transaction per hour. The transaction immediately terminates and decrements the termination counter. In this example, simulation would end after 2 hours of simulated time.

End of job

                              END

must be the last statement of the input deck, which may contain several GPSS jobs.

Clearance of model

                             CLEAR

has two functions: (1) it removes all transactions from the model, clears all statistics accumulated and all save locations, and resets the clock time and all switches; and (2) it creates a new transaction for every GENERATE block. In brief, CLEAR re-initializes the model as it was when loaded but does not reset the eight random-number generators.

CLEAR has a selective option. The user may specify certain savevalues, or ranges of savevalues, which must not be set to zero. In GPSS V, matrices can also be specified. The save locations not to be reset must be specified beginning in column 19, as in the following examples.

EXAMPLES:

    (1)   CLEAR   X1,X7,X20-X25

        will not reset fullword saves X1, X7, and X20 to X25.

    (2)   CLEAR   XH1-XH10

        will not reset halfword saves 1 to 10.

Clearance of accumulated statistics

                RESET

erases all statistics and sets the relative clock to zero without modifying the model status. The transactions, saves, and so on are unaltered.

    RESET has a selective option. The user may specify certain entities, or ranges of entities, which should not be affected by the RESET statement. The entities that may be excepted are facilities, storages, queues, user chains, and tables, for which the corresponding mnemonics are Fj, Sj, Qj, CHj, and TBj.

EXAMPLE:

                RESET   F1,S1-S5,Q3,CH1

        would reset all statistics except those relating to facility 1, storages 1 to 5, queue 3, and user chain 1.

6.2 Block-Definition Statements

In GPSS fixed format, the card layout of block-definition statements is:

    2   8   19

    LABEL   OPERATION   OPERANDS

For every block we will indicate the instruction, with the operands which may be used and the graphical symbol suggested for the block. Remember that when an operand is not used its absence must be indicated by a comma if it is followed by another operand. We also describe the operations performed by the block and give examples of the possible operands.

6.2.1 Transaction-oriented blocks

Creation and destruction of transactions

                        GENERATE   A,B,C,D,E,F,G

Operation:

This block creates transactions that enter the model in the next sequential block. The intergeneration time between successive transactions is computed using operands A and B. The generation time of the first transaction is equal to the C-operand value if nonzero or to the value computed the first time by operands A and B.

The GENERATE block only computes the time of the generation of the next transaction when the current transaction leaves the GENERATE block. Therefore, if a block that can refuse entry to a transaction immediately follows the GENERATE block, it can block the generation process and thus bias the intergeneration times.

Operands:

A: The mean intergeneration time. This is constant if no B-operand is defined.

B: The spread or, if a function, the multiplying function modifier. The spread must be less than or equal to the mean.

EXAMPLES:

(1)   GENERATE   50

specifies a constant intergeneration time of 50 time units.

(2)   GENERATE   50,10

specifies an intergeneration time which is a random number uniformly distributed between $50 - 10$ and $50 + 10$, that is, between 40 and 60.

(3)   GENERATE   50,FN$EXPON

specifies an intergeneration time equal to 50 multiplied by the value of the function EXPON. If this function is the inverse of the cumulative distribution function of the exponential distribution [see Section D.2 (appendix), example 2], this instruction generates transactions according to a Poisson distribution with mean arrival rate of $\frac{1}{50}$ transaction per time unit (or exponential inter-arrival time with mean 50).

(4) The next two instructions are equivalent:

GENERATE   1,FN$TIME
GENERATE   FN$TIME

C: The initialization interval, that is, the time of the generation of the first transaction. This field is a way to delay the operations of the GENERATE block for a specified time.

D: The creation limit. It is the total number of transactions to be generated by the GENERATE block. When this number is reached, the block ceases operation. This is one way to limit the duration of simulation. In this case with no TERMINATE/START limitation, the simulation would end with the error message: "no new event in the system."

E: The priority level (0 to 127) of the generated transactions. If the E-field is not specified, the default priority is 0.

F: The number of parameters to be attached to each transaction (1 to 100).
If not specified, 12 halfword parameters are assigned by default.

G: The parameter type; H for halfwords, F for fullwords.

EXAMPLES:

(1)   GENERATE   2,,200,100,,10,F

will generate 100 transactions, one every 2 time units, the first at time 200.
Ten fullword parameters will be allocated to every transaction.

(2)   GENERATE   20,5,1000,,1,2,H

will generate transactions with a uniformly distributed intergeneration time
of 15 to 25 after the first transaction, which will be generated at time 1000.
Their priority will be 1 and they will have two halfword parameters.

Remark on GPSS V: In GPSS V, the F to I operands are used for defining the
number of parameters of every type (fullword, halfword, byte, and floating point)
needed. They may be coded in any order.

EXAMPLES:

(1)   GENERATE   100,,,,,10PF,4PB

allocates to each generated transaction ten fullword parameters and four byte
parameters.

(2)   GENERATE   100,,,,,1PL,4PH

allocates one floating point and four halfword parameters to each transaction.
A maximum of 255 parameters of each type is allowed. If no F to I operand
is specified, then 12 halfword parameters are assigned by default. If no parameters are needed, code a zero as F-operand.

                        TERMINATE   A

Operation:

This block destroys the entering transaction.

Operand:

A: *(optional)* The number of units by which the run termination count must be
reduced. This counter is specified in the A-field of the START card (see
Section 6.1, START). As already mentioned, if the A-field is omitted from a
TERMINATE statement, the run termination count is unaltered. The
A-field may be a SNA, so that the amount by which the count is reduced
may vary.

EXAMPLES:

(1)   TERMINATE   P1

The number of units by which the count is reduced is the value of parameter 1 of the transaction.

(2)   TERMINATE   X10

The number of units is the present value of save location 10.

Time delay

ADVANCE   A,B

Operation:

This block provides the means to delay transactions. When a transaction enters the ADVANCE block, the time that it will remain in the block is computed using operands A and B. If the result is zero, the transaction continues to the next sequential block.

Operands:

A: The mean time.

B: The spread or, if a function, the function modifier.

The rules for computing the time delay are the same as for the GENERATE block.

EXAMPLES:

(1)   ADVANCE   100

The transaction will spend 100 time units in this block before it proceeds to the next sequential block.

(2)   ADVANCE   100,P1

The transaction will spend a random time, uniformly distributed between $100 - P1$ and $100 + P1$, in this block. The spread P1 is the current contents of parameter 1 of the transaction.

(3)   ADVANCE   FN*2

The time delay is obtained by computing the value of the function, the number of which is the value of parameter 2 of the transaction.

Access to or handling of attributes

ASSIGN   A,B,C

Operation:

This block is used to enter numerical values into or modify the contents of a transaction parameter.

Operands:

A: The parameter number. If followed by $+$ or $-$, the value specified by the B- and C-operands will be added to or subtracted from it, respectively. If no sign is present the value will replace the current contents of the parameter.

B: The value to be stored, added, or subtracted.

C: (*optional*) The number of a multiplying function modifier. If present, the function defined by this number is computed and multiplied by the B-operand. The resulting number, truncated to the nearest integer, is stored, added, or subtracted.

EXAMPLES:

(1)   ASSIGN   1,FN10

stores the current value of function 10 in parameter 1.

(2)   ASSIGN   2+,X*3

adds the contents of the save location whose number is the contents of parameter 3 of the transaction to parameter 2.

(3)   ASSIGN   2,P3,1

stores the value obtained by multiplying the contents of parameter 3 of the transaction by the value of function 1 in parameter 2.

In GPSS V, if different parameter types are used, the type of the parameter must be specified in the D-operand: PF, PH, PB, or PL for fullword, halfword, byte, or floating point, respectively.

PRIORITY   A,B

Operation:

This block is used to set the priority of the transaction to a specified value. The existing transaction priority, either assigned by the GENERATE block E-operand or another PRIORITY block, is replaced by the value of the A-operand.

Operands:

A: The value, between 0 and 127, of the priority to be assigned.

EXAMPLES:

(1)   PRIORITY   2

assigns priority 2 to the transaction.

(2)   PRIORITY   X*1

> assigns priority equal to the value of the save location whose number is given by parameter 1 of the transaction.

B: (*optional*) May be coded as BUFFER. Its effect will be discussed in Section 7.2.3.

6.2.2 Equipment-oriented blocks

Facility

The following four blocks are used to modify the status of a facility. A facility is a permanent entity which can accommodate only one transaction at a time. It can be free, seized (normal busy status), or preempted (priority busy status).

   SEIZE   A

Operation:

This block tests the status of facility A. It refuses entry to the transaction if the facility is not free. If the transaction enters the block, the facility is immediately seized and the transaction proceeds to the next block. The facility would then refuse entry to subsequent transactions trying to seize it, until it is released by the seizing transaction.

Operand:

A: The name or number of the facility.

   RELEASE   A

Operation:

This block releases the facility, which makes it available to be seized by a transaction. This block never refuses entry to a transaction, but the facility must be released by the same transaction that seized it. Whenever a transaction tries to release a facility that it did not seize, an execution error occurs.

Operand:

A: The name or number of the facility.

   PREEMPT   A,B,C,D,E

Operation:

This block tests if the transaction can preempt facility A. If no, the transaction is refused; if yes, the transaction is accepted by the block and facility A is preempted. The simplest nontrivial situation is when facility A is being seized. When the seizing transaction is interrupted, the interrupting or preempting transaction takes control of the facility. When it reaches the RETURN block, the original seizing transaction will regain control of the facility for the outstanding service time.

When the B-operand is used, the PREEMPT block operates in the priority mode (using also the C-, D-, and E-operands). This case will be discussed in Section 7.2.2.

Operands:

A: The facility name or number.

B: (*optional*) May be coded as PR (priority) to show that the PREEMPT block must operate in priority mode.

C: (*optional*) An address to which the preempted transaction can be sent when preempted.

D: (*optional*) The number of a parameter in which the remaining service time of the preempted transaction can be stored.

E: (*optional*) May be coded as RE (remove), indicating that the preempted transaction has to be removed from the facility.

RETURN   A

Operation:

This block removes the preempting transaction from the facility. This block never refuses entry to a transaction, but the facility must be returned by the transaction that preempted it. Otherwise, an execution error would occur.

Operand:

A: The name or number of the facility.

EXAMPLES:

(1)

```
            .
            .
            .
        SEIZE        P2
        ADVANCE      50
        RELEASE      P2
```

Seize the facility whose number is the value of parameter 2, stay in the ADVANCE block, and therefore retain the facility for 50 time units, and then release the facility.

(2)   .
                             .
                             .

NORMA   SEIZE   CPU
         ADVANCE   P1
         RELEASE   CPU

Normal processing: seize facility CPU for P1 time units and then release CPU.

                             .
                             .
                             .

PRIOR   PREEMPT   CPU
         ADVANCE   10
         RETURN   CPU

Priority processing: facility CPU, if seized, is preempted, kept for 10 time units, and returned to the seizing transaction. If free, it is preempted and returned after 10 time units.

Storage. The next two blocks are used to modify the status of a storage. A storage is a permanent entity that can accommodate several transactions at the same time. Its capacity is defined by the user by means of the STORAGE statement (see Section 6.3, "Entity-Definition Statements").

ENTER   A,B

Operation:

This block tests if the transaction can be accepted by the storage. If so, the transaction enters the ENTER block, the storage contents are increased by the number of units specified by the B-operand, and the transaction proceeds to the next block. If not, the transaction has to wait in the preceding block until enough room is available for it in the storage.

Operands:

A: The storage name or number.

B: (*optional*) The number of units of storage requested by the transaction. If the B-operand is not specified, this number is assumed to be 1.

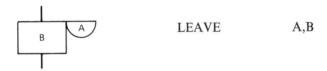

LEAVE   A,B

Operation:

This block removes the transaction from storage A and increases available storage by the number of units specified in the B-operand. This block never refuses entry to a transaction.

Operands:

A: The storage name or number.

B: (*optional*) The number of units of storage to be freed. This number must be smaller than the present contents of the storage. If the B-operand is not specified, the number of units is assumed to be 1.

EXAMPLES:

(1)

```
               .
               .
               .
         ENTER          BUFFE,P1
         ADVANCE        100
         LEAVE          BUFFE,P1
               .
               .
```

tests if there are at least P1 available units in storage BUFFE. If so, the transaction is accepted by the ENTER block, spends 100 time units in the ADVANCE block, and then makes P1 places available when entering the LEAVE block.

(2)

```
               .
               .
               .
         ENTER          PARK
         ADVANCE        120,20
         LEAVE          PARK
               .
               .
               .
```

tests if one place is available in PARK. If so, the transaction is accepted by the ENTER block; the available space in storage PARK is reduced by 1 unit. After waiting in the ADVANCE block, the transaction enters the LEAVE block, which causes the transaction to leave the storage and one place to be made available in PARK.

Queue. The following two blocks are used to modify the status of a queue. A queue is a permanent entity analogous to a storage with unlimited capacity. None of the blocks can refuse entry to a transaction.

QUEUE   A,B

Operation:

This block makes the transaction a member of queue A and adds to its contents the number of units specified by the B-operand (1 if B not specified). The transaction then proceeds to the next block.

Usually a QUEUE block is followed by a block that may refuse entry to transactions, such as SEIZE, ENTER, or GATE. The time that the transaction spends in the queue (between the QUEUE and DEPART blocks) is recorded automatically and can be tabulated.

Operands:

A: The name or number of the queue.

B: (*optional*) The number of units to be added to the contents of the queue. If not specified, it is assumed to be 1.

DEPART   A,B

Operation:

This block is used to remove a transaction from a queue and to decrease the queue contents by the number of units specified by the B-operand.

Operands:

A: The queue name or number.

B: (*optional*) The number of units to be removed from the queue contents. If not specified, 1 is assumed.

EXAMPLES:

(1)
                .
                .
                .

```
QUEUE      LANE
SEIZE      BOOTH
DEPART     LANE
ADVANCE    5
RELEASE    BOOTH
```
                .
                .
                .

The transaction enters queue LANE and waits, if necessary, to seize facility BOOTH. If able to move to facility BOOTH, it departs from the queue, spends 5 time units in the ADVANCE block and releases the facility.

(2)
.
.
.

QUEUE	LANE
SEIZE	BOOTH
ADVANCE	5
RELEASE	BOOTH
DEPART	LANE

.
.
.

This program is similar to example (1) except that queue LANE now includes the facility. The statistics of queue LANE will be different from those of example (1), because the time in the queue now includes the time spent in the facility. The two examples are illustrated by Figure 6.1.

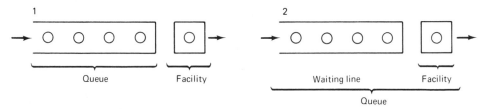

Figure 6.1 Time spent in a queue.

GPSS automatically records and prints the number of transactions that spent zero time in the queue. This information is very useful but is meaningful only in example (1). In example (2) the minimum time in the queue is the time spent in the facility, which is always greater than zero.

6.2.3 Transaction-flow modification

These blocks allow the analyst to direct transactions to a block other than the next sequential one. This is usually achieved by testing the status of components of the model. For example, when a customer arrives at a bank with two cashiers and one is busy, he will usually go straight to the free counter.

Transfer.

TRANSFER   A,B,C,D

Operation:

This block will direct the transaction to a specified location (block), depending on the situation and the transfer mode defined by the A-operand.

Operands:

A: The transfer mode.

1. If omitted (replaced by a comma), the transaction is unconditionally sent to the address specified by the B-operand.

2. BOTH: If the mode is BOTH, the block specified by B is tested; if the transaction is refused by this block, it tries to exit via the block specified by C. If both paths are closed, the transaction remains in the TRANSFER block. The process is repeated at every modification of the clock time.

3. Statistical: If the mode is a decimal fraction, such as 0.25, a random choice is made between addresses B and C. The probability of selecting the next block as C is given by the fraction (here 25 per cent); the probability of selecting the B-address is thus the complement (here 75 per cent). For any particular transaction it is not possible to predict in advance which path will be chosen.

4. SIM (simultaneous mode) is used to select one of two possible paths, depending on the "delay indicator" of the transaction, which may be either set (equal to 1) or reset (equal to 0). If it is 0, the transaction is sent to address B, if 1, to address C.

The delay indicator of a transaction is normally zero until the transaction is refused entry by a block. The indicator is then set to 1 to record that the transaction has been delayed. If several conditions must be satisfied simultaneously before the transaction can proceed, they can be tested one after the other and, at the end, the delay indicator tested using TRANSFER SIM. If it is 0, the transaction is allowed to proceed. If it is 1, meaning that at least one of the conditions had not been satisfied, the transaction is sent back to test all the conditions again.

Other transfer modes are discussed in Section 7.2.3.

B and C: The addresses of a block where the transaction can be sent, depending on the mode specified by the A-operand.

D: An indexing constant used with the ALL transfer mode, to be discussed later.

EXAMPLES:

(1)   TRANSFER   ,LOOP

The transactions are unconditionally sent to block LOOP.

(2)   TRANSFER   .75,NEXT,SEVEN

75 per cent of the transactions, selected at random, are sent to block SEVEN and the remaining 25 per cent go to NEXT. This instruction can also be written as:

TRANSFER   .75,,SEVEN

which implies that the B-field is the next sequential block.

(3)   TRANSFER   BOTH,SERV1,SERV2

The transaction tries to exit to block SERV1; if it is refused, it tries block SERV2. If still refused, it stays in the TRANSFER block.

Another example using the SIM transfer mode is presented at the end of this section after discussion of the GATE and TEST blocks.

Testing.   Blocks GATE and TEST are used to control the flow of transactions based on logical conditions to be tested in the model. These conditions could be the status of equipment, such as facilities or storages, or any other condition between any combination of GPSS attributes. These conditions are not modified by GATE and TEST.

Both blocks can operate in two modes:

Refusal mode: in this case, the transaction is accepted in the block only if the condition is met.

Alternate exit mode: in this case, the transaction is always accepted in the block and immediately sent to the next sequential block if the condition is met, and to an alternate address if the condition is not met.

The difference between the two modes is implied by the use or nonuse of the B-operand to specify an alternate exit address.

                GATE X   A,B

Operation:

The status of the permanent entity specified by the A-operand is tested according to the mnemonics used for X. If a B-operand is specified, the transaction is sent to this address if the condition is not met and to the next sequential block if the condition is met. If no B-operand is specified, the transaction is accepted in the block if the condition is met and refused otherwise.

Operands:

A: The permanent entity name or number.

B: (*optional*) The alternate exit for the transaction when the condition is not satisfied. If the B-operand is not defined, the block operates in refusal mode.

X-Mnemonics.

Facilities:

The mnemonics used in conjunction with facilities are:

U   for facility used (seized or preempted).

NU   for facility not used.

I   for facility interrupted (preempted).

NI   for facility not interrupted (not preempted, that is, either seized or free).

EXAMPLES:

(1)   GATE NU   CPU,WAIT

The transaction will be accepted by the block and sent to the next sequential block if facility CPU is not in use. It will branch to block WAIT if CPU is in use.

(2)   GATE NU   CPU

The transaction will be accepted in the block only if facility CPU is not in use.

Storages:

The mnemonics used in conjunction with storages are:

SF   for storage full.

SNF   for storage not full.

SE   for storage empty.

SNE   for storage not empty.

EXAMPLE:

GATE SNF   BUFFE

The transaction will be accepted by the block only if storage BUFFE is not full.

Other mnemonics available to test the status of switches and the match or non-match status of transactions are discussed in Section 7.2.3. GPSS V can also test the availability or nonavailability of facilities and storages (see Section 7.2.8).

TEST X   A,B,C

Operation:

The condition specified by the logical operator X and the A- and B-operands is tested. If a C-operand is used, the transaction is accepted in the block and sent to the next sequential block if the condition is met. It branches to the address specified by the C-operand if the condition is not met. If no C-operand is used, the block will accept the transaction if the condition is met. It will refuse the transaction otherwise.

Operands:

A and B: The SNAs to be compared using the X-logical operator.

C: (*optional*) The alternate exit address for the transaction when the condition is not met.

X-Logical operator.

E: Equal to. The relation is true only if both arguments are equal.

NE: Not equal to. The relation is true unless the two arguments are equal.

L: Less than. The relation is true only if the A-operand is less than the B-operand.

LE: Less than or equal to. The relation is true if the A-operand is less than or equal to the B-operand.

G: Greater than. The relation is true if the A-operand is greater than the B-operand.

GE: Greater than or equal to. The relation is true if the A-operand is greater than or equal to the B-operand.

EXAMPLES:

(1)   TEST GE   R20,P1

will accept the transaction only if the remaining room in storage 20 is greater than or equal to the value of parameter 1 of the transaction. If the condition is not met, the transaction waits in the previous block.

(2)   TEST L   Q3,10,OUT

The transaction is accepted and sent to the next sequential block if the contents of queue 3 is less than 10 and to block OUT if it is not.

(3)   TEST L   V1,FN3,FAIL

will test whether the value of variable 1 is less than the value of function 3. If true, the transaction enters the TEST block and proceeds to the next sequential block. If false, the transaction is sent to block FAIL.

(4)   In a computer system we want to allow transactions to proceed only if the three facilities CPU, CHA (channel), and CONTR (control unit) are simultaneously available. It is not sufficient to use the following three GATE blocks:

.
.
.

```
ONE        GATE NU      CPU
TWO        GATE NU      CHA
THREE      GATE NU      CONTR
              .
              .
              .
```

It is obvious that such a program segment does not solve the problem. For example, if a transaction arrives and finds CPU and CHA free and CONTR busy, it would wait in block TWO. When CONTR becomes free, the transaction proceeds, but in the meantime CPU or CHA could be seized by another transaction. The above coding does not check these conditions again. The solution to this problem is to use either a TRANSFER in SIM mode, as shown below, or a TEST on a Boolean variable, as shown in Section 7.3.1.

.
.
.

```
ONE        GATE NU       CPU
           GATE NU       CHA
           GATE NU       CONTR
           TRANSFER      SIM,,ONE
              .
              .
              .
```

When the transaction enters the TRANSFER block, its delay indicator is tested. If set, the transaction is sent back to ONE. If reset, then the transaction has gone through the three GATE blocks without delay and can proceed to the next sequential block.

6.2.4 Storage and retrieval of information

The following blocks store information in save locations and matrices. These entities are used in simulation models to retain the values of variables for later use by the simulation program. They never refuse entry to transactions.

SAVEVALUE   A,B,C

Operation:

This block gives access to the save location specified by the A-operand to store, add, or subtract information defined by the B- and C-operands.

Operands:

A: The name or number of the save location. It can be followed by a + or −, indicating that the information specified by the B- and C-operands must be added to or subtracted from the current value of the save.

B: The value to be stored, added, or subtracted.

C: (*optional*) Used to indicate the type of save location referenced: F for fullword, H for halfword. When no C-operand is defined, *fullword* is assumed.

MSAVEVALUE   A,B,C,D,E

Operation:

This block is used to store, add, or subtract information into a matrix savevalue in the same way as the SAVEVALUE block.

Operands:

A: The name or number of the matrix save; it can be followed by a + or −, indicating addition to or subtraction from current contents.

B: The row number of the matrix element.

C: The column number of the matrix element.

D: The value to be stored, added, or subtracted.

E: (*optional*) Used to indicate the type of matrix elements: F for fullword, H for halfword. If no C-operand is defined, *fullword* is assumed.

In GPSS V, there are two additional types of element, denoted by B for byte and L for floating-point save locations and matrices.

EXAMPLES:

(1)   SAVEVALUE   P1,Q3

stores the present length of queue 3 in the save whose number is the value of parameter 1 of the transaction.

(2)   SAVEVALUE   10+,P2,H

adds to halfword save 10 the contents of parameter 2 of the transaction.

(3)   MSAVEVALUE   8,P1,N$XXX,Q*1,H

stores the contents of the queue whose number is the present contents of parameter 1 into halfword matrix 8 in the row specified by parameter 1 of the transaction and the column specified by the number of entries to block XXX.

This procedure allows the user to store information gathered during the simulation and to print it at the end. In matrix 8, for example, we will have the history of the queues specified by parameter 1. If we suppose that P1 can take values 1 to 10 (queues 1 to 10), that we make a loop so as to handle the 10 values successively, and that XXX is the block preceding the loop of MSAVEVALUE concerned, then every time a transaction goes through the loop, the contents of the 10 queues are recorded and will be printed at the end of the simulation. We therefore will have in row 1 the history of queue 1, in row 2 the history of queue 2, and so on. It should be noted that this way of getting transient information is very efficient because it involves no output operation during the simulation.

6.3 Entity-Definition Statements

The format of these statements is the same as for the block-definition statements:

```
2          8               19
LABEL    OPERATION        OPERANDS
```

6.3.1 Storage-definition statement

This statement is used to define the capacity of storages.

Two formats can be used:

The first specifies the capacity of several storages or a range of storages; the second, which was used in the earlier versions of GPSS, specifies single storages.

EXAMPLES:

(1) First format:

```
STORAGE        S1,100/S2-S5,200/S$BUFFE,1500
```

This statement defines the capacities of the storages as shown in Table 6.2.

Table 6.2

Storage Number or Name	Capacity
1	100
2,3,4,5	200
BUFFE	1500

(2) Second format: the label field specifies the storage name or number, the A-operand specifies the capacity.

```
1        STORAGE        100
2        STORAGE        200
.
.
.
BUFFE    STORAGE        1500
```

This form uses six statements instead of one required for the first format shown above.

6.3.2 Variable-definition statement

Variables are computational entities that are evaluated by the simulator when they are referenced. They are identified by Vj or V$NAME, where j (or NAME) is the number (or name) of the variable. There are three types of variable: arithmetic, floating-point, and Boolean. Boolean variables are discussed in Section 7.3.1.

The variable statement has the format:

LABEL VARIABLE	Arithmetic expression for the arithmetic variable.
LABEL FVARIABLE	Arithmetic expression for the floating-point variable.
LABEL	Variable name or number.

No embedded blanks are permitted within the arithmetic expression. The first blank indicates the end of the expression, and everything after is considered as comment.

The elements of a variable may be any SNA, including variables and functions. The available operators are:

$$+ \quad - \quad * \quad / \quad @$$

for addition, subtraction, multiplication, division (truncated to the nearest integer), and modulo division (in which the quotient is discarded and the remainder retained), respectively. Variables are evaluated from left to right, with multiplication and division having precedence over addition and subtraction. Parenthetical expressions have priority.

The difference between the arithmetic and the floating-point variables is as follows. During evaluation of the arithmetic variable each element is evaluated and truncated to an integer. When the final value of the function is evaluated, it is truncated. The elements of a floating-point variable are kept in floating-point form throughout computation, the final value is evaluated, and then it is truncated.

EXAMPLES:

1	VARIABLE	X1+P2
DELAY	VARIABLE	P2+P3/5
2	FVARIABLE	V1/50+V$DELAY@P3

The value of variable 1 is obtained by adding the contents of save location 1 and the value of parameter 2 of the transaction. DELAY is equal to P3/5 (truncated) added to P2.

Note that

10	VARIABLE	(2/3+5)*2

is equal to 10 but

11	FVARIABLE	(2/3+5)*2

is equal to 11.

6.3.3   Function-definition statement

Functions, like variables, are computational entities that are evaluated by the simulator when they are referenced. They allow the user to express functions of one variable in numerical form. The argument can be any SNA, for example, a random number (RNj) for the generation of random variates.

Several types of function can be defined: continuous (C), discrete (D), list (L), discrete attribute valued (E), and list attribute valued (M). The C, D, and L types are illustrated in Figure 6.2(a). For the continuous type, a linear interpolation is performed when the given argument falls between two given points. (The E and M types are discussed in Section 7.3.2.)

The value of a function is truncated after computation *except* when it is used as a function modifier in GENERATE, ADVANCE, and ASSIGN statements or when it is used specifically as a floating-point value. Examples include element of an FVARIABLE, argument of another function, and, in GPSS V, value to be stored in a floating-point parameter or savevalue.

The format of the function definition statement is:

NAME   FUNCTION   A,B

NAME is the function name or number.

Operands:

A: The argument.

B: The type of the function and the number of points specified.

This statement must be immediately followed by entries consisting of numerical values defining all the points of the function by pairs of x, y coordinates separated by a / symbol. In addition, the first numerical value must begin in column 1, the x and y coordinates must be separated by a comma, both coordinates of a point must appear on the same line, the points must be given in ascending order of the argument x, and no information can appear after position 71.

In the case of L (list) type functions, the arguments may be omitted. They are not examined by the GPSS input program because they are supposed to be the successive integers 1, 2, 3, 4, ...

EXAMPLES (FIGURE 6.2):

   (1)   FUNC1   FUNCTION   RN2,C4
                    0,0/.20,.3/.7,.8/1,1
   (2)   FUNC2   FUNCTION   X1,D4
                    5,10/10,40/20,30/30,10
   (3)   FUNC3   FUNCTION   P1,L5
                    ,2/,4/,10/,8/,2

FUNC1 is continuous, defined by four points, and its argument is RN2 (random number 2).

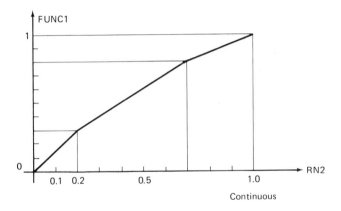

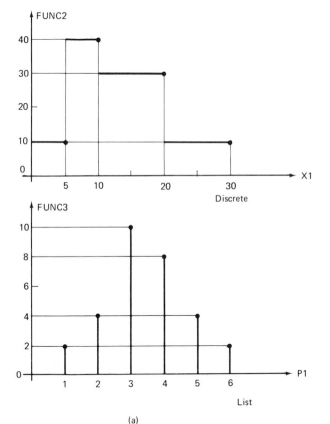

(a)

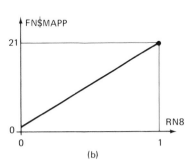

(b)

Figure 6.2(a) Types of GPSS functions. **(b)** Uniform distribution over (1, 20)

Remark: The random numbers generated by the GPSS random-number generators as argument of a function are $0 \leq RNj < 1$ and therefore never reach value 1. This should be taken into account when programming continuous functions. In the above example the value of the function will never be equal to 1.

To amplify this point suppose that we require a mapping function that will produce a uniformly distributed random sequence of the numbers from 1 to 20. It should be programmed as follows [Figure 6.2(b)]:

```
MAPP    FUNCTION        RN8,C2
0,1/1,21
```

Because the greatest value for RN8 is less than 1, the maximum value for the function will be 20.

FUNC2 is a discrete function with four points and its argument is X1, the contents of save location 1.

FUNC3 is a list function with five points, its argument is P1, the contents of parameter 1 of the transaction.

Poisson/exponential distribution. A function that is often used in queueing models is the inverse of the exponential distribution which generates interarrival times corresponding to a Poisson distribution. It is usually defined as C24, continuous with 24 points, which corresponds to $-\ln(1 - r)$ and therefore to a normalized average interarrival time of 1.

```
EXPON   FUNCTION        RN8,C24         EXPON. distr. Mean=1
0.,0/0.1,0.104/0.2,0.222/0.3,0.355/0.4,0.509/0.5,0.69/
0.6,0.915/0.7,1.2/0.75,1.38/0.8,1.6/0.84,1.83/0.88,2.12/
0.9,2.3/0.92,2.52/0.94,2.81/0.95,2.99/0.96,3.2/0.97,3.5/
0.98,3.9/0.99,4.6/0.995,5.3/0.998,6.2/0.999,7.0/0.9997,8.0
```

The following statement will generate transactions with exponentially distributed interarrival times, and an average of 100 time units:

```
GENERATE        100,FN$EXPON
```

The EXPON function is evaluated and used to modify the mean value of 100 by multiplication. The truncated product is taken as the time to generation of the next transaction.

It should be noted that:

(1) the range of the function has been limited to 8, and

(2) the function is evaluated by interpolation between the points given, multiplies the A-operand value, and truncates the result.

Therefore, the distribution of the intergeneration times actually generated during simulation may differ significantly from the theoretical distribution. In particular, if the A-operand is small, it is prudent to reduce the time unit of the model.

For example, if we wish to generate transactions with an average intergeneration time of 3 seconds, it would be bad practice to use the instruction:

```
GENERATE        3,FN$EXPON
```

which implies that the time unit is 1 second.

By changing the time unit to $\frac{1}{100}$ second, we have:

```
GENERATE        300,FN$EXPON
```

which is much better. To illustrate this point, we ran both cases for 10,000 transactions and obtained the following averages for the intergeneration times: $E(t_a) = 2.531$ and $E(t_a) = 300.166$. (This point is discussed further in Section 13.3.)

6.3.4 Save-matrix-definition statement

The save locations and matrices are available for storing information on the model status for later retrieval. They can be used for keeping data accessible to all transactions, to store intermediate results, and to pass information from one GPSS run to the next within the same GPSS job (using the CLEAR control statement with the selective option described in Section 6.1).

The dimensions and type of a matrix save are defined by means of the MATRIX statement:

NAME MATRIX   A,B,C

NAME is the matrix name or number.

Operands:

A: Specifies the type of the matrix: MH for halfwords and MX for fullwords. In GPSS V two further types of matrices may be defined: MB for bytes and ML for floating-point.

B: The number of rows.

C: The number of columns of the matrix.

EXAMPLE:

DELAY MATRIX   MX,3,5

6.3.5 Save and matrix initialization

The contents of save locations and matrices can be modified (replaced, increased, or decreased) by the SAVEVALUE and MSAVEVALUE blocks (see Section 6.2.4) and can also be initialized before a simulation run by using the INITIAL statement:

INITIAL   A,B,C

Operands:

A: The name (or number) of the save location or matrix preceded by its type: X and XH for save locations, MX and MH for matrices, with further types XB, XL, and MB, ML in GPSS V.

B: The value to be stored.

C: (*optional*) A delimiter: / when multiple entries are made in the same INITIAL statement.

EXAMPLES:

(1)   INITIAL   XH1,10

  Save (halfword) 1 is set to 10.

(2)   INITIAL   XH2-XH10,100

Saves (halfword) 2 to 10 are set to 100.

(3)   INITIAL   MX$DELAY(2-3,2-5),20

Elements in rows 2 to 3 and columns 2 to 5 of matrix DELAY are set to 20.
After this initialization, the DELAY matrix has the form shown in Table 6.3.

Table 6.3

	1	2	3	4	5
1	0	0	0	0	0
2	0	20	20	20	20
3	0	20	20	20	20

(4)   INITIAL   MX5-MX10(2-3,2-5),20

Matrices 5 to 10 are initialized to the same values as the matrix DELAY
above.

6.4 Attributes

The 17 attributes listed in this section have been selected from the complete list
because of their importance and convenience to the modeling analyst.

6.4.1 Standard numerical attributes

System attributes.

C1:   Clock time.

RNj: Random number produced by the jth random-number generator. RNj
       is mentioned here because of its importance in modeling, but it is actually
       a computational attribute and therefore mentioned again in Section 6.4.2.

Remark on GPSS V: In addition to the clock time C1, GPSS V has an additional
attribute: AC1, which is the absolute clock time, that is, the time since the beginning
of simulation or since the last CLEAR statement.

Block attributes.

Nj: Total number of transactions that have entered block j.

Wj: Current number of transactions in block j.

It should be noted that:

Nj is the entry count since the beginning of the simulation or the last CLEAR/
RESET operation.

Nj is automatically updated, so it can be used when a one-increment counter is
needed—for example, to number the transactions going through a specific series
of blocks.

EXAMPLES:

(1) Suppose that we need the history of queue number 1. We would like to know the length of the queue at every minute of simulated time. One elegant solution consists of storing the queue length at time 1 in save 1, at time 2 in save 2, etc. At the end of the run, the saves with nonzero contents will be printed. This store operation can be controlled by an "auxiliary clock," as follows:

```
GEN        GENERATE        60
           SAVEVALUE       N$GEN,Q1
           TERMINATE
```

We use N$GEN rather than the N of the SAVEVALUE block because the latter would not include the currently entering transaction. It would therefore be 0 for the first transaction (an illegal save number), 1 for the second, etc.

(2) This idea may be applied to other situations and cases using matrix saves, with the rows corresponding to the values to be saved and the columns to the time values. As an example, store the history of queue 1 in row 1, queue 2 in row 2, etc.

```
GEN        GENERATE        60
           MSAVEVALUE      QUEUE,1,N$GEN,Q1
           MSAVEVALUE      QUEUE,2,N$GEN,Q2
              .
              .
              .
           TERMINATE
```

(3) In certain situations, we may want to number successive transactions cyclically in one parameter, say P1, which should then read: 1, 2, 3, 4, 5, 1, 2, 3, 4, 5, 1, etc. This can be achieved by using one ASSIGN block and one variable as follows:

```
XXX        ASSIGN          1,V1
 1         VARIABLE        N$XXX@5+1
              .
              .
```

When the first transaction enters the ASSIGN block, N$XXX is 0, therefore $V1=1$; when the second transaction enters, $V1=2$, etc., until the fifth transaction enters the block and $V1=5$. When the sixth transaction enters the block, NXXX=5$ and $V1=1$, and the cycle repeats.

Transaction attributes.

Pj: Parameter j of the transaction. The parameter may be halfword or full-word and j may be between 1 and 100.

M1: Transit time of the transaction, or "age"—the difference between the current clock time and the time when the transaction was generated (or last passed a MARK block with no A-operand).

PR: Priority of the transaction (between 0 and 127).

Facility attribute.

Fj: Status of facility j:
           1 if used
           0 if not used

Storage attributes.

Sj: Current contents of storage j.

Rj: Remaining storage units available in storage j.

Queue attribute.

Qj: Current contents of queue j.

Remark on storages and queues: The attributes mentioned above are expressed in units and not in transactions. Remember that one transaction may make several units enter or leave a storage or queue. The count is specified by the B-operand of ENTER, LEAVE, QUEUE, and DEPART.

Save locations and matrices.

Xj: Current contents of fullword save location j.

XHj: Current contents of halfword save location j.

MXj(k,ℓ):   Current contents of element in line k, column ℓ of fullword matrix save j.

MXHj(k,ℓ): Current contents of element in line k, column ℓ of halfword matrix save j.

Remark on GPSS V: Because of the availability of various types of parameter and save and matrix in GPSS V, the following notation applies:

Transaction parameter j: PFj (fullword), PHj (halfword), PBj (byte), and PLj (floating point).

Save j: Xj or XFj (fullword), XHj (halfword), XBj (byte), and XLj (floating point).

Matrix save j: MXj(k,ℓ) (fullword), MHj(k,ℓ) (halfword), MBj(k,ℓ) (byte), and MLj(k,ℓ) (floating point).

6.4.2   Computational entities

Variable.

Vj: Value of the variable j.

Function.

FNj: Value of the function j.

See Sections 6.3.2 and 6.3.3 for detailed information on these entities.

Random number.

RNj: Value of the random number produced by the random-number generator j.

Remark: Like variables and functions, random numbers are not stored as a SNA; they are computed every time they are referenced, using an algorithm that calculates a new value from the previous value.

6.4.3 Standard logical attributes

Facilities.

Uj: Status of facility j:
        1 if used
        0 otherwise

NUj: Status of facility j:
        1 if not used
        0 otherwise

6.5 Indirect Addressing

The usual way of specifying GPSS entities is by their names or numbers, for example:

SEIZE	CPU	Seize facility CPU;
ENTER	WAIT	Enter storage WAIT;
QUEUE	LINE	Enter queue LINE;
ADVANCE	FN$MEAN	Compute the delay, value of the function MEAN, and schedule the transaction accordingly;

or

SEIZE	1	Seize facility number 1;
ENTER	7	Enter storage number 7;
QUEUE	2	Enter queue number 2;
ADVANCE	FN1,FN2	Advance by FN1*FN2.

Reference to GPSS attributes is made in the following way:

Q$WAIT	Current contents of queue WAIT.
S$BUFFE	Current contents of storage BUFFE.
FN$EXPON	Value of function EXPON.
Q10	Current contents of queue 10.
R12	Remaining room in storage 12.

.
.
.

To give greater flexibility and power to GPSS models, the concept of *indirect addressing* was introduced. It allows the user to specify block operands as SNAs and to refer to SNAs whose index numbers are stored in parameters.

In certain problems it may be necessary to repeat a sequence of GPSS blocks several times. For example, suppose that we have transactions of types 1 to 3, coded

as 1, 2, or 3 in parameter 1 and that at a given point in the model we must send transactions of type 1 to facility 1 preceded by queue 1, type 2 to facility 2 and queue 2, etc.

Without indirect addressing, we would require the following type of code:

	TEST E	P1,1,NOT1	Test if type 1 transaction: if not, go to
	QUEUE	1	NOT1; if yes, enter queue 1, seize facility
	SEIZE	1	1, ...
	.		
	.		
	.		
NOT1	TEST E	P1,2,NOT2	Test if type 2 transaction: if not, go to
	QUEUE	2	NOT2; if yes, enter queue 2, seize facility
	SEIZE	2	2, ...
	.		
	.		
	.		
NOT2	TEST E	P1,3,ERROR	Test if type 3 transaction, etc. . . .
	QUEUE	3	
	SEIZE	3	
	.		
	.		
	.		

Indirect addressing reduces these nine blocks to two:

.		
.		
.		
QUEUE	P1	Enter the queue whose number is the value
SEIZE	P1	of parameter 1 and seize the facility whose
.		number is the value of parameter 1.
.		

More generally, almost all operands of GPSS statements may be specified using
GPSS attributes instead of symbolic names or numbers. When there is any doubt
about the permitted forms of an operand, one should consult Appendix B, which lists
all the blocks with their operands and indicates where SNAs can be used.

Transaction parameters can be referenced in three ways:

$$*j$$
$$Pj$$
$$P*j$$

The first two are equivalent. The third has a completely different interpretation: it
means the value of the parameter whose number is the present value of parameter j; for
example: P*3 is the value of the parameter whose number is the value of parameter 3.
If P3=7 and P7=2, then P*3=2. Therefore, with the above parameter values,

$$\text{SEIZE} \qquad \text{P*3}$$

would be equivalent to SEIZE 2.

When referencing *GPSS attributes*, indirect addressing is also possible; for example:

Q∗3:   The contents of the queue whose number is the present value of the transaction parameter 3.

R∗2:   The remaining room in the storage whose number is the present value of P2.

GPSS/360 does not allow the user to define attributes using two levels of indirect addressing. To find the length of the queue whose number is the contents of save location 10, one must first save X10 in a parameter, say P1, by ASSIGN 1,X10. Then one can refer to Q∗1. Examples of utilization of indirect addressing are given in Sections 6.6.2 and 6.6.4.

GPSS V extends these indirect addressing capabilities considerably. The asterisk is used to indicate when indirect addressing is used. The general format for indirect addressing is therefore SNA∗SNAj.

EXAMPLES:

(1)   FN∗XB$NAME is the value of the function whose number is the current value of the byte save location NAME.

(2)   X∗PH5 is the contents of the save location whose number is the contents of halfword parameter 5.

(3)   Q∗XH10 is the contents of the queue whose number is the contents of halfword save 10.

(4)   FN∗FN$FUNCT is the value of the function whose number is the value of function FUNCT.

(5)   ADVANCE MX∗V2(FN∗PH4,2) means advance by a time that is given by the fullword matrix whose number is the value of variable 2, whose row number is the value of the function whose number is halfword parameter 4, and whose column number is 2.

6.6 Programming Examples

6.6.1 SMALL manufacturing and delivery company

The problem. The SMALL company (Figure 6.3) consists of two departments, the manufacturing department, which has one machine producing one type of item, and the packing and delivery department, with one packing machine. Incoming orders for items are fulfilled on a first in–first out (FIFO) basis. The items ordered are taken from the stock produced by the machine and packed by the packing machine.

To avoid an excessive delivery time, the backlog is limited to 10. When this limit is reached, further incoming orders are sent to another company (not considered in this model) until the backlog is decreased by filling the waiting orders.

Statistical data are summarized below.

The time to produce one item varies between 60 and 100 seconds, with uniform distribution.

MANUFACTURING

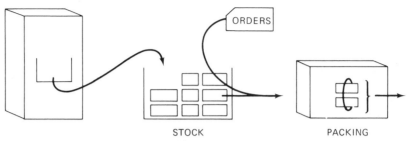

Figure 6.3   The SMALL Company problem.

The mean time between two orders is 300 seconds; the distribution of time is assumed to be exponential.

The number of items required by each order is given by the distribution shown in Table 6.4.

Table 6.4

Percentage	Number of Items
10	4
40	5
30	6
20	7

The packing time per order consists of a fixed time of 90 seconds plus 50 seconds per item to be packed.

The purpose of this model is to determine:

1. The number of orders that have to be sent to another company. This lost business could indicate that another strategy should be tried.
2. The utilization of the packing machine.
3. The average number of orders waiting for fulfillment.
4. The average waiting time for the packing machine.

The GPSS model.   In this problem there are two flows of elements. The first is the creation of items by the machine. The second consists of incoming orders. The interaction between the two flows is indicated by the stock level. Created items increase stock and filled orders decrease stock.

This is represented in GPSS by two streams of transactions which are completely separated. The stock is represented by a storage called STOCK; its capacity is not limited, which means that no storage-definition card is needed. To limit the number of orders accepted, a second storage called REQ is used; its capacity in this trial is set to 10, so that a maximum of 10 orders may wait together.

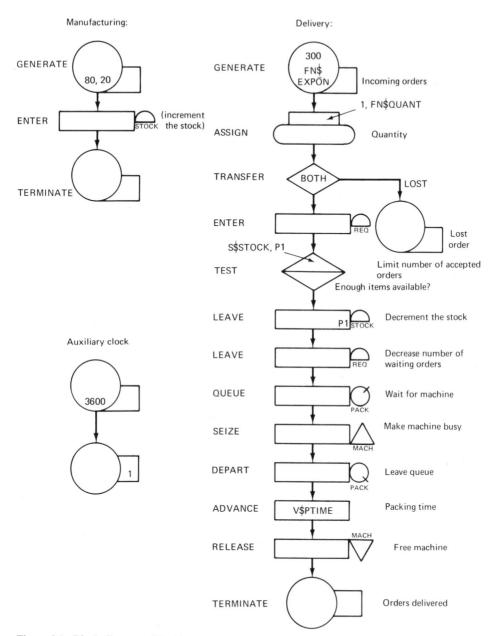

Figure 6.4 Block diagram of the SMALL company.

Figure 6.4 gives the flowchart of the model. Note that storage STOCK is incremented (ENTER STOCK) by one kind of transaction, items, and that it is decremented (LEAVE STOCK) by another, orders.

```
BLOCK                                                                          CARD
NUMBER  *LOC    OPERATION  A,B,C,D,E,F,G                COMMENTS               NUMBER
                SIMULATE                                                         1
                                                                                2
        EXPON FUNCTION   RN8,C24      EXPONENTIAL DISTRIBUTION - MEAN = 1.       3
        0.,0/0.1,0.104/0.2,0.222/0.3,0.355/0.4,0.509/0.5,0.69/0.6,0.915/        4
        0.7,1.2/0.75,1.38/0.8,1.6/0.84,1.83/0.88,2.12/0.9,2.3/0.92,2.52/        5
        0.94,2.81/0.95,2.99/0.96,3.2/0.97,3.5/0.98,3.9/0.99,4.6/0.995,5.3/      6
        0.998,6.2/0.999,7.0/0.9997,8.0                                          7
                                                                                8
        QUANT FUNCTION   RN2,D4                ORDER'S QUANTITY                  9
        .1,4/.5,5/.8,6/1,7                                                      10
                                                                               11
        PTIME VARIABLE   50*P1+90              PACKAGING TIME                   12
                                                                               13
        REQ   STORAGE    10                                                    14
                                                                               15
1               GENERATE   300,FN$EXPON       ORDERS                           16
2               ASSIGN     1,FN$QUANT         QUANTITY PER ORDER               17
3               TRANSFER   BOTH,,LOST                                          18
                                                                               19
4               ENTER      REQ                ACCEPTED ORDERS                  20
5               TEST GE    S$STOCK,P1                                          21
6               LEAVE      STOCK,P1                                            22
7               LEAVE      REQ                                                 23
8               QUEUE      PACK                                                24
9               SEIZE      MACH               PACKAGING MACHINE                25
10              DEPART     PACK                                                26
11              ADVANCE    V$PTIME                                             27
12              RELEASE    MACH                                                28
13              TERMINATE                                                      29
                                                                               30
14      LOST    TERMINATE                     REJECTED ORDERS                  31
                                                                               32
15              GENERATE   80,20              PARTS' CREATION                  33
16              ENTER      STOCK                                               34
17              TERMINATE                                                      35
                                                                               36
18              GENERATE   3600               SIMULATED CLOCK                  37
19              TERMINATE  1                                                   38
                                                                               39
                START      8                                                   40
                                                                               41
                END                                                            42
```

Figure 6.5   GPSS program of SMALL company model.

Figure 6.5 gives the listing of the program. The following remarks amplify some points of detail. The packing time is calculated by the variable PTIME used in block 11: ADVANCE V$PTIME. When a transaction enters that block, the variable V$PTIME is computed using the number stored in parameter 1 of the incoming transaction. The number assigned by block 2 represents the quantity ordered.

Block 3: TRANSFER BOTH,,LOST controls the orders. Each time a transaction enters the block, an attempt is made to go to the next block (ENTER REQ). If the storage REQ is already full, then the transaction is sent to the block with symbolic name LOST (block 14).

The simulation length is controlled by the auxiliary clock (blocks 18 and 19). The START 8 statement, together with the two preceding blocks, specifies that the duration of simulation will be 8 hours (8 times 3600 seconds).

Conclusion and results.   With the input data given above, the following results were obtained:

1. A total of 96 orders were generated, 73 were accepted, 23 were lost.

2. The utilization of the packing machine was 0.807.

3. The average number of orders waiting for fulfillment was 7.960. In general these orders did not wait because of unavailability of the packing machine but because the production rate of the manufacturing machine was too slow.

4. Of 64 transactions handled by the packing machine, 46 did not wait. The average waiting time for the others was 72.611 seconds, which is negligible.

Summary. This simple problem has shown how a model can be considered as two submodels that handle manufacturing and delivery. In each submodel the transactions generated at the beginning are destroyed by different TERMINATE blocks. The two streams of transactions are completely separated. The only interaction is through referencing the contents of storage STOCK. Transactions representing orders have to wait if the contents of that storage is too small. Further, we have seen how to use GPSS variables and the operation of the TRANSFER BOTH block.

6.6.2 Traffic lights

The problem. A two-lane road is being repaired and one lane is closed for 500 meters. Traffic lights must be installed to control the traffic. The traffic intensity is Poisson-distributed, with an average of 300 cars per hour in one direction and 400 in the other. A limit of 40 kilometers per hour is imposed on the 500 meters and we assume it to be observed by all cars.

When a light turns green, the waiting cars start and pass the light line every 2 seconds. A light cycle consists of green in direction 1 (GRE1), both red, green in direction 2 (GRE2), both red. Both traffic lights must be red for 55 seconds to allow cars to leave the repair section.

The problem to be studied is how should GRE1 and GRE2 be chosen to minimize the average waiting time for all cars?

The GPSS model. The first analysis of the problem shows that we have three independent phenomena: traffic from both directions and traffic lights. The model will therefore consist of three groups of blocks.

In the first two parts it is natural to represent the cars by transactions. In the third, the simplest way of treating the problem is to let the green light (or green signal) be the transaction. The lights are then represented by facilities ONE and TWO, which will alternately be seized (green) for the green time and released (red) for 110 seconds plus the green time of the other direction.

The model is quite simple, as shown by the block diagram of Figure 6.6 and the program of Figure 6.7. However, it is vital to process only one transaction at a time in each of the vehicle streams. This is done by using dummy facilities STAR1 and STAR2 for directions 1 and 2, respectively, which can be thought of as the physical places where the first car of the queue is waiting. By seizing the facility and releasing it only after one car is completely processed, we ensure that only one car is handled at a time.

To illustrate this point, suppose that SEIZE STAR1 is placed just before the ADVANCE block. If the light was red at the beginning of simulation and then turned green, the first transaction in the queue would be processed, seize the facility, and stay in the ADVANCE block. At the same clock time, the second transaction of the queue would be processed. As the light is green, it would be accepted, in turn, by the GATE and in the TRANSFER block, where it would wait. The same would happen

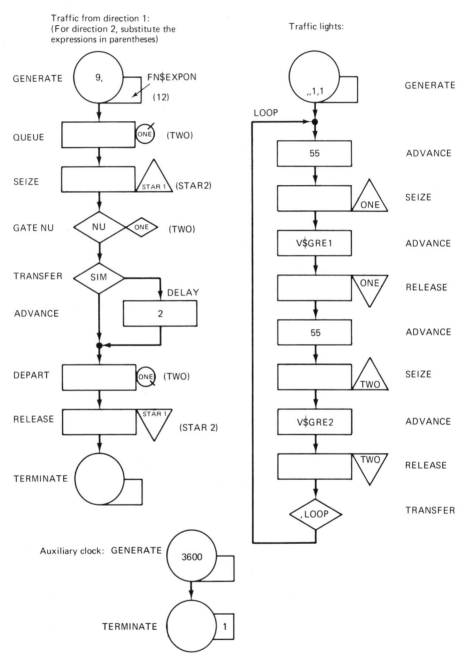

Figure 6.6 Block diagram of traffic lights model.

```
            SIMULATE

* TRAFFIC LIGHTS PROBLEM
*-----------------------

 EXPON FUNCTICN    RN8,C24       EXPONENTIAL DISTRIBUTICN - MEAN = 1.
0.,0/0.1,0.104/0.2,0.222/0.3,0.355/0.4,0.509/0.5,0.69/C.6,0.915/
0.7,1.2/0.75,1.38/0.8,1.6/0.84,1.83/0.88,2.12/0.9,2.3/0.92,2.52/
0.94,2.81/0.95,2.99/0.96,3.2/0.97,3.5/0.98,3.9/0.99,4.6/0.995,5.3/
0.998,6.2/0.999,7.0/0.9997,8.0

 GRE1   VARIABLE    60
 GRE2   VARIABLE    45

* TRAFFIC FROM DIRECTICN 1
*------------------------
        GENERATE    9,FN$EXPCN          GENERATE CARS
        QUEUE       CNE                 ENTER CLELE
        SEIZE       STAR1               SEIZE STARTING PLACE
        GATE U      CNE                 IS LIGHT GREEN?
        TRANSFER    SIM,DIREC,DFLAY     IF CAR WAS STOPPED START, IF NOT
*                                       GC TO DIREC

 DELAY  ADVANCE     2                   START TIME

 DIREC  DEPART      CNE                 LEAVE QUEUE
        RELEASE     STAR1               FREE STARTING PLACE
        TERMINATE                       LEAVE MCDEL

* TRAFFIC FROM DIRECTION 2
*------------------------
        GENERATE    12,FN$EXPON         SAME FROGRAM AS FOR
        QUEUE       TWO                 CIRECTICN 1 WITH QUEUE TWC,
        SEIZE       STAR2               STARTING PLACE STAR2 AND
        GATE U      TWO                 LIGHT TWO
        TRANSFER    SIM,CIR,DEL

 DEL    ADVANCE     2

 CIR    DEPART      TWO
        RELEASE     STAR2
        TERMINATE

* TRAFFIC LIGHTS
*--------------
        GENERATE    ,,1,1               CCNTRCL TRANSACTION: LIGHT
 LOOP   ADVANCE     55                  BOTH LIGHTS RED
        SEIZE       CNE                 LIGHT ONE BECOMES GREEN
        ADVANCE     V$GRE1              GREEN TIME 1
        RELEASE     ONE                 LIGHT ONE TURNS TO RED
        ADVANCE     55                  BOTH LIGHTS RED
        SEIZE       TWO                 LIGHT TWC BECOMES GREEN
        ADVANCE     V$GRE2              GREEN TIME 2
        RELEASE     TWO                 LIGHT TWC TURNS TO RED
        TRANSFER    ,LOOP               BEGIN NEW CYCLE

*AUXILIARY CLCCK
*--------------
        GENERATE    3600                ONE TRANSACTION PER HOUR
        TERMINATE   1                   DECREMENT TERM. TO GO COUNT




        START       1

        CLEAR
 GRE1   VARIABLE    80
 GRE2   VARIABLE    60
        START       1

        CLEAR
 GRE1   VARIABLE    40
 GRE2   VARIABLE    30
        START       1
        ENC
```

Figure 6.7   GPSS program of traffic lights model.

for other queued transactions. Now, if there were 60 in the queue and the green time were 80 seconds, then 40 cars would pass, but, when the light changed to red, 20 cars would still be waiting *in the* TRANSFER *block*. Therefore, having passed the test for the green light but with the light red, they would continue to pass every 2 seconds.

This difficulty arises because GPSS always moves transactions as far as possible through the block diagram at a given point in time. This problem is very general and great care should be taken whenever one transaction must be processed completely before another one can be considered.

After being generated, transactions join the queue, try to seize facility STAR1 or STAR2, representing the starting place and test the light, using the GATE block. If the light is green, we must decide if the car was stopped, and therefore has to spend the 2 seconds starting time, or had just arrived, in which case it could pass without the 2-second delay. This decision is made by using a TRANSFER block in SIM mode. If the transaction had been delayed, either by the SEIZE block because a previous car was starting or by the GATE block because the light was red, its delay indicator (see Section 6.2.3, "Transfer": SIM mode) is set and the TRANSFER block sends it to DELAY. Otherwise, it goes to DIREC where it terminates.

The traffic-light operation is modeled by one transaction representing the green light. It is delayed for 55 seconds (both lights red), seizes facility ONE for a time equal to GRE1, releases it (turning it to red), is delayed for 55 seconds, seizes facility TWO for a time equal to GRE2, releases it (making it red), and loops.

To make the model flexible the green times are specified by two variables GRE1 and GRE2. This allows the user to experiment with various values without changing the model. In the program shown in Figure 6.7, we have made three runs of the same job, taking successive green times of 60 and 45 seconds, 80 and 60, 40 and 30. They are in the ratio 4:3, which is the same ratio as the arrival rates for the two directions. The three runs are separated by CLEAR statements, followed by the new definition of the variables GRE1 and GRE2. Every run was for 1 hour of simulated time using an "auxiliary clock" (GENERATE/TERMINATE with the START statement).

Simultaneous events. The problem of simultaneous events was briefly mentioned in Section 5.5.4. We now consider it in more detail.

Suppose that during the simulation one car is scheduled to arrive in the model (that is, to leave the GENERATE block 1) at the same clock time as the green-light transaction is scheduled to leave the ADVANCE V$GRE1 block. As these two transactions are able to move, they are both in the current-events chain. First, suppose that the transaction representing the car is ahead of the other. It will move successively to the QUEUE, SEIZE, GATE (and be accepted there because the light is green), TRANSFER, and TERMINATE blocks. The other transaction, representing the green light, then moves from the ADVANCE V$GRE1 block to the RELEASE ONE block (turning the light to red) and to the ADVANCE 55 block. The car has passed the light at the same instant as it turned red.

Second, suppose that the two transactions appear in the current-events chain in the reverse order. The transaction representing the light is moved from the ADVANCE into the RELEASE ONE block, thus turning the light to red, is stopped in the ADVANCE 55, and put in the future-events chain. The next transaction (representing the car) is then processed and, because it finds the light red, is not accepted in the GATE block and consequently has to wait.

It is therefore clear that the results depend on the order in which transactions appear in the current-events chain. In one case the car passes as the light turns red, in the other it must stop. One could argue that this also happens in real life. But in many problems we wish to control such events in one way or another, depending, for example, on the country in which the model is used, and therefore on the degree of discipline of the local drivers.

The problem is easily overcome by using the concept of priority. If we decide that no car will start if the light is about to turn red, we impose this condition by assigning a higher priority to the transaction that represents the light than to the transactions that represent the cars. This forces the transaction representing the light to be processed first because the current-events chain is ordered first by priority level and second by BDT, block departure time (see Section 4.6). This can be done by specifying priority 1 in the traffic-lights GENERATE block 19, which would have the form GENERATE ,,1,1,1. Conversely, if we want to allow the car to start when the light is turning to red at the same clock time, we would give priority 1 to the cars and priority zero to the traffic-light transaction.

Indirect addressing. To illustrate the use of indirect addressing, we show an alternative GPSS model (Figure 6.8) in which we process transactions from both directions in a common program, beginning with COMM. The transactions are generated, the direction (1 or 2) is stored in parameter 1, and the same number, plus 2, is stored in P2, to be used as facility number for the traffic lights: 3 for direction 1, 4 for direction 2. Transactions join queue P1 (1 for direction 1, 2 for direction 2) and try to seize facility P1. If successful, the light (P2) is tested (facility 3 for direction 1, facility 4 for direction 2). Finally, they leave queue P1 and release facility P1.

This simple example shows how indirect addressing can be used to make simulation programs more concise. The technique is very important when coding larger models.

Conclusion and results. The important statistics are the waiting times in queues 1 and 2 that we wish to minimize. In the three runs, we obtained successive results: 80.6 and 102.4 (60 and 45 seconds, green times), 83.1 and 92.9 (80 and 60 seconds), and 162.2 and 303.4 (40 and 30 seconds). These results suggest that further investigations in the 60-to-45-second range should lead to the minimum average waiting time. To do this, we simply change the variables GRE1 and GRE2. Also, when the optimum is found, one may want to simulate the behavior of the system for a longer time or for several time slices to check the stability of the results.

Summary. To construct a valid model for this problem it was important

(1) to recognize that there were three independent phenomena.

(2) to decide which transactions were in the various groups of blocks.

```
        SIMULATE

*  TRAFFIC LIGHTS PROBLEM
*-----------------------

  EXPON FUNCTION    RN8,C24        EXPONENTIAL DISTRIBUTION - MEAN = 1.
  0.,0/0.1,0.104/0.2,0.222/0.3,0.355/0.4,0.509/0.5,0.69/0.6,0.915/
  0.7,1.2/0.75,1.38/0.8,1.6/0.84,1.83/0.88,2.12/0.9,2.3/0.92,2.52/
  0.94,2.81/0.95,2.99/0.96,3.2/0.97,3.5/0.98,3.9/0.99,4.6/0.995,5.3/
  0.998,6.2/0.999,7.0/0.9997,8.0

  GRE1  VARIABLE   60
  GRE2  VARIABLE   45

*  TRAFFIC FROM DIRECTION 1
*------------------------
        GENERATE   9,FN$EXPON
        ASSIGN     1,1             DIRECTION 1 IN P1
        ASSIGN     2,3             FACILITY 3 (LIGHT 1) IN P2
        TRANSFER   ,COMM

*  TRAFFIC FROM DIRECTION 2
*------------------------
        GENERATE   12,FN$EXPON
        ASSIGN     1,2             DIRECTION 2 IN P1
        ASSIGN     2,4             FACILITY 4 (LIGHT 2) IN P2

*  COMMON TREATMENT USING INDIRECT ADDRESSING
*----------------------------------------------
  COMM  QUEUE      P1              QUEUE 1 OR 2 DEPEND. ON DIRECTION
        SEIZE      P1              STARTING PLACE 1 OR 2
        GATE U     P2              IS LIGHT GREEN? (FAC 3 OR 4)
        TRANSFER   SIM,DIREC,DELAY IF CAR WAS STOPPED START. IF NOT
*                                  LEAVE AND TERMINATE IMMEDIATELY
  DELAY ADVANCE    2               STARTING TIME

  DIREC DEPART     P1              LEAVE QUEUE AND
        RELEASE    P1              FREE STARTING PLACE
        TERMINATE

*  TRAFFIC LIGHTS
*--------------
        GENERATE   ,,1,1           GENERATE ONE SIGNAL (GREEN LIGHT)
  LOOP  ADVANCE    55
        SEIZE      3               LIGHT 1 BECOMES GREEN (FAC 3)
        ADVANCE    V$GRE1          GREEN TIME 1
        RELEASE    3               RED
        ADVANCE    55              BOTH RED
        SEIZE      4               LIGHT 2 BECOMES GREEN (FAC 4)
        ADVANCE    V$GRE2          GREEN TIME 2
        RELEASE    4               RED
        TRANSFER   ,LOOP

*  AUXILIARY CLOCK
*---------------
        GENERATE   3600
        TERMINATE  1

        START      1
```

```
        CLEAR
  GRE1  VARIABLE   80
  GRE2  VARIABLE   60
        START      1

        CLEAR
  GRE1  VARIABLE   40
  GRE2  VARIABLE   30
        START      1
        END
```

Figure 6.8 GPSS traffic lights program, using indirect addressing.

(3) to avoid simultaneously moving several transactions at the same clock time, which could lead to an incorrect model. This problem was solved by using a facility to admit only one transaction between the corresponding SEIZE and RELEASE blocks.

In addition, the use of different priorities for the green light and the cars was proposed as a solution to the difficulties inherent in programming simultaneous events.

6.6.3 Machine repair

The problem. A machine has one essential component that breaks down after a random time (time between failures) found to be uniformly distributed between 400 and 1400 minutes. The machine is serviced by an operator who is also in charge of repairing the parts. The time to repair is uniformly distributed between 400 and 1200 minutes. When the machine breaks down, the operator dismounts the faulty part, which takes a negligible amount of time, and mounts a repaired one. Mounting and adjusting take 10 to 30 minutes. When not occupied in changing parts, the operator repairs the used parts. If the machine breaks down during repairs and a good part is available, the operator stops repairing, replaces the faulty part to restore machine operation, and resumes repairing damaged parts. Before the repaired parts can be used, they must be submitted to a special treatment, which takes 5 minutes.

The problem is to determine how many parts are needed to ensure that the machine will be operational for more than 90 percent of the time. It is also necessary to estimate the busy time of the operator. We wish to simulate the operation of the machine for 8000 hours and test the significance of the results every 2000 hours.

The GPSS model. There are several possible approaches to this problem. The simplest is to represent the parts by transactions; therefore, we will have as many transactions as we have parts. The machine is represented by facility MAC, the operator by facility OPER. The good parts are kept in storage STOCK and the parts to be repaired in queue REP.

It is important to decide how to represent the breakdowns. They occur after random intervals, so we could use either a GENERATE or an ADVANCE block. The GENERATE-block approach poses problems because breakdowns must not be generated when the machine is down or being repaired. This block should therefore be followed by a block that can refuse transactions. If this is the case then when the path is open the transaction immediately leaves the GENERATE block and goes farther, but the distribution of generated transactions is different from that specified. These reflections obviously suggest the use of an ADVANCE block which specifies the time between failures. (In other problems, the times between events may be represented better by a GENERATE block. See the example given in Section 7.6.2.)

The transaction represents a good part when it enters the ADVANCE block and it models a faulty part when it leaves. This technique makes the program very simple. The remaining problem is to ensure that only one part at a time leaves the storage

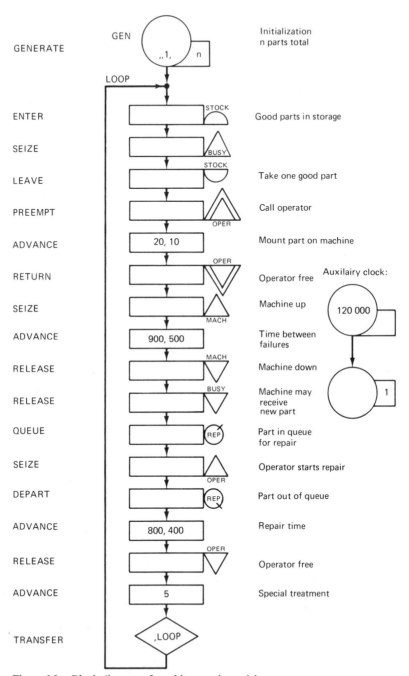

Figure 6.9 Block diagram of machine repair model.

```
BLOCK                                                                           CARD
NUMBER  *LOC    OPERATION  A,B,C,D,E,F,G              COMMENTS                  NUMBER
        *MACHINE REPAIR PROBLEM                                                    1
                                                                                  2
                SIMULATE                                                           3
                                                                                  4
1       GEN     GENERATE   ,,1,2              CREATE GOOD PARTS                    5
2       LOOP    ENTER      STOCK              STORE IN STOCK                       6
3               SEIZE      BUSY               IS MACHINE TO BE REPAIRED?           7
4               LEAVE      STOCK              TAKE ONE GOOD PART                    8
5               PREEMPT    OPER               INTERRUPT OPERATOR                   9
6               ADVANCE    20,10              TO MOUNT THE PART                   10
7               RETURN     OPER               END INTERRUPT                       11
8               SEIZE      MACH               START MACHINE                       12
9               ADVANCE    900,500            TIME BETWEEN FAILURES               13
10              RELEASE    MACH               MACHINE BREAKS DOWN                 14
11              RELEASE    BUSY               HAS TO BE REPAIRED                  15
12              QUEUE      REP                BAD PARTS IN QUEUE REP              16
13              SEIZE      OPER               OPERATOR STARTS REPAIRING           17
14              DEPART     REP                PART OUT OF QUEUE REP               18
15              ADVANCE    800,400            REPAIR TIME                        19
16              RELEASE    OPER               OPERATOR FINISHES                   20
17              ADVANCE    5                  SPECIAL TREATMENT                   21
18              TRANSFER   ,LOOP              BACK INTO GOOD PARTS: STOCK         22
                                                                                 23
        * AUXILIARY CLOCK                                                         24
19              GENERATE   120000             ONE TRANSACTION EVERY 2000 HOURS    25
20              TERMINATE  1                                                      26
                                                                                 27
                START      4,,1               SIMULATION FOR 8000 HOURS WITH      28
        *                                     INTERMEDIATE RESULTS EVERY 200HRS   29
                CLEAR                                                             30
1       GEN     GENERATE   ,,1,3                                                  31
        MULTIPLE DEFINITION OF SYMBOL IN ABOVE CARD                               32
                START      4,,1                                                   33
                END                                                              34
```

Figure 6.10 GPSS program of machine repair model.

STOCK. We therefore introduce a dummy facility, BUSY, which ensures that only one part, either being mounted or in operation, will be on the machine at any time. The BUSY facility may be considered as "machine is either in operation or being repaired."

The block diagram is shown in Figure 6.9 and the source program in Figure 6.10. The best way to follow the program is to start reading at block 8, where the machine begins operation. The transaction (good part) seizes MACH for a time = 900 ± 500. After this time has elapsed, a breakdown occurs; the transaction releases MACH and represents a part to be repaired, which is put in queue REP. As soon as the operator (facility OPER) is free, it will be seized by one transaction waiting in queue REP, for a time equal to 800 ± 400, and then released. After 5 time units spent in the ADVANCE block for the special treatment, the transaction, which now represents a good part, is put in storage STOCK of good parts and waits. When facility BUSY becomes free, which means that the machine breaks down (one transaction entering block 11: RELEASE BUSY), one transaction (if one is currently in the ENTER STOCK block) seizes it, leaves STOCK, and interrupts (PREEMPT block) operator OPER (who might be busy repairing a part) for a time of 20 ± 10 minutes to fit a new part. The transaction then seizes MACH to restart the machine.

At time 1 the first GENERATE instruction creates the number of parts with which we want to operate. In this example we have specified 2 in the D-operand.

The simulation length is controlled by an "auxiliary clock" (blocks 19 and 20), where a transaction is generated and terminated every 2000 hours (120,000 minutes). The START card requests simulation for 8000 hours (4 times 2000) with intermediate printouts at every termination (1 in the C-field), which occurs every 2000 hours.

The next statements, CLEAR, GENERATE, and START, cause a new run to take place, this time with three parts (D-operand of the GENERATE block).

Conclusion and results.   The results of the two runs are summarized in Table 6.5. Only the final results, after 8000 hours of simulation, are given. After these simulation experiments, we see that three parts are needed to give a utilization of MACH above 90 per cent.

Table 6.5

	With Two Parts	With Three Parts
Number of breakdowns	465	511
Average utilization of MACH	0.875	0.954
Average utilization of OPER	0.779	0.865
Average utilization of BUSY	0.895	0.976
Average time per transaction in MACH	904	897

At this point, we can look further into the results and see, for example, that the last experiment showed an average time between failures of 897 (904 in the first case) and a total number of breakdowns of 511 (465 in the first case). These figures suggest that we should investigate the stability of the simulation by looking at intermediate results.

The percentage utilization of MACH for 2000, 4000, 6000, and 8000, respectively, was 0.936, 0.951, 0.950, and 0.954, which indicates good stability.

Summary.   The following important decisions were made for modeling this system:

1. Definition of the transactions. We have decided that the parts were transactions. A different approach would be to have two "control transactions," the first one bringing the machine into operation and stopping it, and the second controlling the repair of damaged parts. The parts might then be represented by units in two save locations, one for the good parts, the other the faulty parts. Such an approach, although different, would lead to a perfectly acceptable model, but it would use more GPSS blocks and probably more machine time.

2. Choice between GENERATE and ADVANCE block for the simulation of breakdowns. In this example the obvious choice was the ADVANCE block.

3. Use of PREEMPT/RETURN to define the operator priority for repairing the machine over off-line repairing of faulty parts.

4. Avoidance of the uncontrolled movement at the same clock time of several transactions. We added the dummy facility BUSY, which ensures that there is only one transaction between the corresponding SEIZE and RELEASE blocks.

6.6.4 Teleprocessing system

The initial problem. A real-time computer serves three terminals which can send four types of message. When they arrive, the messages enter a queue and wait for processing. The queue is handled in arrival order (FIFO). The processing time of each message depends on its source and type, as given in Table 6.6. Statistics of the distributions of interarrival times between messages, which were found to be uniform, are also given in the table. All values are stated in milliseconds (ms).

Table 6.6

Source Number	Interarrival Times	Processing Time
1	4500 ± 2000	350
2	3000 ± 800	320
3	2000 ± 700	240

The distribution of the various types of messages, which is the same for all terminals, is given in Table 6.7, together with the additional processing time required for each type. For example, a message of type 3 from terminal 2 takes a processing time of 570 ± 50 ms.

Table 6.7

Message Type	Frequency	Processing Time
1	30	500 ± 100
2	50	400 ± 100
3	10	250 ± 50
4	10	900 ± 200

Simulate the behavior of the central processing unit (CPU), ignoring the transmission lines and terminal operations. Simulate the system for 10 minutes of operation and record the average waiting time, the average contents of the queue (all message types), the average response time of the system for each source separately (ignoring the transmission time to and from the terminal), and the utilization of the CPU.

The GPSS model. Messages are represented by transactions and each terminal by a GENERATE block. The central processor is facility CPU and all messages waiting to be processed are put in queue 5. The statistics of this queue will give the required information about waiting times of all messages. The simulation duration is controlled by blocks 1 and 2 and the START card. It will stop after 600,000 ms, or 10 minutes.

To get the response time per source we add one queue per terminal (numbers 1 to 3), which is entered when the message is generated and left when processing is completed. The statistics of these queues contain all the information required. When using the full language, we will see that a TABULATE block can be used instead of the three queues mentioned (see Section 7.2.6).

First (simple) approach. The block diagram is shown in Figure 6.11 and the listing of the program in source code is given in Figure 6.13. There are three streams of blocks which correspond to the three terminals, all of which are identical except for the blocks:

QUEUE and DEPART, where the queue number is the same as the terminal number.

ADVANCE blocks, which specify the additional processing time, which is a function of terminal number. This similarity suggests replacement of the three streams by a common one and use of indirect addressing for those items which vary from one stream to another.

The stream for each terminal is straightforward. The messages are created by the GENERATE block, enter the appropriate terminal queue, enter the common queue 5, and try to seize the CPU. When a transaction is accepted by the SEIZE block, it departs from the general queue 5 and goes to the ASSIGN block, where the message type (1, 2, 3, or 4) is generated as the random variable specified by the function TYPE and assigned to halfword parameter 2 of the transaction by the ASSIGN instruction. Then it reaches the first ADVANCE block, where the time specified is FN1,V1, which specifies a uniform distribution with mean FN1 and spread $\pm$ V1. Variable 1 is defined as function 2. (*Note*: It is not possible to use FN2 in the B-operand because it would multiply the value of the A-operand.) Both FN1 and FN2 are discrete list-type random variables, depending on argument P2, which contains the message type. FN1 is the mean process time and FN2 the spread. FN1, FN2, and TYPE are shown in Figure 6.12.

After completing this processing time, the transaction enters the second ADVANCE block for additional processing time, depending on the message source; the transaction then releases the CPU, leaves queue 5, and terminates (see Figure 6.13).

To simulate the system for 10 minutes, we use an "auxiliary clock" (blocks 1 and 2), which generates one transaction at time 600,000, which equals 10 minutes. This transaction terminates immediately, thus decrementing the terminations-to-go counter (START statement A-field) and ends the simulation run.

Second approach: indirect addressing. The similarities between the programs for the three terminals suggest the use of the indirect-addressing capability of GPSS to condense the program. Parameter 1 of the transactions will contain the number of the terminal generating the message. We replace the three instruction streams by one common stream where references to the terminal number are given by parameter 1.

For each terminal (see the block diagram of Figure 6.14) there is a GENERATE block labeled for further modifications GEN1, GEN2, and GEN3, followed by the

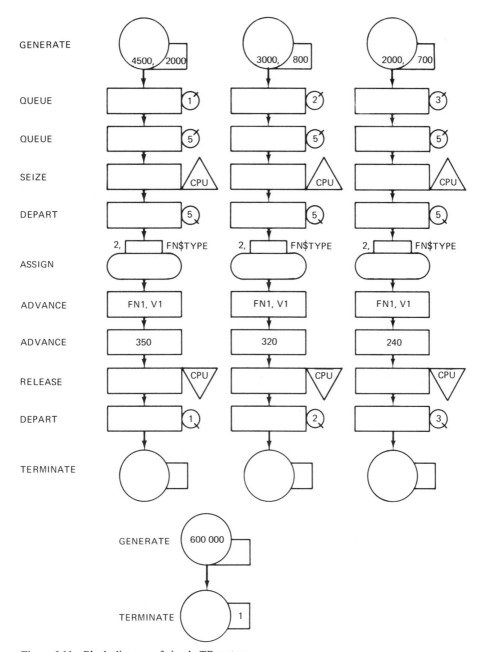

Figure 6.11 Block diagram of simple TP system.

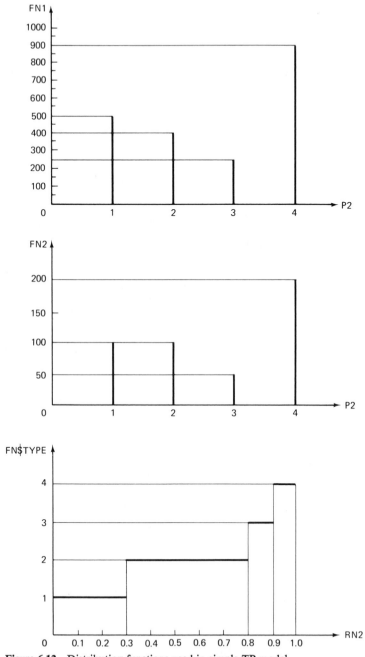

Figure 6.12 Distribution functions used in simple TP model.

```
BLCCK                                                                              CARC
NUMBER  *LCC    CFERATICN  A,B,C,C,E,F,G              COMMENTS                      NUMBER
                SIMULATE                                                              1
                                                                                     2
        *FUNCTIONS ANC VARIABLES                                                     3
            1     FUNCTICN   P2,L4                                                    4
        1,500/2,4CC/3,25C/4,90C                                                       5
            2     FUNCTION   P2,L4                                                    6
        1,100/2,100/3,50/4,200                                                        7
            TYPE  FUNCTICN   RN2,D4                                                   8
        .3,1/.8,2/.9,3/1,4                                                            9
            1     VARIABLE   FN2                                                      10
                                                                                     11
        *AUXILIARY CLCCK                                                             12
1               GENERATE   600000                                                   13
2               TERMINATE  1                                                        14
                                                                                     15
        *FIRST TERMINAL                                                             16
3               GENERATE   45C0,2CCC              GENERATE TRANSACTICNS              17
4               QUEUE      1                      IN QUEUE 1(TERMINAL 1)             18
5               QLEUE      5                      IN COMMON CUEUE                    19
6               SEIZE      CPU                    SEIZE THE CPU                      20
7               DEPART     5                      CUT OF COMMCN QLELE                21
8               ASSIGN     2,FN$TYFE              ASSIGN MESSAGE TYPE TC P2          22
9               ADVANCE    FN1,V1                 PROC. TIME DEPENC. CN MESS. TYPE   23
10              ACVANCE    350                    PRCC. TIME FCR TERMINAL 1          24
11              RELEASE    CPU                    RELEASE THE CPU                    25
12              DEPART     1                      CUT OF QUEUE 1                     26
13              TERMINATE                         DESTRCY MESSAGE                    27
                                                                                     28
        *SECONC TERMINAL                                                            29
14              GENERATE   3000,800                                                 30
15              CUEUE      2                      IN QUEUE 2 (TERMINAL 2)            31
16              QUEUE      5                                                         32
17              SEIZE      CPU                                                       33
18              DEPART     5                                                         34
19              ASSIGN     2,FN$TYFE              ASSIGN MESSAGE TYPE TC P2          35
20              ADVANCE    FN1,V1                                                    36
21              ADVANCE    320                    PROC. TIME FOR TERMINAL 2          37
22              RELEASE    CPU                                                       38
23              DEPART     2                      CUT OF QUEUE 2                     39
24              TERMINATE                                                           40
                                                                                     41
        *THIRC TERMINAL                                                             42
25              GENERATE   2000,70C                                                 43
26              QUEUE      3                      IN CUEUE 3(TERMINAL 3)             44
27              QUEUE      5                                                         45
28              SEIZE      CPL                                                       46
29              DEPART     5                                                         47
3C              ASSIGN     2,FN$TYFE              ASSIGN MESSAGE TYPE TO P2          48
31              ADVANCE    FN1,V1                                                    49
32              ADVANCE    240                    PROC. TIME FCR TERMINAL 3          50
33              RELEASE    CPL                                                       51
34              DEPART     3                      CUT CF QUEUE 3                     52
35              TERMINATE                                                           53
                START      1                                                        54
                ENC                                                                 55
```

Figure 6.13 GPSS program of simple TP program.

ASSIGN block, which stores the terminal number in parameter 1, and an unconditional TRANSFER block to send all transactions to block CONT (continuation) for processing.

The transaction joins the queue with number specified by P1, and proceeds in the same way as in the previous program. The second ADVANCE block specifies a processing time defined by function 3 (Figure 6.15). This function has argument P1 because the time considered depends on the terminal that generates the message.

It is clear that block QUEUE P1 (or QUEUE PH1 in GPSS V) creates one queue each time a transaction with a new value of P1 enters. As we have agreed that the values would be 1, 2, and 3, these three numbers are reserved. If we used other queues with symbolic names, it would be necessary to reserve these three numbers to avoid use by the compiler. This would be done by using the EQU statement. As previously stated, blocks QUEUE P1 and DEPART P1 can be replaced by one TABULATE block (see Section 7.2.6) and the associated table-definition statements.

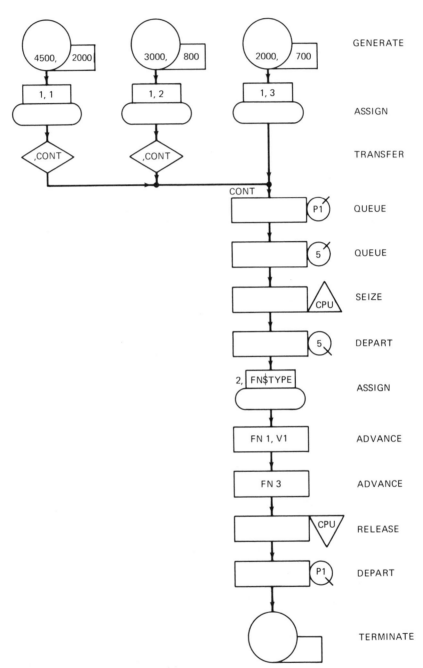

Figure 6.14 Block diagram of TP model with indirect addressing.

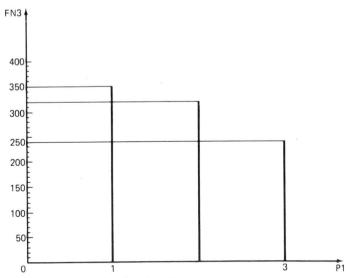

Figure 6.15 Processing time function.

Extensions of the previous system. Knowing the results of the initial problem, referred to subsequently as case *a*, we want to study the following possible modifications and extensions of the system.

Case b: add one terminal, number 4. The interarrival times for this terminal are to be 2000 ± 500 and the total message processing time 150 ± 100 ms.

Case c: give a higher priority to terminal number 4. Messages arriving from this terminal are put at the front of the queue but do not interrupt the processing of the message currently being handled by the CPU.

Case d: evaluate the effect on the response times for the various terminals if the messages from terminal 4 interrupt the processing of other messages when they reach the CPU. In particular, does the response time for terminal 4 improve significantly with this strategy?

Case e: finally, for the last case only, estimate the overall effect of having all exponentially distributed interarrival times (Poisson arrivals) with the same means, instead of uniformly distributed times.

The GPSS model. The block diagram, which is very similar to that of the initial problem, is not shown. We have included all five problems in one program, using indirect addressing; therefore, there are five successive runs. The program listing (source code and assembled program) is given in Figure 6.16. Between two runs the CLEAR statement clears the model and the instructions to be added or to replace existing instructions are inserted before the new START statement.

After the first run, the model is cleared. We then find instructions 21 to 29, which simulate the additional terminal. We have modeled its processing separately for practical reasons, since we will have to modify it for the next runs. As for the other terminals we have the GENERATE block followed by QUEUE 4 (queue 4 is associated with terminal 4). The next blocks are the same as in the main program except that the total processing time for these messages is represented in one ADVANCE block. SEIZE CPU and RELEASE CPU have labels, since we must change these instructions in subsequent runs. The START card starts the simulation and initiates printing of the results.

We then find

CLEAR

GEN4   GENERATE   2000,500,,,1

which replaces the old GEN4 instruction. The new block assigns priority 1 to the transactions, but the transactions created by the other GENERATE blocks have a default priority of zero. The START statement then controls the run in a similar manner to the previous one but with a higher priority for terminal 4.

Figure 6.16 GPSS program of extended TP model.

```
BLCCK
NUMBER   *LCC   OPERATION   A,B,C,D,E,F,G            COMMENTS                              CARD
                SIMULATE                                                                  NUMBER
                                                                                            1
                                                                                            2
                *FUNCTIONS ANC VARIABLES                                                     3
                  1      FUNCTICN    P2,L4                                                   4
                1,500/2,400/3,250/4,500                                                      5
                  2      FUNCTICN    P2,L4                                                   6
                1,100/2,100/3,50/4,200                                                       7
                  3      FUNCTICN    P1,L3                                                   8
                1,350/2,320/3,240                                                            9
                TYPE   FUNCTICN    RN2,D4                                                   10
                .3/1/.8,2/.9,3/1,4                                                          11
                  1      VARIABLE    FN2                                                    12
                                                                                           13
                *AUXILIARY CLCCK                                                            14
     1              GENERATE    600000                                                      15
     2              TERMINATE   1                                                           16
                                                                                           17
                *FIRST TERMINAL                                                             18
     3      GEN1    GENERATE    4500,2000       GENERATE TRANSACTICNS ANC                   19
     4              ASSIGN      1,1             ASSIGN SOURCE TERMINAL NUMBER               20
     5              TRANSFER    ,CCNT           TC PARAMETER 1.                             21
                                                                                           22
                *SECCNC TERMINAL                                                            23
     6      GEN2    GENERATE    3000,800        THEN SEND THEM TC CCNT FCR                  24
     7              ASSIGN      1,2             CCMMCN PROCESSING                           25
     8              TRANSFER    ,CCNT                                                       26
                                                                                           27
                *THIRD TERMINAL                                                             28
     9      GEN3    GENERATE    2000,700                                                    29
    10              ASSIGN      1,3                                                         30
                                                                                           31
    11      CCNT    CUEUE       P1              QUEUE INTO TERMINAL CUEUE                   32
    12              QUEUE       5               ANC IN COMMON QUEUE                         33
    13              SEIZE       CPU                                                         34
    14              DEFART      5                                                           35
    15              ASSIGN      2,FN$TYPE       STCRE TYPE IN PARAMETER 2                   36
    16              ADVANCE     FN1,V1          PROC. TIME CEPENC. CN MESS. TYPE           37
    17              ACVANCE     FN3             PRCC. TIME DEPENC. ON THE SOURCE            38
    18              RELEASE     CPL                                                         39
    19              CEPART      P1                                                          40
    20              TERMINATE                   CESTRCY TRANSACTION                         41
                    START       1               START RUN WITH TERM. 1,2 ANC 3             42
                    CLEAR                       CLEAR THE MCDEL                             43
                                                                                           44
    21      GEN4    GENERATE    2000,500        ADDITICN CF TERMINAL 4                      45
    22              QUEUE       4               WITH THE NORMAL FRCCESSING                  46
    23              QUELE       5                                                           47
    24      PROCE   SEIZE       CPL                                                         48
    25              DEFART      5                                                           49
    26              ADVANCE     150,100                                                     50
    27      PREND   RELEASE     CPL                                                         51
    28              DEPART      4                                                           52
    29              TERMINATE                                                               53
                    START       1               START SEC. RUN WITH 4 TERMINALS            54
            *                                   WITH THE SAME PRICRITY                      55
```

```
          CLEAR                         CLEAR THE MODEL                                  56
                                                                                         57
21       GEN4  GENERATE   2000,500,,,1  TERM.4 GEN. TRANS. WITH PRIOR. 1                 58
MULTIPLE DEFINITION OF SYMBOL IN ABOVE CARD
                START      1            START THIRD RUN                                  59
          CLEAR                         CLEAR THE MODEL                                  60
                                                                                         61
24       PROCE PREEMPT    CPU           INTRODUCE PREEMPTING BY TRANSACT.               62
MULTIPLE DEFINITION OF SYMBOL IN ABOVE CARD
27       PREND RETURN     CPU           FROM TERMINAL 4                                  63
MULTIPLE DEFINITION OF SYMBOL IN ABOVE CARD
                START      1            START FOURTH RUN WITH PREEMPTION                 64
          CLEAR                         CLEAR THE MODEL                                  65
                                                                                         66
          EXPON FUNCTION  RN8,C24       EXPONENTIAL DISTRIBUTION - MEAN = 1.            67
  0.,0/0.1,0.104/0.2,0.222/0.3,0.355/0.4,0.509/0.5,0.69/0.6,0.915/                      68
  0.7,1.2/0.75,1.38/0.8,1.6/0.84,1.83/0.88,2.12/0.9,2.3/0.92,2.52/                      69
  0.94,2.81/0.95,2.99/0.96,3.2/0.97,3.5/0.98,3.9/0.99,4.6/0.995,5.3/                    70
  0.998,6.2/0.999,7.0/0.9997,8.0                                                         71
3        GEN1  GENERATE   4500,FN$EXPON INTRODUCE EXPONENTIAL INTERARRIV.               72
MULTIPLE DEFINITION OF SYMBOL IN ABOVE CARD
6        GEN2  GENERATE   3000,FN$EXPON TIMES FOR THE FOUR TERMINALS                    73
MULTIPLE DEFINITION OF SYMBOL IN ABOVE CARD
9        GEN3  GENERATE   2000,FN$EXPON                                                  74
MULTIPLE DEFINITION OF SYMBOL IN ABOVE CARD
21       GEN4  GENERATE   2000,FN$EXPON,,,1                                             75
MULTIPLE DEFINITION OF SYMBOL IN ABOVE CARD
                START      1            START LAST RUN: PREEMPTION BY                    76
     *                                  TERMINAL 4 AND EXPON. INTERARRIV.               77
     *                                                                                   78
          REPORT                                                                         79
          EJECT                                                                          80
CLO       TITLE      ,                                                                   81
          SPACE      3                                                                   82
BLO       TITLE      ,                                                                   83
          SPACE      2                                                                   84
FAC       TITLE      ,                                                                   85
          SPACE      2                                                                   86
QUE       TITLE      ,                                                                   87
          EJECT                                                                          88
          END                                                                           89
```

Figure 6.16 (continued)

We then find another CLEAR statement with the two instructions

          PROCE   PREEMPT   CPU

which overwrites

                SEIZE   CPU

and

          PREND   RETURN   CPU

which overwrites

                RELEASE   CPU

The next run therefore includes the preempt resume strategy for messages from terminal 4.

In the last run, the four GENERATE blocks are replaced by statements specifying the exponential function, which is defined just before it is invoked. The last START statement controls the last run.

Results and conclusions. The results of the five runs are given in Figures 6.17 to 6.21; they were obtained using GPSS/360. The program as it is presented in Figure 6.16 may be run without modification using GPSS V.

For all runs the simulated time was 10 minutes.

To simplify the discussion, the output data in which we are interested has been summarized in Table 6.8. Case *a* shows a CPU utilization of 77.1 per cent. This utilization increases to between 85.7 and 88.4 with four terminals. Giving a priority of 1 to the messages coming from terminal 4 considerably reduces the response time but increases the response times of the other terminals. To appraise the relative advantages of cases *c* and *d*, additional information should be provided, especially regarding the cost of such procedures and the value attached to the reduction of the response time for terminal 4. Until such information is available, we can only conclude

Table 6.8 SUMMARY OF RESULTS

Case	Number of Messages Processed	Utilization of CPU (%)	Response Times				Average Waiting Time	
			1	2	3	4	Total	Excluding Zero Entries
a	618	77.1	1.12	1.04	0.96	—	0.27	0.49
b	926	87.1	1.30	1.19	1.12	0.82	0.50	0.66
c	939	88.4	1.37	1.31	1.27	0.48	0.47	0.60
d	926	87.3	1.41	1.36	1.29	0.15	0.35	0.70
e	902	85.7	2.68	2.56	2.41	0.16	1.19	1.94

```
RELATIVE CLOCK      600000  ABSCLUTE CLOCK      600000


BLOCK CCLNTS
BLOCK CURRENT    TOTAL    BLOCK CLRRENT    TOTAL   BLOCK CURRENT   TOTAL   BLOCK CURRENT   TOTAL   BLOCK CURRENT   TOTAL
   1     0         1        11     0       618
   2     0         1        12     0       618
   3     0       130        13     0       618
   4     0       130        14     0       618
   5     0       130        15     0       618
   6     0       195        16     1       618
   7     0       195        17     0       617
   8     0       195        18     0       617
   9     0       293        19     0       617
  10     0       293        20     0       617


FACILITY       AVERAGE        NUMBER       AVERAGE        SEIZING      PREEMPTING
              UTILIZATION     ENTRIES      TIME/TRAN     TRANS. NO.    TRANS. NO.
   CPU          .771           618         749.370          6


QUEUE    MAXIMUM     AVERAGE     TCTAL    ZERC    PERCENT    AVERAGE     SAVERAGE    TABLE    CURRENT
        CONTENTS    CONTENTS    ENTRIES  ENTRIES   ZEROS   TIME/TRANS  TIME/TRANS   NUMBER  CONTENTS
   1       1         .243        130                .0     1123.215    1123.215
   2       1         .338        195                .0     1042.271    1042.271               1
   3       2         .466        293                .0      955.378     955.378
   5       2         .276        618      276     44.6      268.731     485.602
SAVERAGE TIME/TRANS = AVERAGE TIME/TRANS EXCLUDING ZERC ENTRIES
```

Figure 6.17

RELATIVE CLOCK   600000   ABSCLUTE CLOCK   600000

BLOCK CCUNTS

BLOCK	CURRENT	TOTAL	BLOCK	CURRENT	TOTAL	BLOCK	CURRENT	TOTAL	BLOCK	CURRENT	TOTAL	BLOCK	CURRENT	TOTAL
1	0	1	11	0	630	21	0	296						
2	0	1	12	C	630	22	0	296						
3	0	131	13	0	630	23	0	296						
4	0	131	14	0	630	24	C	296						
5	0	131	15	C	630	25	0	296						
6	0	200	16	0	630	26	C	296						
7	0	200	17	0	630	27	C	296						
8	0	200	18	C	630	28	0	296						
9	0	299	19	C	630	25	0	296						
10	0	299	20	C	630									

FACILITY	AVERAGE UTILIZATION	NUMBER ENTRIES	AVERAGE TIME/TRAN	SEIZING TRANS. NC.	PREEMPTING TRANS. NC.
CPU	.871	926	564.875		

QUEUE	MAXIMUM CONTENTS	AVERAGE CONTENTS	TOTAL ENTRIES	ZERO ENTRIES	PERCENT ZEROS	AVERAGE TIME/TRANS	$AVERAGE TIME/TRANS	TABLE NUMBER	CURRENT CONTENTS
1	1	.284	131		.0	1304.274	1304.274		
2	2	.397	200		.C	1191.104	1191.104		
3	2	.560	299		.0	1123.792	1123.792		
4	2	.402	296		.0	816.107	816.107		
5	4	.772	926	221	23.8	500.634	657.571		

$AVERAGE TIME/TRANS = AVERAGE TIME/TRANS EXCLUDING ZERO ENTRIES

Figure 6.18

RELATIVE CLOCK   600000   ABSOLUTE CLOCK   600000

BLOCK CCUNTS

BLOCK	CURRENT	TOTAL	BLOCK	CURRENT	TOTAL	BLOCK	CURRENT	TOTAL	BLOCK	CURRENT	TOTAL	BLOCK	CURRENT	TOTAL
1	0	1	11	C	640	21	C	299						
2	0	1	12	0	640	22	0	255						
3	0	134	13	0	640	23	0	299						
4	0	134	14	0	640	24	0	299						
5	0	134	15	0	640	25	0	299						
6	0	204	16	0	640	26	0	299						
7	0	204	17	0	640	27	0	255						
8	0	204	18	0	640	28	0	299						
9	0	302	19	C	640	29	0	299						
10	0	302	20	C	640									

FACILITY	AVERAGE UTILIZATION	NUMBER ENTRIES	AVERAGE TIME/TRAN	SEIZING TRANS. NO.	PREEMPTING TRANS. NO.
CPU	.884	939	565.375		

QUEUE	MAXIMUM CONTENTS	AVERAGE CONTENTS	TOTAL ENTRIES	ZERO ENTRIES	PERCENT ZEROS	AVERAGE TIME/TRANS	$AVERAGE TIME/TRANS	TABLE NUMBER	CURRENT CONTENTS
1	2	.305	134		.0	1367.119	1367.119		
2	2	.445	204		.0	1311.137	1311.137		
3	3	.637	302		.0	1266.155	1266.155		
4	1	.237	299		.0	477.468	477.468		
5	5	.741	939	198	21.0	473.822	600.431		

$AVERAGE TIME/TRANS = AVERAGE TIME/TRANS EXCLUDING ZERO ENTRIES

Figure 6.19

RELATIVE CLOCK   600000 ABSOLUTE CLOCK   600000

BLOCK COUNTS

BLOCK	CURRENT	TOTAL	BLOCK	CURRENT	TOTAL	BLOCK	CURRENT	TOTAL	BLOCK	CURRENT	TOTAL	BLOCK	CURRENT	TOTAL
1	0	1	11	0	630	21	0	296						
2	0	1	12	0	630	22	0	296						
3	0	131	13	0	630	23	0	296						
4	0	131	14	0	630	24	0	296						
5	0	131	15	0	630	25	0	296						
6	0	198	16	1	630	26	0	296						
7	0	198	17	0	629	27	0	296						
8	0	198	18	0	629	28	0	296						
9	0	301	19	0	629	29	0	296						
10	0	301	20	0	629									

FACILITY	AVERAGE UTILIZATION	NUMBER ENTRIES	AVERAGE TIME/TRAN	SEIZING TRANS. NO.	PREEMPTING TRANS. NO.
CPU	.873	926	565.934	11	

QUEUE	MAXIMUM CONTENTS	AVERAGE CONTENTS	TOTAL ENTRIES	ZERO ENTRIES	PERCENT ZEROS	AVERAGE TIME/TRANS	$AVERAGE TIME/TRANS	TABLE NUMBER	CURRENT CONTENTS
1	2	.308	131		.0	1413.221	1413.221		
2	2	.449	198		.0	1362.156	1362.156		
3	3	.648	301		.0	1292.866	1292.866		1
4	1	.076	296		.0	154.145	154.145		
5	5	.545	926	461	49.7	353.217	703.395		

$AVERAGE TIME/TRANS = AVERAGE TIME/TRANS EXCLUDING ZERO ENTRIES

Figure 6.20

RELATIVE CLOCK   600000 ABSOLUTE CLOCK   600000

BLOCK COUNTS

BLOCK	CURRENT	TOTAL	BLOCK	CURRENT	TOTAL	BLOCK	CURRENT	TOTAL	BLOCK	CURRENT	TOTAL	BLOCK	CURRENT	TOTAL
1	0	1	11	0	627	21	0	275						
2	0	1	12	0	627	22	0	275						
3	0	134	13	0	627	23	0	275						
4	0	134	14	0	627	24	0	275						
5	0	134	15	0	627	25	0	275						
6	0	198	16	0	627	26	1	275						
7	0	198	17	0	627	27	0	274						
8	0	198	18	0	627	28	0	274						
9	0	295	19	0	627	29	0	274						
10	0	295	20	0	627									

FACILITY	AVERAGE UTILIZATION	NUMBER ENTRIES	AVERAGE TIME/TRAN	SEIZING TRANS. NO.	PREEMPTING TRANS. NO.
CPU	.857	902	570.702	8	

QUEUE	MAXIMUM CONTENTS	AVERAGE CONTENTS	TOTAL ENTRIES	ZERO ENTRIES	PERCENT ZEROS	AVERAGE TIME/TRANS	$AVERAGE TIME/TRANS	TABLE NUMBER	CURRENT CONTENTS
1	5	.599	134		.0	2682.111	2682.111		
2	6	.844	198		.0	2559.934	2559.934		
3	8	1.185	295		.0	2411.023	2411.023		
4	2	.074	275		.0	161.919	161.919		1
5	12	1.786	902	350	38.8	1188.503	1942.083		

$AVERAGE TIME/TRANS = AVERAGE TIME/TRANS EXCLUDING ZERO ENTRIES

Figure 6.21

128

that strategy *d* (priority with preempt/resume) is the most interesting, because the response time of terminal 4 is small, less than one-third of strategies *b* or *c*. The last case shows an increase in all response times due to the exponential interarrival times. But even then, the response time of terminal 4 is still very low.

Statistical considerations:

It is obvious that the above experiments are only introductory to a complete study, especially because only one run has been performed for each case and the transmission lines have been omitted.

When comparing the various cases, we should remember that the differences between two of them are caused mainly by two factors:

1. The strategy concerned (number of terminals, priority rule, distribution of interarrival times).
2. The random-number sequence used in the various parts of the model where random variables are introduced either explicitly in functions TYPE 1,2,3 or implicitly in GENERATE and ADVANCE blocks.

As we use the CLEAR statement between successive runs, the random-number generators are not reset and therefore produce a different sequence of random numbers for each run. To compare the net effects of changing the strategy, we should work with the same random-number series. This could be done by running every case as a single job (reloading GPSS reinitializes the random-number generators) or initializing each run with an RMULT statement, discussed in Section 7.1.1. This statement, placed before the CLEAR statement, would reinitialize the random-number generators before every run. But even in this case, great care should be taken to ensure that changes in coding do not alter the effect of the random-number stream. Another way to obtain consistency of input would be to create a transaction jobtape (see Section 7.2.1) and run it against the various strategies to be investigated.

It is also important to note that the utilization of the CPU is very high (more than 80 per cent), so the response times are random variables that are very highly autocorrelated. Therefore, several runs should be made and other action may be necessary to obtain small confidence intervals for the various average waiting times and response times.

6.6.5 Four-disk system

The problem. A computer system has one channel to which four disk drives are connected. The application considered has an average of 20 file requests per second (Poisson arrivals). It has been observed that the requests are random over the four drives with an equal probability for each.

We make the following hypotheses. When a file request is issued by the program in the CPU, it is queued until the channel and the arm of the requested disk drive are both free. When this condition is met, the arm is seized for a time (called *seek time*) equal to 75 ms average and uniformly distributed. During the seek time, the channel is free. Further, we neglect the time during which the channel is busy issuing the seek command. When the seek is complete, we wait until the channel is free. Then the information is transferred from the disk to the CPU (channel service time), which takes an average time of 36 ms, exponentially distributed. When this time has elapsed, the channel and the arm (disk) are freed.

When several requests are competing for the channel, we give priority to requests to start a seek operation over those to execute a data transfer, which is accomplished by using priority. Note that only one request, either to start a seek or a transmit operation, is accepted per disk.

We require statistics of the waiting queue and waiting times of the requests before being accepted (waiting for channel and arm), the total service time, which is seek time, plus wait time for the channel and channel service time. For the latter, we want both the average and the standard deviation. The results will provide a basis for further analyses such as changing the priorities of the requests and adding (or suppressing) one disk.

The GPSS model.   It is quite natural to model file requests as transactions. The disks, or rather the arms, will be facilities 1 to 4 with which queues 1 to 4 will be associated. The channel will be represented by facility CHAN, and its queue for transactions waiting to transmit information will also be called CHAN. Further, we introduce a dummy storage, ARMS (capacity 4) to gather global statistics on the four arms.

As we use symbolic and numeric entities in our model for facilities CHAN1,2,3,4 and queues CHAN1,2,3,4, we must indicate this fact to the compiler. Instead of merely reserving four numbers, we use an EQU (equate) statement to show that we want to reserve numbers 1 to 10 for both facilities and queues. Our program would therefore be valid for up to 10 disks, with minimal modification to function 2, which is used to select which disk to access.

The time unit of the program is 1 ms.

The program is shown in Figure 6.22. It starts with the GENERATE block, which creates the file requests, with an average interarrival time of 50 ms exponentially distributed, priority of 3 and 4 parameters. Parameter 1 will contain the number of the disk to be accessed, parameter 2 the seek time, parameter 3 the channel service time, and parameter 4 an intermediate clock time.

The first three parameters are not absolutely necessary for this problem but are introduced purposely to show what would be done in larger, similar models and also in case we wish to make antithetic runs using the same program, by replacing the functions by their antithetic (see Section 14.3). Note that parameter 1 is used for indirectly addressing the arm number, used for both facilities and queues. This simplifies the program slightly.

After we have assigned values to parameters 1, 2, and 3, the transaction is queued (QUEUE block) and the availability of the arm and the channel is tested by means of the two GATE blocks (6 and 7) and the TRANSFER SIM(8), which allows a transaction to proceed to the next block only if its delay indicator is reset.

```
BLCCK                                                                                  CARD
NUMBER   *LOC    OPERATION   A,B,C,D,E,F,G                COMMENTS                     NUMBER
                 SIMULATE                                                                1
         CHAN    EQU         10,F,Q                                                      2
                                                                                        3
         1       FUNCTION    RN8,C24               EXPONENT. DISTR. MEAN = 1             4
0.,0/0.1,0.104/0.2,0.222/0.3,0.355/0.4,0.509/0.5,0.69/0.6,0.915/                         5
0.7,1.2/0.75,1.38/0.8,1.6/0.84,1.83/0.88,2.12/0.9,2.3/0.92,2.52/                         6
0.94,2.81/0.95,2.99/0.96,3.2/C.97,3.5/0.98,3.9/0.99,4.6/0.995,5.3/                       7
0.998,6.2/0.999,7.0/0.9997,8.0                                                           8
                                                                                        9
         2       FUNCTION    RN8,C2      ARM SELECTION  4 ARMS                          10
0,1/1.,5                                                                                11
                                                                                       12
         ARMS    STORAGE     4                                                          13
                                                                                       14
1                GENERATE    50,FN1,,,3,4,F   EXPONENTIAL ARRIVALS PR=3,4PARAM          15
2                ASSIGN      1,FN2            ARM NUMBER                                16
3                ASSIGN      2,75,1           SEEK TIME EXPCNENTIAL MEAN = 75           17
4                ASSIGN      3,36,1           CHANNEL SERVICE EXPONENTIAL MEAN=         18
5                QUEUE       *1               WAIT FCR ARM                              19
6        AAA     GATE NU     *1               AND CHANNEL                               20
7                GATE NU     CHAN                                                       21
8                TRANSFER    SIM,,AAA         IF BOTH FREE PROCESS, IF NCT WAIT         22
9                SEIZE       *1               SEIZE ARM                                 23
10               ENTER       ARMS             STORAGE ARMS RECORD OVERALL STATS         24
11               DEPART      *1                                                         25
12               MARK        4                                                          26
13               ADVANCE     *2               START SEEK                                27
14               PRIORITY    2                LOWER THE PRIORITY TC 2                   28
15               CUEUE       CHAN             WAIT FOR CHANNEL SERVICE                  29
16               SEIZE       CHAN                                                       30
17               DEPART      CHAN                                                       31
18               ADVANCE     *3               CHANNEL SERVICE TIME                      32
19               RELEASE     CHAN                                                       33
20               RELEASE     *1               RELEASE ARM                               34
21               LEAVE       ARMS                                                       35
22               TABULATE    TSARM            TABULATE TOTAL SERVICE TIME               36
         TSARM   TABLE       MP4,50,5C,20                                               37
23               TERMINATE   1                                                          38
                 START       5000                                                       39
                                                                                       40
                 ENC                                                                    41
```

Figure 6.22 GPSS program of 4 disk system.

When the transaction can proceed, it seizes the arm (block 9) and enters storage ARMS to update the storage statistics. The transaction then leaves the queue (DEPART block) and enters the MARK block (number 12, to be discussed later), which places the current clock time in parameter 4. Tabulation of the transit time spent by the transaction between this point and the end of the program gives statistics of total service time. To model the seek operation the transaction then enters the ADVANCE block (13) for a mean time of 75 ms specified in parameter 2, modified by function 1 (exponential distribution). When this time has elapsed, the transaction must queue for the channel, QUEUE block (15).

However, we must remember that transactions waiting in queues 1 to 5, to seize arms 1 to 5 and the channel, are competing with requests that have completed their seek. All these transactions are merged on the current-events chain, which, as we have seen in Section 5.4.1, is sorted by (1) priority and (2) block departure time (BDT).

As we wish to process the incoming requests first, we must lower the priority of transactions that have completed the seek operation. This is done by block 14, which lowers the priority of the transactions to 2. The transaction then queues and, when the channel becomes free, seizes it (block 16), leaves the queue (block 17), and spends the channel service time (block 18) contained in parameter 3. It then releases the channel and the arm (blocks 19 and 20) and leaves storage ARMS (block 21). Before termination the transaction enters the TABULATE block (22), discussed in Section

7.2.6. The function of this block is to record in a histogram, specified by the TABLE statement TSARM, the total service time previously mentioned.

The histogram gives the distribution of the times observed and, in particular, the mean and standard deviation.

Conclusion and results. In this section we consider how the model might be made more realistic. In a real problem, it is obvious that more realistic functions than the exponential should be used. For example, the channel service time is probably uniformly distributed between the time to transmit the information from the disk and the same time plus the time for a complete rotation of the disk. This extra time is called *rotational delay*.

Further, the seek time can be evaluated more precisely if we suppose that an arm remains where it is after a read operation. Its next travel time will therefore depend on the difference between the new position and the previous position. If the probability to select any cylinder is uniform, we must compute the travel distance as the difference of two random variables uniformly distributed between two values.

We will discuss this problem to illustrate the use of random variates in a simulation model, as discussed in Appendix D. Suppose that the cylinder numbers can vary between 0 and N. Let x be the cylinder number of the old arm position and y the new position. The seek time will be a function of the number of cylinders to cross, that is, of the absolute value of the difference $y - x$. We have

$$\Pr\left(|x - y| \le n\right) = 1 - \frac{(N - n)^2}{N^2}$$

This probability is given by the shaded area of Figure 6.23(a).

If the seek time t is a linear function of n [Figure 6.23(b)], then $t = a + bn$ or $n = (1/b)(t - a)$. Therefore, the cumulative distribution of t is:

$$F(t) = \Pr\left(t_{\text{seek}} \le t\right) = 1 - \frac{(N - (t - a)/b)^2}{N^2}$$

$$= 1 - \left\{\frac{N - (t - a)/b}{N}\right\}^2$$

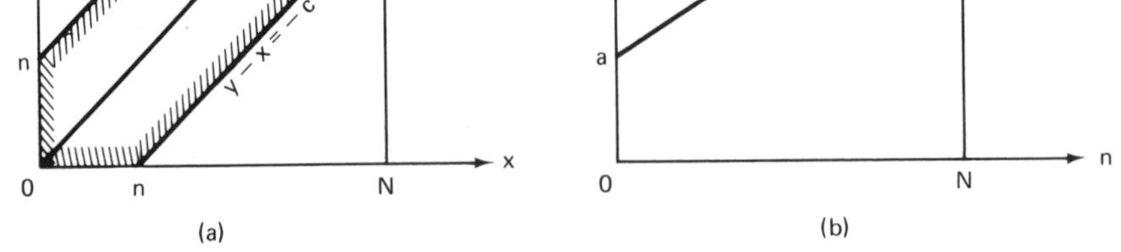

(a)   (b)

Figure 6.23

As discussed in Appendix D, we set $F(t) = r$, where r is a random number uniformly distributed between 0 and 1, and we solve for t. To compute t, we solve the equation $F(t) = r$ for t and obtain:

$$t = a + bN(1 - \sqrt{1 - r})$$

To use this distribution in a GPSS model, it is necessary to tabulate a few values in order to obtain a suitable approximation and to introduce the table obtained as a continuous function whose argument is RNj, one of the eight GPSS random-number generators.

One run with 5000 processed transactions produced the following information, where times are expressed in milliseconds:

1. Average waiting time for all transactions: 224.3
   (Obtained as the average of the average waiting times
   in queues 1 to 4).
2. Average total service time (seek + wait + channel service):   133.4
   (Given by the storage ARMS statistics or the table ARMS).
3. Standard deviation of the total service time: 93.1
   (Given in the table ARMS).
4. Average utilization of the arms: 0.667
   (Given by the statistics of the storage ARMS).

These results show that the system can operate normally under the conditions given in the problem. The utilization of the disks is approximately 70 per cent, which is acceptable.

Summary. This example presented no special difficulties, and its nature is ideal for GPSS modeling. We have seen how priority may be used to impose a given order of processing when several kinds of transactions compete for the same equipment, even if they are not in the same queue. We also used the SIM transfer mode to check simultaneous conditions. Further, note that the utilization of both indirect addressing and of symbolic names necessitated an equate statement in order to reserve certain numbers for facilities and queues.

6.7 Conclusion

In this chapter we have shown, by means of examples, the versatility of a GPSS subset. A modular approach to learning the language is thereby justified: the analyst can make practical use of GPSS and proceed to more advanced models in stages, using more instructions as the need arises.

Never forget that a simulation study has value only if the results are delivered on schedule. A working model that uses elementary code is always preferable to a sophisticated program that does not run properly or on time.

The next chapter is devoted to the complete GPSS language and discusses all instructions not included in the present subset.

7 The Complete GPSS Language

In Chapter 6 we showed how a subset of GPSS can solve various simulation problems. But when solving practical problems modeling requirements may be difficult to satisfy with the subset.

For example, if we have a queue, we might be interested in the distribution of queueing times rather than the average waiting time, which is achieved by using the QTABLE statement. In addition, we might want the distribution of times spent by the transactions between two given points in a system, which is obtained by using the TABULATE and MARK blocks.

Other requirements depend on the way GPSS handles transactions. One may wish, for example, to organize a queue in a special order or, more generally, to manipulate transactions in a different way from the GPSS discipline. This can be done by using one or more user chains. Or, if one wants, one can manipulate related sets of transactions using the GROUP entity.

Although the most important aspects of the language are the blocks we will treat the topics in this chapter in the same order as in Chapter 6. The blocks, Section 7.2, are presented in the same order as in Section 6.2.

7.1 Control Statements

7.1.1 Initialization of the random-number generators

RMULT   A,B,C,D,E,F,G,H

Operation and Operands:

This statement allows the user to modify the random-number sequences produced by the eight random-number generators. The A to H fields specify the initial seeds of random-number generators 1 to 8, respectively. Seeds must be odd and have one to five digits, with a default value of unity.

If used for the initial run, the RMULT card should precede all block statements. If used for subsequent runs, it should be placed immediately before the CLEAR statement, to avoid creation of transactions using the old seed when one or more GENERATE blocks call for random-number sampling.

EXAMPLES:

(1)   RMULT   ,,,,3

     initializes the multiplier of RN5 to 3 and does not change the others.

(2)   SIMULATE
                       GENERATE
                          .
                          .
                          .
                       TERMINATE
                       START   100
                       RMULT   1,1,1,1,1,1,1,1
                       CLEAR
                       START   100

    The first START statement causes one run to take place using the eight standard initial multipliers. The RMULT statement reinitializes all the seeds to 1 so that the second START statement causes a second run to take place with the same random-number sequence as the first.

7.1.2 Reallocation of entities

           REALLOCATE   A,B,C,D,. . .

Operation:

This statement changes the standard allocation of GPSS entities, which is specified by the PARM argument of the Operating System EXEC card. This feature helps the programmer to use available storage effectively. The need for many entities of one type can be met by the storage released by requesting fewer entities of other types.

Operands:

The operands are paired fields that list, in order, a mnemonic to specify the GPSS entity and the corresponding number of entities.

EXAMPLE:

           REALLOCATE   XAC,100,QUE,10

    provides for 100 transactions and 10 queues.

7.1.3 Saving and reading-in models

The SAVE/READ feature allows the user to store the existing model with current statistics at a given time and subsequently to restart the simulation from that point. It is useful as a "checkpoint/restart procedure," for example with models using a lot of computer time. In such cases, one might wish to save the model at certain time intervals to be able to restart the simulation from the last saved model and thus avoid having to repeat the whole simulation run. Another situation in which this feature will be used is during initial runs when it is not yet known how long the simulation run should be to reach equilibrium. A first run is made and the model is saved. Later it is always possible to continue the simulation for a new period, save the model, analyze the results, and determine if they are stable. The device on which the model has to be saved (and from which it will be read) must be specified in the operating system procedure. An example will be found in Appendix A (see the DRDSAVE DD statement).

GPSS V allows the specification of different devices and data sets for the SAVE and READ instructions. They are specified, respectively, by the DRDSAVEO (output) and DRDSAVEI (input) DD statements.

SAVE   A

Operation:

When this statement is read by GPSS, the model is saved in its current state on the device specified by the user. GPSS will then read the next control statement.

Operand:

A: (*optional*) Used as a signal. If not present, the model is saved as the first file of the data set. If necessary, the tape will be rewound before the model is saved, or the pointer to a direct access device data set will be positioned at the beginning of the data set. If A contains an alphameric character, the model is saved at the current place on the data set.

EXAMPLES:

```
(1)              START       1000
                 SAVE
                 START       1000
                 SAVE
                 START       1000
                 SAVE
                 END
```

After every run of 1000, the model is saved, but each new SAVE command *replaces* the previous saved results.

(2)	START	1000
	SAVE	A
	START	1000
	SAVE	A
	START	1000
	SAVE	A
	END	

At the end of simulation three models are saved in files 1, 2, and 3 on the device specified: file 1 after 1000, file 2 after 2000, and file 3 after 3000 terminations.

READ   A

Operation:

This statement will read the model from the device specified by the user in the operating system procedure. It immediately follows the SIMULATE statement and must itself be followed by a START statement, which will control the simulation run. When a model is read in, modifications to it can be made before starting the simulation. This means that such statements can appear between the READ and START statements.

Remark: Modifications must be specified in absolute format and, if block definition statements are included, should be preceded by the ABS and followed by the ENDABS statements. In absolute format, blocks and other entities are specified numerically, which circumvents the normal operation of assigning sequential block numbers. See GPSS V manual, page 356, [G.12].

Operand:

A: (*optional*) Used to specify the number of files to be skipped before reading the model. If not specified, the first file of the data set will be read.

EXAMPLES:

(1)	SIMULATE	
	READ	
	START	1000
	END	

causes the first file to be read and a run of 1000 made.

(2)	SIMULATE	
	READ	3
	START	1000
	END	

causes the fourth file, skipping the first three, to be read in and a run of 1000 to be made.

7.1.4   Batching GPSS jobs

JOB

Operation:

This statement is used to separate successive **GPSS** models submitted as parts of the same job stream. It removes the existing model from the CPU and transfers control to the assembly phase of GPSS, which will read in the next model and assemble and run it.

7.1.5   Rewinding jobtapes

A jobtape is a transaction file that has been prepared either by the GPSS WRITE statement or by other means (see JOBTAPE in Section 7.2.1 and WRITE in Section 7.2.6).

REWIND   A

Operation:

This statement causes the tape specified by A to be rewound (or the data set to be repositioned at its beginning).

Operand:

A: Specifies the jobtape concerned; it may be JOBTA1, JOBTA2, or JOBTA3.

7.1.6   Output editor

The output editor may be used in all cases in which a special report is wanted in place of the standard output.

REPORT

Operation:

This statement, which has no operand, must be placed after the last START statement of a GPSS job. It suppresses standard output and requests the services of the GPSS output editor. The REPORT statement is followed by the output editor statements needed to produce the desired report (see Section 8.1). In the case of an error in the output editor statements which prevents the production of the requested report, the standard output is produced.

7.1.7   GPSS V additional statements

GPSS V has two features not offered by the previous versions: LOAD and AUXILIARY.

LOAD   A,B,C,...

Operation and Operands:

This statement specifies that the modules identified by the A, B, C, . . . fields must be resident in main storage. This is a way to improve the efficiency of the simulator when it is known, for instance, that certain GPSS, or user written, nonresident modules are invoked frequently, in particular when using PRINT or TRACE blocks.

AUXILIARY   A,B,C,D,E

Operation and operands:

This statement permits the user to specify those GPSS entities which must be placed on an auxiliary storage device. This feature allows the user to run large models that cannot be contained in main memory. It can be used for most entities. The A, B, . . . fields specify the type of entity, the number to be made resident, the number to be placed on auxiliary storage, and other information specifying the method of storage.

This feature is most important because it removes constraints on the size of GPSS program which can be run on a specific computer.

7.2 Block-Definition Statements

7.2.1 Transaction-oriented blocks

Creation and destruction of transactions. We explained in Section 6.2.1 how transactions can be created by GENERATE blocks. We may have other needs, for example:

From one transaction, create several others and make them members of the same family. For this purpose, the SPLIT block was designed.

Create a transaction stream that can be run against various models. This can be done with the JOBTAPE block.

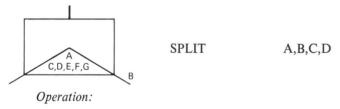

SPLIT   A,B,C,D

Operation:

This block creates the number of copies of the entering parent transaction specified by the A-operand. The copies, together with their parent, become members of the same family, or *transaction assembly set.* The parent transaction continues to the next sequential block and the copies go to the address specified by B.

All properties of the parent are transmitted to the copies: priority, parameter values (see D below), and mark time, but not the block-departure time, which remains zero until an ADVANCE block is reached. The N (total block count) and W (current block count) of the SPLIT block are incremented by 1 for each parent and copy

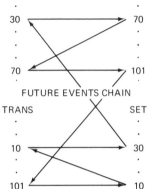

Figure 7.1 Assembly set linkage.

transaction. W is decremented by one unit, as each transaction leaves the SPLIT block.

The transaction assembly sets may be manipulated by other blocks, such as MATCH, GATHER, GATE M, GATE NM, and ASSEMBLE, which are discussed later in this section.

Operands:

A: The number of copies to be created.

B: The address for copy transactions. This address is computed for each copy.

C: A parameter number to be used for the serialization of the copies. If, for example, parameter 2 is specified and P2 of the parent transaction contains 5, the copies will be numbered 6, 7, 8, 9, . . . in parameter 2.

D: The number of parameters to be assigned to each copy transaction. If blank, the copies have the same number of parameters as the parent. The parameter contents of the copies are identical to those of the parent transaction. If copies have more parameters than the parent, the additional parameters are all set to zero.

In GPSS V, this operand, as well as E, F, and G, are used to specify the number of parameters of each type to be assigned to the copies: kPx, where k = number of parameters and x = type, which may be F (fullword), H (halfword), B (byte), or L (floating point). If D- to G-operands are omitted, the copies receive the same number of parameters as the parent.

The relationship between members of an assembly set is recorded by means of a linkage displayed in the current- and future-events chains. An example is given in Figure 7.1, where a set consisting of one parent and three copies is shown. The four transactions concerned have the numbers 30, 70, 10, and 101 and are connected by a cyclic chain. If one of these is split, the new copies become members of the same set.

JOBTAPE   A,B,C,D

Operation:

This block initiates the entry of transactions from a previously prepared data set. It operates in a similar way to the GENERATE block except that the interarrival times are stored and transaction properties may be recorded in the JOBTAPE.

If operands B, C, and D are omitted, the JOBTAPE statement is a control statement used to position the data set at the record following the next END OF FILE JOBT record found in the data set. Usually a single file of transactions is used, so this option will not be discussed.

Operands:

A: The name of one of three jobtapes: JOBTA1, JOBTA2, or JOBTA3. The corresponding data sets must be defined in the operating-system procedure (see DJBTAP1–3 DD cards in Appendix A) and created by using either the GPSS WRITE statement or some other means (see Section 7.2.6 WRITE).

B: The label of the block where the transactions must go.

C: The offset time, that is, the time relative to the start of the simulation run at which the first transaction is to enter the model. If this field is omitted (or equal to zero), the first transaction enters the model at time 1. The following transactions will enter the model according to the recorded interarrival times between transactions 2 and 1, 3 and 2, ...

D: A scaling factor, between 1 and 999999, by which the transaction interarrival times and transit times recorded on the jobtape will be multiplied. When not specified, this scaling factor is assumed to be 1. This operand is very useful when changing the time unit of the model.

EXAMPLE:

JOBTAPE   JOBTA2,BEGIN,480

will cause the transactions recorded on the data set JOBTA2 to be read in, the first one at time 480 and the subsequent ones according to the interarrival times stored in the transaction records.

The next block discussed destroys transactions. It can be considered as complementary to the SPLIT block. It retains the first transaction in the block and destroys all the others.

ASSEMBLE   A

Operation:

This block causes the first transaction to wait until a specified number of transactions of the same assembly set have arrived, after which it leaves the ASSEMBLE block. The attributes of the outgoing transaction are therefore those of the first arrival of the assembly set. This is realized by counting and destroying the transactions that arrive after the first member of an assembly set. When the count is reached, all the transactions to be assembled have arrived and the original transaction proceeds to the next sequential block. When waiting for the other transactions the initial arrival is in a matching status; that is, its matching indicator is set. This condition can be tested by the GATE on match/no match block (see Section 7.2.3). When the assemble operation is complete, the match indicator of the transaction is reset.

Operand:

A: The number of transactions to be assembled.

EXAMPLE:

In a computer a message has to be processed by the CPU and needs an input/output (I/O) operation which can be done concurrently. This is simulated by splitting the message transaction. The original seizes the CPU, advances, releases the CPU, and waits in the ASSEMBLE block until the copy has performed the I/O operation. The copy simulates the I/O operation by seizing the access arm modeled by facility ARM, seizing the channel, spending time in an ADVANCE block to simulate the actual I/O operation, releasing the channel, releasing the access arm, and entering the ASSEMBLE block to allow the original transaction to proceed. The block diagram is shown in Figure 7.2 and the program is as follows:

```
              SEIZE           CPU
              SPLIT           1,PCA
              ADVANCE         V1
              RELEASE         CPU
      PAE1    ASSEMBLE        2
                 .
                 .
                 .
              TRANSFER        ,CONT
                 .
                 .
                 .
      PCA     SEIZE           ARM
              ADVANCE         V2
              SEIZE           CHA
              ADVANCE         V3
              RELEASE         CHA
              RELEASE         ARM
              TRANSFER        ,PAE1
```

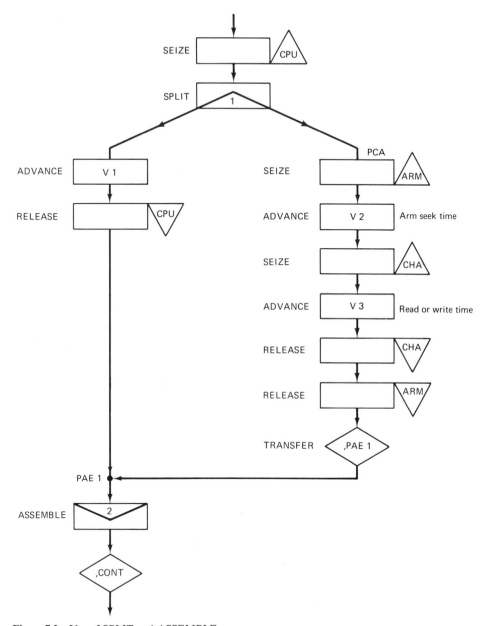

Figure 7.2 Use of SPLIT and ASSEMBLE.

In such examples the user must ensure that V2 + V3 > V1 or the wrong transaction might win. To avoid this chance split three ways and send the master transaction to the assemble block without delay.

Access to or handling of attributes. In Chapter 6 we saw how to modify priority with the PRIORITY block and parameter contents with the ASSIGN block. The next two blocks also modify transaction attributes: MARK and INDEX.

MARK   A

Operation:

This block either replaces the MARK time of the transaction by the current clock time C1 (when no A-operand is specified) or places C1 in the parameter specified by the A-operand.

Operand:

A: (*optional*) The number of the parameter in which to store the value of C1.

The *mark time* is the time when the transaction originally entered the model. Its common use is to evaluate or to tabulate the *transit time* M1 (which is computed by GPSS as C1 — mark time) (see the example given in Section 7.2.6 under TABULATE). Therefore, the MARK block, when used without the A-operand, modifies the transit time M1. When the original mark time and intermediate transit times are desired, one can use MARK A to tabulate the intermediate transit time as MPj, relative to the parameter j specified by the A-operand. If several intermediate transit times are required, then several MARK blocks can be used with different parameters.

INDEX   A,B

Operation:

This block allows the user to add a specified value to a parameter and to store the result in parameter 1 of the transaction.

Operands:

A: The parameter whose contents have to be increased by the value of the B-operand. The contents of the A-operand parameter are not modified unless it is parameter 1.

B: The value to be added to the A-operand parameter.

EXAMPLES:

(1)   INDEX   2,FN3 Add the value of FN3 to P2
                                            and store the result in P1.

| (2) | | INDEX | 1,1 | Add 1 to P1. |
| (3) | | INDEX | 1,5 | Add 5 to P1. |

Remark: The operations of the INDEX block can be performed by ASSIGN blocks but less efficiently. For instance, the first example would need two ASSIGN blocks or utilization of a variable:

| | ASSIGN | 1,V1 |
| 1 | VARIABLE | P2+FN3 |

Synchronization of transactions. In this paragraph we describe the blocks used to synchronize transactions of the same assembly set. These blocks are

MATCH   for the synchronization of two transactions.

GATHER   for the synchronization of *n* transactions.

ASSEMBLE (discussed earlier).

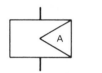

MATCH   A

Operation:

This block synchronizes the progress of two transactions of an assembly set by delaying one until the other has reached a specified point in the block diagram, after which both transactions can continue. The transactions that must match are one arriving at the MATCH block and another arriving at a conjugate MATCH block specified by the A-operand. The first arrival at a MATCH block waits until another has arrived at the conjugate block. The conjugate block can be the block itself. In this case the MATCH block has the same function as a GATHER block with a count of 2. Pairs of transactions from several assembly sets may be synchronized simultaneously at the same pair of MATCH blocks. It is also possible for several pairs of transactions from the same assembly set to be synchronized simultaneously at different pairs of MATCH blocks.

When a transaction is waiting for the conjugate, its matching indicator is set. It is reset when the match is made. This condition can be tested by the GATE match/no match block (see Section 7.2.3).

Operand:

A: The label, or number, of the conjugate MATCH block.

EXAMPLE:

In a manufacturing process transactions are split and enter queues for facilities FAC1 and FAC2. For the process to start, the first member of the pair must get control of FAC1 and the second of FAC2.

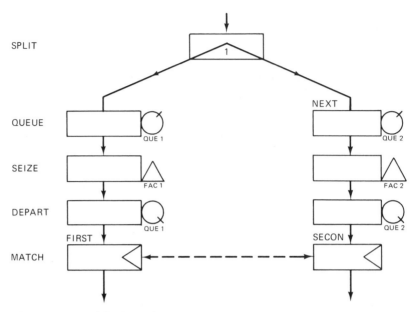

Figure 7.3   Use of SPLIT and MATCH.

The block diagram is represented in Figure 7.3. The program is

	GENERATE	1320,500
	SPLIT	1,NEXT
	QUEUE	QUE1
	SEIZE	FAC1
	DEPART	QUE1
FIRST	MATCH	SECON
	.	
	.	
	.	
NEXT	QUEUE	QUE2
	SEIZE	FAC2
	DEPART	QUE2
SECON	MATCH	FIRST
	.	
	.	
	.	

When a transaction enters a MATCH block, the system checks for its duplicate at the other MATCH block. If none has arrived, the transaction must wait. If a matching transaction is present, then both transactions are allowed to proceed.

Remark: The principle of matching is to remove from the current-events chain a transaction that does not find its conjugate at the other MATCH block and to place it in an interrupt status on the matching chain. This transaction is returned to the current-events chain when another transaction enters a MATCH block that refers to the current MATCH block.

Matching conditions can be tested and used to control the flow of transactions. This is done by GATE blocks with the options M (match) and NM (no match), which are discussed and illustrated in Section 7.2.3.

GATHER   A

Operation:

This block is similar to the ASSEMBLE block. It collects a specified number of transactions from an assembly set. When they have been gathered, all the transactions proceed to the next sequential block.

When transactions are waiting to be gathered, their match indicator is set. It is reset when they have been gathered. This matching condition can be tested by the GATE block on match/no match condition (see Section 7.2.3).

Operand:

A: The number of transactions of the assembly set to be gathered. This number must be 1 or greater; otherwise, an execution error occurs.

Remark: When the specified number of transactions has been gathered, they are returned to the current-events chain at the end of their respective priority class, in the same order as they arrived at the GATHER block.

7.2.2   Equipment-oriented blocks

Facilities.   Four associated blocks were discussed in Section 6.2.2, SEIZE/ RELEASE and PREEMPT/RETURN. They control a transaction's use of the facility entity. PREEMPT can interrupt the service of a transaction currently seizing the facility.

Sometimes it is necessary to interrupt a transaction which itself had already interrupted another transaction. The PREEMPT statement can do this when used in priority mode, indicated by specifying PR as B-operand.

PREEMPT   A,B,C,D,E

Operation:

This block allows the entering transaction to obtain the use of the facility, specified by the A-operand, if it has higher priority than the transaction having currently gained control of the facility by a PREEMPT block. The situations that must be considered are numerous and depend on the status of the facility:

If the facility is free, it is preempted.

If the facility is seized, it is preempted and the seizing transaction is put into interrupt status.

If the facility is already preempted and if the priority of the arriving transaction is greater, it preempts the facility, and the transaction that was in the facility is put into interrupt status. If the priority of the arriving transaction is lower, it is refused by the block.

The preempted transaction is interrupted until the preempting transaction returns the facility by entering a RETURN block. It then regains control and finishes its service time unless another option has been specified by the C-, D-, and E-operands.

The priority of a transaction may be 0 to 127, so it is possible to have 127 interrupted transactions in contention for the same facility, or 128 if the first interrupted transaction had seized the facility. The preempted transactions are put in a push-down list and removed one after the other in LIFO order (Last In–First Out). All interrupted transactions are recorded as in contention for the facility unless specified otherwise by the E-operand. Some examples of typical situations are given after the discussion of the RETURN block.

Operands:

A: The facility name or number.

B=PR: Indicates that the block operates in priority mode.

C: The address for the preempted transaction.

D: The number of a parameter in which to store the remaining time that the transaction must spend in the current ADVANCE block.

E=RE: A signal to remove the transaction from the facility. If blank (that is, not used), the interrupted transaction remains in contention for the facility.

RETURN   A

Operation:

This block removes the preempting transaction from the facility. If no other transaction is in interrupt status, the facility is made available. Otherwise, the last interrupted transaction gets the control of the facility.

Operand:

A: The name or number of the facility.

EXAMPLES:

(1)   In a computer, an I/O error causes the termination of the jobs currently being processed. Jobs with different priorities are processed; therefore multilevel interrupts may occur (Figure 7.4).

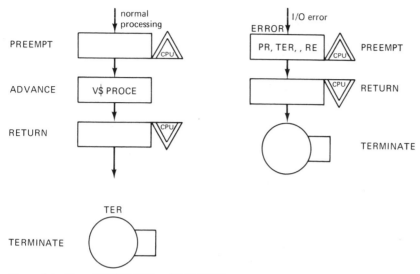

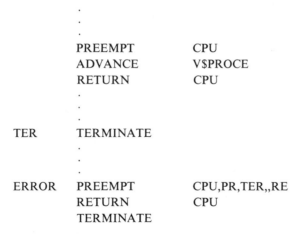

Figure 7.4   Use of PREEMPT and RETURN.

The processing is represented by the classical series of blocks PREEMPT, ADVANCE, and RETURN. The I/O error is simulated by the arrival of a transaction of higher priority at the ERROR PREEMPT block, which interrupts the transaction currently being processed, removes it from the facility, and sends it to TER, where it is terminated. Note that the number of terminated jobs during the whole simulation run will be given automatically as the N attribute of the TERMINATE block.

```
            .
            .
            .
        PREEMPT         CPU
        ADVANCE         V$PROCE
        RETURN          CPU
            .
            .
            .
TER     TERMINATE
            .
            .
            .
ERROR   PREEMPT         CPU,PR,TER,,RE
        RETURN          CPU
        TERMINATE
```

(2)   This program is similar to that of example 1, but we tabulate the remaining service time of interrupted jobs. The one difference is that the PREEMPT block stores the remaining service time in parameter 2 and the TER block tabulates these values (see Section 7.2.6) before terminating the transaction (Figure 7.5).

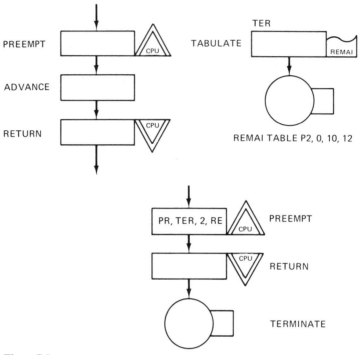

Figure 7.5

```
                        .
                        .
                        .

    TER        TABULATE          REMAI
               TERMINATE
    REMAI      TABLE             P2,0,10,12
                        .
                        .
                        .
```

The TABULATE block produces a table of values of P2, which contains the remaining service time. The REMAI TABLE indicates that P2 is to be tabulated, the end of the first interval class is zero, the value of the interval is 10, and the total number of intervals is 12. We assume that the ADVANCE time is less than 100.

(3) In a computer system, where a job can be interrupted by another with higher priority, the interrupted job must restart from the beginning (recycling). We require the distribution of the remaining times when interrupted.

This is achieved (Figure 7.6) by sending the interrupted job to the INTER block, where the remaining service time is tabulated. The transaction is sent back to the ADVANCE block, where the whole process will be restarted. Note that the transaction will not be accepted in the ADVANCE block ADV until the corresponding interrupt is released. This function is performed automatically by GPSS.

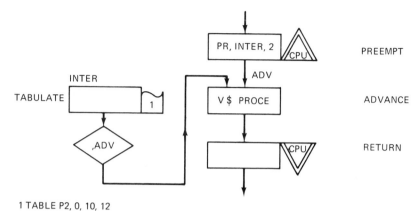

1 TABLE P2, 0, 10, 12

Figure 7.6

	PREEMPT	CPU,PR,INTER,2
ADV	ADVANCE	V$PROCE
	RETURN	CPU
	.	
	.	
	.	
INTER	TABULATE	1
	TRANSFER	,ADV
1	TABLE	P2,0,10,12

(4) A computer system processes jobs with different priorities. When a job is interrupted, it waits until the higher-priority job is processed; then processing continues from where the interrupt occurred. We want to tabulate the remaining process times when interrupted.

In this case (Figure 7.7), we need to tabulate, so we use the C-operand. Therefore, we must send the interrupted transaction back to the ADVANCE block, but the time it will spend in this block must be the time remaining when the interrupt occurred. One method is to use ADVANCE P2 and to store the original (total) processing time in P2 before the transaction enters the facility.

	ASSIGN	2,V$PROCE
	PREEMPT	CPU,PR,INTER,2
ADV	ADVANCE	P2
	RETURN	CPU
	.	
	.	
	.	
INTER	TABULATE	REMAI
	TRANSFER	,ADV
REMAI	TABLE	P2,0,10,12

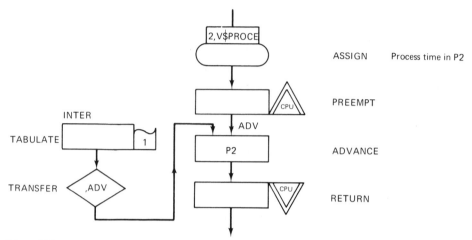

Figure 7.7

Remarks:

1. The PREEMPT block is very useful to model complicated situations. Its use is rather simple although its implementation is quite complicated, owing to the numerous cases that have to be considered.

2. In GPSS V there are several types of parameters, so the D-operand of the PREEMPT statement must be coded accordingly.

Switches. The LOGIC block is used to modify the status of a switch. The status of the switch can be tested elsewhere in the model by GATE blocks.

LOGIC X   A

Operation:

This block sets the logic switch specified by the A-operand to the status specified by the X-mnemonics.

Operand:

A: The switch name or number.

X-mnemonics:

S: Set the logic switch.

R: Reset the logic switch.

I: Invert the logic switch. (This is a flip-flop operation which changes set to reset or reset to set.)

If a switch is already in the state specified by the X-mnemonic, the LOGIC block performs no operation.

EXAMPLES:

(1)	LOGIC I	17	If logic switch 17 is set, then reset it; if reset then set it.
(2)	LOGIC S	LIGHT	Set switch LIGHT.

Counting and scanning of permanent entities.   Two instructions are available

(1) to count the number of entities, such as facilities, storages, queues, and save locations, satisfying a given condition.

(2) select from one of those classes one entity with a given property.

One may need to know, for example, the number of facilities within a given range which are not in use, the number of full storages, the number of queues with contents exceeding a given number, the most used facility, the queue with minimum contents, and so on.

                    COUNT X   A,B,C,D,E

Operation:

This block counts the number of entities satisfying the condition defined by the conditional or logical operator X and places the count in the parameter specified by the A-operand.

Operands:

A: The number of the transaction parameter in which the count will be placed.

B: The lower limit of the range of the specified entity to be tested.

C: The upper limit.

D: The value with which the standard numerical attributes specified in the C-field will be compared when the X conditional operator is L, LE, E, NE, G, or GE.

E: The entity attribute to be counted. It can be any standard numerical attribute except attributes of transactions and of matrix savevalues: MXj or MHj (and MBj or MLj in GPSS V).

X-Operator:

X is a conditional or logical operator and may be

A conditional operator: E for equal, NE for not equal, L for less than, LE for less than or equal, G for greater than, GE for greater than or equal.

A logical operator in the case of facilities, storages, and switches. In this case, the D- and E-operands are not used. The following operators are available.

Facilities.

U   for used.

NU   for not used.

I   for interrupted.

NI   for not interrupted.

EXAMPLES:

   (1)   COUNT NU   1,5,14

Count the number of facilities between 5 and 14 not currently in use. Store the count in parameter 1.

   (2)   COUNT GE   2,5,14,800,FR

Count the number of facilities between 5 and 14 which have a current utilization (FR) greater than or equal to 80 per cent (see Section 7.4.1, where FR is discussed). Store the result in parameter 2.

Storages.

SF   for storage full.

SNF   for storage not full.

SE   for storage empty.

SNE   for storage not empty.

EXAMPLE:

COUNT SF   3,1,10

Count the number of full storages between 1 and 10. Store the count in P3.

Switches.

S   for set. COUNT will count the number of switches set.

R   for reset.

EXAMPLE:

COUNT S   2,1,100

Count the number of set switches between 1 and 100 and store this value in P2.

SELECT X   A,B,C,D,E,F

Operation:

This block selects *the first entity* of the specified range which meets the condition defined by the conditional or logical operator X and places its number in the parameter specified by the A-operand. If no entity meets the required condition, the transaction is sent to the block specified by the F-operand.

Operands:

Operands A, B, C, D, and E have the same meaning as for the COUNT block, but the result, placed in the parameter specified by the A-operand, is the number of the first entity found to meet the specified condition.

A: The number of the transaction parameter in which the number of the selected entity will be placed.

B,C,D,E: Have the same meaning as for the COUNT block above.

F: (*optional*) An alternative block for the transaction if no entity in the given range meets the specified condition.

X-operator:

Has the same meaning as for the COUNT block with two additional logical operators: MIN for minimum and MAX for maximum.

EXAMPLES:

(1) Select the queue, from 1 to 10, with minimum contents and queue the transaction there.

.
.
.

      SELECT MIN 1,1,10,,Q   Select the minimum length queue and place
      QUEUE   P1   its number in P1; then go to queue P1.

(2) Select the facility, from 1 to 15, with maximum utilization and place its number in P2.

      SELECT MAX 2,1,25,,FR   (See Section 7.4.1.)

(3) Select the first queue, from 1 to 5, with contents less than or equal to 5 and place its number in P4.

      SELECT LE   4,1,5,,5,Q

(4) Select and seize the first free facility between 1 and 10.

      SELECT NU   1,1,10   Select first free facility, store its number in P1,
      SEIZE   P1   and seize it.

Remark: These two blocks operate correctly only if there is at least one free facility. This condition should be checked before performing the operation, for example by allowing at most 10 transactions to seize facilities 1 to 10.

(5) Select and seize the free facility, between 1 and 5, with minimum utilization.
      This cannot be done with only 2 blocks because it is not possible to select directly on two facility attributes. We could, for instance, save the variable

IDLTI in save locations and select the one corresponding to the maximum value stored, assuming that at least one facility is free:

```
               .
               .
               .
          ASSIGN        2,5           Prepare the loop;
BACK      SAVEVALUE     P2,V$IDLTI    Save the value of IDLTI for
          LOOP          2,BACK        every facility, 5 to 1, in X*2;
          SELECT MAX    2,1,5,,X      Select the maximum value and
          SEIZE         P2            save its number in P2;
                                      Seize the corresponding facil-
                                      ity.
IDLTI     VARIABLE      (1−F*2)(1000−FR*2)
```

This variable has two factors:

(1) $(1-F*2)$, which is equal to 1 if the facility whose number is the contents of P2 is idle, 0 if the facility is in use; and

(2) $(1000-FR*2)$, which represents the proportion of idle time. FR is the standard numerical attribute for the facility utilization in parts per thousand.

It is easier to select the facility with maximum idle time because of the need to eliminate busy facilities.

The above solution has the disadvantage of being slow. Every time a transaction has to seize a facility, we evaluate five variables, store them in save locations, and only then perform the select operation. We can speed the process by defining five variables (variable n associated with facility n) and reduce the program segment to two instructions:

```
               .
               .
               .
          SELECT MAX    2,1,5,,V      Select the variable, 1
          SEIZE         P2            to 5, which has max-
               .                      imum value and seize
               .                      the     corresponding
               .                      facility.
1         VARIABLE      (1−F1)*(1000−FR1)   One variable is de-
2         VARIABLE      (1−F2)*(1000−FR2)   fined per facility. It
3         VARIABLE      (1−F3)*(1000−FR3)   is equal to zero if
4         VARIABLE      (1−F4)*(1000−FR4)   the facility is busy
5         VARIABLE      (1−F5)*(1000−FR5)   and proportional to
                                            the idle time if the
                                            facility is free.
```

7.2.3 Transaction-flow modification

In Chapter 6 we discussed the simplest modes of the TRANSFER block, the GATE (on facility and storage), and the TEST blocks. This section and Section 7.2.4 present additional features that are extremely useful for modeling: transfers, testing, loops, buffer, and user chains.

It is important to note that the blocks BUFFER, PRIORITY, with the BUFFER option, and LINK/UNLINK, which refer to user chains, are different from the blocks previously discussed. They allow the user to override the normal GPSS order of operation. In the case of BUFFER, the user can change the order of processing transactions. User chains, LINK and UNLINK blocks, let the analyst deactivate and reactivate transactions as required. Owing to the importance of user chains, this subject is treated separately in Section 7.2.4.

Some other blocks include branching options but their main function is not to modify the flow of transactions. They all have an alternate exit address where the transaction is sent when a condition is not met. These blocks are:

SELECT (discussed in Section 7.2.2)

ALTER, EXAMINE, REMOVE, and SCAN (which refer to the group entity, discussed in Section 7.2.5).

FUNAVAIL (discussed in Section 7.2.8).

PREEMPT in priority mode allows the user to direct preempted transactions to a specified block.

Transfers.

TRANSFER   A,B,C,D

Operation:

This block directs transactions to a specific location, depending on the transfer mode defined by the A-operand.

Operands:

A: The transfer mode.

B, C, and D: Have different meanings, depending on A, which are discussed separately for every mode.

Transfer modes—unconditional, BOTH, statistical, and SIM—were discussed in Section 6.2.3. Additional modes are discussed below.

1. ALL: The transaction tries to branch to the block specified by the B-operand. If it cannot, it attempts successively to branch to $B+D$, $B+2D$, $B+3D$, ..., C. If the transaction fails to find an exit, it stays in the TRANSFER block. The above trials will be repeated, in the same order, when a new scan of the current-events chain is initiated.
   B is the first address tested for exit;
   C is the last address tested for exit;
   D is an indexing factor.

EXAMPLE:

TRANSFER   ALL,FIRST,LAST,5

Try to exit to FIRST; if not possible, try FIRST+5, FIRST+10, . . . , until LAST.

2. PICK: The transaction is sent to an address picked at random, with uniform
   probability, from B, B+1, B+2, . . . , C. The choice is made independent of
   the status of the block selected. If this block refuses the transaction, it waits in
   the TRANSFER block until the blocking condition is removed and then
   moves.

EXAMPLE:

TRANSFER   PICK,50,55

Pick a number between 50 and 55 at random as the next block address.

3. FN (function selection mode): The function identified by the B-operand is
   evaluated and truncated, and the value of the C-operand is added. The C-
   operand may be zero or blank. The result is used as the next address for the
   transaction.

EXAMPLE:

TRANSFER   FN,1

Sends the transaction to the address computed by FN1. This function could be
of type E (see Section 7.3.2), have P1 as argument, and labels as values. In such a
case one could use just one TRANSFER block to direct transactions to various
parts of the model, depending on the value of a parameter.

4. P (parameter): The value of the B-operand is the number of a transaction
   parameter. The value of this parameter added to the C-operand gives the
   next address for the transaction. The C-operand can be zero or blank.

EXAMPLE:

TRANSFER   P,3,X5

The transaction is sent to the address given by P3+X5.

5. SBR (subroutine): The transaction is sent to the address specified by the
   B-operand. The C-operand is the number of a parameter which contains the
   address j of the current TRANSFER block.
        Usually, the B-operand is the first block of the GPSS subroutine to
   which we wish to send the transaction. After the subroutine has been executed,
   the transaction must be returned to the address j+1, the block following the
   TRANSFER SBR. This is done by a TRANSFER in parameter mode.

EXAMPLE:

The main program is:

		.	
		.	
		.	
(j)	TRANSFER	SBR,ROUTI,3	Store j, current
(j+1)	QUEUE		block address, in
	.		P3, and send the
	.		transaction to
	.		ROUTI.

The GPSS subroutine is:

ROUTI	QUEUE	1	First instruction of
	SEIZE	CHAN	the GPSS subrou-
	.		tine.
	.		
	.		
	TRANSFER	P,3,1	Return; transfer to
			P3+1 (=j+1), the
			block following the
			TRANSFER SBR
			block.

The TRANSFER block provides a very important set of instructions. Remembering all the possible transfer modes, the programmer can save considerable time and effort by making programs shorter and more elegant. Sometimes the program will also run faster, but, even if the execution time is unaltered, there are the two advantages of reduced project time and program readability. For example, suppose that the transaction can branch to four different locations, depending on the value of a parameter. This means testing successively for the four values of the parameter and branching, using unconditional TRANSFER blocks. However, a single TRANSFER in function mode can perform the same task.

Testing. The GATE block, introduced in Section 6.2.3, can operate in refusal mode or alternate exit mode. This second mode is implied by the presence of the B-operand, which defines the alternate address to which the transaction is sent when the condition specified by the GATE block is not met.

	GATE X	A,B

Operation:

The status of the entity specified by the A-operand is tested according to the mnemonics used for X. If a B-operand is specified, the transaction is sent to this address if the condition is not met, to the next sequential block if the condition is met. If no

B-operand is specified, the transaction is refused if the condition is not met, accepted if the condition is met.

Operands:

The operands used to test logic switches are:

A: The entity name or number.

B: (*optional*) The alternate exit for the transaction when the condition is not met. If no B-operand is specified, the block operates in refusal mode.

X-Mnemonics:

The mnemonics relating to *facilities* and *storages* were discussed in Section 6.2.3. We discuss mnemonics relating to logic switches and matching status below.

 Switches:

The mnemonics used with switches are:

LR   for logic reset.

LS   for logic set.

Operand A is the switch name or number.

EXAMPLES:

(1)   GATE LR   TRY

The transaction will be accepted by the block if switch TRY is reset, and refused otherwise.

(2)   GATE LS   7,FAIL

The transaction will be directed to FAIL if switch 7 is not set and to the next sequential block if switch 7 is set.

 Matching Status:

Two mnemonics are available to test if another transaction of the same assembly set is or is not in a matching condition at a specified block:

M   for match.

The GATE M condition is true if a transaction of the same assembly set is in matching status at the block specified by the A-operand, false otherwise.

NM   for no match.

The condition is true if no transaction of the same assembly set is in matching status at the block specified by the A-operand, false if one is present.

Operand A is the address of the block to be examined for a matching condition. A transaction might be in a matching condition in a MATCH, GATHER or ASSEMBLE block. This is indicated by the matching indicator of the transaction which is set when a transaction is waiting for the condition to be met and reset when the condition is satisfied.

It can happen that a transaction is at the block specified by the A-operand but not in matching status. This can occur if transactions have been successfully gathered at a GATHER block, their matching indicator thereby being reset, but were refused entry to the next block.

EXAMPLES:

(1)   GATE M   FIRST,OTHER

If another transaction of the same assembly set is waiting in matching status at block FIRST, the transaction is accepted in the GATE block and proceeds to the next sequential block. If no match in block FIRST, the transaction is accepted in the GATE block and moves to block OTHER.

(2)   When the first transaction of an assembly set of 10 transactions arrives at a given point, we store the contents of parameter 1 in the save location whose number is the value of parameter 2. The other transactions must be assembled before the first transaction can proceed.

The block diagram is shown in Figure 7.8 and the program is:

	TRANSFER	BOTH,,ASSEM	Is this transaction the
	GATE NM	ASSEM	first of its assembly set?
	SAVEVALUE	P2,P1	If so, accept the trans-
ASSEM	ASSEMBLE	10	action, save P1 in save
			location P2, and proceed.
			If not, transfer to
			ASSEM.

Figure 7.8   GATE on matching status.

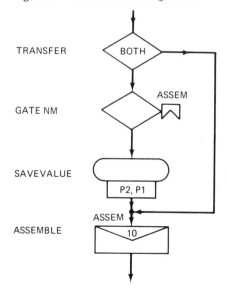

(3) In a manufacturing process two parts issued from a SPLIT block have to reach certain points before the process continues. Part 1 always arrives at block FIRST and must wait for the second part to arrive at either block SECON or THIRD. The order in which parts arrive cannot be predicted.

The problem is solved by using a combination of MATCH and GATE M, as shown in Figure 7.9. The program is:

	.		
	.		
	.		
FIRST	MATCH	ANY	When part 1 arrives, no match is possible. ANY is a block where part 2 cannot be in matching status.
	.		
	.		
	.		
	.		
	.		
	GATE M	FIRST	When part 2 arrives at either GATE
SECON	MATCH	FIRST	block, it must wait until the corresponding part 1 has arrived at FIRST.
	.		It can then enter the GATE block and
	.		proceed to the MATCH block
	GATE M	FIRST	(SECON or THIRD), which allows
THIRD	MATCH	FIRST	both transactions to move.

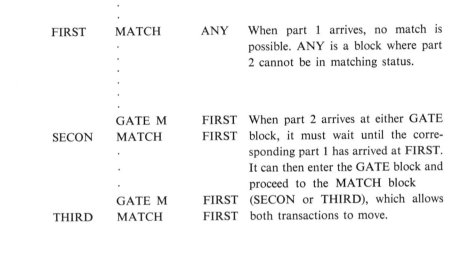

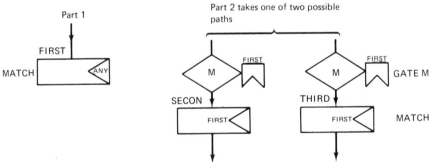

Figure 7.9 / Use of GATE and MATCH.

Loops. It is often necessary for transactions to make a number of loops of a sequence of blocks before they can continue. This can be coded by using a parameter of the transaction to contain the number of loops required and a TEST block to determine when the requested number of loops has been made. This would entail one ASSIGN block to store the total number of loops, another to decrease the count as each loop ended, and a TEST block.

The LOOP block executes the operations of decrementing the parameter contents by 1, testing for looping finished, and transferring the transaction. Therefore, it runs faster on the computer.

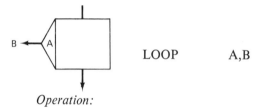

LOOP   A,B

Operation:

The parameter specified by the A-operand is decremented by unity. If the result is zero, the transaction continues to the next sequential block. If nonzero, the transaction is sent to the address specified by the B-operand.

Operands:

A: The parameter controlling the number of loops required. It must be initialized before entering the loop and will be reduced to zero when the transaction leaves the loop.

B: The address to which the transaction branches when the parameter (specified by the A-operand) is nonzero.

EXAMPLE:

Reset save locations 1 to 100 to zero. The program given below is illustrated by Figure 7.10.

	ASSIGN	1,100	Initialize P1 to 100;
SAV	SAVEVALUE	P1,0	Save 0 in XP1 (X100,X99,...X1);
	LOOP	1,SAV	Decrement P1 by 1. If zero,
			go to next sequential block;
			if not, go to SAV.

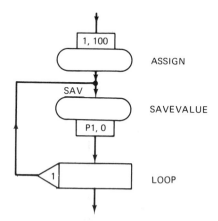

Figure 7.10   Use of the LOOP block.

Buffer.   The blocks discussed so far do not give the user any control over the way transactions are processed by GPSS. The user knows only the properties of the block concerned, the operations it performs, and the two basic rules of GPSS:

1. Transactions are moved automatically by GPSS from block to block until delayed by an ADVANCE block or a logical condition.

2. A block is activated when a transaction enters.

As previously explained, GPSS always moves transactions as far as possible through the block diagram until a stopping condition is encountered. Sometimes the user would like to modify the operation of GPSS, for example by stopping a transaction at a given block (for a zero time) to allow the processing of others. This is made possible by using the BUFFER block.

Consider the following situation. Transactions that represent parts to be manufactured must go five times through a process, represented by facility 1, for 10 time units. When a part has been processed, it is returned to the waiting line, which is organized FIFO, until the fifth pass.

The program that first comes to mind is very simple [see the block diagram of Figure 7.11(a)]

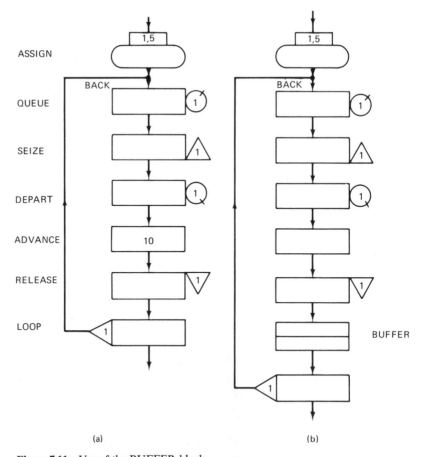

(a)   (b)

Figure 7.11 Use of the BUFFER block.

	ASSIGN	1,5	Assign the number of loops in P1
BACK	QUEUE	1	Enter queue 1 and wait for machine
	SEIZE	1	Seize machine
	DEPART	1	Leave queue
	ADVANCE	10	Processing time
	RELEASE	1	Free machine
	LOOP	1,BACK	Loop if fewer than five times.

In fact, this program is incorrect. Suppose that the clock time is 200 and one transaction arrives in the queue. It takes control of the facility, enters the ADVANCE block, and is scheduled to leave at 210. At 205 another transaction arrives in the queue and must wait because facility 1 is busy. At 210, transaction 1 leaves the ADVANCE block, releases facility 1, goes through the LOOP block and the QUEUE block, and seizes facility 1 again. But we require transaction 2, which arrived in queue 1 at 205 to be processed before the second loop of transaction 1. This difficulty occurs because GPSS moves transactions as far as possible.

To solve the problem we insert a BUFFER block after RELEASE [Figure 7.11(b)]. The transaction is then stopped in the BUFFER block. GPSS tries to move transactions that are ahead of the current one in the current-events chain. It finds transaction 2 and moves it until delayed by the ADVANCE block. Later, but at the same clock time, transaction 1 is moved to the QUEUE block and stops there to wait for facility 1 to be released.

   BUFFER

Operation:

This block, which has no operand, stops processing of the current transaction and reinitializes the scanning of the current-events chain at the start of the chain, first transaction of highest priority. The BUFFER block involves no time delay, so the transaction is always processed by the scan at the same clock time as it initiated the buffer operation.

   PRIORITY   A,BUFFER

Operation:

This block has the combined effects of a PRIORITY and a BUFFER block. It sets the priority of the transaction to the value specified by the A-operand, places the transaction at the back of its priority class, and behaves like a BUFFER block.

Operands:

A: The value, 0 to 127, of the priority to be assigned to the transaction.

B: Coded as BUFFER and makes the PRIORITY block behave like a BUFFER block.

EXAMPLES:

(1) Consider the problem above, where transactions have various priority levels between 1 and 10. The transaction leaving the facility should not be reprocessed immediately, even when it has the highest priority.

    The model of Figure 7.11(b) does not describe the system in all cases. It is clear that if the priority of the current transaction is 10 and all other transactions in the current-events chain have lower priority, the current transaction will be stopped in the buffer block and placed in the current-events chain at the end of its priority class. Therefore, it will be at the front of the current-events chain and immediately processed when the scan is reinitialized.

    To solve the problem we must stop the transaction, ensure that one waiting transaction, if any, is moved from the queue to seize the facility, and then place the current transaction back in the current-events chain at the right place. This is achieved by the PRIORITY with BUFFER option. We reduce the priority to zero after having saved the true value in a parameter, 2 for example. When the transaction is next processed, we restore the priority to its original value and send it back to the queue. The block diagram is not shown because it is the same as Figure 7.11(b), where the BUFFER block is replaced by the three blocks marked with an asterisk in the following program:

```
               .
               .
               .
          ASSIGN      1,5
BACK      QUEUE       1
          SEIZE       1
          DEPART      1
          ADVANCE     10
          RELEASE     1
          ASSIGN      2,PR      *  Save priority in P2;
          PRIORITY    0,BUFFER  *  Reduce priority to 0, and
          PRIORITY    P2        *  Stop the transaction; restore
          LOOP        1,BACK       priority to its original value.
```

(2) In a chemical process we make products 1 and 2. Product 1, type 1 transaction, uses facilities 1 and 2 simultaneously. Product 2, type 2 transaction, uses facility 2 first, then facility 1. The products have equal priority of 3 when waiting for facility 2, but product 2 has a lower priority of 2 for facility 1.

    Figure 7.12 shows model A and model B. Consider model A. Type 1 transactions receive priority 3 in block 100 and wait for facilities 1 and 2 (GATE blocks 101 and 102 followed by TRANSFER SIM 103). Then they seize facilities 1 and 2. Type 2 transactions get priority of 3 in block 200, use

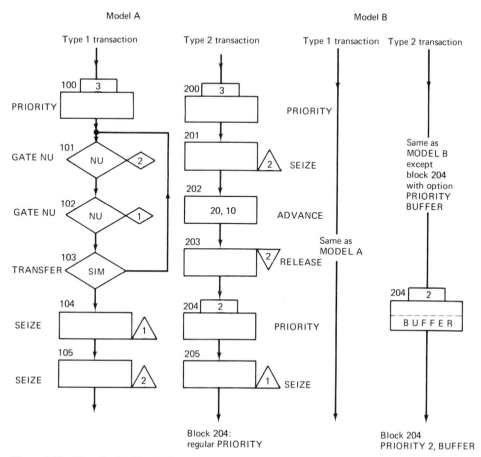

Figure 7.12 Use of a PRIORITY BUFFER block.

facility 2 (blocks 201 to 203), have their priority lowered to 2 in block 204, and seize facility 1 (block 205).

Again, GPSS continues to move a transaction that came from block 203, that is, from facility 2, through blocks 204 and 205, even after having lowered its priority. This transaction would therefore seize facility 1 immediately, even if type 1 transactions, with higher priority, were waiting to seize it.

A valid solution is given in model B, where the only change is to block 204 which is now:

PRIORITY   2,BUFFER

By changing the priority of the transaction at this block, GPSS stops processing it, places it at the end of the type 2 transactions in the current-events chain, and resumes scanning the chain. If it finds any type 1 transactions, the first one moves to blocks 104 and 105 to use facilities 1 and 2. The scan continues and reaches the stopped transaction, which must wait because facility 1 has been seized.

7.2.4   User chains

GPSS user chains allow the analyst to remove transactions from the model and return them when required. Two blocks are available for these operations: LINK, which sends (or links) a transaction to a user chain, and UNLINK, which returns it to the current-events chain from the user chain.

The user chain is a queue in the "real" sense that the entity is physically delayed until served. The GPSS queue block indicates that the transaction is in a waiting state but does not delay it, for example, a passenger on stand-by for a flight.

We introduce the user chain by considering the example of a simple queue with one server [Figure 7.13(a)] from three points of view: the computation involved, the queueing organization, and the overall organization.

When a transaction attempts to seize facility FAC1 and finds it busy, it is removed from the current-events chain and placed on a delay chain associated with the facility. When the facility is released, all the transactions waiting for the facility are removed from the delay chain and put back on the current-events chain. The scan begins and

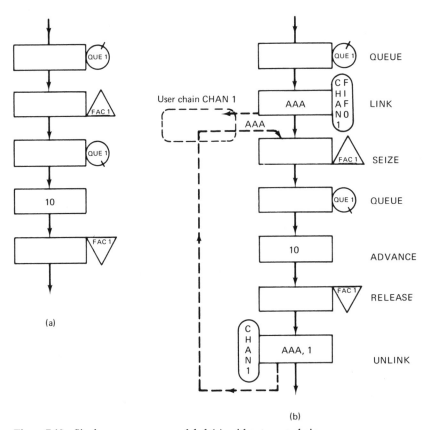

Figure 7.13   Single server queue modeled (a) without user chain, and (b) with user chain.

each of the transactions attempts to seize the facility; only the first succeeds, however, and all the others are replaced on the delay chain.

Such a procedure becomes very time-consuming when many transactions are queueing. Further, the moment when a trial must be made to move one transaction to the facility is known exactly: it is when, and only when, a transaction reaches the RELEASE block. Before this time it is useless to try to move a transaction to seize the facility because the facility is already seized.

One of the advantages of the user chain is that it can remove transactions from the model until they are able to move. In the meantime they are made inactive and put into a reservoir of transactions waiting to be recalled.

A second important aspect of user chains is that of queueing organization. Previously, we could order queues only by priority level and FIFO discipline because of GPSS implementation. Sometimes, the user needs to organize the transactions in queues based on other criteria. One possibility might be, before entering the queue, to replace the priority of the transaction by the new ordering criterion. This would entail changing priority after saving it in a parameter to be restored later—a tedious procedure. The user chain provides the ideal solution because it can be organized to suit the user's needs.

The third advantage of the user chain is that it enables the user to manipulate transactions in a different way from the standard GPSS implementation.

Figure 7.13(b) represents an improved solution to the problem through use of a user chain called CHAN1, with the LINK and UNLINK blocks. When a transaction enters queue QUE1, it is sent to facility FAC1 if free and to user chain CHAN1 otherwise. Therefore, GPSS will never find a transaction waiting for FAC1 during the scan of the current-events chain. When a transaction leaves the ADVANCE block, it releases FAC1 and, at the same clock time, removes one transaction from the user chain and sends it to the SEIZE block. The queue statistics of QUE1 are unaffected because they are based on the time spent by transactions between the QUEUE and DEPART blocks. In addition to these statistics, GPSS also records and prints statistics of the user chain. In this example the queue and the user chain statistics are the same, because transactions enter and leave both queue and user chain at the same clock time.

Every user chain has a *link indicator*, which is used to control the operations of the LINK/UNLINK blocks.

LINK   A,B,C

Operation:

This block directs transactions either to the user chain specified by the A-operand or to the address specified by the C-operand, depending on the status of the user chain link indicator.

If the link indicator is reset, it is set and the transaction is sent to the block specified by the C-operand; if the link indicator is set, it remains unchanged and the transaction is linked to the user chain.

When no C-operand is specified, the transaction is unconditionally linked to the user chain.

Operands:

A: The name or number of the user chain.

B: The ordering of transactions in the user chain:
FIFO: The transaction is placed at the back of the user chain.
LIFO: The transaction is placed at the front of the user chain.
Pj: The transaction is merged onto the user chain according to the value of Pj in ascending order, (transactions with the smallest values of Pj first in the chain). If an entering transaction has Pj equal to another already on the chain, it is merged behind it.

C: (*optional*) The address for transactions finding the link indicator reset.

UNLINK   A,B,C,D,E,F

Operation:

This block removes transaction(s) from a user chain either unconditionally, when operands D and E are not specified, or based on the condition defined by the D- and E-operands, and sends the unlinked transaction(s) to the block specified by the B-operand.

If the user chain is empty, the link indicator of the chain is reset.

If the user chain is not empty, transactions are removed from the user chain until the count specified by the C-operand is reached or all transactions on the chain have been examined, or the chain is empty.

If one transaction, at least, could be unlinked, the transaction continues to the next sequential block.

If no transaction could be unlinked, the transaction is sent to the block specified by the F-operand or to the next sequential block if no F-operand is specified.

Operands:

A: The user chain name or number.

B: The address for the unlinked transaction(s).

C: The number of transactions to be unlinked from the user chain.

D and E: (*optional*) Used to specify a condition to be met by the transaction(s) to be unlinked; see below.

F: (*optional*) The address for the unlinking transaction when (1) the user chain is found to be empty or (2) the condition to unlink a transaction is not met by any transaction on the chain.

D: may be (1) a numerical value meaning a parameter number.
                     (2) the word **BACK**
                     (3) a Boolean variable: BVj.
          1. Parameter number of the transactions on the user chain:
             If no E-operand is used, the value of the specified parameter of the entering transaction is matched with the value of the same parameter of the transactions on the user chain.
             If an E-operand is specified, its value is matched with the value of the parameter (specified by the D-operand of the entering transaction) of the transactions of the user chain. In both cases, those transactions satisfying the matching condition are unlinked.
          2. BACK. The transactions are removed from the back of the user chain. The E-operand must be blank.
          3. BVj. The variable is evaluated for every transaction on the user chain and the transactions are unlinked only if BVj=1. If parameters are referenced in the Boolean variable, they refer to parameters of the transactions on the user chain. The E-operand must be blank.

E: The value to be matched with the value of parameters of transactions on the user chain. The parameter number is specified by the D-operand.

EXAMPLES:

(1)   LINK   CHAIN,FIFO

Unconditionally link transactions to the user chain CHAIN.

(2)   LINK   SET,LIFO,ALTER

If the link indicator of the user chain SET is reset, go to ALTER and set the link indicator. Otherwise, link the transaction at the front of the user chain SET.

(3)   UNLINK   SET1,RETUR,1,BV7,,UNSUC

Unlink the first transaction from user chain SET1 for which BV7 is equal to 1. Continue in sequence until one is found; if none is found, branch to UNSUC. If user chain SET1 is empty, the link indicator is reset and the transaction goes to UNSUC.

(4)   UNLINK   SET1,RETUR,ALL,2,12,UNSUC

Unlink from user chain SET1 and send all transactions whose parameter 2 has value 12 to RETUR. If none is found, go to UNSUC; otherwise, go to the next sequential block. If SET1 is empty, reset link indicator and go to UNSUC.

The concept of user chains is extremely useful for many problems, both for the reasons mentioned at the beginning of this paragraph and for the power of the logic that it provides. For example, let us consider a model of a teleprocessing system in outline. We can divide the model roughly into three submodels.

1. Generation of the input and preprocessing. This would simulate the generation of messages at the terminals and transmission to the central computer.
2. Processing of the messages—that is, execution of the application program.
3. Control program management for the whole system—that is, deciding when waiting messages should be processed and in which order, operating conditions, and so on.

These submodels should normally be independent because it might be necessary to change one. Modularity reduces the need to recheck the entire model each time. It is well known in programming that making the slightest modification to a big program, entails a great risk of creating special conditions and side effects. The bigger the program, the more difficult it is to estimate such interferences.

For example, if the input and processing submodels have been completed, the study concerns the control program, and questions such as the following must be answered: What is the best order for processing the waiting transactions? Should we process them when they arrive or should they be batched? If batched, what size should the batch be? How should a batch be organized? Each question requires one or more simulation runs and modification of the control program which provides the link between the input and the processing submodels. An outline of the coding is shown below:

Input program.

	GENERATE		Create messages at terminal 1; assign their parameter values, for instance, terminal number—to P1
	TRANSFER	,COM	Transfer to COM
	GENERATE		Same for terminals 2, 3, ...
	.		
	TRANSFER	,COM	
	.		
COM	QUEUE	P1	Queue the messages in the queue whose number is P1; execute some activities.
	LINK	WAIT,FIFO	Send the transaction to the user chain WAIT.

Processing program.

PROC	SEIZE	CPU	Seize the central
	DEPART	P1	processing unit and
	.		continue processing.
	.		
	.		
	TERMINATE		Destroy the
			message or associated task.

Control program.   This program has to remove transactions from the user chain WAIT and send them to PROC for processing.

	GENERATE	,,1,1	Generate one control
			transaction;
LOOP	.		Check the status of the
	.		computer, the user
	.		chain WAIT, and the
			various queue contents.
			Decide which
	.		transaction(s) should be
	.		removed from the
	.		user chain;
	UNLINK	WAIT,PROC,..	Unlink the transaction(s)
	TRANSFER	,LOOP	and send to the
			processing program;
			Restart the control loop.

Another strategy would be to send unlinked transactions to a series of blocks defined within the control program where they could be sorted or combined before branching to the processing program. These blocks would be logically separated from those used by the control transaction.

When using this control loop strategy, one should be careful to avoid an endless loop. If there is no ADVANCE block in the control program, the control transaction might loop in zero simulated time. This could happen in the first example if the computer were free with no message waiting, which would mean an unsuccessful unlink operation and therefore a branch to the block specified by the F-operand of the UNLINK block. One possible strategy is to put a GATE block in the loop to stop the transaction when no message is waiting. The controlling switch would be located in either the input model or the processing submodel.

It should be noted that this problem occurs because control of the model has deliberately been given to the control program, and thus to the transaction flowing through it, rather than letting the message transactions control the behavior of the model. The latter strategy is also feasible but changes the philosophy because every event would then be caused by the messages arriving in the system. We believe that the first approach (1) is closer to the real-world problems and (2) leads to better and more flexible models.

7.2.5   Group entity

In many simulation models, transactions represent items that can be categorized by common properties. For example, if transactions represent parts in an inventory model, the parts can be classified by weight, price, or length of time in stock. In a transportation model, such as a subway or elevator system, the transactions may represent the passengers who can be categorized by destination point. Attributes such as weight, price, and destination are usually stored in transaction parameters which can be changed by an ASSIGN block. However, this provides access to only one transaction at a time. In some situations it might be necessary to modify attributes of all transactions of a given class—for example, if one wanted to change the price of all the parts with given weight, independent of their present status in the current-events or future-events chains.

The GROUP entity and associated blocks allow the user to classify transactions and to transfer and reference attributes of transactions which are members of a given group. Any reference to members of a group is independent of the status of individual members. If transactions form a group, they all can be referenced, regardless of where they are on the future-events chain, current-events chain, or on a user chain. The blocks associated with the group entity enable the user to change attribute values such as priority or parameter values of all transactions in the group. Therefore, this is a means for transactions to communicate with others.

Groups operate in one of two modes: *transaction mode* or *numeric mode*. The members of transaction mode groups are transactions. The members of numeric mode groups are numbers; thus a numeric mode group is a list of numerical values. A group in transaction mode is organized on a FIFO basis. Therefore, when removing one or more transactions from a group, those which first joined the group will be removed first.

Five blocks are associated with the group entity:

JOIN, REMOVE, EXAMINE, SCAN, ALTER

The first three operate in either transaction or numeric mode. SCAN and ALTER operate only in transaction mode. The mode is determined by the first group reference, and subsequent group operations must conform to that mode. An execution error occurs if an attempt is made to use a group in the wrong mode.

JOIN   A,B

Operation:

The transaction, or the numeric value specified by the B-operand, is made a member of the group on a FIFO basis.

Operands:

A :   The name or number of the group.

B :   The numeric value to be made member of the group in numeric mode. If this operand is blank, the block operates in transaction mode.

EXAMPLES :

(1)   JOIN   FARM

The transaction is made a member of the group FARM.

(2)   JOIN   P2,V$PRICE

The variable PRICE is evaluated and its value is made a member of the numeric-mode group whose number is the present contents of P2.

                       REMOVE   A,B,C,D,E,F

Operation:

This block removes one or more elements from the group. Removal can be unconditional or based on the value of transaction attributes. An alternate exit may be specified for the transaction when the transaction or the numeric value specified is not a member of the group.

Operands:

A :   The name or number of the group.

B :   (*in transaction mode*) The number of transactions to be removed from the group. It may be 1,2,..., ALL.

C :   (*in numeric mode*) The value to be removed from the group.

D :   (*used in transaction mode with the E-operand*) The transaction attribute used for comparison to determine if a transaction should be removed from the group. This may be PR (priority) or a parameter number.

E :   (*used in transaction mode with the D-operand*) The SNA against which the transaction attribute will be compared.

F :   (*optional*) The address for the transaction when:
    1. It is not a member of the group (transaction mode without specification of the B-, C-, D-, and E-operands).
    2. The numerical value (in numeric mode) specified by the C-operand is not a member of the group.
    3. No transaction meets the condition specified (when B-, D-, and E-operands used), in particular when the group is empty.
    4. The count specified by the B-operand cannot be satisfied.

   If the F-operand is not used, the transaction always proceeds to the next sequential block, independent of the result of the REMOVE operation.

   If the A-operand only (or A- and F-operands only) are used, the transaction concerned is the one arriving in the REMOVE block.

   If B, D, and E are used, those transactions which satisfy the conditions specified by the B, D, and E fields are removed from the group.

EXAMPLES:

(1)   REMOVE   FARM

   If the transaction is a member of the group FARM, it is removed. The transaction continues to the next sequential block.

(2)   REMOVE   FARM,,,,,NOT

   Same as (1), but if it was not a member of FARM, it proceeds to the block NOT.

(3)   REMOVE   FARM,ALL,,1,3,NOONE

   All the transactions of the group FARM which have their parameter 1 equal to 3 are removed. If none is found with this property, the transaction proceeds to NOONE.

(4)   REMOVE   SET,V$SCORE

   The variable SCORE is evaluated and its value removed from the numeric-mode group SET.

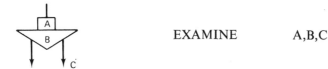

                         EXAMINE   A,B,C

Operation:

This block directs the transaction to one of two paths based on group membership. If the transaction or the numeric value is a member of the group, it proceeds to the next sequential block.

Operands:

A: The name or number of the group.

B: (*in numeric mode*) The value to test for membership of the group.

C: The alternate exit for the transaction if it is not a member (transaction mode) or if the B-operand numerical value is not a member (numeric mode).

EXAMPLES:

(1)   EXAMINE   FARM,,OUT

   If the transaction is a member of FARM, go to the next sequential block; if not, go to OUT.

(2)   EXAMINE   SET,X10,NOO

If the value of X10 is a member of SET, go to the next sequential block; if
not, go to NOO.

The following two blocks, SCAN and ALTER, are used only in transaction
mode:

SCAN   A,B,C,D,E,F

Operation:

This block provides the following capabilities:

1. It determines whether a transaction with certain attribute values is a member
   of a group.
2. It transfers attribute values of a member of a group which meets certain
   conditions to the transaction at the SCAN block.
3. It modifies the subsequent transaction flow if no member of the group is found
   to meet the specified condition.

Operands:

A: The name or number of the group.
B: The transaction attribute, PR or parameter number, which is to be examined.
C: Specifies the value with which the transaction attribute is to be compared.
D: Specifies, when the match is found, which attribute of the transaction of
    the group is to be placed in the parameter specified by the E-operand of the
    transaction in the SCAN block.
E: Specifies the parameter number where the attribute of the transaction found
    from the group must be stored.
F: The alternate exit for the transaction when no match is found. If no F-
    operand is specified, the transaction proceeds to the next sequential block.

If the D- and E-operands are not used, the operation is a simple scan followed by
a branch for the controlling transaction (next sequential block or F-operand), depending on the result of the scan. If all the fields are used, the operations are as above,
with the added possibility of passing information from the transaction found on the
chain to the controlling transaction.

EXAMPLES:

(1)   SCAN   FARM,PR,2,1,3,NONE

Scan the group FARM to find the first transaction with a priority of 2. Store
its parameter 1 in parameter 3 of the controlling transaction and proceed to
the next sequential block. If none is found, go to NONE.

(2)   SCAN   SET,1,*1,,,NONE

Scan the group SET for a transaction with parameter 1 equal to the contents of parameter 1 of the controlling transaction.

(3)   SCAN   FARM,*1,X1,*1,1,NONE

Scan the group FARM for a transaction whose parameter specified by parameter 1 of the controlling transaction is equal to X1. Copy this parameter (*1) into parameter 1 of the controlling transaction and proceed to the next sequential block. If none is found, go to NONE.

ALTER   A,B,C,D,E,F,G

Operation:

This block provides the following capabilities:

1. It modifies a given attribute of one, several, or all transactions of a group either unconditionally or if some other attribute meets a specified condition.
2. It modifies subsequent transaction flow if the group is empty or if no member is found to match the specified condition.

Operands:

A: The name or number of the group.

B: The number of transactions to be altered. It may be 1, 2, . . . , or ALL.

C: The attribute of transactions of the group to be altered. It may be PR (priority) or a parameter number.

D: The value to replace the attribute specified by the C-operand.

E: The transaction attribute (PR or parameter number) which is to be matched with the value specified by the F-operand.

F: The value to be matched by the transaction attribute specified by the E-operand before the alteration specified by the B-, C-, and D-operands takes place.

G: The alternate exit for the transaction when the group is empty or has no member matching the condition specified.

If operands E and F are not used, the alteration is unconditional.

EXAMPLES:

(1)   ALTER   FARM,2,PR,1

Alter the priority of the first two members of the group FARM to 1.

(2)   ALTER   FARM,ALL,2,P2,PR,0,NONE

Set parameter 2 of all transactions of the group FARM whose priority is zero to the value of the contents of parameter 2 of the controlling transaction.

If none is found, go to NONE. This operation consists of copying parameter 2 value of the controlling transaction into the same parameter of all transactions matching the condition.

An example of utilization of the GROUP entity is given in Section 7.6.3.

An added feature of GPSS V increases the power and flexibility of the three instructions REMOVE, SCAN, and ALTER. These instructions may be completed by a conditional operator, which may be G (greater than), GE (greater than or equal to), L (less than), LE (less than or equal to), E (equal to), NE (not equal to), MIN (minimum), or MAX (maximum). If no conditional operator is specified, E (equal to) is assumed.

EXAMPLES:

(1)   REMOVE LE   GOOD,ALL,,PR,3,NONE

Remove from the group GOOD all transactions whose priority is less than or equal to 3. If no transactions are found, go to NONE; otherwise to the next sequential block.

(2)   ALTER LE   WAIT,ALL,PR,0,1PB,10

Assign priority 0 to all transactions of the group WAIT whose byte parameter 1 is less than or equal to 10.

(3)   SCAN L   BALL,10PF,X3,PR,6PB,NONE

Scan the group BALL for the first transaction with the value of fullword parameter 10 less than the value of fullword save location 3. Copy its priority into byte parameter 6 of the entering transaction. If none is found, send transaction to NONE.

7.2.6 Accumulation and printing of information

We have previously discussed the need for simulation languages to produce a standard output report and we noted that the user must also be able to specify particular forms of output to meet special requirements. These possibilities are discussed below. The report generator is described in Section 8.1.

The following statements are available with the standard GPSS output: TABULATE, TABLE definition statement, PRINT, TRACE/UNTRACE, and WRITE.

                              TABULATE   A,B

Operation:

This block causes an entry to be made in the table specified by the A-operand. The nature of the tabulation depends on the TABLE definition statement associated with the TABULATE block.

Operands:

A: The table name or number. Every table must be defined by a table definition statement.

B: (*optional*) A number of units (weighting factor) to be added to the class of the distribution table in which the argument is placed. If omitted, 1 is assumed.

The operation of the TABULATE block cannot be discussed without the TABLE definition statement so we include this statement now, rather than in Section 7.3.3, although it does not follow the logical structure of this chapter.

TNAME   TABLE   A,B,C,D,E

Operation:

This definition statement is used to specify the argument of the table whose name or number is given in the label-field, here TNAME. The definition includes the range and width of the frequency classes. This statement may be placed anywhere in the program.

Operands:

A: The table argument. Every time a transaction enters a TABULATE block which references this table, the argument is computed and its value is entered in the corresponding frequency class. If the table is to operate in difference mode, a minus ($-$) sign should be coded as the rightmost character. In this mode the entry will be the difference between the current argument value and its preceding tabulated value.

B: The upper limit of the lowest frequency class.

C: The width of the frequency classes.

D: The number of frequency classes. If this number does not agree with the numerical values obtained during the simulation, it will be noted in the results: every value greater than the last interval will be put in the *overflow* class and the average of this class will be given. If several classes have zero entries after a certain class, an appropriate statement will be printed.

E: (*used only when operating in arrival rate mode*) The arrival rate time interval.

Operands B, C, and D are best explained by Figure 7.14.

The following results are automatically accumulated and printed: table name or number, mean argument, standard deviation, the sum of arguments, and, for every frequency class, the upper limit of the class, the observed frequency in units, the same in percent, the cumulative percentage, the cumulative remainder, the multiple of mean, and the deviation from mean. An example is given in Figure 7.15.

EXAMPLES:

(1) *Transit times:*

	TABULATE	HISTO
HISTO	TABLE	M1,0,5,20

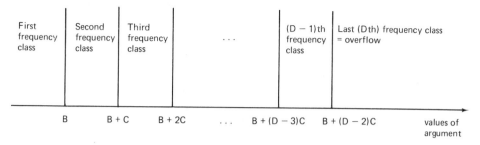

First frequency class	Second frequency class	Third frequency class		$\cdots$	$(D-1)$th frequency class	Last $(D$th) frequency class = overflow

B   B + C   B + 2C $\cdots$ B + (D − 3)C   B + (D − 2)C   values of argument

B = Upper limit of the first frequency class
C = Size of frequency classes
D = Number of frequency classes

Figure 7.14 Table frequency classes.

```
TABLE  HISTO
ENTRIES IN TABLE            MEAN ARGUMENT        STANDARD DEVIATION         SUM OF ARGUMENTS
       1000                    51.894                   25.750                  51895.000        NON-WEIGHTED

        UPPER        OBSERVED       PER CENT      CUMULATIVE        CUMULATIVE       MULTIPLE        DEVIATION
        LIMIT        FREQUENCY      OF TOTAL      PERCENTAGE        REMAINDER        OF MEAN         FROM MEAN
            0               0           .00              .0            100.0          -.000          -2.015
            5               6           .59              .6             99.3           .096          -1.821
           10              61          6.09             6.6             93.2           .192          -1.626
           15              41          4.09            10.7             89.1           .289          -1.432
           20              43          4.29            15.0             84.8           .385          -1.238
           25              49          4.89            19.9             80.0           .481          -1.044
           30              47          4.69            24.6             75.3           .578           -.850
           35              52          5.19            29.8             70.1           .674           -.656
           40              58          5.79            35.6             64.3           .770           -.461
           45              49          4.89            40.5             59.4           .867           -.267
           50              70          6.99            47.5             52.4           .963           -.073
           55              57          5.69            53.2             46.7          1.059            .120
           60              52          5.19            58.4             41.5          1.156            .314
           65              61          6.09            64.5             35.4          1.252            .508
           70              62          6.19            70.7             29.2          1.348            .703
           75              63          6.29            77.0             22.9          1.445            .897
           80              60          5.99            83.0             16.9          1.541           1.091
           85              53          5.29            88.3             11.6          1.637           1.285
           90              63          6.29            94.6              5.3          1.734           1.479
     OVERFLOW              53          5.29           100.0              .0
AVERAGE VALUE OF OVERFLOW            93.07
```

Figure 7.15 Example of a table.

Make an entry to the table HISTO. Table mode is M1, thus the transit time of the transaction is tabulated (see Section 7.2.1: under "Access to or handling of attributes"). The first frequency class is 0, the frequency class width is 5, and we specify 20 classes. Figure 7.15 shows the frequency table HISTO after 1000 entries have been made in the table.

(2) In the example presented in Section 6.6.4 we had to compute the average response time of the system for each source separately. Therefore, we defined three queues which were accumulating the required statistics and we noted that the three queues could be replaced by one TABULATE block. Consider the program using indirect addressing (see Figure 6.16), which can be modified by inserting a tabulate block after the instruction RELEASE CPU:

TABULATE   P1

This block makes an entry in the table specified by parameter 1, which contains the terminal number. We must also define the following three tables:

1	TABLE	M1,400,200,20
2	TABLE	M1,400,200,20
3	TABLE	M1,400,200,20

We take 400 as the upper limit of the first frequency class because the minimum processing time is 440, which is shown by the input data, message type 3 from terminal 3. We define frequency classes of 200 ms width and we allow for 20 classes. In this way, we get the response times per source from the average value of the table and also the complete distributions of these times together with their statistical parameters.

(3) *Interarrival times:* suppose that we need the distribution of times between arrivals of successive transactions at a given place. We insert a TABULATE block and define the argument of the corresponding table PASSA to be IA, interarrival time. The table is then coded:

     PASSA   TABLE   IA,0,10,21

We assume that the minimum value is 0, to include the case of two transactions arriving at the same simulated time, and that the maximum is 200. In this mode, the value entered in the table is the time interval since the previous reference to the table. No entry is made for the first transaction entering the TABU-LATE block. (The distribution of interarrival times is valuable for debugging simulation models; it provides a simple check on how the program generates transactions or ADVANCE time distributions.)

(4) *Arrival rates:* at the end of a manufacturing model, the transactions produced by a machine are terminated. They come out with a random pattern, so we want to know the arrival rate distribution in parts per minute. We suppose that the time unit of the model is 1 second and we know that this rate may vary from 0 to 20 parts per minute.

Before terminating the transaction, we pass it through a TABULATE block referring to the table RATE, which is then coded:

     RATE   TABLE   RT,0,1,21,60

RT means that the table operates in arrival-rate mode. The E-operand 60 specifies time slices of 60 seconds; that is, an entry is made in the table every 60 seconds. The frequency classes range from 0 to 20 transactions per minute with frequency class width of 1.

The important difference from the other modes is that one entry is made in the table for every time interval passed instead of every transaction. This table mode is very useful when arrival rates are required.

(5) *Relative transit times:* it is sometimes necessary to tabulate not only the transit time M1 but also one or more intermediate transit times, such as those spent by transactions between various parts of the system. For this purpose we use the combination MARK/TABULATE. The MARK block is used to store the value of the clock, in a parameter, when the transaction passes the first point. The TABULATE block will then tabulate the time difference between (1) the passage at the second point and (2) the value stored in the referenced parameter:

             .
             .
             .

     MARK   1   Store the clock time when the
     .   transaction passes the MARK
     .   block in P1
     .

	TABULATE	TRTIM	Make entry in table
TRTIM	TABLE	MP1,0,10,10	TRTIM; Tabulate the transit time MP1, (clock time − P1).

If the distribution of other intermediate transit times is needed, the same procedure may be applied using parameters 2, 3, . . . and specifying MP2, MP3, . . . in the corresponding tables.

(6) *Other arguments:* any argument may be entered in a table. Suppose, for example, that we have parts (transactions) whose type 1 to 50 is stored in parameter 3 and which are mixed up during a process. At a given point we want to construct a distribution table of the types of parts. This is done by a TABULATE block with the table definition:

TYPES	TABLE	P3,1,1,51

Enter the value of P3 in the corresponding frequency class.

(7) *Queue histograms:* queue statistics automatically accumulated and printed include average time spent by transactions in the queue and the same average excluding transactions that did not wait. Sometimes this information is insufficient and we may need the distribution of queue delay times. In such cases a TABULATE block is not necessary. A QTABLE statement will suffice.

The QTABLE statement is coded in a similar way to the TABLE statement except that the A-operand specifies the queue name or number:

NAME	QTABLE	A,B,C,D

Operands:

A: The queue name or number.

B: The upper limit of the lowest frequency class.

C: The size of the frequency classes.

D: The number of classes.

The table printed is similar to the other statistical tables.

	PRINT	A,B,C,D

Operation:

This block causes a partial output of the standard GPSS simulation statistics.

Operands:

A: The lower limit of the entity to be printed.

B: The upper limit of the entity to be printed.

C: A mnemonic that defines the information desired.

The mnemonics shown in Table 7.1 are available. In addition, GPSS V will print byte and floating-point savevalues and matrix savevalues: XB, XL, MB, and ML.

Table 7.1

Mnemonic	Output	Mnemonic	Output
C*	Clock time (absolute and relative)	LG	Logic-switches status
		G	Current members of groups
B or N or W*	Block statistics	T	Table statistics
F	Facility statistics	MOV*	Current-events chain
S	Storage statistics	FUT*	Future-events chain
Q	Queue statistics	I*	Interrupted chain
X, XF or blank	Savevalue (fullwords)	MAT*	Matching-status chain
XH	Savevalue (halfwords)	U	User-chain statistics
MX	Matrix savevalue (fullwords)	CHA	User-chain listing
MH	Matrix savevalue (halfwords)		

When using the mnemonics not marked with '*', the A- and B-operands should be specified. If not, the entire range of the particular entity involved will be printed.

D: A paging indicator. If this operand contains any alphameric character, a page will not be skipped preceding every PRINT operation. If blank, a page will be skipped before every PRINT operation.

EXAMPLES:

(1)   PRINT   S,1,10

Print the storage statistics for storages 1 to 10.

(2)   PRINT   MOV

Print the current-events chain.

(3)   PRINT   F

Print the facility statistics for all facilities.

The amount of printing can increase very rapidly because a printing operation occurs whenever a transaction goes through the PRINT block; one must therefore be very cautious about using this block. As this block is frequently used for debugging, it is discussed again in Section 8.3.8.

Tracing features. Sometimes it is necessary to check a program step-by-step to justify the model. The tracing feature has been provided for this purpose.

                    TRACE

Operation:

This block sets the tracing indicator of the transaction. When a transaction with its trace indicator set enters a block, two lines of output are produced which contain:

First line: transaction number, previous block number, new block number, clock time, remaining run termination count.

Second line: normal transaction printout as described in the current-events chain.

If more than four parameters are associated with the transactions, more lines are printed—one additional line per group of four additional parameters. As the amount of printing produced by tracing can be enormous, one should normally avoid using this feature.

Figure 8.11 (Section 8.3.10), is an example of the output produced by TRACE.

UNTRACE

Operation:

This block resets the trace indicator of the transaction. If it was already reset, the block has no effect.

WRITE   A

This block differs from the blocks discussed so far in that it plays no role in the behavior of a model. It is used to build a transaction file for subsequent use.

Operation:

The WRITE block writes, on the data set specified by the A-operand, all the information associated with the entering transaction. This data set can be read subsequently by the JOBTAPE statement (see Section 7.2.1) to enter the transactions into the model.

When a transaction enters a WRITE block, the following information is recorded: interarrival time from the previous transaction (0 for the first transaction), transit time, priority, and number of parameters and their values. The transaction then proceeds to the next sequential block.

Operand:

A: the name of the data set: JOBTA1, JOBTA2, or JOBTA3. The data-set characteristics must be defined by a control card, described in Appendix A.

This WRITE block can be very useful in situations when a complicated program must be run to build the transaction pattern to be input to a model. If the model is liable to be changed but the same input should be used again, then it is convenient to record the transaction pattern by means of the WRITE feature during the first run. Later, the jobtape so obtained can be run against the various models studied. This has the advantage of isolating the influence of possible changes in the input from the consequences of a change in the model.

Remark: It is not obligatory to use the GPSS WRITE instruction for creating a jobtape. One can also create it by using another language, provided that the format of the jobtape is used.

7.2.7   Special blocks

Three blocks that have more sophisticated uses are CHANGE, EXECUTE, and HELP. CHANGE and EXECUTE are associated with block entities. The HELP block, which provides an interface between GPSS and other programming languages, is treated separately in Section 8.2.

CHANGE   A,B

Operation:

This block provides a means of changing one block of a model into another one *during a simulation run.*

Operands:

A: The number or name of the block to be changed.

B: The number or name of the block to replace the block specified by the A-operand.

EXAMPLE:

```
                          .
                          .
                          .
        1        GENERATE        100,FN$EXPON
                          .
                          .
                          .
        10       ADVANCE         0
                          .
                          .
                          .
                 CHANGE          1,10
```

will replace block 1 (GENERATE) by block 10 (ADVANCE). This is one way of killing a GENERATE block.

EXECUTE   A

Operation:

This block will cause execution of the operations of the block specified by the A-operand. The transaction, after completion of this operation, will proceed to the next sequential block, unless the executed block directs the transaction to another address.

Operand:

A: The name or number of the block to be executed.

When executing a block, the transaction remains in the EXECUTE block until all operations are completed. Delays for ADVANCE with a nonzero time, seizing a busy facility, and waiting on a matching condition are at the EXECUTE block, not at the block being executed. The execution of a GENERATE block is not allowed and will result in an execution error if attempted.

7.2.8 Facility and storage availability and unavailability

In GPSS V the concept of *availability* and *unavailability* of facilities and storages has been introduced as a standard feature.

In many simulation applications equipment may be unavailable at certain periods because of breakdowns or normal breaks, such as nights or lunch periods. Such situations can be modeled by stopping transactions in front of all facilities and storages, for example by preempting the facilities and filling the storages, which prevents them from entering SEIZE or ENTER blocks. The disadvantage of such procedures is that the statistics relating to the facilities and storages will include this pseudo-utilization, so that the effective utilization during normal running is not known directly.

The available and unavailable blocks have been added to GPSS V to solve this problem. The statistics automatically accumulated by GPSS V for facilities and storages are given separately for total available time, total nonavailable time, and total time.

Four new logical attributes have been added to allow the user to refer to facility and storage states and, for example, to test their status using the GATE block:

FVj (facility j available):   1 if facility j is available
                                  0 if facility j is unavailable

FNVj (facility j unavailable):   1 if facility j is unavailable
                                  0 if facility j is available

SVj (storage j available):   1 if storage j is available
                                  0 if storage j is unavailable
SNVj (storage j unavailable):   1 if storage j is unavailable
                                  0 if storage j is available.

Facilities.

FUNAVAIL   A,B,C,D,E,F,G,H

Operation:

This block makes a facility, or a range of facilities, unavailable. If a specified facility is already unavailable, this block has no effect.

Operands:

A: The facility, or range of facilities, to be made unavailable. A facility is specified by its name or number, a range by the lower and upper limits—for example 10–15, meaning facilities 10 to 15.

If no other operand is specified, the facility is made unavailable to all transactions including that currently in use, which is interrupted, and those waiting to seize or preempt until the facility is again made available.

The B-, C- and D-operands apply to the transaction, if any, currently seizing or preempting the facility.

The E- and F-operands apply to those transactions which are in a preempted status (interrupted) at the time the facility becomes unavailable.

The G- and H-operands apply to those transactions which are waiting to seize or preempt the facility at the time it becomes unavailable. They do not affect transactions waiting at GATE I or GATE NI blocks.

B: Specifies what must be done with the transaction currently in the facility:
1. Unspecified: Causes the transaction in the facility to be interrupted until the facility becomes available again.
2. CO: Allows the transaction to continue using the facility during the unavailable period until its service ends by going through a RELEASE or RETURN block.
3. RE: Removes the transaction from the facility. The removed transaction attempts to enter the block specified by the C-operand.

C: The alternate exit for the transaction using the facility at the time it is made unavailable. This operand is required when RE is specified as B-operand. (The case when C is specified and the B-operand is CO is not discussed here.)

D: The number of a parameter of the transaction using the facility where the outstanding time that the transaction has to spend on the future-events chain can be stored.

E: Specifies the handling of previously preempted transactions:
   1. Unspecified: Causes the preempted transactions to wait until the facility is available again.
   2. CO: Allows all these transactions to use the facility when it is returned in priority order.
   3. RE: Removes them from contention for use of the facility. These transactions attempt to enter the block specified by the F-operand.

F: The alternate exit for preempted transactions when RE is specified as E-operand.

G: Specifies what must be done with the transactions waiting to seize or preempt the facility:
   1. Unspecified: Causes the transactions to wait until the facility is again available when they again contend for the facility.
   2. CO: Allows all these transactions to use the facility when it is released or returned in priority order.
   3. RE: Removes them from contention for use of the facility. They attempt to enter the block specified by the H-operand.

H: The alternate exit for the transactions waiting to seize or preempt the facility at the time it becomes unavailable. This operand is required when RE is specified as G-operand.

Options B to H apply only to transactions that are at the facility when it is made unavailable. Other transactions are placed on delay chains.

                    FAVAIL   A

Operation:

This block makes the facility, or range of facilities, specified by the A-operand available. It cancels all effects caused by the previous FUNAVAIL block. If the facility is already available, this block has no effect.

Operand:

A: The facility or range of facilities to be made available.

EXAMPLE:
                         FAVAIL   5—10
      Make facilities 5 to 10 available.

                         GATE XX   A,B

Operation:

This block operates in the usual way (see Section 7.2.3) but allows testing of the two new logical attributes FV and FNV, specified as XX:

FV: Facility available. The condition is true if the facility specified by the A-operand is available, false otherwise.

FNV: Facility not available. The condition is true if the facility is not available, false otherwise.

Storages.

SUNAVAIL   A

Operation:

This block causes a storage, or range of storages, to become unavailable. It will then refuse entry to transactions until it becomes available again.

Operand:

A: The storage, or range of storages, to be made unavailable.

When a storage is made unavailable and the storage is not empty, it continues to be used until the contents are decremented to zero by transactions entering a LEAVE block.

SAVAIL   A

Operation:

This block makes a storage, or range of storages, available. If the storage is already available, this block has no effect.

GATE XX   A,B

Operation:

As above, this block allows testing of the two new logical attributes SV and SNV.

SV: Storage available. This condition is true if the storage specified by the A-operand is available, false otherwise.

SNV: Storage not available. The condition is true if the storage specified by the A-operand is not available, false otherwise.

7.3 Entity-Definition Statements

Entity-definition statements for the GPSS subset were discussed in Section 6.3. In the present chapter we present other entities so that Chapters 6 and 7, together, review the complete GPSS language. The entities considered in this section are Boolean variables, functions of types E, M, and S, and statistical tables.

7.3.1 Boolean variable-definition statement

A Boolean variable, BVj or BV$name, is a Boolean combination of standard numerical and standard logical attributes, including other variables. It is defined and used in the same way as the arithmetic variables but, instead of computing an arithmetic value, the Boolean variable tests one or more logical conditions. Its result is either true ($= 1$) if the condition is met or false ($= 0$) if not met. The Boolean variable-definition statement reads:

Label BVARIABLE logical expression

Label is the Boolean variable name or number.

Three types of operators and attributes are allowed in Boolean variable expressions: conditional operators, logical attributes, and Boolean operators.

Conditional operators. The conditional operators are the same as those previously discussed for the TEST block in Section 6.2.3. They allow the user to make algebraic comparisons between SNAs. The conditional operators are:

'E'	equal to	'NE'	not equal to
'L'	less than	'LE'	less than or equal to
'G'	greater than	'GE'	greater than or equal to

EXAMPLES:

(1)   ONE   BVARIABLE   V5'GE'6

The Boolean variable ONE is 1 (true) if variable $5 \geq 6$; 0 (false) otherwise.

(2)   17   BVARIABLE   FN$TYPE'E'4

The Boolean variable 17 is 1 (true) if the function TYPE is equal to 4; 0 (false) otherwise.

Logical attributes. All standard logical attributes are listed in Section 7.4.3.

Boolean operators. The Boolean operators are:

"and"   represented by   *
"or"   represented by   +

The "and" operator tests if *both* conditions are met; the "or" operator tests if *either or both* of the conditions are met.

EXAMPLES:

(1)   1   BVARIABLE   FNU10*V1'GE'5

Boolean variable 1 is 1 if facility 10 is not used and variable $1 \geq 5$.

(2)   2   BVARIABLE   (FNU1+FNU2)*SNF$BUFFE

Boolean variable 2 is 1 if facility 1 or facility 2 is not used and if storage BUFFE is not full.

(3) In example 4 of Section 6.2.3, we wanted to allow transactions to proceed only if facilities CPU, CHA, and CONTR were simultaneously available. This can be achieved by a TEST in refusal mode on the Boolean variable CHECK:

.
.
.

```
       TEST  NE          BV$CHECK,0
```
.
.
.

```
CHECK   BVARIABLE       FNU$CPU*FNU$CHA*FNU$CONTR
```

The Boolean variable CHECK is 1 if all three factors are 1, which means that none of the three facilities is in use.

In addition to these obvious utilizations, Boolean variables are very useful for modeling situations such as:

Removal of transactions from a user chain (UNLINK block), based on some characteristics of transactions in the chain.

Scanning of groups (SCAN block) or altering transactions (ALTER block) of groups based on logical considerations.

EXAMPLE:

```
        UNLINK          CHAIN,ADDR,ALL,BV$SELEC
SELEC   BVARIABLE       P1'E'2+P1'E'X$EXTRA
```

This block unlinks all transactions from the user chain CHAIN which have parameter 1 either equal to 2 or to the contents of the save location EXTRA.

7.3.2 Function-definition statements

Several function types were considered in Section 6.3.3. Two additional types are discrete attribute-valued and list attribute-valued functions. These functions allow the user to define the function values as attributes instead of numerical values.

Discrete attribute-valued function. The discrete attribute-valued function is similar to the D (discrete) type except that the values of the functions may be any SNA. This fact is indicated by E as function type in the function-definition statement.

EXAMPLE:

```
INDIR   FUNCTION        P1,E4
5,V1/10,V2/15,V3/50,FN3
```

Discrete attribute-valued function with four points. Argument is P1. If $P1 \leq 5$, the value of function INDIR is obtained by evaluating variable 1; if $5 < P1 \leq 10$, then V2 is evaluated; if $10 < P1 \leq 15$, V3 is evaluated; if $15 < P1 \leq 50$, then FN3 is evaluated.

List attribute-valued function. The list attribute-valued function is similar to the L (list) type except that the values of the function may be any SNA. The function type is indicated by an M in the function-definition statement. The arguments can be omitted; they are taken by GPSS to be the successive integers 1, 2, 3. . . .

EXAMPLE:

        LIST   FUNCTION   P2,M5
        ,V1/,V2/,FN3/,5/,X10

        List attribute-valued function, argument P2. The value is equal to variable 1 if P2 = 1; variable 2 if P2 = 2; function 3 if P2 = 3; 5 if P2 = 4; and X10 if P2 = 5.

Discrete and list attribute-valued functions can be extremely useful in many situations. One interesting example is the evaluation of a function z of two variables, say x and y. In such cases, one can express z as being type E, with x as argument. For every value of x, say x_1, we specify the value of the function to be another function z_1, which is the cut of the surface $z = f(x, y)$ by the plane $x = x_1$. In other terms, these functions z_1 give the values z as a function of y for the particular value x_1 considered.

Entity function. The main purpose of the entity, or S type, function is to enable the user to specify symbolic entities within a function. One function can be used to assign the same numeric value to multiple entity types, and can, in many cases, eliminate the need for EQU statements, see Section 7.5.1.

7.3.3 Statistical tables

The statistical tables that can be specified in GPSS were discussed with the TABULATE block (see Section 7.2.6). Several examples are given in that section and additional cases appear in Chapters 9 and 10. Three SNAs associated with tables are accessible to the user. They are discussed in Section 7.4.1.

7.4 Attributes

In Chapter 6 we discussed a few attributes. We omitted from our discussion all those listed in the rightmost column of Table 6.1. In this section most of these other attributes are discussed, in the same order as they appear in Table 6.1. However, some GPSS V attributes are considered separately in Section 7.4.4.

Remarks: All attributes are updated and maintained by GPSS during simulation according to the rules implemented by the simulator. The definitions given below are simplified expressions that should be understood as being true for a single run. Thus FCj, facility j count, or the number of entries to facility j, means the number of transactions that entered the facility since the beginning of the simulation run, or, if CLEAR/RESET statements were used, since the last CLEAR or RESET statement. The same applies to all averages computed over one run.

In all discussions that follow we have used j as the number of the GPSS entity concerned. This number can be replaced by a symbolic name if the entity concerned is so defined. For example, FR$MACH and QM$WAIT instead of FRj and QMj, respectively.

7.4.1   Standard numerical attributes

Transaction attributes.

MPj: Transit time relative to parameter j. It is computed as the difference between the clock time and the contents of Pj. Pj must have been previously marked by a MARK block with j specified in its A-operand.

As discussed in Section 7.2.1, this is a way to tabulate transaction transit times between two points of a model. An example of such utilization is given in Section 7.2.6 (example 5 under TABULATE).

Facility attributes.

FRj: Utilization of facility j in parts per thousand. Thus if utilization were 0.75 or 75 per cent, FR would be 750.

FCj: Number of entries for facility j.

FTj: Average time the transactions used facility j. When invoked, the computed value will be truncated. If, for example, FTj were 17.45, the value obtained would be 17.

In addition to these numerical attributes, standard logical attributes are associated with facilities (see Section 7.4.3).

Storage attributes.

SRj: Utilization of storage j (in parts per thousand).

SCj: Number of entries for storage j.

SAj: Average contents of storage j. When invoked, this value is truncated.

SMj: Maximum contents of storage j.

STj: Average time each transaction used storage j. When utilized, the value is truncated.

In addition to these numerical attributes, standard logical attributes are associated with storages (see Section 7.4.3).

Queue attributes.

QCj: Number of entries in queue j.

QAj: Average contents of queue j. When invoked, the value is truncated.

QMj: Maximum contents of queue j.

QZj: Number of zero entries in queue j, that is, the number of transactions that went through the queue without waiting.

QTj: Average time spent by transactions in queue j. When utilized, the value is truncated.

QXj: Average time spent by transactions in queue j, excluding zero entries. When invoked, the value is truncated (GPSS V only).

Group attribute.   Each group has one SNA:

Gj: Number of items of group j (number of transactions if transaction mode, number of values if numeric mode).

User chain attributes.   Each user chain has five SNAs:

CHj: Current number of transactions on user chain j.

CAj: Average number of transactions on user chain j. When invoked, the value is truncated.

CMj: Maximum number of transactions on user chain j.

CCj: Total number of transactions linked to user chain j.

CTj: Average time spent by transactions on user chain j, truncated.

Table attributes.   Each table has three SNAs:

TCj: Number of entries in table j.

TBj: Mean of the argument values accumulated in table j. It is computed as the sum of the arguments divided by the number of entries TCj.

TDj: Standard deviation of table j, which is the standard deviation of the argument values accumulated.

7.4.2 Computational entities

Variable.

BVj: Value of the Boolean variable j.

See Section 7.3.1 for details.

Function.

FNj: Value of the function j.

See Section 6.3.2 for C, D, and L types; Section 7.3.2 for details of E, M, and S types.

7.4.3 Standard logical attributes

Transactions.   There are two standard logical attributes associated with transactions and used in GATE M (match) and GATE NM (no match) blocks to control the flow of transactions (see Section 7.2.3, GATE: "Matching Status").

Mj: Where j is the number of a MATCH, ASSEMBLE, or GATHER block. Mj is 1 (true) if another member of the assembly set of the transaction currently being processed in a GATE M block is in matching status at block number j. It is 0 (false) otherwise.

NMj: Where j is the number of a MATCH, ASSEMBLE, or GATHER block. NMj is true if no other member of the assembly set of the transaction currently being processed at a GATE NM block is in matching status at block j.

Facility. Each facility has four standard logical attributes which may take two values,

FUj: Facility in use:
           1 if facility j in use (seized or preempted)
           0 if facility j not in use

FNUj: Facility not in use:
           1 if facility j not in use (neither seized nor preempted)
           0 if facility j in use

FIj: Facility interrupted:
           1 if facility j preempted
           0 if facility j not preempted

FNIj: Facility not interrupted:
           1 if facility j not preempted
           0 if facility j preempted

These logical attributes are used in Boolean variables (see Section 7.3.1).

When the status of a facility is tested by means of a GATE block, the leading F of the attributes is omitted. The attributes are then Uj, NUj, Ij, and NIj (see Section 6.2.3, GATE: "Facilities"). They correspond exactly to those listed above.

Storage. Each storage has four standard logical attributes which may take two values: true (1) or false (0).

SEj: Storage empty:
           1 if storage j is empty
           0 if storage j is not empty

SNEj: Storage not empty:
           1 if storage j is not empty
           0 if storage j is empty

SFj: Storage full:
           1 if storage j is full
           0 if storage j is not full

SNFj: Storage not full:
           1 if storage j is not full
           0 if storage j is full

These logical attributes are used in Boolean variables (see Section 7.3.1) and in GATE on storages (see Section 6.2.3). Note that for a storage of capacity 1, SEj=SNFj and SFj=SNEj. In this case we can compare it with a facility. We then have NUj=SEj and Uj=SFj.

Logic switch. Each logic switch has two standard logical attributes which may take two values: true (1) or false (0).

LRj: Logic reset:
           1 if the logic switch j is reset
           0 if the logic switch j is set

LSj: Logic set:
            1 if the logic switch j is set
            0 if the logic switch j is reset

These logical attributes are used in Boolean variables (See Section 7.3.1) and in GATE blocks on logic switches (see Section 7.2.3).

7.4.4 Additional attributes in GPSS V

System attributes. In addition to C1 (clock time) and RNj (random numbers), mentioned in Section 6.4.1, two additional attributes are available:

AC1:   Absolute clock time. This the value of the absolute clock, which records the time elapsed since the beginning of the simulation or since the last CLEAR operation. Therefore, in the case of one run containing several RESET operations both absolute and relative clock times are accessible.

TG1:   Number of terminations to go to satisfy the current start count.

Facility and storage attributes. The GPSS V concepts of unavailability and availability for facilities and storages provide four additional standard logical attributes, two for facilities and two for storages (see Section 7.2.8).

Facility:

FVj: Facility available:
            1 if facility j is available
            0 if facility j is not available

FNVj: Facility not available:
            1 if facility j is not available
            0 if facility j is available

Storage:

SVj: Storage available:
            1 if storage j is available
            0 if storage j is not available

SNVj: Storage not available:
            1 if storage j is not available
            0 if storage j is available

These logical attributes are used in Boolean variables (see Section 7.3.1), and may also be used as mnemonics XX in GATE XX blocks. The GATE block then tests the condition specified by XX.

EXAMPLES:

(1)   GATE FV   CPU

will accept the transaction if facility CPU is available.

(2)   GATE SV   PARK,OUT

The transaction is accepted in the block and proceeds to the next sequential block if storage PARK is available; it goes to OUT if PARK is not available.

7.5 Assembly Control Statements

In this section we discuss the EQU statement and the MACRO facility, which are very useful features for the advanced modeler. They are service functions that reduce the task of program organization. Both of them are used later in this book.

7.5.1 The equivalence statement

$$\text{NNNN} \qquad \text{EQU} \qquad \text{A,B,C}$$

Service:

This statement is used to direct the assembly program to assign a specific number (A-operand) to the symbolic name NNNN (label field) for entities of types specified by the B-, C-, ... operands.

Operands:

NNNN: (*label field*) The symbolic name to be used.
A: Indicates the value to be given to NNNN.
B, C, ... :   Indicate which types of entity with the symbolic name NNNN are referred to by the EQU statement. The mnemonics that may be used are:

F:	Facilities	*Save locations*	
S:	Storages	X or XF:	fullword
Q:	Queues	H or XH:	halfword
T:	Tables	XB:	byte
V:	Variables	XL:	floating point
L:	Logic switches	*Save matrices*	
C:	User chains	M or MX:	fullword
Z:	Functions	Y or MH:	halfword
B:	Boolean variables	MB:	byte
G:	Groups	ML:	floating point

EXAMPLES:

(1)   WAIT   EQU   7,F

The facility symbolically called WAIT will be facility 7.
In the program, the instruction

                    SEIZE   WAIT

will be assembled as

                    SEIZE   7

(2)   LINE   EQU   10,F,Q

The LINE symbol for both facility and queue will be equal to 10.
The instruction

                    DEPART   LINE

will be assembled as

DEPART   10

It is also possible to identify and reserve a sequence of GPSS entities by using a number in parenthesis.

EXAMPLE:

ARMS   EQU   11(5),F,Q

The symbolic name ARMS will be assigned the value 11 for both facilities and queues, and five values will be reserved, the numbers 11 to 15. Reference to ARMS+1 will imply number 12, and so on.

The EQU statement must be used when the same program includes both symbolic names and indirect addressing (numeric values) to ensure that the necessary numeric values are reserved by the assembly program.

7.5.2 The macro facility

When a GPSS program contains several sequences of blocks which are very similar, it is possible to avoid repeated writing of these sequences by using the MACRO statement:

NNNN   MACRO   A,B,C,D,E,F,G,H,I,J

Service:

This statement makes the assembly program generate the series of instructions which constitute the macro using the arguments A, B, C, ...

Operands:

NNNN: The name of the macro called by the statement. It must be defined in the program by means of the STARTMACRO/ENDMACRO statements discussed below.

A, B, C, . . . , J: The arguments to be substituted in the macro. They may be substituted for the location field, the operation code, or the operands.

Two control statements are required to define each macro:

NNNN   STARTMACRO

        .
        .
        .

ENDMACRO

The STARTMACRO statement indicates the beginning of the macro-definition statements and assigns the name NNNN to it. The ENDMACRO statement indicates the end of the macro-definition statements.

Within the macro-definition statements arguments are identified by the special character #, followed by a single letter (A through J), which corresponds to the arguments (1 to 10) in the MACRO statement.

EXAMPLES:

(1) FIRST   STARTMACRO
               QUEUE   #A
               SEIZE   #B
               DEPART   #A
               ADVANCE   #C
               RELEASE   #B
               ENDMACRO

Within a GPSS program, the statement

FIRST   MACRO   1,2,50

will generate the following instructions:

               QUEUE   1
               SEIZE   2
               DEPART   1
               ADVANCE   50
               RELEASE   2

(2) SECON   STARTMACRO
    #A   #B   #C
               SEIZE   #D
               #E   #C
               ADVANCE   #F
               RELEASE   #D
               ENDMACRO

Within the program the statement

SECON   MACRO   LOOP,QUEUE,MAN,MACH,DEPART,100

will generate the following instructions:

LOOP   QUEUE   MAN
          SEIZE   MACH
          DEPART   MAN
          ADVANCE   100
          RELEASE   MACH

These examples show how the MACRO facility can be used to reduce the amount of source code. It may be used often because, in most models, we find that similar series of GPSS blocks occur frequently. However, the user should exercise caution because each macro reference increases the in-line coding and therefore the size of the program. When long sequences of blocks are repeated many times, the size of the program can be minimized by writing a subroutine called by TRANSFER SBR.

7.6 Programming Examples

7.6.1 Assembly line

The problem. Let us assume that to produce a certain item three successive operations are required. Each operation is performed by a different kind of machine. Consider a small shop having only three machines, one for each operation. The system to be modeled consists of incoming parts, three processing machines, and a waiting line before each machine (Figure 7.16). The object of the simulation is to study different scheduling strategies for the parts waiting for service. The simplest one would be FIFO. We will try a more complicated one: "the next part to be processed is the one from those waiting that has the *shortest processing time.*" We will restrict ourselves to this strategy and suggest that the reader try others to compare them with the one described here.

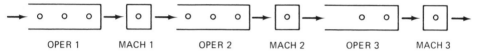

OPER 1   MACH 1   OPER 2   MACH 2   OPER 3   MACH 3

Figure 7.16 Assembly line.

Let us assume that:

1. The mean time between two incoming parts is 120 seconds and that the distribution of the interarrival times is exponential.
2. The processing time on machine 1 is 50 seconds, on machine 2 is 70 seconds and on machine 3 is 60 seconds multiplied by a random factor which is equal to:

$$
\begin{array}{lll}
0.5 & \text{in} & 20\% \text{ of the cases} \\
1.0 & \text{in} & 50\% \text{ of the cases} \\
1.5 & \text{in} & 20\% \text{ of the cases} \\
2.0 & \text{in} & 10\% \text{ of the cases}
\end{array}
$$

The GPSS model. To model the shortest-processing-time-first discipline, we use three user chains, OPER1, OPER2, and OPER3. The ranking order of transactions within these user chains will be based on the values of P5, P6, and P7, which contain the processing times for machines 1, 2, and 3, respectively.

In the program of Figure 7.17, transactions are generated and processing times are assigned to P5, P6, and P7. The C-operand in the assign blocks (2, 3, and 4) is the number of the function modifier. The B-operand is multiplied by the value of that function. If the transaction cannot seize facility MACH1 (block 6), it is linked to user chain OPER1, depending on the value of P5. The transaction with the smallest value of P5 will be at the beginning of the user chain and the one with the largest value of P5 at the end. If facility MACH1 is free, the incoming transaction seizes it for P5 time units (blocks 7 and 8). Then the transaction proceeds to the UNLINK block (9). The user chain OPER1 is tested to determine whether it is empty.

```
BLCCK                                                                              CARC
NUMBER  *LCC   OPERATION  A,B,C,C,E,F,G              COMMENTS                       NUMBER
               SIMULATE                                                            1
        1      FUNCTION   RN1,C4           PROCESSING TIME DISTRIBUTION            2
        .2,.5/.7,1/.9,1.5/1,2                                                      3
                                                                                   4
        EXPON FUNCTION    RN8,C24      EXPONENTIAL DISTRIBUTION - MEAN = 1.        5
        0.,0/0.1,C.104/0.2,0.222/0.3,0.355/0.4,0.509/0.5,0.69/0.6,0.915/          6
        0.7,1.2/0.75,1.38/0.8,1.6/0.84,1.83/0.88,2.12/0.9,2.3/0.92,2.52/          7
        C.94,2.81/0.95,2.99/0.96,3.2/0.97,3.5/0.98,3.9/0.99,4.6/0.995,5.3/        8
        0.998,6.2/0.999,7.0/C.9997,8.0                                            9
                                                                                   10
1              GENERATE   120,FN$EXPON        PARTS ARRIVALS                      11
2              ASSIGN     5,50,1              PRCCESSING TIME 1                    12
3              ASSIGN     6,70,1              PROCESSING TIME 2                    13
4              ASSIGN     7,60,1              PROCESSING TIME 3                    14
5              LINK       OPER1,P5,PRCC1      RANKED ON SHCRTEST PRCC.            15
        *                                     TIME 1                             16
                                                                                   17
6       PROC1 SEIZE       MACH1               FIRST MACHINE                       18
7              ACVANCE    P5                                                       19
8              RELEASE    MACH1                                                    20
9              UNLINK     OPER1,PRCC1,1       IF PART IN CHAIN OPER1              21
        *                                     UNLINK,SEND TC PRCC1               22
10             LINK       OPER2,P6,PRCC2      PUT IN CHAIN CPER2                  23
                                                                                   24
11      PROC2 SEIZE       MACH2               SECCND MACHINE                      25
12             ACVANCE    P6                                                       26
13             RELEASE    MACH2                                                    27
14             UNLINK     CPER2,PROC2,1       IF PART IN CHAIN2                   28
        *                                     UNLINK,SEND TC PROC2               29
15             LINK       OPER3,P6,PRCC3                                          30
                                                                                   31
                                                                                   32
16      PROC3 SEIZE       MACH3                                                   33
17             ACVANCE    P7                  THIRD MACHINE                       34
18             RELEASE    MACH3                                                    35
19             UNLINK     OPER3,PROC3,1       IF PART IN CHAIN CPER3             36
        *                                     UNLINK,SEND TC PROC3              37
                                                                                   38
20             TABULATE   1                   FREQ. CISTR. CF PROC. TIME         39
21             TERMINATE  1                                                       40
                                                                                   41
        1      TABLE      M1,100,20,3C        TABLE CEFINITION PRCC.TIME         42
        *                                     TIME-STANDARD TRANS.TIME          43
                                                                                   44
               START      1000                PRCCESSING OF 1000 PARTS           45
               ENC                                                                46
```

Figure 7.17 Assembly line; first GPSS program.

If the user chain is not empty, the first transaction is removed from the front of the chain and sent to the PROC1 block. The transaction that entered the UNLINK block proceeds to the next block (10).

If the user chain is empty, the transaction proceeds to block 10.

The operations simulated by blocks 10 to 14 and then 15 to 19 are the same as those for 5 to 9 described above. They concern user chains OPER2 and OPER3, respectively. These three series of blocks are combined in the next program, using indirect addressing (Figure 7.18).

Before the transaction in block 21 is destroyed, its transit time from creation to the current time is recorded in table 1, which increments the corresponding frequency class by one. Table 1 is defined by the TABLE definition statement to have 30 classes each, with an interval of 20 units, the upper limit of the lowest interval being 100. The argument tabulated is M1, the transit time. The run termination count is set to 1000 (START statement), and each transaction arriving in a TERMINATE block decrements this count by one so that simulation will end after 1000 transactions have reached the TERMINATE block.

It is possible, by using indirect addressing, to avoid the repetition of similar block sequences (5 to 9, 10 to 14, and 15 to 19) of the first version of the GPSS model; see Figure 7.18.

```
BLCCK                                                                              CARD
NUMBER  *LCC   OFERATION  A,B,C,C,E,F,G              COMMENTS                       NUMBER
               SIMULATE                                                               1
        1      FUNCTICN   RN1,D4              PROCESSING TIME DISTRIBUTION             2
        .2,.5/.7,1/.9,1.5/1,2                                                         3
                                                                                     4
        EXPON  FUNCTION   RN8,C24    EXPONENTIAL DISTRIBUTION - MEAN = 1.             5
        0.,0/0.1,0.104/0.2,0.222/0.3,0.355/0.4,0.509/0.5,0.69/0.6,0.915/             6
        0.7,1.2/0.75,1.38/0.8,1.6/0.84,1.83/0.88,2.12/0.9,2.3/0.92,2.52/             7
        0.94,2.81/0.95,2.99/0.96,3.2/0.97,3.5/0.98,3.9/0.99,4.6/0.995,5.3/           8
        0.998,6.2/0.999,7.0/0.9997,8.0                                               9
        PTIME  FUNCTION   P1,L3                                                      10
        1,50/2,70/3,60                                                              11
1              GENERATE   120,FN$EXPCN        LOOP COUNTER                           12
2              ASSIGN     2,3                 MACHINE COUNTER                        13
3       ALIN   ASSIGN     1+,1                PROCESSING TIME                        14
4              ASSIGN     3,FN$PTIME,1        RANKED ON SHORTEST                     15
5              LINK       *1,*3,PROC          PROCESSING TIME                        16
        *                                                                           17
                                                                                    18
6       PROC   SEIZE      *1                                                         19
7              ADVANCE    *3                                                         20
8              RELEASE    *1                                                         21
9              UNLINK     *1,PROC,1                                                  22
10             LOCP       2,ALIN                                                     23
11             TABULATE   1                   FREQ. CISTR. OF PROC. TIME             24
12             TERMINATE  1                                                          25
                                                                                    26
        1      TABLE      M1,100,20,30                                               27
               START      1000                                                       28
               ENC                                                                   29
```

Figure 7.18 Assembly line; second GPSS program.

Parameter 2 is used as a loop counter, which is set to 3 by block 2. P1 contains the number of the machine currently referred to by the transaction and P3 the processing time, which is defined as the function PTIME whose argument is P1.

User chains and facilities are not identified symbolically; they are assigned the numbers 1, 2, and 3, respectively, for each stage of the processing. Each time a transaction enters the LOOP block (10), the contents of parameter 2 is decremented by one; if its value is nonzero, the transaction goes to block ALIN (3); when it is zero, the transaction proceeds to the next sequential block (11).

At first glance, the use of indirect addressing may seem to make the program difficult to read. But after a detailed analysis, the advantages of using indirect addressing soon become evident.

Results and conclusions.   From the statistics produced by GPSS, we can extract the results shown in Table 7.2 and 7.3.

Table 7.2

User Chain	Average Time per Transaction	Maximum Contents
1 (OPER1)	53.080	5
2 (OPER2)	83.210	4
3 (OPER3)	42.737	3

Table 7.3

Facility	Average Utilization
1 (MACH1)	.447
2 (MACH2)	.630
3 (MACH3)	.530

and from table 1 of the GPSS program the following information is obtained: in 95.5 per cent of the cases the transit time was less than 540 seconds. A meaningful study would compare these results with those obtained by different sequencing strategies. However, as our purpose was not to solve a practical problem but to show different features of GPSS with the help of an example, we leave further analysis to the reader.

Summary. The assembly-line problem illustrates one application of user chains (different ranking orders of waiting lines). User chains are also very useful for structuring models into separate submodels, the link between models being the user chain. For example, in one submodel transactions are placed on a user chain by a LINK block, where they remain until transactions in another submodel remove them by an UNLINK block.

7.6.2 Inventory control

The problem. We want to study an inventory in which only one type of part is considered. The requests, for one part at a time, have been found to be Poisson distributed with a mean interarrival time of 10 days. The replenishment rule is to place a new order, for the constant reorder quantity ROQ, as soon as the stock falls to the reorder point, ROP. The lead time is uniformly distributed with an average LTAVE and spread RANGE. If the request cannot be satisfied, it is queued until the part can be delivered. Currently, the parameters used are ROP = 4 units: ROQ = 6 units: LTAVE = 30 days: and RANGE = 5 days.

We simulate the behavior of the inventory to determine:

1. During what percentage of the time the stock is empty.
2. During what percentage of the time the stock is empty with waiting requests (the out-of-stock situation). This percentage should be reduced to less than 1.5 per cent by changing ROP and ROQ if necessary.

The GPSS model. The parts are represented by transactions. They are generated using the exponential distribution for the interarrival times, Poisson arrivals. The stock is represented by storage STOCK. We have to compute the percentage of times during which particular situations occur. We therefore introduce two dummy facilities called ZERO, for stock at zero level, and OOS, for out of stock for zero level and request(s) waiting. We seize these facilities as long as the STOCK is empty. Parameters ROP and ROQ are stored in save locations initialized before simulation starts.

The block diagram (Figure 7.19) and the program (Figure 7.20) are largely self-explanatory. The following remarks amplify the documentation.

After being generated, a request is put on queue REQ to gather statistics of the waiting times and, in particular, the number of transactions that do not wait, which represent requests that are satisfied immediately. The normal processing is then to proceed to block CONT where the transaction seizes facility OOS. If STOCK is not empty, meaning that the request can be satisfied, the transaction releases the facility immediately, STOCK is reduced by one unit, and the test is made to see if it is necessary

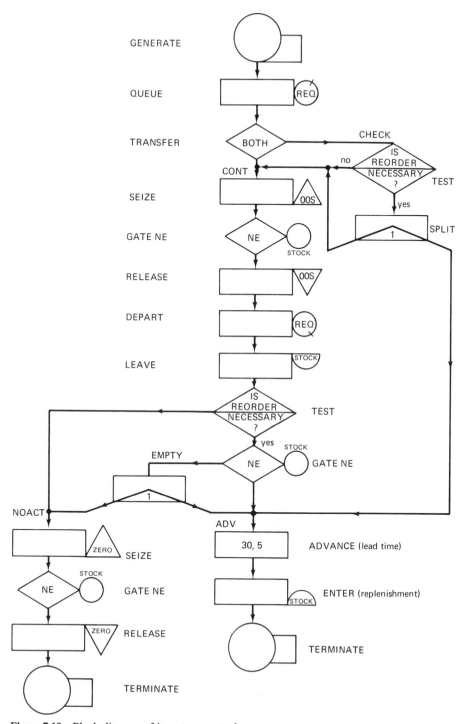

GENERATE

QUEUE   REO

TRANSFER   BOTH   CHECK

IS REORDER NECESSARY ?   no   TEST

CONT

SEIZE   OOS

GATE NE   NE   STOCK

yes

1   SPLIT

RELEASE   OOS

DEPART   REO

LEAVE   STOCK

IS REORDER NECESSARY ?   TEST

yes   STOCK

EMPTY   NE   GATE NE

1

NOACT   ADV

ZERO   SEIZE   30, 5   ADVANCE (lead time)

STOCK   NE   GATE NE   STOCK   ENTER (replenishment)

ZERO   RELEASE

TERMINATE   TERMINATE

Figure 7.19 Block diagram of inventory control program.

```
            SIMULATE

* SIMPLE INVENTORY PROBLEM
*------------------------
            INITIAL     X$ROP,4                 REORDER POINT IS INITIALLY 4
            INITIAL     X$ROQ,6                 REORDER QUANTITY IS 6

1           VARIABLE    N$ADV*X$ROQ+S$STOCK-C$REQ
* VARIABLE 1 EXPRESSES: QUANTITY ON ORDER + ON HAND - WAITING REQUESTS

EXPON FUNCTION          RN8,C24         EXPONENTIAL DISTRIBUTION - MEAN = 1.
0.,0/0.1,0.104/0.2,0.222/0.3,0.355/0.4,0.509/0.5,0.69/0.6,0.915/
0.7,1.2/0.75,1.38/0.8,1.6/0.84,1.83/0.88,2.12/0.9,2.3/0.92,2.52/
0.94,2.81/0.95,2.99/0.96,3.2/0.97,3.5/0.98,3.9/0.99,4.6/0.995,5.3/
0.998,6.2/0.999,7.0/0.9997,8.0

            GENERATE    1,,FN$EXPON              GENERATE REQUESTS
            QUEUE       REQ                      QUEUE TO RECORD WAITING TIMES
            TRANSFER    BOTH,CONT,CHECK          IF OUT OF STOCK, GO TO CHECK

CONT        SEIZE       OOS                      SEIZE DUMMY OUT OF STOCK FACILITY
            GATE SNF    STOCK                    IF ONE PART AVAILABLE GO ON
            RELEASE     OOS                      RELEASE THE OUT OF STOCK FACILITY
            DEPART      REQ                      OUT OF WAITING REQUESTS QUEUE
            LEAVE       STOCK                    DELIVER THE REQUESTED PART
            TEST LE     V1,X$ROP,NOACT           IF NO REORDER, GO TO NOACT
            GATE SNF    STOCK,EMPTY

ADV         ADVANCE     30,5                     RECORD:LEAD TIME FOR REPLENISHMENT
            ENTER       STOCK,X$ROQ              REPLENISHMENT
            TERMINATE

EMPTY       SPLIT       1,ADV
NOACT       SEIZE       ZERO                     SEIZE THE DUMMY FACILITY ZERO
            GATE SNF    STOCK                    IF ONE PART AVAILABLE, GO ON
            RELEASE     ZERO                     RELEASE THE ZERO FACILITY
            TERMINATE

CHECK       TEST LE     V1,X$ROP,CONT            IF NO REORDER, GO TO CONT
            SPLIT       1,ADV                    RECORD.: CREATE & SEND COPY TO ADV
            TRANSFER    ,CONT                    SEND ORIGINAL TRANSACTION TO CONT.

            GENERATE    1440
            TERMINATE   1

            START       1
            CLEAR       X$ROQ
            INITIAL     X$ROP,5
            START       1
            END
```

Figure 7.20   GPSS inventory program.

to reorder. The condition tested is: on hand plus on order minus waiting requests must be greater than reorder point (X$ROP). If less than or equal (reorder necessary), the transaction goes to the ADVANCE block, which delays it for the replenishment lead time. The transaction at this level may be considered as the replenishment order. When the lead time has elapsed, the storage STOCK is increased by X$ROQ units and the transaction is terminated. If no reorder is required, the transaction goes to NOACT and seizes facility ZERO, to record the time the stock is empty. If parts are still available, the transaction immediately releases the facility and terminates.

Now suppose that the STOCK were zero. One transaction has seized facility ZERO and one request is generated. It arrives at the TRANSFER block and seizes the OOS facility. If a new request comes, it is sent by the TRANSFER block to CHECK, where we test if a reorder should be placed. If not, the transaction is scheduled to go back to CONT, waiting to be served. If so, two actions must take place: one order must be placed and the request must wait to be served. This is done with the SPLIT block. The original transaction is sent to CONT and one copy, the reorder transaction, is sent to ADV, which represents the lead time.

The simulation is made for 10,000 days, using an auxiliary clock as usual. We can make several successive runs by using the CLEAR control statement. In the program displayed, the model is cleared (with the exception of the save ROQ), ROP is changed to 5 units, and a new run is requested by the START statement. Additional runs may be requested in a similar manner.

Results and conclusion.   The two figures for the utilization of facilities ZERO and OOS are interesting. With ROP = 4 and ROQ = 6, they were, respectively, 6.6 and 3.9 per cent. With ROP = 5, ROQ = 6, they were 3.5 and 1.8 per cent. In both cases more than 1000 requests were generated. Additional trials showed that the percentage of the out-of-stock time is 0.9 per cent for ROP = 6 and ROQ = 5 and 0.8 per cent for ROP = 7 and ROQ = 5.

This information should be sufficient to allow management to formulate decisions, in particular, concerning the incentive to be attached to a decrease in the out-of-stock percentage.

7.6.3   Simple factory model

The problem.   We wish to estimate the performance of a factory with three production lines. On each line three operations are performed consecutively. For each operation a machine is available.

Parts enter in batches of 50 every 360 ± 20 minutes. These parts are dispatched to a line based on the following distribution:

Forty per cent to line 1,

Forty five per cent to line 2, and

Fifteen per cent to line 3.

The mean processing times in minutes, for each line, are shown in Table 7.4.

Table 7.4

	Line		
Operation	1	2	3
1	6	7	10
2	9	10	14
3	8	8	16

These processing times are uniformly distributed over the range: mean ± 2.

Because the processing operations are very delicate, an operator will render a line inoperative relatively frequently. It has been noticed that such failures occur every 720 ± 180 minutes. The failure affects any of the lines with equal probability. The time to repair a line is 60 ± 10 minutes.

When a line failure occurs, the following operations are necessary:

Parts currently being processed at any machine must be purged from their present operation, and after a delay of 150 ± 20, owing to some inspection operations, they join the queue before the machine to be processed again.

Parts waiting at the first stage of processing are not affected by the failure.

Parts waiting for processing at the second and third operation continue the normal processing but are marked for possible inspection at completion.

The GPSS model. The GPSS model consists of two sections. In the first, shown in the first two parts of Figure 7.21, transactions representing parts are generated, dispatched to one of the three lines, and processed. Parameter 2 of the transaction gives the line number and parameter 3 the number of the current operation. The nine facilities representing the machines and the queue before each machine are numbered as shown in Table 7.5. The current facility and queue number is stored in parameter 1 of the part transactions.

Table 7.5

		Line	
Operation	1	2	3
1	1	2	3
2	4	5	6
3	7	8	9

Once a line number has been assigned, a transaction also joins a group with the same number. These groups give access to the values of the parameters of all the transactions on a down line, regardless of which chain they are on.

When a failure occurs, the three machines of a down line become inoperative by preemption of the corresponding facilities. Parameter 4 of part transactions currently seizing one of the preempted facilities is set to 2. This shows that processing has been interrupted. Parameter 4 of part transactions waiting in a queue of the down line for the second or third operation is set to 1.

The change in the value of parameter 4 of these transactions is made by using an ALTER block. Parameter 5 is used to distinguish between transactions being processed, P5 = 1, and waiting transactions, P5 = 0.

In the second section of the GPSS model, shown in the third part of Figure 7.21, transactions representing line failures are generated. The number identifying the failed line is stored in parameter 1 of these transactions. The priority of line-failure transactions is set to 1. Such transactions preempt all the facilities of the line and alter the value of parameter 4 of the part transactions of the corresponding line.

The block

> PREEMPT   *1,PR,RECJC,,RE

specifies that the preempted part transaction will be sent to the block RECJC and (mnemonic RE) will not be in contention for the facility at the end of the interruption.

The block

> ALTER   *1,ALL,4,1,5,0

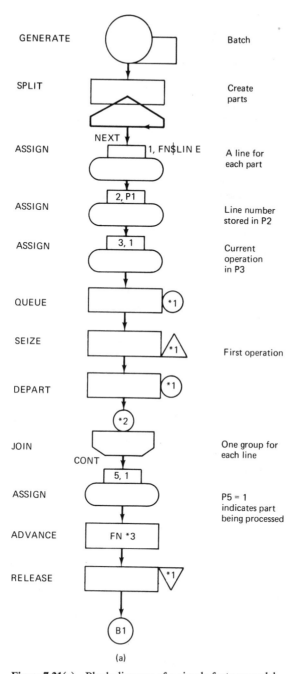

GENERATE		Batch
SPLIT		Create parts
ASSIGN	NEXT 1, FN$LINE	A line for each part
ASSIGN	2, P1	Line number stored in P2
ASSIGN	3, 1	Current operation in P3
QUEUE	*1	
SEIZE	*1	First operation
DEPART	*1	
	*2	
JOIN		One group for each line
ASSIGN	CONT 5, 1	P5 = 1 indicates part being processed
ADVANCE	FN *3	
RELEASE	*1	
	B1	

(a)

Figure 7.21(a) Block diagram of a simple factory model.

209

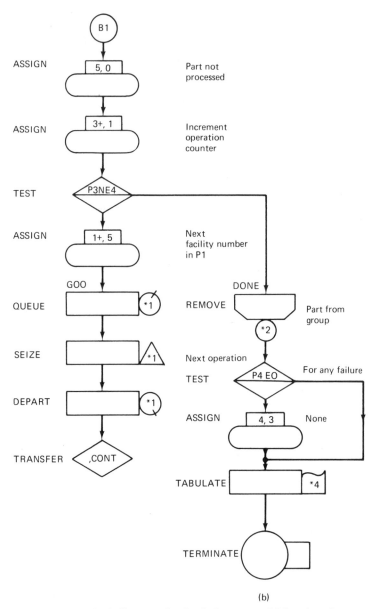

Figure 7.21(b) Block diagram of a simple factory model (continued).

sets the value of parameter 4 to 1 for all transactions belonging to the group number ∗1 whose value of parameter 5 is zero.

The importance of the group concept is shown by this example. It is possible to communicate with all transactions belonging to a group, in our case to modify the value of a parameter, regardless of the status of the transactions at the time of modification.

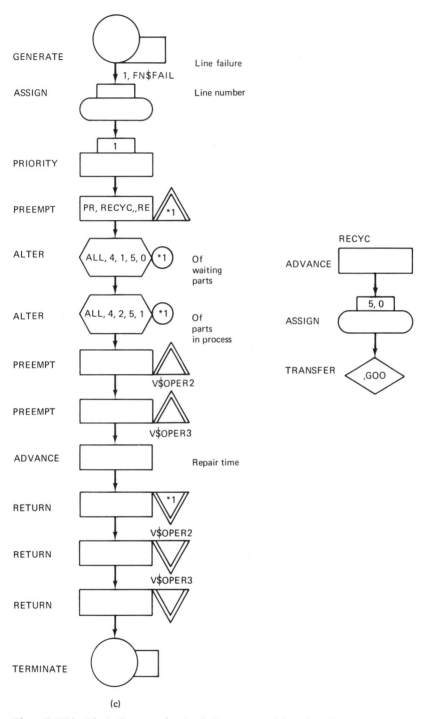

GENERATE		Line failure
ASSIGN	1, FN$FAIL	Line number
PRIORITY	1	
PREEMPT	PR, RECYC,,RE *1	
ALTER	ALL, 4, 1, 5, 0 *1	Of waiting parts
ALTER	ALL, 4, 2, 5, 1 *1	Of parts in process
PREEMPT	V$OPER2	
PREEMPT	V$OPER3	
ADVANCE		Repair time
RETURN	*1 V$OPER2	
RETURN	V$OPER3	
RETURN		
TERMINATE		

RECYC

ADVANCE		
ASSIGN	5, 0	
TRANSFER	,GOO	

(c)

Figure 7.21(c) Block diagram of a simple factory model (concluded).

In the simple model shown in Figure 7.22, we use functions 1, 2, and 3 to specify the processing times on the three lines, function LINE to assign a line number to the part transactions, and function FAIL to assign a line number to the line-failure transactions. Tables 1 and 2 give the number of parts affected by a line failure during a waiting phase and a processing phase, respectively, and also their transit times. The same sort of information is given by Table 3 for parts not affected by a line failure. Variables OPER2 and OPER3 determine the numbers of the facilities representing second and third stage machines of a given line. They are used by the failure transactions.

Results and conclusion. From the results provided by GPSS, after 1000 parts have been processed, we extract the data shown in Tables 7.6 and 7.7. During the 7669 minutes of the simulation 1000 parts were processed. There were 11 failures, involving 8 parts in process and 11 waiting for operation at the second and third stages.

Table 7.6

Facility	Average Utilization
1	0.334
2	0.455
3	0.235
4	0.483
5	0.627
6	0.320
7	0.437
8	0.510
9	0.356

Table 7.7

Queue	Maximum Contents	Average Contents	Per Cent Zeros[a]	Average Time per Transaction	$Average Time per Transaction[b]
1	26	3.096	4.6	61.835	64.877
2	29	4.971	4.1	83.433	87.052
3	11	0.874	13.0	41.658	47.907
4	9	1.400	6.2	27.903	29.759
5	8	1.924	5.0	32.295	34.006
6	3	0.302	14.8	14.339	16.833
7	2	0.053	60.4	1.075	2.717
8	1	0.014	86.2	0.238	1.730
9	2	0.134	19.7	6.370	7.938

[a]The percentage of transactions that spend zero time in the queue.

[b]Average time per transaction excluding zero entries.

```
BLOCK
NUMBER  *LOC    OPERATION  A,B,C,D,E,F,G              COMMENTS                        CARD
                SIMULATE                                                              NUMBER
                                                                                       1
        *   JOBSHOP BATCH                                                              2
        *                                                                              3
        *                     FACILITIES 1-3 ARE FOR OPERATIONS 1                      4
        *                     FACILITIES 4-6 ARE FOR OPERATIONS #2                     5
        *                     FACILITIES 7-9 ARE FOR OPERATIONS # 3                    6
                                                                                       7
                                                                                       8
        1    FUNCTION    P3,L3                PROCESSING TIME LINE 1                    9
        1,6/2,9/3,8                                                                    10
        2    FUNCTION    P3,L3                PROCESSING TIME LINE 2                    11
        1,7/2,10/3,8                                                                   12
        3    FUNCTION    P3,L3                PROCESSING TIME LINE 3                    13
        1,10/2,14/3,16                                                                 14
        FAIL FUNCTION    RN1,D3               ASSIGN LINE # FOR FAILURES               15
        .333,1/.6667,2/1,3                                                             16
                                                                                       17
        LINE FUNCTION    RN1,D3               TO ASSIGN A LINE #                       18
        .4,1/.85,2/1,3                                                                 19
                                                                                       20
        CPER2 VARIABLE   P1+3                 FACILITIES OPERATION # 2                  21
        CPER3 VARIABLE   P1+6                 FACILITIES OPERATION # 3                  22
        1    TABLE       M1,150,30,20                                                  23
        2    TABLE       M1,150,30,20                                                  24
        3    TABLE       M1,0,30,20                                                     25
                                                                                       26
1            GENERATE    360,20                                                        27
2            SPLIT       49,NEXT              CREATE PARTS                             28
3    NEXT    ASSIGN      1,FN$LINE            LINE NUMBER FOR PARTS                    29
4            ASSIGN      2,P1                 LINE # STORED IN P2                      30
5            ASSIGN      3,1                  # OF CURRENT OPERATION IN P3             31
6            QUEUE       *1                   QUEUE FOR FIRST PROCESSING              32
7            SEIZE       *1                   FIRST OPERATION'S FACILITY             33
8            DEPART      *1                                                            34
9            JOIN        *2                   JOIN GROUP,ONE PER LINE                 35
10   CONT    ASSIGN      5,1                  INDICATES THAT PART IS IN PROC.         36
11           ADVANCE     FN*2,2                                                        37
12           RELEASE     *1                                                            38
13           ASSIGN      5,0                  INDICATES THAT PART NOT IN PROC.        39
14           ASSIGN      3+,1                 INCREMENT COUNTER FOR NEXT OPER.        40
15           TEST NE     P3,4,CONT            ANOTHER OPERATION ?                     41
16           ASSIGN      1+,3                 NO. OF NEXT FACILITY                    42
17   GOO     QUEUE       *1                                                           43
18           SEIZE       *1                                                           44
19           DEPART      *1                                                           45
20           TRANSFER    ,CONT                NEXT OPERATION                          46
21   DONE    REMOVE      *2                   REMOVE PART FROM GROUP                  47
22           TEST E      P4,0,TAB             TEST FOR ANY FAILURE                    48
23           ASSIGN      4,3                  NONE                                    49
24   TAB     TABULATE    *4                                                           50
25           TERMINATE   1                    END OF PROCESSING                       51
                                                                                       52
        *                                                                              53
26   RECYC   ADVANCE     150,20                                                       54
                                                                                       55
27           ASSIGN      5,0                                                           56
28           TRANSFER    ,GOO                 RECYCLING FOR CURRENT OPERATION         57
        *                                                                              58
        *    LINE FAILURES                                                             59
                                                                                       60
29           GENERATE    720,180                                                      61
30           ASSIGN      1,FN$FAIL            ASSIGN LINE NO.                         62
31           PRIORITY    1                    LINE FAILURE HAS PRIORITY ON            63
        *                                     PARTS                                    64
                                                                                       65
32           PREEMPT     *1,PR,RECYC,,RE                                              66
33           ALTER       *1,ALL,4,1,5,0       SET P4 OF WAITING XACTS TO 1            67
34           ALTER       *1,ALL,4,2,5,1       SET P4 OF XACTS IN PROC.TO 2            68
                                                                                       69
35           PREEMPT     V$OPER2,PR,RECYC,,RE                                         70
36           PREEMPT     V$CPER3,PR,RECYC,,RE                                         71
37           ADVANCE     60,10                TIME TO REPAIR                          72
38           RETURN      *1                                                           73
39           RETURN      V$CPER2                                                      74
40           RETURN      V$CPER3              RETURN ALL FACILITIES                   75
41           TERMINATE                                                                76
                                                                                       77
                                                                                       78
        *                                                                              79
             START       1000                                                         80
             END                                                                      81
```

Figure 7.22 GPSS program listing (simple factory model).

Once such a model is built it is possible to investigate the influence of changes in line distribution, processing times, failure rates, and so on.

Summary. This problem has illustrated a possible use of the group entity and its associated blocks JOIN, REMOVE, and ALTER. The group entity gives a means of classifying transactions and/or other entities. It allows the user to communicate with transactions belonging to the group and to manipulate their attributes at the same time, regardless of their position and status in the model.

7.7 A Re-examination of the GPSS Control Program

We have described the basic modeling concepts of GPSS and the blocks that are available. It is also necessary to consider some important internal aspects of GPSS operation which can affect the formulation of complex models. The interpretation of GPSS blocks as a simulation model depends on the logic of the GPSS control program.

We know that to schedule transactions in correct sequence the control program maintains a clock and scans two chains, the current-events chain and the future-events chain. Because of the relationship of the scan to the various block operations, a good understanding of that scanning function is definitely required. The three main phases of the scanning operation are:

1. Update the clock to the next most imminent block departure time, BDT, and transfer all transactions with that BDT from the future-events chain to the current-events chain.

2. Scan the current-events chain sequentially for the first potentially active transaction.

3. Try to move that transaction into some new block.

For expediency, we use the same abbreviations as in Chapter 5:

XAC   for transaction.
FUT   for future-events chain.
CUR   for current-events chain.
C1   for clock time.
BDT   for block departure time.

Phase 1: clock updating. Figure 7.23 summarizes the operations of the clock-updating phase. The organization of the FUT in ascending order of time at which a transaction is scheduled to leave the chain puts the transaction with the most imminent BDT at the front.

Phase 2: current-events chain scan. The control program must keep track of everything that happens in the system. It must maintain records of the status of every entity, it must monitor status changes, and it must convey their effects to every element concerned. To do this, two types of status indicators are maintained. They play a vital role during the scan of the CUR.

The first indicator is called the *status-change flag*, which may be either on (set) or off (reset). The status-change flag, associated with the CUR, is used to determine

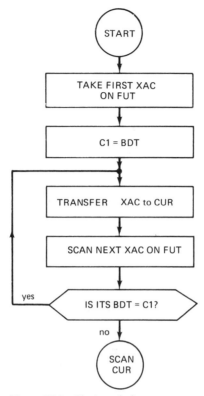

Figure 7.23 Clock updating.

the position of the CUR scan—either at the next sequential XAC or at the beginning of the CUR.

In addition, each transaction has a *scan-status indicator*. If its scan indicator is on (set), the transaction is in *inactive*, or delayed, status and will be ignored by the CUR scan. If its scan indicator is off (reset), the transaction is in a *potentially active* status and when the control program reaches the transaction, it will attempt to move it.

Figure 7.24 illustrates the operation of the CUR scan.

Phase 3: transaction move. When the GPSS scan has found a transaction that is potentially active because its scan indicator is off, the control program attempts to move it (see Figure 7.25). There are two possibilities: (1) the transaction *cannot* enter the next block, and (2) the transaction *can* enter the next block.

Transaction Cannot Enter Next Block:

Two situations are possible, depending upon the operation of the block denying entry.

1. Blocks SEIZE, PREEMPT, ENTER, or any GATE block, except M and NM.
   If the transaction is unable to obtain the use of an entity (for example, facility unavailable, or storage full), the scan indicator of the transaction is

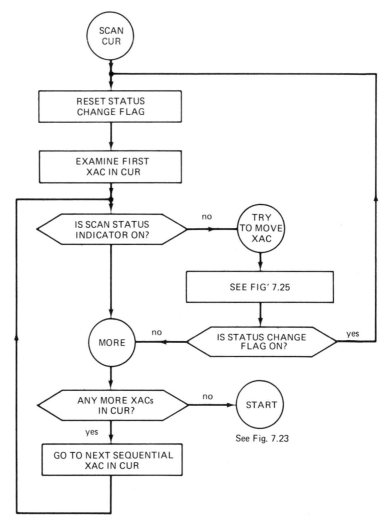

Figure 7.24 Current events chain scan.

set. This indicates that the transaction is now inactive and is in a delayed status. The transaction is placed on a delay chain. A *delay chain* is a list of transactions that cannot be moved until the status of the entity that caused the deactivation of the transaction (called a unique blocking condition) is changed. Members of the same delay chain are deactivated by the same unique blocking condition. They are reactivated only after the corresponding blocking condition is removed. This reactivation feature increases the speed of the GPSS scan.

2. Entry is denied:
   a. By a TEST block, which involves the testing of a relation (E, NE, L, LE, G, GE) between two SNAs.

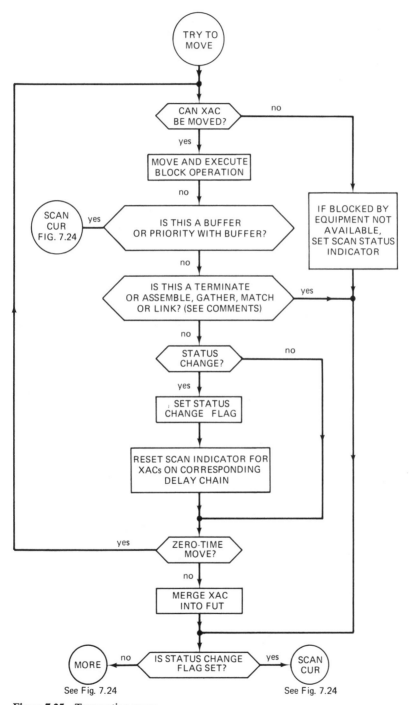

Figure 7.25 Transaction move.

b. By a GATE M or NM block, which references matching conditions of assembly-set members at a specified block.

c. Within TRANSFER (BOTH or ALL selection).

In this case the scan indicator of the transaction is *not set* and the transaction is *not linked* to a delay chain. The GPSS scan tries to advance these blocked transactions every time they are encountered. Therefore, such blocked transactions can increase the running time of the model.

Transaction Can Enter Next Block:

The transaction can enter the next block if the next block is:

1. A BUFFER block or PRIORITY block with a BUFFER option; the transaction is abandoned and the CUR is scanned again from the first transaction, as described in Figure 7.24.

2. A TERMINATE or an ASSEMBLE block where a member of the same assembly set is already waiting; the transaction is destroyed.

3. A LINK block; the transaction is placed on a user chain if the link indicator is set.

4. An ASSEMBLE block (and the transaction is the first one to enter it) or a GATHER block or a MATCH block (and the transaction finds no matching transaction in the conjugate MATCH block); the transaction is placed in an interrupt matching condition.

Setting the status-change flag. It is important to note that various block types cause the status-change flag to be set. After it has finished moving the current transaction, the GPSS scan tests the status-change flag. If the flag is set, then the CUR is scanned again from the first transaction (see Figure 7.25). If the flag is reset, the next sequential transaction in the CUR is examined.

There are essentially four types of conditions under which the status-change flag is set:

1. The flag is unconditionally set by a SEIZE, RELEASE, PREEMPT, RETURN, ENTER, LEAVE, LOGIC, FAVAIL, FUNAVAIL, SAVAIL, or SUNAVAIL block, which changes the status of a logic switch, facility, or storage. This unconditional setting ensures that all transactions being delayed by SEIZE, PREEMPT, ENTER, and GATE blocks will be moved if the entity status change removes the blocking condition.

2. The flag is set by the completion of matching, assembling, or gathering operations in MATCH, ASSEMBLE, or GATHER blocks.

3. The flag is set by a PRIORITY block, but if the PRIORITY block has a BUFFER option, the GPSS scan returns to the beginning of the current-events chain, thereby resetting the status-change flag.

4. A transaction(s) is removed from a user chain by an UNLINK block.

Conclusion. The preceding description of the scanning function shows clearly that:

1. A transaction is moved through as many zero-time blocks as possible.
2. The GPSS scan does not necessarily test the status-change flag after each block move.
3. Any change of an attribute of any GPSS entity is made only by moving a transaction through a block.

The preceding paragraphs have presented the underlying logical structure of the GPSS control program. The reader is advised to review the detailed simulation given in Chapter 5.

8 Special Features and Debugging

In this chapter we discuss two additional features of GPSS: (1) the REPORT program (Section 8.1), which allows the user to produce reports that differ in form or contents from the standard GPSS output and includes a feature for plotting graphs; and (2) the HELP block (Section 8.2), which gives the user the possibility of using Fortran or PL/I subroutines within a GPSS program. We also discuss the problems of debugging GPSS programs (Section 8.3), which may be useful during the frustrating phase of program testing.

8.1 REPORT Program

A standard output is automatically produced by GPSS at the end of every simulation run. However, a user who is not completely satisfied with either the contents of the standard output or the way in which the information is presented, can call for the services of the GPSS output editor. This is performed by the REPORT statement, which should appear after the last START statement and before the END statement of the program.

REPORT

Service:

This statement, which has no operand, suppresses the production of the standard output and gives control to the GPSS output editor. The information that will be produced depends on the statements that follow REPORT. In particular, it is possible to produce graphical representation of SNAs by the GRAPH statement. Such a graphical representation is sometimes very useful, as it gives a visual picture of the general behavior of the variable concerned. When an error in the output editor statements is encountered which prevents production of the requested report, the standard output is supplied.

8.1.1 List of statements available with REPORT

The following statements are available in the output editor. Their format is discussed in more detail in Section 8.1.2 and the graphic output statements GRAPH, ORIGIN, X, Y, and STATEMENT in Section 8.1.3:

OUTPUT: Requests the standard output suppressed by the REPORT statement.

TITLE: Selects the entity type for which statistics are to be printed and titles the corresponding section.

INCLUDE: Selects from an entity type the statistics to be printed.

FORMAT: Prints statistics relating to different entity types on the same line.

TEXT: Allows mixing of numeric output with alphanumeric data in sentence form.

EJECT: Skips to a new page before executing additional output requests.

SPACE: Skips a specified number of lines.

GRAPH: Indicates that a graphical output is required and specifies the entity SNA to be plotted.

ENDGRAPH: Indicates the end of a GRAPH program.

Between GRAPH and ENDGRAPH, the following statements must appear:

ORIGIN: To specify where the origin of the graph must be printed.

X: To specify the x-axis of the graph.

Y: To specify the y-axis of the graph.

Further, the user may insert one or more STATEMENT instructions to include alphanumeric information with the graph.

To summarize:

1. When a special output is wanted, include a REPORT statement after the last START statement of the program.

2. If the standard output must also be printed, include the OUTPUT statement.

3. If all statistics of a given entity type are to be printed, use the TITLE statement. Specify as A-operand the number of the entity concerned or leave it undefined for printing all of them.

4. If selected statistics are desired of one entity type per line, use the INCLUDE statement.

5. To mix numeric output with alphanumeric data in sentence form, use the TEXT statement.

6. If a graphical representation is required, use the GRAPH and ENDGRAPH statements with the necessary ORIGIN, X, Y and optional STATEMENT statements in between.

8.1.2 Statements format

OUTPUT

Service:

This statement, which has no operand, causes printing of the standard output. When REPORT is used, the utilization of OUTPUT is recommended during the debugging of programs, so that, if the output produced by the REPORT program is not quite in the form required, the complete output is available.

type   TITLE   A,B

Service:

This statement selects the entity type for which statistics are to be produced.

Operands:

type: (*label field*) Indicates the entity type associated with this TITLE statement (the mnemonics available are listed below).

A: Is the name or number of the entity specified in the label field for which statistics are required. If A is omitted (comma in column 19), the entire output statistics for the entity type are printed.

B: Is the title to be printed before the statistics. The length must not exceed 124 characters. If it extends beyond column 71 of the TITLE statement, a nonblank character should appear in column 72 of TITLE to show continuation to the next card image.

The mnemonics available for the label field are:

CLO:	Clock statistics	SAV:	Fullword savevalue contents
BLO:	Block statistics	HSAV:	Halfword savevalue contents
FAC:	Facility statistics	MSAV:	Matrix savevalue contents
STO:	Storage statistics	HMSA:	Halfword matrix savevalue contents
QUE:	Queue statistics	CHA:	User chain statistics
TAB:	Table statistics	GRO:	Group statistics

In GPSS V, four modes are available for save locations and matrices; the corresponding mnemonics to be used are shown in Table 8.1.

Table 8.1

Mode	Save Locations	Save Matrices
Byte mode	BSV	BMS
Halfword	HSV	HMS
Fullword	FSV	FMS
Floating point	LSV	LMS

                        type   INCLUDE   range/n1,n2,n3,...

Service:

This statement selects the statistics to be printed within entity type.

Operands:

type: (*label field*) Indicates the entity type concerned. The same mnemonics
             are available as for TITLE.

range: Indicates the range of the entities to be printed. For instance, F5–F15:
             facilities 1 to 15, or symbolically F$BEGIN-F$END, where the
             number of facility BEGIN must be smaller than the number of facility
             END.

n1,n2,...:   Indicate the columns of the standard output to be selected. It is
             therefore possible to select and print one or more columns instead of
             printing the whole line as it appears in the standard output.

For example, the statistics for tables in the standard output are the following.
The column numbers are preceded by T (for table):

T1   table name or number.
T2   number of entries in table, nonweighted.
T3   mean argument, nonweighted.
T4   standard deviation, nonweighted.
T5   sum of arguments, nonweighted.
T6   number of entries in table, weighted.
T7   mean argument, weighted.
T8   standard deviation, weighted.
T9   sum of arguments, weighted.
T10   upper limit.
T11   observed frequency.
T12   per cent of total.
T13   cumulative percentage.
T14   cumulative remainder.
T15   multiple of mean.
T16   deviation from mean.

Suppose that we want to print table number, number of entries, mean argument,
and standard deviation for tables 1 to 3. We would specify:

                TAB   INCLUDE   T1-T3/1,2,3,4

The INCLUDE statement can be used together with the TITLE Statement. If
an INCLUDE statement immediately follows a TITLE statement referring to the
same entity type (label field), the arguments of the INCLUDE statement are used to

```
NUMBER OF ENTRIES, RESPCNSE TIME AVERAGE ANC ST.DEV
------------------------------------------------------
TABLE   1
ENTRIES IN TABLE            MEAN ARCUMENT        STANDARC CEVIATION
          130                  1123.215                  393.000
TABLE   2
ENTRIES IN TABLE            MEAN ARCUMENT        STANDARD CEVIATION
          194                  1C45.C87                  411.000
TABLE   3
ENTRIES IN TABLE            MEAN ARCUMENT        STANDARC CEVIATION
          293                   955.378                  372.000
```

Figure 8.1

print the statistics associated with the TITLE statement. Note that the same effect is obtained by using the combination TEXT/INCLUDE (see the TEXT statement later in this section). For instance, the following statements:

	TEXT	NUMBER OF ENTRIES,RESPONSE TIME
		AVERAGE and ST.DEV
TAB	INCLUDE	T1-T3/1,2,3,4

would produce the output shown in Figure 8.1. If one of the columns T10 to T16 is stipulated, the tables are printed in the usual form, with all frequency classes, but with only the requested columns.

The contents of the various columns for entities other than tables are given in Table 8.2. In the INCLUDE statement, they should be preceded by the letter, or letters, appearing in the column title: for example, Q3 for the third column of the queue statistics, CH5 for the fifth column of the user chain statistics, and so on.

Table 8.2

Column Number	Facilities (F)	Storages (S)	Queues (Q)	User Chains (CH)
1	Name or number	Name or number	Name or number	Name or number
2	Average utilization	Capacity	Maximum contents	Number of entries
3	Number of entries	Average utilization	Average contents	Average time per trans
4	Average time per trans	Average utilization	Number of entries	Current contents
5	Seizing trans number	Number of entries	Number of zero entries	Average contents
6	Preempting trans number	Average time per trans	Percent zero entries	Maximum contents
7	—	Current contents	Average time per trans	—
8	—	Maximum contents	Same excluding zero entries	—
9	—	—	Assoc. table number	—
10	—	—	Current contents	—

EXAMPLE:

Print the average utilization and average service time for the machines represented by facilities 1 to 5. The following statements:

FAC	TITLE	,STATISTICS FOR MACHINES 1 TO 5
FAC	INCLUDE	F1-F5/1,2,4

would produce the output shown in Table 8.3.

Table 8.3 STATISTICS FOR MACHINES 1 TO 5

Facility	Average Utilization	Average Time per Transaction
1	0.268	27.252
2	0.542	32.563
3	0.427	31.056
4	0.492	29.654
5	0.364	30.070

For the following entity types it is sufficient for the B-operand of the INCLUDE statement to specify the range of members to be included in the output. This will cause the standard output for the entity type to be printed but only for the requested members of the type:

SAV	INCLUDE	,Xn1-Xn2	save locations
HSAV	INCLUDE	,XHn1-XHn2	halfword save locations
MSAV	INCLUDE	,MXn1-MXn2	save matrices
MHSAV	INCLUDE	,MHn1-MHn2	halfword save matrices
GRO	INCLUDE	,Gn1-Gn2	groups

Here n1 and n2 specify by number or name the range of the entities to be printed.

EXAMPLE:

SAV	INCLUDE	,X5-X10

Instructs the editor to print complete statistics for save 5 to 10.

In GPSS V, the same applies to the entity types listed below:

FSV	INCLUDE	,Xn1-Xn2	fullword save locations
HSV	INCLUDE	,XHn1-XHn2	halfword save locations
FMS	INCLUDE	,MXn1-MXn2	fullword save matrices
HMS	INCLUDE	,MHn1-MHn2	halfword save matrices
LSV	INCLUDE	,XLn1-XLn2	floating-point save locations
BSV	INCLUDE	,XBn1-XBn2	byte save locations
LMS	INCLUDE	,MLn1-MLn2	floating-point save matrices
BMS	INCLUDE	,MBn1-MBn2	byte save matrices

n	FORMAT	range/xn1,yn2,zn3,...

Service:

This statement prints on the same line selected statistics from various entity types.

Operands:

n: Specifies the print column for the first column of statistics. The spacing between subsequent columns is not controllable. If n is omitted, printing starts in column 1.

range: Indicates the range of entities concerned—for example, 1-10.

xn1,yn2,zn3,...:   Specify the type of entity (x, y, z, . . .) and the associated column number (n1, n2, n3, . . .) to be printed. It is therefore possible to extract from the standard output statistics of particular interest and to gather them on the same line. The entries that can be used are listed in Table 8.4.

Table 8.4

Facilities	Save locations
F1 name or number	X1 name or number (fullword)
F2 average utilization	X2 contents (fullword)
F3 number of entries	XH1 name or number (halfword)
F4 average time per transaction	XH2 contents (halfword)
Queues	Storages
Q1 name or number	S1 name or number
Q2 maximum contents	S3 average contents
Q3 average contents	S4 average utilization
Q4 number of entries	S5 number of entries
Q5 zero entries	S6 average time per transaction
Q6 percent zero entries	S7 current contents
Q7 average time per transaction	S8 maximum contents
Q8 same without zero entries	
Q10 current contents	
User chains	Tables
CH1 name or number	T1 name or number
CH2 number of entries	T2 number of entries nonweighted
CH3 average time per transaction	T3 mean argument nonweighted
CH4 current contents	T4 standard deviation nonweighted
CH5 average contents	T6 number of entries weighted
CH6 maximum contents	T7 mean argument, weighted
	T8 standard deviation, weighted

Remark on GPSS V: For save locations, the following entries can be used, in addition to those mentioned above:

XB1 name or number (byte)   XL1 name or number (floating point)

XB2 contents (byte)   XL2 contents (floating point)

EXAMPLE:

We want to print a table for facilities and queues 1 to 5 with reference number, number of entries in the facility, average time per transaction, average queue length, and average time spent in the queue. This is accomplished by the statement:

FORMAT   1–5/F1,F3,F4,Q3,Q7

which prints the following results:

1	105	27.251	1.275	42.527
2	101	31.492	1.312	51.392
.	.	.	.	.
.	.	.	.	.
.	.	.	.	.
5	103	32.548	1.542	48.253

No column heading is printed when using the FORMAT statement. Appropriate titles can be inserted by using the TEXT statement or by inserting a comment line, * in column 1, before the FORMAT statement.

n   TEXT   text#data/format#

Service:

This statement causes the printing of mixed text and data.

Operands:

n: The starting position for printing. If omitted, 1 is assumed.

text#data/format#:   Specifies what must be printed. The text to be printed starts in column 19 and continues to column 71. If necessary, a continuation line can be specified by a non-blank character in column 72 of the first statement. Data of the simulation model to be printed are distinguished from text by preceding and following the information with the character #. These data and their desired output format are separated by the character /.

The entries that may be specified as *data* are numbered as in the case of the FORMAT statement discussed above, except that the name or number of the entity referred to is specified.

The valid entries are listed below. In all cases, n is the name or number of the referenced entity and j is the column number:

Facilities:	Fn,j	where j = 2, 3, or 4
Storages:	Sn,j	where j = 3, 4, 5, 6, 7, or 8
Queues:	Qn,j	where j = 2, 3, 4, 5, 6, 7, 8, or 10
Tables:	Tn,j	where j = 2, 3, 4, 6, 7, or 8
User chains:	CHn,j	where j = 2, 3, 4, 5, or 6
Save locations:	Xn,2	
	XHn,2	

The *format* is defined by:

A series of x's, representing digits.

An optional decimal point.

An optional instruction to move the decimal point to the left (L) or to the right (R) by k digits.

EXAMPLES:

(1) Examples of internal data, format, and printed data are shown in Table 8.5 .

Table 8.5

Internal Data	Format in TEXT	Printed Data
12345	2Lxxx.xx	123.45
12345	2Lxxx.x	123.4
12.34	2Lx.xxxx	0.1234
1.234	3Rxxxxx	1234
1.234	2Rxxx.x	123.4
123.45	1Rxxxx.x	1234.5

(2) TEXT   AVERAGE WAITING TIME IS # Q1,7/3Rxxxxx#MSEC.

If for queue 1 the average time in seconds is 10.372 in storage, the line printed would be:

AVERAGE WAITING TIME IS 10372 MSEC.

(3) Suppose that the results of queue 1 are: average length = 1.742, average time per transaction = 142.346, and maximum queue length = 5. Also suppose the total utilization of the system (represented by facility 10) to be 0.764. The following statements:

TEXT   OVERALL SYSTEM UTILIZATION IS #F10,2/2Rxx.x# %,
TEXT   AVERAGE QUEUEING, TIME IS # Q1,7/xxx.x# SEC,
TEXT   QUEUE IS #Q1,3/x.xx# AVERAGE AND Q1,2/x# MAXIMUM#

would produce:

OVERALL SYSTEM UTILIZATION IS 76.4 %,
AVERAGE QUEUEING TIME IS 142.3 SEC,
QUEUE IS 1.74 AVERAGE AND 5 MAXIMUM.

EJECT

Service:

This statement produces a skip to the beginning of a new page.

SPACE   A

Service:

This statement produces a skip of one to three lines.

Operand:

A: Specifies the number of lines to be skipped.

8.1.3 Graphic output

We can obtain a graphic representation by using the GRAPH statement followed, in order, by the statements: ORIGIN,X,Y,STATEMENT(s),ENDGRAPH.

GRAPH   A,B,C,D

Service:

This statement is used to produce one graph, to specify the entity attribute to be plotted, range of entities, and printing character to be used.

Operands:

A: Specifies the entity attribute to be plotted (see Table 8.6).
B: The lower limit of the range of the entities, specified as A-operand, to be plotted, or the table name or number if A is one of the table attributes marked with an asterisk in Table 8.6.
C: The upper limit of the entity range.
D: The character to be used for plotting the graph. If left blank, an asterisk is assumed.

The A-operand may be one of the SNAs shown in Table 8.6.

Table 8.6

Facilities			Save locations	
	FR	utilization	X	contents (fullword)
	FC	entry count	XH	contents (halfword)
	FT	average time per transaction	Storages	
User chains			SR	utilization
	CA	average contents	SA	average contents
	CH	current contents	S	current contents
	CM	maximum contents	SM	maximum contents
	CC	entry count	SC	entry count
	CT	average time per transaction	ST	average time per transaction
Queues			Tables	
	QA	average contents	TC	entry count
	Q	current contents	TB	mean
	QM	maximum contents	TS	standard deviation
	QC	entry count	* TF	observed frequencies
	QZ	zero entries	* TP	percent of total
	QT	average time per transaction	* TD	cumulative percent
	QX	same excluding zero entries	* TR	cumulative remainder
Groups			Blocks	
	G	current contents	N	entry count

EXAMPLES:

(1)   GRAPH   TP,TSARM

Plot the percentage frequencies observed in table TSARM.

(2)   GRAPH   TD,TSARM

Plot the cumulative percentage frequencies observed in table TSARM.

(3)   GRAPH   FR,1,20

Plot the utilization of facilities 1 to 20.

(4)   GRAPH   QM,5,10

Plot the maximum queue contents of queues 5 to 10.

ORIGIN   A,B

This statement must immediately follow the GRAPH statement.

Service:

This statement specifies where the origin of the graph is to be located. The available area for the graph is 60 rows and 132 columns.

Operands:

A: Specifies the row where the X-axis is to be printed.

B: Specifies the column where the Y-axis is to be printed.

The A- and B-operands are chosen according to the size of the graph, taking into account observations that might appear below the X-axis or to the left of the Y-axis.

X   A,B,C,D,E,F,G

Service:

This statement specifies whether the X-axis has to be labeled, whether symbols or numerics have to appear below the X-axis, the width of the rectangle to be plotted for the SNA of the member of the entity class being plotted, the spacing between these rectangles, and the combination of frequency classes in case of table attributes.

Operands:

Two formats are available for the X-statement: format 1, associated with all SNAs, except those marked with an asterisk in Table 8.6 (TF, TP, TD, and TR), and format 2, associated with TF, TP, TD, and TR.

Format 1 has the following operands:

A: Specifies whether symbolics or numerics appear in the X-axis label. SYM means symbolics; if not specified, numerics are assumed.

B: Specifies the width, including end points, of the rectangle to represent the value of the SNA to be plotted. If omitted, 1 is assumed.

C: Specifies the space between two successive rectangles.

D,E,F: Not used.

G: The X-axis label indicator: if NO, no indication will be printed.

Format 2 refers to table SNAs only:

A: Not used.

B: Specifies the width, including end points, of the rectangles for the frequency classes when plotting TF or TP. Not used when plotting TR or TD.

C: Specifies the spacing between rectangles (TF or TP) or points (TR, TD).

D: The upper limit of the lowest frequency class to be plotted.

E: Specifies the number of frequency classes of the table to be included per X-axis increment. If not specified, 1 is assumed.

F: Specifies the number of increments to be plotted on the X-axis.

G: The X-axis label indicator: if NO, no indication will be printed.

When the E-operand specifies multiple frequency classes, if the E-operand is n, the D-operand should be at least the upper limit of the nth frequency class of the table.

$$Y \qquad\qquad A,B,C,D$$

This statement must immediately follow the X-statement.

Service:

This statement specifies the lower limit of values for the Y-axis, the number of increments and the number of rows per increment.

Operands:

A: Specifies the lower limit of the Y-axis.

B: Specifies the size of each Y increment.

C: Specifies the number of increments to be included in the Y-axis.

D: Specifies the number of rows to be allocated for each Y increment.

Examples are given at the end of this section, after the ENDGRAPH statement.

$$\text{col} \qquad \text{STATEMENT} \qquad A,B,C$$

Service:

This statement allows the user to write information on graphs. Any number of STATEMENT statements may be used for a given graph. They must appear in ascending order of the row in which they have to be printed.

Operands:

col: (*label field*) Specifies the column in which printing should start. If no entry made, column 1 is assumed.

A: Specifies the row number for printing.

B: The number of characters that make up the statement.

C: The information to be printed. If it extends beyond column 71, a 1 must be coded in column 72 and the statement continued in column 1 of the next line.

ENDGRAPH

is the last statement associated with graph specifications. It must follow the last STATEMENT line associated with a graph.

EXAMPLES:

Several examples of graphs are given below. They refer to the four-disk system discussed in Section 6.6.5. The REPORT program (1) gathers all results on one page and (2) requests the plotting of the following three graphs:
1. Maximum queue lengths for queues 1 to CHAN.
2. Frequencies of TSARM: total service time for the arms, which consists of seek time, wait time, and channel service time.
3. Cumulative distribution of TSARM.
The complete program is shown in Figure 8.2 and the corresponding results in Figures 8.3 to 8.6.

The REPORT program starts after the START statement of the program (Figure 8.2). An EJECT ensures printing of results on a new page. Then we request the following statistics to be printed on one page: clock, blocks, facilities, storages, queues, and tables separated by one space (Figure 8.3). Then we request the three graphs mentioned above.

The first graph, in format 1, must be printed using the + character. This is specified in the C-operand of the GRAPH statement. The origin is on row 20, column 10. The X-statement requests symbolic labeling of the axis, a width of 3 for the rectangles representing the values to be plotted and a space of 4 characters between successive rectangles. The Y-statement requests the Y-origin to be at 0, the Y-increment to be 1, with 15 increments and 1 row per increment.

One comment must be written beginning in column 19 and row 1; it is 22 characters long. The graph produced is shown in Figure 8.4.

The second graph, in format 2 (Figure 8.5), plots the frequencies of TSARM using the standard character, the asterisk. The origin is on row 40, column 10. The X-statement requests rectangles of width 1 separated by 3 characters, specifies the upper limit of the lowest class to be 50, that 1 frequency class must be included per X-increment and that we want 12 classes. The Y-statement is self-explanatory: starting value 0, increment 1, 35 increments, and 1 row per increment.

The third graph, shown in Figure 8.6, is in format 2 also and plots the cumulative frequencies of the above distribution.

Additional examples of REPORT and GRAPH can be found in the programs discussed in Chapters 9 and 10. They show graphs of the utilization of facilities and table frequencies.

8.2 HELP Block

Sometimes it is convenient to incorporate routines written in PL/I, FORTRAN, or Assembler Language, in a GPSS model—for example, when the model requires extensive computations and data handling.

```
BLOCK
NUMBER  *LOC    OPERATION  A,B,C,D,E,F,G              COMMENTS                    CARD
                                                                                 NUMBER
                SIMULATE                                                         1
        CHAN    EQU        10,F,Q                                                2
                                                                                 3
        1       FUNCTION   RN8,C24              EXPONENT. DISTR. MEAN = 1         4
0.,0/0.1,0.104/0.2,0.222/0.3,0.355/0.4,0.509/0.5,0.69/0.6,0.915/                 5
0.7,1.2/0.75,1.38/0.8,1.6/0.84,1.83/0.88,2.12/0.9,2.3/0.92,2.52/                 6
0.94,2.81/0.95,2.99/0.96,3.2/0.97,3.5/0.98,3.9/0.99,4.6/0.995,5.3/               7
0.998,6.2/0.999,7.0/0.9997,8.0                                                   8
                                                                                 9
        2       FUNCTION   RN8,C2     ARM SELECTION  4 ARMS                       10
0,1/1.,5                                                                          11
                                                                                 12
        ARMS    STORAGE    4                                                      13
                                                                                 14
1               GENERATE   50,FN1,,,3,4,F   EXPONENTIAL ARRIVALS PR=3,4PARAM      15
2               ASSIGN     1,FN2      ARM NUMBER                                  16
3               ASSIGN     2,75,1     SEEK TIME EXPONENTIAL MEAN = 75             17
4               ASSIGN     3,36,1     CHANNEL SERVICE EXPONENTIAL MEAN=36         18
5               QUEUE      *1         WAIT FOR ARM                                19
6       AAA     GATE NU    *1         AND CHANNEL                                 20
7               GATE NU    CHAN                                                   21
8               TRANSFER   SIM,,AAA   IF BOTH FREE PROCESS, IF NOT WAIT           22
9               SEIZE      *1         SEIZE ARM                                   23
10              ENTER      ARMS       STORAGE ARMS RECORD OVERALL STATS.          24
11              DEPART     *1                                                     25
12              MARK       4                                                      26
13              ADVANCE    *2         START SEEK                                  27
14              PRIORITY   2          LOWER THE PRIORITY TO 2                     28
15              QUEUE      CHAN       WAIT FOR CHANNEL SERVICE                    29
16              SEIZE      CHAN                                                   30
17              DEPART     CHAN                                                   31
18              ADVANCE    *3         CHANNEL SERVICE TIME                        32
19              RELEASE    CHAN                                                   33
20              RELEASE    *1         RELEASE ARM                                 34
21              LEAVE      ARMS                                                   35
22              TABULATE   TSARM      TABULATE CHANNEL PLUS SERVICE TIME          36
        TSARM   TABLE      MP4,50,50,20                                           37
23              TERMINATE  1                                                      38
                START      1000                                                   39
                                                                                 40
                REPORT     TO GATHER ALL RESULTS ON ONE PAGE                      41
                EJECT      AND TO PLOT CHARACTERISTICS OF ARMS                    42
        CLO     TITLE      ,CLOCK TIME AT END OF SIMULATION                       43
                SPACE      1          SPACE ONE LINE                              44
        BLO     TITLE      ,                                                      45
                SPACE      1          SPACE ONE LINE                              46
        FAC     TITLE      ,STATISTICS FOR EVERY ARM AND CHANNEL (FACILITIES)     47
                SPACE      1          SPACE ONE LINE                              48
        STO     TITLE      ,STATISTICS FOR ALL ARMS                              49
                SPACE      1                                                      50
        QUE     TITLE      ,STATISTICS FOR EVERY ARM AND CHANNEL (QUEUES)         51
                SPACE      1                                                      52
        TAB     TITLE      ,TOTAL TIME FOR ARMS (SEEK+WAIT+CHANNEL)               53
                EJECT                                                             54
                GRAPH      QM,1,CHAN,+ SAMPLE FORMAT 1 GRAPH - MAX QUEUES         55
                ORIGIN     20,10                                                  56
                X          SYM,3,4    SYMBOLIC NAMES                              57
                Y          0,1,15,1                                               58
        19      STATEMENT  1,22,MAXIMUM QUEUE LENGTHS                             59
                ENDGRAPH                                                          60
                EJECT                                                             61
                GRAPH      TP,TSARM   EXAMPLE OF A TABLE FREQ. GRAPH              62
                ORIGIN     40,10                                                  63
                X          ,1,3,50,1,12,TSARM                                     64
                Y          0,1,35,1                                               65
        19      STATEMENT  1,28,FREQUENCY FUNCTION OF TSARM                       66
        41      STATEMENT  43,25,TIMES IN MILLISECONDS                            67
                ENDGRAPH                                                          68
                EJECT                                                             69
                GRAPH      TD,TSARM   EXAMPLE OF A TABLE CUM. DISTR.              70
                ORIGIN     55,10                                                  71
                X          ,1,3,50,1,20,TSARM                                     72
                Y          0,2,50,1                                               73
        19      STATEMENT  1,28,CUMULATIVE DISTR. OF TSARM                        74
                ENDGRAPH                                                          75
                END                                                              76
```

Figure 8.2 Sample program with graphs.

233

RELATIVE CLOCK   50966   ABSOLUTE CLOCK   50966

BLOCK COUNTS

BLOCK	CURRENT	TOTAL	BLOCK	CURRENT	TOTAL	BLOCK	CURRENT	TOTAL
1	0	1008	11	0	1003	21	0	1000
2	0	1008	12	0	1003	22	0	1000
3	0	1008	13	0	1003	23	0	1000
4	0	1008	14	0	1003			
5	4	1008	15	3	1003			
6	0	1009	16	0	1000			
7	0	1009	17	0	1000			
8	1	1009	18	0	1000			
9	0	1003	19	0	1000			
10	0	1003	20	0	1000			

STATISTICS FOR EVERY ARM AND CHANNEL (FACILITIES)

FACILITY	AVERAGE UTILIZATION	NUMBER ENTRIES	AVERAGE TIME/TRAN	SEIZING TRANS. NO.	PREEMPTING TRANS. NO.
1	.650	241	137.547	10	
2	.690	264	133.375	20	
3	.657	260	128.819	23	
4	.627	238	134.302		
CHAN	.696	1000	35.497		

STATISTICS FOR ALL ARMS

STORAGE	CAPACITY	AVERAGE CONTENTS	AVERAGE UTILIZATION	ENTRIES	AVERAGE TIME/TRAN	CURRENT CONTENTS	MAXIMUM CONTENTS
ARMS	4	2.625	.656	1003	133.416	3	4

STATISTICS FOR EVERY ARM AND CHANNEL (QUEUES)

QUEUE	MAXIMUM CONTENTS	AVERAGE CONTENTS	TOTAL ENTRIES	ZERO ENTRIES	PERCENT ZEROS	AVERAGE TIME/TRANS	$AVERAGE TIME/TRANS	TABLE NUMBER	CURRENT CONTENTS
1	12	1.522	242	36	14.8	320.545	376.562		1
2	10	1.264	265	29	10.9	243.147	273.025		1
3	6	.895	262	36	13.7	174.221	201.973		2
4	7	.753	239	38	15.8	160.690	191.069		1
CHAN	3	.473	1003	498	49.6	24.067	47.891		3

$AVERAGE TIME/TRANS = AVERAGE TIME/TRANS EXCLUDING ZERO ENTRIES

TOTAL TIME FOR ARMS (SEEK+WAIT+CHANNEL)

TABLE TSARM

ENTRIES IN TABLE	MEAN ARGUMENT	STANDARD DEVIATION	SUM OF ARGUMENTS	
1000	133.524	93.062	133525.000	NON-WEIGHTED

UPPER LIMIT	OBSERVED FREQUENCY	PER CENT OF TOTAL	CUMULATIVE PERCENTAGE	CUMULATIVE REMAINDER	MULTIPLE OF MEAN	DEVIATION FROM MEAN
50	161	16.09	16.0	83.9	.374	-.897
100	299	29.89	45.9	54.0	.748	-.360
150	179	17.89	63.8	36.1	1.123	.177
200	156	15.59	79.4	20.5	1.497	.714
250	93	9.29	88.7	11.2	1.872	1.251
300	46	4.59	93.3	6.6	2.246	1.788
350	31	3.09	96.4	3.5	2.621	2.326
400	23	2.29	98.7	1.2	2.995	2.863
450	5	.49	99.2	.7	3.370	3.400
500	5	.49	99.7	.2	3.744	3.937
550	1	.09	99.8	.1	4.119	4.475
600	0	.00	99.8	.1	4.493	5.012
650	1	.09	100.0	.0	4.868	5.549

REMAINING FREQUENCIES ARE ALL ZERO

Figure 8.3 Results: clock, block, facility, storage, queue, and table statistics

Figure 8.4 Graph of the maximum queue lengths.

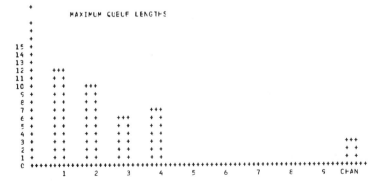

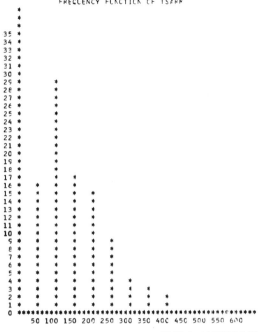

TIMES IN MILLISECONDS **Figure 8.5** Graph of the frequencies of TSARM.

Figure 8.6 Graph of the cumulative distribution of TSARM.

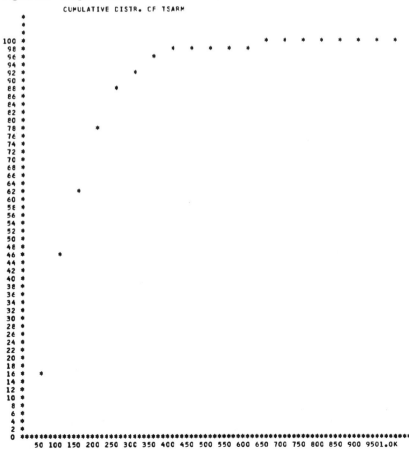

CUMULATIVE DISTR. OF TSARM

8.2.1 The basic GPSS HELP block—Assembler Language

The GPSS HELP block enables the user to call routines written in Assembler Language from a GPSS program. The HELP block can have up to seven operands: A, B to G. The first, A, gives the name of the HELP routine: the others, B to G, are SNA values to be passed to this HELP routine.

HELP routine users must observe the following rules:

1. The contents of all registers must be saved on entry to the HELP routine. Registers must be restored before returning to GPSS. The first executable instruction of the HELP routine must be:

$$\text{SAVE} \qquad (14,12)$$

2. A base register must be assigned for use by the HELP routine. General register 12 is suggested—for example:

$$\begin{array}{ll} \text{BALR} & 12,0 \\ \text{USING} & *,12 \end{array}$$

3. The last instruction in the HELP routine must be:

$$\text{RETURN} \qquad (14,12)$$

The RETURN instruction returns control to the GPSS execution phase and sends the transaction to the next sequential block.

The HELP block subroutine sets up a 25-word table consisting of the decoded B- to G-operands, the address of control words, and the address of various subroutines, and passes the starting address of the table in general register 10 to the HELP routine. These words may be referenced by using, for example, the base-displacement method.

Table 8.7 contains some available values with their displacement from address in general register 10. The purpose of each routine given in the table is as follows:

ADDCUR: To add a transaction to the current-events chain at the end of its priority class.

SUBCUR: To remove a transaction from the current-events chain.

ADDFUT: To insert a transaction into the future-events chain.

SUBFUT: To remove a transaction from the future-events chain.

ADDINT: To place a transaction in interrupt status.

SUBINT: To remove a transaction from interrupt status.

Refer to the GPSS User's Manual for further details [G.10].

8.2.2 GPSS V HELP routines—Fortran and PL/I

The GPSS V HELP routines should be used when FORTRAN or PL/I routines are frequently required with GPSS programs. In addition to the HELP block used with Assembler Language, GPSS V provides three routines, HELPA, HELPB, and

Table 8.7

Item	Displacement
B-operand value	0
C-operand value	4
D-operand value	8
E-operand value	12
F-operand value	16
G-operand value	20
Address of control words	24
Address of ADDCUR routine	28
Address of SUBCUR routine	32
Address of ADDFUT routine	36
Address of SUBFUT routine	40
Address of ADDINT routine	44
Address of SUBINT routine	48

HELPC, to communicate with FORTRAN routines and three, HELPAPL1, HELPBPL1, and HELPCPL1, to communicate with PL/I routines.

The general format of these blocks is:

$$\text{HELPX} \qquad \text{A,B,C,D,E,F,G}$$

Operation:

X is to be replaced by one of the following codes:

$$\text{A,B,C}$$
$$\text{APL1,BPL1,CPL1}$$

Operands:

A: Gives the name of the HELP routine.

B to G: SNA values to be passed to the HELP routine.

The mode of operation of these blocks is summarized in Table 8.8.

Techniques for coding HELP routines

FORTRAN help blocks.   FORTRAN help routines should be coded as subroutines with the following formats, depending on the HELP block used.

If block HELPA is used, code as follows:

```
SUBROUTINE      XX——X(IVALUE)
DIMENSION       IVALUE(6)
.
.
.
RETURN
END
```

Table 8.8 OPERATION MODES OF THE HELPX BLOCKS

Block Name		Type of Communication	Data Transmission
Fortran	PL/I		
HELPA	HELPAPL1	One-way from GPSS to help routine	SNA values passed by the B–G operands; GPSS passes the starting address of the six full-words containing the SNA values
HELPB	HELPBPL1	Two-way to and from help routine	Via fullword or floating-point savevalues whose numbers are given by the B–G operands; GPSS passes to the FORTRAN or PL/I routine the addresses of the savevalue
HELPC	HELPCPL1	One-way from GPSS to help routine Two-way to and from help routine.	SNA values passed by the B–G operands GPSS constructs an entity address argument list. The addresses of attributes associated with each entity are passed in an argument list defined in the FORTRAN subroutine or via an array defined in the PL/I routine.

XX——X is the name of the FORTRAN subroutine.

IVALUE gives the address of a six-word area containing the values of the B- to G-operand SNAs. The only significance of the name IVALUE is that it identifies the format of the information passed to the FORTRAN routine, that is, fullword (four bytes) integer data. Any valid FORTRAN symbol conveying the same information is allowed.

Within the FORTRAN routine, the user can obtain the decoded SNA values of the B- to G-operands by referencing the array IVALUE, with the appropriate subscript.

EXAMPLE:

$$KLONG = IVALUE(4)$$

places the E-operand SNA value in the FORTRAN variable KLONG.

If block HELPB is used, code as follows:

```
        SUBROUTINE XX——X (IX1,IX2,IX3,IX4,IX5,IX6)
        .
        .
        .
        RETURN
        END
```

XX——X is the name of the FORTRAN subroutine.

IX1,IX2, . . .IX6 contain the addresses of the fullword savevalues referenced in the B- to G-operands. The only significance of the FORTRAN variable names IX1,IX2——IX6 is that they identify the format of the information passed to the FORTRAN routine, that is, fullword (four bytes) integer data. It should also be noted that if the user desires to address floating-point savevalues, the FORTRAN variable names used must begin with the letters A through H or O through Z. These variable names identify the floating-point (single precision) format of the information being passed to the FORTRAN subroutine. Any valid FORTRAN symbol conveying the same information is allowed.

Within the FORTRAN routine, the contents of specific fullword or floating-point savevalues can be obtained and/or replaced by using the names of the corresponding arguments.

If the HELPB block in a GPSS model were coded:

$$\text{HELP} \qquad \text{EXAMPL,2,15,16,17,18,19}$$

and within the FORTRAN subroutine:

```
SUBROUTINE EXAMPL(IX1,IX2,IX3,IX4,IX5,IX6)
.
.
.
IX1=IX1+70
.
.
.
RETURN
END
```

the content of fullword savevalue 2 is incremented by 70.

If block HELPC is used, code as follows:

```
SUBROUTINE XX——X(IVALUE,ISAVEF,ISAVEH,IFAC,ISTO,FSTO,IQUE,
* FQUE,ILOG,ITAB,FTAB,IUSE,IUSEF,FUSE,IMAX,IMAXB,IMAXH,IMAXBH,
* FSAVEL,IMAXL,FMAXBL)
INTEGER*2 ISAVEH,ILOG,IUSE,IMAXBH
REAL*8 FQUE,FUSE,FTAB
REAL*4 FSTO,FSAVEL,FMAXBL
DIMENSION IVALUE(6),ISAVEF(2),ISAVEH(2),IFAC(2),ISTO(2),FSTO(2),
* IQUE(2),FQUE(2),ILOG(2),ITAB(2),FTAB(2),IUSE(2),IUSEF(2),FUSE(2),
* IMAX(2),IMAXB(2),IMAXH(2),IMAXBH(2),FSAVEL(2),IMAXL(2),FMAXBL(2)
.
.
.
RETURN
END
```

XX——X is the name of the FORTRAN subroutine. The arguments IVALUE, ISAVEF, ISAVEH, etc., are FORTRAN array names that may be used to reference attributes of GPSS entities as defined in Table 8.9.

IVALUE conveys the same information as in HELPA.

Matrix savevalues may also be referenced but require special consideration outside the scope of this description (see [G.12]).

Access to the attributes. GPSS entity information is stored internally in arrays not directly compatible with FORTRAN array structure. To gain access to the attributes of a specific GPSS entity, it is necessary, therefore, to specify an array name that corresponds to the referenced entity type (as given in Table 8.9 under "Reference Word") and an index J, which defines the number of that entity as well as the type of information required.

The index J is given by the following formula:

$$J = K*(N-1) + L$$

K and L are indexing constants given in Table 8.9 for each entity type.

N is the index number of a specific entity type, for example facility 5 or queue 8.

This formula is applicable for savevalues (fullword, halfword, and floating-point), facilities, storages, queues, logic switches, tables, and user chains.

EXAMPLE:

Within the FORTRAN subroutine it is possible to place the current contents of storage 4 in variable ICONT by writing:

$$N = 4$$
$$K = 11$$
$$L = 1$$
$$J = K*(N-1) + L$$
$$ICONT = ISTO(J)$$

PL/I help blocks. The use of three modes of PL/I HELP block operations (HELPAPL1, HELPBPL1, and HELPCPL1) requires special knowledge which goes beyond the scope of this presentation. For example, the parameter that a PL/I routine receives from GPSS should be described to PL/I as a character string, although that parameter is in reality a list of addresses of those variables which the HELP routine can reference; this is a requirement for communicating between Assembler Language and PL/I. Such details assume a working knowledge of PL/I, so we refer the reader to the IBM Manuals [G.12] and [G.13].

8.2.3 HELPC block and statistical evaluation of simulation results

The problem. Compute the confidence interval of the average waiting time of customers in a single GPSS queue, single server, with exponential interarrival time and constant service time. The computations have to be done during a single computer

Table 8.9 REFERENCE INFORMATION FOR HELPC ROUTINES CODED
IN FORTRAN

Entity	Attribute	Indexing Constants		Reference Word	FORTRAN Mode	FORTRAN Length (bytes)
		K	L			
SAVEVALUE (fullword)	Contents	1	1	ISAVEF	INTEGER	4
SAVEVALUE (halfword)	Contents	1	1	ISAVEH	INTEGER	2
SAVEVALUE (floating point)	Contents	1	1	FSAVEL	REAL	4
Facility	Cumulative time integral	7	2	IFAC	INTEGER	4
	Clock time of last status change	7	3	IFAC	INTEGER	4
	Entry count	7	6	IFAC	INTEGER	4
Storage	Current contents of storage	11	1	ISTO	INTEGER	4
	Number of available units in storage	11	2	ISTO	INTEGER	4
	Cumulative time integral	11	3	FSTO	REAL	4
	Clock time storage last changed status	11	5	ISTO	INTEGER	4
	Entry count	11	6	ISTO	INTEGER	4
	Maximum storage contents	11	7	ISTO	INTEGER	4
Queue	Clock time queue last changed status	8	1	IQUE	INTEGER	4
	Total entry count	8	2	IQUE	INTEGER	4
	Number of zero-delay entries	8	5	IQUE	INTEGER	4
	Cumulative time integral	4	2	FQUE	REAL	8
	Current contents of queue	8	6	IQUE	INTEGER	4
	Maximum contents	8	7	IQUE	INTEGER	4
Logic switch	Logic switch status	3	1	ILOG	INTEGER	2
Table	Sum of arguments in table	8	1	FTAB	REAL	8
	Sum of squared arguments	8	2	FTAB	REAL	8
	Sum of weighted values	8	3	FTAB	REAL	8
	Sum of weighted squared values	8	4	FTAB	REAL	8
	Number of entries	16	10	ITAB	INTEGER	4
User chain	Number of transactions on user chain	12	3	IUSE	INTEGER	2
	Maximum number of transactions on user chain	12	4	IUSE	INTEGER	2
	Total number of transactions on user chain	6	3	IUSEF	INTEGER	4
	Clock time of last status change	6	4	IUSEF	INTEGER	4
	Cumulative time integral	3	3	FUSE	REAL	8

run of a GPSS model, according to the procedure of Mechanic and McKay, summarized in Section 14.3.

The GPSS model. Figure 8.7 shows how two FORTRAN subroutines, BATCH1 and CONFID, are called by HELPC blocks from within the GPSS model. The listing of the GPSS model is given in Figure 8.8.

Following are general descriptions of BATCH1 and CONFID (Figure 8.9).

Subroutine BATCH1:

This subroutine computes and stores, in floating-point savevalues, the sum of squares of batch means of a function of a discrete argument, from a single sample of data. The GPSS block that calls this subroutine is:

$$\text{HELPC BATCH1,I1,I2,I3,I4}$$

I1 :   First size of batches.

I2 :   Number of batch sizes.

I3 :   GPSS SNA whose confidence interval is to be found.

I4 :   Value of the discrete argument of the function I3.

The number of floating-point savevalues used is $2*I2 + 1$.

The purpose of XL(1) is to compute the overall average; and of XL(2) to XL$(1+I2)$ is to compute, for each batch size, the batch means; and of XL$(2+I2)$ to XL$(2*I2+1)$ is to compute the square of these batch means.

Subroutine CONFID:

This subroutine computes and prints the confidence interval.

The GPSS block calling this subroutine is:

$$\text{HELPC CONFID,I1,I2,I3}$$

I1 :   First size of batches.

I2 :   Number of batch sizes.

I3 :   Size of the sample of data.

The printed results consist of the sizes of batches, the estimated variances of the batch mean values, the correlation coefficients between successive batches, and the confidence interval.

How to use the FORTRAN subroutines.   To use these subroutines, first compile and link-edit them in one load module, BATCH1 and CONFID being the entry points of that load module. Second, store the load module in a data set which has to be concatenated with the data set containing the GPSS load modules at execution time. A description of the OS (operating system) control statements required for these operations can be found in [G.13].

Sample of results.   Correlation coefficients for two sample sizes are given in Table 8.10.

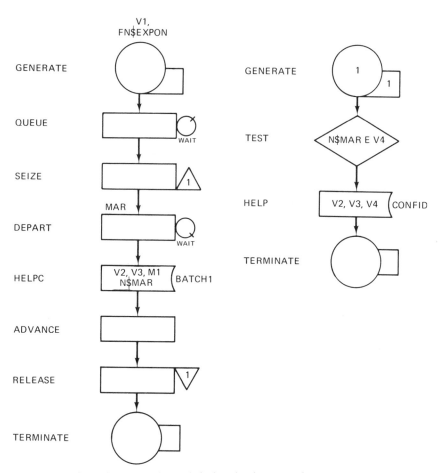

Figure 8.7 Block diagram of the statistical evaluation example.

```
            SIMULATE
            LOAD        BATCH1
    1       VARIABLE    150
    2       VARIABLE    1
    3       VARIABLE    5
    4       VARIABLE    25600
    EXPON FUNCTION      RN8,C24        EXPONENTIAL DISTRIBUTION - MEAN = 1.
    0.,0/0.1,0.104/0.2,0.222/0.3,0.355/0.4,0.509/0.5,0.69/0.6,0.915/
    0.7,1.2/0.75,1.38/0.8,1.6/0.84,1.83/0.88,2.12/0.9,2.3/0.92,2.52/
    0.94,2.81/0.95,2.99/0.96,3.2/0.97,3.5/0.98,3.9/0.99,4.6/0.995,5.3/
    0.998,6.2/0.999,7.0/0.9997,8.0
    DEB   GENERATE      V1,FN$EXPON
          QUEUE         WAIT
          SEIZE         1
    MAR   DEPART        WAIT
          HELPC         BATCH1,V2,V3,M1,N$MAR
          ADVANCE       100
          RELEASE       1
          TERMINATE
          GENERATE      1,,,1
          TEST E        N$MAR,V4
          HELPC         CONFID,V2,V3,V4
          TERMINATE     1
          START         1
          END
```

Figure 8.8 GPSS model.

```
      SLBROUTINE BATCH1(IV,I1,I2,I3,I4,I5,I6,I7,I8,I9,
     1I1C,I11,I12,I13,I14,/I15/,I16,/I17/,>L)
      CIMENSION IV(6),XL(2)
C COMPUTATION CF CONFIDENCE INTERVALS - MECHANIC AND MCKAY'S
C PROCEDURE
C THIS SUBROUTINE COMPUTES AND STORES THE SUM OF SQUARES CF BATCH
C MEANS OF A FUNCTION OF A DISCRETE ARGUMENT(EX:WAITING TIME OF
C TRANSACTIONS),FROM A SINGLE SAMPLE CF DATA
C GPSS BLOCK TC CALL THIS SUBROUTINE:
C          HELPC   BATCH1,I1,I2,I3,I4
C          I1=FIRST SIZE CF BATCHES
C          I2=NUMBER CF BATCH SIZES
C          I3=SNA WHOSE CONFIDENCE INTERVAL IS TC BE FCUND
C          I4=VALUE CF THE DISCRETE ARGUMENT OF THE FUNCTION I3
C NUMBER OF USED FLOATING POINT SAVEVALUES:1 TO 2*I2+1
C
      IC=IV(4)
      NB=IV(2)
      ISZ=IV(1)
      XL(1)=XL(1)+IV(3)
      CC 100 I=1,NB
      IF(ID-(IC/ISZ)*ISZ)100,10,100
   10 XAI=(XL(1)-XL(I+1))/ISZ
      XL(I+NB+1)=XL(I+NB+1)+XAI*XAI
      XL(I+1)=XL(1)
  100 ISZ=ISZ*4
      RETURN
      END
      SUBROUTINE CONFID(IV,I1,I2,I3,I4,I5,I6,I7,I8,I9,
     1I1C,I11,I12,I13,I14,/I15/,I16,/I17/,XL)
      DIMENSION IV(3),XL(2),NBS(11),RC(10),XNUA(1C)
C COMPUTATION CF CONFIDENCE INTERVALS - MECHANIC AND MCKAY'S
C PROCEDURE
C THIS SUBROUTINE IS TC BE USED WITH THE SLBROUTINE BATCH1
C IT COMPUTES THE CONFIDENCE INTERVAL OF A FUNCTION OF A
C DISCRETE VARIABLE,FROM A SINGLE SAMPLE OF DATA DIVIDED
C INTC BATCHES
C GPSS BLOCK TC CALL THIS SUBROUTINE:
C          HELPC   CONFID,I1,I2,I3
C          I1=FIRST SIZE CF BATCHES
C          I2=NUMBER OF BATCH SIZES (MAXIMUM NUMBER=10 CF DIMENSION
C             STATEMENT)
C          I3=SIZE CF THE SAMPLE
C
      NB=IV(2)
      XAV=XL(1)/IV(3)
      NSA=IV(3)/IV(1)
      NBS(1)=IV(1)
      CC 100 I=1,NB
      XNUA(I)=(XL(I+NB+1)-XAV*XAV*NSA)/((NSA-1)*NSA)
      NBS(I+1)=NBS(I)*4
  100 NSA=NSA/4
      NB1=NB-1
      IC=0
      CC 200 I=1,NB1
      ID=ID+1
      RC(I)=(XNUA(I+1)/XNUA(I)-1)/3
      IF(RC(I)-0.05)250,200,200
  200 CONTINUE
      IC=ID+1

  250 WRITE(6,1000)(NBS(I),I=1,NB)
      WRITE(6,2000)(XNUA(I),I=1,NB)
      WRITE(6,3000)(RC(I),I=1,ID)
 1000 FORMAT(1H1,//40X,'COMPUTATION OF A CONFIDENCE INTERVAL',
     1/40X,'-----------------------------------',/////5X,
     2'SIZE OF BATCHES',/10I12)
 2000 FORMAT(1H0,4X,'ESTIMATED VARIANCES CF THE MEAN VALUE'/10E12.3)
 3000 FORMAT(1H0,4X,'CORRELATION COEFFICIENTS BETWEEN SUCCESSIVE BATCH
     1ES'/10F12.4)
      IF(ID-NB)400,300,400
  300 WRITE(6,4000)
 4000 FORMAT(1H0,//'    NO SOLUTION AVAILABLE'/4X,
     1'--------------------')
      CC TO 999
  400 FNU=1.96*SQRT(XNUA(ID+1))
      X1=XAV-FNU
      X2=XAV+FNU
      WRITE(6,5000)X1,X2
 5000 FORMAT(1H0,//'    CONFIDENCE INTERVAL:',2E12.4/4X,
     1'--------------------')
  999 RETURN
      END
```

Figure 8.9   Subroutines BATCH1 and CONFID.

Table 8.10

	Sample Sizes	
	10,240	25,600
Average interarrival time	150	150
Service time	100	100
Lowest correlation coefficient	−0.003	0.023
Confidence interval	93.1/115.9	97.8/111

Comments. The purpose of this example was to show a practical case where FORTRAN routines can be useful within a GPSS model and to illustrate, in broad outline, how the communication is done with these routines. However, the reader is advised to review this example after reading Chapter 14 and understanding the details of the Mechanic and McKay procedure. The subroutine CONFID, as given above, tests only whether or not the correlation coefficient (rho) is smaller than 0.05.

8.3 Debugging GPSS Programs

Debugging is often the most difficult activity associated with programming and it requires a high degree of imagination. In the early days of programming digital computers, the importance of debugging was usually overlooked. In fact, many programmers did not anticipate that errors would occur.

If the users of electronic computers accept that it is difficult to debug computer programs in general, they will certainly agree that debugging simulation programs, especially those representing large random models, is even more difficult. This is sufficient reason to have good debugging tools or methods built into simulation languages and systems.

Before discussing some of the tools available for debugging, we want to stress that it is only one element in the chain of activities involved in a simulation study, from the moment the problem is posed until sufficient information has been obtained to make final recommendations to the decision makers. These activities may be described as: analysis of the problem, choice of a method (in our case simulation), choice of a programming language (general-purpose or simulation language), detailed modeling, programming in machine-readable form, debugging and verification of the program, validation and adjustment of the model, simulation, analysis and critique of the results, and preparation of the final report. We have previously observed that the time and effort involved in these activities may be significantly different if a general-purpose programming language, such as Fortran or PL/I, or a simulation language such as GPSS is used.

GPSS has many practical advantages, in particular because of its compactness: a GPSS program may be considerably shorter, than a program written in another language. For most programmers, writing in a more compact language means a smaller chance of making errors and consequently less time and effort to find and correct them. It is also easier for the implementor of the language to introduce numerous and powerful diagnostics into the system, both at compile time and during execution.

The next sections present several ideas for debugging GPSS programs which though simple have proved to be very useful to the numerous students to whom we have taught GPSS both at the elementary level, such as that of the subset presented in Chapter 6, and at an advanced level, using the full language with sophisticated programming techniques.

8.3.1   Divide programs into modules

Large programs should always be divided into small independent or semi-independent modules which can be tested independently of one another. New modules should be incorporated into the model only when they are working correctly.

8.3.2   Use the diagnostics

It is surprising how many users do not read the diagnostics carefully or do not try to interpret them completely. GPSS produces two types of diagnostics: (1) at compile time (*assembly program errors* and *input errors*) and (2) during program execution (*execution errors*). Some of the errors detected are severe and the diagnostics do not allow simulation to start. Some diagnostics just warn the user but allow simulation to continue. All diagnostics produced are numbered. A complete list is given in [G.10]. Every error number is accompanied by a few words explaining the type of error.

Examples of compile-time diagnostics.

MULTIPLE DEFINITION OF SYMBOL IN ABOVE CARD.

This is a warning that does not prevent the simulation from starting. It tells the user that there might be an error, but that the program could still execute. This occurs, for example, when blocks, specified by their label name, are redefined between successive runs during the same simulation, that is, between successive START statements.

ERROR IN ABOVE CARD—INPUT ERROR 250: Illegal SNA mnemonic.

This diagnostic statement is completed by a message placed at the end of the model which reads: ERROR IN ABOVE ASSEMBLY—SIMULATION DELETED.

ERROR NUMBER 44: Syntax error in above card.

When this message is obtained, it is sometimes necessary to relate it to the previous statement. For example, if a function were defined with 10 points and only 9 are given, the system tries to find the tenth point in the next statement. If this is a legal instruction, it is considered as an error by the compiler, which is looking for numerical values, and it is therefore flagged with error number 44.

Examples of execution-time diagnostics. All execution-time diagnostics, in addition to the cause of the error, indicate the clock time, the number of the transaction causing the error, the block in which it is, the block it was attempting to enter, and the value of the termination count. In addition, as already mentioned, the standard output and the status printout are produced. We therefore find, in the current-events chain, the transaction that caused the error with all its attributes such as BDT, priority, and parameter values.

ERROR 599: Common core storage exceeded.

This message occurs when the memory is full, that is, when too many transactions have been generated and stay in the model. This can be due to several types of programming error, some of which we mention here.

GENERATE block with zero, intergeneration time. This is probably a keying error—either the A-operand was omitted or a blank character, (which is interpreted by GPSS as no operand specified) appeared in column 19. The condition could also arise if the intergeneration time were too short.

Another type of error may cause a blockage of the model which prevents transactions from proceeding farther. It may be caused by a permanent entity that is made busy and never released—for example, facility SEIZED and never RELEASED, or storage ENTERED without the corresponding LEAVE block.

Such a blockage may also occur when a specific condition is encountered which makes the release of the blocking condition impossible (even when it is programmed). The following paragraph illustrates such a situation (Figure 8.10). It is a segment extracted from an actual simulation.

In a teleprocessing system messages arriving from one terminal (GENERATE block) are queued (QUEUE WAIT). The CPU is interrupted (PREEMPT CPU), the transaction leaves the queue (DEPART WAIT), enters a buffer (ENTER BUF), which can contain 20 messages, uses the CPU for one ms (ADVANCE 1), and releases the CPU (RETURN CPU). The normal processing continues later by the combination: SEIZE CPU, . . . , RELEASE CPU. Finally the buffer is freed (LEAVE BUF), and the transaction is destroyed (TERMINATE).

At first glance this program looks correct. But during execution, the diagnostic message: "Error 599, common core storage exceeded" was printed. Looking at the statistics printed and in particular at the queue WAIT, we found the following figures:

Total number of zero entries:	450
Current queue contents:	210
Total number of entries:	660

This queue is thus exhibiting very peculiar behavior: either the transactions go through it without waiting or they stay in it. Having noticed this phenomenon we try to interpret it physically and we can reasonably suppose that, as soon as one transaction waits in the queue, the system is locked so that the transaction cannot proceed. This diagnosis having been made, we must find the reason for the blockage and it is

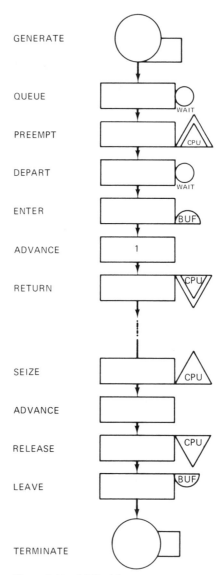

GENERATE

QUEUE

PREEMPT

DEPART

ENTER

ADVANCE

RETURN

SEIZE

ADVANCE

RELEASE

LEAVE

TERMINATE

Figure 8.10 Self-locking system.

indeed not difficult to discover. Although the interrupt simulated by PREEMPT CPU, ADVANCE1, RETURN CPU is very short (1 unit of time), between the PREEMPT and RETURN blocks we find the block ENTER BUF. This block will refuse entry to a transaction when BUF is full. But when this happens, the CPU is preempted; therefore, the transaction seizing the CPU is interrupted, cannot release it, and consequently cannot enter the block LEAVE BUF, which would have released some space in the storage BUF and allowed the transaction to ENTER the storage BUF and to return the CPU. This model can really be called "self-locking" because it locks itself when a particular situation is encountered and cannot unlock itself.

Another very common error that may cause saturation of the model is the improper use of indirect addressing together with symbolic names. Again, this case is best explained with an example:

A computer system receives messages from one terminal. These have to be processed and need information from one of three disks. A read request for a disk is queued in a queue corresponding to the disk, which is represented as a facility. To shorten the program we use indirect addressing. The three disks are called facilities 1, 2, and 3 and their associated queues 1, 2, and 3. The queue number and the number of the disk to be accessed are stored in parameter 1 of the transactions.

If we look at the program we find instructions such as QUEUE P1 (enter the queue whose number is in P1), QUEUE CPU, SEIZE CPU, SEIZE P1, and so on. At compile time symbolic names are converted to numeric values. So, when the instruction QUEUE CPU is encountered, CPU will be converted to 1 and the queue CPU will be queue 1; in the same way CPU will be facility 1; and so on. This is obvious because the compiler has no indication of the fact that queue and facility numbers 1 to 3 should be reserved for indirect addressing. The result of such confusion is obvious: facility 1 is a unique facility representing the CPU *and* disk 1. Therefore, when disk 1 is used, the CPU is seized.

Note that this problem is immediately resolved by using the EQU statement to reserve the numbers 1 to 3 for queues and facilities: DISK EQU 1(3),F,Q.

ERROR 401: no new event in system.

This error means that the model is empty and therefore that nothing more can happen. Such cases occur when the number of transactions to be generated and therefore introduced into the model is limited, for example by using the D-operand of the GENERATE statement. GPSS moves the transactions through the block diagram until both the current-events and the future-events chains are empty when the message is printed.

ERROR 616: Transaction parameter zero referenced.

This error occurs frequently when people are learning GPSS and using the ASSIGN instruction. Its A-operand is a *parameter number* so that it is coded, for example:

ASSIGN   3,10

to assign 10 to parameter 3.
We may make the error by writing:

ASSIGN   P3,10

which refers to the parameter whose number is the contents of P3. If P3=0, then we try to reference parameter 0, which does not exist.

8.3.3   Check the generated distributions

In random models samples of random variables are generated, for example, in
GENERATE or in ADVANCE blocks. Such samples are obtained by means of GPSS
functions. When using such functions for the first time, it is prudent to check that the
values produced correspond to those required.

Such a check can easily be made by inserting a TABULATE statement at a
suitable place in the program. Suppose, for instance, that we generate transactions
with a complicated interarrival distribution. If we insert a TABULATE block right
after the GENERATE block, we can tabulate the interarrival times observed. These
should have a distribution close to the given one.

Such checks are very simple and they give more confidence in the model being
developed. They should always be included when new functions are introduced.

8.3.4   Anticipate results

Although the need to anticipate results was mentioned earlier (in Chapter 3),
it is so important that we repeat it here. When submitting a simulation program to the
computer, we may have one of two attitudes: (1) we may decide to wait until the results
are available and read them; or (2) we may anticipate the results in an approximate
fashion, for example by simplifying the model or by crude reasoning.

When adopting the first attitude, we will find many reasons to justify the results
of the run even if they appear somewhat strange. If, on the contrary, we adopt the
second attitude, we have estimated a ball-park figure in advance, say between 150
and 400. If the result produced is 500, then we know there is an error, which may
be either in the rough evaluation of the range mentioned or in the program, *but*, we
are now forced to explain the discrepancy.

We believe strongly that the latter attitude should always be adopted. It gives us
more chance of building correct models and, in case of errors, puts us in a much
better position to locate mistakes.

8.3.5   Make short runs

When debugging a program, we must understand what is happening in the model
and be able to reproduce a run; that is, we must be able either to check that the initializing procedure works correctly by using the same random numbers or to establish
that repeated runs with different random numbers produce coherent results.

There are several ways to produce successive short runs:

START *statement C-operand:* this feature allows the user to obtain intermediate
results at each so-called snap interval specified by the C-operand (see Section
6.1: "Limitation of the Simulation Length").

Successive utilization of the START *and* CLEAR *statements:* as discussed
previously, CLEAR reinitializes a GPSS model as it was when loaded, with the
exception of the random-number generators. This causes several runs to be made
with different random-number sequences but starting with an empty model each
time.

Successive utilization of the START *and* RESET *statements:* RESET erases all statistics accumulated up to the point where it is read. This causes the run to continue but with new statistics to be taken on the various segments of this run.

Combined utilization of START, RESET, *and* CLEAR *statements.*

8.3.6 Glance at the results

When looking at the standard output of a GPSS run, even very quickly, we may discover special situations that may be due to an error. We now discuss some of the points to watch.

Block statistics. For every block, the number of entries (N) and the current number of transactions in the block (W) are given. Both those blocks with N=0 and those with a large value for N are suspect. The first have never been reached by transactions. This may be due to a special situation that occurred during the run, but possibly the group of blocks cannot be reached because of a programming error. For instance, this group begins without label after an unconditional TRANSFER.

Those blocks with a high N value show a loop through which the transactions go a number of times. If this number is incorrect, it is easy to find the reason and to remedy it. In those cases in which a loop exists and no information is printed at the end of the simulation run because the job terminated after the time allowed in the job card had elapsed, we recommend that the user add one GENERATE and one TERMINATE block to stop the simulation after a reasonable time. The standard output will then show where the loop is.

However, this procedure can fail in the case of a timeless loop, where transactions cycle endlessly without updating the simulated clock. The simple remedy is to use the GPSS V run time feature, which specifies the host computer time after which the run is terminated, with output, even if the simulation has not ended. Ensure that the specified run time is less than the time imposed by the operating system of your installation.

Blocks with nonzero W values may also give interesting information. When such blocks are QUEUE or ADVANCE blocks, for instance, it is normal to find several transactions. If on the other hand we find several transactions in a RELEASE or LEAVE block, this fact should be studied and may lead to the discovery of an error. An example is given in Section 13.2.2.

Facility and storage statistics. For facilities and storages, the average utilization is printed. When the utilization is either 0 or 1 (which means, in practice, close to 1, for instance 0.998), this fact is suspect.

A utilization of 0 means that all transactions remain in the facility (or storage) for a zero time; that is, they enter and leave at the same clock time. In such cases, why use a facility (or storage) that is apparently useless? In practice such a situation can be caused by a logical error.

A utilization of 1 means that the entity is used all the time. This facility (or storage) is therefore a bottleneck in the system modeled, a fact that should be investigated further. Several conditions may cause this situation:

(1) SEIZE without corresponding RELEASE block (or an unreachable one), ENTER without corresponding LEAVE block, or a self-locking program (see the example in Section 8.3.2).

(2) An error in the definition of the times (either interarrival times too short, or service times too long, or both); or other programming errors.

Even if no programming error is present, the model cannot operate in the way proposed and has to be changed.

Queue and storage statistics.   For queues and storages, GPSS prints the maximum contents and the actual contents. When these two values are equal, we should make a careful check. It is usually an indication that the queue is building up constantly and that the system would saturate if simulation continued. The same applies to storages.

The reasoning behind this hypothesis is based on the fact that, when stopping the simulation at a given moment, more or less randomly, the probability of finding the actual queue contents identical with the maximum contents is extremely small. When this situation is encountered, a further indication is the average queue length (or average storage contents); if it is approximately half the current contents, we have an additional reason to suspect that the queue (or storage) is building up.

The reason for such a situation may be either that the model is correct and therefore the system is not viable and is unable to handle the load or that the model is incorrect and must therefore be modified.

Figure 8.11   Part of a status printout.

```
THIS IS SNAP      1 OF      2

RELATIVE CLOCK         14400  ABSOLUTE CLOCK        14400
BLOCK CCUNTS
BLOCK CURRENT     TOTAL   BLOCK CURRENT    TOTAL    BLOCK CURRENT     TOTAL    BLOCK CURRENT     TOTAL    BLOCK CURRENT     TOTAL
    1      0       165      11      1        34
    2      0       165      12      0        33
    3      0       165      13      0       159
    4      0       165      14      0         4
    5      2       165      15      0         4
    6      0       163
    7      0       163
    8      3        37
    9      0        34
   10      0        34


CURRENT EVENTS CHAIN
TRANS       BDT  BLCCK   PR  SF   NBA    SET   MARK-TIME      P1         P2         P3         P4    SI TI DI CI MC  PC PF
   16     13179     8            9     16     12682          0          0          0          0   1     1  2
                                                            0          0          0          0
                                                            0          0          0          0
    6     13721     8            9      6     13413          0          0          0          0   1     1  2
                                                            0          0          0          0
   11     14392     8            9     11     13924          0          0          0          0   1     1  2
                                                            0          0          0          0
                                                            0          0          0          0


FUTURE EVENTS CHAIN
TRANS       BDT  BLCCK   PR  SF   NBA    SET   MARK-TIME      P1         P2         P3         P4    SI TI DI CI MC  PC PF
   12     14483                  1     12      -165          0          0          0          0           4
                                                            0          0          0          0
                                                            0          0          0          0
    2     14491     5            6      2     14157          0          0          0          0           4
                                                            0          0          0          0
   14     14584    11           12     14     12590          0          0          0          0        1  4
                                                            0          0          0          0
                                                            0          0          0          0
    3     14682     5            6      3     14345          0          0          0          0           4
                                                            0          0          0          0
                                                            0          0          0          0
    5     18000                 14      5        -4          0          0          0          0           4
                                                            0          0          0          0
                                                            0          0          0          0
```

8.3.7 Use the status printout

The status printout is comprised of the lists of the current-events chain, the future-events chain, and other chains kept by the simulator during simulation. It gives the full, detailed description of the status of the model at the time it is produced (see Figure 8.11). The status printout is produced:

1. Automatically in case of an execution error.
2. At the end of a simulation run if the D-operand of the START statement is not blank: START 1000,,,1, for example.
3. Through the utilization of a PRINT block specifying the chain concerned:

PRINT	MOV	for the current-events chain.
PRINT	FUT	for the future-events chain.
PRINT	I	for the interrupt chain.
PRINT	MAT	for the matching status chain.

The information contained in these lists allows the user to see and therefore check where every transaction is (block number), its block departure time, the next block address, its priority, its parameter values, and its indicators. It is therefore possible to understand in detail the reasons for the system being in its current status. A careful perusal of these lists is usually sufficient to explain the trouble to be eliminated from the program and to take the necessary corrective action.

Analysis of the status printout generally speeds up debugging a model considerably, both in the machine time used as well as in the total time spent.

8.3.8 Use the PRINT block

If the previously mentioned methods have failed to locate the error in the program, more information must be obtained.

The PRINT block, previously discussed in Section 7.2.6, will print information during simulation. This printing is performed every time a transaction enters the PRINT block. The information to be printed is specified in the A-, B-, and C-operands and will depend on the problem encountered. If, for example, we do not understand the behavior of a queue, then we would print the statistics of that queue, plus, possibly, the current- and future-events chains.

One should be very cautious about using the PRINT block because (1) it will produce a lot of output if too many transactions go through it, and (2) it is time-consuming.

Remark on GPSS V: When the PRINT block is extensively used in GPSS V, it is recommended that the LOAD feature be used to minimize the computer time used. This feature makes specified modules resident in main storage.

Use of the PRINT block can be a somewhat complex matter. Initial use of the block depends on the type of error detected; it may be that:

1. An abnormal situation arises in the model when a specific situation is encountered, or
2. A problem occurs in a certain part of the model, or
3. The problem occurs at a given time, or
4. We have no idea of what is happening, but we think that the model goes wrong when the queue contents grow beyond a specified amount.

In case (1), we would include a PRINT statement at the very place where we suspect that the error occurs, for example when a specific branch of a TEST is taken by the transaction. We would then request the printing of the current- and future-events chains, for instance, or of any other statistics we may find useful. If we suspect that many transactions will follow this path, we can execute the PRINT block once, and immediately thereafter, by using the CHANGE block, we can replace it by a dummy block, such as ADVANCE 0.

Case (2) is more difficult. In such a situation we could include PRINT statements on all the paths that arrive at the critical part of the model and maybe also on the paths leaving that part. So, every time that this part of the model is reached by a transaction, some information is produced.

Case (3) is easier. We can generate a transaction at the time when we know the error occurred, using a GENERATE block with this time specified as off-set and create just one transaction, followed by one PRINT block that will produce the vital information at this time.

Case (4) is also easy. We can generate a transaction, then stop it by a TEST block, testing the contents of the queue until it reaches the value specified. The TEST is followed by the PRINT block that would produce the requested information.

The information printed by the PRINT block may very often be produced in a much more efficient and elegant way by using the SAVEVALUE block. Examples are given in the next section.

8.3.9 Use the SAVEVALUE block

As mentioned above, we frequently face the need to record information during the simulation in order to understand what is happening and to take corrective action or to observe the time-dependent behavior of the system as the main purpose of the simulation. Instead of printing the information at the moment when something is happening, we might take advantage of the fact that GPSS, at the end of a simulation run, automatically prints the contents of the save locations and matrices that have nonzero contents. It is thus quite natural to use the SAVEVALUE and MSAVEVALUE blocks to store the information of interest in save locations and matrices. The results are the same as for using PRINT, but the operations are much faster because no intermediate input/output activity is required.

EXAMPLES:

(1) We want to record the contents of the queue WAIT every 20 seconds. We add to our program the following instructions:

```
GEN              GENERATE        20
                 SAVEVALUE       N$GEN,Q$WAIT
                 TERMINATE
```

At time 20, the queue contents will be saved in X1, at 40 in X2, at 60 in X3, etc. We have only to check that we will have enough save locations for the length of the simulated run.

(2)   When a transaction goes through the block SPECI, we want to know the transit time of the transaction, its parameter 3 value, and its priority. We can define a MATRIX: TEST with row 1 containing the transit time, row 2 the parameter 3 value, and row 3 the priority; the columns will correspond to the respective values when the first, second, third, . . . , transaction goes through the MSAVE-VALUE blocks:

```
SPECI            . . . . . .
                 MSAVEVALUE      TEST,1,N$SPECI,M1
                 MSAVEVALUE      TEST,2,N$SPECI,P3
                 MSAVEVALUE      TEST,3,N$SPECI,P
```

(3)   Every time that the contents of queue WAIT is greater than or equal to 10 and the contents of storage 1 is greater than or equal to 150 bytes, we want to record the clock time, the storage utilization, its average and maximum contents, and the average time spent in it by the transactions. This can be done by the addition of the following blocks once the transactions enter queue WAIT:

```
TTT      TEST NE    BV1,0,RECOR           If BVARIABLE1 is 1,
           .                              go to RECOR,
           .                              otherwise, go to
           .                              normal sequence.
RECOR    MSAVEVALUE STATI,1,V1,C1         save clock time
         MSAVEVALUE STATI,2,N$RECOR,SR1   storage utilization
         MSAVEVALUE STATI,3,N$RECOR,SA1   average contents
         MSAVEVALUE STATI,4,N$RECOR,SM1   maximum contents
         MSAVEVALUE STATI,5,N$RECOR,ST1   average time per transaction
         TRANSFER   ,TTT+1                back to normal sequence
           .
           .
           .

1        VARIABLE   N$RECOR+1             necessary because
                                         N$RECOR does not yet
                                         count current transaction
                                         in RECOR.

1        BVARIABLE  Q$WAIT'GE'10*S1'GE'150
                                         BV1 is 1 only if WAIT
                                         contains 10 or more and
                                         STORAGE 1 150 or more.
```

These instructions fill the matrix STATI, one column after the other, every time the condition is met (that is, when BVARIABLE 1 is equal to 1). At the end of the run all information needed will therefore be available in a practical and condensed form.

These examples are sufficient to illustrate the great flexibility offered by the SAVEVALUE and MSAVEVALUE blocks. Again, using them constitutes a very efficient and elegant way of producing information during the simulation without adding significantly to the computer time used.

8.3.10 Use the TRACE feature

The utilization of the trace feature should be the last step to take and only when all other methods have failed. However, it is obviously a very powerful tool because, when a transaction is "traced," every one of its movements is described in detail, including transaction number, number of the block it is leaving, block number to which it goes, clock time, priority, and parameter values. An example of the tracing output is presented in Figure 8.12. Tracing is controlled by the tracing indicator of the transaction. This indicator is set when the transaction goes through a TRACE block and reset when it enters an UNTRACE block.

Looking again at the situation described in Section 8.3.8, we could use the tracing feature as follows:

In case (1), we can insert a TRACE block where we suspect the error occurs. Then all transactions reaching this point will be traced until they terminate. If we want to suppress the tracing from a given point, an UNTRACE block (or several, if many paths are possible) can be inserted. If we suspect that too many transactions will go through this part of the model, we will need to reduce the quantity of output. This can be done, for instance, by limiting the number of times the TRACE block is executed (given by the N of the TRACE block) and stopping the simulation.

In case (2), a TRACE block should be inserted on all paths leading to the part of the model that is suspect. For the same reason as above, the UNTRACE block should be inserted on all paths going from the part concerned.

In case (3), we can add to the model a GENERATE block, creating only one transaction, follow it by a TRACE block, and send this transaction into the network of blocks. This transaction will then be traced through the whole model.

Case (4) is similar to case (3) except that the GENERATE block is followed by a TEST in refusal mode, as in example 3 of Section 8.3.9. The transaction is stopped until the condition is met, then sent into the model and traced until it terminates or, alternatively, until it reaches an UNTRACE block—if we are sure that the part between the UNTRACE and the TERMINATE blocks works satisfactorily.

As stressed earlier, the trace feature should be manipulated with great care, particularly because of the amount of information produced. As an example, suppose that it is used in a program that has 40 blocks and that 20 transactions are traced from the first to the last block. As shown by Figure 8.12, 5 lines are printed for every

```
RANS    1 FROM   12 TO   13 CLOCK       12 TERMINATIONS TC GC      3
RANS      BCT  BLCCK  PR  SF   NBA   SET  MARK-TIME      P1        P2          P3          P4  SI TI DI CI MC  PC PF
 1         12   12               13    1       1                 3       0           0           7   1    2
                                                                 0       0           6           0
                                                                 1       0           3           0

RANS    1 FROM   13 TO   14 CLOCK       12 TERMINATIONS TC GC      3
RANS      BCT  BLCCK  PR  SF   NBA   SET  MARK-TIME      P1        P2          P3          P4  SI TI DI CI MC  PC PF
 1         12   13               14    1       1                 3       0           0           7   0    2
                                                                 0       0           6           0
                                                                 1       0           3           0

RANS    2 FROM    9 TO   10 CLCCK       12 TERMINATICNS TC GC      2
RANS      BCT  ELCCK  PR  SF   NBA   SET  MARK-TIME      P1        P2          P3          P4  SI TI DI CI MC  PC PF
 2         10    9               10    2      10                 3       0           0           7     1  1  2
                                                                 0       0           6           0
                                                                 1       0           3           0

RANS    2 FROM   10 TO   11 CLOCK       12 TERMINATICNS TO GO      2
RANS      BCT  BLCCK  PR  SF   NBA   SET  MARK-TIME      P1        P2          P3          P4  SI TI DI CI MC  PC PF
 2         10   10               11    2      10                 3       0           0           7     1  1  2
                                                                 0       0           6           0
                                                                 1       0           3           0

RANS    2 FROM   11 TO   12 CLCCK       12 TERMINATIONS TO GO      2
RANS      BDT  BLCCK  PR  SF   NBA   SET  MARK-TIME      P1        P2          P3          P4  SI TI DI CI MC  PC PF
 2         10   11               12    2      10                 3       0           0           7     1  1  2
                                                                 0       0           6           0
                                                                 1       0           3           0

RANS    2 FROM   12 TO   13 CLCCK       18 TERMINATIONS TO GO      2
RANS      BDT  BLCCK  PR  SF   NBA   SET  MARK-TIME      P1        P2          P3          P4  SI TI DI CI MC  PC PF
 2         18   12               13    2      10                 3       0           0           7   1    2
                                                                 0       0           6           0
                                                                 1       0           3           0

RANS    2 FROM   13 TO   14 CLCCK       18 TERMINATIONS TO GO      2
ANS       BDT  BLCCK  PR  SF   NBA   SET  MARK-TIME      P1        P2          P3          P4  SI TI DI CI MC  PC PF
 2         18   13               14    2      10                 3       0           0           7   1    2
                                                                 0       0           6           0
                                                                 1       0           3           0

RANS    3 FROM    8 TO    9 CLCCK       28 TERMINATIONS TO GC      1
RANS      BCT  BLCCK  PR  SF   NBA   SET  MARK-TIME      P1        P2          P3          P4  SI TI DI CI MC  PC PF
 3         28    8                9    3      28                 3       0           0           7   1    2
                                                                 0       0           6           0
                                                                 1       0           3           0

RANS    3 FROM    9 TO   10 CLCCK       28 TERMINATIONS TO GC      1
RANS      BDT  BLCCK  PR  SF   NBA   SET  MARK-TIME      P1        P2          P3          P4  SI TI DI CI MC  PC PF
 3         28    9               10    3      28                 3       0           0           7   1    2
                                                                 0       0           6           0
                                                                 1       0           3           0
```

Figure 8.12 Sample tracing printout.

movement of a transaction. If we print 50 lines per page, the above program would produce $40 \times 20 \times 5/50 = 80$ pages.

8.3.11 Conclusion

In this section we have presented a few methods that we have found efficient for debugging GPSS programs. Our list is obviously not exhaustive but contains most of the ideas that may be used during this difficult phase.

Our experience with students and other practitioners of GPSS, especially with nonprogrammers, has shown that a significant number of errors is caused by simultaneous events, that is, events that take place at the same clock time. In certain types of problem, the fact that simultaneous events may occur in an unpredictable order is not important, but in others it may be critical. The user of GPSS and other discrete simulation languages must remember that everything in the model is moving in parallel. If, at certain places, simultaneous events must take place in a specific order, they should be programmed accordingly. Such problems may occur, for example, when using the SPLIT block. The transactions created by the SPLIT block are put on the current-events chain at the end of the corresponding priority class. If other transactions appeared in the chain after the presently processed transaction, they could be processed before the newly created ones, which might result in errors if the order of processing is important. Such situations are obviously the responsibility of the user who, in complex situations, should use the PRIORITY or the PRIORITY BUFFER blocks to resolve the problem.

9 Simulation of an Automatic Warehouse

9.1 The System

9.1.1 Introduction

In this chapter we consider a simple model of an automatic warehouse. We show how the model can be elaborated to simulate more complicated operating disciplines and thus become an aid in designing a projected warehouse. As the argument proceeds, the reader will see that clear definition of the system being modeled and simulation techniques are equally important, that is, the input data and the "rules of the game."

A warehouse is a building used for storing products until they are required. Goods are normally placed on standard-sized trays, called *pallets*. Movement of pallets means movement of the goods on those pallets. Shelves or *racks* are divided into *bins*, each of which can accommodate one pallet. Racks are arranged vertically in *corridors*. In large warehouses items can easily be stored in the wrong location, which makes quick retrieval difficult. Fully automated warehouses under computer control make such operations more efficient.

9.1.2 Description of the warehouse

The warehouse is built for handling standard-sized pallets and has bins of $1 \times 1 \times 1$ meter (m) which can hold one pallet with its load. The weight of one loaded pallet may vary from 50 to several hundred kilograms.

The warehouse, shown in Figure 9.1, consists of three principal parts: a shipping and a receiving bay; a conveyor; and the warehouse itself, that is, racks of bins.

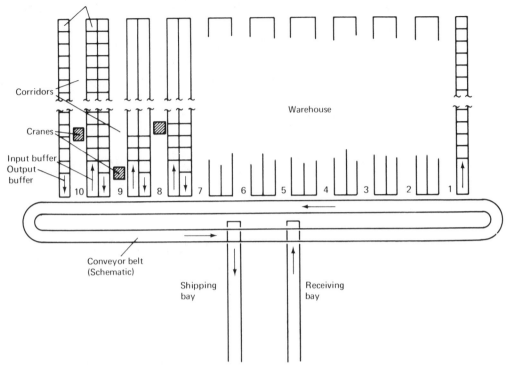

Figure 9.1 General layout of the warehouse.

The *warehouse* has 10 corridors. Each corridor has a stacker crane, which moves pallets in and out of the two adjacent racks. The length of a corridor is 50 m and the height 10 m. Therefore, a rack has 500 bins in which 500 pallets can be stored. Thus, a crane has access to 1000 bins (left and right rack) and the total capacity of the 10 corridors is 10,000 pallets.

The *conveyor* connects the receiving and shipping bays with the rack area. It is a continuous mechanism designed on two levels which moves the pallets between the warehouse corridors on the upper level and the shipping/receiving bays on the lower level. The connections between the two levels are made by two elevators. Figure 9.2 illustrates the organization of the conveyor and a corridor.

The *shipping and receiving bays* provide access to and from the conveyor belt. They are the interface between the warehouse and the outside world, which we can consider as the trucks and railcars that transport goods to and from the warehouse. In most warehouses there are several shipping and receiving bays which can be operated in either way, depending on the priorities associated with current operations. In this example we model one shipping and one receiving bay.

9.1.3 Warehouse operations

Incoming goods. When pallets arrive at the receiving bay, either by truck or railcar, they are unloaded, and after the necessary operations of identification, checking, and data transfer to the computer are performed, the pallets are put in the bay.

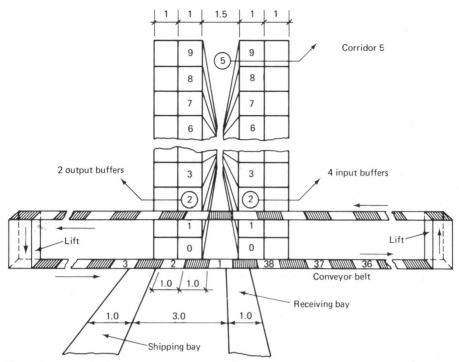

Figure 9.2 Organization of the conveyor and one corridor.

The transfer to the conveyor is under computer control. The pallets are put on the conveyor (lower level) at fixed intervals when the first free place is detected. They are then transported to the assigned corridor, where they are taken from the conveyor (upper level) and put into the input buffer. The crane of this corridor receives the order to pick the pallet from the input buffer and move it to the assigned bin.

Outgoing goods. When a pallet is required, it is picked from its bin by the crane and moved to the output buffer. It waits until a free place is found on the conveyor and is loaded on the conveyor (upper level), which transports it to the shipping bay (lower level). It is then loaded on a truck or railcar and leaves the warehouse.

Cranes and buffers. The input and output *buffers* of a corridor are the interface between the conveyor, which rotates with a uniform speed, and the bins served by the crane, which operates asynchronously with respect to the conveyor. In other words, several pallets are unloaded from the conveyor before the crane is available to pick and place them in their bin. The size of the input buffer is quite critical. If too small, a pallet assigned to a given corridor may find the buffer full and therefore have to stay on the conveyor for a whole cycle, until it is again in front of the same corridor. The occurrence of these incidents should be minimized. On the other hand, too large a buffer reduces the capacity by the corresponding amount; therefore it must be as small as possible. Although less critical, an output buffer must be available to accommodate outgoing pallets taken from the bins if they must wait for a free position on the conveyor belt. The crane is not allowed to pick a new pallet from a bin if no place is available in the output buffer.

The corridor crane receives its instructions from the computer, for example type of operation to be performed and bin location. If the operation is to store a pallet in a bin, the signal to the crane is given when the pallet leaves the main conveyor and enters the corridor input buffer. If the operation is retrieval of a pallet, the crane picks it from the bin and stows it in the output buffer. An automatic device then moves the pallet from the buffer to the conveyor as soon as a free place is detected. In both buffers the pallets are treated in arrival order (FIFO).

The crane operates on incoming or outgoing pallets, depending on its physical location after it has completed the previous operation. If the crane has just deposited an outgoing pallet in the buffer, it will pick up a pallet (if any waiting) from the input buffer and take it to its bin. If its last operation was to stow an incoming pallet in a bin, the crane will be directed to pick an outgoing pallet from a bin if such a request is pending.

Conveyor.   The conveyor connects the shipping and receiving bays with the corridor buffers. It is a continuously moving belt transport on two levels. The lower level serves the shipping and receiving bays, the upper level (2 m higher) serves the corridors. Two elevators connect the two levels at either end. Their operation is automatic and they do not disrupt the movement of the pallets; we can therefore consider the conveyor as a loop on which pallets are transported between the corridors and the shipping bay or between the receiving bay and the corridors.

Corridor and bin assignment.   The assignment of a bin location to an incoming pallet is specified by corridor number and bin location. The special problem of assignment of the corridor to a pallet is not included in our model. We assign corridor 1 to pallet 1, corridor 2 to pallet 2, and so on. In a real system this assignment might be unacceptable for the following reasons:

1. Some products could be inflammable, which would entail the creation of special corridors equipped for fire protection.
2. Arrival and departure of pallets may be made in trains or batches, which introduces further complications, especially for grouping all pallets with the same product in one receiving bay when there are several such bays in the system.
3. Picking a pallet with a given product could be based on a complicated algorithm, such as the position of the pallets that are currently the closest to the buffers or those in the warehouse for the longest time.

Although these complexities are not built into our model, their addition would not be difficult. However, we think that their inclusion would complicate the coding and would add very little to the purpose of this example.

The model does not simulate the 1000 bins individually. Instead we consider four *zones* of equal volume where the products are stored according to turnover. The most frequently required items are stored in zone 1, closest to the conveyor, the least frequently required ones in zone 4, farthest from the conveyor. Hence, when generating a pallet, we assign bin location by:

1. Generating the corridor number: successive integers 1 to 10 for input, uniformly distributed random numbers between 1 and 10 for output.

2. Generating the two coordinates of the bin based on the zone arrangement considered and the frequencies of zone accesses given in the problem (see Section 9.2.2). Initially, the zones are vertical slices. We shall see how this can be modified, based on the results of the simulation study.

9.2   The Problem

9.2.1   Problem description

The problem is to simulate the operation of the warehouse to check if the whole system can operate satisfactorily, especially during peak hours.

It will be necessary to define the size of the input/output buffers (to avoid having too many pallets remaining for an additional cycle on the conveyor) and the geometric partition of the four zones (initially vertical slices). It might also be advisable or necessary to modify the initially assumed speeds of the cranes both horizontally and vertically. Moreover, it might become obvious that additional shipping or receiving bays would be required for handling the load. Finally, the FIFO strategy of processing the pallets in buffers might be questioned.

Not all these aspects can be covered here. We shall present one model and explain how certain alternatives can be made to investigate the effects of changes to the system. In particular, we want to estimate the maximum rates of arrival and departure of pallets which the system can handle.

9.2.2   Numerical data

The following initial values for input data may be modified, with the exception of data about the building.

Warehouse.   The warehouse has 10 corridors, each 50 m long; 10 m high; and 3.5 m wide (left and right racks, 1 m; crane space, 1.5 m). Total width of the warehouse is 35 m.

The input buffer has four pallets, the output buffer, two pallets, and ordering of buffers is FIFO.

There are four zones of equal volume. The products are allocated to the four zones based on turnover. The frequencies of requests for the four zones are:

zone 1:   40%
zone 2:   30%
zone 3:   20%
zone 4:   10%

Zones are initially bounded by vertical cross sections.

Conveyor. The length (upper and lower parts) of the conveyor is 35 m (without lifts). The distance between the upper and lower levels is 2 m; the elevators are built so that they do not disrupt the movement of pallets. The total capacity of the conveyor is 38 pallets; the main conveyor speed, 20 meters per minute (m/min); the distance between two pallets, 1 m; and the minumum time between the passage of two pallets is 6 seconds (s).

Cranes. The mean crane speed is: horizontal, 10 m/min; vertical, 1 m/min. When a crane has deposited a pallet in the output buffer, it will take one (if present) from the input buffer and stow it in the assigned bin. If the last operation was stowing a pallet in a bin, it will pick a pallet from a bin and bring it to the output buffer if a request is pending.

Bays. The distance between the left lift and the shipping bay is 15 m; the distance between the receiving bay and the right lift, 15 m; and the distance between the shipping and receiving bay, 3 m.

The model does not simulate the operations at the bays in detail. We treat the receiving bay as a queue where pallets wait for a free place on the conveyor and assume that the shipping bay can always accept outgoing pallets.

Traffic intensity. By "traffic intensity" we mean the input/output frequencies. Anticipated peak hours are of two types:

1. More pallets received than requested:
   average input rate: 2 pallets/min
   average output rate: 1 pallet/min

2. More pallets requested than received:
   average output rate: 3 pallets/min
   average input rate: 1 pallet/min

In all cases, arrivals of incoming pallets or requests for outgoing ones are Poisson distributed; that is, interarrival times are exponentially distributed. The simulation will not consider individual bins. We generate the coordinates of the bins for incoming and outgoing pallets as random numbers uniformly spread over intervals corresponding, respectively, to the four zones of the warehouse. These numbers are used to compute the traveling time for the crane. We could obviously go further in the refinement of the model, but we notice that in real life the computer will always choose the bin location that is as close as possible to the buffer within a zone. In this way, the strategy adopted above is conservative, at least as long as the warehouse is not almost completely full. When this is the case, the average traveling time for the cranes could increase because of incoming pallets being placed in the furthest bins. The situation should be studied carefully. In our model, this could be modeled easily by modifying the statistical functions used for bin-number allocation.

9.3 The GPSS Model

9.3.1 Correspondence between system elements and GPSS entities

Time units. The times are all expressed in $\frac{1}{10}$ s.

Pallets. Pallets are represented by transactions. Parameters are used for indirect addressing of the conveyor, corridor, crane, and bin positions.

Shipping and receiving bays. Shipping and receiving bays are not modeled. We observe the queue at the receiving bay and use a logic switch to control the serial movement of the input pallets from the receiving bay to the conveyor.

Conveyor. The pallets are separated by a distance of 1 m. Consequently, there is room for 38 pallets, which are numbered 1 to 38 and are represented by 38 facilities. Such a facility will be seized when the place is occupied by a pallet. When a pallet cannot leave the conveyor, because the buffer of the receiving corridor is full, it stays on the conveyor for a whole cycle. The degree of utilization of the conveyor is measured by the utilization of the 38 facilities and the statistics relating to three queues representing input pallets, output pallets, and cycling pallets on the conveyor.

Buffers. The input and output buffers of the corridors are represented by storages. The cranes always operate at the last position of the buffers, farthest from conveyor. The pallets move automatically in the buffers with the speed of the conveyor. A logic switch is used to control the serial movement of pallets from the output buffer to the conveyor.

Cranes. Cranes are represented by facilities but, to ease the modeling of the operations and gathering of statistical information, the following entities have been assigned to a crane:

1. Two facilities that measure the total time the crane is moving with a pallet and the total time the crane is moving with or without a pallet. These two values give a useful indication of system performance.
2. Two logic switches to control the logic of crane operation: alternately move an input and an output pallet.
3. One save location to store the crane position.
4. Two queues in addition to the three queues defined for the conveyor. The first records the time a pallet waits in its bin to be picked by the crane. The second records the additional waiting time of crane and pallet in front of a possibly full buffer.
5. Several functions and variables are used to compute the crane displacement time.

9.3.2 Parameters and save locations

Transaction parameters.

P1: Reference value used for computation of other parameters.

P2: Corridor number (1 to 10), used for indirect addressing of:
     crane facility, moving with a pallet
     output buffer storage
     crane logic switch for output
     queue of output pallet waiting for crane.

P3:   Corridor number +10 (11 to 20), used for indirect addressing of:
        crane facility, moving with or without pallet
        input buffer storage
        crane logic switch for input
        crane position save
        queue of output pallets in front of output buffer.

P4:   Corridor number +20 (21 to 30), used for indirect addressing of the output buffer logic switch, to conveyor.

P6:   Conveyor place (21 to 58), used for indirect addressing of the conveyor-place facilities.

P8:   Bin position, horizontal (1 to 50).

P9:   Bin position, vertical (0 to 9).

P10:   Combined bin positions (10*P8+P9).

Save locations.

X1:   Conveyor speed: time interval between two pallet places.

X2: $\frac{1}{4}$ of X1.

X3:   Crane speed, horizontal: time interval from one bin to the next.

X4:   Crane speed, vertical.

X5:   Input buffer length.

X6:   Output buffer length.

X7:   Mean interarrival times of input pallets.

X8:   Mean interarrival time of output pallets.

X11–20: Crane position, horizontal and vertical coordinates combined; see the variable POSIT.

9.3.3 Functions and variables

Functions.

EXPON: Exponential cumulative distribution function (inverted).

CORID: Corridor number for output pallets (uniform distribution 1 to 10).

POSHA: Horizontal bin position.

POSVA: Vertical bin position.
         POSHA and POSVA are specific to each type of zone allocation and will be discussed in detail later.

ABS1:   Absolute value of horizontal crane displacement.

ABS2:   Absolute value of vertical crane displacement.
         These functions compute the movement time for the cranes.

CORNR: Auxiliary "positive" function. Function = argument if greater than 0; otherwise, 0.

Variables.

CORI: Corridor number for input pallet, assigned serially: 1 for first pallet, 2 for second, ..., 10 for tenth, 1 for eleventh, and so on. CORI is computed as (ASSIGN block count)(mod 10) + 1.

ROUND: Time for a full cycle of the conveyor belt: ROUND = 38*X1.

IBUF: Time to move from first to last position in input buffer.

OBUF: Same for output buffer.

POSIT: Combination of the two coordinates of a bin: POSIT = 10*P8+P9.

IBUFP: Combination of the coordinates of a pallet in input buffer: IBUFP = 10*X5+2.

OBUFP: Combination of the coordinates of a pallet in output buffer: OBUFP = 10*X6+2.

CONIC: Conveyor time from receiving bay to corridor, P2: CONIC = (31+7*P2)*X2.

CONCO: Conveyor time from corridor, P2, to shipping bay: CONCO = (108−7*P2)*X2.

CONVI: Conveyor-place number at the receiving bay: CONVI = (clock time/X1)(mod 38)+21.

WAITI: Wait time at receiving bay until the next conveyor-place passage: WAITI = X1−1−(clock time)(mod X1).

CONVC: Conveyor-place number in front of a corridor; it is computed by means of a time offset to the shipping bay: CONVC = ((clock time + CONCO)/X1)(mod 38)+21.

WAITC: Wait time at a corridor until the next conveyor place passes: WAITC = X1−1−(clock time + CONCO)(mod X1).

CONXT: Next sequential conveyor place number: CONXT = (P6−20)(mod 38)+21.

HORIZ: Horizontal crane moving time between actual position and bin location: HORIZ = (crane save/10−P10/10)*X3.

VERTI: Vertical crane moving time between actual position and bin location: VERTI = (crane save(mod 10)−P10(mod 10))*X4.

VHDIF: Difference between vertical and horizontal crane moving times. It will be used to compute TCRAN when horizontal and vertical movements are combined. VHDIF = ABS2 (VERTI)−ABS1 (HORIZ).

TCRAN: Time for crane movement. In the initial program it is the sum of the horizontal and vertical displacement times. When both movements are combined, this function will be modified accordingly.

9.3.4 Numerical values

Input buffer length: X5=4.

Output buffer length: X6=2.

Conveyor speed: 20 m/min, X1=60; minimum time between passage of
                        two pallets.
Crane speeds: horizontal: 10 m/min, X3=60;
                        vertical: 1 m/min, X4=600.
Initial crane position: output buffer.
Input rate: 2 pallets/min, X7=300.
Output rate: 1 pallet/min, X8=600.

Further investigations should be made; in particular, the behavior of the system
should be studied to indicate the maximum input rates that could be accepted for the
corresponding output rates of 1 pallet/min and 3 pallets/min. The approximate
frequencies for the "peak hours" are:

1. output rate: 1 pallet/min
   input rate: 2 pallets/min
2. output rate: 3 pallets/min
   input rate: 1 pallet/min

The warehouse must be able to handle these loads.

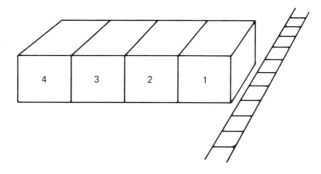

Figure 9.3 Zone allocation.

The zone allocation considered is shown in Figure 9.3. Frequencies of requests
are given in Table 9.1.

Table 9.1

Zone	1	2	3	4
Frequency (%)	40	30	20	10

9.3.5 Flowchart and program

General flowchart. The flowchart (see Figure 9.4), represents in general terms
the various operations that have to be performed on incoming and outgoing pallets
modeled by the transactions. When studying such a flowchart, one should always
remember that the processing of pallets in the model is quasi-parallel, so that at a
given time many transactions at various stages of processing are present in the model.

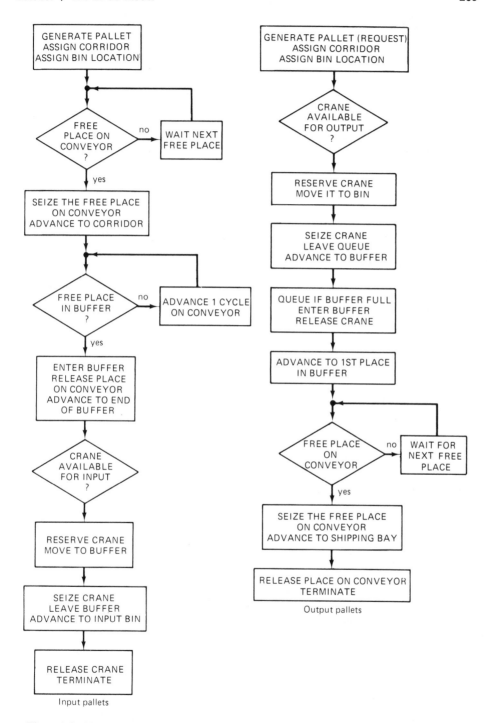

Figure 9.4 Movement of pallets.

The GPSS program.   The GPSS flowchart for input pallets is given in Figure 9.5. The flowchart for output pallets, which has a very similar form, is not shown. We now discuss the details of the GPSS program listed in Figure 9.6.

EQU Statements:

The EQU statement is used to reserve specific numerical values for the symbols defined on the left-hand side by the label field. For instance, the statement CONVR EQU 21(38),F associates facility number 21 with the symbol name CONVR and reserves the 38 consecutive numbers 21 to 58 for facilities. They correspond to the 38 facilities that constitute the conveyor. In the same way, the other EQU statements allocate numerical values to storages, switches, queues, and save locations.

Functions:

CORID uses the random-number generator RN7 to produce the corridor number, an integer distributed between 1 and 10 with a uniform probability.

POSHA generates the horizontal bin number of the pallet. It is:

Uniformly spread within a zone, which is represented by a continuous-type function.

Distributed in the four zones as specified by the stastistics of the problem:
   40% (argument between 0 and 0.4) in zone 1 (values 1 to 12)
   30% (argument between 0.4 and 0.7) in zone 2 (values 13 to 24)
   20% (argument between 0.7 and 0.9) in zone 3 (values 25 to 37)
   10% (argument between 0.9 and 1) in zone 4 (values 38 to 50).

The ordinate values are always increased by one unit to take care of the truncation which is made after the function is evaluated by linear interpolation between two successive values.

POSVA generates the vertical bin number, which is between 0 and 9, uniformly distributed.

POSHA and POSVA will be replaced for experiments with other zone-partition strategies in the warehouse. For these later experiments, we will first use functions POSHU and POSVU and then POSHO and POSVO, which will be discussed later.

ABS1 and ABS2 are used to take the absolute value of their argument, which is the difference between the position of the crane (horizontal and vertical) and a bin, multiplied by the time to move from one position to the next. They are used to evaluate the moving time of the crane: TCRAV in the original problem (when the cranes move first horizontally, then vertically), TCRAN later (when cranes can move in both directions simultaneously). TCRAV is the sum of the times for the horizontal and vertical displacements. TCRAN is equal to the maximum of the two. Note that in order to change from one strategy to the next, it is only necessary to change these variables in the ADVANCE statements that simulate the displacements of the cranes (blocks 37, 41, 63, and 67). If this seems too complicated, one could use another variable, for example in the ADVANCE blocks, and define it as TCRAV for the first strategy and as TCRAN for the second. The statements for the first strategy would

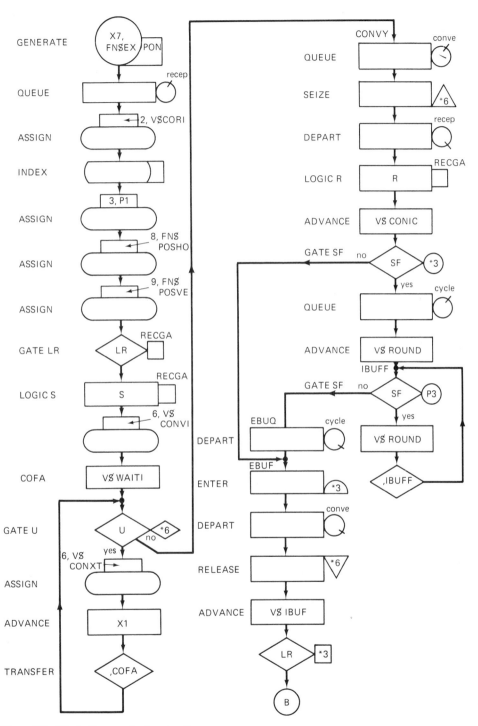

Figure 9.5 Block diagram for input pallets.

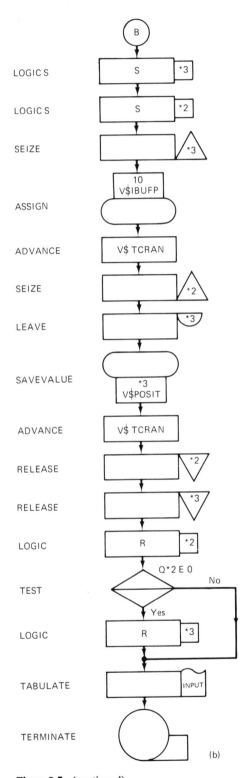

LOGIC S	S *3
LOGIC S	S *2
SEIZE	*3
ASSIGN	10 V$IBUFP
ADVANCE	V$ TCRAN
SEIZE	*2
LEAVE	*3
SAVEVALUE	*3 V$POSIT
ADVANCE	V$ TCRAN
RELEASE	*2
RELEASE	*3
LOGIC	R *2
TEST	Q*2 E 0 No / Yes
LOGIC	R *3
TABULATE	INPUT
TERMINATE	

(b)

Figure 9.5 (continued)

```
BLCCK
NUMBER  *LCC   OPERATION  A,B,C,D,E,F,G            COMMENTS                    CARD
                SIMULATE                                                       NUMBER
               EXPON FUNCTION   RN8,C24        EXPONENTIAL DISTRIBUTION - MEAN = 1.   1
         0.,0/0.1,0.104/0.2,0.222/0.3,0.355/0.4,0.505/C.5,0.69/0.6,0.915/           2
         0.7,1.2/0.75,1.38/0.8,1.6/0.84,1.83/C.88,2.12/0.9,2.3/0.92,2.52/           3
         0.94,2.81/C.95,2.99/0.96,3.2/0.97,3.5/0.98,3.9/0.99,4.6/0.995,5.3/         4
         0.998,6.2/0.999,7.0/0.9997,8.0                                             5
         ************************************************                          6
         *                                              *                          7
         *      SIMULATION OF AN AUTOMATIC WAREHOUSE     *                          8
         *                                              *                          9
         ************************************************                         10
                                                                                  11
         *** TRANSACTION PARAMETERS ***********************                       12
         *-----------------------------------------------                        13
                                                                                  14
         *    1    WORKING PARAMETER                                              15
         *    2    CORRIDOR NUMBER                                                16
         *    3    P2+10                                                          17
         *    4    P2+20                                                          18
         *    5                                                                   19
         *    6    CONVEYOR PLACE NUMBER                                          20
         *    7                                                                   21
         *    8    STCRE POSITION HCRIZONTAL (1-50)                               22
         *    9    STCRE POSITION VERTICAL    (0-5)                               23
         *   10    STCRE POSITION COMBINED   (10*HCR + VERT)                      24
                                                                                  25
         *** SPECIAL SAVEVALUE *****************************                       26
         *-----------------------------------------------                        27
         *    1    TIME OF MOUVEMENT FCR 1 CONVEYOR PLACE                         28
         *    2    1/4 OF X1                                                      29
         *    3    CRANE TIME HCRIZONTAL FCR 1 BIN PLACE                          30
         *    4    CRANE TIME VERTICAL                                            31
         *    5    INPUT BUFFER LENGTH                                            32
         *    6    OUTPUT BUFFER LENGTH                                           33
         *    7    MEAN INTERARRIVAL TIME OF INPUT PALLETS                        34
         *    8    MEAN INTERARRIVAL TIME OF OUTPUT PALLETS                       35
         *  11-20  CRANE POSITION (COMBINED AS P10)                              36
                                                                                  37
         *** ECUATIONS **********************************                         38
                                                                                  39
         CRANN  EQU      1(10),F               CRANES MCVING PALLETS             40
         CRANE  EQU      11(10),F              CRANES BUSY                       41
         CONVR  EQU      21(38),F              CONVEYOR PLACES                   42
         OBUFS  EQU      1(10),S               OUTPUT BUFFERS                    43
         IBUFS  EQU      11(10),S              INPUT BUFFERS                     44
         CSTO   EQU      1(10),L               CRANE STATUS FOR OUTPUT           45
         CSTI   EQU      11(10),L              CRANE STATUS FCR INPUT            46
         CBUSW  EQU      21(10),L              GATE IN OUTPUT BUFFER             47
         CRAPO  EQU      11(10),X              CRANE POSITION (COMBINED)         48
         CPAL   EQU      1(10),Q               CRANE OUTPUT-PALLET QUEUE         49
         CFALB  EQU      11(10),C              OUT-BUFFER OUT-PALLET QUEUE       50
         CONVE  EQU      21,Q                  INPUT-PALLET CONVEYCR BELT Q      51
         CONVO  EQU      22,Q                  OUTPUT-PALLET CONVEYOR BELT Q     52
         CYCLE  EQU      23,Q                  CYCLING TRANS. ON CONVEYO         53
         *                                                                       54
                                                                                  55
         *** FUNCTIONS *******************************************                 56
         *                                                                       57
         CORID  FUNCTION   RN7,C2             CORRIDOR FCR CUTPUT PALLET        58
         0,1/1,11                                                                59
         POSHA  FUNCTION   RN7,C5             HORIZONTAL POSITION OF PALLET     60
         0,1/.4,13/.7,25/.9,38/1,51                                             61
         POSVA  FUNCTION   RN7,C2             VERTICAL POSITION OF PALLET       62
         0,0/1,10                                                               63
         POSHU  FUNCTION   RN7,C2             HORIZONTAL PCS OF PALLET (ALTER)  64
         0,1/1,51                                                               65
         POSVU  FUNCTION   RN7,C5             VERTICAL PCS OF PALLET (ALTER)    66
         0,0/.4,2.5/.7,5/.9,7.5/1,10                                            67
         PCSHC  FUNCTION   RN7,C5             HORIZONTAL POS OF PALLET (ALTER 2)68
         0,1/.63,26/.84,36.3/.95,43.3/1,51                                      69
         PCSVE  FUNCTION   RN7,C5             VERTICAL PCS OF PALLET (ALTER 2)  70
         0,0/.63,5/.84,7.1/.95,8.6/1,10                                         71
         ABS1   FUNCTION   V$HORIZ,C3         ABS VALUE CF HORIZ CRANE MCVEMENT 72
         -10000,10000/0,0/10000,10000                                           73
         ABS2   FUNCTION   V$VERTI,C3         ABS VALUE OF VERTIC CRANE MOVEMEN 74
         -10000,10000/0,0/10000,1000C                                           75
         CORNR  FUNCTION   V$VHDIF,C3         TO COMP MAXIMUM (Y=X IF >0)       76
         -10000,0/0,0/10000,10000                                               77
         *                                                                       78
         *** VARIABLES *******************************************                 79
         *                                                                       80
         CCRI   VARIABLE   N$ASS2@10+1 CORRIDOR # FOR INPUT-PALLET              81
         ROUND  VARIABLE   X1*38              TIME FOR FULL CONV BELT MOVEMENT  82
         IBUF   VARIABLE   X5*X1              TIME TO LAST PLACE IN INPUT BUFFE 83
         OBUF   VARIABLE   (X6-1)*X1          TIME TC FIRST PLACE IN CUTPUT BUF 84
         POSIT  VARIABLE   10*P8+P9           COMBINED PALLET POSITION          85
         IBUFP  VARIABLE   10*X5+2            CCMB. PALLET POS IN INPUT BUFFER  86
         OBUFP  VARIABLE   10*X6+2            CCMB. PALLET POS IN CUTPUT BUFFER 87
```

Figure 9.6 GPSS program for warehouse model.

```
        CONIC VARIABLE    (31+7*P2)*X2   TIME FROM INPUT DOCK TO CORRIDOR        88
        CONCO VARIABLE    (108-7*F2)*X2  TIME FROM CORRIDOR TO OUTPUT DOCK       89
        CCNXT VARIABLE    (P6-20)a38+21  NEXT CONVEYOR PLACE #                   90
        WAITI VARIABLE    X1-1-C1aX1    INPUT DOCK WAIT TIME FOR NEXT CONV PLACE 91
        CCNVI VARIABLE    (C1/X1)a38+21  CONVEYOR PLACE # AT INPUT DOCK          92
        WAITC VARIABLE    X1-1-(C1+V$CCNCO)aX1   WAIT TIME FCR NEXT CONVEYOR     93
        *                                        PLACE AT CORRIDOR              94
        CONVC VARIABLE    ((C1+V$CONCO)/X1)a38+21 CCNV. PLACE # AT CORRIDOR      95
        HORIZ VARIABLE    (X*3/10-P10/10)*X3     HORIZ. DIFF CRANE - PALLET      96
        VERTI VARIABLE    (X*3a10-P10a10)*X4     VERT. DIFF CRANE - PALLET       97
        VHDIF VARIABLE    FN$ABS2-FN$ABS1        TIME DIFFER. VERT TC HCRIZ      98
        TCRAN VARIABLE    FN$ABS1+FN$CCRNR       TIME FOR CRANE CISPLACEMENT     99
        TCRAV VARIABLE    FN$ABS1+FN$ABS2        DITO (ALTER FOR 1 DIR)          100
        *                                                                       101
        *                                                                       102
        *** TABLES ***************************************                      103
        *                                                                       104
        INPUT TABLE       M1,0,1000,30 TOTAL TRANSIT TIME FOR INPUT PALLETS     105
        OUTPU TABLE       M1,0,1000,30 TOTAL TRANSIT TIME FOR OUTPUT PALLETS    106
        *                                                                       107
        *** INPUT PALLETS ********************************                      108
 1      *                                                                       109
 1             GENERATE   X7,FN$EXFCN GENERATE INPUT PALLETS                    110
 2             QUEUE      RECEP        INPUT DOCK QUEUE                          111
 3      ASS2   ASSIGN     2,V$CORI     DESTINATION CORRIDOR OF PALLET           112
 4             INDEX      2,10         P1=P2+10                                 113
 5             ASSIGN     3,P1         PARAMETER 3 = PAR.2 + 10                 114
 6             ASSIGN     8,FN$POSHO   STORE HCRIZ POS OF PALLET                115
 7             ASSIGN     9,FN$POSVE   STORE VERTIC POS CF PALLET               116
        *                                                                       117
 8             GATE LR    RECGA        CNLY 1 PALLET CAN MOVE TO CCNVEYO        118
 9             LOGIC S    RECGA        CLOSE GATE                               119
10             ASSIGN     6,V$CCNVI    CCNV. PLACE # AT DOCK                    120
11             ADVANCE    V$WAITI      WAIT FOR THIS CCNV. PLACE                121
        *                                                                       122
12      CCFA   GATE U     *6,CONVY     IS THIS CONV. PLACE EMPTY?               123
13             ASSIGN     6,V$CCNXT    NO CF FOLLCWING PLACE                    124
14             ADVANCE    X1           WAIT FCR NEXT PLACE                      125
15             TRANSFER   ,CCFA        GO TC EMPTY TEST                         126
        *                                                                       127
16      CONVY  QUEUE      CONVE        QUEUE PALLET CNTO CONVEYOR               128
17             SEIZE      *6           PUT PALLET ONTO DETERM.PLACE             129
18             DEPART     RECEP        LEAVE INPUT DOCK QUEUE                    130
19             LOGIC R    RECGA        OPEN GATE FOR NEXT PALLET                131
20             ADVANCE    V$CONIC      TIME TO GET TO CORRIDOR                  132
        *                                                                       133
21             GATE SF    *3,EBUF      TEST IF INPLT BUFFER FULL                134
22             QUEUE      CYCLE        Q. OF CYCLING TRANSACTIONS               135
23             ADVANCE    V$ROUND      FULL. TIME FCR 1 CCNV.CYCLE              136
24      IBUFF  GATE SF    *3,EBUQ      TEST IF INPUT BUFFER IS FULL             137
25             ADVANCE    V$ROUND      FULL. TIME FOR 1 CONV.CYCLE              138
26             TRANSFER   ,IBUFF       GC TO BUFFER TEST                        139
27      EBUQ   DEPART     CYCLE        LEAVE CYCLING QUEUE                      140
        *                                                                       141
28      EBUF   ENTER      *3           CORRIDCR INPUT BUFFER                    142
29             DEPART     CONVE        LEAVE CONV.BELT QUEUE                    143
30             RELEASE    *6           FREE OCCUP. CONV.PLACE                   144
31             ADVANCE    V$IBUF       MIN.TIME IN INPUT BUFFER                 145
        *                                                                       146
32             GATE LR    *3           IS CRANE AVAIL. FOR INPUT                147
33             LOGIC S    *3           INDICATE CRANE BUSY FOR INPUT            148
34             LCGIC S    *2           INDICATE CRANE BUSY FOR OUTPUT           149
        *                                                                       150
35             SEIZE      *3           RESERVE CRANE FOR INPUT PALLET           151
36             ASSIGN     10,V$IBUFP   P10=PRESENT PALLET POSITION              152
37             ADVANCE    V$TCRAN      TIME TO MOVE CRANE TC INP.BUFFER         153
38             SEIZE      *2           TAKE CRANE TO MOVE TO BIN POS            154
39             LEAVE      *3           LEAVE CORRIDOR INP.BUFFER                155
40             SAVEVALUE  *3,V$PCSIT   BIN POS WHERE PALLET IS STCRED           156
41             ADVANCE    V$TCRAN      MOVE CRANE WITH PALLET TO BIN POS        157
42             RELEASE    *2           FREE CRANE                               158
43             RELEASE    *3           FREE CRANE                               159
44             LOGIC R    *2                                                    160
45             TEST E     Q*2,0,QNE    TEST IF THERE IS CUT PUT PALLET          161
46             LCGIC R    *3           NO. INCICATE CRANE AVAIL.FOR INPU        162
47      QNE    TABULATE   INPUT        TAB FCR TOTAL TRANSIT TIME               163
48             TERMINATE               TAKE PALLET OUT CF SYSTEM                164
                                                                               165
        *** OUTPUT PALLETS ****************************************             166
                                                                               167
49             GENERATE   X8,FN$EXFCN  GENERATE OUTPUT PALLET                   168
50             ASSIGN     2,FN$CORID   DETERMINE CORRID. NBR.                   169
51             INDEX      2,10         P1=P2+10                                 170
52             ASSIGN     3,P1         PARAM 3 = PARAM 2 + 10                   171
53             INDEX      2,20         P1=P2+20                                 172
54             ASSIGN     4,P1         PARAM 4 = PARAM 2 + 20                   173
55             ASSIGN     8,FN$POSHO   HORIZ. POS CF OUTPUT PALLET              174
56             ASSIGN     9,FN$PCSVE   VERTIC.POS CF OUTPUT PALLET
```

Figure 9.6 (continued)

```
57              QUEUE       *2              PALLET IN OUT QUEUE FCR CRANE              175
58              GATE LR     *2              IS CRANE AVAIL. FCR OUTPUT?                176
59              LOGIC S     *2              INDICATE CRANE BUSY FOR OUTPUT             177
60              LOGIC S     *3              INDICATE CRANE BUSY FCR INPUT              178
                                                                                       179
                                                                                       180
61              SEIZE       *3              RESERVE CRANE FOR OUTPUT PALLET            181
62              ASSIGN      10,V$POSIT      P10=ACTUAL PALLET PCSITION                 182
63              ADVANCE     V$TCRAN         MOVE CRANE TO OUTPUT PALLET                183
64              SEIZE       *2              TAKE CRANE TC MCVE TO BUFFER               184
65              DEPART      *2              LEAVE QUEUE CF CRANE                       185
66              SAVEVALUE   *3,V$CBUFP      CRANE POS + OUTPUT BUFFER                  186
67              ADVANCE     V$TCRAN         MOVE CRANE WITH PALLET TO BUFFER           187
                                                                                       188
68              CUEUE       *3              QUEUE IF BUFFER IS FULL                    189
69              ENTER       *2              MOVE PALLET INTO BUFFER                    190
70              DEPART      *3              LEAVE OUTPLT BUFFER QUEUE                  191
71              RELEASE     *2              FREE CRANE                                 192
72              RELEASE     *3              FREE CRANE                                 193
73              LCGIC R     *3              INDICATE CRANE AVAIL. FOR INPUT            194
74              GATE SE     *3,SNE          IS INPUT BUFFER EMPTY?                     195
75              LOGIC R     *2              YES. INDICATE CRANE AVAIL. FCR CUT         196
                                                                                       197
76      SNE     ADVANCE     V$CBUF          MIN.TIME IN CUTPUT BUFFER                  198
77              GATE LR     *4              ONLY 1 PALLET CAN MCVE TC CCNV.BE          199
78              LOGIC S     *4              CLOSE THE GATE                             200
79              ASSIGN      6,V$CCNVC       P6=CONV.PLACE NBR.                         201
80              ADVANCE     V$WAITC         WAIT FOR NEXT CONV.PLACE                   202
                                                                                       203
81      CCFO    GATE U      *6,CCNFC        IS THIS CONV. PLACE EMPTY?                 204
82              ASSIGN      6,V$CCNXT       NO. NEXT CCNV. PLACE NR.                   205
83              ADVANCE     X1              WAIT FCR NEXT PLACE                        206
84              TRANSFER    ,COFO           GO TC EMPTY TEST                           207
85      CONFO   QUEUE       CONVC           CCNV.QUEUE FCR CUTPUT PALLETS              208
86              SEIZE       *6              PUT PALLET ONTO CCNV.PLACE                 209
87              LEAVE       *2              LEAVE OUTPUT BUFFER                        210
88              LOGIC R     *4              OPEN GATE FCR NEXT PALLET IN BUFF          211
89              ADVANCE     V$CONCO         TIME TO GET TC OUTPLT DOCK                 212
                                                                                       213
90              RELEASE     *6              FREE CCNV. PLACE                           214
91              DEPART      CONVO           LEAVE CONV. QUEUE FCR OUTPUT PALL          215
92              TABULATE    CUTPU           TABUL. TOTAL TRANS.TIME OUTPUT PA          216
93              TERMINATE                   TAKE PALLET CUT CF SYSTEM                  217
                                                                                       218
                                                                                       219
        *** DEFINITIONS *************************************************              220
                                                                                       221
                STCRAGE     S1-S10,2/S11-S20,4                                         222
                INITIAL     X1,60/X2,15/X3,30/X4,150/X5,4/X6,2                         223
                INITIAL     X7,200/X8,6CC                                             224
                INITIAL     X11-X20,22                                                225
                                                                                       226
        *** TIME CONTROL ***********************************************              227
                                                                                       228
94              GENERATE    36000                                                     229
95              TERMINATE   1                                                         230
                START       1,NP                                                      231
                RESET                                                                  232
                START       8                                                        233
                                                                                       234
        *** REPORT SECTION *********************************************              235
                REPORT                                                                236
                EJECT                                                                 237
        CLO     TITLE       ,C L C C K   S T A T I S T I C S                          238
                SPACE       4                                                         239
        BLO     TITLE       ,B L C C K   C O U N T S                                  240
                EJECT                                                                  241
        *I N P U T   D O C K   C U E U E                                              242
                SPACE       1                                                         243
        QUE     INCLUDE     Q$RECEP/1,2,3,4,5,6,7,8,10                                244
                SPACE       4                                                         245
        *C O N V E Y O R   B E L T   C L E U E S                                      246
                SPACE       1                                                         247
        QUE     INCLUDE     C$CCNVE-C$CYCLE/1,2,3,7,10                                248
                SPACE       4                                                         249
        *C O N V E Y O R   B E L T   U T I L I Z A T I C N                            250
                SPACE       1                                                         251
        FAC     INCLUDE     F21-F58/1,2,3,4                                           252
                EJECT                                                                 253
        *I N P U T   B U F F E R S                                                    254
                SPACE       1                                                         255
        STO     INCLUDE     S11-S20/1,2,3,4,5,6,7,8                                   256
                SPACE       4                                                         257
        *C L T P L T   B U F F E R S                                                  258
                SPACE       1                                                         259
        STO     INCLUDE     S1-S10/1,2,3,4,5,6,7,8                                    260
                SPACE       4                                                         261
        *C R A N E   U T I L I Z A T I C N      - M O V I N G -                       262
                SPACE       1                                                         263
        FAC     INCLUDE     F11-F20/1,2,3,4                                           264
                SPACE       1
```

Figure 9.6   (continued)

```
*                                 - O C C U P I E D -                              265
          SPACE      1                                                            266
FAC       INCLUDE    F1-F10/1,2,3,4                                               267
          EJECT                                                                   268
*O U T P U T        PALLETS BEFCRE GETTING   C R A N E                            269
          SPACE      1                                                            270
CUE       INCLUDE    C1-C10/1,2,3,4,7,10                                          271
          SPACE      4                                                            272
*O U T P U T        PALLETS WAITING FCR OUTPUT   B U F F E R                      273
          SPACE      1                                                            274
QUE       INCLUDE    C11-Q20/1,4,5,6,7,8                                          275
          SPACE      4                                                            276
*C R A N E    P C S I T I C N S                                                   277
          SPACE      1                                                            278
SAV       INCLUDE    ,X11-X20                                                     279
          EJECT                                                                   280
*TOTAL    T R A N S . T I M E   FCR   I N P U T   PALLETS                         281
          SPACE      1                                                            282
TAB       INCLUDE    T1/1,2,3,4,5,10,11,12,13,15,16                               283
          EJECT                                                                   284
*TOTAL    T R A N S . T I M E   FCR   O U T P U T   PALLETS                       285
          SPACE      1                                                            286
TAB       INCLUDE    T2/1,2,3,4,5,10,11,12,13,15,16                               287
          EJECT                                                                   288
          GRAPH      FR,21,50                                                     289
          ORIGIN     52,8                                                         290
          X          ,1,3,,,,NC                                                   291
          Y          ,0,,1,10,5                                                   292
30        STATEMENT  57,40,C C N V E Y C R   U T I L I Z A T I O N                293
          ENDGRAPH                                                               294
          EJECT                                                                   295
          GRAPH      FR,11,20                                                     296
          ORIGIN     52,8                                                         297
          X          ,1,3,,,,NO                                                   298
          Y          ,0,,1,10,5                                                   299
15        STATEMENT  55,44,C R A N E   U T I L I Z A T I C N   MOVING             300
          ENDGRAPH                                                               301
          EJECT                                                                   302
          GRAPH      FR,1,10                                                      303
          ORIGIN     52,8                                                         304
          X          ,1,3,,,,NC                                                   305
          Y          ,0,,1,10,5                                                   306
15        STATEMENT  57,46,C R A N E   U T I L I Z A T I C N   CCCUPIED           307
          ENDGRAPH                                                               308
          EJECT                                                                   309
          GRAPH      TP,INPUT,,I                                                  310
          ORIGIN     52,8                                                         311
          X          ,1,3,0,1,30,NC                                              312
          Y          0,2,25,2                                                     313
34        STATEMENT  53,5, 6CCC                                                   314
58        STATEMENT  53,5,12000                                                   315
82        STATEMENT  53,5,18CCC                                                   316
106       STATEMENT  53,5,24CCC                                                   317
20        STATEMENT  57,44,T R A N S . T I M E  FOR  I N P U T  PALLETS           318
          ENDGRAPH                                                               319
          EJECT                                                                   320
          GRAPH      TP,OUTPU,,O                                                  321
          ORIGIN     42,8                                                         322
          X          ,1,3,0,1,30,NC                                              323
          Y          0,2,20,2                                                     324
34        STATEMENT  43,5, 6CCC                                                   325
58        STATEMENT  43,5,12CCC                                                   326
82        STATEMENT  43,5,18000                                                   327
1C6       STATEMENT  43,5,24000                                                   328
20        STATEMENT  47,46,T R A N S . T I M E  FOR  C L T P L T  PALLETS         329
          ENDGRAPH                                                               330
          EJECT                                                                   331
          ENC                                                                     332
```

Figure 9.6 (continued)

read XXX VARIABLE V$TCRAV, and for the second, XXX VARIABLE V$TCRAN.

In fact, this method of programming is preferable. It does not involve modifications to the actual program, which is always a potential source of errors.

Program for Input Pallets:

In the first paragraph (blocks 1 to 7), we generate pallets with interarrival times exponentially distributed with an average of X7, which can therefore be modified by changing the contents of save 7, and then assign the corridor number to P2, this value plus 10 to P3, and the horizontal and vertical positions of the bin to P8 and P9. Then the pallet finds a free place on the conveyor. First, we compute the number of this place and the time for the conveyor to bring it exactly in front of the receiving bay. Then GATE block 12 asks if the conveyor place is free; if so, the pallet is put in queue CONVE to record how long the pallet is on the conveyor and then put in an ADVANCE block, to spend the time to the corridor. If the buffer is not full (block 21), the pallet enters, departs from the queue, and the conveyor place is released. Then the pallet is moved to the end of the buffer, where it waits until the crane is available. If the buffer is full, the pallet is put on a new queue, CYCLE, and scheduled to make a complete cycle on the conveyor (blocks 22 and 23). It then tests if there is a free place in the buffer and, if not, starts another cycle.

If the conveyor place in front of the bay is occupied (GATE block 12), the pallet waits for the next place to pass in front of the bay and checks if it is free (blocks 13 to 15).

When the crane is available for input (logic switch reset as tested by the GATE block 32), it is immediately made busy and facility P3 (recording crane busy time with or without a pallet) is seized. The present position of the pallet (horizontal and vertical combined) is assigned to P10 and the crane is moved to the input buffer (ADVANCE block 37). When this time has elapsed, facility P2 (recording crane busy time with a pallet) is seized, a place is made available in the buffer (block 39), the location of the bin where the pallet is to be stored is put in save location P3 (block 40), and the crane is moved to that location (block 41). When the traveling time has elapsed, the two facilities used for the crane are released, switch P2 is reset to indicate that the crane is available for an output operation, and we check for an output request pending (block 45). If not, switch P3 is reset, thus making the crane again available for input. The TABULATE block 47 gathers, in table INPUT, the statistics of the total time (transit time) spent by the pallet from its arrival at the receiving bay to its storage in the bin.

Program for Output Pallets:

The program for output pallets is quite similar to that for input pallets so we discuss only a few details. In the first paragraph (blocks 49 to 58), the request is generated with corridor and bin location, the parameters are prepared, and the pallet is put in queue P2, where it waits for the crane to be available. When this occurs, the necessary operations are performed and the pallet is put in the output buffer; queue P2 records the waiting time, if any, in front of the buffer, and a test is made (block 74), to decide if the crane has to make an input operation or, if no pallet is waiting in the input buffer, has to be made available for another output operation. The pallet is moved to the end of the buffer and will take the first available place on the conveyor. When a place is found, the pallet is put in queue CONVO (recording the time the pallet is on the conveyor), a place is made available in the output buffer, and the pallet is moved to the shipping bay. Its time in the system—difference between order and delivery time—is recorded in the table OUTPU.

Time Control:

We use an auxiliary clock to generate a transaction every hour. In our experiments we have simulated the system for 1 hour as an initialization period, reset the statistics, and run the experiment for 8 hours. This can easily be changed.

Report Program:

This section of the program is optional because all information of interest is printed at the end of the run. It has been added to illustrate some features provided by the GPSS report generator:

1. It selects the entities for which information is requested and the order of appearance.
2. It selects the statistics to be printed with the titles specified by the user.
3. It plots, in graphical form, the utilization figures for the conveyor and the cranes.

This report program produces a very convenient output document, part of which has been reproduced as Figure 9.7.

9.4 Experiments and Results

During the simulation experiments we soon found that the size of the output buffers was adequate with two places and that the size of the input buffers was insufficient only when the cranes could not follow. We could have increased their size considerably without resolving the difficulty. The problems to be studied were clearly (1) the crane movements and speed, (2) the zone allocation, and (3) the conveyor speed.

The strategy to follow was dictated by the problem environment: first, find acceptable rules for zone allocation and for the operation of the cranes which do not raise the costs of the warehouse; then, if necessary, investigate additional improvements by modifying the technical data of cranes and conveyor. However, increases in the speed would possibly increase the capital and maintenance costs of the equipment. Such considerations could lead to a reappraisal of the cost effectiveness of the project.

9.4.1 Choice of zone allocation

Vertical slices (functions POSHA and POSVA). The run with the initial data and zone allocation (see Figure 9.3) showed that the system could not handle the input pallet rate. After 30 minutes of simulated time, the cranes were fully busy, the input buffers full, more and more pallets were cycling on the conveyor, and the queue of pallets on the receiving bay was growing. No problem was encountered for the output pallets, because every one could be moved after an input pallet was brought in.

Horizontal slices. The zone allocation was changed from vertical to horizontal slices (see Figure 9.8) with zone 1 (most frequently accessed) at the conveyor level and zone 4 (least frequently accessed) at the top. With this allocation, using the functions POSHU and POSVU, the results were slightly better, but the system could still not handle the traffic.

RELATIVE CLOCK   288000 ABSOLUTE CLOCK   324000

BLOCK COUNTS

BLOCK	CURRENT	TOTAL	BLOCK	CURRENT	TOTAL	BLOCK	CURRENT	TOTAL	BLOCK	CURRENT	TOTAL	BLOCK	CURRENT	TOTAL
1	0	1425	11	0	1425	21	0	1421	31	4	1421	41	3	1420
2	0	1425	12	0	1681	22	0	4	32	0	1422	42	0	1420
3	0	1425	13	0	256	23	0	4	33	0	1422	43	0	1420
4	0	1425	14	0	256	24	0	6	34	0	1422	44	0	1420
5	0	1425	15	0	256	25	0	2	35	0	1422	45	0	1420
6	0	1425	16	0	1425	26	0	2	36	0	1422	46	0	1045
7	0	1425	17	0	1425	27	0	4	37	6	1422	47	0	1420
8	0	1425	18	0	1425	28	0	1421	38	0	1420	48	0	1420
9	0	1425	19	0	1425	29	0	1421	39	0	1420	49	0	499
10	0	1425	20	8	1425	30	0	1421	40	0	1420	50	0	499

BLOCK	CURRENT	TOTAL	BLOCK	CURRENT	TOTAL	BLOCK	CURRENT	TOTAL	BLOCK	CURRENT	TOTAL	BLOCK	CURRENT	TOTAL
51	0	499	61	0	501	71	0	503	81	0	637	91	0	504
52	0	499	62	0	501	72	0	503	82	0	134	92	0	504
53	0	499	63	0	501	73	0	503	83	0	134	93	0	504
54	0	499	64	0	503	74	0	503	84	0	134	94	0	8
55	0	499	65	0	503	75	0	60	85	0	503	95	0	8
56	0	499	66	0	503	76	0	503	86	0	503			
57	1	499	67	0	503	77	0	503	87	0	503			
58	0	501	68	0	503	78	0	503	88	0	503			
59	0	501	69	0	503	79	0	503	89	1	503			
60	0	501	70	0	503	80	0	503	90	0	504			

INPUT DOCK QUEUE

QUEUE	MAXIMUM CONTENTS	AVERAGE CONTENTS	TOTAL ENTRIES	ZERO ENTRIES	PERCENT ZEROS	AVERAGE TIME/TRANS	$AVERAGE TIME/TRANS	CURRENT CONTENTS
RECEP	4	.204	1425	16	1.1	41.352	41.822	

CONVEYOR BELT QUEUES

QUEUE	MAXIMUM CONTENTS	AVERAGE CONTENTS	AVERAGE TIME/TRANS	CURRENT CONTENTS
CONVE	15	5.198	1047.693	8
CONVO	6	1.837	1047.710	1
CYCLE	1	.047	3420.000	

CONVEYOR BELT UTILIZATION

FACILITY	AVERAGE UTILIZATION	NUMBER ENTRIES	AVERAGE TIME/TRAN
CONVR	.207	56	1065.000
22	.182	54	973.073
23	.209	60	1007.016
24	.176	51	997.352
25	.183	50	1057.199
26	.191	56	982.517
27	.180	51	1016.764
28	.190	52	1056.365
29	.194	51	1057.666
30	.195	54	1042.500
31	.167	48	1007.833
32	.197	55	1033.908
33	.196	52	1086.922
34	.212	56	1095.000
35	.171	43	1147.325
36	.184	50	1061.399
37	.183	52	1014.230
38	.182	47	1117.340
39	.173	45	1111.333
40	.131	36	1051.250
41	.203	56	1048.125
42	.145	39	1074.589
43	.136	42	937.476
44	.204	59	1000.677
45	.206	60	991.750
46	.216	59	1058.898
47	.137	38	1041.710
48	.179	48	1079.687
49	.214	60	1029.233
50	.212	54	1131.944
51	.201	49	1183.775
52	.187	54	999.462
53	.172	49	1015.714
54	.172	47	1058.616
55	.183	50	1055.099
56	.165	48	992.187
57	.178	48	1070.937
58	.203	55	1066.618

Figure 9.7 GPSS output.

I N P U T   B U F F E R S

STORAGE	CAPACITY	AVERAGE CONTENTS	AVERAGE UTILIZATION	ENTRIES	AVERAGE TIME/TRAN	CURRENT CONTENTS	MAXIMUM CONTENTS
IBUFS	4	.971	.242	143	1957.167	1	4
12	4	.504	.126	143	1016.636		2
13	4	.553	.138	144	1106.097	2	3
14	4	.644	.161	143	1298.265	2	4
15	4	.518	.129	143	1045.104		3
16	4	.559	.139	143	1126.349		2
17	4	.615	.153	143	1239.979	1	3
18	4	.600	.150	143	1209.377	1	3
19	4	.567	.141	143	1142.797	2	3
20	4	.714	.178	142	1448.253	1	3

O U T P U T   B U F F E R S

STORAGE	CAPACITY	AVERAGE CONTENTS	AVERAGE UTILIZATION	ENTRIES	AVERAGE TIME/TRAN	CURRENT CONTENTS	MAXIMUM CONTENTS
CBUFS	2	.025	.012	66	110.515		2
2	2	.015	.007	42	109.642		1
3	2	.022	.011	56	114.071		1
4	2	.019	.009	51	108.666		1
5	2	.011	.005	33	96.060		1
6	2	.020	.010	54	108.555		1
7	2	.015	.007	42	104.428		1
8	2	.024	.012	68	104.602		1
9	2	.011	.005	34	93.500		1
10	2	.018	.009	57	95.017		1

C R A N E   U T I L I Z A T I O N   - M O V I N G -

FACILITY	AVERAGE UTILIZATION	NUMBER ENTRIES	AVERAGE TIME/TRAN
CRANE	.831	209	1145.818
12	.718	186	1112.741
13	.783	199	1134.366
14	.806	193	1203.419
15	.700	176	1145.560
16	.783	198	1140.151
17	.750	186	1161.451
18	.785	211	1072.606
19	.700	175	1152.856
20	.807	199	1168.205

- O C C U P I E D -

FACILITY	AVERAGE UTILIZATION	NUMBER ENTRIES	AVERAGE TIME/TRAN
CRANN	.500	208	692.307
2	.407	186	630.806
3	.460	198	669.656
4	.461	192	692.656
5	.384	176	625.825
6	.447	198	651.211
7	.414	185	645.237
8	.468	210	642.714
9	.380	175	625.376
10	.467	198	680.454

O U T P U T   PALLETS BEFORE GETTING   C R A N E

QUEUE	MAXIMUM CONTENTS	AVERAGE CONTENTS	TOTAL ENTRIES	AVERAGE TIME/TRANS	CURRENT CONTENTS
CPAL	5	.640	66	2794.651	
2	4	.237	43	1592.674	1
3	3	.277	56	1426.852	
4	2	.247	51	1394.941	
5	2	.133	33	1166.666	
6	4	.332	54	1770.888	
7	3	.229	42	1572.452	
8	3	.450	68	1508.705	
9	2	.157	34	1337.970	
10	4	.328	57	1661.350	

Figure 9.7 (continued)

O U T P U T   PALLETS WAITING FOR OUTPUT   B U F F E R

QUEUE	TOTAL ENTRIES	ZERO ENTRIES	PERCENT ZEROS	AVERAGE TIME/TRANS	$AVERAGE TIME/TRANS
OPA	66	66	100.0	.000	.000
12	42	42	100.0	.000	.000
13	56	56	100.0	.000	.000
14	51	51	100.0	.000	.000
15	33	33	100.0	.000	.000
16	54	54	100.0	.000	.000
17	42	42	100.0	.000	.000
18	68	68	100.0	.000	.000
19	34	34	100.0	.000	.000
20	57	57	100.0	.000	.000

C R A N E   P O S I T I O N S

CONTENTS OF FULLWORD SAVEVALUES (NON-ZERO)

SAVEVALUE NR.	VALUE	NR.	VALUE	NR.	VALUE	NR.	VALUE	NR.	VALUE
CRAPO	26	12	274	13	188	14	15	15	253
16	189	17	227	18	253	19	388	20	421

TOTAL   T R A N S . T I M E   FOR   I N P U T   PALLETS

TABLE INPUT

ENTRIES IN TABLE	MEAN ARGUMENT		STANDARD DEVIATION		SUM OF ARGUMENTO	
1420	2993.523		1069.000		4250804.000	NON-WEIGHTED
UPPER LIMIT	OBSERVED FREQUENCY	PER CENT OF TOTAL	CUMULATIVE PERCENTAGE	MULTIPLE OF MEAN	DEVIATION FROM MEAN	
0	0	.00	.0	-.000	-2.800	
1000	0	.00	.0	.334	-1.864	
2000	156	10.98	10.9	.668	-.929	
3000	695	48.94	59.9	1.002	.006	
4000	400	28.16	88.0	1.336	.941	
5000	101	7.11	95.2	1.670	1.876	
6000	44	3.09	98.3	2.004	2.812	
7000	13	.91	99.2	2.338	3.747	
8000	2	.14	99.3	2.672	4.683	
9000	3	.21	99.5	3.006	5.618	
10000	4	.28	99.8	3.340	6.554	
11000	1	.07	99.9	3.674	7.489	
12000	0	.00	99.9	4.008	8.425	
13000	1	.07	100.0	4.342	9.360	

REMAINING FREQUENCIES ARE ALL ZERO

TOTAL   T R A N S . T I M E   FOR   O U T P U T   PALLETS

TABLE OUTPU

ENTRIES IN TABLE	MEAN ARGUMENT		STANDARD DEVIATION		SUM OF ARGUMENTO	
504	3597.323		1596.000		1813051.000	NON-WEIGHTED
UPPER LIMIT	OBSERVED FREQUENCY	PER CENT OF TOTAL	CUMULATIVE PERCENTAGE	MULTIPLE OF MEAN	DEVIATION FROM MEAN	
0	0	.00	.0	-.000	-2.253	
1000	0	.00	.0	.277	-1.627	
2000	39	7.73	7.7	.555	-1.000	
3000	156	30.95	38.6	.833	-.374	
4000	167	33.13	71.8	1.111	.252	
5000	72	14.28	86.1	1.389	.878	
6000	38	7.53	93.6	1.667	1.505	
7000	13	2.57	96.2	1.945	2.132	
8000	7	1.38	97.6	2.223	2.758	
9000	5	.99	98.6	2.501	3.385	
10000	2	.39	99.0	2.779	4.011	
11000	0	.00	99.0	3.057	4.638	
12000	3	.59	99.6	3.335	5.264	
13000	2	.39	100.0	3.613	5.891	

REMAINING FREQUENCIES ARE ALL ZERO

Figure 9.7 (continued)

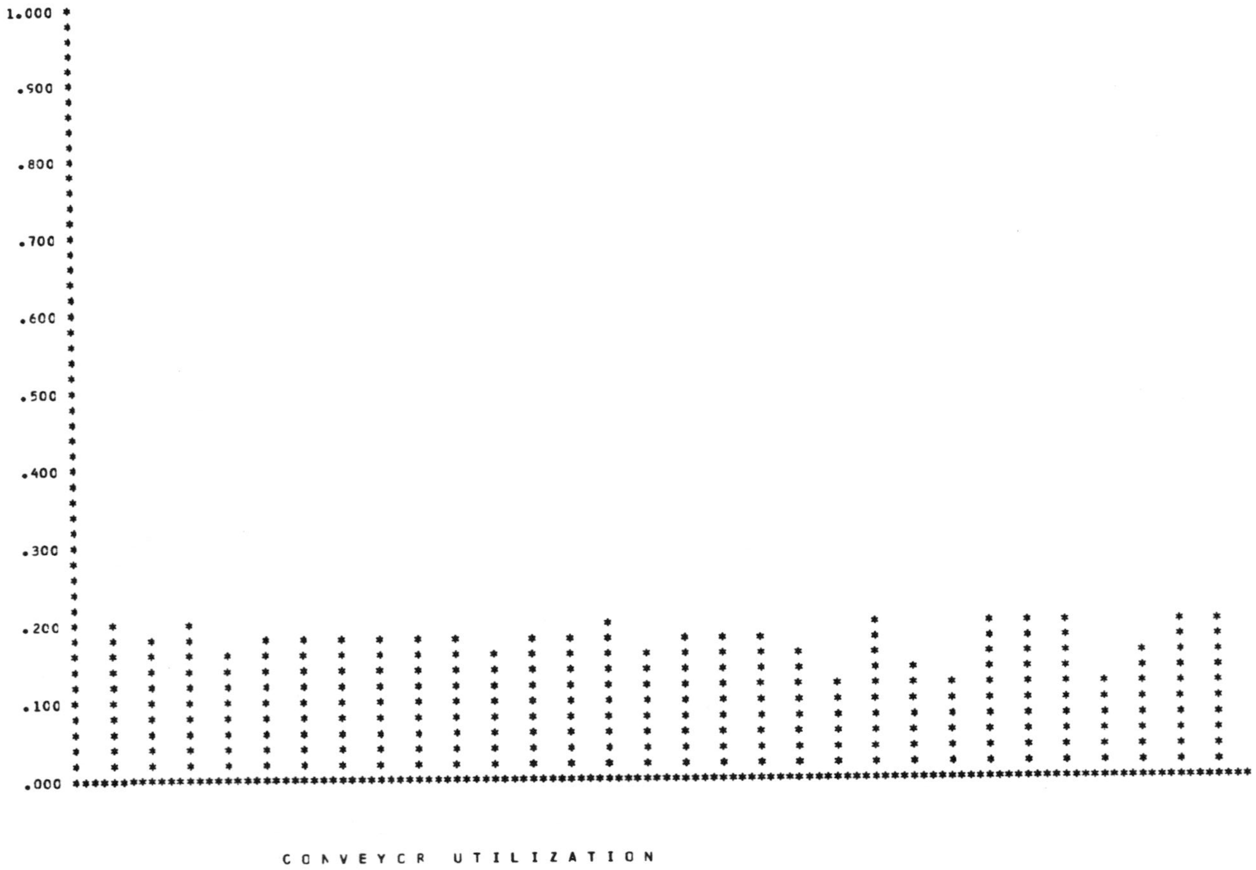

CONVEYOR UTILIZATION

Figure 9.7 (continued)

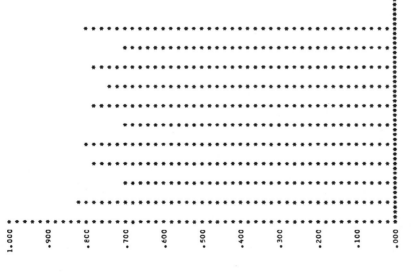

Figure 9.7 (continued)

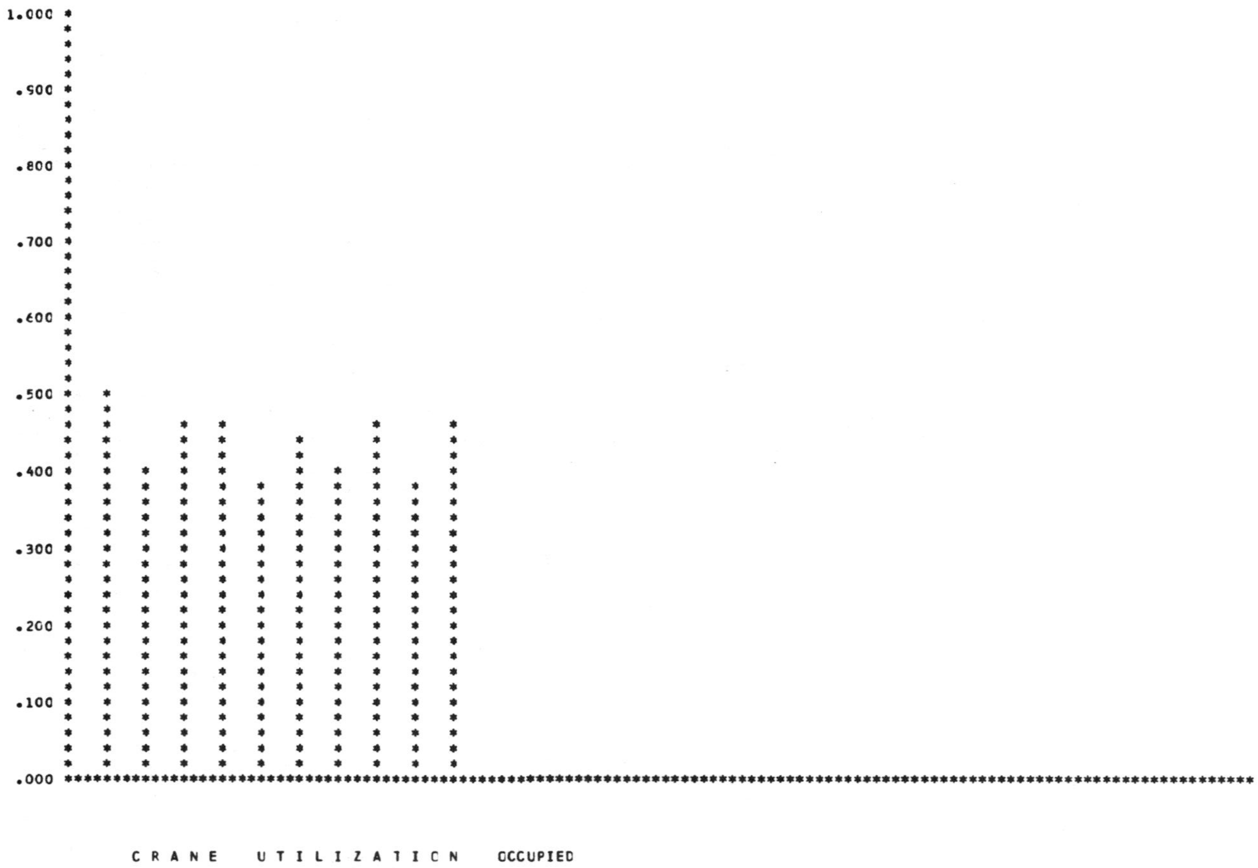
1.000
.900
.800
.700
.600
.500
.400
.300
.200
.100
.000
C R A N E   U T I L I Z A T I O N   OCCUPIED

Figure 9.7 (continued)

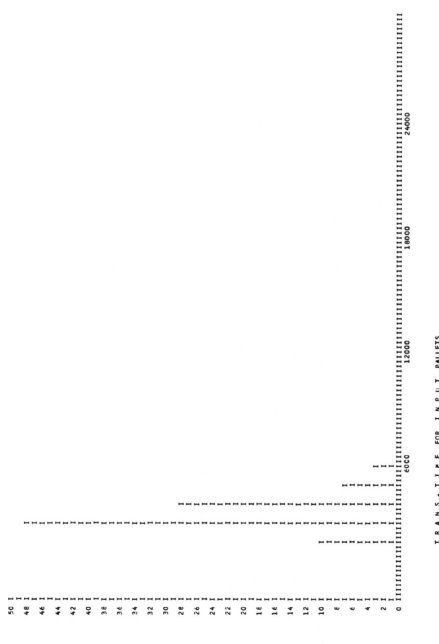

T R A N S . T I M E FOR I N P U T PALLETS

Figure 9.7 (continued)

285

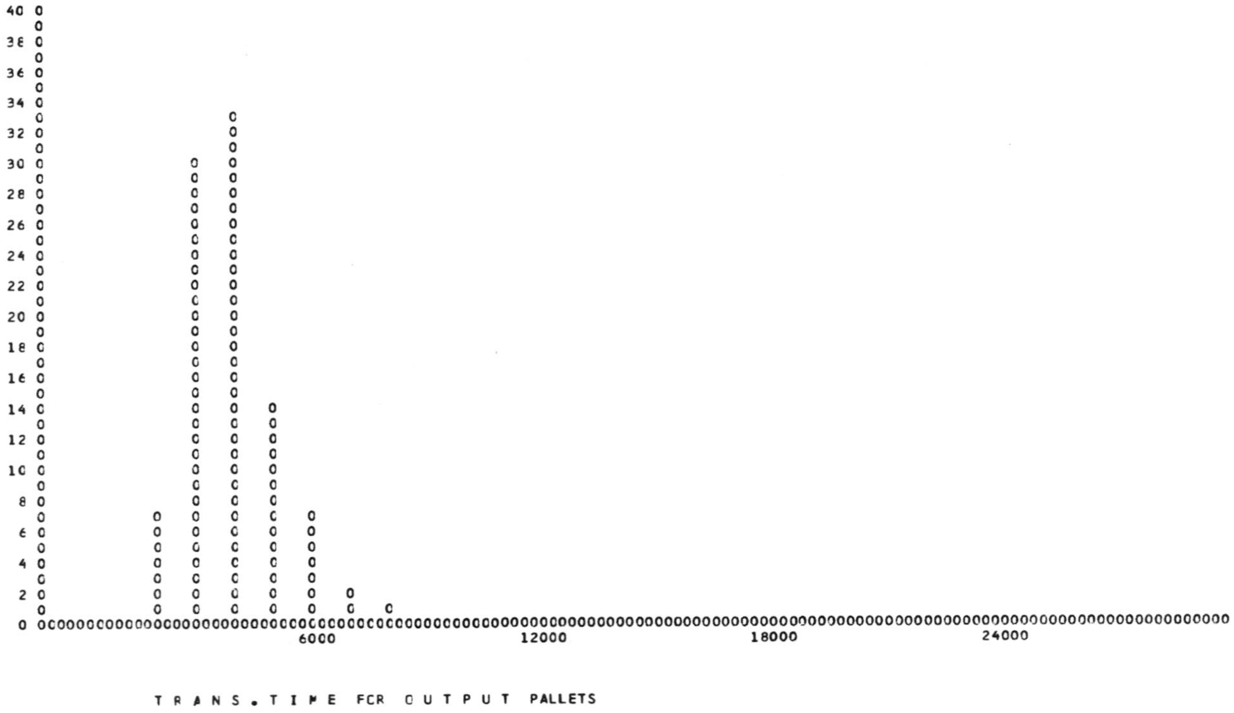

TRANS.TIME FCR OUTPUT PALLETS

Figure 9.7 (continued)

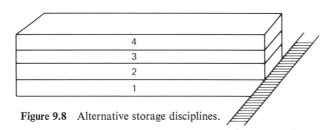

Figure 9.8 Alternative storage disciplines.

Combined zones.   A new scheme was then defined based on the time to access the bins: zone 1 the closest to the conveyor, zone 4 the farthest (see Figure 9.9). This led to slightly better results, but the cranes were still too slow to handle the traffic. It was then decided to continue the study with this last zone allocation and explore possible variations. Before these considerations, we discuss the way in which this zone allocation was introduced into the model. The functions used for the generation of horizontal and vertical bin positions were, respectively, POSHO and POSVE (see the program, Figure 9.6).

POSHO is a continuous function with RN7 as argument. If the argument is between 0 and 0.63, we get a bin number between 1 and 25, uniformly distributed; if between 0.63 and 0.84, the bin number is between 26 and 36; and so on.

POSVE is also a continuous function with RN7 as argument. For the same values of the argument as for POSHO, we get the values 0 to 4, 5 to 7, 7 to 8, and 8 to 9.

As the drawings for RN 7 are independent of each other, there is a probability of 0.4 (0.63×0.63) of finding a combined bin position such as:

horizontal position: 1 to 25

vertical position: 0 to 4   in zone 1

It can be seen that the same reasoning applies to zones 2, 3, and 4, with the respective cumulative probabilities of 0.7, 0.9 and 1.0.

It should be noted here that the approach taken is somewhat schematic. In a real problem the exact layout of the warehouse should be simulated and we could for instance, when the exact rules of operations for the cranes are known, compute the necessary traveling time for each bin. The zones could then be allocated by arranging the warehouse according to these exact traveling times, which is done quite easily by changing the statistical functions POSHO and POSVE.

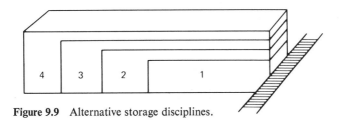

Figure 9.9 Alternative storage disciplines.

9.4.2 Cranes

Crane movement. In the initial model movements of the cranes were serial: first a horizontal move, then a vertical move. The total time was computed as the sum of the horizontal and vertical traveling times. The function TCRAV was used.

The next attempt was made with simultaneous crane movements. The function TCRAN is equal to the longer of the two displacement times.

The improvement obtained was still insufficient and the system could not handle the specified traffic. It was then decided that for the rest of the study we would keep to simultaneous movements of the cranes.

Crane speed. The results obtained with the initial crane speeds clearly indicated that the cranes were the bottleneck of the system, so it was necessary to speed them up. The new speeds chosen were:

horizontal speed: 20 m/min, so that X3=30
vertical speed: 4 m/min, so that X4=150

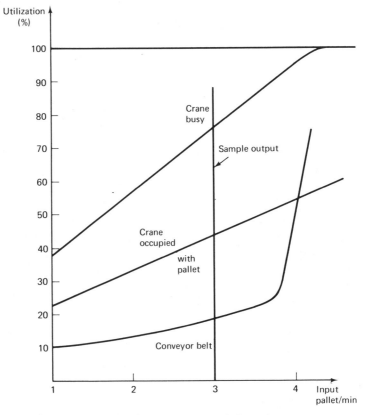

Figure 9.10 Average utilization of conveyor belt and cranes (with pallet or moving) for 1 output pallet/min.

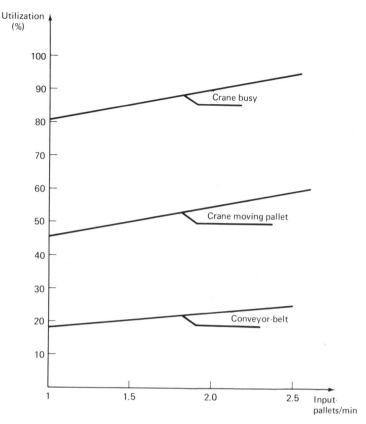

Figure 9.11 Average utilization of conveyor belts and cranes (with pallet and moving) for 3 output pallets/min.

X3 and X4 are the time intervals, in tenths of a second, between two bins. As the relation between the two speeds is different, ($\frac{1}{5}$ instead of $\frac{1}{10}$), the zone allocation should have been modified along the lines discussed at the end of Section 9.4.1. We did not do so because we felt this would bring no new information for understanding the program and also because the influence of such a change is negligible compared with the other aspects discussed.

9.4.3 Results

The results of the various experiments using these data showed that the system was able to handle the load given in the initial data. Detailed throughput measurements were then made for the various fixed values of the output rate, keeping the input rate as a variable. We finally represented the critical variables of the warehouse as a function of the input rate for two cases: output rate = 1 pallet/min and output rate = 3 pallets/min. Figure 9.10 shows the average utilization of the cranes, with or without pallet, and of the conveyor for output rate = 1 pallet/min. Figure 9.11 shows the same variables for output rate = 3 pallets/min.

One output pallet per minute (Figure 9.10). The utilization of the cranes grows linearly with the input rate. This is true for crane busy with or without pallet and crane busy with pallet. The conveyor utilization rises smoothly up to the input rate of 3.7 pallets/min and then rises extremely steeply, reaching 50 per cent for the input rate of 4 pallets/min compared with 17 per cent for 3 pallets/min. This increasing utilization is obviously caused by the cranes which are no longer able to handle the incoming pallets (95 per cent total utilization). The input buffers fill and the pallets begin to cycle on the conveyor: 3.5 pallets on average cycling for 3.75 input pallets/min and 25 pallets for 4 input pallets/min.

For this input rate of 4 pallets/min we observe a utilization of cranes with pallets of 54 percent. The queue at the receiving bay grows rapidly when the rate is greater than 4 input pallets/min. For 4 pallets/min we observed a maximum queue length of 16 pallets. Therefore, for this output rate, 1 pallet/min, the *input rate of 4 pallets/min* is the upper limit for the crane and conveyor speeds chosen.

Three output pallets per minute (Figure 9.11).   The crane and conveyor utilizations grow linearly with the input rate. The utilization of cranes is better than before: it reaches 60 per cent (with pallets) for 2.5 input pallets/min. For this rate the total throughput (total number of processed pallets) comes to 5.5 as compared to 5.0 for 1 output and 4 input pallets/min. So the overall utilization of the warehouse is "better" in this case.

On the other hand, the processing time for output pallets is much higher than for 1 output pallet/min. If the input rate is increased beyond 2.5, the system breaks down because the number of waiting output pallets gets too large.

Therefore, for this output rate of 3 pallets/min, the *upper limit is 2.5 input pallets/min.*

9.5 Conclusions

The results obtained so far can be summarized as follows:

1. For the speeds chosen: conveyor   20 m/min
   cranes horizontal   20 m/min
   cranes vertical   4 m/min

2. Simultaneous horizontal and vertical crane movements.

3. Combined zone allocation based on time to access the bins.

4. Input buffers, four places; output buffers, two places. This number of places was found to be satisfactory.

5. The upper limits of operation of the warehouse for 1 and 3 output pallets/min were:

   1 output pallet/min: 4   input pallets/min *maximum*
   3 output pallets/min: 2.5 input pallets/min *maximum*

In the case of 1 output and 4 input pallets/min, there should be enough room at the shipping and receiving bay to contain 20 pallets waiting for a place on the conveyor.

This is the end of our current study.

In practice, it is quite obvious that having developed the model, we would investigate further to get a better balanced system. In particular, we would explore the following:

1. Other values for conveyor and crane speeds.
2. The effect of adding other shipping and receiving bays, possibly separating the input and output functions.
3. Changing the cranes, so that they could move two pallets at a time.
4. Reducing the crane speeds, but increasing the size of the input buffers. This might be feasible if peak traffic occurs for only a short time.

Obviously for every such alternative the financial implications should be evaluated and presented to management. This information will then allow management to make the final decision by comparing the planned performance of the warehouse with its overall cost.

When the warehouse is constructed, the model could continue to be used because the real operation will almost certainly show aspects that were not anticipated. Further simulation experiments could then investigate the best strategy to be used with the characteristics of the machines installed. It might happen that the statistics on which the zone partition was made are changed and that a new arrangement would improve the operation. Furthermore, the output operation might be complicated by new constraints, such as multiple pallets grouped for large orders. In such a case one might want them all to come together to the shipping bay to reduce the number of vehicles waiting to transport goods from the warehouse. This in turn raises the problem of shipping-bay design, which was excluded from our model.

To sum up, the design model is just the first step in a continuing process of appraisal to obtain the most efficient operation of the warehouse.

10 Simulation of a Subway Transportation System

This chapter is based on a study made at the Institute for Transportation Sciences of the École Polytechnique Fédérale de Lausanne, Switzerland [10.1]. This institute (ITEP) has been engaged for several years in research work relating to all kinds of transportation problems and has used simulation and GPSS extensively for studying problems such as:

> *In road transportation:* simulation of general crossroads, of chains of crossroads with synchronized signals, of traffic flows, and the like.

> *In railway systems:* simulation of the maintenance of the lines, of the traffic throughput, of the stability of the schedule, and so on.

From these studies we have chosen the model discussed below because it is a very interesting and practical problem which could be simplified sufficiently to be presented realistically in this chapter. We would like to note that this model relates to a real transportation system presently under investigation for extension and modernization. Part of the model presented here was reworked by Guette and Vinet, two students at the IBM European Systems Research Institute. We want to thank the management of the ITEP and these students very sincerely for allowing their work to be used in this chapter. The model is written in GPSS V to illustrate some of the special features offered by this version of GPSS.

10.1 The System

10.1.1 Introduction

A subway is a transportation system that consists of a double-track line going from one end station, terminus, to another via intermediate stations. At each station waiting passengers enter the train if there is room. They stay on the train until it reaches their destination station, where they get off. Between stations the line is divided into sections equipped with traffic lights that operate according to safety regulations. The train movements are constrained to follow the published schedule and are physically controlled by the traffic signals.

Trains operate in two directions and, because of the geography of the region the times between stations may vary with the direction. For this reason and in order to keep our model very general, we have defined two stations for each real station: one in each direction. This would allow us to model complicated situations in which, for example, trains going one way could bypass one or more stations. In the same way, the sections of track between stations have been considered separately for each direction.

In the model given here, single-track sections have not been considered because they complicate the logic of the model and would not increase the interest of the program.

Two movement patterns have been considered: *normal*, when the train is *on schedule; accelerated,* when it is *behind schedule.*

10.1.2 Description of the subway

The subway studied is a double-track line going from terminus 1 to terminus 2, through intermediate stations. Trains can be stored at each terminus until they are scheduled to start. During the day trains may be suppressed for a certain period of time. Such suppressions can occur only at a terminus.

The schedule of train departures is controlled at each end of the line. When the trains are on schedule, the time delay between the departure of two consecutive trains is determined by the published timetable. When the trains are behind schedule, the frequency of departures is increased and the time between successive trains is fixed by the safety regulations, until the departure time coincides with the theoretical schedule. When a train is behind schedule, its movement will be specified by the accelerated pattern.

Passengers at each station are generated according to the distribution function specified, in our case Poisson distribution. The average arrival rate varies for each station and with the time of the day.

10.1.3 Train movements

The line between two stations is divided into *sections*. The number of sections between stations may vary along the line. Each section may contain only one train. Access to a section is controlled by a signal that is red if a train is in the section, amber if a train is in the next section, and green otherwise (Figure 10.1). When a train passes the signal n, it sets the signal for the section n to red and the signal for section $n - 1$ to amber. The signal $n - 2$ would normally be set to green, except if there is a train in section $n - 1$ (see Figure 10.1, case b). When signal n is amber, the train will stop at the end of section n, independent of the color of the next signal.

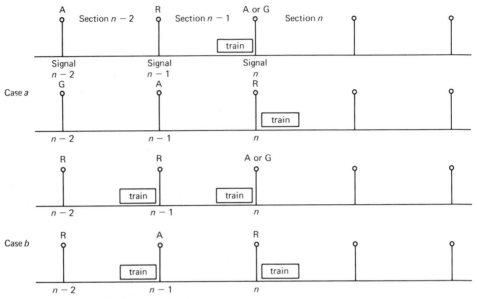

Figure 10.1 Schematic diagram of train movements.

When the signal is green, the train will not stop. Thus, if the light is green at any section, the train can go for at least two sections.

The time spent in a station consists of the times to open and close the doors plus the time for passengers to get in or out.

A train always waits at the station until the scheduled departure time. When it leaves, it will follow the normal movement pattern. If it leaves the station behind schedule, it then adopts an accelerated movement pattern to try to get back on schedule.

At a terminus the starting of a train is controlled by a traffic light. This light is green when a train is due to leave and turned to red as soon as the train starts.

10.1.4 Passenger entry and exit

Passengers arrive at stations according to a random pattern. The average arrival rate is different for every station and may vary during the day. Passenger destination points are also random; their distribution is different for every station but kept constant in this model. It is a relatively minor modification to vary the destination distribution with the time of day.

Passengers waiting at a station enter the train if there is room and stay on the train until it reaches their destination.

10.2 The Problem

10.2.1 Problem description

The problem is to simulate the operations of the subway with the main objective of studying the stability of the schedule. This stability will depend on the time reserves included in the theoretical schedule which determine the possibility that trains behind schedule can get back on schedule by adopting the accelerated movement pattern. Obviously this will also depend on the values of the data chosen for operating the system. The model has been built to produce the following statistical information:

Time behind schedule when trains arrive at each terminus.

Time ahead of or behind schedule when trains are ready to leave each station after all necessary operations have been performed: door opening and closing and time for passengers to get on and off. In the case of being behind schedule, how often can the trains be brought back onto schedule? What are the maximum times that trains get behind schedule?

Train statistics—that is, the percentage of time during which trains are running, the overall average utilization, and the average utilization between stations. These questions are important, for example during low traffic hours.

Passenger statistics—that is, the average number of passengers waiting at each station and average waiting time. Are these times smaller than an acceptable threshold? Statistics are also needed on the average number of passengers left at each station because a train is full.

As the model is so flexible, it can also be used to study the influence of factors such as:

Train capacity: should it be constant or vary during the day?

Train frequencies (schedule) and their relation with train capacities: is it better to have more frequent, short trains or less frequent, longer trains?

In addition to the aspects mentioned above, we believe that this model may also be used to evaluate the reserve capacity of the total system, the consequences of adding one or more intermediate stations, increasing the number of passengers at certain stations, and changing the frequency of trains, their speed characteristics for normal and accelerated movement patterns, and so on.

10.2.2 Numerical data

The following values have been used to run the program, which is presented in Figure 10.10.

Stations. The line consists of four stations (see Figure 10.2), which have been numbered:

$$1 \text{ to } 4 \text{ for direction } 1,$$
$$5 \text{ to } 8 \text{ for direction } 2.$$

Sections. Between every two stations, we have three sections. Sections are numbered:

$$1 \text{ to } 10 \text{ for direction } 1,$$
$$11 \text{ to } 20 \text{ for direction } 2.$$

Sections 1 and 11 have a special role: they are used by the trains to change direction from one track to the other.

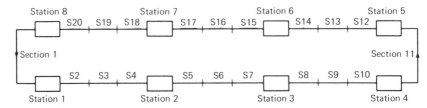

Figure 10.2 Schematic diagram of the simulated line.

Remark: The above numbering is not stated explicitly in the program. In fact, the number of stations and the number of sections are specified by save locations in order to maintain the generality of the model.

Train schedule. The train schedule is constant: one train every five min.

Station operations. The total time spent by the train in a station is equal to: door opening and closing time, 5 s; and mean time for passengers to get on or off, 0.3 s per passenger.

Train movement pattern. The time for every section may take eight values, depending on the color of the section signal and the status of the train in the previous section, stopped or not stopped (see Figure 10.3), and the type of movement pattern followed. These times are given in Table 10.1. Although these times are supposed to be equal for each section in this example, they are implemented in the program using eight different functions, numbered 1 to 8, to allow for the possibility of defining any value for every section of the line, including sections 1 and 11.

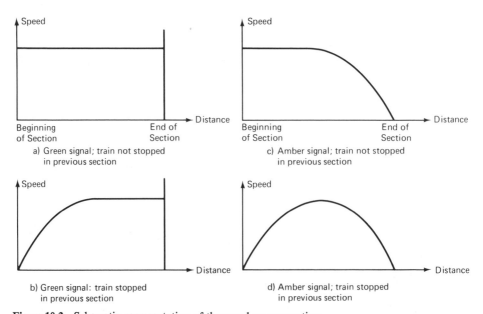

Figure 10.3 Schematic representation of the speed on one section.

Table 10.1 TIME FOR ONE SECTION

Input Signal	Status of Train in Previous Section	Normal Pattern (s)	Accelerated Pattern (s)
Green	Running	60	45
Green	Stopped	90	60
Amber	Running	90	60
Amber	Stopped	120	90

Track changing. The time to change tracks has been taken as 180 s, independent of the color of the signals.

Theoretical schedule. Using the above figures one can see that the minimum traveling time for one direction is 15 min. This minimum time is obtained by adding the section times for sections 1 to 10 or 11 to 20 and supposing that between two stations, the three signals are successively green, green, and amber. Therefore, the minimum total traveling time is 90 s (green, train stopped) plus 60 s (green, train running) plus 90 s (amber, train running).

Arrival rates and destination points of passengers. The arrival rates have been taken as constant during the day and are given, in numbers of passengers per hour, by Table 10.2. As stations 1 and 8, 2 and 7, 3 and 6, and 4 and 5 are the same, the "real" total number of passengers generated, for both directions, at each station (1 to 4) is that given in Table 10.3.

Table 10.2. ORIGIN–DESTINATION DISTRIBUTION (PASSENGERS PER HOUR)

Origin Station	Destination Station						Total
	2	3	4	6	7	8	
1	333	333	333				1000
2		250	250				500
3			333				333
5				333	333	333	1000
6					250	250	500
7						333	333
Total	333	583	916	333	583	916	

Table 10.3

Station	1	2	3	4
Passengers/hour	1000	833	833	1000

Train capacity. The train capacity is constant: 200 passengers.

Number of trains. In the sample program we started the simulation with six trains in each direction and 20 s later three trains were put in reserve at each terminus. Thus the effective number of trains in the simulation was six.

10.3 The GPSS Model

10.3.1 Correspondence between system elements and GPSS entities

Time unit. The time unit for the model is $\frac{1}{10}$ s.

Trains. Trains are represented by transactions. Parameters are used for indirect addressing of train storage number, section number, station number, and number of passengers going to next stations. Other parameters are used for movement pattern adopted and status of train on previous section, stopped or not stopped. Each train is associated with a storage that collects statistics of train utilization automatically.

Terminus. At the beginning of the simulation trains are generated at each terminus by one GENERATE block and put in a storage that represents the sidings. The departure of a train is controlled by the start signal, which is controlled by the schedule. The scheduling transaction sets the start signal. When the train starts, it immediately resets the start signal, leaves the siding (storage), and checks the input signal of the starting station; if not red, it starts, otherwise, it waits.

When trains must be suppressed (temporarily taken out of service), they are linked to a user chain, one per terminus. They can be unlinked when required.

Passengers. Passengers are represented by transactions. One parameter is used to record the station number. The destination point is not attached to the transaction: it is generated when the passenger enters the train. It should be noted that other strategies could be followed, for instance, define one transaction per station to generate the passengers, which could then be represented by units accumulated in a storage, a queue, or a save location. Alternatively, passengers could be kept in user chains until they can get into a train. Such alternatives are discussed in Section 10.5.

Stations. Stations are not represented as such by GPSS entities in this model except for the input traffic light, which controls the movement of trains; that is, it refuses a train when red. This signal is common for the section on which the station is and for the station itself. The queue of passengers waiting at a station j is represented by queue j. Passengers are entered in the queue when they arrive and immediately terminated. They are later extracted from the queue by the train transactions, which will accept waiting passengers (units in a queue) up to the number of vacant places remaining on the train. For every station a switch is set at the beginning of simulation, to start generating passengers at a given constant time before the arrival of the first train.

Line. The line is divided into sections, each of which may contain only one train. It is represented by function 9: the argument is the section number and the function is the station number, or zero if there is no station on this section. A section is represented by the traffic light (switch) which controls its access; it refuses entry to a train when red.

Traffic light.   The traffic light controlling access to a section is represented by a switch which is set when the light is green or amber, reset when red. The color green or amber when the switch is set is decided in the program by looking at the next signal, which, if set, means that the current signal is green, and if reset, means that the current signal is amber.

Train movement.   When a train has started from a terminus, it always tries to move to the next section with or without a station. On reaching the input signal, the switch is tested: if reset, the train waits; if set, the train passes the signal, resets it, and sets the preceding one. If the section includes a station, the program executes the station operations: passengers for this station get off and waiting passengers at the station get on until the train is full. For each passenger, the destination point is generated using the appropriate distribution function, and the train parameter that contains the number of passengers for this point is increased by unity.

Time is allowed for opening and closing doors; then a test is made to decide if the train is ahead of or behind schedule. If ahead, it waits until the scheduled departure time and moves according to the normal movement pattern. The waiting time is tabulated in the table WAIT. If behind time, the train immediately leaves the station and adopts the accelerated movement pattern until the next station. The time behind schedule when leaving the station is tabulated in the table RET.

Train scheduling.   Departure of a train from a terminus is controlled by a transaction generated at every scheduled departure time. This transaction sets the departure signal, which will be reset by the train when starting. If the starting signal is already set, which means that the preceding train has not yet left and therefore is behind schedule, the transaction waits and will set the signal as soon as it is reset by the starting train. This ensures that no starting signal is lost and that one train will start, even if behind schedule, for every scheduled departure. Time behind schedule for trains leaving the terminus is tabulated in table RET1 for terminus 1, and RET2 for terminus 2.

10.3.2 Parameters and save locations

Transaction parameters.   Transaction parameters have all been defined as fullword to simplify the understanding of the program and the expression of some of the variables. This is not mandatory. In real applications their length is chosen according to their contents. For example, section and station numbers could be defined by byte parameters.

Train parameters.

PF1:   Train number.

PF2:   Current station number; if 0, the section has no station.

PF3:   Section number, updated just before entering the section.

PF4:   Actual cumulated schedule.

PF5:   Type of movement pattern:
                          0 normal,
                          1 accelerated.

PF6:   Status of train on the last section:
                          1 if not stopped,
                          2 if stopped.

PF7:   Number of passengers boarding the train.

PF11–PF (10+X1):   Number of passengers going to various destination
                          points (one parameter per destination point).

Passenger parameters.

PF2:   Station number where passengers arrive. This parameter is used to deter-
       mine:
       (1) the user chain number, and
       (2) the switch number for starting the generation of passengers.

Scheduling transaction parameters.

PF1:   Theoretical (scheduled) departure time.

Save locations.   The following six save locations are used to define characteristics
of the line under study; they must be initialized before starting the simulation:

X1:   Number of stations. The line is double-track, so X1 is twice the actual
       number of stations. This is because, in the model, we represent one real
       station by two distinct stations, one for each direction.

X2:   Number of sections. This number is also twice the real number of sections.

X3:   Opening and closing times of doors.

X4:   Time to board the train, per passenger.

X5:   Time to leave the train, per passenger.

X7:   Number of trains started at one terminus at the beginning of the simula-
       tion. The same number is started at the other terminus.

The next save locations are used during the simulation:

X8:   Scheduled departure time of the train at terminus 1.

X9:   Scheduled departure time of the train at terminus 2.

X10:   Number of trains to be suppressed at terminus 1.

X11:   Number of trains to be suppressed at terminus 2.

The last two values are specified dynamically by means of SAVEVALUE instructions (see Figure 10.7) under the control of train suppression, which may be executed
at any time during the day. Several train suppressions may take place during the
simulation. If such suppressions are programmed when one is not sure that X10 and
X11 are equal to zero (last trains suppressed), one should change the SAVEVALUE

instructions presently in the program so that they would add to X10 and X11, respectively, rather than store in them the new numbers of trains to be suppressed.

X12:   Working location used to store at one station the number of the function to be used when embarking passengers to generate their destination points.

10.3.3 Variables and functions

Variables.

$V1=10+PF2$:	Parameter number (of the train) containing the number of passengers for station PF2.
$V2=X3+PF5*X5+PF7*X4$:	Time spent by the train in station (door opening and closing times plus time for passengers to get on and off).
$V3=FN13-PF4$:	Time to wait in the station (for trains ahead of schedule).
$V4=PF3-1$:	Section $N-1$ traffic light number.
$V5=PF3+1$:	Section $N+1$ traffic light number.
$V6=4*PF5+PF6$:	Number of the function giving the section traveling time when the section signal is green.
$V7=4*PF5+PF6+2$:	Number of the function giving the section traveling time when the section signal is amber.
$V8=PF2+X2$:	Number of the switch controlling passenger arrivals at station PF2.
$V9=FN13-PF3$:	Time interval between the setting of switches controlling passenger arrivals in two consecutive stations.
$V10=20+PF2$:	Number of the table giving the utilization of trains in station PF2.
$V11=10+PF2$:	Number of the table giving the number of passengers left in station PF2.
$V12=N\$STEL+X7$:	Number of the train leaving terminus 2.
$V15=C1-X8$:	Time behind schedule for trains leaving terminus 1.
$V16=C1-X9$:	Time behind schedule for trains leaving terminus 2.
$V17=X2/2+1$:	First signal for trains leaving terminus 2 (equal to the first section number).
$V19=X1/2$:	Station number of terminus 2 (terminus 1 is station 1).

V22=PF2+X2+X1/2:	Number of the switch controlling passenger arrivals at station PF2+X1/2.
V23=X1/2:	Half the total number of stations (real number of stations).
V24=11+X1+PF2:	Number of the function giving the passenger-destination-point distribution for station PF2.
V25=10+FN*X12:	Number of the train parameter containing the number of passengers going to the stations beyond the current one.
CAPAC:	Train capacity.
UTILI=(S*PF1/V$CAPAC)*100:	Percentage occupation of the train at a given time.

Functions.

FN1–FN8 :   Train movement pattern functions. The argument is the section number. The function gives the section traveling time for each section.

The eight functions are for the various cases (see Figure 10.3) to be considered:

　　type of movement pattern, normal or accelerated;

　　color of the input signal, green or amber; and

　　status of train on previous section, stopped or not stopped.

The function number is given for all cases by Table 10.4.

Table 10.4 Section Traveling Time Functions

	Normal Pattern	Accelerated Pattern
Green		
Train not stopped	FN1	FN5
Train stopped	FN2	FN6
Amber		
Train not stopped	FN3	FN7
Train stopped	FN4	FN8

FN9:	Function gives the position of the stations. The argument is the section number; the function is the station number on the corresponding section, or 0 if no station on the section.
FN10:	Time interval between train departures at terminus 1. The argument is the time of the day.
FN11:	Time interval between train departures at terminus 2. The argument is the time of the day.

FN12:Erlang 1 (exponential) distribution function with random number argument. Used for generating Poisson-distributed passenger interarrival times.

FN13:Theoretical cumulative schedule. This function is used to determine the time ahead of or behind schedule when a train is leaving a station.

FN14 to FN(11+X1):Average passenger interarrival times, one function per station. The argument is the time of the day.

FN(11+X1+PF2):Distribution functions (one per station PF2) of the passenger destination points.

10.3.4 Statistical tables

To get detailed information about the behavior of the model, the following statistical tables are built up during the simulation:

1 to X1:Time behind schedule at station (one per station).

11 to 10+X1:Number of passengers left in station (one per station).

21 to 20+X1:Train utilization when leaving the station (one per station).

RET1/2:Time behind schedule when trains arrive at terminus 1 or 2.

WAIT:Time trains have to wait at stations (when ahead of schedule).

The passenger waiting time at stations is given by the queue statistics corresponding to the station concerned. If the standard queue statistics produced by GPSS are not sufficient, one can associate one QTABLE with each queue to produce all requested statistical information, including the maximum waiting time.

10.3.5 Numerical values

The numerical values used in this example are those given in Section 10.2.2; therefore:

$X1=8$:Two times four stations.

$X2=20$:Sections.

$X3=50$:Door opening and closing times, 5 s.

$X4=X5=3$:Average time to get on or off, 0.3 s per passenger.

$X7=6$:Six trains are introduced in the model for each direction.

V\$CAPAC=200:Train capacity.

Cumulative theoretical schedule. The two schedules considered are shown in Table 10.5. Changing this schedule means modifying FN13. We studied both schedules and coded function data for both in the program, but for each run we suppressed one data line by inserting an asterisk in card column 1, which made it into a comment.

Passenger interarrival times. The average passenger interarrival times are defined by functions 14, 15, and 16 for stations 1, 2, and 3, and 17, 18, and 19 for

Table 10.5

| Station | Cumulative Time—(s) (When Leaving Stations) | |
Number	Normal Schedule	Reduced Schedule
1 and 5	60	60
2 and 6	360	300
3 and 7	660	540
4 and 8	960	780

stations 5, 6, and 7, respectively. These values, based on the origin–destination distribution given in Table 10.2, are, respectively:

3.6 s for stations 1 and 5 (functions 14 and 17)

7.2 s for stations 2 and 6 (functions 15 and 18)

10.8 s for stations 3 and 7 (functions 16 and 19).

These are kept constant during the day, but other patterns can easily be introduced into the above functions.

10.3.6 Flowchart and program

The flowchart and the program have been broken down into several modules, each describing a distinct part or function of the model. They are gathered into three sections:

Train sequence:

Train generation at each terminus

Station operations

Train movement in one section

Train suppression

Passenger sequence:

Generation of passengers

Signal to start generation of passengers at stations

Train scheduling and suppression:

Scheduling train departure from terminus

Control of train suppression

We have completed the flowcharts (Figures 10.4 to 10.9) with as many details as possible to increase their readability and to give the reader the choice, when studying the model, of looking either at the flowcharts or at the program. The program (Figure 10.10) contains many comments that explain the function of the instructions.

Train generation at each terminus. The flowchart is shown in Figure 10.4. The program consists of instructions 1 to 35 (Figure 10.10). As it is the same for both

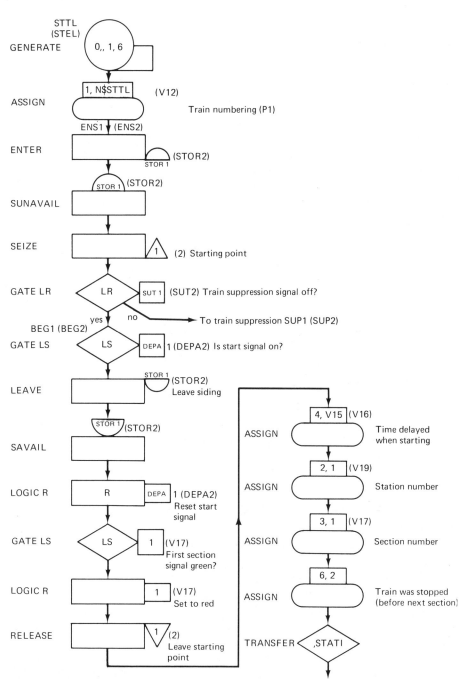

Figure 10.4 Train generation at each terminus. The symbols or values in the blocks refer to starting station (terminus 1), those in the brackets to end station (terminus 2).

termini, we discuss only the first. The symbols and values in the block diagrams correspond to the starting station (terminus 1), those in brackets to the end station (terminus 2).

The total number of trains to be introduced at terminus 1 is defined as the D-operand of the GENERATE block (number 1). The intergeneration times are zero. The trains are numbered in parameter 1 (block 2), enter storage STOR1, which represents the siding, and are made unavailable. This availability/unavailability feature allows us to get statistics on the percentage of time that the trains are busy traveling or idle at either terminus. This information will be used when investigating the number of trains which should be put into service at various times during the day. Then we find instruction 5, SEIZE 1, which ensures that between this point and block 13, RELEASE 1, only one transaction can be processed. [This point was previously discussed in the traffic (Section 6.6.2) and the machine repair (Section 6.6.3) problems.] Here we must avoid several trains passing the train-suppression test at block 6. When the transaction enters block 6 (GATE LR SUT1,SUP1), the switch SUT1 (suppression terminus 1) can be set only by the sequence: control of train suppression (blocks 155 to 162).

If the signal is reset (no train to be suppressed), the transaction tests if the start signal (DEPA1) is set (meaning that one train should start). If so, the train leaves the siding (block 8), is made available, and resets the start signal immediately. There is no possible ambiguity because the starting signals (see Figure 10.9 and instructions 139 to 154 of the program) are queued and ensure that one train will start for every signal. The train then checks if the traffic light of station 1 is not red (block 12) and releases facility 1 so that another train may execute the above sequence of operations. Then, before going to the station, the time behind schedule when starting (if any) is stored in parameter 4, the station number in parameter 2, the section number in parameter 3, and the code indicating the train status before entering the next section in parameter 6. As the train is in a station, it is stopped (2 in parameter 6). The train transaction now enters the station.

The sequence for terminus 2 is the same except that we use variables 17 (to specify the number of the station input signal) and 19 (for the station number).

Station operations. The flowchart is shown in Figure 10.5, (a) and (b) and the program consists of blocks 36 (STATI) to 75. The following operations are performed successively.

Passengers for this station get off. Waiting passengers get on until all are on board or the train is full, their destination points are generated, and the parameters containing the number of passengers for the next stations updated accordingly. The clock time is compared with the theoretical schedule: if the train is ahead of schedule, it waits until the scheduled departure time; if behind schedule, it leaves immediately and adopts the accelerated movement pattern. We then test if the train has reached a terminus; if so, the train enters the siding and is made unavailable. If not, the train enters the next section.

When a train transaction enters block 36, STATI, its parameters contain the following information (see Section 10.3.2):

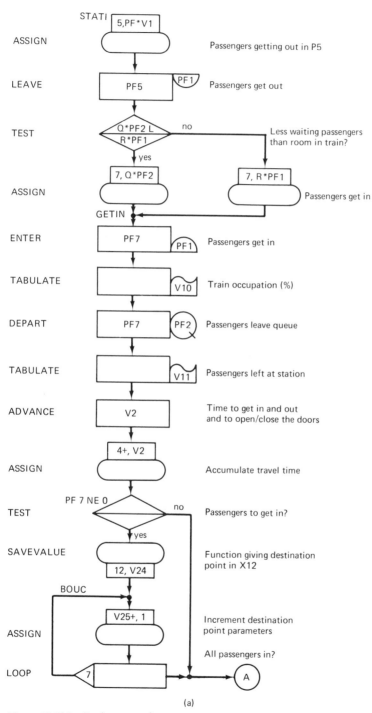

STATI ASSIGN 5,PF*V1 — Passengers getting out in P5

LEAVE PF5 PF1 — Passengers get out

TEST Q*PF2 L R*PF1 — no — Less waiting passengers than room in train?

ASSIGN 7, Q*PF2 — yes

ASSIGN 7, R*PF1 — Passengers get in

GETIN

ENTER PF7 PF1 — Passengers get in

TABULATE V10 — Train occupation (%)

DEPART PF7 PF2 — Passengers leave queue

TABULATE V11 — Passengers left at station

ADVANCE V2 — Time to get in and out and to open/close the doors

ASSIGN 4+, V2 — Accumulate travel time

TEST PF 7 NE 0 — no — Passengers to get in?

SAVEVALUE 12, V24 — yes — Function giving destination point in X12

BOUC

ASSIGN V25+, 1 — Increment destination point parameters

LOOP 7 — All passengers in?

A

(a)

Figure 10.5(a) Station operations.

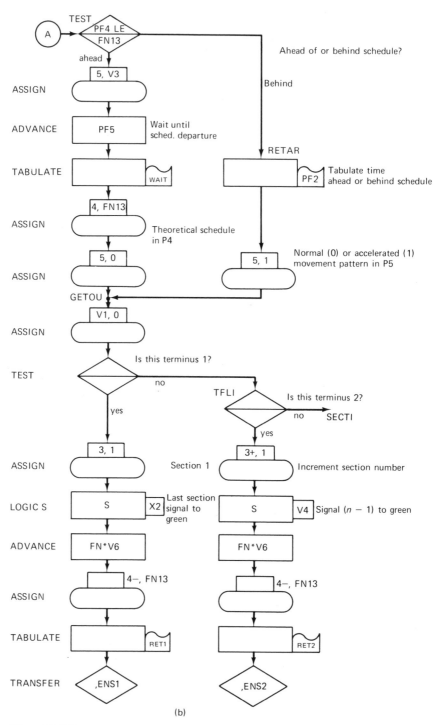

Figure 10.5(b)

PF1:   Train number and number of the associated storage.

PF2:   Station number.

PF3:   Section number.

PF4:   Accumulated traveling time.

PF6:   2, for train stopped at the station.

PF11 to 18:   Number of passengers going to various destination points.

The STATI block (36) finds the number of passengers for this station in the parameter whose number is V1 and stores it in parameter 5. The LEAVE block (37) removes the passengers from the train storage. The TEST instruction (38) checks if there are more passengers waiting in the station queue (Q*PF2) than there are places available in the train (R*PF1). The minimum of these numbers is stored in parameter 7 (block 39 or 41). Then this number of passengers is entered in the storage (block 42: ENTER). We then tabulate the train occupation (block 43) in tables 21 to 28. For this purpose, we enter the value of the variable UTILI, which is the current value of the utilization expressed as a percentage.

The DEPART block (44) removes the passengers from the station queue, and the TABULATE block (45) tabulates the number of passengers left at the station in table V11, tables 11 to 18. The train then waits in the station for the period necessary to open and close the doors and for passengers to get off and on (block 46: ADVANCE V2).

Parameter 4 is updated (cumulative traveling time) and we test if passengers are getting on (block 48: TEST). If this is the case, we store V24, the number of the distribution function to be used at this particular station to compute the destination of passengers waiting at this station, in save location 12. There is obviously one function per station (numbers 20 to 26). In this model, these functions are independent of the time of day.

The transaction now enters the loop consisting of blocks 50 and 51 (ASSIGN and LOOP), which will be executed once for every passenger (the total number of loops is contained in PF7), which computes the destination using the function whose number is contained in X12, and which adds the passenger (one unit) to the corresponding train parameter (destination point plus 10).

When all passengers have been handled, the transaction goes to A [top of Figure 10.5(b)], where we check (block 52: TEST) if the train is behind schedule. If so, the transaction goes to RETAR, where (blocks 59 and 60) we assign 1 to parameter 5 (for accelerated movement pattern) and tabulate the time behind schedule in the table (1 to 8) corresponding to this station. If the train is ahead of schedule it waits (blocks 53 and 54: ASSIGN and ADVANCE) the necessary time for scheduled departure, and we tabulate (block 55: TABULATE) this wait time in a unique table: WAIT. Note that we could also have one table per station, but we did not feel it to be necessary. The scheduled time is stored in P4 (block 56: ASSIGN), 0 is stored in P5 (for normal running pattern), and the transaction goes to GETOU (block 61), where the parameter containing the number of passengers for this station is reset.

We then test if the station is terminus 1 at block 62: TEST. If so, the section number is set to 1 and the last section signal is set to green. The train moves from one track to the other (block 65: ADVANCE), the time behind schedule is tabulated (blocks 66 and 67: ASSIGN and TABULATE) in table RET1, and the train is sent to the siding. If the station is not terminus 1, we test (block 69: TEST) if it is terminus 2. If so, the same operations are performed as for terminus 1, using the appropriate numbers for the section, traffic light, and table. If the station is neither terminus 1 nor terminus 2, the transaction is sent from block 62 (first TEST) to TFLI (second TEST) and to SECTI (block 76), where the block sequence for train movement in a section begins.

Train movement in one section. The flowchart is given in Figure 10.6, and the program consists of blocks 76 (SECTI) to 91 (TRANSFER).

First, the section number (in parameter 3) is increased by unity (block 76: ASSIGN) and we store the value of function 9 in parameter 2. The value is zero if there is no station in this section; otherwise, it is equal to the station number. Then the input signal for this section is tested (block 78: GATE). If set (not red), the train "enters" the section that sets the signal to red and the previous one to not red (blocks 79 and 80: LOGIC). If there is a station, (parameter 2 (nonzero)), the train must stop and, therefore, the transaction goes to the amber section. If no station is on the section, the signal is tested (block 82: GATE). If green, the transaction proceeds to spend the traveling time (block 83: ADVANCE) specified by the function whose reference number is given by variable 6 (see Table 10.3). This time is added to parameter 4 to give the cumulative traveling time (block 84: ASSIGN) and parameter 6 is set to 1 to show that the train was not stopped at the end of this section. The train is then sent to SECTI to go to the next section. When there is a station or the signal is amber, the transaction continues to block 87: AMBER, where the section traveling time given by the function whose reference number is given by variable 7 is spent. This time is added to parameter 4 to obtain the cumulative traveling time. Parameter 6 is set to 2 to indicate that the train was stopped on this section, and a test is made (block 90) to direct the transaction either to SECTI (next section) or to STATI for the station operations.

Train suppression. The flowchart is given in Figure 10.7, and the program consists of blocks 119 (SUP1) to 138.

The signal to suppress trains is switch SWT1 for terminus 1 and SWT2 for terminus 2. The number of trains to be suppressed is given by X10 and X11, respectively. When several trains have to be suppressed, alternate ones are taken out of service. This strategy is implemented by using logical switch SWT1 (SWT2 for terminus 2), which, if reset, causes the train to be suppressed and, if set, not to be suppressed until save location 10 (or 11) is reduced to zero.

SUP1 (block 119) tests switch SWT1. If reset, the train must be suppressed, so X10 is reduced by 1. Facility 1, which represents the starting point and which was seized by block 5 is released, and the transaction tests for additional trains to be suppressed (block 122). If not, the suppression switch, SUT1, is reset (block 123) and

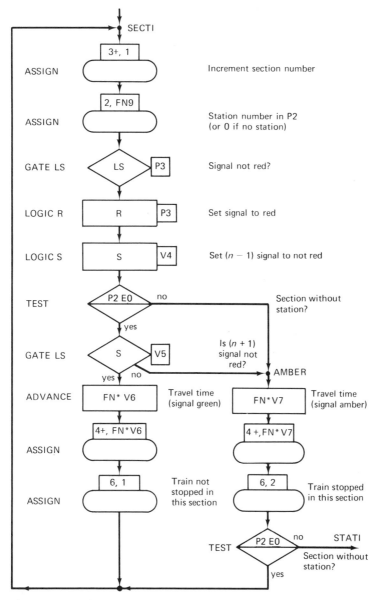

Figure 10.6 Train movements in one section.

the train is suppressed, by linking to user chain RES1. If more trains must be suppressed, the transaction is sent to TER1 (block 125), where switch SWT1 is set so that the next train will remain in service, and the current train is suppressed by linking to user chain RES1 as above.

When switch SWT1 is set (block 119), meaning that the train must not be

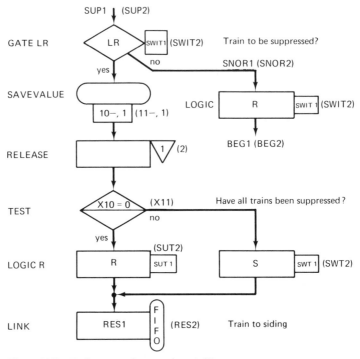

Figure 10.7 Train supression terminus 1 (2).

suppressed, the transaction goes to SNOR1 (block 127), where SWT1 is reset and the train proceeds to BEG1 (block 7), which is the instruction following the test for train suppression.

The program for terminus 2 is analogous and is not further discussed. The block diagram is the same as for terminus 1, using the names indicated in parentheses.

Generation of passengers. The flowchart is given in Figure 10.8(a), and the program consists of blocks 103 to 118.

For each station passengers are generated by a GENERATE block with mean intergeneration time given by a function (with reference number 14 for station 1, 15 for station 2, . . . , 19 for station 7) and function modifier which is the inverse of the exponential cumulative distribution function. The station number assigned to the priority of the transaction by the GENERATE block is assigned to parameter 2, the priority is set to 1, and the signal to start generation of passengers is tested (block 116). If this signal is closed (it opens every day only a certain time before the arrival of the first train), the passengers are terminated. Otherwise, they enter the appropriate station queue (block 117) and are terminated.

It is important to note that by using the station queues in this way, each time that a train transaction removes units from these queues, we get the warning error message: "execution error number 854: transaction entering a DEPART block is not a member of this queue. Simulation continues." This is to be expected because of the use we make of these queues. Remember that we chose this solution to avoid having too many transactions (passengers waiting at all stations) in the system. Considering passengers as units in the queues solved the problem. This aspect will be discussed further in Section 10.5.

Signals to start generation of passengers at stations. In our model we have started the generation of passengers at every station a certain (constant) time before the scheduled departure time of the first train. For this purpose we define a switch (numbers 21 to 28) for each station input signal. Passengers are generated only when it is set: otherwise they are terminated. These switches are set by the subprogram, consisting of blocks 92 to 102; the flowchart is represented in Figure 10.8(b).

One control transaction is generated (block 92: GENERATE) at time 1 and loops blocks 96 to 101 for a number of times equal to the real number of stations

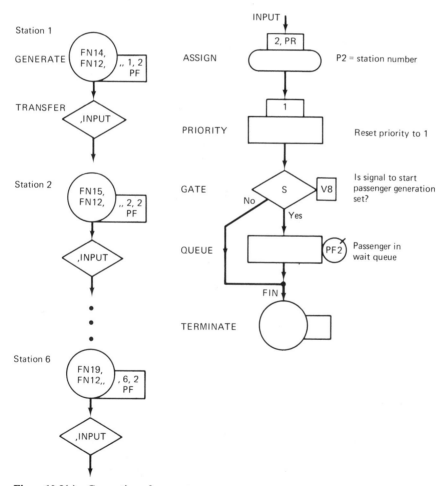

Figure 10.8(a)   Generation of passengers.

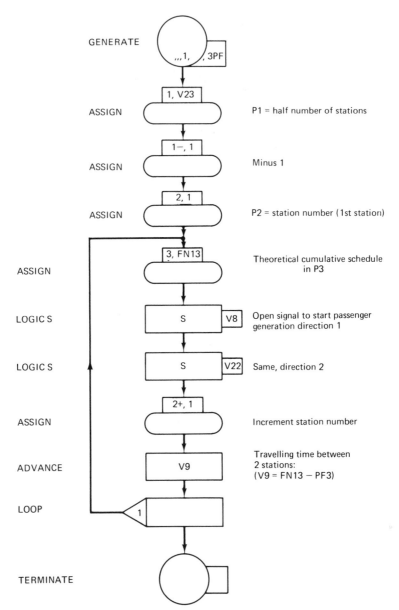

GENERATE

,,,1,   3PF

ASSIGN   1, V23   P1 = half number of stations

ASSIGN   1−, 1   Minus 1

ASSIGN   2, 1   P2 = station number (1st station)

ASSIGN   3, FN13   Theoretical cumulative schedule
                              in P3

LOGIC S   S   V8   Open signal to start passenger
                              generation direction 1

LOGIC S   S   V22   Same, direction 2

ASSIGN   2+, 1   Increment station number

ADVANCE   V9   Travelling time between
                              2 stations:
                              (V9 = FN13 − PF3)

LOOP   1

TERMINATE

Figure 10.8(b)   Signal to start generation of passengers at stations.

minus one. This is done by using the two ASSIGN blocks 93 and 94. The starting
station number (1) is stored in parameter 2 (block 95). The section traveling time is
assigned to parameter 3. The signals to start the generation of passengers at stations
1 and 5 are opened (blocks 97 and 98). The station number is increased by one unit
(block 99). The transaction is then delayed (block 100) for a time corresponding to

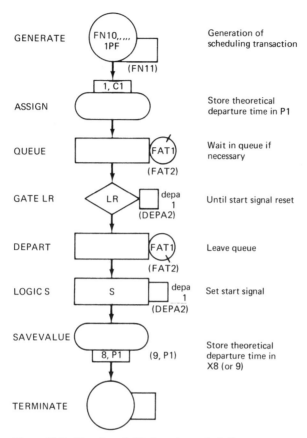

GENERATE — Generation of scheduling transaction

ASSIGN — Store theoretical departure time in P1

QUEUE — Wait in queue if necessary

GATE LR — Until start signal reset

DEPART — Leave queue

LOGIC S — Set start signal

SAVEVALUE — Store theoretical departure time in X8 (or 9)

TERMINATE

Figure 10.9 Terminus 1 (2) departure scheduling.

the theoretical schedule (variable 9) and the same operations take place successively for all stations.

Scheduling train departure from terminus. The departure of trains from the terminus is controlled by scheduling transactions generated according to the time-table. The flowchart is given in Figure 10.9 and the program consists of blocks 139 to 154. We discuss only the program for terminus 1, because that for terminus 2 is analogous.

One transaction is generated for each departure scheduled according to function 10, which gives the time interval between two successive trains as a function of the time of the day. In our example we kept this interval constant at 5 min, or 3000 time units. The theoretical departure time is stored in parameter 1 (block 140) and the transaction is queued to allow for the case where several departure signals have been generated but not satisfied. If (block 142) the departure signal (switch DEPA1) is red (reset), it is set (block 144) after the signal has left the queue; the theoretical signal is then stored in X8 (block 145). Note that when the start signal is set, only a train leaving terminus 1 can reset it (by going through block 10: **LOGIC R DEPA1**) (see Figure 10.10).

```
BLOCK                                                                                      STATEMENT
NUMBER  *LOC    OPERATION   A,B,C,D,E,F,G,H,I        COMMENTS                               NUMBER
                SIMULATE    12                                                                 1
                UNLIST      ABS                      SUPPRESS ABSOLUTE LISTING                  2
         *                                                                                     3
         *   TIME UNIT = 1/10 SECOND                                                           4
         *                                                                                     5
         *    EQUIVALENCES                                                                     6
         *                                                                                     7
        STAT1  EQU          1(8),Q                   STATIONS                                  8
        SWIT   EQU          1(28),L                  SWITCHES                                  9
        FOES   EQU          20(6),Z                  FUNCTIONS                                10
        TRAIN  EQU          1(12),S                  TRAIN STORAGES                           11
        TABLE  EQU          11(18),T                 TABLES                                   12
         *                                                                                    13
         *    INITIALIZATIONS                                                                 14
         *                                                                                    15
                INITIAL     LS1-10/LS11-20                                                    16
                INITIAL     X1,8                     NUMBER OF STATIONS                       17
                INITIAL     X2,20                    NUMBER OF SECTIONS                       18
                INITIAL     X3,50                    DOOR OPENING AND CLOSING TIME           19
                INITIAL     X4,3                     TIME TO GET IN PER PASSENGER            20
                INITIAL     X5,3                     TIME TO GET OUT PER PASSENGER           21
                INITIAL     X7,6                     1/2 NB OF TRAINS                        22
         *                                                                                    23
         *    STORAGE CAPACITY DEFINITIONS                                                    24
         *                                                                                    25
                STORAGE     S1-S12,200               TRAIN CAPACITY = 200                    26
                STORAGE     S$STOR1,12/S$STOR2,12                                            27
         *                                                                                    28
         *    VARIABLES                                                                       29
         *                                                                                    30
          1    VARIABLE     PF2+10                   PARM NUMBER CONTAINING THE NUMBER       31
                                                     OF PASSENGERS PER DESTINATION           32
          2    VARIABLE     X3+PF5*X5+PF7*X4         TIME SPENT IN STATION                   33
          3    VARIABLE     FN13-PF4                 WAITING TIME IN STATION FOR TRAINS      34
         *                                           AHEAD OF SCHEDULE                       35
          4    VARIABLE     PF3-1                    SIGNAL N-1                              36
          5    VARIABLE     PF3+1                    SIGNAL N+1                              37
          6    VARIABLE     4*PF5+PF6                FUNCTION NUMBER SECTION                 38
         *                                           TRAVELING TIME GREEN LIGHT             39
          7    VARIABLE     4*PF5+PF6+2              FUNCTION NUMBER SECTION                 40
         *                                           TRAVELING TIME AMBER SIGNAL            41
          8    VARIABLE     PF2+X2                   SIGNAL NR. FOR PASSENG. ARRIV.          42
          9    VARIABLE     FN13-PF3                 TIME DELAY BETWEEN SETTING SIGNALS      43
         *                                           FOR PASSENGERS ARRIVALS                44
         10    VARIABLE     20+PF2                   TABLE NR. UTILIZATION OF TRAINS         45
         *                                           PER STATION                            46
         11    VARIABLE     10+PF2                   TABLE NUMBER PASSENGERS LEFT            47
         *                                           IN STATION                             48
         12    VARIABLE     N$STEL+X7                TRAIN NUMBER STARTING AT TERM.2         49
         15    VARIABLE     C1-X8                    TIME TRAINS DELAYED TERMINUS 1          50
         16    VARIABLE     C1-X9                    TIME TRAINS DELAYED TERMINUS 2          51
         17    VARIABLE     X2/2+1                   1ST SIGNAL NUMBER TERMINUS 2            52
         19    VARIABLE     X1/2+1                   STATION NUMBER TERMINUS 2               53
         22    VARIABLE     PF2+X2+X1/2              SIGNAL NUMBER FOR PASSENGERS            54
         *                                           ARRIVALS DIRECT. TERM.2-TERM.1         55
         23    VARIABLE     X1/2                     HALF NUMBER OS STATIONS                 56
         24    VARIABLE     11+X1+PF2                FUNCTION NR. FOR DISTRIBUTION           57
         *                                           OF DESTINATION POINTS                  58
         25    VARIABLE     10+FN*X12                PARM. NUMBER CONTAINING THE NUMBER      59
         *                                           OF PASSENG. FOR STATION FN*V24         60
         26    VARIABLE     PF4-FN13                                                         61
        CAPAC  FVARIABLE    200                      TRAIN CAPACITY                          62
        UTILI  FVARIABLE    (S*PF1/V$CAPAC)*100      UTILIZAT. OF TRAINS TIMES 100           63
         *                                                                                    64
         *    TABLES                                                                          65
         *                                                                                    66
          1    TABLE        V26,0,300,10             TIME BEHIND SCHEDULE STATION 1          67
          2    TABLE        V26,0,300,10             TIME BEHIND SCHEDULE STATION 2          68
          3    TABLE        V26,0,300,10             ----------------------------- 3         69
          4    TABLE        V26,0,300,10             ----------------------------- 4         70
          5    TABLE        V26,0,300,10             ----------------------------- 5         71
          6    TABLE        V26,0,300,10             ----------------------------- 6         72
          7    TABLE        V26,0,300,10             ----------------------------- 7         73
          8    TABLE        V26,0,300,10             TIME BEHIND SCHEDULE STATION 8          74
         11    TABLE        Q1,5,5,10                PASSENGERS LEFT STATION 1               75
         12    TABLE        Q2,5,5,10                PASSENGERS LEFT STATION 2               76
         13    TABLE        Q3,5,5,10                PASSENGERS LEFT STATION 3               77
         14    TABLE        Q4,5,5,10                PASSENGERS LEFT STATION 4               78
         15    TABLE        Q5,5,5,10                PASSENGERS LEFT STATION 5               79
         16    TABLE        Q6,5,5,10                -----------------------6                80
         17    TABLE        Q7,5,5,10                -----------------------7                81
         18    TABLE        Q8,5,5,10                PASSENGERS LEFT STATION 8               82
         21    TABLE        V$UTILI,0,10,12          TRAIN UTILIZATION STATION 1             83
         22    TABLE        V$UTILI,0,10,12          ---------------------------2            84
```

Figure 10.10 GPSS model of subway system.

```
 23    TABLE     V$UTILI,0,10,12      --------------------------3                85
 24    TABLE     V$UTILI,0,10,12      --------------------------4                86
 25    TABLE     V$UTILI,0,10,12      --------------------------5                87
 26    TABLE     V$UTILI,0,10,12      --------------------------6                88
 27    TABLE     V$UTILI,0,10,12      --------------------------7                89
 28    TABLE     V$UTILI,0,10,12      TRAIN UTILIZATION STATION 8                90
 RET1  TABLE     PF4,0,300,5          TIMES TRAINS DELAYED TERMINUS 1            91
 RET2  TABLE     PF4,0,300,5          TIMES TRAINS DELAYED TERMINUS 2            92
 WAIT  TABLE     PF5,0,100,5          TRAIN WAIT TIMES AT STATIONS               93
 *                                                                              94
 *   FUNCTIONS                                                                  95
 *                                                                              96
 1     FUNCTION  PF3,D20       GREEN LIGHT,NO STOP,NORMAL PATTERN               97
1,1800/2,600/3,600/4,600/5,600/6,600/7,600/8,600/9,600/10,600/11,1800/          98
12,600/13,600/14,600/15,600/16,600/17,600/18,600/19,600/20,600                  99
 *                                                                             100
 2     FUNCTION  PF3,D20        GREEN,STOPPED,NORMAL PATTERN                    101
1,1800/2,900/3,900/4,900/5,900/6,900/7,900/8,900/9,900/10,900/11,1800/          102
12,900/13,900/14,900/15,900/16,900/17,900/18,900/19,900/20,900                  103
 *                                                                             104
 3     FUNCTION  PF3,D20        AMBER,NO STOP, NORMAL PATTERN                    105
1,1800/2,900/3,900/4,900/5,900/6,900/7,900/8,900/9,900/10,900/11,1800/          106
12,900/13,900/14,900/15,900/16,900/17,900/18,900/19,900/20,900                  107
 *                                                                             108
 4     FUNCTION  PF3,D20        AMBER,STOPPED,NORMAL PATTERN                     109
1,1800/2,1200/3,1200/4,1200/5,1200/6,1200/7,1200/8,1200/9,1200/10,1200/         110
11,1800/12,1200/13,1200/14,1200/15,1200/16,1200/17,1200/18,1200/19,1200/        111
20,1200                                                                         112
 *                                                                             113
 5     FUNCTION  PF3,D20        GREEN,NO STOP,ACCELERATED PATTERN                114
1,1800/2,450/3,450/4,450/5,450/6,450/7,450/8,450/9,450/10,450/11,1800/          115
12,450/13,450/14,450/15,450/16,450/17,450/18,450/19,450/20,450                  116
 *                                                                             117
 6     FUNCTION  PF3,D20        GREEN,STOPPED,ACCELERATED PATTERN                118
1,1800/2,600/3,600/4,600/5,600/6,600/7,600/8,600/9,600/10,600/11,1800/          119
12,600/13,600/14,600/15,600/16,600/17,600/18,600/19,600/20,600                  120
 *                                                                             121
 7     FUNCTION  PF3,D20        AMBER,NO STOP,ACCELERATED PATTERN                122
1,1800/2,600/3,600/4,600/5,600/6,600/7,600/8,600/9,600/10,600/11,1800/          123
12,600/13,600/14,600/15,600/16,600/17,600/18,600/19,600/20,600                  124
 *                                                                             125
 8     FUNCTION  PF3,D20        AMBER,STOPPED,ACCELERATED PATTERN                126
1,1800/2,900/3,900/4,900/5,900/6,900/7,900/8,900/9,900/10,900/11,1800/          127
12,900/13,900/14,900/15,900/16,900/17,900/18,900/19,900/20,900                  128
 **                                                                            129
 9     FUNCTION  PF3,D20              STATION NUMBER OR 0 IF NO STATION         130
1,1/2,0/3,0/4,2/5,0/6,0/7,3/8,0/9,0/10,4/11,5/12,0/13,0/14,6/15,0/16,0/         131
17,7/18,0/19,0/20,8                                                             132
 **                                                                            133
 *                                                                             134
 * FUNCTION 10 IS FOR TERMINUS 1, FUNCTION 11 FOR TERMINUS 2                    135
 10    FUNCTION  C1,C2                    TIME INTERVAL BETWEEN                  136
0,3000/360000,3000                                                              137
 11    FUNCTION  C1,C2                    2 CONSECUTIVE TRAINS                   138
0,3000/360000,3000                                                              139
 12    FUNCTION  RN8,C24            ERLANG 1                                     140
0.,0/0.1,0.104/0.2,0.222/0.3,0.355/0.4,0.509/0.5,0.69/0.6,0.915/               141
0.7,1.2/0.75,1.38/0.8,1.6/0.84,1.83/0.88,2.12/0.9,2.3/0.92,2.52/               142
0.94,2.81/0.95,2.99/0.96,3.2/0.97,3.5/0.98,3.9/0.99,4.6/0.995,5.3/            143
0.998,6.2/0.999,7.0/0.9997,8.0                                                  144
 *                                                                             145
 13    FUNCTION  PF2,D8               CUMULATED THEORETICAL SCHEDULE            146
1,600/2,3600/3,6600/4,9600/5,600/6,3600/7,6600/8,9600                           147
*1,600/2,2300/3,6300/4,9300/5,600/6,3300/7,6300/8,9300                          148
*1,600/2,3000/3,5400/4,7800/5,600/6,3000/7,5400/8,7800                          149
 *                                                                             150
 * PASSENGERS INTERARRIVAL TIMES, 1 FUNCTION PER STATION                        151
 *                                                                             152
 14    FUNCTION  C1,C2               PASSENG. INTERARRIV. TIMES                 153
0,36/360000,36                                                                  154
 15    FUNCTION  C1,C2               STATION 2                                  155
0,72/360000,72                                                                  156
 16    FUNCTION  C1,C2               STATION 3                                  157
0,108/360000,108                                                                158
 17    FUNCTION  C1,C2               STATION 5                                  159
0,36/360000,36                                                                  160
 18    FUNCTION  C1,C2               STATION 6                                  161
0,72/360000,72                                                                  162
 19    FUNCTION  C1,C2               STATION 7                                  163
0,108/360000,108                                                                164
 *                                                                             165
 * DESTINATION POINTS DISTRIBUTION FUNCTIONS, 1 PER STARTING STATION            166
 *                                                                             167
 20    FUNCTION  RN1,D3              STATION 1                                  168
.333,2/.667,3/1.,4                                                              169
```

Figure 10.10 (continued)

```
     21  FUNCTION   RN1,D2          STATION 2                        170
  .5,3/1.,4                                                          171
     22  FUNCTION   RN1,D2          STATION 3                        172
  C.,4/1.,4                                                          173
     24  FUNCTION   RN1,D3          STATION 5                        174
  .333,6/.667,7/1.,8                                                 175
     25  FUNCTION   RN1,D2          STATION 6                        176
  .5,7/1.,8                                                          177
     26  FUNCTION   RN1,D2          STATION 7                        178
  C.,8/1.,8                                                          179
  *                                                                  180
  *  END OF FUNCTIONS                                                181
  *                                                                  182
  *                                                                  183
  *  TRAINS SEQUENCE                                                 184
  *                                                                  185
  *    TERMINUS 1                                                    186
  *                                                                  187
1     STTL  GENERATE  0,,1,6,,18PF                                   188
2           ASSIGN    1,N$STTL,,PF    P1 = TRAIN NUMBER              189
3     ENS1  ENTER     STOR1           GARAGE TERMINUS 1              190
4           SUNAVAIL  PF1             TRAIN STORAGE MADE UNAVAILABLE  191
5           SEIZE     1               TRAIN IN STARTING PLACE        192
6           GATE LR   SUT1,SUP1       TRAINS TO BE SUPPRESSED?       193
7     BEG1  GATE LS   DEPA1           START SIGNAL GREEN?            194
8           LEAVE     STOR1           TRAIN LEAVES GARAGE            195
9           SAVAIL    PF1             TRAIN STORAGE MADE AVAILABLE   196
  *         MARK                      TRAIN STARTING TIME - WAS USED FOR DEBUGGING   197
10          LOGICR    DEPA1           SET START SIGNAL TO RED        198
11          GATE LS   1               IS STATION INPUT SIGNAL GREEN? 199
12          LOGICR    1               SET IT TO RED                  200
13          RELEASE   1               TRAIN ENTERS STATION           201
14          ASSIGN    4,V15,,PF       P4=TIME DELAYED WHEN STARTING  202
15          ASSIGN    2,1,,PF         P2=STATION NUMBER              203
16          ASSIGN    3,1,,PF         P3=SECTION NUMBER              204
17          ASSIGN    6,2,,PF         STOP AT BEGINNING OF SECTION   205
18          TRANSFER  ,STATI                                         206
  *                                                                  207
  *    TERMINUS 2                                                    208
  *                                                                  209
19    STEL  GENERATE  0,,1,6,,18PF                                   210
20          ASSIGN    1,V12,,PF       P1 = TRAIN NUMBER              211
21    ENS2  ENTER     STOR2           GARAGE TERMINUS 2              212
22          SUNAVAIL  PF1             TRAIN STORAGE MADE UNAVAILABLE 213
23          SEIZE     2               TRAIN IN STARTING PLACE        214
24          GATE LR   SUT2,SUF2       TRAINS TO BE SUPPRESSED?       215
25    BEG2  GATE LS   DEPA2           START SIGNAL GREEN?            216
26          LEAVE     STOR2           TRAIN LEAVES GARAGE            217
27          SAVAIL    PF1             TRAIN STORAGE MADE AVAILABLE   218
  *         MARK                      TRAIN STARTING TIME - WAS USED FOR DEBUGGING   219
28          LOGICR    DEPA2           START SIGNAL SET TO RED        220
29          GATE LS   V17             IS STATION INPUT SIGNAL GREEN? 221
30          LOGICR    V17             SET IT TO RED                  222
31          RELEASE   2               TRAIN ENTERS STATION           223
32          ASSIGN    4,V16,,PF       P4=TIME DELAYED WHEN STARTING  224
33          ASSIGN    2,V19,,PF       P2=STATION NUMBER              225
34          ASSIGN    3,V17,,PF       P3=SECTION NUMBER              226
35          ASSIGN    6,2,PF          STOP AT BEGINNING OF SECTION   227
  *                                                                  228
  *    STATION OPERATIONS                                            229
  *                                                                  230
36    STATI ASSIGN    5,PF*V1,,PF     NBR.OF PASS.GOING OUT IN P5    231
37          LEAVE     PF1,PF*V1       PASSENGERS GET OUT             232
38          TEST L    C*PF2,R*PF1,TREMP PASSENG. NBR.<AVAILABLE ROOM? 233
39          ASSIGN    7,Q*PF2,,PF     P7=NB OF PASSENG. GETTING IN   234
40          TRANSFER  ,GETIN                                         235
41    TREMP ASSIGN    7,R*PF1,,PF     P7=NB.OF PASSENGERS GETTING IN 236
42    GETIN ENTER     PF1,PF7         P7 PASSENGERS IN TRAIN P1      237
43          TABULATE  V10             TABLES TRAIN UTILIZ. PER STATION 238
44          DEPART    PF2,PF7         PASS. EXTRAC. FROM WAIT QUEUE  239
45          TABULATE  V11             TAB. PASSENG. LEFT IN STATION  240
46          ADVANCE   V2              TIME TO GET IN AND OUT         241
47          ASSIGN    4+,V2,,PF       P4=CUMULATIVE TRAVELING TIME   242
48          TEST NE   PF7,0,TEG       PASSENGERS TO GET IN?          243
49          SAVEVALUE 12,V24          DESTIN. POINT FUNCT. IN X12    244
50    BCUC  ASSIGN    V25+,1,,PF      INCREM. DESTIN. POINT BY 1     245
51          LOOP      7PF,BCUC                                       246
52    TEG   TEST LE   PF4,FN13,RETAR  BEHIND SCHED. WHEN LEAVING STAT? 247
53          ASSIGN    5,V3,,PF        AHEAD: WAIT TIME IN STATION IN P5 248
54          ADVANCE   PF5             WAIT TIME                      249
55          TABULATE  WAIT            TABULATE WAIT TIME             250
56          ASSIGN    4,FN13,,PF      THEOR. SCHED. IN P4            251
57          ASSIGN    5,0,,PF         NORMAL PATTERN                 252
58          TRANSFER  ,GETOU                                         253
59    RETAR ASSIGN    5,1,,PF         ACCELERATED PATTERN            254
60          TABULATE  PF2             TABUL. TIME BEHIND SCHED. IN STATIONS 255
61    GETOU ASSIGN    V1,0,,PF        PASSENG.NBR FOR THIS STATION=0 256
```

Figure 10.10 (continued)

```
62            TEST E     PF2,X1,TFLI        IS THIS TERMINUS 1?             257
63            ASSIGN     3,1,,PF            SECTION 1                       258
64            LOGICS     X2                 LAST SECTION SIGNAL TO GREEN    259
65            ADVANCE    FN*V6              CHANGE TRACK                    260
66            ASSIGN     4-,FN13,,FF        COMPUTE TIME BEHIND SCHEDULE    261
67            TABULATE   RET1               TABULATE THIS TIME              262
68            TRANSFER   ,ENS1              BACK TO GARAGE                  263
69   TFLI     TEST E     PF2,V23,SECTI      IS THIS TERMINUS 2?             264
70            ASSIGN     3+,1,,PF           INCREMENT SECTION NUMBER        265
71            LOGICS     V4                 SIGNAL N-1 SET TO GREEN         266
72            ADVANCE    FN*V6              CHANGE TRACK                    267
73            ASSIGN     4-,FN13,,PF        COMPUTE TIME BEHIND SCHEDULE    268
74            TABULATE   RET2               TABULATE THIS TIME              269
75            TRANSFER   ,ENS2              BACK TO GARAGE                  270
                                                                           271
      *                                                                    272
      *  TRAIN MOVEMENT BETWEEN STATIONS (ON ONE SECTION)                  273
      *                                                                    274
76   SECTI    ASSIGN     3+,1,,PF           NEXT SECTION                    274
77            ASSIGN     2,FN9,,FF          STATION NR OF THIS SECTION      275
78            GATE LS    PF3                INPUT SIGNAL SECTION N NOT RED? 276
79            LOGICR     PF3                SIGNAL N SET TO RED             277
80            LOGICS     V4                 SIGNAL N-1 SET TO NOT RED       278
81            TEST E     PF2,0,AMBER        SECTION WITH A STATION?         279
82            GATE LS    V5,AMBER           SIGNAL N AMBER?                 280
83            ADVANCE    FN*V6              TIME FOR GREEN SECTION          281
84            ASSIGN     4+,FN*V6,,PF                                       282
85            ASSIGN     6,1                NO STOP AT SIGNAL N+1           283
86            TRANSFER   ,SECTI             TO NEXT SECTION                 284
87   AMBER    ADVANCE    FN*V7              TIME FOR AMBER SECTION          285
88            ASSIGN     4+,FN*V7,,PF                                       286
89            ASSIGN     6,2,,PF            STOP AT SIGNAL N+1              287
90            TEST E     PF2,0,STATI        SECTION WITH A STATION?         288
91            TRANSFER   ,SECTI             TO NEXT SECTION                 289
                                                                           290
      *                                                                    291
      *  END TRAINS SEQUENCE                                               292
      *                                                                    293
      *  TIME DELAYS FOR ARRIVALS OF PASSENGERS AT STATIONS                294
      *                                                                    295
92            GENERATE   ,,,1,,3PF                                         296
93            ASSIGN     1,V23,,PF          P1=1/2 NB OF STATIONS           297
94            ASSIGN     1-,1,,PF           -1 (NO PASSENG. GENER. LAST STAT.) 298
95            ASSIGN     2,1,,PF            P2=STATION NUMBER               299
96   DEC      ASSIGN     3,FN13,,PF         P3=TRAVEL TIME FOR THE SECTION  300
97            LOGICS     V8                 DIR.1 PASSENG.START SIGNAL GREEN 301
98            LOGICS     V22                DIR.2 PASSENG.START SIGNAL GREEN 302
99            ASSIGN     2+,1,,PF           INCREMENT STATION NUMBER        303
100           ADVANCE    V9                 THEOR. SCHEDULE BETWEEN STATIONS 304
101           LOOP       1PF,DEC                                           305
102           TERMINATE                                                    306
      *                                                                    307
      *  PASSENGERS GENERATION                                             308
      *                                                                    309
103           GENERATE   FN14,FN12,,,1,2PF   STATION 1                     310
104           TRANSFER   ,INPUT                                            311
105           GENERATE   FN15,FN12,,,2,2PF   STATION 2                     312
106           TRANSFER   ,INPUT                                            313
107           GENERATE   FN16,FN12,,,3,2PF   STATION 3                     314
108           TRANSFER   ,INPUT                                            315
109           GENERATE   FN17,FN12,,,5,2PF   STATION 5                     316
110           TRANSFER   ,INPUT                                            317
111           GENERATE   FN18,FN12,,,6,2PF   STATION 6                     318
112           TRANSFER   ,INPUT                                            319
113           GENERATE   FN19,FN12,,,7,2PF   STATION 7                     320
      *                                                                    321
      *  COMMON SEQUENCE FOR ALL STATIONS                                  322
      *                                                                    323
114  INPUT    ASSIGN     2,PR,,PF           P1=STATION NUMBER              324
115           PRIORITY   1                  RESET PRIORITY TO 1            325
116           GATE LS    V8,FIN             IS STATION INPUT SIGNAL GREEN? 326
117           QUEUE      PF2                PASSENG. IN STAT. WAIT QUEUE   327
118  FIN      TERMINATE                                                   328
      *                                                                    329
      *                                                                    330
      *  TRAIN SUPPRESSION                                                 331
      *                                                                    332
      *  TERMINUS 1                                                        333
      *                                                                    334
119  SUP1     GATE LR    SWT1,SNOR1         SUPPRESS EVERY OTHER TRAIN     334
120           SAVEVALUE  10-,1              X10=NB. OF TRAINS TO BE SUPPRESSED 335
121           RELEASE    1                  FREE STARTING PLACE           336
122           TEST E     X10,0,TER1                                       337
123           LOGICR     SUT1               END TRAIN SUPPRESSION          338
124           LINK       RES1,FIFO          TRAIN IN RESERVE              339
125  TER1     LOGIC S    SWT1               NEXT TRAIN WILL NOT BE SUPPRESSED 340
126           LINK       RES1,FIFO          TRAIN IN RESERVE              341
127  SNOR1    LOGIC R    SWT1               NEXT TRAIN WILL BE SUPPRESSED 342
128           TRANSFER   ,BEG1              BACK TO NORMAL PROCESS        343
```

Figure 10.10   (continued)

```
        *                                                              344
        *    TERMINUS 2                                                345
        *                                                              346
129     SUP2 GATE LR    SWT2,SNOR2        SAME SEQUENCE AS FOR TERMINUS 1    347
130          SAVEVALUE  11-,1                                          348
131          RELEASE    2                                              349
132          TEST E     X11,0,TER2                                     350
133          LOGICR     SUT2                                           351
134          LINK       RES2,FIFO                                      352
135     TER2 LOGIC S    SWT2                                           353
136          LINK       RES2,FIFO                                      354
137     SNOR2 LOGIC R   SWT2                                           355
138          TRANSFER   ,BEG2                                          356
        *                                                              357
        * TERMINUS 1 DEPARTURE SCHEDULING                              358
        *                                                              359
139          GENERATE   FN10,,,,,1PF      1 TRANSACTION/THEOR. DEPART.TIME  360
140          ASSIGN     1,C1,,PF          P1=THEOR. DEPARTURE TIME     361
141          QUEUE      FAT1              QUEUE TRAIN                  362
142          GATE LR    DEPA1             IS START SIGNAL RED?         363
143          DEPART     FAT1              LEAVE QUEUE                  364
144          LOGICS     DEPA1             SET START SIGNAL TO GREEN    365
145          SAVEVALUE  8,PF1             THEOR. DEPART. TIME IN X8    366
146          TERMINATE                                                 367
        *                                                              368
        * TERMINUS 2 DEPARTURE SCHEDULING                              369
        *                                                              370
147          GENERATE   FN11,,,,,1PF      SAME PROGRAM FOR DIRECTION 2  371
148          ASSIGN     1,C1,,PF                                       372
149          QUEUE      FAT2                                           373
150          GATE LR    DEPA2                                          374
151          DEPART     FAT2                                           375
152          LOGICS     DEPA2                                          376
153          SAVEVALUE  9,PF1                                          377
154          TERMINATE                                                 378
        *                                                              379
        * CONTROL OF TRAIN SUPPRESSION                                 380
        *                                                              381
        * DIRECTION 1                                                  382
155          GENERATE   200,,,1           TRAIN SUPPRESSION STARTING TIME  383
156          LOGICS     SUT1              SET SUPPRESS SIGNAL          384
157          SAVEVALUE  10,2              NBR. OF TRAINS TO BE SUPP. IN X10  385
158          TERMINATE                                                 386
        *                                                              387
        * DIRECTION 2                                                  388
159          GENERATE   200,,,1                                        389
160          LOGICS     SUT2                                           390
161          SAVEVALUE  11,2                                           391
162          TERMINATE                                                 392
        *                                                              393
        *                                                              394
        * AUXILIARY CLOCK                                              395
        *                                                              396
163          GENERATE   36000                                         397
164          TERMINATE  1                                              398
        *                                                              399
        * INJECTION OF ADDITION. PASSENGERS AT STATIONS 1,2,3         400
        * WITH INTERARRIVAL TIMES OF 5 SEC., EXPONENTIAL. DISTR.      401
        *                                                              402
165          GENERATE   50,FN12,,,1,2PF                               403
166          TRANSFER   ,INPUT                                        404
167          GENERATE   50,FN12,,,2,2PF                               405
168          TRANSFER   ,INPUT                                        406
169          GENERATE   50,FN12,,,3,2PF                               407
170          TRANSFER   ,INPUT                                        408
             START      4                                             409
        *                                                              410
        * REPORT SECTION                                               411
        *                                                              412
             REPORT                                                    413
             EJECT                                                     414
        CLO  TITLE      ,                                              415
             SPACE      3                                              416
        BLO  TITLE      ,                                              417
             SPACE      3                                              418
        FSV  TITLE      ,FULLWORD SAVEVALUES                          419
             EJECT                                                     420
        TAB  TITLE      ,AVERAGE TIME BEHIND SCHEDULE AT STATIONS     421
        TAB  INCLUDE    T1-T8/1,2,3,4                                 422
             SPACE      3                                              423
        TAB  TITLE      ,AVERAGE TIME BEHIND SCHEDULE AT TERMINUS 1 AND 2  424
        TAB  INCLUDE    T$RET1-T$RET2/1,2,3,4                         425
             SPACE      3                                              426
        TAB  TITLE      ,TRAIN AVERAGE WAITING TIME AT STATIONS (AHEAD OF SCHE  427
        DULE)                                                          428
        TAB  INCLUDE    T$WAIT/1,2,3,4                                429
             EJECT                                                     430
```

Figure 10.10   (continued)

```
STO    TITLE      ,AVERAGE TRAIN OCCUPATION (%) ANC GARAGE STATISTICS AC        431
T TERMINUS 1 ANC 2                                                              432
       SPACE      3                                                             433
TAB    TITLE      ,AVERAGE TRAIN UTILIZATICN WHEN LEAVING STATION               434
TAB    INCLUDE    T21-T28/1,2,3,4                                               435
       EJECT                                                                    436
CUE    TITLE      ,PASSENGER STATISTICS AT STATIONS: MAXIM. AND AVERAGEC        437
LENGTH, AVERAGE WAITING TIME                                                    438
CLE    INCLUDE    C1-C8/1,2,3,4,7,10                                            439
       SPACE      3                                                             440
TAB    TITLE      ,AVERAGE NUMBER CF PASSENGERS LEFT AT STATIONS                441
TAB    INCLUDE    T11-T18/1,2,3,4                                               442
       EJECT                                                                    443
       ENC                                                                      444
```

Figure 10.10   (continued)

10.4   Experiments and Results

It is obvious that many investigations can be made with the model described, but we have decided to limit ourselves to those which are standard and thus demonstrate the flexibility of the model, particularly the ease of making modifications to study other aspects of the system.

We have simulated the system for periods of 4 hours. We feel this to be sufficient to obtain reliable results which are unaffected by the starting period.

We have studied the influence of three factors:

1. the number of trains kept in service;
2. the train schedule: normal or reduced schedule (see Table 10.5);
3. additional passengers at stations 1, 2, and 3, Poisson-distributed, with various average interarrival times, 2, 5, and 10 s.

We discovered that considerable differences were produced so we also investigated an "intermediate" schedule between the two discussed. The corresponding values as well as the values of the reduced schedule can be found under function 13 in the listing of the program, with an asterisk in column 1 so that these lines are considered as comments when not used.

10.4.1   Three trains running in each direction

The investigations showed that the trains consistently left the terminus behind schedule—on the average, approximately 3.5 min late. Owing to the accelerated movement pattern adopted, this time could be reduced so that the trains could arrive on time at the terminus. It is obvious that such operation is not acceptable. The reduced schedule improved the situation somewhat in that the total train turnaround was faster (average time behind schedule when leaving was about 1.0 min).

In both situations, additional passengers at stations 1, 2, and 3 increased the times behind schedule slightly. With the normal schedule and an average intergeneration time of 10 s, some passengers were left in stations 1 and 2 (average number 0.2 in station 1 and 2.8 in station 2), whereas with the accelerated schedule no passengers were left. With an average intergeneration time of 5 s, the situation became much worse: the average number left in station 1 was 3.5 with normal schedule and 0.4 with accelerated schedule; and in station 2, 112.4 with normal schedule and 29.6 with accelerated schedule.

Another very interesting point was the percentage availability of the storages (trains), which indicate the percentage of time that the trains were used. In all the cases considered above they were greater than 94 per cent. It was then decided to add one train in both directions and thus suppress two trains in each direction in our model.

10.4.2   Four trains running in each direction

During the experiments performed with a total of eight trains, the utilization of the trains, given by the percentage availability, was between 87 and 93 per cent, normal schedule, and 75 and 82 per cent, accelerated schedule.

With the normal schedule no late running was observed and the maximum contents of the trains was 126. With the accelerated schedule, an interesting phenomenon appeared: trains on schedule at the terminus were alternately late and early at successive stations. This confirmed that the accelerated movement pattern allows trains to catch up a certain amount of time but also drew our attention to the fact that it might be overcorrecting. This is certainly a point for further study. This result was also one of the reasons for experimenting with an "intermediate schedule," mentioned at the beginning of Section 10.4.

With the normal schedule and with additional passengers (average interarrival time of 10 s) at stations 1, 2, and 3, no problems were encountered. The maximum train content was 177. No train was behind schedule. When applying the accelerated schedule, we observed that times behind schedule at all stations, except the termini, were alternately large and small. No passengers were left waiting at stations. With additional passengers with an average interarrival time of 5 s, we observed the following results, which are presented in Figure 10.11.

The average time behind schedule and number of times was 3.1 s at station 3 (26 times), 3.6 at station 4 (6 times), and zero at all other stations. The average time behind schedule at terminus 1 was zero; at terminus 2 was 5 s. The difference in the times for station 4 (terminus 2) is caused by the fact that in the first tables (time behind schedule at stations) we make an entry only when the train is behind schedule, whereas at the terminus every train makes an entry (which is zero if the train is not behind schedule). The average waiting time at stations when ahead of schedule was 26 s.

With additional passengers at stations 1, 2, and 3 and with an average interarrival time less than 5 s, the queues increase, the trains are full when leaving these stations, and the system can no longer absorb the increased load. If such a case should really occur one should investigate a change of the train frequencies (interval shorter than 5 min), or, more simply, apply a reduced schedule, as discussed earlier.

10.4.3   Further experiments

Although we ended our experiment at this point, the above account is sufficient to demonstrate the flexibility of the model.

The reader may want to investigate other properties of the system such as:

RELATIVE CLOCK   144000   ABSOLUTE CLOCK   144000

BLOCK COUNTS

BLOCK	CURRENT	TOTAL	BLOCK	CURRENT	TOTAL	BLOCK	CURRENT	TOTAL	BLOCK	CURRENT	TOTAL	BLOCK	CURRENT	TOTAL
1	0	6	11	0	47	21	0	50	31	0	47	41	0	36
2	0	6	12	0	47	22	0	50	32	0	47	42	0	364
3	0	50	13	0	47	23	0	50	33	0	47	43	0	364
4	0	50	14	0	47	24	1	50	34	0	47	44	0	364
5	0	50	15	0	47	25	0	47	35	0	47	45	0	364
6	1	50	16	0	47	26	0	47	36	0	364	46	0	364
7	0	47	17	0	47	27	0	47	37	0	364	47	0	364
8	0	47	18	0	47	28	0	47	38	0	364	48	0	364
9	0	47	19	0	6	29	0	47	39	0	328	49	0	276
10	0	47	20	0	6	30	0	47	40	0	328	50	0	22671

BLOCK	CURRENT	TOTAL	BLOCK	CURRENT	TOTAL	BLOCK	CURRENT	TOTAL	BLOCK	CURRENT	TOTAL	BLOCK	CURRENT	TOTAL
51	0	22671	61	0	364	71	0	44	81	0	828	91	0	0
52	0	364	62	0	364	72	0	44	82	0	552	92	0	1
53	0	332	63	0	44	73	0	44	83	0	552	93	0	1
54	0	332	64	0	44	74	0	44	84	0	552	94	0	1
55	0	332	65	0	44	75	0	44	85	0	552	95	0	1
56	0	332	66	0	44	76	0	828	86	0	552	96	0	3
57	0	332	67	0	44	77	0	828	87	6	276	97	0	3
58	0	332	68	0	44	78	0	828	88	0	270	98	0	3
59	0	32	69	0	320	79	0	828	89	0	270	99	0	3
60	0	32	70	0	44	80	0	828	90	0	270	100	0	3

BLOCK	CURRENT	TOTAL	BLOCK	CURRENT	TOTAL	BLOCK	CURRENT	TOTAL	BLOCK	CURRENT	TOTAL	BLOCK	CURRENT	TOTAL
101	0	3	111	0	2000	121	0	2	131	0	2	141	0	47
102	0	1	112	0	2000	122	0	2	132	0	2	142	0	47
103	0	4124	113	0	1358	123	0	1	133	0	1	143	0	47
104	0	4124	114	0	23579	124	0	1	134	0	1	144	0	47
105	0	1599	115	0	23579	125	0	1	135	0	1	145	0	47
106	0	1999	116	0	23579	126	0	1	136	0	1	146	0	47
107	0	1287	117	0	23210	127	0	1	137	0	1	147	0	47
108	0	1287	118	0	23579	128	0	1	138	0	1	148	0	47
109	0	4130	119	0	3	129	0	3	139	0	47	149	0	47
110	0	4130	120	0	2	130	0	2	140	0	47	150	0	47

BLOCK	CURRENT	TOTAL	BLOCK	CURRENT	TOTAL	BLOCK	CURRENT	TOTAL	BLOCK	CURRENT	TOTAL	BLOCK	CURRENT	TOTAL
151	0	47	161	0	1									
152	0	47	162	0	1									
153	0	47	163	0	4									
154	0	47	164	0	4									
155	0	1	165	0	2993									
156	0	1	166	0	2993									
157	0	1	167	0	2791									
158	0	1	168	0	2791									
159	0	1	169	0	2897									
160	0	1	170	0	2897									

FULLWORD SAVEVALUES

NUMBER	CONTENTS	NUMBER	CONTENTS	NUMBER	CONTENTS	NUMBER	CONTENTS	NUMBER	CONTENTS	NUMBER	CONTENTS
1	8	2	20	3	50	4	3	5	3	7	6
8	141000	9	141000	12	22						

AVERAGE TIME BEHIND SCHEDULE AT STATIONS

TABLE   3

ENTRIES IN TABLE	MEAN ARGUMENT	STANDARD DEVIATION	
26	30.846	20.187	NON-WEIGHTED

TABLE   4

ENTRIES IN TABLE	MEAN ARGUMENT	STANDARD DEVIATION	
6	36.000	12.535	NON-WEIGHTED

AVERAGE TIME BEHIND SCHEDULE AT TERMINUS 1 AND 2

TABLE   RET1

ENTRIES IN TABLE	MEAN ARGUMENT	STANDARD DEVIATION	
44	-.000	.000	NON-WEIGHTED

TABLE   RET2

ENTRIES IN TABLE	MEAN ARGUMENT	STANDARD DEVIATION	
44	4.909	13.207	NON-WEIGHTED

MAIN AVERAGE WAITING TIME AT STATIONS (AHEAD OF SCHEDULE)

TABLE   WAIT

ENTRIES IN TABLE	MEAN ARGUMENT	STANDARD DEVIATION	
332	260.406	173.000	NON-WEIGHTED

Figure 10.11   Condensed output from subway simulation.

AVERAGE TRAIN OCCUPATION (%) AND GARAGE STATISTICS AT TERMINUS 1 AND 2

STORAGE	CAPACITY	AVERAGE CONTENTS	ENTRIES	AVERAGE TIME/UNIT	-AVERAGE TOTAL TIME	UTILIZATION DURING- AVAIL. TIME	UNAVAIL. TIME	CURRENT STATUS	PERCENT AVAILABILITY	CURRENT CONTENTS	MAXIMUM CONTENTS
TRAIN	200	94.822	2885	4732.882	.474	.507	.000	A	93.3	84	200
3	200	92.184	2871	4623.667	.460	.504	.000	A	91.2	110	200
5	200	94.909	2893	4724.125	.474	.531	.000	A	89.2	96	200
6	200	91.815	2819	4690.105	.459	.527	.000	NA	87.1		200
7	200	94.798	2968	4599.367	.473	.507	.000	A	93.3	200	200
9	200	95.160	2899	4726.859	.475	.521	.000	A	91.2	200	200
11	200	88.907	2842	4504.804	.444	.458	.000	A	89.1	165	200
12	200	84.240	2494	4863.929	.421	.483	.000	NA	87.0		200
STOR1	12	2.391	50	6887.878	.199				100.0	3	6
STOR2	12	2.390	50	6883.558	.199				100.0	3	6

AVERAGE TRAIN UTILIZATION WHEN LEAVING STATION

TABLE   21
ENTRIES IN TABLE   MEAN ARGUMENT   STANDARD DEVIATION
     47   73.425   5.496   NON-WEIGHTED

TABLE   22
ENTRIES IN TABLE   MEAN ARGUMENT   STANDARD DEVIATION
     46   98.608   2.644   NON-WEIGHTED

TABLE   23
ENTRIES IN TABLE   MEAN ARGUMENT   STANDARD DEVIATION
     45   92.555   4.824   NON-WEIGHTED

TABLE   24
ENTRIES IN TABLE   MEAN ARGUMENT   STANDARD DEVIATION
     44   -.000   .000   NON-WEIGHTED

TABLE   25
ENTRIES IN TABLE   MEAN ARGUMENT   STANDARD DEVIATION
     47   42.404   5.378   NON-WEIGHTED

TABLE   26
ENTRIES IN TABLE   MEAN ARGUMENT   STANDARD DEVIATION
     46   48.978   4.421   NON-WEIGHTED

TABLE   27
ENTRIES IN TABLE   MEAN ARGUMENT   STANDARD DEVIATION
     45   37.799   4.804   NON-WEIGHTED

TABLE   28
ENTRIES IN TABLE   MEAN ARGUMENT   STANDARD DEVIATION
     44   -.000   .000   NON-WEIGHTED

PASSENGER STATISTICS AT STATIONS: MAXIM. AND AVERAGE LENGTH, AVERAGE WAITING TIME

QUEUE	MAXIMUM CONTENTS	AVERAGE CONTENTS	TOTAL ENTRIES	AVERAGE TIME/TRANS	CURRENT CONTENTS
STAT1	172	74.357	7116	1504.699	145
2	155	62.468	4687	1919.241	140
3	120	42.469	4033	1516.406	120
5	109	42.830	4130	1493.347	75
6	53	20.443	1951	1508.917	36
7	40	13.648	1293	1520.074	23

AVERAGE NUMBER OF PASSENGERS LEFT AT STATIONS

TABLE TABLE
ENTRIES IN TABLE   MEAN ARGUMENT   STANDARD DEVIATION
     47   -.000   .000   NON-WEIGHTED

TABLE 12
ENTRIES IN TABLE   MEAN ARGUMENT   STANDARD DEVIATION
     46   14.665   15.847   NON-WEIGHTED

TABLE 13
ENTRIES IN TABLE   MEAN ARGUMENT   STANDARD DEVIATION
     45   .311   1.425   NON-WEIGHTED

TABLE 14
ENTRIES IN TABLE   MEAN ARGUMENT   STANDARD DEVIATION
     44   -.000   .000   NON-WEIGHTED

TABLE 15
ENTRIES IN TABLE   MEAN ARGUMENT   STANDARD DEVIATION
     47   -.000   .000   NON-WEIGHTED

TABLE 16
ENTRIES IN TABLE   MEAN ARGUMENT   STANDARD DEVIATION
     46   -.000   .000   NON-WEIGHTED

TABLE 17
ENTRIES IN TABLE   MEAN ARGUMENT   STANDARD DEVIATION
     45   -.000   .000   NON-WEIGHTED

TABLE 18
ENTRIES IN TABLE   MEAN ARGUMENT   STANDARD DEVIATION
     44   -.000   .000   NON-WEIGHTED

Figure 10.11   (continued)

Varying the schedule further.

Changing the accelerated movement pattern.

Changing the train frequencies and the train capacities during the day.

Simulating accidents or incidents: train breakdowns can be simulated very easily by using red signals and examining the time necessary to bring the system back to stability.

Studying the allocation of passengers to stations during peak hours. For example, if too many passengers are generated at station 2, instead of waiting too long they might decide to walk to another station where they might wait for a shorter time. This alternative obviously depends on the distances to adjacent stations and on the exact location from which they are generated.

Replacing the adopted simple accelerated movement pattern by a more sophisticated one: for example, testing the situation, ahead of or behind schedule, for every section rather than at every station.

In the next section, we discuss some modeling aspects which are very important for the overall efficiency of the simulation study.

10.5 Alternative Modeling Strategies

10.5.1 Passenger representation

When designing the first version of the model, we had decided that the passengers, after being generated at the station, would be linked on a user chain waiting to enter a train. When unlinked from the user chain by a train transaction, they would be used for producing statistics, for instance on their waiting time, and immediately destroyed (terminated). This form of modeling would have had the advantage of keeping the passenger transactions in existence until entering the train. It would allow the program to specify the destination for every passenger and could include rules for selecting how passengers enter the train, which might be more sophisticated and more realistic than the FIFO strategy. The disadvantages would be the main storage used (all live transactions in the model need storage), the computer time used for linking and unlinking transactions, and, in consequence of the first point, the danger of running out of main storage (that is, of producing the GPSS error 599: common storage exceeded and job canceled).

In our desire for this model to be able to explore a wide spectrum of cases, we ran a great risk of aborting with the error 599. We therefore suggested the change of strategy, which was implemented in the model: Passengers are generated, entered in the queue corresponding to the station, and terminated. When a train enters a station, it extracts from the queue the number of units computed (either to fill the train or to empty the queue). As the train transaction which goes through the DEPART block is not a member of the queue (it never entered it), the warning message "execution error 854" is produced but does not stop the simulation. Another argument in favor of this strategy is that we were more interested in the schedule and its stability than in the passenger statistics.

If, for any reason, we want to manipulate the passengers as transactions, we would recommend making first investigations using our model, to save computer running time. When stable cases for further analysis have been identified, then it is justifiable to modify the model, that is, replace the queues by user chains and the DEPART block in the train sequence by an UNLINK block. This new model would then be used for the specific investigations.

10.5.2 Passenger generation

Another question that may be asked is: Why generate one transaction per passenger? One could replace the GENERATE, QUEUE, and TERMINATE blocks of the current strategy by an ADVANCE block (to simulate the time between successive arrivals), a QUEUE (as before), and a TRANSFER block back to the ADVANCE block. In this way, we would generate and have present in the model only one transaction per station. This transaction would "generate" a passenger every time it goes through the loop, but it would save the computer time used for creation and destruction of passenger transactions.

Another modification would be to suppress the GATE block, used to start generating passengers a given time before the arrival of the first train, by using the offset (C-operand) of the GENERATE blocks for all stations, but this would have the disadvantage of making later alterations to the model somewhat complex.

10.5.3 Station operations

The model, as implemented, does not allow passengers, who arrive during the time that the train is in the station, to board. It is like the Paris metro, whose access doors are closed when the train arrives. One can change this discipline with the following modification.

When the train is ahead of schedule by an amount greater than a given time, program an ADVANCE block with a time equal, for instance, to the time ahead of schedule minus $(R*PF1)*X4$, which is the time that would be needed to fill the remaining room on the train. This would guard against the risk of delaying an early train until it is behind schedule. After this ADVANCE block, the transaction would loop back to block 38 to admit those passengers who have arrived during the interim. A further modification would be needed: the ADVANCE time V2 of block 46 should be split into several parts so as to separate the time for passengers to descend, door opening, the time for passengers to enter, and, finally the door closing time.

10.5.4 Program debugging

The program is not large—170 blocks, but even in this case debugging must not be neglected (see Section 8.3). In our model, we first tested the train movements without passengers. The easiest way to do so was to replace block 114 by a TERMINATE block. The MARK instructions were used, (after blocks 9 and 27) to associate the starting time from the terminus with each train.

When the trains were modeled correctly, train suppression was introduced. When this extension was working properly, the passengers were generated and included in the model.

The programmed tables may seem to be too numerous. They were introduced to produce the information necessary to understand and check the behavior of the model. It is clear that we could use a single table to gather the times behind schedule at stations, as we did for the waiting times, but this would have hidden, for example, the fact that trains could be behind schedule at alternate stations.

10.6 Conclusions

The model presented in this chapter is simple but flexible enough to allow easy experimentation with many of the variables and parameters of the problem. We have shown that it is not the only possible modeling philosophy and we have discussed some alternatives in Section 10.5. Our strategy was directed by the results required and also by the overall efficiency of the model. One could obviously simplify the model by suppressing some of the tables produced and thus gather fewer statistics.

The field of public transportation is ideal for GPSS modeling. However, we have also tried to show that even so, one has to be prepared to make abstractions and avoid systematic application of a one-to-one correspondence between the problem studied and the model. For example, the traffic signals, which may be green, amber, or red, have not been represented as such but their effect on the system is simulated by a combination of two successive red or not red signals.

The model includes most of the commonly used GPSS features, including a REPORT to gather all model statistics in a condensed form on three pages.

Reference

10.1. Jean Greyfie de Bellecombe, Système de transports urbains collectifs (STUC): Etudes des circulations sur une ligne du réseau lausannois par simulation. Epreuves pratiques de diplôme, Lausanne EPF-L, 1971. (Unpublished.)

11 Simulation of a Job Shop

11.1 Introduction: Job Shop Scheduling

A *job shop* [11.2] is a manufacturing plant consisting of a set of machines operating independently. This set of machines may be divided into subgroups of machines which have the same characteristics. A *job* is a unit of output produced by a series of operations performed on machines in a specified sequence. This sequence is called the *routing* or the *technological sequence* of the job.

When scheduling jobs through the shop, the objective is to ensure that the operations are done in the proper sequence, while meeting such criteria as minimizing late deliveries, maximizing utilization of equipment, or minimizing in-process inventories.

In recent years there has been extensive research in the area of job shop scheduling [11.3] and [11.4], and the problem continues to intrigue analysts who cannot see why a system with such a simple structure may be so difficult to deal with until they have made their own studies [11.5].

There are two classes of job shop problem:

(1) the *static case*, in which all the jobs are on hand at time zero.

(2) the *dynamic case*, in which job arrivals vary with time.

Particularly in the latter case the complexity of the interactions among the many parts of the system make simulation techniques more suitable than analytic.

The aspects of job shop operations most extensively examined are the dispatching, or scheduling, rules. Many jobs can compete for an available machine, and rules to resolve conflicts must be defined. Many scheduling rules have been suggested, including:

328

1. *First in–first out* (FIFO):   the job with the earliest arrival time in the queue is selected.

2. *Highest priority:* each job is assigned a priority on arrival. The job with highest priority gets the machine first.

3. *Shortest processing time:* the job that requires minimum machine time is chosen from the queue of waiting jobs.

4. *Smallest remaining job slack:* the job that has minimum job slack is selected. The job slack, or remaining free time, is defined as the due date, minus the current time, minus the sum of the remaining processing times for that job. Thus this is the job most likely to be late.

5. *Earliest job due date:* the job with the earliest due date is chosen. This is similar to (4) above but does not include processing time in the scheduling rule.

The advantage of using simulation to evaluate these and other rules [11.1] or combination of rules, lies in its experimental flexibility. Simulation allows the user to evaluate alternative operating policies under reasonably realistic conditions without the necessity of simplifications usually required to obtain a tractable analytic model.

11.2 The System

The job shop considered in this study has the following characteristics:

N different groups of machines are available. Each group is treated as an independent work center. All machines in a given group are identical. Jobs waiting at any machine group form a single queue and are processed on the first available machine.

An operation is the processing of a particular job on a given machine. Once started, an operation continues until completed.

The dynamic problem is considered: job arrival is stochastic. It is assumed that batches of M different jobs are released to the shop according to a known probabilistic distribution.

On arrival, each job is assigned a routing. Each job may be processed more than once on a specified machine.

The sum of setup time and run time on a given machine is known as *processing time*. Transit time required to move jobs from a given machine group to any other machine group is also included in the processing time.

Before being scheduled, each job is assigned a due date proportional to the total work involved.

The number of machines within each group is fixed, so the only decisions required during the processing involve assignment of jobs to machines. The dispatching rules examined are those described in the introduction above: (1) first in–first served, (2) highest priority, (3) shortest processing time, (4) smallest remaining job slack, and (5) earliest job due date.

11.3 Model Requirements

The following simulator was designed to demonstrate the nature of job shop problems and to show the computational feasibility and efficiency of GPSS for handling job shop experiments. The model is based partly on practical experience and partly on theoretical work similar to that described in [11.1] and [11.5].

The simulation was designed for use in advanced simulation courses. A major requirement was that it should be as flexible as possible to permit various experiments on predetermined systems and also to allow for easy modification of the system itself. Numerous scheduling rules should be appraised, independently or combined, and system conditions, such as job-arrival pattern or job-processing times, should be varied to study the effect of varying traffic on different strategies.

Although very flexible, the model should be simple enough for a user to understand its structure quickly and thus be able to use it and to modify it without delay.

11.4 Numerical Characteristics

We describe two particular job shop configurations from the numerous cases that were modeled. The purpose of these descriptions is to show first how the model was implemented in GPSS and second how changes can be made.

The first shop consists of four groups of machines processing ten job types. A description of the job routings is shown in matrix form in Table 11.1. Each row contains information about a different job type. Column 11 specifies the number of operations required by the job, and columns 1 to 5 give the numbers of the machine groups in the sequence in which they are used by the job. Columns 6 to 10, not used here, allow the sequence to be extended to 10 operations without modification of the matrix size.

Table 11.1 ROUTING FOR FIRST JOB SHOP

	Column						
Row	1	2	3	4	5	...	11
1	1	4	2	3	4	—	5
2	4	3	1	2	—	—	4
3	4	1	2	—	—	—	3
4	3	4	2	1	—	—	4
5	2	1	3	4	1	—	5
6	2	3	4	1	—	—	4
7	1	3	4	2	—	—	4
8	3	4	1	2	3	—	5
9	4	1	2	3	—	—	4
10	2	1	4	3	—	—	4

Further, each job belongs to one of two processing classes. The matrix of Table 11.2 contains information about the processing times in minutes; first row for jobs of class 1, second row for jobs of class 2. The columns represent the machine groups. For example, line 2 and column 3 gives the processing time on machines of group 3 for jobs belonging to class 2.

Table 11.2 PROCESSING TIMES

		Group		
Class	1	2	3	4
1	10	20	30	40
2	15	30	40	45

Different numbers of machines for each group, called *capacity*, are mentioned in our discussion of the GPSS implementation. One of the configurations is summarized in Table 11.3.

Table 11.3 CAPACITY OF THE FIRST JOB SHOP

Group	1	2	3	4
Number	2	2	3	3

The numerical characteristics of the second job shop considered are summarized in Tables 11.4 to 11.6. The second shop consists of five groups of machines and eleven types of jobs.

Table 11.4 ROUTING FOR SECOND JOB SHOP

				Column				
Row	1	2	3	4	5	6	...	11
1	1	4	2	3	4	—	—	5
2	4	3	1	2	—	—	—	4
3	4	1	2	—	—	—	—	3
4	3	4	2	1	5	—	—	5
5	2	1	3	4	1	5	—	6
6	2	3	4	1	—	—	—	4
7	1	3	4	2	—	—	—	4
8	3	4	1	2	3	5	—	6
9	4	1	2	3	—	—	—	4
10	2	1	4	3	—	—	—	4
11	1	3	2	—	—	—	—	3

Table 11.5 PROCESSING TIMES

	Group				
Class	1	2	3	4	5
1	10	20	30	40	20
2	15	30	40	45	25

Table 11.6 CAPACITY OF THE SECOND JOB SHOP

Group	1	2	3	4	5
Number	2	2	3	3	1

11.5   The GPSS Model

11.5.1   Correspondence between system elements and GPSS entities

A group of machines is represented by a storage whose capacity is the number of machines in that group.

A waiting line before a group of busy machines is simulated by three GPSS entities: a queue, a group, and a user chain, with reference numbers corresponding to the machine-group number. The queue collects statistics. The GPSS group entity allows the programmer to use the SCAN block to find particular characteristics of the waiting transactions such as the smallest remaining job slack or the earliest job due date. These characteristics are used to schedule a job on the first free machine.

The user chain contains transactions which are waiting for service. Thus only transactions corresponding to jobs being processed are not on a user chain.

11.5.2   Model overview

The GPSS model consists of three submodels called *job scheduling* (Figure 11.1), *job processing* (Figure 11.3) and *job creation* (Figure 11.4). Two types of transaction are used. The first represents the jobs and the second the control transactions which schedule the jobs competing for a free machine.

Job-scheduling submodel (Figure 11.1).   At the beginning of the simulation a control transaction is generated for each group of machines. Each control transaction is used for finding which transaction should be scheduled when a machine of its group becomes free.

Two or more of the scheduling rules mentioned in Section 11.1 may be used simultaneously, so the control transaction first examines all the job transactions waiting in the corresponding user chain. It extracts the required information such as highest priority, shortest processing time, smallest remaining job slack, longest time

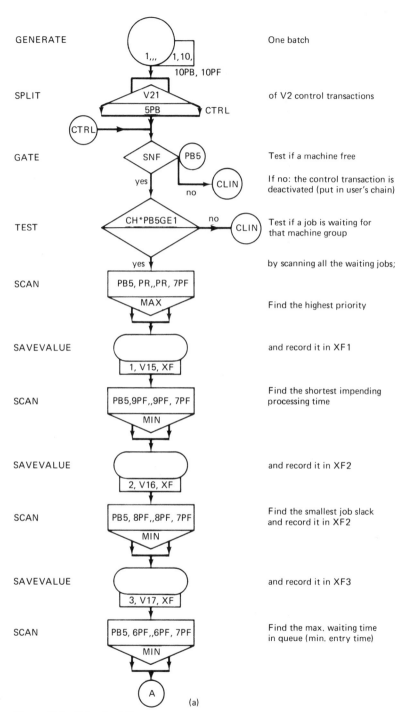

Figure 11.1 Job scheduling.

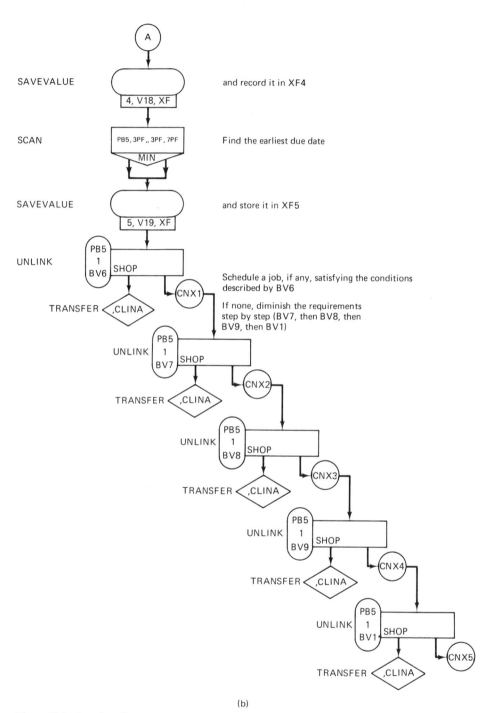

Figure 11.1 (continued)

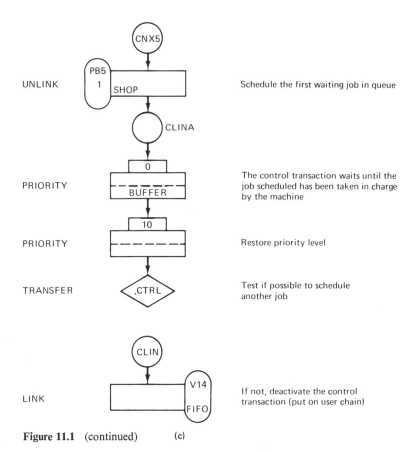

Figure 11.1 (continued)   (c)

in queue, or earliest job due date and stores it in savevalues. Each value is then multiplied by its corresponding effectiveness factor [shown later in the program listing as GPSS variables 5 to 9 (Figure 11.5)] to screen the scheduling rules which are not used in a given run.

Next, find one transaction, if any, that satisfies the active conditions or scheduling rules of the first set of conditions (defined by Boolean variable BV6 in Figure 11.5). If none, the second set of screening criteria is tried (BV7), and so on, as summarized in Figure 11.2, until one job transaction can be scheduled. This job transaction is unlinked from its user chain and sent to the job-processing submodel.

Afterwards the control transaction tests if at least one other job transaction is waiting and a machine is available. If so, the procedure is repeated. As soon as one of the conditions (at least one job transaction waiting and one machine available) is not satisfied, the control transaction is linked to a user chain and thus deactivated.

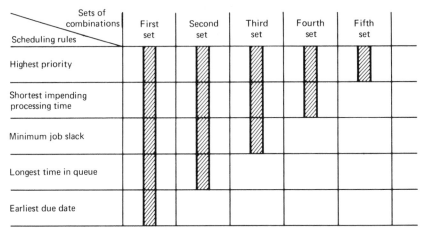

Figure 11.2 Screening criteria.

Job-processing submodel (Figure 11.3).   When the job transaction is sent to the job-processing submodel it is removed from the group and the queue where it was waiting for a free machine. After being processed, it notifies the control transaction that a machine has been freed. The number of remaining operations to be performed is then tested: if the number is zero, statistics are tabulated and the job transaction is destroyed. If at least one operation remains, its impending machine number, the processing time, and the job slack are updated. The job transaction then enters the next queue, joins the next group of waiting jobs, notifies the corresponding control transaction of its arrival, and is linked to a user chain to wait for scheduling.

Job-creation submodel (Figure 11.4).   The job-creation submodel generates batches of job transactions. Each batch contains one transaction of the different types specified. Each transaction is assigned the sequence of operations corresponding to its type and all the necessary information such as due date and priority. Each job transaction enters the assigned queue and joins its group, then signals its arrival to the control transaction before being linked to a user chain.

11.5.3 Program description

The listing of the GPSS program appears in Figure 11.5. The model simulates the second job shop described in Section 11.4. The following SNAs (standard numerical attributes) have been used.

Byte msavevalue 1 and fullword msavevalue 1.   Byte msavevalue 1 contains the routing information defined in Table 11.4. Fullword msavevalue 1 contains the processing times given in Table 11.5. Both msavevalues are initialized by INITIAL statements (statements 67 to 85) and are retained unaltered for reference only.

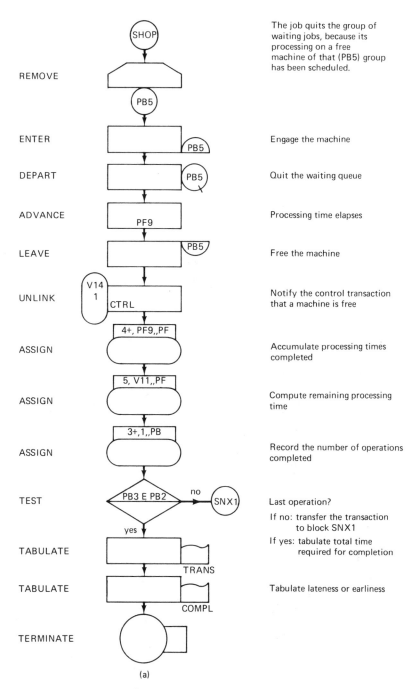

		The job quits the group of waiting jobs, because its processing on a free machine of that (PB5) group has been scheduled.
REMOVE	SHOP	
	PB5	
ENTER	PB5	Engage the machine
DEPART	PB5	Quit the waiting queue
ADVANCE	PF9	Processing time elapses
LEAVE	PB5	Free the machine
UNLINK	V14 1 CTRL	Notify the control transaction that a machine is free
ASSIGN	4+, PF9,,PF	Accumulate processing times completed
ASSIGN	5, V11,,PF	Compute remaining processing time
ASSIGN	3+,1,,PB	Record the number of operations completed
TEST	PB3 E PB2 → no SNX1	Last operation?
	yes	If no: transfer the transaction to block SNX1
TABULATE	TRANS	If yes: tabulate total time required for completion
TABULATE	COMPL	Tabulate lateness or earliness
TERMINATE		

(a)

Figure 11.3 Job processing.

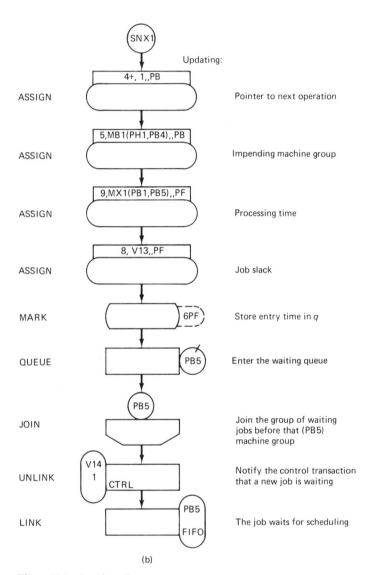

Figure 11.3 (continued)

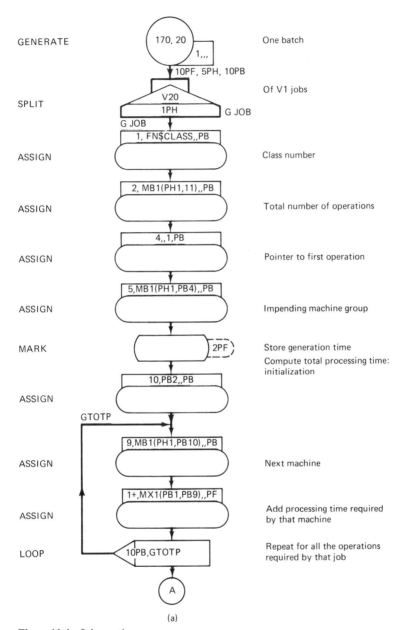

GENERATE	170, 20 1,,,	One batch
	▼ 10PF, 5PH, 10PB	
SPLIT	V20 1PH G JOB G JOB	Of V1 jobs
ASSIGN	1, FN$CLASS,,PB	Class number
ASSIGN	2, MB1(PH1,11),,PB	Total number of operations
ASSIGN	4,,1,PB	Pointer to first operation
ASSIGN	5,MB1(PH1,PB4),,PB	Impending machine group
MARK	2PF	Store generation time
ASSIGN	10,PB2,,PB	Compute total processing time: initialization
ASSIGN	GTOTP 9,MB1(PH1,PB10),,PB	Next machine
ASSIGN	1+,MX1(PB1,PB9),,PF	Add processing time required by that machine
LOOP	10PB,GTOTP	Repeat for all the operations required by that job
	A	

(a)

Figure 11.4 Job creation.

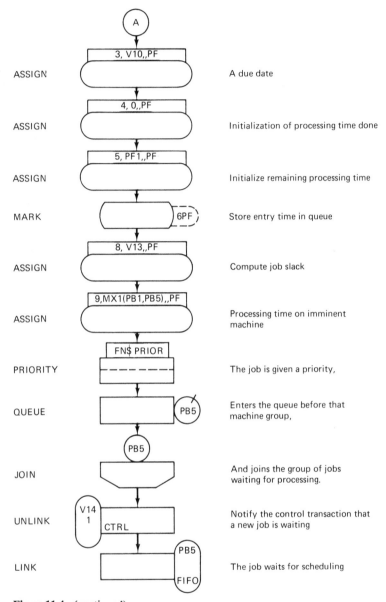

	3, V10,,PF	A due date
ASSIGN		
	4, 0,,PF	Initialization of processing time done
ASSIGN		
	5, PF1,,PF	Initialize remaining processing time
ASSIGN		
MARK	6PF	Store entry time in queue
	8, V13,,PF	Compute job slack
ASSIGN		
	9,MX1(PB1,PB5),,PF	Processing time on imminent machine
ASSIGN		
PRIORITY	FN$ PRIOR	The job is given a priority,
QUEUE	PB5	Enters the queue before that machine group,
	PB5	
JOIN		And joins the group of jobs waiting for processing.
UNLINK	V14 1 CTRL	Notify the control transaction that a new job is waiting
LINK	PB5 FIFO	The job waits for scheduling

Figure 11.4 (continued)

Storages. The capacity of the job shop (Table 11.6) is defined by the STORAGE statement (number 44).

Parameters. Job Transactions

Byte parameters:

PB1:	Class number.
PB2:	Total number of operations.
PB3:	Number of operations already completed.

```
                         * * *   G P S S   V  -  C S   V E R S I O N   * * *
                            *** IBM PROGRAM PRODUCT 5734-XS2 (V1M2) ***
                                                                             STATEMENT
                                                                              NUMBER
       REALLOCATE FAC,1,STO,30,QUE,3C,FUN,1C,CCM,27500                           1


BLOCK                                                                        STATEMENT
NUMBER  *LOC   OPERATION  A,B,C,D,E,F,G,H,I          COMMENTS                  NUMBER
               SIMULATE                                                          2
        *                                                                        3
        *      DEFINE USER'S OPTIONS                                             4
        *                                                                        5
        *              VARIABLES                                                 6
        *                                                                        7
        1      VARIABLE   11                 # OF DIFFER. JOBS                    8
        2      VARIABLE   5                  # OF GROUPS OF MACHINES              9
        3      VARIABLE   6                  MAX. # OF OPERATIONS                10
        4      VARIABLE   2                  FACTOR FOR DUE DATE CALCUL.         11
        *              EFFECTIVENESS FACTORS                                    12
        *              USED IN SCREENING CRITERIA                               13
        5      VARIABLE   0                  HIGHEST PRIORITY (1|0)              14
        6      VARIABLE   20                 SHORTEST IMMIN. OPER. (1|20)        15
        7      VARIABLE   1                  REMAIN. JOB SLACK (1|20)            16
        8      VARIABLE   2C                 LONGEST TIME IN Q (1|20)            17
        9      VARIABLE   2C                 EARLIEST DUE DATE (1|20)            18
        *                                                                       19
        *              DON'T FORGET TO CHANGE MB1 AND MX1 IF NECESS.            20
        *                                                                       21
        10     VARIABLE   PF2+PF1*V4         DUE DATE                           22
        11     VARIABLE   PF1-PF4            REMAIN. PROCESS. TIME              23
        *      V12 NOT USED                                                     24
        13     VARIABLE   PF3-PF5            JOB SLACK                          25
        14     VARIABLE   V2+PF5             CTRL XAC CHAIN #                   26
        15     VARIABLE   V5*PF7                                                27
        16     VARIABLE   V6*PF7             FOR SCREENING CRITERIA             28
        17     VARIABLE   V7*PF7                                                29
        18     VARIABLE   V8*PF7                                                3C
        19     VARIABLE   V9*PF7                                                31
        20     VARIABLE   V1-1                                                  32
        21     VARIABLE   V2-1               SPLIT( CTRL XACS)                  33
        *                                                                       34
        TERM1  VARIABLE   PF3-C1             JOB DURATION (TOTAL)               35
        *                                                                       36
        *                                                                       37
        *                                                                       38
        *                                                                       39
        1      MATRIX     MB,11,11           TECHNOLOGICAL MATRIX               40
        *                                    (OPERATIONS SEQUENCE)              41
        1      MATRIX     MX,2,5             TIME/OPER.                         42
        *                                                                       43
               STORAGE    S1-S2,2/S3-S4,3/S5,1                                  44
        *      JOB COMPLETION TABLE RECORDS THE DISTRIBUTION OF                 45
        *      JOB EARLINESS (+) OR LATENESS (-) RELATIVE TO DUE DATE           46
        COMPL  TABLE      V$TERM1,-100,20,20                                    47
        TRANS  TABLE      M1,130,2C,2C       TRANSIT TIME DISTR.                48
        *                                                                       49
        *                                                                       5C
        PRIOR  FUNCTION   RN1,C2             JOB PRIORITY                       51
       .8,1/1.,2                                                                52
        CLASS  FUNCTION   RN1,C2             JOB CLASS                          53
       .5,1/1.,2                                                                54
        *                                                                       55
        *                                                                       56
        1      BVARIABLE  (PR'GE'XF1)        HIGHEST PRIORITY                   57
        2      BVARIABLE  (PF9'LE'XF2)       SHORTEST IMMIN. PROC. TIME         58
        3      BVARIABLE  (PF8'LE'XF3)       MIN. JOB SLACK                     59
        4      BVARIABLE  (PF6'LE'XF4)       LONGEST TIME IN Q                  60
        5      BVARIABLE  (PF3'LE'XF5)       EARLIEST DUE DATE                  61
        6      BVARIABLE  BV1*BV2*BV3*BV4*BV5                                   62
        7      BVARIABLE  BV1*BV2*BV3*BV4                                       63
        8      BVARIABLE  BV1*BV2*BV3                                           64
        9      BVARIABLE  BV1*BV2                                               65
        *                                                                       66
               INITIAL    MB1(1,1),1/MB1(2-3,1),4/MB1(4,1),3/MB1(5-6,1),2       67
               INITIAL    MB1(7,1),1/MB1(8,1),3/MB1(9,1),4/MB1(10,1),2          68
               INITIAL    MB1(1,2),4/MB1(2,2),3/MB1(3,2),1/MB1(4,2),4           69
               INITIAL    MB1(5,2),1/MB1(6-7,2),3/MB1(8,2),4                    7C
               INITIAL    MB1(9-1C,2),1                                         71
               INITIAL    MB1(1,3),2/MB1(2,3),1/MB1(3-4,3),2/MB1(5,3),3         72
               INITIAL    MB1(6-7,3),4/MB1(8,3),1/MB1(9,3),2/MB1(10,3),4        73
               INITIAL    MB1(1,4),3/MB1(2,4),2/MB1(3,4),0/MB1(4,4),1          74
               INITIAL    MB1(5,4),4/MB1(6,4),1/MB1(7-8,4),2                    75
               INITIAL    MB1(9-1C,4),3                                         76
               INITIAL    MB1(1,5),4/MB1(4,5),5/MB1(5,5),1/MB1(8,5),3          77
```

Figure 11.5 Job shop scheduling. Listing of the GPSS program.

```
              INITIAL     MB1(1,11),5/MB1(2,11),4/MB1(3,11),3/MB1(4,11),5         78
              INITIAL     MB1(5,11),6/MB1(6-7,11),4/MB1(8,11),6/MB1(9-10,11),4    79
              INITIAL     MB1(5,6),5/MB1(8,6),5                                   80
              INITIAL     MB1(11,1),1/MB1(11,2),3/MB1(11,3),2/MB1(11,11),3        81
      *       PROCESSING TIME/CLASS/OPERATION                                     82
              INITIAL     MX1(1,1),10/MX1(1,2),20/MX1(1,3),30/MX1(1,4),40         83
              INITIAL     MX1(1,5),20/MX1(2,5),25                                 84
              INITIAL     MX1(2,1),15/MX1(2,2),30/MX1(2,3),40/MX1(2,4),45         85
      *                                                                          86
      *                                                                          87
      *               JOB PARAMETERS                                             88
      *       PB1:CLASS # (FN$CLASS)                                             89
      *       PB2:TOT # OF OPERATIONS (MX1(PH1,11))                              90
      *       PB3:# OF OPERATIONS ALREADY DONE                                   91
      *       PB4:PTER IMMINENT(CURRENT) OPERATION                              92
      *       PB5:CURRENT MACHINE GROUP                                          93
      *       PB6-PB8:NOT USED                                                   94
      *       PB9-PB10: FOR COMPUTATIONS                                         95
      *                                                                          96
      *       PH1:SEQUENTIAL JOB # (1 TO V1)                                     97
      *                                                                          98
      *       PF1:TOT. PROCESSING TIME                                           99
      *       PF2:TIME OF GENERATION                                            100
      *       PF3:DUE DATE (V10)                                                101
      *       PF4:SUM OF PROC. TIMES OF OPERATIONS DONE                         102
      *       PF5:REMAINING PROC. TIME (V11)                                    103
      *       PF6:TO STORE ENTRY TIME IN CURRENT Q                              104
      *       PF7:NOT USED                                                      105
      *       PF8:JOB SLACK (V13)                                               106
      *       PF9:PROC. TIME                                                    107
      *                                                                          108
      *               JOB CREATION                                              109
1             GENERATE    170,20,1,,,10PF,5PH,10PB                               110
      *       V1 JOBS                                                           111
2             SPLIT       V20,GJOB,1PH         # IN PH1                          112
3      GJOB   ASSIGN      1,FN$CLASS,,PB       CLASS #                           113
4             ASSIGN      2,MB1(PF1,11),,PB    TOT.NBER OF OPERATIONS            114
5             ASSIGN      4,1,,PB              IMMINENT OPERATION                115
6             ASSIGN      5,MB1(PF1,PB4),,PB   CURRENT MACHINE GROUP             116
      *                                                                          117
7             MARK        2PF                  GENERATION TIME                   118
      *       SUM OF PROC. TIMES                                                119
8             ASSIGN      1,0,,PF                                                120
9             ASSIGN      10,PB2,,PB                                             121
10     GTOTP  ASSIGN      9,MB1(PF1,PB10),,PB                                    122
11            ASSIGN      1+,MX1(PB1,PB9),,PF                                    123
12            LOOP        10PB,GTOTP                                             124
      *                                                                          125
13            ASSIGN      3,V10,,PF            DUE DATE                          126
14            ASSIGN      4,0,,PF                                                127
15            ASSIGN      5,PF1,,PF            REMAINING PROC. TIME              128
      *                                                                          129
16            MARK        6PF                  ENTRY TIME IN CURRENT Q           130
17            ASSIGN      8,V13,,PF            JOB SLACK                         131
18            ASSIGN      9,MX1(PB1,PB5),,PF   PROC. TIME                        132
19            PRIORITY    FN$PRIOR             PRIORITY                          133
20            QUEUE       PB5                                                    134
21            JOIN        PB5                                                    135
22            UNLINK      V14,CTRL,1           ACTIVATE CTRL XAC                 136
23            LINK        PB5,FIFO                                               137
      *                                                                          138
      *                                                                          139
      *               JOBSHOP                                                   140
      *                                                                          141
24     SHOP   REMOVE      PB5                                                    142
25            ENTER       PB5                                                    143
26            DEPART      PB5                                                    144
27            ADVANCE     PF9                  PROC. TIME                        145
28            LEAVE       PB5                                                    146
29            UNLINK      V14,CTRL,1                                             147
30            ASSIGN      4+,PF9,,PF           SUM PROC. TIMES DONE              148
31            ASSIGN      5,V11,,PF            REMAINING PROC. TIME              149
32            ASSIGN      3+,1,,PB             # OF OPER. DONE                   150
33            TEST E      PB3,PB2,SNX1                                           151
34     STER   TABULATE    TRANS                                                 152
35            TABULATE    COMPL                                                 153
36            TERMINATE                        JOB COMPLETED                     154
      *                                                                          155
37     SNX1   ASSIGN      4+,1,,PB             PTR NEXT OPERATION                156
38            ASSIGN      5,MB1(PH1,PB4),,PB   MACHINE GROUP #                   157
39            ASSIGN      9,MX1(PB1,PB5),,PF   PROCESSING TIME                   158
40            ASSIGN      8,V13,,PF            JOB SLACK                         159
41            MARK        6PF                  ENTRY TIME IN Q                   160
42            QUEUE       PB5                                                    161
43            JOIN        PB5                                                    162
44            UNLINK      V14,CTRL,1           ACTIVATE CTRL XAC                 163
45            LINK        PB5,FIFO                                               164
```

Figure 11.5 (continued)

```
          *                                                                          165
          *                                                                          166
          *                  CCNTRCL TRANSACTICN                                      167
          *                                                                          168
          *                  PARAMETERS                                              169
          *      PF7:USEC IN V15 TC V19                                              17C
          *      PB5:MACHINE CROUP #                                                 171
          *      PB1C:FCR CCMPUTATICNS                                               172
          *                                                                          173
46               GENERATE    1,,,1,1C,1CFB,1CFF                                      174
47               SPLIT       V21,CTRL,5PH            # IN PB5                        175
          *                                                                          176
48     CTRL      GATE SNF    PB5,CLIN               MACHINE FREE ?                   177
49               TEST GE     CH*PB5,1,CLIN          JOB IN Q ?                       178
          *                  SCAN VALUES CF JCB XAC PARAM (MIN/MAX)                  179
          *                  PUT IN PF7 CTRL XAC                                     18C
          *                                                                          181
5C               SCAN  MAX   PB5,PR,,PR,7PF         PRIORITY                         182
51               SAVEVALUE   1,V15,XF                                                183
52               SCAN  MIN   PB5,9PF,,9PF,7PF       PRUC. TIME                       184
53               SAVEVALUE   2,V16,XF                                                185
54               SCAN  MIN   PB5,8PF,,EPF,7PF       JOB SLACK                        186
55               SAVEVALUE   3,V17,XF                                                187
          *                                                                          188
56               SCAN  MIN   PB5,6PF,,6PF,7PF       MIN ENTRY TIME IN Q              189
          *                                                                          190
57               SAVEVALUE   4,V18,XF               MAX TIME IN C (MIN ENTRY TIME)   191
58               SCAN  MIN   PB5,3PF,,3PF,7PF       EARLIEST DUE DATE                192
59               SAVEVALUE   5,V19,XF                                                193
          *                                                                          194
          *                  UNLINK JOB SATISFYING THE HIGHEST CRITERIA              195
          *                                                                          196
6C               UNLINK      PB5,SHCF,1,BV6,,CNX1                                    197
61               TRANSFER    ,CLINA                                                  198
62     CNX1      UNLINK      PB5,SHCF,1,BV7,,CNX2                                    199
63               TRANSFER    ,CLINA                                                  2CC
64     CNX2      UNLINK      PB5,SHCF,1,EVB,,CNX3                                    201
65               TRANSFER    ,CLINA                                                  202
66     CNX3      UNLINK      PB5,SHCP,1,BV9,,CNX4                                    203
67               TRANSFER    ,CLINA                                                  204
68     CNX4      UNLINK      PB5,SHCF,1,EV1,,CNX5                                    205
69               TRANSFER    ,CLINA                                                  206
          *                                                                          2C7
7C     CNX5      UNLINK      PB5,SHCF,1                                              2C8
71     CLINA     PRICRITY    0,BUFFER                                               209
72               PRICRITY    10                                                      21C
73               TRANSFER    ,CTRL                                                   211
          *                                                                          212
74     CLIN      LINK        V14,FIFC               THAT CTRL XAC WAITS FOR          213
          *                                         REACTIVATION                     214
          *                                                                          215
          *                  CLCCK                  CONTROL SIMULATICN'S LENGTH       216
75               GENERATE    36C                                                     217
76               TERMINATE   1                                                       218
                 START       50,,,1                                                  219
                 ENC                                                                 220
```

Figure 11.5 (continued)

PB4:	Index pointing to the impending operation.
PB5:	Current machine group.
PB6 to PB8:	Not used.
PB9 and PB10:	Used for various computations.

Halfword parameter:

PH1: Job type; used as row index for byte msavevalue 1.

Fullword parameters:

PF1: Contains the sum of all processing times for the job.

PF2: Time of generation.

PF3: Due date.

PF4: Sum of processing times of operations already performed.

PF5: Remaining processing time.

PF6:   Entry time in current queue.

PF7:   Not used.

PF8:   Job slack.

PF9:   Current processing time.

Parameters.   Control Transactions

Byte parameters:

PB5:   Number of the machine group being controlled.

PB10:   Used for computations.

Fullword parameter:

PF7:   Used for computations by variables 15 to 19.

The other parameters are not used.

Functions.

PRIOR: Discrete function used to assign priority to a job transaction.

CLASS: Discrete function used to assign a class number (either 1 or 2) to a job transaction.

Variables.

V1:	Defines the number of different types of job.
V2:	Defines the number of machine groups.
V3:	The maximum number of operations in a sequence.
V4:	The proportionality factor to compute a due date.
V5 to V9:	Specify which scheduling rule or combination of scheduling rules is to be used. A value of unity indicates that the corresponding rule is used. A value of 20 indicates that the rule shall not be effective, except for V5, where a zero is required.
V5:	For the highest priority. Zero indicates that this scheduling rule is not effective.
V6:	Shortest impending operation.
V7:	Shortest remaining job slack.
V8:	Longest time in queue.
V9:	Earliest due date.
V10:	Computes a due date.
V11:	Computes the remaining processing time.
V12:	Not used.
V13:	Computes the job slack.
V14:	Gives the user chain number to deactivate the control transaction. Each machine group has a corresponding user chain for the control transaction of that group.

V15 to V19:   Used for computation of the screening criteria (see discussion below). The computed values are stored in XF1 to XF5, respectively.

V20:   Used in SPLIT (statement 112) to generate a batch of V1 job transactions.

V21:   Used in SPLIT (statement 175).

V$TERMI: Computes job duration (used in table COMPL).

Boolean variables.

BV1 to BV9:   Used to represent the sets of conditions of Figure 11.2 which must be satisfied by a scheduled transaction.

For example, BV9 corresponds to the fourth set of Figure 11.2. A transaction is unlinked if its priority is greater than or equal to the highest priority in a group of waiting transactions AND its impending processing time is less than or equal to the shortest impending processing time.

Fullword savevalues.

XF1:   To store the current highest priority in a group of waiting job transactions.

XF2:   The shortest impending processing time.

XF3:   The minimum job slack.

XF4:   The longest time in queue.

XF5:   The earliest due date.

Tables.

COMPL: Table of frequencies of times ahead of or behind job due date. A negative value means that the job was completed late (computed by V$TERMI).

TRANS: Frequency table of transit times. Job durations including waiting times.

Comments on the program listing.   The job-creation submodel begins at statement 110 and ends at statement 137; the job-processing submodel begins at statement 142 and ends at statement 164; and the job-scheduling submodel begins at statement 174 and ends at statement 214.

To combine scheduling rules as mentioned in Section 11.5.2, several computation steps are required (statements 182 to 211). First, a control transaction scans all the job transactions waiting in the user chain that it controls and seeks the following values: highest priority, minimum impending processing time, shortest job slack, earliest entry time in queue, and earliest due date. These values are multiplied by the corresponding effectiveness factors (variables 5 to 9), and the resulting values are stored in fullword savevalues XF1 to XF5.

For example (statement 182), the highest-priority value of the waiting job transactions is found and stored in fullword parameter 7 of the control transaction;

then that value is multiplied by variable V5, whose value is either zero or one; if zero, it indicates that the user does not want to schedule the job according to the value of the priority. The result of the multiplication is stored in XF1, statement 183. The contents of XF1 is then used in Boolean variable 1, which itself is used in BV6 to BV9, which define the screening criteria (see Section 11.5.2).

A job transaction that satisfies the specified scheduling rule—that is, for which one of the corresponding Boolean variables BV6 to BV9 gives a value of unity—is unlinked from the user chain and sent to the job-processing submodel (statement 142).

After selecting a job transaction, the control transaction waits until the job transaction has been effectively unlinked by GPSS and sent to the job-processing submodel. This is achieved by the PRIORITY 0,BUFFER block, (statement 209), which suspends processing of the control transaction and reinitiates the GPSS scan at the start of the current-events chain.

11.6 Experiments and Results

In this section we give a brief discussion of some significant results obtained from various experiments.

Table 11.7 summarizes the output of the program of Figure 11.5 after 18,000 time units. For that run the numerical characteristics of Tables 11.4 to 11.6 have been used, with a job generation rate of one batch every 170 ± 20 time units, uniformly distributed. The "shortest remaining job slack" scheduling rule has been tested, V7=1, V6–V9=20 and V5=0.

Table 11.7 Job Shop Scheduling

Selected Results: Storages

Storage	Capacity	Average Contents	Entries	Average Time per Unit	Average Total Time	Current Contents	Maximum Contents
1	2	0.883	1275	12.478	0.441	—	2
2	2	1.617	1169	24.911	0.808	2	2
3	3	2.267	1168	34.943	0.755	3	3
4	3	2.754	1169	42.417	0.918	3	3
5	1	0.399	317	22.681	0.399	—	1

Selected Results: Queues

Queue	Maximum Contents	Average Contents	Total Entries	Zero Entries	Zeros (%)	Average Time per Transaction	$Average Time per Transaction[a]	Current Contents
1	4	0.177	1275	926	72.6	2.512	9.180	—
2	4	0.453	1169	592	50.6	6.976	14.135	—
3	5	0.441	1171	664	56.7	6.784	15.670	3
4	5	1.194	1170	259	22.1	18.377	23.602	1
5	2	0.062	317	233	73.5	3.552	13.404	—

[a]Average time per transaction, excluding zero entries.

Table 11.7 (continued)

SELECTED RESULTS: TRANS TABLE

Entries in table	Mean argument	Standard deviation
1,165	157.987	53.500

Upper Limit	Observed Frequency	Per Cent of Total	Cumulative Percentage	Cumulative Remainder
130	355	30.47	30.4	69.5
150	194	16.65	47.1	52.8
170	176	15.10	62.2	37.7
190	164	14.07	76.3	23.6
210	99	8.49	84.8	15.1
230	67	5.75	90.5	9.4
250	44	3.77	94.3	5.6
270	26	2.23	96.5	3.4
290	18	1.54	98.1	1.8
310	18	1.54	99.6	0.3
330	4	0.34	100.0	0.0

Remaining Frequencies are all zero.

Let us now change the structure of the system, according to Tables 11.1 to 11.3, to obtain ten different types of jobs instead of eleven, four groups of machines instead of five, and a maximum number of operations of five instead of six. What modifications are needed in the program of Figure 11.5?

One has first to change the values of variable 1 (now 10), variable 2 (now 4), and variable 3 (now 5). Second, the STORAGE definition card (statement 44) is altered to the values of Table 11.3. Then, with INITIAL statements, the byte matrix savevalue 1 content is changed according to Table 11.1. The job-arrival rate (statement 110) may also be changed: now uniformly distributed between 160 and 200.

If the jobs are scheduled according to the "shortest impending operation time" rule, V5=0, V6=1, V7–V9=20, the statistics given in Table 11.8 are gathered after 18,000 time units.

If the jobs are scheduled according to the combined rules "smallest remaining job slack" and "earliest due date," V7 and V9=1, V5=0, V6 and V8=20, the results, shown in Table 11.9, show some improvements; compare both tables TRANS, for example.

Table 11.8 JOB SHOP SCHEDULING

SELECTED OUTPUT: STORAGES

Storage	Capacity	Average Contents	Entries	Average Time per Unit	Average Total Time	Current Contents	Maximum Contents
1	1	0.762	1102	12.457	0.762	1	1
2	2	1.386	1002	24.908	0.693	1	2
3	2	1.934	1002	34.747	0.967	2	2
4	3	2.597	1102	42.431	0.865	3	3

Table 11.8   (continued)

Selected Output: Queues

Queue	Maximum Contents	Average Contents	Total Entries	Zero Entries	Zeros (%)	Average Time per Transaction	$Average Time per Transaction[a]	Current Contents
1	4	0.543	1103	380	34.4	8.869	13.531	1
2	5	0.352	1002	595	59.3	6.328	15.579	—
3	7	1.498	1003	132	13.1	26.899	30.975	1
4	5	0.842	1105	375	33.9	13.730	20.783	3

[a]Average time per transaction, excluding zero entries.

Selected Output: TRANS Table

Entries in table	Mean argument	Standard deviation
998	178.043	59.437

Upper Limit	Observed Frequency	Per Cent of Total	Cumulative Percentage	Cumulative Remainder
130	211	21.14	21.1	78.8
150	162	16.23	37.3	62.6
170	134	13.42	50.8	49.1
190	159	15.93	66.7	33.2
210	111	11.12	77.8	22.1
230	63	6.31	84.1	15.8
250	46	4.60	88.7	11.2
270	26	2.60	91.3	8.6
290	30	3.00	94.3	5.6
310	22	2.20	96.5	3.4
330	9	0.90	97.4	2.5
350	12	1.20	98.6	1.3
370	6	0.60	99.2	0.7
390	4	0.40	99.6	0.3
410	1	0.10	99.7	0.2
430	0	0.00	99.7	0.2
450	1	0.10	99.8	0.1
470	0	0.00	99.8	0.1
490	1	0.10	100.0	0.0

Remaining frequencies are all zero.

Table 11.9 Job Shop Scheduling

Selected Output: Storages

Storage	Capacity	Average Contents	Entries	Average Time per Unit	Average Total Time	Current Contents	Maximum Contents
1	1	0.762	1102	12.457	0.762	1	1
2	2	1.386	1003	24.891	0.693	2	2
3	2	1.934	1002	34.756	0.967	2	2
4	3	2.598	1102	42.440	0.866	3	3

Table 11.9 (continued)

SELECTED OUTPUT: QUEUES

Queue	Maximum Contents	Average Contents	Total Entries	Zero Entries	Zeros (%)	Average Time per Transaction	$Average Time per Transaction[a]	Current Contents
1	5	0.599	1103	403	36.5	9.786	15.421	1
2	5	0.370	1003	595	59.3	6.644	16.333	—
3	6	1.488	1002	131	13.0	26.733	30.754	—
4	4	0.744	1105	414	37.4	12.123	19.387	3

[a]Average time per transaction, excluding zero entries.

SELECTED OUTPUT: TRANS TABLE

Entries in table	Mean argument	Standard deviation
998	177.434	54.000

Upper Limit	Observed Frequency	Per Cent of Total	Cumulative Percentage	Cumulative Remainder
130	186	18.63	18.6	81.3
150	152	15.23	33.8	66.1
170	139	13.92	47.7	52.2
190	147	14.72	62.5	37.4
210	138	13.82	76.3	23.6
230	73	7.31	83.6	16.3
250	59	5.91	89.5	10.4
270	42	4.20	93.7	6.2
290	33	3.30	97.0	2.9
310	19	1.90	98.9	1.0
330	6	0.60	99.5	0.4
350	3	0.30	99.8	0.1
370	0	0.00	99.8	0.1
390	1	0.10	100.0	0.0

Remaining frequencies are all zero.

11.7 Conclusions

The simulation of a job shop provides a means of evaluating different scheduling rules under different experimental conditions. The problems described above did not represent actual shops. Therefore, the resulting model has been somewhat stylized for the sake of clarity. However, because of its flexibility, we believe that such a model is a valuable tool for advanced simulation and industrial engineering courses because it helps the students to understand the problems arising in experimental investigation and in the comparative evaluation of priority disciplines in production scheduling.

Other modifications that could be tried include:

1. A composite priority rule as described in [11.1].
2. Simulation of machine breakdowns.

3. Different arrival patterns; for example, a different probability distribution for each type of job.

4. An optimum-seeking search program designed to vary parameter values automatically within specified limits.

References

11.1. J. C. EMERY, "Job Shop Scheduling by Means of Simulation and an Optimum-Seeking Search," *Proceedings of the Third Conference on Applications of Simulation, Los Angeles, 1969*, Association for Computing Machinery, New York, 1969.

11.2 R. C. MEIER, W. T. NEWELL, and H. L. PAZER, *Simulation in Business and Economics*, Prentice-Hall, Englewood Cliffs, N.J., 1969.

11.3. C. L. FRANKLIN, "The Current State of Research in Job Shop Scheduling," *Proceedings of the Third Conference on Applications of Simulation, Los Angeles, 1969*, Association for Computing Machinery, New York, 1969.

11.4. S. ASHOUR and S. D. WASWANI, "A GASP Simulation Study of Job Shop Scheduling," *Simulation*, Vol. 18, No. 1, 1972.

11.5. R. W. CONWAY, W. L. MAXWELL, and L. W. MILLER, *Theory of Scheduling*, Addison-Wesley, Reading, Mass., 1967.

12 Simulation of a Teleprocessing System

The following model may seem rather intricate at first sight, so we suggest that the reader try to follow through the GPSS coding in stages. This example might well provide basic material for a case study in an advanced simulation course. After an introductory overview of the program, students would learn by running it on a computer, studying the results, altering some system parameters, and observing the effect. More complex modifications could then be tried, such as extending the hardware and modeling more application programs.

12.1 The System

12.1.1 Introduction

The purpose of this chapter is to describe the use of GPSS as a tool for analyzing the performance of teleprocessing systems. To do this, the fundamental features of a real-time data-base/data-communication system will be considered. Such a system is represented in Figure 12.1. It must control many messages arriving at random from remote terminals and must provide data management for each application (integrated data base).

In a teleprocessing system, the number of interactions among the system elements can be very large, so that it is very difficult to determine the overall dynamic system performance of a complex installation. Simulation is one of the techniques that can be used to study the system operation.

We must emphasize that the computer timings and the teleprocessing system chosen for this example have been selected for illustrative purposes only. They are realistic but do not represent a specific system.

TERMINALS   COMPUTER   DATA BASE

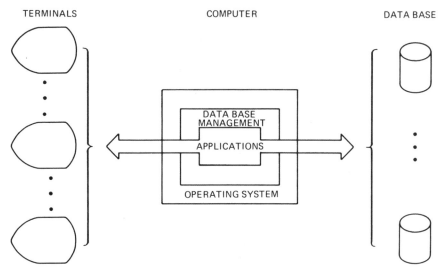

Figure 12.1 Components of a teleprocessing system.

12.1.2 System description

Hardware (see Figure 12.2). The following hardware is used:

CPU (central processing unit) plus main storage of 96K bytes.

3 disk drives, called, respectively, DRV1, DRV2, and DRV3.

3 communication lines.

30 terminals, displays with 2000 characters, divided into four groups (A, B, C, and D) (see Table 12.1 for characteristics).

Channel and control function for disk storage units.

Communication line adapter.

The CPU to be simulated is not complex. All CPU timings are fictitious but consistent and are expressed in milliseconds (ms). Other CPU performances may be simulated by changing a factor called V$MODEL (see Section 12.3.1). The disks have characteristics given by the GPSS function ARMMV (Section 12.3.3).

Software. The detailed features of the operating system are not simulated explicitly; they are implicitly included in the relevant timings within the model. We are interested in modeling the following management facilities in more detail: multitasking, storage allocation, program management, and the application programs.

Multitasking. We describe here some of the features that have been modeled. A transaction consists of the transmission and the complete processing of a message. When a message is read into the CPU, a *task is initiated* to process the message. This task is simply a unit of work for the CPU. Thus an application program that corresponds to the type of the incoming message will be executed. To do this, the application program must be in main computer storage. If the program is not in main storage, then it must be loaded (see "Storage Allocation and Management").

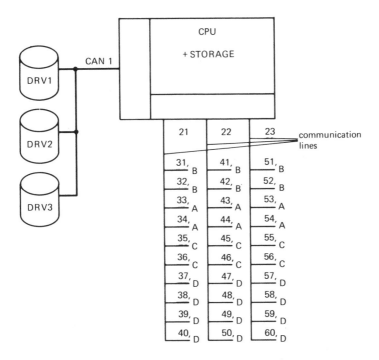

Terminals (number and group)

Figure 12.2 Teleprocessing system hardware.

Multiple transactions are processed concurrently; this is called *multitasking*. In fact, only one task is processed at any time, but many tasks may share the resources and thus give the impression of simultaneous processing. Each task relinquishes control of the CPU when the task makes a request for an input/output (I/O) operation. The task cannot resume processing until the I/O operation is complete. Requests for a serially usable resource are queued if the resource is currently busy servicing a prior request. The number of active tasks is limited by the amount of storage available. It is also possible to specify that only a certain number of transactions can be processed concurrently.

Storage allocation and management. The acquisition and release of main storage for the application programs and for the control programs is modeled.

A "storage cushion," which represents a certain amount of storage, is acquired at the beginning; this corresponds to the initialization of a real system. The cushion is held in reserve until all available storage is in use.

When a request for storage cannot be met because all available storage is in use, the following procedure is modeled:

1. An attempt is made to free the storage occupied by programs that are no longer active.
2. If this is insufficient, the storage cushion is used and the creation of new tasks is suspended.

3. If the space is still insufficient, the request is queued.

4. As soon as a task completes, the storage freed is used to recreate the cushion.

5. When the cushion becomes available again, new transactions may be initiated.

Program management. This part of the model simulates the multiprogramming capability by dynamic program management with a real-time program fetch capability.

Application programs are loaded from the disk into main storage, as required. They remain resident in main storage even when idle, unless system storage resources become overloaded. In this case, idle programs are deleted from main storage.

Each program's location on disk or in main storage, as well as the status of all programs, is maintained in a table.

A single copy of an application program can be used to process several transactions concurrently. This assumes that the system uses re-entrant code.

The functional applications to be modeled are data entry and file updating, inquiry, and broadcasting. They are described in detail in the next section.

12.2 The Problem

12.2.1 Problem description

The problem is to study the performance of the system described in Section 12.1. The numerical data are given in Section 12.2.3.

We wish to determine:

1. The utilization of the components: CPU, channels, drives, main storage, and lines.

2. The time available for possible background jobs. This can be done by comparing total simulated time with total time during which no task was in the system.

3. The number of transactions that cannot enter the system and must wait because of insufficient main storage.

4. The number of times a program is rolled out owing to shortage of main storage.

5. The response times to an inquiry.

Two kinds of response times are considered:

Terminal operator response time: this is the time from keying "End of message" to receipt of the first character of the reply.

Control program response time: this is the time from the arrival of the message at the CPU to the termination of the corresponding task. This time therefore includes: task initiation and termination, program linkage, and processing.

12.2.2 The transactions

Seven different types of transactions, denoted, respectively, as types 1, 2, 3, 12, 14, 9, and 10, are processed. Table 12.1 defines their characteristics, such as originating terminal and interarrival time. The functional applications modeled are data entry, inquiry, end of inquiry, and broadcasting.

Data entry.   Modeled by transactions of types 1, 2, and 3 coming from terminal groups A, B, and C, respectively. Each transaction involves a reply, in conversational mode. Transactions of type 1 involve a second reply.

Inquiry.   A selective retrieval of information from a data base (master file), simulated by transactions of types 12 and 14 coming from terminal groups B and D, respectively. Each transaction involves a reply in conversational mode.

End of inquiry.   Transaction 9 is generated by simulating the terminal-operator message ("LOOK") to the CPU that he has finished looking at the reply to his inquiry. As a result a message obtained from a file called FILEX is sent to the terminal.

Broadcasting.   A transaction of type 10 is generated by the system as a result of processing a transaction of type 1. A message is sent to all but the originating terminal. If a terminal from group B or D is in inquiry (INQ) mode, no message is sent.

12.2.3   Numerical data

Characteristics of the transactions.   In Table 12.1 XACT means transaction, MSG message, and the entry, Interarrival Time, specifies the mean time between

Table 12.1

Terminal Group	XACT Type	In/ Out	MSG Length	Interarrival Time or Reply (R)	Conversation (C) or Unsolicited (U)
Data entry					
A	1	In	40	180 s	—
A	1	Out	80	R	C
A	1	Out	80	R	U
B	2	In	40	240 s	—
B	2	Out	80	R	C
C	3	In	40	300 s	—
C	3	Out	80	R	C
Inquiry					
B	12	In	30	600 s	—
B	12	Out	2000	R	C
D	14	In	30	600 s	—
D	14	Out	500	R	C
End of inquiry					
B	9	In	10	After "LOOK"	—
B	9	Out	1000	R	C
D	9	In	10	After "LOOK"	—
D	9	Out	1000	R	C
Broadcasting					
A	10	Out	80		
B	10	Out	80		
C	10	Out	80		
D	10	Out	80		

arrivals. The interarrival times are defined for *one* terminal of the group. Inter-arrival time for all terminals of a group is used in the GPSS GENERATE block and is calculated using the variables XACTx, where x = type = 1, 2, 3, B, or D.

File description. Table 12.2, FILEM, and Table 12.3, MFLDR, specify the distribution of the files on the three disk drives, DRV1, DRV2, and DRV3. The tables are stored in GPSS matrices in the model. Table 12.4 summarizes the contents of each drive.

Table 12.2 FILEM MATRIX

FILE		Not Used	From CYL	To CYL	Block Size	Number of Packs
Number	Name	1	2	3	4	5
1	MAIN	All files:	111	135	2200	1
2	BMAIN	assume	111	135	2200	1
3	PAGE	random-access	108	109	2000	1
4	FILEX	organization	108	109	1000	1
5	LOG		136	160	100	1
6	BLOG		136	160	100	1
7	LIB DIRECTORY		98	98	256	1
8	LIB PGMS		99	100	Program size	1
9	DESTINATION		110	110	100	1

Table 12.3 MFLDR MATRIX

File Number	File Name	Disk Allocation
1	MAIN	1
2	BMAIN	2
3	PAGE	3
4	FILEX	2
5	LOG	1
6	BLOG	3
7	DIREC.	2
8	PGMS	3
9	DEST.	1

Table 12.4

DRV1 Files	DRV2 Files	DRV3 Files
1	2	3
5	4	6
9	7	8

12.2.4 Application programs

The seven types of transaction are processed by seven application programs called SBRx, where x = 1, 2, 3, 9, 10, 12, and 14. Thus type 1 transactions use application program SBR1; type 2 transactions, SBR2; and so on.

The following broad flowcharts define the program operations. Note that a model of an application program is an abstraction which consists of processing data (in a GPSS ADVANCE block) and of I/O operations.

The *subroutine INSBR* used by the application programs is described in Figure 12.3; the subroutine *SBR1*, used to process transactions of type 1, in Figure 12.4; and subroutines SBR2 and SBR3, which process type 2 and type 3 transactions, respectively, in Figure 12.5. The other subroutines are analogous in form, and the reader will find them in the listing of the program at the end of this chapter.

Remark: A READ/WRITE operation means INPUT or OUTPUT of one block of data, the length of which depends on the file concerned. Block lengths are specified in the matrix FILEM (Table 12.2).

12.2.5 Other considerations

Several terminals are connected to each line, which is known as *multidropping*. Lines are assumed to be half-duplex. Only one terminal per line is active at any time. See Figure 12.2.

No polling/addressing mechanism is included in the model. The in/out message obtains the line as soon as it becomes free (FIFO queue).

A transaction always waits for the completion of a disk I/O operation.

Whenever an output message is to be sent to a terminal, an internal concurrent task is created. The original transaction proceeds further without waiting; this is translated in GPSS by a SPLIT block and by the fact that the original GPSS transaction proceeds in its flow without waiting for the completion of the transmission of the output message.

12.3 The GPSS Model

12.3.1 Correspondence between system elements and GPSS entities

Time units. The time unit is given by the value of the GPSS variable MODEL, as shown in Table 12.5. This allows for simulation of different CPUs without changing the model.

Table 12.5

V$MODEL	Time Unit (ms)
10	1
5	2
20	$\frac{1}{2}$

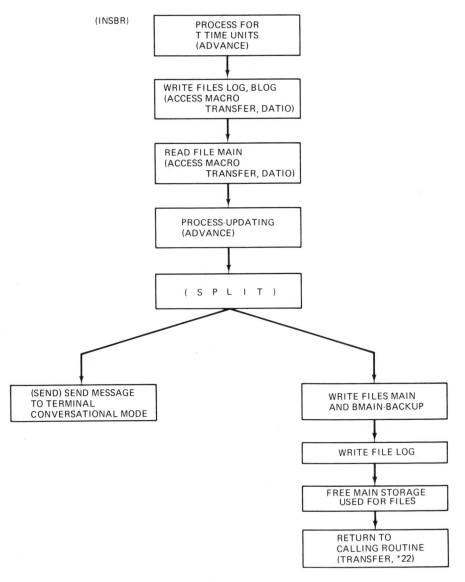

(INSBR)

PROCESS FOR
T TIME UNITS
(ADVANCE)

WRITE FILES LOG, BLOG
(ACCESS MACRO
        TRANSFER, DATIO)

READ FILE MAIN
(ACCESS MACRO
        TRANSFER, DATIO)

PROCESS-UPDATING
(ADVANCE)

(S P L I T)

(SEND) SEND MESSAGE
TO TERMINAL
CONVERSATIONAL MODE

WRITE FILES MAIN
AND BMAIN-BACKUP

WRITE FILE LOG

FREE MAIN STORAGE
USED FOR FILES

RETURN TO
CALLING ROUTINE
(TRANSFER, *22)

Note:

GPSS symbolic block numbers and GPSS blocks used to perform an operation
are written in capitals between parentheses.

Figure 12.3 Subroutine INSBR. *Note:* GPSS symbolic block
numbers and GPSS blocks used to perform an operation are
written in capitals between parentheses.

358

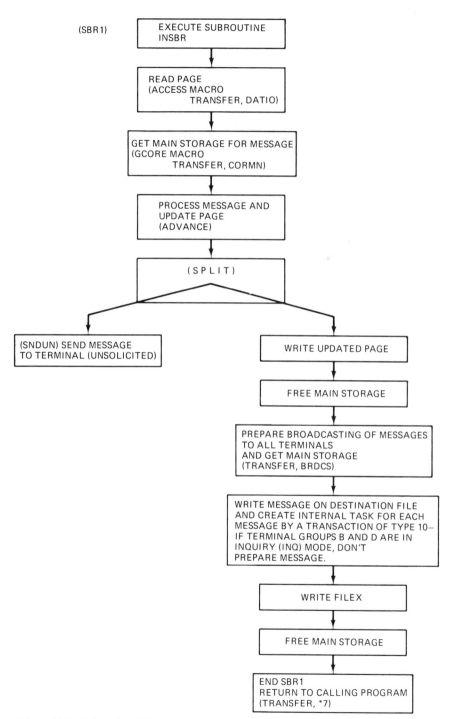

Figure 12.4 Subroutine SBR1.

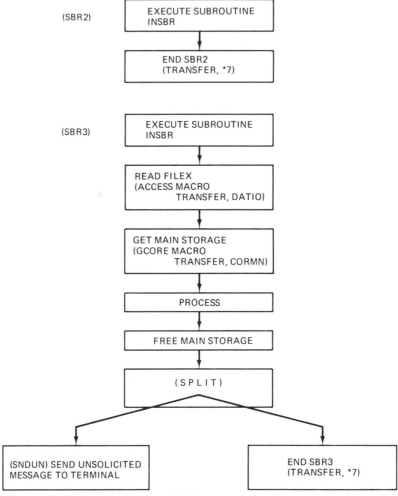

Figure 12.5 Subroutines SBR2 and SBR3.

All non-CPU timing variables are multiplied by V$MODEL/10, so different CPUs may be simulated by changing the relationship between CPU and I/O operations, which involves changing the value of the GPSS variable MODEL.

Facilities. Facilities are used to model CPU, channels, disk drives, and communication lines.

Storages. Storages are used to model application programs, entry counters, main storage, counter for "no active task in core," and terminals.

For each application program we define a storage to count the number of tasks simultaneously executing this program. The storage ACTIV counts the number of tasks currently active in the system.

Each terminal is associated with a storage of capacity 1, storages 31 to 60. This allows the unsolicited message to compete for a terminal when it becomes available. A transaction enters the storage after its generation, when the operator starts to key in. This transaction leaves the storage after the reply has been received at the terminal and the operator has finished looking at it.

The storage CORE models main storage utilization dynamically in bytes.

Queues. Queues are used to gather statistics on transactions waiting for disk drives, channels, communication lines, transmission of message to CPU, and task creation.

12.3.2   Parameters, matrices, and savevalues

Transaction parameters.

P1:   Cylinder number (used in subroutine DATIO).

P2:   File Number (DATIO).

P3:   Drive number (for the file request handled by DATIO).

P4:   Program number (used in subroutines STATE and QUIT).

P7:   Return address after execution of a subroutine SBRx.

P8:   CORMN subroutine return address when called from SBRx, DATIO, and STATE.

P9:   Transaction type given at generation time.

P10: Return address for STATE, QUIT.

P11: Working parameter used in CORMN.

P12: DATIO return address.

P13: $= 0$: I/O request for a file on the *same* drive;
      $= 1$: I/O request for a file on a *new* drive;
           specified in SBRx and STATE, (used in DATIO).

P14: Amount of core for core management.

P15: $= 0$: indicates that no core needed for buffer;
      $= 1$:   core needed for buffer;
           specified in SBRx and STATE (used in DATIO).

P16: File organization specified in SBRx and STATE (used in DATIO).
      $= 0$:   read sequentially;
      $= 1$:   read randomly from one of the cylinders on which the file is located;
      $= x$:   read from cylinder x.

P17: Number of the originating terminal.

P18: Number of the communication line to which the terminal is connected.

P19: Mark time for file request.

P22: Return address from subroutine INSBR.

P23: Mark time for "terminal operator response time" tabulation.

P24: Number of rotational delays required, passed to DATIO by SBRx to model the access method.

P25: Channel number to which the drive is connected, given by DATIO.

Matrices.   Matrices used in subroutine DATIO are:

ARMPO: Indicates the current arm position for each drive.

FILEM: Describes each file (row number); specifies the cylinder numbers for the beginning (column 2) and the end (column 3) of the file, the block size (column 4), and the number of drives on which the file is distributed (column 5). Column 1 is not used in this model.

MFLDR: Defines on which drives the files are located:

      row number: file number
      column 1:   first drive
      column 2:   second drive
      .
      .
      .

Remark: The number of drives required by a file is specified in matrix FILEM (Table 12.2).

The matrix used in subroutines STATE and QUIT is:

PROGD: Row number equals the application program number.

      column 1:   main storage requirement for the program (in bytes)
      column 2:   current status of the program
      0:              not in main storage
      1:              in main storage but not in use
      2:              in main storage and in use
      3:              now being loaded

The matrix used in SBR10 is:

MTR: Describes terminal status.

      1:              inquiry mode

Savevalues.

ACTIV: Number of times there was no active task in the system.

LOCAT: Saves the last position of the arm.

NOPOL: Number of transactions that have to wait because no storage was available.

LLL: Saves the terminal number to which a message is being broadcast.

12.3.3   Functions and variables

Functions.

ARMMV: Defines the seek time in either the forward or reverse direction for the number of cylinders that the access

	mechanism traverses. Argument is V$SPAN = number of cylinders to be traversed.
BFSZ:	To get extra storage for inquiry: number of bytes minus 100 needed for output message according to transaction type.
CHAN:	Assigns a channel number to each disk drive.
EXPON:	Exponential cumulative distribution function (inverted).
KEY:	Keying time.
LINE:	Assigns a line to each terminal according to the configuration.
LKT:	Time needed by the operator to study the output message according to the transaction time.
SBR:	Assigns an application program (SBRx), according to transaction type.
TGA,TGB,TGC,TGD:	Assign a terminal number to a generated transaction according to the terminal groups A, B, C, and D. The terminals must be numbered consecutively, starting with number 30.
TRIN:	Input transaction transmission time.
TROUT:	Output transaction transmission time.

Variables. Variables used in subroutine DATIO are:

AMOVE:	Computes the seek time, using FN$ARMMV.
DLY:	Computes rotational delay using RN2.
DRIVE:	Picks a drive number for an I/O request using RN2.
LACAA:	Specifies the first cylinder of a file.
LOCA:	Gets specific cylinder for the I/O request.
READ:	Defines the CPU time taken by the control program for file management, task switching, and setup.
SPAN:	Computes the number of cylinders to be traversed by the access mechanism.

Variables used in subroutine CORMN are:

GETM,FREEM:	CPU timing for GET/Main and FREE/Main routines, respectively.

Variables used for task generation/termination are:

CLNUP:	CPU timings for task termination.
CUSHN,TASK:	Minimum storage necessary for task initiation.
TASKT:	CPU timing for task initiation.

Variables used to describe the teleprocessing network are:

KEYT: Computes the time needed to key a transaction
                                    message as a function of the transaction type.

LOOK: Time needed to look at the output message as
                                    function of the message type.

MAX: Serial number of the storage associated with
                                    the last terminal.

TIBUF: Input buffer length, storage needed for incom-
                                    ing messages.

TNOA,TNOB,TNOC,TNOD: Specify the number of terminals for each class.

TOBUF: Output buffer length, storage needed for out-
                                    going messages as function of the message type.

TRASI,TRASO: Input and output transmission time, according
                                    to the transaction type, respectively.

XACTx (x=1,2,3,B,D):   mean interarrival time between the messages of
                                    a group.

Additional variables are:

CINTR: Interruption and interference time.

LINK: Link time, used in subroutine STATE.

MPT9:   Gives a TABLE Number, according to transaction type.

12.3.4   Tables available for output

FLREQ: Response time for disk I/O request.

ACTIV: Tabulates and accumulates the elapsed time during which there is no
         task in the system.

$\left\{\begin{array}{l}21,22,23:\\29,30:\\32:\\34:\end{array}\right.$ Tabulate for each transaction type the *operator-response time*, which is defined as the duration between "end of message keying" and "start of answer display."

$\left\{\begin{array}{l}1,2,3:\\9,10:\\12:\\14:\end{array}\right.$ Tabulate for each transaction the *control-program response time*, which is defined as the time from the arrival of the message in the CPU to the task termination. This includes: task initiation, program linkage, processing, and task termination.

ALL: Tabulates control-program response time for all the transactions.

12.3.5   Program description

The complete program listing is given in Figure 12.9.

Model overview. The model, divided into submodels or modules, consists of two types of routine: support routines and main routine. The purpose of the support routines is to model storage management, file management, program management facilities, and auxiliary features. The main routine models the generation of messages, their flow through the system, their handling by the control and the application programs.

Support routines. These routines are called from several places; before a call is executed by a TRANSFER block, the return address must be stored in a specified parameter.

CORMN: Simulates storage management. If insufficient storage is available, all programs that are in main storage but not in use are rolled out. When entering CORMN, the facility CPU is seized and remains in that state at the end of CORMN. The arguments are:

> P8:   return address
> P14:   amount of storage required

DATIO: Simulates file management and handles all disk I/O requests. It gets main storage via CORMN if required. When an I/O request is initiated for a task, the CPU is released for other tasks. After the request is completed, the task originating the I/O request must compete for CPU. The arguments are:

> P2:   file number
> P12:   return address
> P15:   0: if storage for buffer is not required
>   1: if storage for buffer is required
> P16:   0: read sequentially
>   1: read from random cylinder (one of the cylinders over which the specified file is distributed)
>   X: read from cylinder X
> P13:   0: read from the same drive as previously
>   1: the number of the drive is taken randomly from the drives on which the specified file is to be found.
> P24:   1 or 2: the number of rotational delays

STATE: Simulates program management and is used when the task is initiated. It tests the status of the specified application program; if the program is not in main storage, it loads it via DATIO in two disk operations: one to read the directory, the second to read the actual program. The arguments are:

> P4:   program number
> P10:   return address

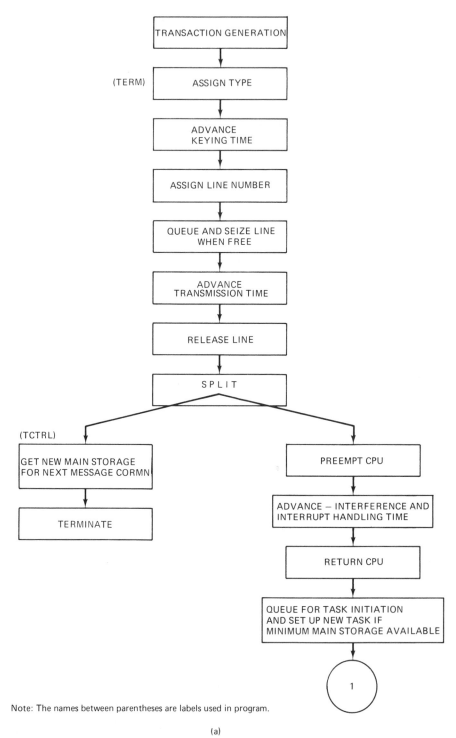

Note: The names between parentheses are labels used in program.

(a)

Figure 12.6(a) Main routine.
Note: The names in parentheses are labels used in the program.

366

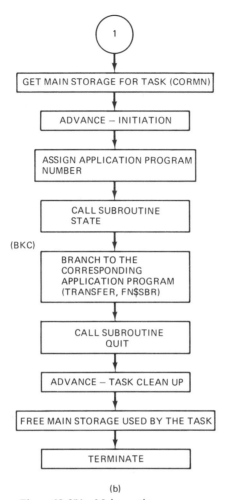

(b)

Figure 12.6(b) Main routine

QUIT : Simulates the program management operation of task termination. It tests if the terminated program must be rolled out and changes the program status if necessary. The arguments are:

P4 : program number

P10 : return address

Auxiliary routines.

ATASK : Traces and tabulates the elapsed time during which no task is active in the system.

CLOCK : Controls the simulated time.

Main routine. The main routine is described in Figure 12.6(a) and (b).

Routine SEND (Figure 12.7). The SEND routine transmits solicited messages (replies to inquiries) back to the terminal. After the operator has studied the reply, the terminal is freed.

367

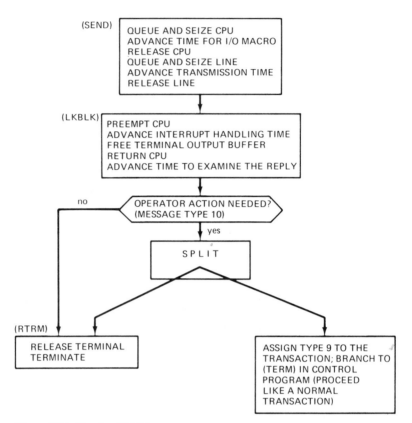

(SEND)

QUEUE AND SEIZE CPU
ADVANCE TIME FOR I/O MACRO
RELEASE CPU
QUEUE AND SEIZE LINE
ADVANCE TRANSMISSION TIME
RELEASE LINE

(LKBLK)

PREEMPT CPU
ADVANCE INTERRUPT HANDLING TIME
FREE TERMINAL OUTPUT BUFFER
RETURN CPU
ADVANCE TIME TO EXAMINE THE REPLY

OPERATOR ACTION NEEDED?
(MESSAGE TYPE 10)

no

yes

SPLIT

(RTRM)

RELEASE TERMINAL
TERMINATE

ASSIGN TYPE 9 TO THE
TRANSACTION; BRANCH TO
(TERM) IN CONTROL
PROGRAM (PROCEED
LIKE A NORMAL
TRANSACTION)

Figure 12.7 Routine SEND.

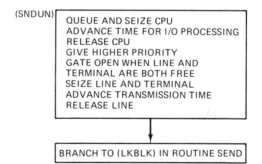

(SNDUN)

QUEUE AND SEIZE CPU
ADVANCE TIME FOR I/O PROCESSING
RELEASE CPU
GIVE HIGHER PRIORITY
GATE OPEN WHEN LINE AND
TERMINAL ARE BOTH FREE
SEIZE LINE AND TERMINAL
ADVANCE TRANSMISSION TIME
RELEASE LINE

BRANCH TO (LKBLK) IN ROUTINE SEND

Figure 12.8 Routine SNDUN.

Routine SNDUN (Figure 12.8). With this routine an unsolicited message is sent to a terminal. This message has to compete for the terminal as well as for the line.

```
                                                           STATEMENT
                                                            NUMBER
      REALLCCATE CHA,0,BMS,0,LMS,0,LCG,5                        1
   REALLCCATE FAC,40,STO,80,QUE,50,TAB,35,FUN,30,CCM,30000   ******     2

BLCCK                                                      STATEMENT
NUMBER  *LOC   OPERATION  A,B,C,D,E,F,G,H,I      COMMENTS    NUMBER
        *                                                       3
        *                                                       4
        ACCES STARTMACRO                                        5
              ASSIGN    2,#A        FILE NR                      6
              ASSIGN    15,#B       CCRE FCR BUFFER NEEDED CR NCT 7
              ASSIGN    16,#C       IS ACCESS SEQ OR ACCCRDING TC CRG 8
              ASSIGN    13,#E       ACCESS THE SAME DRIVE CR NOT   9
              ASSIGN    24,#F       NR CF ROTATICNAL DELAYS       10
              ASSIGN    12,#D       RETURN-ADCRESS               11
              TRANSFER  ,CATIC                                   12
              ENCMACRC                                          13
        *                                                       14
        GCORE STARTMACRO                                        15
              ASSIGN    14,#A       AMCUNT CF CCRE REQUIRED      16
              ASSIGN    8,#B        RETURN-ADCRESS               17
              TRANSFER  ,CCRWN                                   18
              ENCMACRC                                          19
        *                                                       20
        *     SIMULATICN CF A TELEPRCCESSING SYSTEM             21
        *                                                       22
        ***   TIME UNIT IS   MS/(V$MCDEL*0.1)                   23
        *     EACH TIMING VARIABLE THAT DOES NOT RELATE TC CPU IS 24
        *       MULTIPLIED BY V$MCCEL ANC CIVICEC BY 10         25
        *       ALL CPL TIMINGS (ADVANCE BLCCKS) ARE DUMMY,BUT CCNSISTENT 26
        MODEL VARIABLE  K10         TC REFLECT MEDIUM SIZE COMPUTER 27
        *                                                       28
        *                                                       29
        *     S T C R A G E S                                   30
        *                                                       31
        *     THE FIRST N STORAGES ARE RESERVED TO BE PROGRAM ENTRY CCUNTERS 32
        *     WHERE N IS THE NUMBER CF USER'S PROGRAMS IN THE SYSTEM 33
              STCRAGE   S1-S14,100                              34
        PRG1  ECU       1,S                                     35
        PRG2  ECU       2,S                                     36
        PRG3  EQU       3,S                                     37
        PRG9  ECL       9,S                                     38
        PRG10 EQU       10,S                                    39
        PRG12 EQU       12,S                                    40
        PRG14 EQU       14,S                                    41
        ACTIV EQU       18,S   NC CF ACTIVE TASKS IN CORE       42
        **  STORAGES 31-60  ARE TERMINALS ACTING AS FACILITIES  43
              STCRAGE   S31-S60,1                               44
        *                                                       45
        *     DYNAMIC CORE                                      46
        *                                                       47
        CCRE  STCRAGE   70000      MAIN CCRE STCRAGE            48
        *                                                       49
        *     F A C I L I T I E S                               50
        *     THE FIRST N FACILITIES ARE RESERVEC TO BE DRIVES ON THE SYSTEM 51
        *     N CORRESPONDS TO THE NUMBER CF RCWS IN THE MATRIX ARMPO 52
        CRV1  ECU       1,F,Q                                   53
        CRV2  EQL       2,F,C                                   54
        CRV3  EQU       3,F,Q                                   55
        CRV4  ECU       4,F,Q                                   56
        DRV5  EQL       5,F,C                                   57

        CRV6  ECL       6,F,Q                                   58
        CAN1  EQU       12,F,Q                                  59
        CAN2  FQU       13,F,Q                                  60
        *  FACILITIES 21-30 ARE CCMMUNICATICN LINES            61
        *                                                       62
        *     V A R I A B L E   C E F I N I T I C N S           63
        *     FCR D A T I C                                     64
        *                                                       65
        CRIVE VARIABLE  RN2*MH$FILEM(P2,5)/1000+1               66
        READ  VARIABLE  K8          FILEMGT,2,TASK SWITCH,1,SETUP,5 67
        LOCA  VARIABLE  V$LACAA+RN3*(MH$FILEM(P2,3)-MH$FILEM(P2,2)+1)/1000 68
        LACAA VARIABLE  MH$FILEM(P2,2)    FIRST CYL CF FILE     69
        AMOVE VARIABLE  FN$ARMMV*V$MCDEL/10    TIME FOR SEEK    70
        SPAN  VARIABLE  X$LCCAT-MH$ARMFC(P3,1)  SEEK DISTANCE   71
        CLY   VARIABLE  V$MCDEL*RN2*25/100C0+1  RCT.TIME 1-25 MS 72
        CTRAN VARIABLE  V$MCCEL*MH$FILEM(P2,4)/3120+1           73
        *                                                       74
        CETM  VARIABLE  K2          GET MAIN TIME               75
        FREEM VARIABLE  K1          FREE MAIN TIME              76
        *                                                       77
        LINK  VARIABLE  K1          LINK TIME (SLBR STATE)      78
        CINTR VARIABLE  K1               INTERRUPT AND INTERFERENCE TIME 79
        *                                                       80
```

Figure 12.9   A teleprocessing system. The GPSS program.

```
      TRMTB VARIABLE   (V$TNOA+V$TNOB+V$TNOC+V$TNOD)*7C     TERM TABLES         81
      CUSHN VARIABLE   K5000    STORAGE CUSHION REQUIRMENTS                     82
      TASK  VARIABLE   K4C0C       BYTES                                        83
      TASKT VARIABLE   K5              TIME FCR TASK INITIATION                  84
      CLNUP VARIABLE   K8       TASK CLEAN UP TIME                              85
      TIBUF VARIABLE   10C         TERMINAL INPUT BUFFER LENGTH                 86
      TCBUF VARIABLE   100+FN$BFSZ  TERMINAL OUT BUF LENGTH. REG+INQ ANSWER     87
**                                                                             88
**     TNO*  =  NC CF TERMINALS CF GRCLP *                                      89
**     SEE STORAGE DECLARATICNS                                                 90
      MAX   VARIABLE   K60      LAST SERIAL NC CF TERMINAL                      91
      TNOA  VARIABLE   6                                                        92
      TNOB  VARIABLE   6                                                        93
      TNOC  VARIABLE   6                                                        94
      TNOD  VARIABLE   12                                                       95
*     XACT*  =  INTER ARRIVAL TIME CF ALL TERMINALS CF GRCLP *                  96
      XACT1 VARIABLE   180*100C*V$MODEL/(10*V$TNOA)                             97
      XACT2 VARIABLE   24C*10CC*V$MCCEL/(1C*V$TNCB)                             98
      XACT3 VARIABLE   300*100C*V$MCDEL/(10*V$TNOC)                             99
      XACTB VARIABLE   600*100C*V$MCDEL/(10*V$TNOB)                            100
      XACTD VARIABLE   6CC*10CC*V$MCCEL/(10*V$TNCD)                            101
*                                                                             102
      KEYT  VARIABLE   V$MCDEL*FN$KEY/1C       KEY IN TIME                     103
      LCCK  VARIABLE   V$MODFL*FN$LKT/1C   LCCK TIME                           104
      TRNSI VARIABLE   V$MCCEL*FN$TRIN/1C     INP TRANS TIME                   105
      TRNSC VARIABLF   V$MCCEL*FN$TRCUT/10    OUT TRANS TIME                   106
      MPT9  VARIABLE   P9+20            XACT TABLE NC.                         107
**                                                                            108
*       F U N C T I C N    C F F I N I T I C N S                              109
*                                                                            110
      ARMMV FUNCTION   V$SPAN,C5                                              111
      -199,135/-1,25/0,0/1,25/1S9,135                                         112
*                                                                            113
      EXPCN FUNCTION   RN5,C24                                                114
                                                                             115
      .0    0    .1   .104 .2   .222 .3   .355 .4   .509 .5   .69            115
      .6   .915  .7   1.2  .75  1.38 .8   1.6  .84  1.83 .88  2.12           116
      .9   2.3   .92  2.52 .54  2.81 .95  2.99 .96  3.2  .97  3.5            117
      .98  3.9   .99  4.6  .995 5.3  .998 6.2  .999 7.0  .9997 8.0           118
*                                                                            119
*                                                                            120
      SBR   FUNCTION   P9,M14      MLLTIPLE SWITCH                            121
      1,SBR1/2,SBR2/3,SBR3/4,SBRC/5,SBRO/6,SBRO/7,SBRO                        122
      8,SBRC/9,SBR9/10,SBR10/11,SBRO/12,SBR12/13,SBRO/14,SBR14               123
*                                                                            124
      CHAN  FUNCTICN   P3,C3                                                  125
      1,12/2,12/3,12                                                          126
**                                                                           127
******** A S S I G N  TERMINALS  NO TO TRANSACTIONS                          128
**  STCRAGES   31-60   ARE TERMINALS                                         129
*                                                                            130
      TGA   FUNCTION   RN4,C6                                                 131
      0.17,33/0.23,34/0.49,43/0.66,44/0.83,53/1.00,54                        132
      TGB   FUNCTION   RN4,D6                                                 133
      0.17,31/0.33,32/0.49,41/0.66,42/0.83,51/1.00,52                        134
      TGC   FUNCTION   RN4,D6                                                 135
      0.17,35/0.23,36/0.49,45/0.66,46/0.83,55/1.0C,56                        136
      TGD   FUNCTICN   RN4,C12                                               137
      C.09,37/0.17,38/0.25,39/0.33,40/C.41,47/0.49,48/0.58,49/0.66,50        138
      0.74,57/0.83,58/0.91,59/1.00,6C                                        139
**                                                                           140
******* A S S I G N  TERMINALS  TC L I N E S                                 141
****ASSIGN LINE TO TERM. FRCM CCNF.LIST                                      142
*   FACILITIES 21-30 ARE CCMMUNICATICN LINES                                 143
**  STORAGES  31-60  ARE TERMINALS                                           144
*                                                                            145
      LINE  FUNCTICN   P17,C3                                                 146
      40,21/50,22/60,23                                                      147
**                                                                           148
***KEY IN TIME                                                               149
      KEY   FUNCTICN   P9,C4                                                  150
      3,20000/9,1000/10,0/14,1500C                                           151
******TIME TC LOCK AT MES. BEFCRE RESPCNSE                                   152
      LKT   FUNCTICN   P9,D5                                                  153
      3,2000/9,20000/10,2000/12,60000/14,30000              **              154
*****  INPUT XACT TIME + 2*MCDEM TURN AROUND TIME                            155
      TRIN  FUNCTICN   P9,D4                                                 156
      3,630/9,300/10,0/14,600                                                157
****   CUT XACT TIME + 3*MCCEM TURN ARCUND TIME                              158
      TROUT FUNCTION   P9,D5                                                 159
      3,100C/9,C9450/1C,450/12,1745C/14,4500               **               160
      BFSZ  FUNCTICN   P9,C5       FUNCTICN TO GET EXTRA CORE FOR INQ        161
      8,0/9,1000/10,0/12,2000/14,500                 **                     162
*                                                                            163
*      M A T R I X    C E F I N I T I C N S                                  164
*                                                                            165
*      THE FOLLCWING MATRIX DESCRIBES THE CURRENT PCSITICN CF DISK ARM       166
*      RCW I FCR CRIVE I                                                     167
```

Figure 12.9   (continued)

```
*                                                                          168
 ARMPO  MATRIX       H,7,1                                                 169
*                                                                          170
*       THE FOLLCWING MATRIX DESCRIBES THE ATTRIBUTES OF EACH PROGRAM      171
*                                                                          172
*       (RCWS)   RCW N+1 IS ENC CF LIST                                    172
*       CCL 1 = CCRE REC FCR PRCGRAM                                       173
*       CCL 2 = CURRENT STATLS CF PRCGRAM                                  174
*                0= NCT IN CCRE                                            175
*                1= IN CORE BLT NCT IN LSE                                 176
*                2= IN CORE ANC IN LSE                                     177
*                3= NCW BEINC LCACEC                                       178
*                                                                          179
 FROGC  MATRIX       H,15,2                                                180
        INITIAL     MH$PRCGC(1,1),10000                                    181
        INITIAL     MH$PRCGC(2,1),2CCC                                     182
        INITIAL     MH$PROGC(3,1),3000                                     183
        INITIAL     MH$PROGC(9,1),2000                                     184
        INITIAL     MH$PRCGC(10,1),2CCC                                    185
        INITIAL     MF$PRCGC(12,1),30CC                                    186
        INITIAL     MH$PRCGC(14,1),2500                                    187
*                                                                          188
*********F I L E S ::::                                                    189
*****1=MAIN                                                                190
****2=BMAIN                                                                191
**** 3=PAGE                                                                192
**** 4=FILE X                                   **                         193
*** 5=LOG                                                                  194
**** 6=BLCG                                                                195
**** 7=PRCG.CIRECTORY                                                      196
*** 8=PROGRAMS                                                             197
**** 9=DESTINATIONS FOR BRCCCASTING                                       198
*       THE FOLLCWING MATRIX DESCRIBES THE ATTRIBUTES OF EACH FILE(RCW)    199
*       COL 1 = FILE TYPE       NOT LSED                                   200
*       CCL 2 = FIRST CYLINCER CF FILE      EQUALLY CISTRIBLTED CN EACH    201
*       COL 3 = LAST CYLINCER OF FILE       CRIVE                          202
*       COL 4 = BLOCK LENGTH                                               203
*       CCL 5 = NR CF CRIVES ON WFICH THE FILE IS DISTRIBLTED              204
 FILEM  MATRIX       H,9,5                                                 205
*                                                                          206
        INITIAL     MH$FILEM(1,2),111/MH$FILEM(1,3),135                    207
        INITIAL     MH$FILEM(1,4),2200/MH$FILEM(1,5),1                     208
        INITIAL     MH$FILEM(2,2),111/MH$FILEM(2,3),135                    209
        INITIAL     MH$FILEM(2,4),2200                                     210
        INITIAL     MH$FILEM(2,5),1                                        211
        INITIAL     MH$FILEM(3,2),1C8                                      212
        INITIAL     MH$FILEM(3,3),109                                      213
        INITIAL     MH$FILEM(3,4),2000                                     214
        INITIAL     MH$FILEM(3,5),1                                        215
        INITIAL     MH$FILEM(4,2),108                                      216
        INITIAL     MH$FILEM(4,3),109                                      217
        INITIAL     MH$FILEM(4,4),1000                        **           218
        INITIAL     MH$FILEM(4,5),1                                        219
        INITIAL     MH$FILEM(5,2),136/MH$FILEM(5,3),160                    220
        INITIAL     MH$FILEM(5,4),100                                      221
        INITIAL     MH$FILEM(5,5),1                                        222
        INITIAL     MH$FILEM(6,2),136/MH$FILEM(6,3),160                    223
        INITIAL     MH$FILEM(6,4),10C/MH$FILEM(6,5),1                      224
        INITIAL     MH$FILEM(7,2),098/MH$FILEM(7,3),098                    225
        INITIAL     MH$FILEM(7,4),0256/MH$FILEM(7,5),1                     226
        INITIAL     MH$FILEM(8,2),0SS                                      227
        INITIAL     MH$FILEM(8,3),100                                      228

        INITIAL     MH$FILEM(8,4),2000                                     229
        INITIAL     MH$FILEM(8,5),1                                        230
        INITIAL     MF$FILEM(9,2),11C                                      231
        INITIAL     MH$FILEM(9,3),110                                      232
        INITIAL     MH$FILEM(9,4),1CC                                      233
        INITIAL     MH$FILEM(9,5),1                                        234
**                                                                         235
*       THE FOLLCWING MATRIX DESCRIBES CN WHICH DRIVE THE FILES            236
*       (RCWS) ARE SITUATEC                                                237
*       CCL 1 = FIRST CRIVE                                                238
*       COL 2 = SECOND CRIVE                                               239
*                                                                          240
 MFLCR  MATRIX       H,9,2                                                 241
*                                                                          242
        INITIAL     MH$MFLCR(1,1),1                                        243
        INITIAL     MH$MFLCR(2,1),2                                        244
        INITIAL     MH$MFLCR(3,1),3                                        245
        INITIAL     MH$MFLCR(4,1),2                                        246
        INITIAL     MH$MFLCR(5,1),1                                        247
        INITIAL     MH$MFLCR(6,1),3                                        248
        INITIAL     MH$MFLCR(7,1),2                                        249
        INITIAL     MH$MFLCR(8,1),3                                        250
        INITIAL     MH$MFLCR(9,1),1                                        251
**                                                                         252
**  TERMINAL STATUS  ..  SET 1 FCR INC MCCE                                253
**     VALIC TERMINALS ARE 31-6C                                           254
```

Figure 12.9 (continued)

```
       *                                                              255
       MTR    MATRIX      H,80,1                                      256
       *                                                              257
       *      T A B L E   D E F I N I T I O N S                       258
       *                                                              259
       ** TABLES 1-15 FOR XACT TYPE CIRCULATION IN CPU               260
       ** MOVEMENT OF ORIGINAL XACT FROM POINT IT ENTERS CPU         261
       **               TILL IT IS KILLED BY THE SYSTEM              262
       1      TABLE       M1,1000,250,55                              263
       2      TABLE       M1,200,100,55                               264
       3      TABLE       M1,0,50,50                                  265
       5      TABLE       M1,0,50,50                                  266
       10     TABLE       M1,100,100,55                               267
       12     TABLE       M1,0,50,50                                  268
       14     TABLE       M1,0,50,50                                  269
       ALL    EQU         16,T                                        270
       ALL    TABLE       M1,250,250,55                               271
       **                                                             272
       ** TABLES 21-35 FOR XACT CIRCULATION TIME                     273
       ** FROM END OF KEY IN TO START LOOKING AT THE ANSWER          274
       21     TABLE.      MP23,2500,250,55                            275
       22     TABLE       MP23,1500,250,55                            276
       23     TABLE       MP23,1500,250,55                            277
       29     TABLE       MP23,15000,250,55                           278
       30     TABLE       MP23,1500,250,55                            279
       32     TABLE       MP23,15000,250,55                           280
       34     TABLE       MP23,4500,250,55                            281
       **                                                             282
       FLREC  EQU         17,T                                        283
       FLREQ  TABLE       MP19,10,10,55        .DATIC. TIMING        284
       ACTIV  EQU         18,T                                        285

       ACTIV  TABLE       MP2,250,250,55                              286
       **                                                             287
       *                                                              288
       *      THE  D A T I O  SUBROUTINE HANDLES ALL DISK I/O REQUESTS  289
       *      WHEN ENTERING DATIO,THE CPU MUST BE SEIZED             290
       *      WHEN RETURNING FROM DATIO,THE CPU IS RELEASED          291
       *      THE ARGUMENTS:P12= RETURN-ADDRESS                      292
       *                    P2 = FILE NR                             293
       *                    P15= 0  CORE FOR BUFFER NOT NEEDED       294
       *                       = 1  CORE FOR BUFFER NEEDED           295
       *                    P16= 0  READ SEQUENTIAL                  296
       *                       = 1   READ ON RANDOM CYL OF FILE      297
       *                       = X   READ ON THIS SPECIFIC CYL OF FILE 298
       *                    P13= 0   READ ON THE SAME DRIVE          299
       *                       = 1   READ ON RANDOM DRIVE OF FILE    300
       *                    P24= 1OR2 NR OF ROTATIONAL DELAYS        301
1      DATIO  MARK        19                                          302
2             TEST E      P13,1,BUF   IS IT THE SAME DRIVE ?         303
3             ASSIGN      3,V$DRIVE   NO,WHICH DRIVE? 1ST,2ND,3ND ETC ? 304
4             ASSIGN      3,MH$FLDR(P2,P3) PICK UP THE DRIVE         305
       *                                                              306
5      BUF    TEST E      P15,1,SETUP IS BUFFER FOR THE READ NEEDED ? 307
       GCORE  MACRO       MH$FILEM(P2,4),SETUP YES,BUFFER LNGTH=BLOCK LNGTH 308
6             ASSIGN      14,MH$FILEM(P2,4)                          308
7             ASSIGN      8,SETUP                                    308
8             TRANSFER    ,CCRMN                                     308
9      SETUP  ADVANCE     V$READ      SETUP READ (INCLUDES INTERRUPT HANDLING) 309
10            RELEASE     CPU                                        310
       *                                                              311
11            ASSIGN      25,FN$CHAN                                 312
12            QUEUE       *3          QUEUE FOR CHANNNEL AND DISK    313
13     GTE    GATE NU     *3                                         314
14            GATE NU     *25                                        315
15            TRANSFER    SIM,SEQ1,GTE                               316
16     SEQ1   DEPART      *3                                         317
17            SEIZE       *3          SEIZE THE DISK                 318
18            TEST E      P16,0,SPEC  IS THIS A SEQ READ?            319
19            TEST E      MH$ARMPC(P3,1),P1,SEQ2 Y,WAS THE ARM STOLEN? 320
20            TRANSFER    ,ROTAV      NO                             321
21     SEQ2   SAVEVALUE   LOCAT,MH$ARMPC(P3,1) YES,SAVE CUR POS OF ARM 322
22            MSAVEVALUE  ARMPO,P3,1,P1,H   NEW POSITION            323
23            TRANSFER    ,SEEK                                      324
24     SPEC   SAVEVALUE   LOCAT,MH$ARMPC(P3,1)   SAVE CUR POS OF ARM 325
25            TEST NE     P16,1,RANDM IS THIS A SPECIFIC READ ?     326
26            MSAVEVALUE  ARMPO,P3,1,P16,H   NEW POSITION OF ARM    327
27            ASSIGN      1,MH$ARMPC(P3,1)    SAVE IT,USED IF NXT READ SEQ 328
28            TRANSFER    ,SEEK                                      329
       *                                                              330
29     RANDM  MSAVEVALUE  ARMPO,P3,1,V$LOCA,H  NEW POSITION OF ARM  331
30            ASSIGN      1,MH$ARMPC(P3,1)    SAVE IT               332
       *                                                              333
31     SEEK   ADVANCE     V$AMOVE     SEEK TIME                     334
32     ROTAV  QUEUE       *25         QUEUE FOR THE CHANNEL AND SEIZE IT 335
33            SEIZE       *25                                        336
34            DEPART      *25                                        337
35     TRA1   ADVANCE     V$CLY       ROTATIONAL DELAYS             338
36            LOOP        24,TRA1                                    339
```

Figure 12.9 (continued)

```
 37         *                                                           340
 38         ADVANCE    V$DTRAN                                          341
 38         RELEASE    *25         RELEASE THE CHANNEL                  342
 39         RELEASE    *3          RELEASE TH DISK                      343
 40         TABULATE   FLREQ                                            344
 41         TRANSFER   ,*12                                             345
            *                                                           346
            *                                                           347
            *    WHEN ENTERING CORMN  THE CPU IS SEIZED                 348
            *    WHEN RETURNING FRCM  CCRMN THE CPU IS STILL SEIZED     349
            *    IF CORE NOT AVAILABLE,ALL INCCRE-NOTUSED PGMS ARR RCLLEC OUT  350
            *    THE ARGUMENTS:P8 = RETURN-ADDRESS                      351
            *              P14= AMCLNT CF CCRE REQUIREC                 352
            *                                                           353
 42 CCRMN   TEST L     R$CORE,F14,ENTR   IS THERE ENOUGH CCRE          354
 43 CORLP   ASSIGN     11+,K1            NC,ADD 1 TC PROGRAM TABLE INDEX 355
 44         TEST NE    MH$PROGC(P11,1),KC,EXIT  IF END CF LIST,CC TC EXIT 356
 45         TEST E     MH$PROGC(F11,2),K1,CCRLP  IS PRG IN CORE+NOT IN USE 357
 46         LEAVE      CORE,MH$FRCGC(P11,1)      Y,RCLL IT OUT          358
 47         MSAVEVALUE PROGC,P11,2,KC,H  SET STATUS,NOT IN CCRE        359
 48         ADVANCE    V$FREEM                                          360
 49         TRANSFER   ,CCRLP                                           361
            *                                                           362
 50 EXIT    TEST CE    R$CORE,P14,RELS                                  363
 51 ENTR    ENTER      CCRE,P14                                         364
 52 ENDGO   ADVANCE    V$GETM                                           365
 53         ASSIGN     11,KO                                            366
 54         TRANSFER   ,*8                                              367
            *                                                           368
            *    IF THERE WASN'T ENOUGH CCRE                            369
            *                                                           370
 55 RELS    RELEASE    CPU                                              371
 56         QUEUE      CCRE                                             372
 57         ENTER      CCRE,P14                                         373
 58         DEPART     CORE                                             374
 59         SEIZE      CPU                                              375
 6C         TRANSFER   ,ENCGC                                           376
            *                                                           377
            *    SUBROUTINE  S T A T E  TESTS THE STATUS OF THE PRCGRAM 378
            *    IF PROGRAM IS NOT IN CORF,IT WILL BE LCADED            379
            *    WHEN RETURNING FROM THE SLBRCLTINE,THE PRCGRAM WILL BE 380
            *    IN CORE,ANC THE CPU WILL STILL BE SEIZED               381
            *    THE ARGUMENTS:P4 = PRCGRAM NR                          382
            *              P10= RETLRN-ADDRESS                          383
            *                                                           384
 61 STATE   ADVANCE    V$LINK      LINK TIME                            385
 62         TEST NE    MH$PROGC(P4,2),K3,GATER IS PROG BEING LOADED?    386
 63         TEST E     MH$PROGC(P4,2),KC,BLD2  NO,IS PRCG IN CORE?      387
            *                                                           388
            *    NC,WE MLST BRING IT IN                                 389
            *                                                           390
 64         MSAVEVALUE PROGC,P4,2,K3,H   INDICATE PROG IS BEING LOADED  391
 65         ADVANCE    1           INITIATE LOAC                        392
            *                                                           393
            *    READ CIRECTCRY (FILE 7)                                394
            *                                                           395
    ACCES   MACRC      7,1,1,BLB,1,1                                    396
 66         ASSIGN     2,7                                              396
 67         ASSIGN     15,1                                             396
 68         ASSIGN     16,1                                             396
 69         ASSIGN     13,1                                             396
 70         ASSIGN     24,1                                             396
 71         ASSIGN     12,BLB                                           396
 72         TRANSFER   ,CATIC                                           396
            *                                                           397
            *    READ PRCGRAM FROM THE LIBRARY (FILE 8)                 398
            *                                                           399
 73 BLB     MSAVEVALUE FILEM,8,4,MH$FRCGC(P4,1),H    SET REC-LENGTH     400
 74         SEIZE      CPU                                              401
    ACCES   MACRC      8,1,1,BLC1,1,1                                   402
 75         ASSIGN     2,8                                              402
 76         ASSIGN     15,1                                             402
 77         ASSIGN     16,1                                             402
 78         ASSIGN     13,1                                             402
 79         ASSIGN     24,1                                             402
 8C         ASSIGN     12,BLC1                                          402
 81         TRANSFER   ,CATIC                                           402
 82 BLC1    SEIZE      CPU                                              403
 83         LEAVE      CORE,MH$FILEM(7,4)  FREE CORE OF DIRECTORY RECCRC 404
 84         ADVANCE    V$FREEM                                          405
 85         TRANSFER   ,BLD2                                            406
 86 GATER   RELEASE    CPU                                              407
 87         GATE SNE   *4          WAIT TILL PRCG-LOAC IS FINISHED      408
 88         SEIZE      CPU                                              409
 89 BLD2    MSAVEVALUE PRCGC,P4,2,2,H    INDICATE,PROGRAM IS IN CORE+IN USE 410
 90         ENTER      *4          ACC 1 TO PROGR ACTIVITY COUNT        411
```

Figure 12.9 (continued)

```
91              TRANSFER   ,*10                                                          412
    *                                                                                    413
    *       SUBROUTINE  Q U I T  TESTS, WHETHER CR NCT TC RCLL CUT                        414
    *       THE PROGRAM WHEN ITS EXECUTION IS TERMINATED                                 415
    *       THE PROGRAM STATUS IS ADJUSTED                                               416
    *       THE CPU IS SEIZED WHEN ENTERING THE ROUTINE,AND IS STILL                     417
    *       SEIZED WHEN RETURNING FROM IT                                                418
    *       THE ARGUMENTS:P4 = PROGRAM NR                                                419
    *                     P1C= RETURN-ADDRESS                                            420
    *                                                                                    421
92      CUIT  LEAVE      *4,K1       REDUCE PROGR ACTIVITY CCUNT BY 1                     422
93            TEST E     S*4,K0,NXTPG  IS ACTIVITY CCUNT ZERC?                            423
94            TEST E     QSCORE,KC,RCLL   YES,ARE WE SHORT ON STCRAGE?                    424
95            TEST E     CSTASK,K0,RCLL                                                   425
96            MSAVEVALUE PRCGD,P4,2,K1,H  NC,NC CNE NEEDS CCRE,CHANGE STATUS              426
97            TRANSFER   ,NXTPG          (IN CORE,NOT IN USE),RETURN                     427
98      RCLL  MSAVEVALLE PRCGD,P4,2,0,H   INDICATE STATUS NOT IN CORE                    428
99            ADVANCE    VSFREEM                                                         429
100           LEAVE      CCRE,MHSFRCGD(P4,1)  FREE CORE CF PROGRAM                       430
1C1     NXTPG TRANSFER   ,*10            RETURN                                          431
    *                                                                                    432
    *                                                                                    433
    *                                                                                    434
    *       TRACE AND TABULATE ELAPSED TIME THERE IS                                     435
    *       NO ACTIVE TASKS IN THE SYSTEM                                                436
    *                                                                                    437
102     ATASK GENERATE   ,,,1,,,F                                                        438
103     TCR   GATE SE     ACTIV       NC TASK IN THE SYSTEM                              439
                                                                                         440
104           MARK       2           MARK THE TIME                                       440
105           GATE SNE   ACTIV       NEW TASK IN THE SYSTEM                              441
1C6           TABULATE   ACTIV  ELAPSED TIME THERE WAS NC TASK IN THE SYSTEM             442
107           SAVEVALUE  ACTIV+,1   NR CF TIMES THIS HAPPENED                            443
1C8           TRANSFER   ,TCR                                                            444
    *                                                                                    445
    *       VARIABLE CCRE RECUIRMENTS                                                    446
    *                                                                                    447
1C9     CORE  GENERATE   ,,,1        RESERVE 1 TERMINAL INPUT BUFFER (100)               448
11C           ENTER      CCRE,K3CC   PER LINE (3)                                        449
111           ENTER      CCRE,K15CC0    FOR THE MONITOR                                  450
112           ENTER      CORE,K6C00   BASIC STANDARD MODULES                            451
113           ENTER      CORE,VSTRMTB  TERMINAL TABLES                                   452
114           TERMINATE                                                                  453
    *                                                                                    454
    *       THE  F R A M E  OF THE CPU MCDELL                                            455
    *       MSGS ARE GENERATED ACCCRCING TO XACT TYPE AND TERM GROUP                     456
    *       IF CORE IS NOT AVAILABLE TC START TASKS POLLING STOPS                        457
    * THIS IS NOT SIMULATED.MSGS WHICH  CCULD BE DELAYED BY THE ABOVE ACT                458
    *   ARE CCUNTED BY THE BLCCK ==KILL                                                  459
    *       MSGS QUEUE FOR TERMINAL AND LINE FCR TRANSMISICN.                            460
    *       GPSS XACT PASS SPLIT BLCCK:                                                  461
    *       THE O R I G I N A L XACT IS MARKED AT THIS TIME,AS WE ARE                    462
    *       INTERESTED IN THE DURATICN CF THE PRCCESSING,WHICH STARTS NCW                463
    *       THE C F F S P R I N G  XACT CCRRESPONDS TC TERMINAL CONTRCL,                 464
    *       THE HIGH PRICRITY(6) SYSTEM TASK, WHCSE DUTY IS TC GET CORE                  465
    *       FCR THE NEXT INPUT MSG CN THIS LINE                                          466
    *       NB. THERE IS NO SYNCHRCNIZATION BETWEEN GETTING THE CORE AND                 467
    *       ALLCWING FOR A SECCND MSG CN THIS LINE                                       468
    **  NC RETRANSMISICN DUE TC LINE ERRCRS                                             469
    *                                                                                    470
    **   TRANSACTICN GENERATICN                                                          471
    *                                                                                    472
    **  XACT TYPE 1 . TERMINAL GRCUP A .                                                 473
115           GENERATE   VSXACT1,FNSEXPCN,,,,25,F                                        474
116           ASSIGN     17,FNSTGA   CRIGINATING TERMINAL                                475
117           ASSIGN     9,1   XACT TYPE                                                 476
118           TRANSFER   ,PRCC                                                           477
    *                                                                                    478
    **  XACT TYPE 2 TERM GRCUP B                                                         479
119           GENERATE   VSXACT2,FNSEXPCN,,,,25,F                                        480
120           ASSIGN     9,2                                                             481
121           ASSIGN     17,FNSTCB                                                       482
122           TEST E     MHSMTR(P17,1),0,ACTB   TEST IF INC MCDE                         483
123           TRANSFER   ,PROC                                                           484
124     ACTB  TERMINATE   INQ MCDE . CCNT SEND XACT                                      485
    *                                                                                    486
    ***XACT 3  TERM GRCUP C                                                              487
125           GENERATE   VSXACT3,FNSEXPCN,,,,25,F                                        488
126           ASSIGN     9,3                                                             489
127           ASSIGN     17,FNSTCC                                                       490
128           TRANSFER   ,PRCC                                                           491
    *                                                                                    492
    **XACT 12 TERM  GROUP BBBB                                                           493
129           GENERATE   VSXACTB,FNSEXPCN,,,,25,F                                        494
130           ASSIGN     9,12                                                            495
131           ASSIGN     17,FNSTGB                                                       496
                                                                                         497
132           MSAVEVALUE MTR,P17,1,K1,H   INCUIRY STATE                                  497
133           TRANSFER   ,PROC                                                           498
```

Figure 12.9   (continued)

```
                *                                                                    499
                ****XACT 14TERM GROUP DDDD                                           500
134             GENERATE     V$XACTD,FN$EXPON,,,,25,F                                501
135             ASSIGN       9,14                                                    502
136             ASSIGN       17,FN$TGD                                               503
137             MSAVEVALUE   MTR,P17,1,K1,H        INQURY MODE                       504
138             TRANSFER     ,PRCC                                                   505
                *                                                                    506
139      KILL   SAVEVALUE    NOPOL+,1                                                507
         *   ONE SHOULD PUT HERE SOME DELAY TO ALLOW FOR 'STOP POLL'                 508
140             TRANSFER     ,CONT                                                   509
                *                                                                    510
                ***   P-18 LINE   ,,  P-17 TERMINAL                                  511
141      PROC   ADVANCE      0                                                       512
                *                                                                    513
142      TERM   QUEUE        TERM       GENERAL C                                    514
143             ENTER        *17  KEY IN STARTS. TERM SEIZED UNTILL END OF REPLY(S   515
144             DEPART       TERM                                                    516
145             ADVANCE      V$KEYT                                                  517
         **   MSG READY TO BE TRANSFERED BY LINE                                     518
146             MARK         23         TABULATION IN TABLES 21-35                   519
147             TEST GE      R$CORE,V$CUSHN,KILL   TEST IF AT LEAST CUSHION AVAIL.    520
148      CONT   ADVANCE      0                                                       521
149             ASSIGN       18,FN$LINE      ASSIGN LINE NO                          522
150             QUEUE        *18                                                     523
151             SEIZE        *18  LINE FOR TRANSMISSION                              524
152             DEPART       *18                                                     525
153             ADVANCE      V$TRNSI                                                 526
154             RELEASE      *18                                                     527
155             SPLIT        1,TCTRL                                                 528
         **   MARK TIME FOR XACT  IN CPL                                             529
156             MARK                                                                 530
157             PREEMPT      CPU                                                     531
158             ADVANCE      V$CINTR                                                 532
159             RETURN       CPU                                                     533
                *                                                                    534
                *                                                                    535
160      NOLOD  QUEUE        TASK        SIMULATE STORAGE CUSHICN,                   536
161             ENTER        CORE,V$CUSHN   DON'T START ,UNLESS CUSHION AVAILABLE    537
162             SEIZE        CPU         SET UP NEW TASK                             538
163             LEAVE        CORE,V$CLSHN                                            539
164             DEPART       TASK                                                    540
                *                                                                    541
165             ENTER        ACTIV       ADD 1 TO  ACTIV TASK COUNT                  542
         GCORE   MACRO       V$TASK,EKA    GET CORE FOR TASK                         543
166             ASSIGN       14,V$TASK                                               543
167             ASSIGN       8,BKA                                                   543
168             TRANSFER     ,CORMN                                                  543
169      EKA    ADVANCE      V$TASKT         TASK INITIATION                         544
170             ASSIGN       4,P9          PROGRAM NR= MSG TYPE                      545
171             ASSIGN       10,BKC                                                  546
172             TRANSFER     ,STATE                                                  547
         *    PROGRAM IS IN CORE NOW                                                 548
                *                                                                    549
173      BKC    ASSIGN       7,BKB         DC MSG PROCESSING                         550

                **                                                                   551
                *********G O T O  **S B R PROCESSING****                             552
174             TRANSFER     ,FN$SBR                                                 553
                **                                                                   554
175      BKB    ASSIGN       10,BKD        QUITS THE PROGRAM,AND ROLLS IT            555
176             TRANSFER     ,QUIT         OUT IF NECCESSARY                         556
177      BKD    ADVANCE      V$CLNUP       TASK CLEAN UP TIME                        557
178             LEAVE        CORE,V$TASK   FREE TASK CORE                            558
179             ADVANCE      V$FREEM                                                 559
180             LEAVE        ACTIV         SUBTRACT 1 FROM ACTIV TASK COUNT          560
181             RELEASE      CPU                                                     561
182             TABULATE     *9     TABLES 1-15  XACT IN CPU                         562
183             TABULATE     ALL    TABLES 1-15  XACT IN CPU                         563
184             TERMINATE                                                           564
                *                                                                    565
         *      TERMINAL CONTROL GETS CCRE FOR THE NEXT INPUT MSG FROM LINE          566
         *                                                                          567
185      TCTRL  PRIORITY     6                                                       568
186             SEIZE        CPU                                                     569
         GCORE   MACRO       V$TIBUF,TCT                                             570
187             ASSIGN       14,V$TIBLF                                              570
188             ASSIGN       8,TCT                                                   570
189             TRANSFER     ,CORMN                                                  570
190      TCT    RELEASE      CPU                                                     571
191             TERMINATE                                                           572
                *                                                                    573
                *                                                                    574
         *      ROUTINE FOR MSG TRANSMISSION FROM CPU,TO THE TERMINAL,AND            575
         *      FREEING OUTPUT BUFFER.   STATISTICS                                  576
         *                                                                          577
192      SEND   ADVANCE      0                                                       578
                **                                                                   579
```

Figure 12.9 (continued)

```
153           SEIZE     CPU                                                     580
154           ADVANCE   3        WRITE TC TERMINAL MACRO                        581
155           RELEASE   CPU                                                     582
156           QUEUE     *18                                                     583
157           SEIZE     *18                                                     584
198           DEPART    *18                                                     585
199           ADVANCE   V$TRNSC       TRANSMISSION TIME                         586
200           RELEASE   *18                                                     587
      *    INTERRUPT FRCM LINE= END CF TRANSFER                                 588
201           TABULATE  V$MPTS        XACT CYCLE CCNVERSATICN MCDE              589
2C2   LKBLK   PREEMPT   CPU              INTERRUPT                              590
203           ADVANCE   V$CINTR                                                 591
204           LEAVE     CORE,V$TCBUF       FREE TERMINAL CUTPLT BUFFER          592
205           ADVANCE   V$FREEM                                                 593
2C6           RETURN    CPL                                                     594
207           ADVANCE   V$LCCK    LCCK AT ANSWER FRCM CPU                       595
208           TEST LE   P9,K10,SINC  TEST IF INC TYPE XACT                      596
2C9   RTRM    LEAVE     *17       RELEASE TERMINAL                              597
21C           TERMINATE                                                         598
      *                                                                         599
      *    PREPARE INTERNAL XACT TYPE 9 TO SEND A PAGE TC TERM                  600
      *    AFTER CPERATCR FINISHED TC LOCK AT INC REPLY                         601
211   SINQ    SPLIT     1,SINCR                                                 602
212           TRANSFER  ,RTRM                                                   603
213   SINCR   ASSIGN    9,9       XACT TYPE=ENC OF INQ                          604

214           TRANSFER  ,TERM    SAME PRCCEDURE AS REGULAR XACT                 605
      *                                                                         606
      *    UNSOLICITEC MSG SHOULC QUEUE FOR TERMINAL AND LINE                   607
      *                                                                         608
215   SNDUN   ADVANCE   0                                                       609
216           SEIZE     CPU                                                     610
217           ADVANCE   1        RESET FCLL                                     611
218           ADVANCE   3                                                       612
219           RELEASE   CPL                                                     613
220           PRIORITY  6        BRCADCASTING MSG.  ADDRESSING HAS PRICRITY     614
221   TESTP   GATE SE   *17                                                     615
222           GATE NU   *18          TEST LINE                                  616
223           TRANSFER  SIM,PFREE,TESTP                                         617
224   PFREE   ENTER     *17    TERM                                            618
225           QUEUE     *18                                                     619
226           SEIZE     *18                                                     620
227           DEPART    *18                                                     621
228           ADVANCE   V$TRNSC                                                 622
229           RELEASE   *18                                                     623
230           TRANSFER  ,LKBLK                                                  624
      *                                                                         625
      ******* S B R 0 ******    FCR ERRCR CETECTION                            626
231   SBRO    TERMINATE                                                         627
      **                                                                        628
      ******  S B R 1 *********                                                 629
      *                                                                         630
232   SBR1    ADVANCE   1                                                       631
233           ASSIGN    22,BACK1        SET RETURN ADDR                         632
234           TRANSFER  ,INSBR                                                  633
235   BACK1   ADVANCE   0                                                       634
      ACCES   MACRO     3,1,1,SBR1C,1,1        RC TERM PAGE                     635
236           ASSIGN    2,3                                                     635
237           ASSIGN    15,1                                                    635
238           ASSIGN    16,1                                                    635
239           ASSIGN    13,1                                                    635
240           ASSIGN    24,1                                                    635
241           ASSIGN    12,SBR1C                                                635
242           TRANSFER  ,DATIC                                                  635
243   SBR1C   SEIZE     CPU                                                     636
      GCORE   MACRO     V$TCBUF,SBR1K        MSG BUF FOR MSG                    637
244           ASSIGN    14,V$TCBUF                                              637
245           ASSIGN    8,SBR1K                                                 637
246           TRANSFER  ,CORMN                                                  637
247   SBR1K   ADVANCE   2                                                       638
      **           SEND UNSOLICITEC MSG . UPCATE TC TERMINAL                    639
248           SPLIT     1,SNDUN                                                 640
      ACCES   MACRC     3,0,P1,SBR1H,1,2    WT UPCATED PAGE                     641
249           ASSIGN    2,3                                                     641
250           ASSIGN    15,0                                                    641
251           ASSIGN    16,P1                                                   641
252           ASSIGN    13,1                                                    641
253           ASSIGN    24,2                                                    641
254           ASSIGN    12,SBR1H                                                641
255           TRANSFER  ,DATIC                                                  641
256   SBR1H   SEIZE     CPU                                                     642
257           LEAVE     CORE,MH$FILEM(3,4)                                      643
258           ADVANCE   V$FREEM                                                 644

259           TRANSFER  ,BRCCS                                                  645
      * SUBRCUTINE TO HANDLE BRCADCASTING NSGS- RC PAGE,UPDATE,SEND MSG         646
      * WT PAGE,WT BPAGE                                                        647
      **    ENTER THIS SUBRCUTINE WHEN CPU SEIZEC                               648
      * IF TERMINAL IN INC MCDE CCNT SENC MSG                                   649
```

Figure 12.9 (continued)

```
                  *     ORIGINATING TERM NO IN P-17                              650
26C       ERDCS SAVEVALUE LLL,31      INITIAL VALUE=FIRST TERM NO                651
          CCORE MACRO     MH$FILEM(3,4),IGCA                                     652
261             ASSIGN    14,MF$FILEM(3,4)                                       652
262             ASSIGN    8,IGCA                                                 652
263             TRANSFER  ,CCRMN                                                 652
264       IGCA  ADVANCE   0                                                      653
          CCORE MACRC     MH$FILEM(4,4),IGCB                        **           654
265             ASSIGN    14,MH$FILEM(4,4)                                       654
266             ASSIGN    8,IGCB                                                 654
267             TRANSFER  ,CCRMN                                                 654
268       IGCB  ADVANCE   0                           **                         655
          CCORE MACRC     V$TCBUF,TSTME                                          656
265             ASSIGN    14,V$TCBLF                                             656
27C             ASSIGN    8,TSTME                                                656
271             TRANSFER  ,CCRMN                                                 656
          *     DCN'T SFND MSG TC SAME TERMINAL                                  657
272       TSTME TEST NE   X$LLL,P17,BRC1                                         658
273             ADVANCE   3                                                      659
          *     TEST IF TERM IN INC MODE.IF YES:PROCCED                          660
          *        IF NOT:GC TC ERCAC,TC PREPARE UNSOLICITED MSG(TYPF 10)        661
274             TFST E    MH$MTR(X$LLL,1),1,BRCAC                                662
275       ERA5  ADVANCE   C                                                      663
          ACCES MACRO     4,0,1,BRC,1,2     WT FILE X              **            664
276             ASSIGN    2,4                                                    664
277             ASSIGN    15,0                                                   664
278             ASSIGN    16,1                                                   664
279             ASSIGN    13,1                                                   664
28C             ASSIGN    24,2                                                   664
281             ASSIGN    12,BRC                                                 664
282             TRANSFER  ,DATIC                                                 664
283       BRC   SEIZE     CPU                                                    665
284       BRC1  ADVANCE   0                   FCINTER FCR BRANCH FRCM TCP        666
285             TEST L    X$LLL,V$MAX,ENDLF                                      667
286             SAVEVALUF LLL+,1                                                 668
287             TRANSFER  ,TSTME                                                 669
          *                                                                     670
288       ENDLF LEAVE     CORE,MH$FILEM(3,4)                                     671
289             LEAVE     CORE,MH$FILEM(4,4)                       **            672
29C             LEAVF     CORE,V$TCBUF                                           673
291             ADVANCE   V$FREEM                                               674
292             TRANSFER  ,*7    RETLRN                                          675
          *                                                                     676
293       BROAC ADVANCE   2                                                     677
          ACCES MACRO     9,0,1,BRE,1,1   WT MAIN BRCADCASTING MSG              678
294             ASSIGN    2,9                                                   678
295             ASSIGN    15,0                                                  678
296             ASSIGN    16,1                                                  678
297             ASSIGN    13,1                                                  678
298             ASSIGN    24,1                                                  678
299             ASSIGN    12,BRE                                                678
30C             TRANSFER  ,CATIC                                                678

301       BRE   ADVANCE   C                                                     679
302             SPLIT     1,NWTSK          PREPARE TC SEND MSG                  680
303             SEIZE     CPU                                                   681
304             TRANSFER  ,ERA5                                                 682
          *    PRIORITY SHCULD BE RETAINED IN CRDER TC FORCE THIS XACT GO FIRST 683
          *        AND GET THE CORRECT VALLE CF  X$LLL                          684
3C5       NWTSK PRICRITY  7                                                     685
3C6             ASSIGN    17,X$LLL SAVE TERM NC                                 686
307             ASSIGN    9,1C    XACT TYPE=LPCATE LINE IN PAGE                 687
3C8             PRICRITY  0    RESET PR                                         688
          ******SET TIMF HERE  BECALSE IT CC NCT CCMF VIA LINE                  689
309             MARK                                                            690
31C             TRANSFER  ,NOLCG                                                691
          **                                                                    692
          ******* S B R 2   *********                                           693
311       SBR2  ADVANCE   1                                                     694
312             ASSIGN    22,BACK2         SET RETURN ADCR                      695
313             TRANSFER  ,INSBR                                                696
314       BACK2 TRANSFER  ,*7   RETLRN FRCM SER                                 697
          **                                                                    698
          ******* S B R 3   *********                                           699
315       SBR3  ADVANCF   0                                                     700
316             ASSIGN    22,BACK3         SET RETLRN ADCR                      701
317             TRANSFER  ,INSBR                                                702
318       BACK3 ADVANCE   C                                                     703
          ACCFS MACRO     4,1,1,SBR3A,1,1    RD FILE X         **               704
319             ASSIGN    2,4                                                   704
32C             ASSIGN    15,1                                                  704
321             ASSIGN    16,1                                                  704
322             ASSIGN    13,1                                                  704
323             ASSIGN    24,1                                                  704
324             ASSIGN    12,SBR3A                                             704
325             TRANSFER  ,CATIC                                               704
326       SBR3A SEIZE     CPU                                                  705
          CCORE MACRC     V$TCBUF,SBR3B         FCR CLT MSG                     706
327             ASSIGN    14,V$TCBLF                                           706
```

Figure 12.9 (continued)

```
328              ASSIGN     8,SBR3B                                           706
329              TRANSFER   ,CCRMN         .                                  706
330      SBR3B   ADVANCE    2                                                 707
331              LEAVE      CORE,MHSFILEM(4,4)                       **       708
332              ADVANCE    VSFREEM                                           709
333              SPLIT      1,SNDUN         SEND UNSOLICITED MSG              710
334              TRANSFER   ,*7                                              711
         **                                                                  712
         ******  I N S E R    SUBFCTINE        **********                    713
         ** ARRIVE HERE FROM SBR 1,2,3                                       714
         * CCNT RELEASE INP MSG BUF. USE IT FCR CUT MSG                      715
         **                                                                  716
335      INSBR   ADVANCE    2,1    INP MSG CHK                               717
         **                                                                  718
         ACCES   MACRO      5,0,1,SBR1A,1,1    LCG INP XACT                  719
336              ASSIGN     2,5                                              719
337              ASSIGN     15,0                                             719
338              ASSIGN     16,1                                             719
339              ASSIGN     13,1                                             719
340              ASSIGN     24,1                                             719
341              ASSIGN     12,SBR1A                                         719
342              TRANSFER   ,DATIC                                           719
343      SBR1A   SEIZE      CPU                                              720
         ACCES   MACRO      6,C,P1,SBR1B,1,2    WRITE BLOG                   721
344              ASSIGN     2,6                                              721
345              ASSIGN     15,0                                             721
346              ASSIGN     16,P1                                            721
347              ASSIGN     13,1                                             721
348              ASSIGN     24,2                                             721
349              ASSIGN     12,SBR1B                                         721
350              TRANSFER   ,DATIO                                           721
351      SBR1B   SEIZE      CPU                                              722
         ACCES   MACRO      1,1,1,SBR1C,1,1     READ MAIN FILE              723
352              ASSIGN     2,1                                              723
353              ASSIGN     15,1                                             723
354              ASSIGN     16,1                                             723
355              ASSIGN     13,1                                             723
356              ASSIGN     24,1                                             723
357              ASSIGN     12,SBR1C                                         723
358              TRANSFER   ,DATIC                                           723
359      SBR1C   SEIZE      CPU                                              724
360              ADVANCE    5,2    FRCCESS                                   725
         **             SEND REPLY TC TERMINAL. INP BUF IS USED FOR CUTPUT  726
361              SPLIT      1,SEND    CCNVERSATICN MCCE. REPLY TC MSG        727
         ACCES   MACRC      1,0,P1,SBR1C,1,2      WRITE UPCATED MAIN FILE    728
362              ASSIGN     2,1                                              728
363              ASSIGN     15,0                                             728
364              ASSIGN     16,P1                                            728
365              ASSIGN     13,1                                             728
366              ASSIGN     24,2                                             728
367              ASSIGN     12,SBR1C                                         728
368              TRANSFER   ,CATIC                                          728
369      SBR1C   SEIZE      CPU                                              729
         ACCES   MACRC      2,0,P1,SBR1E,1,2    WRITE BMAIN                 730
370              ASSIGN     2,2                                              730
371              ASSIGN     15,0                                             730
372              ASSIGN     16,P1                                            730
373              ASSIGN     13,1                                             730
374              ASSIGN     24,2                                             730
375              ASSIGN     12,SBR1E                                         730
376              TRANSFER   ,CATIC                                          730
377      SBR1E   SEIZE      CPU                                              731
378              LEAVE      CORE,MHSFILEM(1,4)                              732
379              ADVANCE    VSFREEM                                          733
         ACCES   MACRO      5,1,1,SBR1F,1,2    WT CUT LCG                   734
380              ASSIGN     2,5                                              734
381              ASSIGN     15,1                                             734
382              ASSIGN     16,1                                             734
383              ASSIGN     13,1                                             734
384              ASSIGN     24,2                                             734
385              ASSIGN     12,SBR1F                                         734
386              TRANSFER   ,CATIC                                          734
387      SBR1F   SEIZE      CPU                                              735
388              LEAVE      CORE,MHSFILEM(5,4)                              736
389              ADVANCE    VSFREEM                                          737
390              TRANSFER   ,*22    RETURN FRCM SUB                         738
         **                                                                  739
         *                                                                   740
                                                                             741
         ****  S B R 9                                                       742
         * TERMINAL  ..END CF INC INSPECTICN.. MSG                          743
         *                                                                   744
391      SBR9    ADVANCE    1                                                745
         ACCES   MACRC      4,1,1,BXX,1,1  RC FILE X TO SEND TC TERM   **   745
392              ASSIGN     2,4                                              745
393              ASSIGN     15,1                                             745
394              ASSIGN     16,1                                             745
395              ASSIGN     13,1                                             745
396              ASSIGN     24,1                                             745
```

Figure 12.9 (continued)

```
357          ASSIGN      12,BXX
358          TRANSFER    ,DATIO                                                    745
359   BXX    SEIZE       CPU                                                       746
400          MSAVEVALUE  MTR,P17,1,KO,H   RESET TERM MODE                          747
      **** CORE RELEASED BY SEND ***                                              748
401          SPLIT       1,SEND                                                    749
402          TRANSFER    ,*7    RETURN                                            750
      *                                                                           751
      ***** S B R 1 0    *****                                                    752
      **   SEND  BROADCASTING  MSGS                                               753
      *                                                                           754
403   SBR10  ADVANCE     1                                                        755
      ACCES MACRO        9,1,1,SEADA,1,1   RD MSG                                 756
404          ASSIGN      2,9                                                      756
405          ASSIGN      15,1                                                     756
406          ASSIGN      16,1                                                     756
407          ASSIGN      13,1                                                     756
408          ASSIGN      24,1                                                     756
409          ASSIGN      12,SEADA                                                 756
410          TRANSFER    ,DATIO                                                   756
411   SEADA  SEIZE       CPU                                                      757
      *    CHK IF TERMINAL IN ING MODE AND DON'T SEND MSG                         758
412          TEST E      MH$MTR(P17,1),0,NOMSG     BR IF TERMINAL IN ING MODE     759
      *    USE DESTINATION FILE BUF AREA FOR OUTPUT MSG                           760
413          SPLIT       1,SNDUN         SEND MSG                                 761
414          TRANSFER    ,*7    RETURN                                           762
415   NOMSG  LEAVE       CORE,V$TCBUF     RELEASE BUFFER                         763
416          ADVANCE     V$FREEM                                                  764
417          ADVANCE     1                                                        765
418          TRANSFER    ,*7                                                      766
      *                                                                           767
      ******* S B R 1 2   *****                                                   768
      **   INC  FROM  TERM  GROUP  B                                              769
      *                                                                           770
419   SBR12  ADVANCE     2,1                                                      771
420          LEAVE       CORE,V$TIBUF     RELEASE INP XACT AREA                   772
421          ADVANCE     V$FREEM                                                  773
      ACCES MACRO        1,1,1,BSB,1,1   RD MAIN                                  774
422          ASSIGN      2,1                                                      774
423          ASSIGN      15,1                                                     774
424          ASSIGN      16,1                                                     774
425          ASSIGN      13,1                                                     774
426          ASSIGN      24,1                                                     774
427          ASSIGN      12,BSB                                                   774
428          TRANSFER    ,DATIO                                                   774
429   BSB    SEIZE       CPU                                                      775
      GCORE MACRO        V$TOBUF,BSB1                                             776
430          ASSIGN      14,V$TOBLF                                               776
431          ASSIGN      8,BSB1                                                   776
432          TRANSFER    ,CORWN                                                   776
433   BSB1   ADVANCE     2,1                                                      777
434          LEAVE       CORE,MH$FILEM(1,4)                                       778
435          ADVANCE     V$FREEM                                                  779
436          ADVANCE     1                                                        780
437          SPLIT       1,SEND     SEND MSG CONV MODE              **            781
438          TRANSFER    ,*7    RETURN                                           782
      **                                                                          783
      ***S B R 14   INC. FROM TERM. GROUP CCCCC                                   784
      *                                                                           785
439   SBR14  ADVANCE     2,1                                                      786
440          LEAVE       CORE,V$TIBUF     RELEASE INP XACT AREA                   787
441          ADVANCE     V$FREEM                                                  788
      ACCES MACRO        1,1,1,SBD1,1,1                                           789
442          ASSIGN      2,1                                                      789
443          ASSIGN      15,1                                                     789
444          ASSIGN      16,1                                                     789
445          ASSIGN      13,1                                                     789
446          ASSIGN      24,1                                                     789
447          ASSIGN      12,SBD1                                                  789
448          TRANSFER    ,DATIO                                                   789
449   SBD1   SEIZE       CPU                                                      790
450          ADVANCE     1                                                        791
      ACCES MACRO        1,0,1,SBD2,1,1                                           792
451          ASSIGN      2,1                                                      792
452          ASSIGN      15,0                                                     792
453          ASSIGN      16,1                                                     792
454          ASSIGN      13,1                                                     792
455          ASSIGN      24,1                                                     792
456          ASSIGN      12,SBD2                                                  792
457          TRANSFER    ,DATIO                                                   792
458   SBD2   SEIZE       CPU                                                      793
      GCORE MACRO        V$TOBUF,SBD3                                             794
459          ASSIGN      14,V$TOBLF                                               794
460          ASSIGN      8,SBD3                                                   794
461          TRANSFER    ,CORWN                                                   794
462   SBD3   ADVANCE     2,1                                                      795
463          LEAVE       CORE,MH$FILEM(1,4)                                       796
464          ADVANCE     V$FREEM                                                  797
```

Figure 12.9   (continued)

```
465              ACVANCE      1                                              798
466              SPLIT        1,SENC    SENC MSG CONV MCDE                   799
                                                                            800
467              TRANSFER     ,*7                                           801
       *                                                                    802
       *         THE  C L C C K                                             803
       *                                                                    804
468              GENERATE     100000                                        804
469              TERMINATE    1                                             805
                 START        24                                           806
                 ENC                                                        8C.7
```

Figure 12.9   (continued)

12.4   Experiments and Results

12.4.1   Analyzing the results of the model

The following procedure is suggested for analyzing the results of the model:

1. Examine savevalue NOPOL, which contains the number of transactions that could not enter the system because of lack of main storage, for a low value compared with the total number of the generated transactions.

2. Compare total simulated time with total time during which there was no task in the system (from table ACTIV) to obtain a measure of the total system utilization and available time for background jobs. The formula for total system utilization is $U_s = T_a/T$, where T_a = total simulated time minus total time during which there was no task in the system, and T = total simulated time.

3. Check the utilization of CPU, DRIVES, and CHANNELS. Find their effective utilization, which is U_m/U_s, where U_m = the measured utilization for the test and U_s = the total system utilization for the test.

4. The effective utilization gives a measure of how much of the effective potential is already used.

5. Check the average main storage utilization and the statistics of the main storage queue. Check the number of times it was necessary to roll out a program because of a shortage of main storage, and check the number of times there was a need to load a program from the disk.

6. Check file-request table and response-time tables.

7. Check line utilization to determine how much of the network potential was effectively utilized.

12.4.2   Simulation runs: condensed results

Tables 12.6 to 12.9 summarize the results of the simulation runs (see input data in Section 12.2.3):

Run A: Basic transaction rate; 30 terminals (Table 12.1).

Run B: High transaction rate (150% of basic); 30 terminals.

Run C: Basic transaction rate; 5 lines, 50 terminals.

Table 12.6 RESOURCE UTILIZATION (U) AND AVERAGE SERVICE TIME $E(t_s)$:
FACILITIES AND STORAGES

	A		B		C	
Resource	U	$E(t_s)$	U	$E(t_s)$	U	$E(t_s)$
CPU	0.063	9.0	0.085	8.9	0.148	9.0
Core storage	0.70	—	0.71	—	0.670	—
Channel	0.072	20.5	0.10	20.7	0.168	20.4
DRV1	0.042	19.7	0.059	20.9	0.96	18.6
DRV2	0.056	48.5	0.076	48.3	0.13	47.7
DRV3	0.012	48.6	0.018	51.7	0.02	53.5
[a]LINES (AVR)[b]	0.39	925	0.53	950	0.44	800
[a]Term's A[c] (AVR)	0.24				0.29	5000
[a]Term's B (AVR)	0.35				0.39	7850
[a]Term's C (AVR)	0.16				0.23	3920
[a]Term's D (AVR)	0.15				0.21	5030

[a]Includes waiting time for other system resources.

[b]AVR, average.

[c]Term's A, Type A terminals.

Table 12.7 AVERAGE WAITING TIME FOR WAITING TRANSACTIONS ($\$E(t_w)$),
UNDER \$AVERAGE TIME/TRANS IN GPSS OUTPUT:
QUEUES

Queue for Resource	A			B			C		
	MAX[a]	%ZERO[b]	$\$E(t_w)$	MAX	%ZERO	$\$E(t_w)$	MAX	%ZERO	$\$E(t_w)$
Channel	2	88.5	10.6	2	88.3	11.5	2	87.6	11.5
DRV1	4	69.0	14.8	5	67.1	17.2	4	60.6	18.7
DRV2	2	91.0	28.3	2	86.3	32.0	3	82.0	28.8
DRV3	2	93.0	21.0	2	89.0	19.0	1	84.2	18.7
(INP transaction terminal)	4	79.4	16,200.0	7	68.0	24,800.0	6	71.3	17,282.0
Lines (AVR)	4	95.0	5,600.0	5	91.5	5,965.0	5	94.0	6,950.0
Task initiation	15	12.0	52.0	30	12.0	102.0	—	—	—

[a]MAX, maximum content.

[b]%ZERO, percent zero entries, that is, the percentage of transactions that were *not* actually delayed.

Table 12.8 MULTITASKING MEASUREMENTS OF STORAGES: NUMBER OF CONCURRENT USERS AND AVERAGE SERVICE TIME

Resource	A		B		C	
	Maximum Users	Number Entries	Maximum Users	Number Entries	Maximum Users	Number Entries
Active tasks in core	8	2570	8	3426	—	6150
U_s[a]	0.125	—	0.176	—	0.276	—
Users						
PRG1	2	86	2	119	3	132
PRG2	1	51	2	71	1	86
PRG3	1	38	2	69	1	74
PRG9	1	73	1	101	2	111
PRG10	8	2248	8	2963	9	5631
PRG12	1	22	1	30	1	34
PRG14	1	52	1	73	1	81
ROLL[b]	6	2570	14	3426	32	6150

[a]U_s, total system utilization (see Section 12.4.1).
[b]Number of times it was necessary to roll out programs compared with the total use of all programs.

Table 12.9 SYSTEM RESPONSE TIMES (ms)

Table	A (30 Terminals)		B (30 Terminals)		C (50 Terminals)	
	AVR	95%	AVR	95%	AVR	95%
FLREQ (I/O request)	44.0	90.0	47.8	95.0	51.5	100.0
Response time for the operator						
XACT 1	3,225.0	10,750.0	6,660.0	20,500.0	6,490.0	20,500.0
XACT 3	5,015.0	15,000.0	5,034.0	15,000.0	7,230.0	22,500.0
XACT 14	9,140.0	20,000.0	10,350.0	25,000.0	9,740.0	27,800.0
Response time of control program						
XACT 1	3,080.0	4,000.0	3,134.0	4,400.0	5,080.0	7,750.0
XACT 3	505.0	750.0	575.0	950.0	570.0	850.0
XACT 14	150.0	200.0	160.0	240.0	213.0	280.0

12.5 Conclusions

The simulation results show clearly that the given number of messages does not overload the computer. There is considerable CPU capacity left to handle batch jobs. However, adding batch jobs may load the channel and cause longer waiting times for disks.

This model was designed for teaching purposes and, therefore, it is a deliberate simplification of the real system. In particular:

Polling-addressing is not considered. The current model assumes free running lines, with FIFO queueing discipline. This should be changed to reflect a real polling-addressing situation.

No special transient data management is considered.

Task management is handled by the GPSS monitor routine.

The DATIO model does not present the various possibilities of file management.

The model also shows that the analyst who wishes to apply modeling to the design of computer systems must fully understand the hardware, the control program software, and the application programs to be modeled. Simulation of computer systems is time-consuming and costly. The analyst must strive for a realistic compromise between the level of detail in the model and the cost of the study, consistent with the objective of producing meaningful results as quickly as possible.

13 General Appraisal of GPSS

In this chapter we review GPSS. We begin with some general remarks on its value as a simulation language and then present, in some detail, a list of common errors, hints on programming and debugging, and specific programming aspects that affect the running time of GPSS models.

13.1 The Case for GPSS

In our economic system it is becoming increasingly important to be able to study and understand a new concept or a new system, such as a programming language, in the minimum possible time. Two major advantages of GPSS are that it is easy to learn and simple to use.

First, one can study a limited subset of the whole language and solve practical problems with just that subset. One can then extend the subset progressively by adding new statements, which will lead to more elegant and efficient solutions of existing problems and allow the user to model more complicated systems.

Second, the names of the available statements, which are the components of the language, correspond closely with the ideas used in simulation. This both reduces learning time and enables the simulation programmer to return to a GPSS program after an interruption and reacquaint himself easily with the program. Its readability is a special advantage whenever several people must work on the same problem, either simultaneously or successively, or when someone outside the group takes over an existing or partially completed program. GPSS has been designed for the practitioner and from some points of view might not entirely satisfy the purist; but, as we say to our students, "It works and it works well."

As previously mentioned, the most important aspect of problem solving today is the total time spent—from the moment when the problem is posed to the moment when conclusions are ready to be presented to management. This total time consists of several parts: recognition that the problem is one that lends itself to simulation, detailed analysis, block diagram, program in a machine-readable language, debugging and program verification, model validation, simulation, analysis of results, and preparation of the final report.

The choice of programming language will depend on the above factors. In general, GPSS users find that GPSS minimizes project time by releasing them from repetitive clerical tasks, which, in other languages, must often be programmed.

Detailed analysis and *block diagramming* are simplified in GPSS because of the analogies between the concepts used in problem formulation and those available in GPSS and because of the compactness of the language. A model formulated in GPSS is significantly shorter than a corresponding high-level language program. In addition, other simulation languages, such as SIMSCRIPT, SIMULA, or SIMPL/I, tend to use more instructions than GPSS. For example, all the declarations necessary in these languages are performed by the GPSS compiler and are therefore implicit in the language.

Debugging and *program verification* are reduced in GPSS by the numerous diagnostics available at compile time and during execution. Further, the compactness of the language means fewer statements, which implies fewer errors. Another, less conventional notion is the high probability that the program will run and produce usable results. In almost all cases, the analyst obtains results which can be used to plan the next stage of the project. The problem of initializing the model, which means removing the transient statistics accumulated during the warm-up period of modeling, is achieved easily by using the RESET statement.

Validation and *simulation* consist of two important and distinct activities: human work and machine work. Modifications to the program and even to the model are made easily in GPSS by adding or replacing statements. The system is interpretive, so no compilation is necessary: a GPSS compilation consists mainly of translating symbolic names and addresses into numerics and producing the diagnostics, which is a very fast process. The machine time used for a single run is usually longer than for other simulation languages, but it would be misleading to compare only running times. In simulation work one rarely compiles a program in its final form. Usually modifications are made between runs to examine different properties of the system. A simulation program, even more than other computer programs, is continually evolving. These reflections explain why an interpretive system has some advantages over classical compile-load-and-go systems. It allows the user to make several simulation runs, even with changes to the model, by introducing modifications to the program between successive START statements, possibly combined with CLEAR or RESET statements.

A significant advantage of GPSS lies in the functions that are performed automatically. These include clock mechanism and sequencing of events, implicit declarations, implicit tests on blocks such as SEIZE, ENTER, and PREEMPT, automatic accumulation of statistics, and printing.

The report generator is easy to use and can produce both numerical results and graphs without extensive programming. Modification of the results produced or the form of presentation is easy.

Finally, we mention a significant advantage which is not really technical: it is usually possible for a GPSS user to make contact with people studying similar problems. The large number of users of GPSS has resulted in a corresponding accumulated know-how through organized conferences and a number of published articles. This possibility of exchanging information and experiences has proved very useful in eliminating duplication of effort.

The disadvantages of using GPSS lie in the very advantages that we have discussed above.

Because of its simple concepts, the user must make an effort to express the problems to be solved in terms of the available GPSS entities: transactions and blocks. Sometimes this may seem to be a stringent limitation of the language.

Because GPSS performs many functions automatically, the user may find too much rigidity in its structure. There may seem to be insufficient means to interact with the simulator during the simulation, for example by changing the order of processing transactions, changing the way GPSS accumulates statistics, and so on. Such actions may be somewhat difficult to perform with the basic GPSS language; however, by using transaction priority, the BUFFER and PRIORITY BUFFER blocks, the group entity, and user chains (LINK, UNLINK), many situations can be modeled in suitable detail. All that is necessary is a thorough understanding of the GPSS scanning mechanism, in particular, the way in which it handles the chains of transactions.

Data input is not flexible. It is usually performed by filling save locations and matrices or by means of the JOBTAPE statement, where input data are contained in parameters of the jobtape transactions. If the simulation uses large amounts of input data, organized in a data bank for instance, the programmer may decide to use the HELP block to call a routine in another language that has file-handling capabilities, such as FORTRAN or PL/I, to perform those operations too tedious to program in GPSS. This sort of strategy should be used in exceptional cases only, however, and should not become standard programming practice.

13.2   Practical Modeling and Programming Hints

When starting to model a system, the observation of a few simple, but important, rules can considerably reduce the time required for programming and debugging. These hints are listed below, not necessarily in order of importance.

13.2.1   General rules

Choose meaningful symbolic names for all entities where possible. This increases the legibility of the program.

Define the role of the transactions clearly in relation to their attributes, such as parameters, priority, and type. The list of transaction parameters, with their meaning and their function in the system, should be continuously updated. It is advisable to include the list as comments in the actual program (see, for example, the program in Chapter 10).

Clearly define all the GPSS entities used in the model with regard to their meaning in the problem, what they represent, and, if necessary, how they are used. Entities include facilities, storages, queues, save locations, and matrices. Pay special attention when using indirect addressing.

Estimate the total number of transactions which will be present at any time in the model. Is this number reasonable? If it is too large, can it be reduced by changing the structure of the model? Can transactions be replaced by a count in save locations, units in storages or queues?

Write the program in such a way that it has a high probability of executing and producing some results. This can be achieved, for example, by dividing a large model into several submodels, by using the run time feature of GPSS V, or by printing intermediate, transient results during the first runs.

Always include comments in the program, either directly as lines with an asterisk in column 1 or in the statements. This is abundantly illustrated in all the programming examples given in this book. We suggest that all comments begin in the same column to increase their legibility.

Make use of all the features of the language (see Section 8.3 for practical suggestions for debugging). For instance, if the behavior of a particular queue is very important, we may wish to tabulate it as seen by a transaction arriving in the queue also as seen when leaving it. This can be achieved by the following instructions, which use two TABULATE blocks with corresponding TABLE definition statements:

```
              .
              .
              .
              QUEUE       WAIT
              TABULATE    ARRIV
              SEIZE       MACH
              DEPART      WAIT
              TABULATE    DEPAR
              .
              .
              .

      ARRIV   TABLE       Q$WAIT,0,1,20
      DEPAR   TABLE       Q$WAIT,0,1,20
              .
              .
              .
```

If the full history of the queue is required as well as the general queue statistics, a suitable record can be accumulated in SAVEVALUE or MSAVEVALUE blocks. If we wish to tabulate values other than queue contents, we specify the requirements in the TABLE definition statement.

Remember the different types of GPSS block and the various ways in which they can be viewed. This aspect is considered in the next section.

Avoid unnecessary blocks. If a GPSS program includes instructions such as SAVEVALUE 10+,1, one may usually suppress it. In fact, this is just a counter and we know that the N attribute of every GPSS block provides and maintains such a counter, automatically.

Keep control of the movement of transactions. Make sure that they are always at a place where they can really be, and avoid situations in which the location of transactions is undefined. This warning may seem self-evident, but it is most important when modeling situations such as those described in the next section. In addition, avoid simultaneous movement of several transactions where only one transaction should be handled at a time. Such a situation is illustrated in the traffic problem of Section 6.6.2.

Make sure that transactions, of either the same or different types, *are processed in the required order.* This point is particularly important in cases in which transactions are created at GENERATE and SPLIT blocks or reactivated at an UNLINK block. For instance, when copies of transactions are created by a SPLIT block, the original transaction continues to be processed until it reaches a block from which it cannot proceed immediately. The copies are put in the current-events chain and there is no guarantee that they will be processed immediately after the transaction that created them. If the order of processing is important, then it should be programmed, by using priority, for example.

Avoid programming zero-time loops: see Section 13.2.2, "Blocks Where a Time Delay May Be Specified."

Avoid writing self-locking programs. These programs block themselves when specific conditions occur in the model and cannot be released (see the example given in Section 8.3.2, Figure 8.10).

In addition to the above points, also consult Section 8.3, which contains further considerations.

13.2.2   Various ways to look at GPSS blocks

When deciding which GPSS blocks to use in a model, we can consider the blocks from various points of view, depending on the precise entity or operation that we want to simulate.

Five approaches that we have found helpful are listed below. They will help the user to produce a better model which avoids the types of error mentioned above.

Functional aspects.   We consider the blocks by the function or operation which they perform—the approach taken in Chapters 6 and 7, where we divided the blocks into transaction-oriented, equipment-oriented, and so on. We discuss only the following aspect: those blocks which may create or destroy transactions. The blocks concerned are GENERATE, SPLIT, and JOBTAPE for creation and TERMINATE and ASSEMBLE for destruction. For example, when using SPLIT, remember that copies are placed on the current-events chain at the end of their priority class. When using

ASSEMBLE, remember that the properties of the outgoing transaction are those of the first transaction of the assembly set which entered the block.

Blocks able to refuse entry to transactions. Some blocks may refuse entry to transactions unless a specific condition is met: SEIZE and ENTER will refuse entry to a transaction if the facility is busy or if there is insufficient room in the storage. These blocks therefore include implicit tests. PREEMPT will refuse entry to a transaction if the facility is already preempted or, in priority mode, if the arriving transaction does not have higher priority than the transaction currently preempting the facility. GATE and TEST in *refusal mode* may obviously refuse transactions.

Thus we see that few of the available blocks can refuse transactions. They should be used whenever we wish to control the flow of transactions precisely.

Consider the following example. Suppose that we have a factory where one queue (WAIT) is followed by two facilities. Transactions leave the queue when facility 1 (FAC1) is free. When the service time (variable SERV1) ends, they go to facility 2 (FAC2). When the second service (variable SERV2) ends, they leave FAC2 and go out. We suppose that *there is no room between* FAC1 *and* FAC2.

The following sequences of blocks show, on the left, an incorrect program, and, on the right, the correct one:

```
         .                              .
         .                              .
         .                              .
   QUEUE     WAIT              QUEUE     WAIT
   SEIZE     FAC1              SEIZE     FAC1
   DEPART    WAIT              DEPART    WAIT
   ADVANCE   V$SERV1           ADVANCE   V$SERV1
   RELEASE   FAC1              SEIZE     FAC2
   SEIZE     FAC2              RELEASE   FAC1
   ADVANCE   V$SERV2           ADVANCE   V$SERV2
   RELEASE   FAC2              RELEASE   FAC2
         .                              .
         .                              .
         .                              .

   incorrect sequence          correct sequence
```

Although the model given by the left-hand sequence is incorrect, it would run and produce results. There would be no error diagnostics because the incorrect coding is capable of logical interpretation. When a transaction has finished its service time in FAC1, it leaves the ADVANCE V$SERV1 block and enters RELEASE FAC1, *which releases* FAC1. If FAC2 is still in use, the transaction is refused by SEIZE FAC2 and therefore remains in block RELEASE FAC1. We thus have a situation in the GPSS model which does not correspond to real life: the transaction has left FAC1 and is not in FAC2; its location is undefined. The right-hand sequence, on the other hand, is correct: before the transaction releases FAC1, block SEIZE FAC2 ensures that FAC2 can be seized; only then can FAC1 be released.

Another situation to avoid is blocking transactions at a GENERATE block. If a refusal block follows a GENERATE block, it can alter the intergeneration times specified by the A- and B-operands, because the time of generation of the next transaction will be computed by the two operands when the current transaction is able to leave the GENERATE block and proceed to the next block.

Blocks where a time delay may be specified. Only two blocks can contain timing information to delay or schedule transactions: GENERATE and ADVANCE. Therefore, whenever a time delay, service time, travel time, or minimum wait time has to be modeled, one of these two blocks must be used. This point is stressed in the machine-repair model of Section 6.6.3 and the inventory model of Section 7.6.2.

Further, if a program contains a loop with no ADVANCE block, it is a zero-time loop. A transaction entering such an instruction sequence would loop indefinitely, until stopped by the operating-system timer or the run timer of GPSS V. Such a situation may arise when a control loop is programmed to monitor all operations within the model. Some programmers add an ADVANCE 1 block to the loop to guard against this condition, but we prefer a logical procedure, such as setting up a switch that stops the transaction until the conditions for the transaction to proceed are met. This procedure is usually more difficult to implement, but it is a much cleaner method which, in most cases, will avoid wasting computer time.

Blocks where a number of units may be specified. A *number of units* may be specified in the following blocks:

ENTER/LEAVE	for storages
QUEUE/DEPART	for queues
TERMINATE	
TABULATE	

This is not the case for blocks such as GENERATE, UNLINK, REMOVE, or ALTER, where a *number of transactions* may be specified.

The TERMINATE A-operand has a special function connected with the START statement (see Section 6.1). The TABULATE B-operand is a weighting factor associated with the statistical table (see Section 7.2.6).

In the other cases, storages and queues, we must distinguish clearly between *transactions* and *units*. A single transaction arriving at an ENTER block requests the number of units specified by the B-operand. If an insufficient number of units is available in the storage, the transaction is refused.

When entering a LEAVE or DEPART block, the number of units specified in the B-operand is subtracted from the current storage or queue contents. If an attempt is made to subtract more than the current contents, an error message is printed: "425 Attempt to leave a storage by more than current contents" or "428 Attempt to leave a queue by more than current contents."

In all situations in which a transaction may involve several units, use of the B-operands of storages and queues is very useful: order, 1 transaction, for several parts in an inventory; message, 1 transaction, with a variable length in bytes in a teleprocessing system; and so on.

Blocks which set the status flag of the current-events chain. We saw in Section 7.6 that, after a transaction has been processed by the GPSS simulator, the status flag of the current-events chain is tested to decide whether to resume scanning, with the next transaction, if the flag is off, or to restart scanning from the top of the chain if the flag is on.

The flag is set every time the *status of the model is changed* by activating one of the following blocks:

SEIZE,RELEASE,PREEMPT,RETURN:	Change of status of a facility.
ENTER,LEAVE:	Change of status of a storage.
LOGIC:	Change of status of a logic switch.
MATCH:	Change of a matching situation.

It is very important to note that changes in contents of a queue, QUEUE/DEPART, or in a user chain, LINK/UNLINK, or in a group, JOIN/REMOVE, or even the creation by GENERATE/SPLIT or destruction by TERMINATE/ASSEMBLE, are not considered as changes of status of the model. This implies that in practice a GPSS modeler should always make use of facilities, storages, or switches to ensure regular rescanning of the current-events chain.

An example of incorrect programming is:

```
      QUEUE     WAIT        Join the queue WAIT;
      TEST NE   W$ADV,0     Test if block ADV is free;
      DEPART    WAIT        If not, refuse; if so, proceed.
ADV   ADVANCE   10
```

Suppose that the clock time is 200 and that the current-events chain contains three transactions, the first waiting in the queue from time 180, the second leaving the block ADV at time 200, and the third waiting in the queue which it reached at time 200. The scan will find that the first transaction cannot move because the contents of block ADV is not zero; but the second can move and therefore leaves the block ADV. The status flag is not set, so the scan proceeds and finds the third transaction, which is then moved to the TEST and block ADV. The scan is now complete because the status flag has not been set, so the clock time will be advanced to its next value, which is the first time of the future-events chain. In this example, the transaction which should have been processed after transaction 2 was transaction 1; the program contains a logical error.

In conclusion, GPSS models should always contain facilities, storages, or switches, unless the user excludes them for specific reasons. The analyst should always be conscious of potential problems which can arise because of the way in which the scan of the current-events chain is implemented.

13.3 Classical Errors

When modeling systems with a simulation language such as GPSS, one is prone to make certain errors that stem from the philosophy used in implementing a discrete simulation language. The programmer's approach will always be different from the way in which he thinks when coding other types of problem. We have identified some typical errors made by beginners and others made by people who have experience with simulation languages.

Some of the points made here are a recapitulation of previous material (for example, Sections 8.3 and 13.2), but we believe that these remarks are sufficiently important to be presented in a separate section.

Blockage at GENERATE. After a GENERATE block, a block such as SEIZE or ENTER, which can refuse entry to transactions, will modify the average intergeneration time of the generated transactions and will therefore modify the data given in the problem.

Mean of intergeneration time.   Check the mean of the intergeneration or advance times. When a function is specified as B-operand in GENERATE or ADVANCE blocks, the value of the A-operand is multiplied by the value of the B-operand function, and the result, truncated, is used as the intergeneration time or the advance time. If the value of the A-operand is small and the values of the B-operand function are also small, in particular, less than 1, we will find that many zero values are obtained. These zeros occur for all values that were less than 1 before truncation. If this happens at a GENERATE block, simultaneous transactions will be created. Even if this does not cause an execution error, the real mean of the generated values will be smaller than the value specified in the input data.

To illustrate this argument, we ran the following short model which generates transactions according to the exponential distribution, tabulates the interarrival times observed, and terminates.

```
        GENERATE       V1,FN$EXPON
        TABULATE       1
   1    TABLE          IA, . . .
        TERMINATE      1
        START          5000
```

VARIABLE 1 was given successive values of 1, 3, 5, 10, 50, 100, 300, and 1000. The observed means for runs of 5000 transactions each are shown in Table 13.1.

Table 13.1

Value Given	Observed Mean
1	0.596
3	2.583
5	4.597
10	9.667
50	50.364
100	101.220
300	304.644
1000	1013.646

From these results it is obvious that, if the exponential function is used, then the A-operand should never be less than 10, which gave an error in deficit of 3.3 per cent. If the parameters of the problem demand a smaller mean value, then the time unit of the model must be changed. If the required average is 5 seconds, we would take a time unit of one hundredth of a second and the instruction would then be:

GENERATE   500,FN$EXPON

which avoids the difficulty completely. This change of time unit does not alter the computer time used for running the model because the GPSS clock mechanism is based on the time to the next event and not on a fixed time increment.

Self-locking system. A self-locking system is a program which locks itself whenever a particular set of conditions is encountered and is thus unable to continue (see Section 8.3.2, Figure 8.10).

Transaction location undefined. See Section 13.2.2.

Symbolic names and numerics. Confusion arises when both symbolic names and numerics are used for entities, especially when using indirect addressing. An example of such confusion is presented in detail in Section 8.3.2.

Illegal savevalue number. An illegal savevalue number results if one specifies a number that is either zero or larger than the number of savevalues requested. Remember that for every partition size used on a computer system, there is a standard allocation of GPSS entities. This allocation can be changed easily by means of the REALLOCATE statement (see Section 7.1.2). If an attempt is made to use a greater number, an error message is printed and the simulation terminated.

When save location zero is referenced, it is usually because of incorrect or omitted initialization.

Illegal parameter number. Here also, we may address a parameter that does not exist for reasons similar to those given above. In most cases this error is caused by bad use of the ASSIGN instruction. If we write:

ASSIGN   P1,100

instead of

ASSIGN   1,100

we must remember that in the ASSIGN block the A-operand is the *parameter number* concerned and that the C-operand, if used, is the *function number* or name used as modifier.

In the above case we try to assign 100 to the parameter whose number is the contents of P1, which is logically incorrect. If the contents of P1 is either zero or greater than the number of parameters requested, then execution will terminate with an error message.

Illegal function number. An illegal function number occurs, for example, in an ASSIGN instruction if we write:

ASSIGN   1,100,FN1

instead of

ASSIGN   1,100,1

We want to multiply 100 by FN1 and store the value obtained in P1, but what we actually do is to multiply 100, the B-operand, by the value of the function whose number is the value of FN1. If this function were to take the value 7.4, then we would try to evaluate FN7, which may not exist.

Improper use of CLEAR/INITIAL statements.   Another source of error lies in the improper utilization of CLEAR/INITIAL statements when using savevalues in GENERATE blocks. Suppose that we wish to make three runs of the same program and that we require the first transaction to be generated at successive times 100, 200, and 300. For this purpose we use the offset, C-operand, of the GENERATE block and we could store the value in save location 1, say. One may be very tempted to write the following program: '

```
SIMULATE
INITIAL        X1,100
GENERATE       50,FN$EXPON,X1
      .
      .
      .

START          1000
CLEAR
INITIAL        X1,200
START          1000
CLEAR
INITIAL        X1,300
START          1000
```

which, apparently, does what is required: the first run is made with X1=100, the model is cleared, X1 is changed to 200, the second run is controlled by the second START statement, and so on.

Now, remember that the CLEAR statement performs two tasks (see Section 6.1); (1) it clears the model, and (2) it causes the first transaction to be generated by each GENERATE block of the model. Therefore, for the second run, the first transaction will be generated by the instruction

GENERATE   50,FN$EXPON,0

because X1 has been reduced to 0 by the CLEAR statement. Thus it will not be generated, as we thought, at time 200, but at an unpredictable time:50*FN$EXPON.

The correct technique for this problem is to use the selective option of the CLEAR statement:

```
SIMULATE
INITIAL        X1,100
GENERATE       50,FN$EXPON,X1
```

.
.
.

START	1000
INITIAL	X1,200
CLEAR	X1
START	1000
INITIAL	X1,300
CLEAR	X1
START	1000

In this way the following operations occur when a run is terminated:

The results are printed.

The next statement, INITIAL, which causes the initialization of X1, is read.

The CLEAR statement clears the model completely except for X1.

The first transaction is generated *using the new value of X1*.

The START statement is read and the next run takes place.

Synchronization of the transactions.   Many errors in the running of GPSS programs are due to a misunderstanding of the GPSS scan, so that transactions are not processed in the order expected by the user. When faced with such a problem, we must check whether several transactions are scheduled to move at the same clock time, where only one should be allowed to move at a time. This point is explained in detail in the traffic problem of Section 6.6.2, "Simultaneous Events." We must also make a detailed investigation of all parts of the model where SPLIT, MATCH, ASSEMBLE, GATHER, BUFFER, and PRIORITY BUFFER blocks are used.

For example, suppose that we have a model shown schematically by Figure 13.1(a). We want to allow one transaction at a time to be processed by the SPLIT block. To achieve this, we use switch 1, which accepts the transaction if reset and refuses it if set. Immediately after the SPLIT block, we set the switch using the LOGIC S block. This model is incorrect. When a transaction enters the SPLIT block, the current transaction continues to be processed and the new transaction is put in the current-events chain at the end of its priority class. If another transaction is already on the chain, presently in the QUEUE block, it will be processed before the new transaction leaves the SPLIT block. It will then be accepted in the GATE, DEPART, and SPLIT blocks, and so on.

A valid program is shown in Figure 13.1(b), where the LOGIC S block is in the stream of the original transaction and will obviously be activated immediately after the SPLIT block and before any other activity can take place. Remember the basic principle that GPSS always moves transactions as far as possible through the block diagram.

As a general rule, when using SPLIT, always make the original transaction carry out those operations which must be performed immediately. Other actions that may be deferred can be left for the copies.

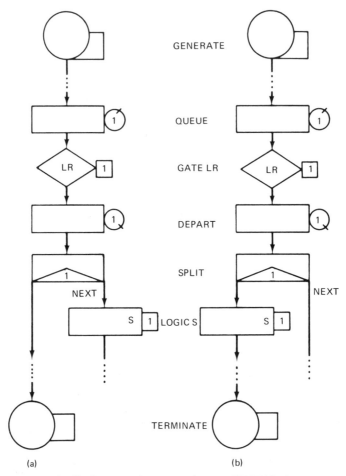

GENERATE

QUEUE

GATE LR

DEPART

SPLIT

NEXT

LOGIC S

TERMINATE

(a)   (b)

Figure 13.1   Single transaction processing at a SPLIT block.

Testing of simultaneous conditions.   This type of error is usually met when first using GPSS. It arises when a succession of GATE or TEST blocks is written without imposing the conditions to be met simultaneously. As discussed earlier, the technique is to use the TRANSFER in SIM mode (see example 4 in Section 6.2.3), or to test a Boolean variable (see example 3 in Section 7.3.1).

Incorrect replacement of statements.   The incorrect replacement of statements between successive runs will lead to error. Between two runs, that is, between successive START statements, we may replace some statements by others so as to run the model with different characteristics. For example, in a computer system we want to study the size of buffer required, represented by a storage, and we want to run the model, taking successive storage sizes of 1000, 1500, and 2000 bytes. We would define the storage with capacity 1000 for the first run, clear the model, add a storage-definition statement to specify capacity of 1500, restart the model for a second run, clear the model, add a storage-definition statement to specify capacity of 2000, and restart the model for the final run.

Sometimes, instead of clearing the model, one wants only to erase the accumulated statistics with the RESET statement, to keep the model in its present form, and then continue simulation after modification of the storage capacity. This is a delicate operation, because we change the capacity of a storage without knowing what its contents were at the end of the run.

The same reasoning applies when modifying blocks: one must avoid replacing blocks by others that would not make sense in the program or that might lead to anomalies in the program logic. As a general rule, it is not advisable to replace blocks that may contain transactions at the end of the run.

Note that the same reasoning applies when using the CHANGE block: one should never replace a block that may contain one or more transactions.

Error with random-number generators. Suppose that we have the following program relating to a computer system:

```
GENERATE  100,FN1      Generate messages
ASSIGN    1,FN2        Assign message length
ASSIGN    2,FN3        Assign number of
                       disk to be accessed.
```

The transactions that represent the messages have a length which may be 200, 400, or 600 characters with a $\frac{1}{3}$ probability for each value. They will cause an access to one of three disks: number 1, 2, or 3, with a probability of $\frac{1}{3}$ for each value. Suppose that functions 2 and 3 are programmed as follows:

```
2    FUNCTION RN2,D3
.333,200/.667,400/1,600
3    FUNCTION RN2,D3
.333,1/.667,2/1,3
```

One could argue that it is dangerous to use RN2 for both functions. In fact, if RN2 is used nowhere else in the program, the generated random numbers are used alternately for FN2 and FN3, which might introduce bias into the program—if, for example, the generated sequence were autocorrelated.

One may try to overcome this potential difficulty by using RN2 as the argument of FN2 and another generator, say RN3 for FN3. If this is done, the situation is worse than before because all random-number generators produce the same series of random numbers when initialized with the same seed. The model would therefore send all short messages to disk 1, intermediate messages to disk 2, and long messages to disk 3. This is an excellent example of good intentions producing disastrous results.

The problem may be very simply overcome by means of the RMULT statement, which allows the user to initialize the multipliers used for the eight random number generators (see Section 7.1.1).

13.4 Program Efficiency

After we have written some GPSS programs and have gained an insight into the working of the simulator, we soon realize that simulation work may use considerable
computer time. It is therefore desirable to reduce the total machine time used as much
as possible. One possible strategy is to write the program so that it executes as quickly
as possible on the computer. Although all programming systems benefit from careful
writing, efficient programming is even more important with simulation languages.

We mention below some aspects of GPSS programming which may affect the
running time of simulation models.

Remember the various ways in which GPSS *blocks can be used* (Section 13.2.2)
and always select the block that best suits the desired function.

Avoid writing useless blocks, such as SAVEVALUE NAME+,1, which is a
counter, (see Section 13.2.1).

Avoid unnecessary recalculations of the same computational entity, such as a
variable. This is illustrated in the following example.

Suppose that we have an ADVANCE block where the time is specified by a
complicated expression V$TIME. Suppose further that we want to tabulate these
values in the table WAIT. We could write the sequence represented in the left-hand
column:

	.			.
	.			.
TABULATE	WAIT		ASSIGN	1,V$TIME
ADVANCE	V$TIME		TABULATE	WAIT
			ADVANCE	P1
	.			.
	.			.
	.			.
WAIT TABLE	V$TIME,0,100,20	WAIT TABLE		P1,0,100,20
	.			.
	.			.
	.			.

In this case, the variable TIME has to be evaluated first during the execution of the
TABULATE block and again in the ADVANCE block. If, instead, we write the
program shown in the right-hand column, the variable TIME is evaluated only once.
Its value is stored in parameter 1 and used in the TABULATE and ADVANCE
blocks.

One should be particularly careful to avoid such coding when writing sections
of programs that are going to be executed many times, such as inner loops of programs.

Avoid using TEST *blocks operating in refusal mode;* whenever possible, substitute
GATE blocks. This is because the comparison that governs entry into the block is
made each time the GPSS scan examines a transaction that has been blocked by the
TEST block. These transactions cannot be deactivated, as in the case of GATE,

SEIZE, and ENTER blocks, because the simulator does not know what is tested by the block.

Avoid letting transactions enter TRANSFER *in* BOTH *or* ALL *mode when no path is available.* In the case of BOTH, it is futile to allow more than two transactions to enter the TRANSFER block because this only increases the scanning time; it is much better to precede the TRANSFER block with an ENTER STOR with STOR of capacity 2, for example, which will allow the required number of transactions to proceed. In the ALL case, the storage used would have a capacity equal to the number of exits from the TRANSFER block.

Avoid insertion of an ADVANCE 1 *block in a control loop.* This block forces the simulated time to be increased in steps of 1 unit and the scanning of the current-events chain to be initialized at every time unit throughout the whole simulation. Although we might want to execute the above control loop frequently, it is a waste of time to do it unnecessarily, especially when nothing has changed in the model. In such control loops, it is advantageous to insert a GATE block to stop the control transaction(s) until the condition to be tested is satisfied.

Avoid creating too many transactions. Consider an *auxiliary clock* where the times are expressed in seconds. We may simulate the model for 4 hours in the following two logically equivalent ways:

(1)	GENERATE	3600	(2) GENERATE	1
	TERMINATE	1	TERMINATE	1
	START	4	START	14400

Although the result, simulate for 4 hours, is the same, the reader should note that, in this part of the model, the simulator will have to do 3600 times as much work in case (2) as in case (1). The overall penalty is even greater because we not only generate 14396 more transactions, which implies updating the block statistics, reducing the terminations-to-go counter, and testing for the end of the simulation, but we force the clock to be increased by 1 unit at each stage and scan the current-events chain unnecessarily.

Do not waste storage when using save locations and matrices. If halfwords are sufficient, use halfwords. When using GPSS V, if bytes suffice, then use bytes.

Specify in GENERATE *blocks* (F- and G-operands in GPSS/360, and further ones in GPSS V), *the exact number and types of parameters required.* Remember that, if not specified, 12 halfword parameters are reserved. In GPSS V, for each parameter type—byte, halfword, fullword, or floating point—request the exact amount needed.

Do not program big tables with many frequency classes unless it is necessary. Remember that every frequency class uses 4 bytes of storage. Frequently, one is tempted to program big tables as a precaution: this may be unjustifiably expensive in storage.

Do not keep too many active transactions in the model. When we suspect queues to be significantly long, the scanning time of the current-events chain can increase prohibitively. Most of this effort is wasted. This is where user chains are vital: they allow the deactivation of all transactions that are known to be unable to proceed, until a condition is met, such as the release of a facility, which will allow only one of them to move. As an example, we ran a very simple model: one queue, one server, Poisson arrivals, and exponential service time, with an average utilization of the server of 90 per cent, and we achieved a reduction of 21 per cent in the running times for the same simulation where the average queue length was 8.

In GPSS V, *when using* PRINT, TRACE, *or* REPORT *extensively, make the appropriate module permanently resident in main storage by using the* LOAD *statement.* In a practical case, a program using PRINT extensively ran in 3.99 minutes; by using the LOAD statement, to make the module DAG06 (see [G. 13]) resident, the total running time was reduced to 2.98 minutes—a saving of 25 per cent.

Always question the philosophy applied in modeling, especially from the point of view of the number of transactions present in the model. Sometimes a change of strategy may reduce the number of transactions by using other entities, such as storages or savevalues.

To summarize: when programming, we should always remember how the utilization of the blocks affects the running time, in particular by carefully planning the work to be done by the GPSS scanning mechanism.

13.5 When To Use GPSS

When the decision to apply simulation to the resolution of a problem is made, the next decision is to choose the programming language. Sufficient arguments have been presented to illustrate the advantages of a simulation language over a general-purpose programming language. The remaining problem is the choice between existing simulation languages. For several years we have given courses in simulation to many types of audience and the following considerations are based on the observations we have made, both during the courses and subsequently when applying simulation to real problems.

No other language can be learned as quickly as GPSS and no other language is so compact. For most other languages one must write longer programs than is usual for GPSS.

It must also be stressed that programming in GPSS does not require previous knowledge or experience of programming. This benefit may be very important when it is essential to solve a problem quickly or when we wish to minimize the total resources used on the project.

For systems easily described in terms of the transaction concept, modeling is usually quite simple. This is the case for traffic problems, such as queueing systems, where dynamic elements flow through the model as vehicles, messages, telephone calls, papers, parts, or people. Traffic problems occur in all areas of human activity, which is one reason why GPSS is so widely used.

GPSS is less useful when it is difficult to think of the problem in terms of transactions flowing through a network of blocks. In such cases, a considerable degree of abstraction may be necessary to express the problem in terms of the GPSS language. However, the advantages obtained from the built-in features of GPSS may well compensate for the difficulties encountered.

If the effort necessary to express the problem in terms of GPSS is too great, it may be that the whole problem is not amenable to GPSS, in which case one would use another simulation language, or it may be that only part of the problem is difficult to express. In such cases, use of the HELP block with the interface in Fortran or PL/I (GPSS V) gives the GPSS user all the additional capabilities of these languages. In our opinion, however, if a significant part of a model has to be written in a statement-oriented language, such as Fortran or PL/I, rather than a block-oriented language, it is better to choose another simulation language, such as SIMPL/I.

A model that does not lend itself to simulation in GPSS is the corporate model, whose basic function is to access data contained in a data bank. Such a model is used for the simulation of such operations as cash flow and plant utilization, for which all the data necessary for the simulation are stored in operational files. This type of model requires not only a simulation language but also a data-bank-access language. For these applications SIMPL/I is the best choice because it offers all features that the user may require: simulation tools, full PL/I power, and access to files.

To illustrate some of the areas in which GPSS has been especially useful, we have listed below a number of examples garnered from various conferences on the application of simulation, organized each year since 1967 by several U.S. organizations, including ACM, IEEE, Simulation Council, and SHARE. See references [1.1] to [1.6].

Industrial systems: Simulation of complex start up operations; design of specific systems, such as a new suspension or braking system for vehicles.

Transportation: Traffic simulation; planning for urban transit systems; ambulance services in a town; complex elevator systems.

Computer and communication systems: Complex computer systems; telecommunication networks; computer networks; information systems.

Manufacturing and material handling: Coal supply to power plants; airport luggage handling systems; coal mine belt design; job scheduling; inventory management.

Aerospace: Simulation of spacecraft and space missions; prelaunch systems and procedures; aircraft performance; guidance systems.

Chemical industry: Plant facility analysis; planning of reactor load; optimization of complex processes.

Health services: Treatment of hospital patients.

Managerial and social sciences: Corporate models; cash-flow prediction; resource allocation for schools and other organizations.

Manpower planning: Staffing; work load modeling; general deployment of labor.

In all these studies, the objective was to optimize some parameter or parameters of the system under study. This means that the performance of the system was examined with the intention of optimizing factors such as price, flexibility, reliability, or availability. The exact objective will vary between different projects, but the general goal is always to achieve the best utilization of available resources.

14 Planning Simulation Experiments

This chapter is intended as a guide to the literature on statistical tools for simulation and is not a self-contained description of those techniques. Our major purpose is to point out that such techniques are essential if justifiable conclusions are to be drawn from results of computer simulation runs. The reader is referred to the cited references for further details on the application of these techniques.

14.1 Simulation and Statistical Tools

Building a model with the help of a specialized language represents only part of the program analyst's work. Simulation of stochastic systems that use statistical sampling requires statistical techniques for the development and use of a computer simulation model. The purpose of this chapter is to give a brief overview of some important statistical aspects of simulation. For a detailed review of these techniques as well as instructions on how to implement them, the reader is advised to consult the references given in the bibliography. We recommend especially the books by Kleijnen [14.1], Naylor [14.3], and Mihram [14.4] and the articles by Fishman and Kiviat [14.5] and Fishman [14.8].

The reader should remember that although knowledge about statistical techniques for simulation experiments is increasing, the practical problem of selecting an appropriate technique for a particular model remains, in addition to the standard problems of empirical research, such as small samples due to the high cost of data and the questionable validity of some data.

We must emphasize that, because simulation is an aid to *decision making*, the analyst must cope with two very severe practical constraints—cost and time:

1. Computer time is not a free gift of nature (Naylor [14.3], p. 23).
2. There are always deadlines and, in order to be useful, simulation results must be given on time.

Faced with these problems, model builders, who generally have no specialized knowledge of statistics, often spend so much time on model development that little time is left for the analysis and criticism of the results. Nonetheless it makes sense to build a model if only to assess its reliability or its validity. This is why there is no alternative to the use of statistical tools. To cope with the two practical problems mentioned above, we can only hope that statisticians will pay increasing attention to the development of tools that can be applied easily to simulation models.

This chapter presents three main aspects of simulation experiments: input-data analysis, statistical reliability, and comparisons of system responses.

14.2 Input-Data Analysis

The statistical properties of each random variable in a model must be determined. A specific form of the distribution must be assumed, for example normal or Poisson, and the distribution parameters must be estimated. When the assumed distribution is a function of two parameters, such as the normal distribution, the parameters are usually estimated from the sample mean and the sample variance. Then the validity of the hypothesis must be checked. Among the "goodness-of-fit" tests that can be used to determine whether the set of data can be accepted as values assumed by a random variable having a given distribution, either the chi-square test or the Kolmogorov–Smirnov non-parametric tests can be used (see Schmidt and Taylor [14.9] or Maisel and Gnugnoli [14.14]).

In the *Kolmogorov–Smirnov test* one first calculates the maximum difference D_n between the hypothetical cumulative distribution function, say $F(x)$, and the sample cumulative distribution function $S_n(x)$, over the intervals for which the sample distribution is tabulated:

$$D_n = \max_x |F(x) - S_n(x)| \tag{14.1}$$

and then one determines whether D_n exceeds a critical value D_n^α, which satisfies the relation

$$\Pr[D_n \leq D_n^\alpha] = 1 - \alpha \tag{14.2}$$

Critical values D_n^α may be found in books on statistics such as Siegel [14.16] or Hoel [14.17].

In the *chi-square test* one uses the fact that the distribution of the quantity

$$\chi^2 = \sum_{i=1}^{n} (O_i - E_i)^2/E_i \tag{14.3}$$

will approach that of a chi-square distribution with $n - 1$ degrees of freedom. This gives a measure of the deviation of observed values from those postulated. $O_1, \ldots, O_n$

are the observed frequencies and $E_1, \ldots, E_n$ the expected, or theoretical, frequencies in each frequency class. The test consists of determining whether the value given by (14.3) exceeds a critical value χ_0^2 obtained from tables of the chi-square distribution (see for instance Maisel and Gnugnoli [14.14]).

14.3 Statistical Reliability

The goals of the model builder are, first, to formulate a model that adequately represents the real system under study and, second, to obtain statistically reliable results. Thus the analyst must plan the experiment so as to be able to quantify confidence in the results. Statements about confidence depend upon the way in which observations have been selected.

A sequence of values produced by a simulation run may be considered as a sequence of observations from a population. The number of observations defines the sample size. The accuracy of the calculated sample mean is usually defined by the length of the confidence interval. To calculate a confidence interval it is necessary to estimate the variance of the sample mean. The problem of determining confidence intervals would be simple if the observations were never correlated.

If we assume that a sample of n *independent* observations $Y_1, \ldots, Y_n$ of a system performance variable Y, such as the length of a waiting line or waiting times, is collected, classical statistics (see Freund [14.18]) may be used and an estimate $\hat{\mu}$ of its true mean μ can be obtained by computing the sample mean:

$$\hat{\mu} = \bar{Y} = \frac{1}{n} \sum_{i=1}^{n} Y_i \qquad (14.4)$$

Further, the Central Limit Theorem states that the sample mean is independent of the distribution being sampled and that it may be considered as a normally distributed random variable. A normal distribution is characterized by its mean μ and its variance σ^2. The mean of the distribution of $\hat{\mu}$ is μ itself:

$$E(\hat{\mu}) = \mu \qquad (14.5)$$

and its variance:

$$\mathrm{Var}\,(\hat{\mu}) = \mathrm{Var}\left(\frac{1}{n} \sum_{i=1}^{n} Y_i\right) = \frac{1}{n^2} \mathrm{Var}\left(\sum_{i=1}^{n} Y_i\right)$$

so that

$$\mathrm{Var}\,(\hat{\mu}) = \frac{1}{n} \mathrm{Var}\,(Y_i) = \frac{\sigma^2}{n} \qquad (14.6)$$

where σ^2 is the variance of an individual observation Y_i.

Then, to find the confidence intervals for the mean μ, construct the standardized random variable

$$Z = \frac{(\bar{Y} - \mu)\sqrt{n}}{\sigma} \qquad (14.7)$$

$\bar{Y}$ is approximately normally distributed, so the distribution of Z is the standard normal distribution with zero mean and unit variance. Hence, from tabulations of the normal distribution, it is possible to find two points, $z_{\alpha/2}$ and $-z_{\alpha/2}$, such that

$$\Pr\left[-z_{\alpha/2} < Z < z_{\alpha/2}\right] = 1 - \alpha \tag{14.8}$$

for any α between 0 and 1; or

$$\Pr\left[\bar{Y} - \frac{\sigma z_{\alpha/2}}{\sqrt{n}} < \mu < \bar{Y} + \frac{\sigma z_{\alpha/2}}{\sqrt{n}}\right] = 1 - \alpha \tag{14.9}$$

Thus there is a probability of $(1 - \alpha) \cdot 100$ percent that the true mean will be found in the interval

$$\left(\bar{Y} - \frac{\sigma z_{\alpha/2}}{\sqrt{n}}, \ \bar{Y} + \frac{\sigma z_{\alpha/2}}{\sqrt{n}}\right)$$

If the value of σ is unknown, which is generally the case in simulation, we replace σ^2 by its estimator S^2, with

$$S^2 = \frac{1}{n-1} \sum_{i=1}^{n} (Y_i - \bar{Y})^2 \tag{14.10}$$

Then the random variable

$$T = \frac{(\bar{Y} - \mu)\sqrt{n}}{S} \tag{14.11}$$

has a Student's t distribution with $(n - 1)$ degrees of freedom.

We can now assert, with a probability of $1 - \alpha$, also called degree of confidence, that

$$\bar{Y} - \left(S \cdot \frac{t_{n-1,\alpha/2}}{\sqrt{n}}\right) < \mu < \bar{Y} + \left(S \cdot \frac{t_{n-1,\alpha/2}}{\sqrt{n}}\right) \tag{14.12}$$

Thus confidence intervals are determined with the aid of tables of the cumulative normal distribution, if the variance σ^2 is known, and with the aid of cumulative Student's t distribution with $(n - 1)$ degrees of freedom, if the variance is estimated with S^2.

Replication of run. The problem is therefore to collect independent observations. An obvious way of obtaining a sample of observations is to repeat the run n times, the mean from each run being treated as one observation. The input specifications of each run are the same, apart from the random-number seed, which is the initial number required in every algorithmic technique to generate pseudo-random numbers. To produce a random sample of n observations, we can use the fact that n independent seed specifications, randomly selected, result in n independent random-response variables. Hence each replication gives a mean value of the observed response of the model. The mean values collected are independent and the formulas quoted above may be used.

Transient phenomenon. However, we may meet a further problem. When collecting data during a run, one generally observes two stages. At the beginning of simulation the model exhibits transient behavior dependent on the starting conditions, and, after a certain simulated time, which varies with the system under study and the starting conditions, a steady state is reached. Such a state is recognized when successive observations of the system's performance variables are statistically indistinguishable.

By using a sequence of START, RESET, ..., START, GPSS statements it is possible to let the simulation run until the steady state is reached, then clear the accumulated statistics and continue the run to analyze the steady-state behavior.

There are no fixed rules to determine when the steady state is attained. A method we have found to be helpful uses the snap feature of the START statement. Statistics are obtained during a simulation run and moving averages of the performance variables computed. Steady state is assumed when the averages no longer change significantly with time.

Decomposition into subruns. Replicating runs sometimes appears to be very wasteful because each replication triggers off a new transient. For this reason some analysts have tried another method to obtain independent observations from a single run by dividing it into n subruns, also called "blocking periods" (see Emshoff and Sisson [14.15]). Averages of performance variables are computed for each subrun and used as observations. But in most situations, if the subrun lengths are insufficient, the observations are autocorrelated. This means that the average calculated in the second of two adjacent subruns depends, in part, on behavior during the first subrun period. The recommended procedures (see Kleijnen [14.1]) for determining the duration of a subrun, to make correlations among subrun averages virtually negligible, are somewhat heuristic.

Confidence limits by the method of Mechanic and McKay. According to Kleijnen [14.1] and others, the method suggested by Mechanic and McKay [14.21] seems attractive because of the iterative way of determining subrun lengths. In short (see [14.21] for details), given $Y_1, \ldots, Y_N$, a sample of N data generated in a single simulation run, form subruns or batches of size a, $b = 4a$, $c = 4b$, ..., s, with $N/s \geq 25$. Compute for each batch size the batch means:

$$Y_{ai} = \frac{1}{a} \sum_{j=1}^{a} Y_{(i-1)a+j} \qquad i = 1, 2, \ldots, [N/a] \qquad (14.13)$$

where $[N/a]$ = the integral part of N/a.

Compute the estimates of the variance of the overall average $\bar{Y}$:

$$(\hat{S}_{aN})^2 = \frac{\hat{\sigma}^2}{N/a} \qquad (14.14)$$

$$\hat{\sigma}_a^2 = \frac{1}{[N/a] - 1} \sum_{i=1}^{[N/a]} (Y_{ai} - \bar{Y})^2 \qquad (14.15)$$

with

$$\bar{Y} = \frac{1}{N} \sum_{i=1}^{n} Y_i \qquad (14.16)$$

Compute estimates of the autocorrelation terms between batch means $\hat{\rho}_{ab}, \hat{\rho}_{bc}, \dots ,$ $\hat{\rho}_{qr}$, where $q = r/4 = s/16$.

The following procedure is used to test if the autocorrelation gets reasonably low: Determine the first

$$\hat{\rho} = \rho_{l, 4l},$$

which is either:

Case 1: in the range $0.05 \le \hat{\rho} < 0.5$ and (a) it is not the first $\hat{\rho}$ in the sequence, (b) it is less than its predecessor, (c) the following $\hat{\rho}$ values, if any, form a monotonically decreasing sequence, with the exception of a last unbroken chain of $\hat{\rho}$ values, which may oscillate as long as they are all ≤ 0.05; *or*

Case 2: less than or equal to 0.05 and all the remaining $\hat{\rho}$ values are also ≤ 0.05. Then calculate the confidence intervals

$$\bar{Y} \pm h\hat{S}_{16l} \tag{14.17}$$

that is, the variance used is calculated from the next largest batch size, $16l$.

The confidence statement now specifies a value of h, say $h = 2$, such that for a given confidence P_h, for example $P_h = 0.95$, the interval $\bar{Y} \pm h\hat{S}_{16l}$ will contain the true mean, μ, with a probability of P_h. The value of h is thus determined from the desired value of P_h using the known relationship between h and P_h for the normal distribution.

The procedure of Mechanic and McKay has several advantages because it permits calculation of the confidence interval *during* a single computer run without storing the entire sequence of data. Programming the calculations is simple and the amount of storage required for the data is small. This procedure is therefore appropriate for incorporation into GPSS models (see also Kleijnen [14.1]).

Estimation of correlation coefficients. Alternative approaches do not consider subruns but estimate correlation coefficients ρ_s between the individual observations.

$$\rho_s = \frac{E\{[Y_t - \mu][Y_{t+s} - \mu]\}}{\sigma^2} \tag{14.18}$$

where Y_t = observation at simulated time t
    Y_{t+s} = observation at simulated time $t + s$
    μ = average output over the simulation run
    σ^2 = variance of an individual observation over the run

Estimations of the correlation coefficients may be found in Fishman [14.6] and Hauser et al. [14.20].

Once ρ_s is estimated, var $(\hat{\mu})$, the variance of the sample mean $\hat{\mu}$, can be estimated by:

$$\text{Var} (\hat{\mu}) = \frac{\sigma^2}{n}\left[1 + 2\sum_{s=1}^{n-1}\left(1 - \frac{s}{n}\right)\rho_s\right] \tag{14.19}$$

If the observations are independent, $\rho_s = 0$ for all s and the formula reduces to (14.6). Conway [14.22] shows that this method provides the minimum variance estimate.

Hauser et al. [14.20] compared the blocking and the autocorrelation methods and found that the blocking method provides results faster than the autocorrelation estimation procedure.

Spectral analysis.   Apart from static measures of the performance of a system, such as means and variances, dynamic measures of steady state can be obtained by spectral analysis, which tests the equivalence of two spectra. For discussion of this technique we refer to Fishman and Kiviat [14.5], Naylor [14.3], and Mihram [14.4]. Note that Emshoff and Sisson [14.15] predict that spectral analysis will have only limited use with simulation models unless some improvements are made in the analytic procedures.

We must point out that many models are constructed for the purpose of studying their transient stage, but as spectral analysis, as well as the procedure of Mechanic and McKay, only apply to steady state, the method of replication of runs must be used. Thus, although the methods based on a single simulation run present advantages in computing time requirements, techniques based on independent observations remain very useful, especially as they do not demand a deeper knowledge of statistics.

Variance-reduction technique: antithetic variates.   Among the various suggested variance-reduction techniques (which include stratified sampling, selective sampling, control variate or regression sampling, and importance sampling; see Kleijnen [14.1], Chapter III), the method of antithetic variates, originally introduced by Hammersley and Morton [14.13], has special appeal because of its simplicity and demonstrated power (see, for example, Andreasson [14.11], Moy [14.12], and Fishman [14.7]). The basic idea is to create *negative correlation* between observations.

As a matter of fact, given two system responses Y_1 and Y_2, the variance of their average is:

$$\text{Var}\,(\bar{Y}) = \text{Var}\,\left(\frac{Y_1 + Y_2}{2}\right)$$

$$= \tfrac{1}{4}[\text{Var}\,(Y_1) + \text{Var}\,(Y_2) + 2\,\text{Cov}\,(Y_1, Y_2)] \qquad (14.20)$$

Thus negative correlation, meaning that $\text{Cov}\,(Y_1, Y_2)$ is negative, decreases the variance of $\bar{Y}$.

Several ways of producing negatively correlated results have been devised. A simple and very useful one follows. If the random-number sequence $r_1, \ldots, r_n$ is used to generate a sequence of events in one *replication*, then the sequence $1 - r_1, \ldots, 1 - r_n$ is used to generate the corresponding sequence of events of the second replication.

In GPSS, the technique for generation of an arbitrarily distributed random variable is via the inverse of the cumulative distribution function, so that if $F_{AT}(t)$ is the cumulative distribution function of arrival time, then

$$t_{i,\,i-1} = F_{AT}^{-1}(r_1)$$

is the interarrival time between the ith and $(i-1)$th arrival. Thus a set $\{r_i\}$ is the input of the GPSS FUNCTION $F_{AT}(t)$, and the $\{F_{AT}^{-1}(r_1)\}$ are output.

The exponential distribution is defined in GPSS by the function EXPON:

EXPON FUNCTION RN8,C24 EXPONENTIAL
*DISTRIBUTION — MEAN = 1.
0.,0/0.1,0.104/0.2,0.222/0.3,0.355/0.4,0.509/0.5,0.69/0.6,0.915/
0.7,1.2/0.75,1.38/0.8,1.6/0.84,1.83/0.88,2.12/0.9,2.3/0.92,2.52/
0.94,2.81/0.95,2.99/0.96,3.2/0.97,3.5/0.98,3.9/0.99,4.6/0.995,5.3/
0.998,6.2/0.999,7.0/0.9997,8.0

The function has been made discrete by breaking the domain (0, 1) of the random numbers generated by RN8 into subintervals and associating a straight-line segment with each subinterval. We need only to subtract each end point of the subintervals used in the piecewise linearization of $F_{\text{EXPON}}^{-1}(\text{RN8})$ from unity to get the linearization of

$$F_{\text{EXPON}}^{-1}(1-\text{RN8})$$

Thus one of the functions is the mirror image of the other (Figure 14.1).

GPSS requires that the independent argument be written in ascending order so the antithetic exponential distribution would be:

AEXPO FUNCTION RN8,C25
*ANTITHETIC EXPONENT. DISTRIB.—MEAN=10.
,8/.0002,8/.001,7/.002,6.2/
.005,5.3/.01,4.6/.02,3.9/.03,3.5/.04,3.2/.05,2.99/
.06,2.81/.08,2.52/.1,2.3/.12,2.12/.16,1.83/.2,1.6/.25,1.38/.3,1.2/
.4,.915/.5,.69/.6,.509/.7,.355/.8,.222/.9,.104/1.0,0

Use of the function AEXPO, to get the antithetic exponential distribution, is the same as using EXPON, but with a prior operation: $1-\text{RN8}$.

Figure 14.1

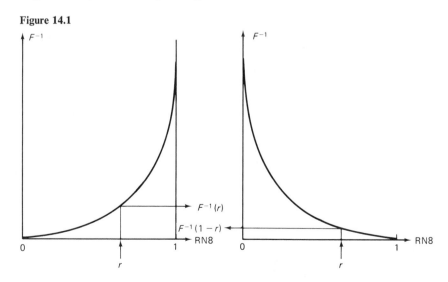

Kleijnen [14.1] points out that, if there are K types of stochastic random variables, such as interarrival times and service times, the best results are obtained when each input variable has its own random-number generator. However, one must be very careful to avoid dangers such as those discussed at the end of Section 13.3, "Error with random-number generators."

14.4 Comparisons of System Responses

Several techniques are available to analyze the output of simulation experiments and to make comparisons of the responses under different environmental conditions, simulated by varying the input parameters.

Analysis of variance, also called *factor analysis*, may be used to study the effect of *qualitative* factors, that is, input specifications that can only vary discretely. Such a specification, called a level of a factor, includes different queueing disciplines, inventory reorder policies, and so on. The analysis of variance can be used to test hypotheses such as the contribution of a factor to the observed results is zero; and the contribution of certain interactions (joint effects of variables) to the observed results is zero (see, for instance, Freund [14.18]).

The significance of *quantitative* factors, that is, continuous input variables, such as service time, can be examined by *regression* techniques. This type of analysis can also be used to determine the functional relationship, for example linear or quadratic, between response and the quantitative factor under consideration. The reader should note that, although these factors are continuous in the actual system, they are processed as discrete variables in the computer simulation model.

Multiple comparison techniques and multiple *ranking procedures*, (see Kendall and Stuart [14.19] or Kleijnen [14.1]) can be used to quantify the relative importance of the influence of the factors.

Besides the determination of the relative importance of alternative policies, a model is usually built to determine the strategy that will provide the best or most suitable solution to the problem. *Response surface methodology* is a technique to find the optimum combination of the levels of n quantitative factors (see Kleijnen [14.1] or Mihram [14.4]).

14.5 Conclusion

This outline of statistical techniques emphasizes the importance of planning simulation experiments in such a way that the analyst can justify a measure of statistical confidence in the results. New developments in this aspect of simulation appear regularly.

References

14.1. J.P.C. KLEIJNEN, *Statistical Techniques and Simulation* Part 1, New York: Marcel Dekker, 1974.

14.2. T. H. NAYLOR and J. M. FINGER, "Verification of Computer Simulation Models," *Management Science*, Vol. 14, 1967, pp. 92–101.

14.3. T. H. NAYLOR, ed., *The Design of Computer Simulation Experiments*, Durham, N.C.: Duke University Press, 1969.

14.4. G. A. MIHRAM, *Simulation, Statistical Foundations and Methodology*, New York: Academic Press, 1972.

14.5. G. S. FISHMAN and P. J. KIVIAT, *Digital Computer Simulation: Statistical Considerations*, RM-5287, Santa Monica, Calif.: Rand Corporation, 1967.

14.6. G. S. FISHMAN, "Digital Computer Simulation, the Allocation of Computer Time in Comparing Simulation Experiments," *Operations Research*, Vol. 16, No. 2, 1968, pp. 280–295.

14.7. G. S. FISHMAN, *Variance Reduction in Simulation Studies*, Report 47, New Haven, Conn.: Yale University, 1971.

14.8. G. S. FISHMAN, "Estimating Sample Size in Computing Simulation Experiments," *Management Science*, Vol. 18, No. 1, 1971, pp. 21–38.

14.9. J. W. SCHMIDT and R. E. TAYLOR, *Simulation and Analysis of Industrial Systems*, Homewood, Ill.: Richard D. Irwin, 1970.

14.10. A. J. BAYES, "A Minimum Variance Sampling Technique for Simulation Models," *Journal of the Association for Computing Machinery*, Vol. 19, No. 4, 1972, pp. 734–741.

14.11. I. J. ANDREASSON, *Antithetic and Control Variate Methods for the Estimation of Probabilities in Simulations*, Report NA-71.74, Stockholm: Royal Institute of Technology, 1971.

14.12. W. A. MOY, *Sampling Techniques for Increasing the Efficiency of Simulations of Queueing Systems*, Evanston, Ill.: Northwestern University, 1965.

14.13. J. M. HAMMERSLEY and K. W. MORTON, "A New Monte Carlo Technique: Antithetic Variates," *Proceedings of the Cambridge Philosophical Society*, Vol. 52, 1956, pp. 449–475.

14.14. H. MAISEL and G. GNUGNOLI, *Simulation of Discrete Stochastic Systems*, Chicago: Science Research Associates, 1972.

14.15. J. R. EMSHOFF and R. L. SISSON, *Design and Use of Simulation Models*, New York: The Macmillan Company, 1970.

14.16. S. SIEGEL, *Nonparametric Statistics for the Behavioral Sciences*, New York: McGraw-Hill, 1956.

14.17. P. G. HOEL, *Introduction to Mathematical Statistics*, New York: John Wiley & Sons, Inc., 1962.

14.18. J. E. FREUND, *Mathematical Statistics*, Prentice-Hall, Englewood Cliffs, N.J., 1962.

14.19. M. G. KENDALL and A. STUART, *The Advanced Theory of Statistics*, Hafner, New York, Vol. I, 1963; Vol. II, 1961; Vol. III, 1966.

14.20. N. HAUSER, N. N. BARISH, and S. EHRENFELD, "Design Problems in a Process Control Simulation," *Journal of Industrial Engineering*, Vol. 17, No. 2, 1966, pp. 79–86.

14.21. H. MECHANIC and W. MCKAY, *Confidence Intervals for Averages of Dependent Data in Simulations II*, Technical Report 17–202, Advanced Systems Development Division, International Business Machines Corporation, Yorktown Heights, N.Y., 1966.

14.22. R. W. Conway, "Some Tactical Problems in Digital Simulation," *Management Science*, Vol. 10, No. 1, 1963.

14.23. R. W. Conway, *An Experimental Investigation of Priority Assignment in a Job Shop*, RM-3789-PR, Rand Corporation, Santa Monica, Calif., 1964.

14.24. J. M. Hammersley and D. C. Handscomb, *Monte Carlo Methods*, Wiley, New York, 1964.

15 The Future of Simulation and Simulation Languages

Simulation is generally considered an expensive tool because most simulation experiments demand a great deal of manpower and computer time. We recall that the following activities form part of *every* simulation: programming, debugging and verification, validation, simulation, and evaluation of the results. It will also be recalled that the cost of the computer time required for simulation experiments always limits the user in:

1. The number of alternative simulation runs which can be made. The user must select those cases which seem to be most promising. Selection is arbitrary because no reasoning has yet been developed to make an optimum choice automatically.

2. The length of the simulation runs to be made. Rarely is there sufficient computer time to simulate all the selected alternatives long enough to obtain the desired confidence intervals.

Further, we expect that the number of problems to be solved in the future will increase, that they will be derived from many diverse areas, and that they will be more complex than those considered today. Thus the requirement for simulation techniques will grow and it becomes imperative to reduce the total cost of simulation studies by all means possible.

From the list of activities given above, there are two principal areas where it is possible to improve the overall efficiency of simulation: (1) in programming, debugging, and validation, and (2) in production runs of the simulation model.

15.1   Programming, Debugging, and Validation

The activities listed in (1) above depend largely on the expertise of the user, we must therefore strive to increase the productivity of human resources.

At the present time, programmer productivity is improved by the built-in features of simulation languages, which automatically provide the user with services that would otherwise have to be programmed manually for every computer model. We briefly recall points previously covered in detail in Chapter 3. The advantages of simulation languages over general-purpose languages are:

> Simulation languages are designed for the use of analysts and other professionals who may not be specialists in computer science.
>
> Languages such as GPSS can be learned quickly.
>
> Many simulation programming features are provided automatically. These include maintenance of a simulated clock, sequencing of events, implicit definition of entities (GPSS), accumulation and printing of statistics, and a comprehensive set of diagnostic messages.

Because these functions are performed automatically the user can concentrate on actual problem solving, without spending time and effort on routine clerical programming.

Our discussion to this point summarizes the current position; however, we must recognize that there is still much room for improvement.

For example, during the past few years there have been dramatic developments in the use of time-sharing, interactive, and conversational computing. The modern computer user wants to communicate directly with the computer via a terminal using a conversational program. What is true of general computing is just as true of simulation. In all phases of computer simulation experiments, such as programming, debugging, and production simulation runs, the analyst would like to work at a computer terminal (possibly a graphic terminal with a visual display) and be able to interact continuously with the model. Thus the user could look at results, correct or modify the code, rerun the model, change parameters and see the effect on model behavior, repeat a run with new starting conditions or a different sequence of random numbers, and so on, without having to leave his desk. The implementation of such man–machine dialogues would take advantage of the different qualities of men and machines by combining them in an optimum way.

Simulation languages should therefore offer these features in the future. For further details on this subject consult the proceedings of the conferences and symposia given in references [1.1] to [1.6]. Each of these symposia contains several papers that deal with this very important topic. In particular, we refer the reader to the article "Approaching a Universal GPSS," by J. Katzke and J. Reitman, in [1.6], which describes the GPSS system developed by the Norden Division of United Aircraft Corporation. This system adds, to the standard version of GPSS V, several useful features for simulating large-scale systems. These extensions include: access to a data base, which cuts the cost of introducing data into the model; use of an on-line display terminal, which allows the user to interact with the model during the simulation run; and flexible output formatting, which gives the user a simple means of selecting, from the standard output, those results in which he is particularly interested. Such developments are definitely helping to improve the overall efficiency of the man–machine combination by allowing the user to make better use of his skills, particularly by giving him more control over computer operations during the execution of the simulation. This should be compared with the current batch approach where the user must wait until he gets all the results from the computer before he can start to analyze the behavior of his model and possibly detect errors in the coding or the logic.

15.2 Production Runs of the Simulation Model

To improve the efficiency of actual simulation, we must try to reduce the cost of using the computer. There are three ways in which such savings might be made:

1. Reduce the number and length of the simulation runs as much as possible. This is a questionable policy, because of the difficulty of choosing the most significant cases from those which we believe to include the optimum. The selection calls for considerable analysis and reasoning, which increases the work of the analyst. Reduction of the run length raises problems with the confidence intervals of the results. To summarize, there is little room for improvement in this area.

2. Improve the efficiency of the simulation program. Here, as in other areas of computing, there is certainly some room for improvement, but we have to recognize that today's simulators are already quite efficient and so we cannot hope for a significant improvement factor in this area.

3. Improve the cost/performance ratio of the electronic computer. This is the most promising alternative because of the fantastic improvement in computer performance which has occurred since its inception. Several years ago, the operation times of very fast machines were expressed in milliseconds. Today, we state their operation times in microseconds or nanoseconds. Experimental circuits with speeds measured in picoseconds already exist; these are hundreds of times faster than those currently used in the fastest computers. This factor will obviously reduce the economic arguments against using simulation techniques for solving problems.

The improvement that we expect in computer efficiency in the coming years really means much more than a reduction in the cost of simulation studies. It will generate a real "explosion" in the sense that many studies that are not feasible today, because of excessive costs and time, will become economical in a few years. Therefore, we will be able to solve today's problems more economically and also tackle larger and more complicated problems which can only be handled successfully by simulation techniques.

The history of electronic computing can be briefly summarized as follows.

Electronic computers were built to solve problems. As machines became available, people discovered that they were so powerful that they could be used to solve more complicated problems. But, as problems grew in size and complexity, they created the need for faster machines, and so it has continued.

In the area of simulation we anticipate a similar kind of development but at a much greater rate. Today we are accustomed to using programming languages on fast computers and we have already identified many problems that could be solved but for the lack of suitable mathematical methods and economical means of simulation. In other words, an enormous backlog of simulation problems exists, ready to be tackled when faster systems become available.

At the beginning of this book we pointed out that simulation was an old technique that had gained new impetus with the advent of the electronic computer. We have discussed why simulation languages are needed and we have illustrated the use of simulation with applications modeled in GPSS V. We have also shown that the current limitations on the use of the technique are largely economic and technological.

We are confident that both these limitations will be removed in the future, and so we predict that simulation is one of the techniques which will benefit most from improvements in technology. The ultimate limit of simulation will depend on the number of professionals who decide to specialize in this field—on their dedication and imagination in tackling the complex problems of the future rather than on the power of the computer.

Appendices

A Operating System Control Cards for GPSS

In this appendix we outline the job control cards and the data sets, or files, required for running a GPSS model on a computer. This information is necessary for a general understanding of the organization of GPSS. The example given in this appendix refers to the requirements for running models under Full Operating System; when using Disk Operating System, consult the systems programmer at your installation.

The GPSS program may be link-edited, that is, stored in machine-readable form for use by the computer, either in a private library of an installation or in the operating system library. For full details of the operations for link-editing GPSS into a program library, see reference [G.13]. In most installations, link-editing of programs is the responsibility of the systems programmer. The information given in this appendix is copied from reference [G.13], with the permission of IBM.

When GPSS has been link-edited, it is usual to store the operating system control statements required for its use in a *catalogued procedure*. A catalogued procedure is a standard set of operating system job control statements which is suitable for executing most applications. Catalogued procedures allow the user to ignore the operating system almost completely.

A.1 GPSS Data Sets Required To Execute GPSS

The execution of a GPSS program requires several data sets. These are defined at execution time, by *data definition*, or DD, statements. The data sets or files are kept, in machine-readable form, on magnetic disks or tapes. The DD statements specify where the data set volume should be mounted, the space required by each of the data sets which reside on a direct access volume, and the disposition of the data set when the simulation run is finished.

The first five of the data sets listed below are mandatory for all GPSS runs. The others are required only when the model uses the capabilities that they represent. All the following data sets are organized sequentially. Each name, such as DOUTPUT, is the ddname of a DD statement.

DOUTPUT: Output data set used by both the GPSS assembly program and the output phase of the simulation program.

DINTERO: Intermediate data set used by the GPSS assembly program.

DSYMTAB: Data set containing a table of the symbols identified by the GPSS assembly program. This data set is subsequently used by the output phase of the simulator.

DINTWORK: Data set created by the GPSS assembly program and used as input to the input phase of the simulator.

DINPUT1:   The normal input data set to the GPSS assembly program or the GPSS UPDATE feature program. If the model is entered in card form, the GPSS model follows the DINPUT1 statement in the input stream. If the model is not entered in card form, DINPUT1 defines the data set that contains the model.

DREPTGEN: The data set that contains the input stream to the GPSS report generator. This data set is prepared by the GPSS assembly program.

DXREFDS: Cross-reference data set required when there are more than 600 symbolic references to GPSS entities when using entity options PARM=A or PARM=B, or 1200 symbolic references when using option PARM=C.

DJBTAP1:   Data set used with GPSS jobtape JOBTA1.

DJBTAP2:   Data set used with GPSS jobtape JOBTA2.

DJBTAP3:   Data set used with GPSS jobtape JOBTA3.

DDNWMAST: The new master data set produced by the GPSS UPDATE feature program.

DDMASTER: The old master data set used as the input data set to the GPSS UPDATE feature program.

DDPUNCH: The optional punched card output associated with the GPSS UPDATE feature program.

DRDSAVEI: Input data set associated with the READ/SAVE feature.

DRDSAVEO: Output data set associated with the READ/SAVE feature.

A.2   Procedure To Execute GPSS

The following statements are mandatory: the JOB statement, the JOBLIB DD-statement, which specifies where the GPSS system resides if not in the SYS1.LINKLIB,

```
//SIMUL       JOB    ACCT.NO.,PROG.NAME,MSGLEVEL=1
//JOBLIB      DD     DSNAME=xxxxxxxx,UNIT=yyy,DISP=SHR,
//                   VOLUME=SER=zzzzzz
//EXEC        EXEC   PGM=DAG01V,PARM=v
//DOUTPUT     DD     SYSOUT=A
//DINTERO     DD     UNIT=SYSDA,SPACE=(TRK,(10,10))
//DSYMTAB     DD     UNIT=SYSDA,SPACE=(TRK,(10,10))
//DREPTGEN    DD     UNIT=SYSDA,SPACE=(TRK,(10,10))
//DINTWORK    DD     UNIT=(SYSDA,SEP=(DINTERO)),
//                   SPACE=(TRK,(10,10))
//DJBTAP1     DD     UNIT=bbb,VOLUME=SER=dummy,LABEL=(,NL)
//DJBTAP2     DD     UNIT=ccc,VOLUME=SER=dummy,LABEL=(,NL)
//DJBTAP3     DD     UNIT=ddd,VOLUME=SER=dummy,LABEL=(,NL)
//DDNWMAST    DD     UNIT=eee,VOLUME=SER=dummy,LABEL=(,NL)
//DDMASTER    DD     UNIT=fff,VOLUME=SER=dummy,LABEL=(,NL)
//DRDSAVEI    DD     UNIT=ggg,VOLUME=SER=dummy,LABEL=(,NL)
//DRDSAVEO    DD     UNIT=hhh,VOLUME=SER=dummy,LABEL=(,NL)
//DDPUNCH     DD     SYSOUT=B
//DINPUT1     DD     *

                    ---------------------
                             |
                         GPSS MODEL
                             |
                    ---------------------
/*
where: xxxxxxxx= name of partitioned data set in which GPSS program
                 modules reside.
       yyy     = unit address of direct access device on which the
                 GPSS program modules reside.
       zzzzzz  = volume serial number of direct access volume to be
                 mounted on yyy.
                 |A|
       v       = |B|   GPSS entity option specified by the user.
                 |C|
bbb    = address of a nine-track tape unit which is being used for
         jobtape, JOBTA1 (bbb must be different from ccc, ddd, eee,
         fff, ggg, and/or hhh).
ccc    = address of a nine-track tape unit to be used for
         jobtape, JOBTA2 (ccc must be different from bbb, ddd, eee,
         fff, ggg, and/or hhh).
ddd    = address of a nine-track tape unit to be used for
         jobtape, JOBTA3 (ddd must be different from bbb, ccc, eee,
         fff, ggg, and/or hhh).
eee    = address of a nine-track tape unit to be used for the new
         master tape (eee must be different from bbb, ccc, ddd, fff,
         ggg, and/or hhh).
fff    = address of a nine-track tape unit to be used for the old
         master tape (fff must be different from bbb, ccc, ddd, eee,
         ggg, and/or hhh).
ggg    = address of a nine-track tape unit to be used for the Read/
         Save input tape (ggg must be different from bbb, ccc, ddd,
         eee, fff, and/or hhh).
hhh    = address of a nine-track tape unit to be used for the Read/
         Save output tape (hhh must be different from bbb, ccc, ddd,
         eee, fff, and/or ggg).
dummy  = the external label associated with the jobtapes, the
         READ/SAVE tapes, and the old and new master tapes.  The
         dummy operand should be different for each tape used.

NOTE:    Although the use of nine-track magnetic tapes is
         illustrated for the data sets DJBTAP1, DJBTAP2, DJBTAP3,
         DDNWMAST, DDMASTER, and DRDSAVEI and DRDSAVEO in this
         example, direct access devices can also be used for any or
         all of these data sets by specifying the appropriate
         parameters in the OS/360 DD statements.  When using direct
         access devices for these data sets, the user is responsible
         for supplying the appropriate DD parameters to save and
         identify the data sets for subsequent use.
```

the EXEC statement, and the DOUTPUT, DINTERO, DSYMTAB, DREPTGEN, and DINTWORK DD-statements. As mentioned in Section 7.1, additional DD-statements are required whenever features such as the SAVE/READ feature or JOBTAPE are used.

The example on page 421, reproduced by courtesy of IBM, shows the form of the job control statements which would be required when running a GPSS model which uses

> three JOBTAPEs
> the UPDATE feature
> the SAVE/READ feature.

If this procedure were catalogued with the name GPSS, the user would submit just three control statements in front of the GPSS model:

//NAME	JOB	· · ·	Job statement for the job.
//E	EXEC	GPSS	Calling the GPSS procedure.
//SYSIN	DD	*	DD card for input.

.
.
.

GPSS MODEL

.
.
.

END

In this way any user may submit GPSS programs requiring a standard set of language features without having a detailed knowledge of the operating system.

B Summary of GPSS Components

BLOCK STATEMENTS
CONTROL AND ENTITY-DEFINITION STATEMENTS
STANDARD NUMERICAL ATTRIBUTES

The following tables provide a list of all the block statements, together with suggested graphical symbols, the control and entity definition statements, and the standard numerical attributes (SNAs) of GPSS. Each listed operand or field contains a brief description of its use and forms of expression that may be used in its specification.

In these tables, k is a constant, SNAj is a SNA specified by j, and SNA*SNAj is a SNA specified by another SNA. The table of SNAs shows the valid ranges of values, blocks that may modify them, and restrictions on their use.

These tables, all of which refer to GPSS V, have been reproduced from [G.12], with the permission of IBM Corporation.

BLOCK STATEMENT FORMATS

OPERATION	A	B	C	D	E
ADVANCE	Mean time ⌈k, SNAj, ⌉ ⌊SNA*SNAj⌋	Spread ⌈k, SNAj, SNA*SNAj or Function modifier FNj, FN*SNAj⌋			
ALTER ⌈G ⌉ GE L LE E NE MIN ⌊MAX⌋	Group no. k, SNAj, SNA*SNAj	Count ALL or k, SNAj, SNA*SNAj	Member attribute to be altered PR or kPx, SNAjPx, SNA*SNAjPx	Value to replace attribute k, SNAj, SNA*SNAj	Matching member attribute ⌈PR or kPx, ⌉ SNAjPx, ⌊SNA*SNAjPx⌋
ASSEMBLE	No. of transactions to assemble k, SNAj, SNA*SNAj				
ASSIGN	Parameter no. or range k, SNAj, SNA*SNAj [±]	SNA value to be assigned k, SNAj, SNA*SNAj†	No. of function modifier ⌈k, SNAj, ⌉ ⌊SNA*SNAj⌋	Parameter type Px	
BUFFER					
CHANGE	"From" block no. k, SNAj, SNA*SNAj	"To" block no. k, SNAj, SNA*SNAj			
COUNT ⌈G, GE ⌉ L, LE E, NE U, NU I, NI SNE, SE SNF, SF ⌊LR, LS⌋	Parameter in which to place count kPx, SNAjPx SNA*SNAjPx	Lower limit k, SNAj, SNA*SNAj	Upper limit k, SNAj, SNA*SNAj	Comparison value if conditional operator is specified ⌈k, SNAj, ⌉ ⌊SNA*SNAj⌋	Mnemonic of SNA to be counted ⌈Any SNA⌉ except MX, MH, ⌊MB, ML⌋

† Block operand where PL, XL, or ML is a valid SNA; [ ] Indicates optional operand;

{ } Indicates that one of the items within the braces must be selected.

424

F	G	H	I	PAGE REFERENCE	BLOCK SYMBOL
				78	
Matching SNA [k, SNAj, SNA*SNAj]	Alternate exit [k, SNAj, SNA*SNAj]			178	
				141	
Note: The parameter type operand may optionally be coded as the C operand if a function modifier is not specified.				78	
				165	
				186	
				153	

BLOCK STATEMENT FORMATS

OPERATION	A	B	C	D	E
DEPART	Queue no. k, SNAj, SNA*SNAj	No. of units ⌈k, SNAj,⌉ ⌊SNA*SNAj⌋			
ENTER	Storage no. k, SNAj, SNA*SNAj	No. of units ⌈k, SNAj,⌉ ⌊SNA*SNAj⌋			
EXAMINE	Group no. k, SNAj, SNA*SNAj	Numeric value-numeric mode ⌈k, SNAj,⌉ ⌊SNA*SNAj⌋	Alternate exit k, SNAj, SNA*SNAj		
EXECUTE	Block no. k, SNAj, SNA*SNAj				
FAVAIL	Facility no. or range k, SNAj, SNA*SNAj				
FUNAVAIL	Facility no. or range k, SNAj, SNA*SNAj	Remove or continue option ⌈RE⌉ ⌊CO⌋	Alternate block no. ⌈k, SNAj,⌉ ⌊SNA*SNAj⌋	Parameter no. ⌈kPx,⌉ SNAjPx ⌊SNA*SNAjPx⌋	Remove or continue option ⌈RE⌉ ⌊CO⌋

Options for controlling
transactions   Options for

† Block operand where PL, XL, or ML is a valid SNA; [ ] Indicates optional operand;

{ } Indicates that one of the items within the braces must be selected.

F	G	H	I	PAGE REFERENCE	BLOCK SYMBOL
				84	
				82	
				176	
				187	
				189	
Alternate block no. $\begin{bmatrix} k, SNAj, \\ SNA*SNAj \end{bmatrix}$	Remove or continue option $\begin{bmatrix} RE \\ CO \end{bmatrix}$	Alternate block no. $\begin{bmatrix} k, SNAj, \\ SNA*SNAj \end{bmatrix}$		188	

preempted transactions

Options for delayed transactions

BLOCK STATEMENT FORMATS

OPERATION	A	B	C	D	E
GATE $\begin{Bmatrix} LS \\ LR \end{Bmatrix}$	Logic switch no. k, SNAj, SNA*SNAj	Next block if condition is false $\begin{bmatrix} k, SNAj, \\ SNA^*SNAj \end{bmatrix}$			
GATE $\begin{Bmatrix} NI \\ I \\ NU \\ U \\ FV \\ FNV \end{Bmatrix}$	Facility no. k, SNAj, SNA*SNAj	Next block if condition is false $\begin{bmatrix} k, SNAj, \\ SNA^*SNAj \end{bmatrix}$			
GATE $\begin{Bmatrix} SE \\ SF \\ SNE \\ SNF \\ SV \\ SNV \end{Bmatrix}$	Storage no. k, SNAj, SNA*SNAj	Next block if condition is false $\begin{bmatrix} k, SNAj, \\ SNA^*SNAj \end{bmatrix}$			
GATE $\begin{Bmatrix} M \\ NM \end{Bmatrix}$	Match block no. k, SNAj, SNA*SNAj	Next block if condition is false $\begin{bmatrix} k, SNAj, \\ SNA^*SNAj \end{bmatrix}$			
GATHER	No. of trans- actions to be gathered k, SNAj, SNA*SNAj				

† Block operand where PL, XL, or ML is a valid SNA; [ ] Indicates optional operand;

{ } Indicates that one of the items within the braces must be selected.

F	G	H	I	PAGE REFERENCE	BLOCK SYMBOL
				160	
				88, 189	
				88, 190	
				160	
				147	

BLOCK STATEMENT FORMATS

OPERATION	A	B	C	D	E
GENERATE	Mean time ⌈k, SNAj, ⌉ ⌊SNA*SNAj⌋	Spread ⌈k, SNAj, SNA*SNAj or Function modifier FNj FN*SNAj ⌋	Initialization interval ⌈k, SNAj, ⌉ ⌊SNA*SNAj⌋	Creation limit ⌈k, SNAj, ⌉ ⌊SNA*SNAj⌋	Priority level ⌈k, SNAj, ⌉ ⌊SNA*SNAj⌋
HELP ⌈HELPA ⌉ HELPB HELPC HELPAPL1 HELPBPL1 ⌊HELPCPL1⌋	Help routine name	B-G operands SNA values to be passed to help routine ⌈k, SNAj, ⌉ ⌊SNA*SNAj⌋ When using HELPB or HELPBPL1, the B-G operands reference either fullword or floating-point savevalues. An XL (floating-point) or XF (fullword) suffix should be used with each of these operands.			
INDEX	Parameter no. kPx, SNAjPx, SNA*SNAjPx	Increment k, SNAj, SNA*SNAj			
JOBTAPE	Jobtape no. ⎧JOBTA1⎫ ⎨JOBTA2⎬ ⎩JOBTA3⎭	Next block for jobtape trans. [k]	Transaction offset time [k]	Scaling factor [k]	
JOIN	Group no. k, SNAj, SNA*SNAj	Numeric value-numeric mode ⌈k, SNAj, ⌉ ⌊SNA*SNAj⌋			
LEAVE	Storage no. k, SNAj, SNA*SNAj	No. of units ⌈k, SNAj, ⌉ ⌊SNA*SNAj⌋			

† Block operand where PL, XL, or ML is a valid SNA; [ ] Indicates optional operand;

{ } Indicates that one of the items within the braces must be selected.

430

F	G	H	I	PAGE REFERENCE	BLOCK SYMBOL

Fullword, halfword, byte & floating point parameters in any sequence   75

⌈kPx,   ⌉ ⌈kPx,   ⌉ ⌈kPx,   ⌉ ⌈kPx,   ⌉
│SNAjPx,   │ │SNAjPx,   │ │SNAjPx,   │ │SNAjPx,   │
⌊SNA*SNAjPx⌋ ⌊SNA*SNAjPx⌋ ⌊SNA*SNAjPx⌋ ⌊SNA*SNAjPx⌋

Note: Operands A—I may be a constant, FNj, Vj, Xj, XFj, XBj, XHj, RNj, C1, AC1, or Nj. Likewise, elements of functions or variables specified are restricted to these SNAs.

236

144

141

174

82

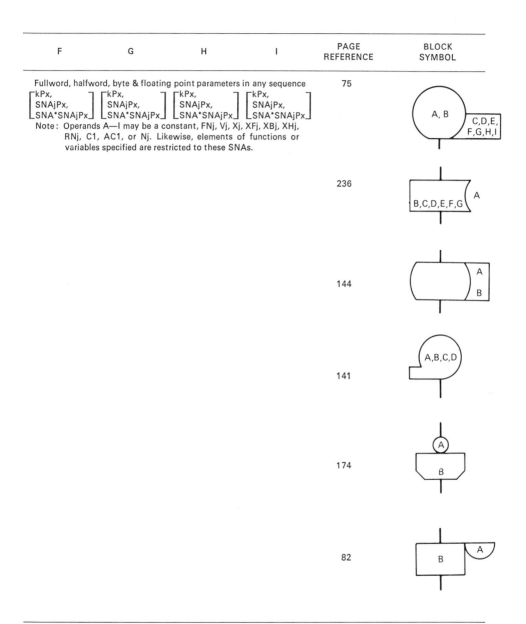

431

BLOCK STATEMENT FORMATS

OPERATION	A	B	C	D	E
LINK	User chain no. k, SNAj, SNA*SNAj	Ordering of chain LIFO,FIFO or parameter number kPx, SNAjPx, SNA*SNAjPx	Alternate block exit ⌈k, SNAj, ⌉ ⌊SNA*SNAj⌋		
LOGIC ⎧S⎫ ⎨R⎬ ⎩I⎭	Logic switch no. k, SNAj, SNA*SNAj				
LOOP	Parameter no. kPx SNAjPx, SNA*SNAjPx	Next block if Pxj ≠ 0 k, SNAj, SNA*SNAj			
MARK	Parameter no. ⌈kPx, ⌉ ⎢SNAjPx, ⎢ ⌊SNA*SNAjPx⌋				
MATCH	Conjugate MATCH block no. k, SNAj, SNA*SNAj				
MSAVEVALUE	Matrix no. or range k, SNAj, SNA*SNAj [±]	Row no. or range k, SNAj, SNA*SNAj	Column no. or range k, SNAj, SNA*SNAj	SNA value to be saved k, SNAj, SNA*SNAj†	Msavevalue type H, MH, MX, MB, ML

† Block operand where PL, XL, or ML is a valid SNA; [ ] Indicates optional operand;

⎧ ⎫ Indicates that one of the items within the braces must be selected.
⎩ ⎭

F	G	H	I	PAGE REFERENCE	BLOCK SYMBOL
				169	
				152	
				163	
				144	
				145	
				91	

BLOCK STATEMENT FORMATS

OPERATION	A	B	C	D	E
PREEMPT	Facility no. k, SNAj, SNA*SNAj	Priority option [PR]	Block no. for preempted transaction ⌈k, SNAj, ⌉ ⌊SNA*SNAj⌋	Parameter no. of preempted transaction ⌈kPx, ⌉ SNAjPx, ⌊SNA*SNAjPx⌋	Remove option [RE]
PRINT	Lower limit ⌈k, SNAj, ⌉ ⌊SNA*SNAj⌋	Upper limit ⌈k, SNAj, ⌉ ⌊SNA*SNAj⌋	Entity mnemonic	Paging indicator ⌈Any ⌉ alphameric ⌊character ⌋	
PRIORITY	Priority no. k, SNAj, SNA*SNAj	Buffer option [BUFFER]			
QUEUE	Queue no. k, SNAj, SNA*SNAj	No. of units ⌈k, SNAj, ⌉ ⌊SNA*SNAj⌋			
RELEASE	Facility no. k, SNAj, SNA*SNAj				

† Block operand where PL, XL, or ML is a valid SNA; [ ] Indicates optional operand;

{ } Indicates that one of the items within the braces must be selected.

F	G	H	I	PAGE REFERENCE	BLOCK SYMBOL
				80, 147	B, C, D, E / A
				183	A – B / C,D
				79, 165	A / B
				84	B A
				80	A

BLOCK STATEMENT FORMATS

OPERATION	A	B	C	D	E
REMOVE {G GE L LE E NE MIN MAX}	Group no. k, SNAj, SNA*SNAj	Count—no. of members to be removed—transaction mode [k, SNAj, SNA*SNAj, ALL]	Numeric value to be removed—numeric mode [k, SNAj, SNA*SNAj]	Member attribute for comparison-transaction mode [PR, or parameter no. kPx, SNAjPx, SNA*SNAjPx]	Comparison SNA [k, SNAj, SNA*SNAj]
RETURN	Facility no. k, SNAj, SNA*SNAj				
SAVAIL	Storage no. or range k, SNAj, SNA*SNAj				
SAVEVALUE	Savevalue no. or range k, SNAj, SNA*SNAj [±]	SNA value to be saved k, SNAj, SNA*SNAj†	Savevalue type X,XF,H,XH, XB, XL		
SCAN {G GE L LE E NE MIN MAX}	Group no. k, SNAj, SNA*SNAj	Member attribute for comparison PR or parameter no. kPx, SNAjPx, SNA*SNAjPx	Comparison value for B operand k, SNAj, SNA*SNAj	Member attribute to be obtained if match is made [PR or parameter no. kPx, SNAjPx, SNA*SNAjPx]	Entering xact parameter no. in which to place D operand value [kPx, SNAjPx, SNA*SNAjPx]

† Block operand where PL, XL, or ML is a valid SNA; [ ] Indicates optional operand;

{ } Indicates that one of the items within the braces must be selected.

F	G	H	I	PAGE REFERENCE	BLOCK SYMBOL
Alternate exit entering xact $\begin{bmatrix} k, SNAj, \\ SNA \cdot SNAj \end{bmatrix}$				175	
				81, 148	
				190	
				90	
Alternate exit $\begin{bmatrix} k, SNAj, \\ SNA \cdot SNAj \end{bmatrix}$				177	

BLOCK STATEMENT FORMATS

OPERATION	A	B	C	D	E
SEIZE	Facility no. k, SNAj, SNA•SNAj				
SELECT ⎡G, GE L, LE E, NE U, NU I, NI SE, SNE SF, SNF LR, LS ⎣MIN, MAX⎦	Parameter in which to place entity number kPx, SNAjPx, SNA•SNAjPx	Lower limit k, SNAj, SNA•SNAj	Upper limit k, SNAj, SNA•SNAj	Comparison value if con- ditional oper- ator is speci- fied ⎡k, SNAj, ⎤ ⎣SNA•SNAj⎦	SNA mnemonic to be examined if conditional operator is specified ⎡Any SNA⎤ except MX, MH, ⎣MB, ML⎦
SPLIT	No. of copies k, SNAj, SNA•SNAj	Next block for copies k, SNAj, SNA•SNAj	Parameter for serial numbering ⎡kPx, ⎤ SNAjPx, ⎣SNA•SNAjPx⎦	No. of fullword, halfword, byte, & ⎡kPx, ⎤ SNAjPx, ⎣SNA•SNAjPx⎦	⎡kPx, ⎤ SNAjPx, ⎣SNA•SNAjPx⎦

Any SNA

OPERATION	A	B	C	D	E
SUNAVAIL	Storage no. or range k, SNAj, SNA•SNAj				
TABULATE	Table no. k, SNAj, SNA•SNAj	Weighting factor ⎡k, SNAj, ⎤ ⎣SNA•SNAj⎦			
TERMINATE	Termination count ⎡k, SNAj, ⎤ ⎣SNA•SNAj⎦				

† Block operand where PL, XL, or ML is a valid SNA; [ ] Indicates optional operand;

{ } Indicates that one of the items within the braces must be selected.

F	G	H	I	PAGE REFERENCE	BLOCK SYMBOL
				80	
Alternate exit $\begin{bmatrix} k, SNAj, \\ SNA \cdot SNAj \end{bmatrix}$				154	
floating-point parameters in any sequence $\begin{bmatrix} kPx, \\ SNAjPx, \\ SNA \cdot SNAjPx \end{bmatrix} \begin{bmatrix} kPx, \\ SNAjPx, \\ SNA \cdot SNAjPx \end{bmatrix}$ except MX, MH, MB, ML				139	
				190	
				179	
				77	

439

BLOCK STATEMENT FORMATS

OPERATION	A	B	C	D	E
TEST ⎧E⎫ ⎪NE⎪ ⎨GE⎬ ⎪LE⎪ ⎪G⎪ ⎩L⎭	First SNA k, SNAj, SNA*SNAj†	Second SNA k, SNAj, SNA*SNAj†	Next block if relation is false ⎡k, SNAj, ⎤ ⎣SNA*SNAj⎦		
TRACE					
TRANSFER	Selection mode	Next block A ⎡k, SNAj, ⎤ ⎣SNA*SNAj⎦	Next block B ⎡k, SNAj, ⎤ ⎣SNA*SNAj⎦	Indexing factor [k]	
	With ALL selection mode a block name or number is the only valid operand				
UNLINK ⎡G⎤ ⎪GE⎪ ⎪L⎪ ⎪LE⎪ ⎪E⎪ ⎣NE⎦	User chain no. k, SNAj, SNA*SNAj	Next block for the unlinked transaction (s) k, SNAj SNA*SNAj	Transaction unlink count ALL or k, SNAj, SNA*SNAj	⎡Parameter no.⎤ kPx, SNAjPx, SNA*SNAjPx, or BACK, or ⎣BVj,BV*SNAj⎦	Match argument ⎡k, SNAj, ⎤ ⎣SNA*SNAj⎦
UNTRACE					
WRITE	Jobtape no. ⎧JOBTA1⎫ ⎨JOBTA2⎬ ⎩JOBTA3⎭				

† Block operand where PL, XL, or ML is a valid SNA; [ ] Indicates optional operand;

{ } Indicates that one of the items within the braces must be selected.

F	G	H	I	PAGE REFERENCE	BLOCK SYMBOL
				88	
				184	
				85, 157	
Next block B $\begin{bmatrix} k, SNAj, \\ SNA^{\bullet}SNAj \end{bmatrix}$				170	
				185	
				185	

CONTROL STATEMENT FORMATS

OPERATION	A	B	C	D	E	F	G	H
AUXILIARY	Entity mnemonic	Total entity allocation k	Number of entity type to reside in core k	Number of entities constituting each direct access record k	Bytes in excess of basic bytes $[k]$			
BVARIABLE		Combinations of elements, attributes, and operators: Elements k, $SNAj$, $SNA•SNAj$		Logical attributes FUj or Fj SFj / $FNUj$ $SNFj$ / FIj SEj / $FNIj$ $SNEj$ / LRj / LSj	Conditional operators 'G' 'NE', 'L' 'LE', 'E' 'GE'	Boolean operators + (or) • (and)		
CLEAR	Savevalues or ranges not to be cleared [X, XF, XH, XB, XL, MX, MH, MB, ML]	Delimiter if multiple entries $[',']$						
END								

[ ] Indicates optional operand ; { } Indicates that one of the items within the braces must be selected.

CONTROL STATEMENT FORMATS

OPERATION	A	B	C	D	E	F	G	H
FUNCTION	Function argument SNAj, SNA*SNAj (any SNA except MX, MH, MB, or ML)	Function type and no. of points $\left.\begin{array}{l}C\\D\\E\\L\\M\\S\end{array}\right\}$ n						

$x_1, y_1/x_2, y_2/$etc.   (Note: Y values cannot be MX, MH, MB, or ML, and X and Y values must start in position 1.)

	A	B	C
INITIAL	Entity or range $\left\{\begin{array}{l}X, XF, XH, XB,\\XL, MX, MH,\\MB, ML, LS\end{array}\right\}$	Value k	Delimiter if Multiple entries [/]

JOB

[ ] Indicates optional operand ;   { } Indicates that one of the items within the braces must be selected.

CONTROL STATEMENT FORMATS

OPERATION	A	B	C	D	E	F	G	H
LOAD	GPSS module or user-written HELP routine to be loaded	Delimiter if multiple entries [']						
MATRIX	Matrix type {MX, MH, MB, ML}	No. of matrix rows k	No. of matrix columns k					
QTABLE	Queue no. k	Upper limit of lowest frequency class k	Frequency class size k	No. of frequency classes k				
READ	No. of files to be skipped [k]							
REALLOCATE	Entity mnemonic to be reallocated	Total no. of that entity k	Delimiter if multiple entries [']					

[ ] Indicates optional operand;   { } Indicates that one of the items within the braces must be selected.

CONTROL STATEMENT FORMATS

OPERATION	A	B	C	D	E	F	G	H
RESET	Entity or range not to be reset [Fj, Qj, Sj, CHj, TBj]	Delimiter if multiple entries [']						
REWIND	Jobtape no. {JOBTA1, JOBTA2, JOBTA3}							
RMULT	Initial multiplier for RN1 [k]	Initial multiplier for RN2 [k]	Initial multiplier for RN3 [k]	Initial multiplier for RN4 [k]	Initial multiplier for RN5 [k]	Initial multiplier for RN6 [k]	Initial multiplier for RN7 [k]	Initial multiplier for RN8 [k]
SAVE	Reposition option [Any alphameric character]							
SIMULATE	Max. run length in minutes [k]	Time expiration option [SAVE REPLY]						

[ ] Indicates optional operand; { } Indicates that one of the items within the braces must be selected.

CONTROL STATEMENT FORMATS

OPERATION	A	B	C	D	E	F	G	H
START	Run termination count k	Printout suppression [NP]	Snap interval [k]	Standard transaction printout [1]				
STORAGE	Storage no. or range Sj	Capacity k	Delimiter if multiple entries [/]					
TABLE	Table argument k, SNAj, SNA*SNAj RT, IA Any SNA except MX, MH, MB, ML	Upper limit of lowest frequency class k	Frequency class size k	No. of frequency class k	Arrival rate time interval for RT mode table [k]			
VARIABLE FVARIABLE	Combinations of elements and arithmetic operators: Elements k, SNAj, SNA*SNAj			Arithmetic Operators + − / . @ (VARIABLE only)				

[ ] Indicates optional operand;   { } Indicates that one of the items within the braces must be selected.

446

STANDARD NUMERICAL ATTRIBUTES

ENTITY	SNA	DEFINITION	RANGE	MODIFIED BY	RESTRICTIONS/REMARKS	EXAMPLE
BLOCKS	Nj	The count of the total number of transactions to enter block j	$2^{24}-1$		Value maintained automatically. The count is updated when a transaction successfully enters the block.	
	Wj	The count of the number of transactions currently waiting at block j	$2^{15}-1$		Value maintained automatically. For blocks followed by a blocking condition such as a GATE or a TEST block which the moving transaction is blocked from entering, Wj includes those transactions waiting to enter either the GATE, or TEST block.	Transactions waiting at an ADVANCE block for advance time to elapse.
FACILITIES	Fj	The in-use status of facility j	0 if not in use 1 if in use	SEIZE, RELEASE, PREEMPT, RETURN	Status maintained automatically. Those using FUNAVAIL and FAVAIL should review the effects of these blocks on the facility in use status.	
	FRj	Utilization in parts per thousand of facility j	0-999		Value computed automatically.	A utilization of .88 would yield FRj = 880.
	FCj	Total number of transactions to enter facility j	$2^{31}-1$		Value maintained automatically.	
	FTj	Average transaction utilization time for facility j	$2^{31}-1$ Truncated to integer*		Value computed automatically.	
FUNCTIONS	FNj	The computed value of function j	$\pm 2^{31}-1$ Truncated to integer except when used as function modifier in GENERATE, ASSIGN or ADVANCE blocks or as the argument of a function*		Defined by FUNCTION definition and follower statements.	
GROUPS	Gj	The current number of members of group j	$2^{15}-1$	JOIN, REMOVE, TERMINATE, ASSEMBLE	Value maintained automatically.	

* Except when used as the Y-value of an E- or M-type function (this does not apply to msavevalues) if a FVARIABLE statement or when saved in a floating-point parameter, savevalue, or msavevalue.

STANDARD NUMERICAL ATTRIBUTES

ENTITY	SNA	DEFINITION	RANGE	MODIFIED BY	RESTRICTIONS/REMARKS	EXAMPLE
MSAVEVALUES	$MXj(a, b)$	The current contents of fullword msavevalue j, row a, column b	$\pm 2^{31}-1$	MSAVEVALUE	Value maintained automatically.	
	$MHj(a, b)$	The current contents of halfword msavevalue j, row a, column b	$\pm 2^{15}-1$	MSAVEVALUE		
	$MBj(a, b)$	The current contents of byte msavevalue j, row a, column b	$\pm 2^{7}-1$	MSAVEVALUE		
	$MLj(a, b)$	The current contents of floating point msavevalue j, row a, column b	$\pm 2^{24}-1$ Without loss of precision. Values may be larger but precision will be lost. Truncated to integer*	MSAVEVALUE	Can be used only as (1) the B operand of an ASSIGN or SAVEVALUE block, (2) the D operand of an MSAVEVALUE block, (3) an element of a FVARIABLE statement, or (4) an operand of a Test block in which two floating-point SNAs are being compared.	
QUEUES	Qj	The current length or number of units in queue j	$2^{31}-1$	QUEUE, DEPART	Value maintained automatically.	
	QAj	Average length or number of units in queue j	$2^{31}-1$ Truncated to integer*		Value computed automatically.	
	QMj	Maximum length or contents of queue j	$2^{31}-1$		Value maintained automatically.	
	QCj	Total number of units to enter queue j	$2^{31}-1$		Value maintained automatically.	
	QZj	Number of units spending zero time in queue j	$2^{31}-1$		Value maintained automatically.	
	QTj	Average time each unit (including zero time units) spent in queue j	$2^{31}-1$ Truncated to integer*		Value computed automatically.	
	QXj	Average time each unit (excluding zero-time units) spent in queue j	$2^{31}-1$ Truncated to integer*		Value computed automatically.	

* Except when used as the Y-value of an E- or M-type function (this does not apply to msavevalues) if a FVARIABLE statement or when saved in a floating-point parameter, savevalue, or msavevalue.

STANDARD NUMERICAL ATTRIBUTES

ENTITY	SNA	DEFINITION	RANGE	MODIFIED BY	RESTRICTIONS/REMARKS	EXAMPLE
SAVEVALUES	Xj or XFj	The current contents of fullword savevalue j	$\pm 2^{31}-1$	SAVEVALUE		
	XHj	The current contents of halfword savevalue j	$\pm 2^{15}-1$	SAVEVALUE		
	XBj	The current contents of byte savevalue j	$\pm 2^{7}-1$	SAVEVALUE		
	XLj	The current contents of floating point savevalue j	$\pm 2^{24}-1$ Without loss of precision. Values may be larger but precision will be lost. Truncated to integer*	SAVEVALUE	Can be used only as (1) the B operand of an ASSIGN or SAVEVALUE block, (2) the D operand of an MSAVEVALUE block, (3) an element in a FVARIABLE statement, (4) an operand of a TEST block in which floating-point SNAs are being compared, (5) the Y-value of an E- or an M-type function, or (6) the argument of a function.	
STORAGES	Sj	The current contents of storage j	$2^{31}-1$	ENTER, LEAVE	Value maintained automatically.	Sj + Rj = Capacity of storage j
	Rj	Number of available units or capacity remaining of storage j	$2^{31}-1$	ENTER, LEAVE	Value maintained automatically.	
	SRj	Utilization in parts per thousand of storage j	0-999		Value computed automatically.	A utilization of .65 would yield SRj = 650
	SAj	Average contents of storage j	$2^{31}-1$ Truncated to integer*		Value computed automatically.	
	SMj	Maximum contents of storage j	$2^{31}-1$		Value maintained automatically.	
	SCj	Total number of units to enter storage j	$2^{31}-1$		Value maintained automatically.	
	STj	Average utilization per unit of storage j	$2^{31}-1$ Truncated to integer*		Value computed automatically.	

* Except when used as the Y-value of an E- or M-type function (this does not apply to msavevalues) if a FVARIABLE statement or when saved in a floating-point parameter, savevalue, or msavevalue.

STANDARD NUMERICAL ATTRIBUTES

ENTITY	SNA	DEFINITION	RANGE	MODIFIED BY	RESTRICTIONS/REMARKS	EXAMPLE
SYSTEM ATTRIBUTES	RNj (1 ≤ j ≤ 8)	A computed random number	An integer value from 0–999 unless used as the argument of a function. In that case a fraction value between 0 and .999999 inclusive.	RMULT, JOB		
	C1	The current value of the relative simulator clock. Clock time relative to last reset or clear operation.	$2^{31}-1$	RESET, CLEAR, JOB	Maintained automatically. Value reset to 0 at start of simulation run and by RESET, CLEAR, or JOB statement.	
	AC1	The current value of the absolute simulator clock. Clock time since start of run or last clear operation.	$2^{31}-1$	CLEAR, JOB	Maintained automatically. Reset to 0 at start of simulation run and by CLEAR or JOB statement.	
	TG1	The number of terminations remaining in the model to satisfy start count.	$2^{31}-1$	START, TERMINATE	Maintained automatically.	
TABLES	TBj	The mean value of table j.	$\pm 2^{31}-1$ Truncated to integer*	TABULATE	Table frequencies are defined by TABLE statement. Value computed automatically.	
	TCj	Total number of entries in table j	$2^{31}-1$		Value maintained automatically.	
	TDj	Standard deviation of table j	$2^{31}-1$ Truncated to integer*		Value computed automatically.	

* Except when used as the Y-value of an E- or M-type function (this does not apply to msavevalues) if a FVARIABLE statement or when saved in a floating-point parameter, savevalue, or msavevalue.

STANDARD NUMERICAL ATTRIBUTES

ENTITY	SNA	DEFINITION	RANGE	MODIFIED BY	RESTRICTIONS/REMARKS	EXAMPLE
TRANSACTIONS	PFj	The current contents of fullword parameter j of the transaction currently being processed	$\pm 2^{31}-1$	ASSIGN, INDEX, LOOP, MARK, SELECT, COUNT May possibly be modified by ALTER, SCAN, SPLIT, PREEMPT		
	PHj	The current contents of halfword parameter j of the transaction currently being processed	$\pm 2^{15}-1$	Same as PFj		
	PBj	The current contents of byte parameter j of the transaction currently being processed	$\pm 2^{7}-1$	Same as PFj with the exception of MARK	Clock time may not be stored in byte parameters.	
	PLj	The current contents of a floating-point parameter j of the transaction currently being processed	$\pm 2^{24}-1$ With no loss of precision. Values may be larger but precision will be lost. Truncated to integer*	ASSIGN	Can be used only as (1) the B operand of either the ASSIGN or SAVEVALUE blocks, (2) the D operand of an MSAVEVALUE block, (3) an element in a FVARIABLE statement, (4) an operand of a TEST block in which two floating-point SNAs are being compared, (5) the Y-value of an E- or an M-type function, or (6) the argument of a function.	
	M1	The transit time of the transaction currently being processed	$2^{31}-1$	MARK	M1 = current absolute clock − mark time of transaction currently being processed.	
	MPjPx	The intermediate transit time of the transaction currently being processed	$2^{31}-1$	MARK, ASSIGN (with C1 or AC1 as B operand)	MPjPx (where x is either F or H only) = current clock − Pxj (Pxj contains clock time placed there by a MARK block.)	MP8PF specifies the parameter containing the clock time to be used in calculating the intermediate transit time.
	PR	Priority of transaction currently being processed	0–127	PRIORITY, ALTER	Priority assigned when transaction created at GENERATE or SPLIT block.	

* Except when used as the Y-value of an E- or M-type function (this does not apply to msavevalues) if a FVARIABLE statement or when saved in a floating-point parameter, savevalue, or msavevalue.

STANDARD NUMERICAL ATTRIBUTES

ENTITY	SNA	DEFINITION	RANGE	MODIFIED BY	RESTRICTIONS/REMARKS	EXAMPLE
USER CHAINS	CHj	The current count of the number of transactions on user chain j	$2^{15}-1$	LINK, UNLINK	Value maintained automatically.	
	CAj	The average number of transactions on user chain j	$2^{15}-1$ Truncated to integer*		Value computed automatically.	
	CMj	The maximum number of transactions on user chain j	$2^{15}-1$		Value maintained automatically.	
	CCj	The total number of transactions on user chain j	$2^{31}-1$		Value maintained automatically.	
	CTj	The average time per transaction on user chain j	$2^{31}-1$ Truncated to integer*		Value computed automatically.	
VARIABLES and BOOLEAN VARIABLES	Vj	The computed value of variable j	$\pm2^{31}-1$ Arithmetic variable or 10^{-78} to 10^{75} if a floating-point variable		Defined by VARIABLE statement.	
	BVj	The computed value of Boolean variable j	1 if statement true, 0 if false		Defined by BVARIABLE statement.	

* Except when used as the Y-value of an E- or M-type function (this does not apply to msavevalues) if a FVARIABLE statement or when saved in a floating-point parameter, savevalue, or msavevalue.

452

C GPSS V: Extensions to GPSS/360

This appendix, which is addressed to the existing GPSS/360 user, summarizes the features of GPSS V which were not available in GPSS/360. Upward compatibility has been maintained between the two versions so that programs written in GPSS/360 may be run under GPSS V.

We consider, in turn, the new features, the new instructions (blocks), and how these are written. Some minor improvements have been made in the operations of the simulator, for instance in the computation of some SNAs, but these will not be presented here. The reader who requires further details is referred to [G.12], where the differences are discussed.

C.1 New Features

Free format: coding of GPSS instructions, control statements or entity-definition statements may be made either in *fixed format*, with label in columns 2 to 6, instruction in columns 8 to 18, and operands from column 19 onward, or free format, which is more convenient for fast typing.

A *run length feature* is specified by the A- and B-operands of the SIMULATE control statement. This allows the user to limit the computer time used for a specific run. If the simulation has not ended when the run time has elapsed, execution is terminated by the run-length feature and the standard printout is produced. The user may specify the action to be taken after the run has terminated in this way. For example, the model can be saved on a secondary storage device for the simulation to be resumed later, or new instructions can be given from the computer console.

Two different data sets are associated with the SAVE/READ feature, one for output and one for input, referred to as DRDSAVEO and DRDSAVEI, respectively, in the DD-statements of the operating system procedure; see Appendix A.

The LOAD *feature* allows the user to make certain GPSS or user-written modules resident in main storage during the simulation. This feature can improve the efficiency of the program considerably, because the modules do not have to be loaded from secondary storage each time they are invoked.

The AUXILIARY *feature* allows the user to store GPSS entities on auxiliary storage. This means that the size of GPSS models is not restricted by the size of main storage partition allocated. Previously, all entities had to be in main storage during execution.

The HELP *feature* provides a simpler interface with either FORTRAN or PL/I thanks to six standard subroutines in GPSS V.

The UNLIST *statement* is now selective, to give users the option of suppressing the compiled (absolute) listing of the program.

The CLEAR *statement* has been extended to operate selectively on all types of save location and matrix.

All data sets associated with GPSS *may be blocked*, which improves the overall operating efficiency.

The *diagnostic capabilities* have been improved to make them more straightforward and understandable than before.

C.2   New Instructions (Blocks) and Extensions of Previous Instructions

Four instructions that have been added to make facilities and storages available or unavailable are:

FAVAIL, FUNAVAIL, SAVAIL, SUNAVAIL

The capabilities of the GATE block have been extended to test the availability (FV, SV) or unavailability (FNV, SNV) of facilities and storages.

The ALTER, REMOVE, SCAN, and UNLINK blocks have been enhanced to include specification of all arithmetic relations, which increases the power and flexibility of these instructions.

C.3   Additional SNAs

Two new attributes have been added:

AC1: absolute clock time, which indicates the time since the start of a GPSS run or the last encountered CLEAR statement, independent of any RESET statements that may have been executed.

TG1: terminations to go count. This counter is initialized by the A-field of the START statement and is decremented each time a transaction enters a TERMINATE block with a nonblank A-operand.

Parameters, saves, and matrices have been extended to include byte and floating-point types, referred to as:

Byte parameter j:	PBj
Floating-point parameter j:	PLj
Byte save location j:	XBj
Floating-point save location j:	XLj
Byte save matrix j:	MBj
Floating-point save matrix j:	MLj

Further, the total *number of parameters* which may be associated with a transaction has been increased from 100 to 1020, to allow for up to 255 parameters of each type.

The capability of specifying four different types of parameter with each transaction has created the need for a notation that is somewhat more complicated than that used in GPSS/360, where parameter j was written Pj. If either fullword or halfword parameters are used exclusively, the previous notation is also valid. When mixed parameter types are used, they are addressed as Pxj, where x is the parameter type: B for byte, H for halfword, F for fullword, and L for floating-point.

When a SNA is identified by a parameter value, the parameter type must be given as a suffix. For example, to refer to the relative transit time, relative to halfword parameter 2, we write MP2PH, where PH is the suffix which specifies that parameter 2 is halfword. The general form is jPx, where j is the parameter number and x is its type. As a consequence, extra operation fields to modify the values of parameters or save locations and matrices have been added to some instructions.

The ASSIGN instruction has a D-operand to specify parameter type. If no function modifier is used, parameter type may be coded as C-operand.

The SAVEVALUE C-operand and MSAVEVALUE E-operand have been added to specify the type of save location and matrix, respectively.

The GENERATE block has fields for specifying the number of parameters of each type to be associated with each transaction. These parameters are specified, as required and in any order, by the F- to I-operands: kPx, where k is the number of parameters of type x.

Indirect addressing has been extended to include all SNAs, using the asterisk symbol. The general form of reference to a SNA is SNA∗SNAj, which is the value of the SNA identified by the value of SNAj.

Operands which refer to parameters have the general form SNA∗SNAjPx, where Px is a suffix that specifies the type of the parameter concerned. See Appendix B for expressions that are valid operands of GPSS blocks.

D Generation of Random Numbers and Random Variates

The examples discussed in this book show the necessity for having an efficient means of generating samples of random variables (variates) defined by their probability function or their distribution function. One commonly used technique is the inverse distribution method, which is described below. Other popular methods, such as the rejection technique and the composition method, are presented in the references (see [D.1]) and will not be discussed here. These methods are based on the generation of random numbers, so we first consider this problem.

D.1 Generation of Random Numbers

The following methods could be used for generating random numbers:

Die throwing: impractical when using a computer.

Physical device: suppose that a computer could pick a voltage known to vary randomly between two limits. The signal could be converted from analog into digital form and used as the value of the random number. This process is not impracticable, but it would raise two types of problem: (1) the sequence of random numbers so generated would not be reproducible, and (2) it would be difficult to ensure that the physical device is functioning properly. Therefore, it would require hardware maintenance.

The need for *reproducibility* of a random-number sequence seems to be a contradiction, because one basic requirement of all random-number generators is that an unpredictable sequence of numbers should be produced. Nevertheless, reproducibility is very important for testing and debugging computer programs. The only way to debug a program using random numbers is to reproduce the same sequence of numbers during every run. There are two ways to approach the problem:

Tables: published tables of random numbers (see [D.2]) could be stored in the computer. When random numbers are required, they would be read in order from the table. This method is not commonly used, probably because it uses considerable storage if kept in main memory or takes computer time to retrieve if put on auxiliary storage. Further, the user is always obliged to use the same source of numbers, which could be an unacceptable limitation. However, this method does ensure reproducibility.

Computer generation: when using computers for simulation, we desire a method that can be programmed easily.

What is needed for simulation work is a random-number sequence with the following four properties:

Uniform distribution over a given interval: usually 0 to 1.

Independence from each other: ideally, there should be no correlation between the numbers produced, that is, between the ith and the $(i + k)$th, where $k = 1$, $2, \ldots, n$. More generally, the series of numbers produced should pass all the statistical tests that the user considers adequate for the particular application.

As long a cycle as possible: the cycle is the sequence of numbers produced before repetition.

Reproducibility: this property is vital for debugging programs. We must be able to repeat runs in order to compare results.

In addition to these mathematical properties we would like the process to be economical in terms of computer time and memory space used. In fact, these last two conditions have strongly influenced the development of those methods now in use.

The general technique is to use a simple algorithm to generate terms of a sequence of pseudo-random numbers, which is called whenever a new random number is required. The sequence is deterministic, but the numbers are called pseudo-random, because they have the statistical properties expected of truly random numbers. Two methods of historical interest were the *mid-square* and the *mid-product* techniques. Later, the Lehmer congruential methods were developed, and most of the simulators now in use employ some variation of the Lehmer multiplicative congruential method.

D.1.1 The mid-square technique

Let r_0 be an arbitrary number. To obtain a new random number, square r_0 and extract the middle digits of the product. For example, if we start with the number 76 and keep two digit numbers, we would get successively:

$$r_0 = 76 \qquad r_0{}^2 = 5776$$
$$r_1 = 77 \qquad r_1{}^2 = 5929$$
$$r_2 = 92 \qquad \text{etc.}$$

The sequence will repeat (cycle) as soon as a number equals one previously generated.

The drawbacks of this method are that the numbers are not uniformly distributed, and if the original value is too small, the sequence quickly degenerates to zeros.

D.1.2   The mid-product technique

Given two numbers r_0 and r_1, the next random number, r_2, is obtained by forming the product $r_0 r_1$ and extracting the middle digits. Thus r_3 would be the middle digits of $r_1 r_2$, etc. If we start with $r_0 = 15$ and $r_1 = 36$, we obtain:

$$r_0 = 15 \quad \text{and} \quad r_1 = 36 \qquad r_0 r_1 = 0540$$
$$r_2 = 54 \qquad\qquad\qquad\qquad r_1 r_2 = 1944$$
$$r_3 = 94 \qquad \text{etc.}$$

The sequence repeats when two successive numbers are obtained which have previously appeared in the same order.

This method proved to be statistically unsatisfactory and was abandoned.

D.1.3   The congruential method

There are several variations of the congruential method. (For details see [D.1], Appendix A.)

The multiplicative congruential, or power residue, method is a special case commonly used in simulators. If r_i, b, and m are constants which, for convenience, we suppose to be positive with $r_i < m$, we obtain the $(i + 1)$th random number by the transformation:

$$r_{i+1} = r_i b(\text{mod } m)$$

The choice of the multiplier b and the radix m, as well as that of the starting number r_0, is most important. They have an effect on the quality of the random numbers produced, in particular on cycle length. The properties that the numbers must possess are discussed in [D.3].

To show the importance of the choice of these numbers, consider the following two examples:

EXAMPLES:

(1)
$$r_0 = 3$$
$$b = 5$$
$$m = 8$$

The sequence of pseudo-random numbers generated is:
$$r_i = 3, 7, 3, 7, 3, \ldots$$
which has a very short cycle.

(2)
$$r_0 = 3$$
$$b = 5$$
$$m = 7$$
$$r_i = 3, 1, 5, 4, 6, 2, 3, 1, \ldots$$

The cycle is much longer despite the fact that we keep only one digit. In fact, we get all possible numbers except 0.

Choice of _m_. To avoid execution of the modulo operation, the choice of _m_ is usually related to the computer-word size. It is chosen as:

10^d for decimal machines, where _d_ is the number of digits in the machine word

2^p for binary machines, where _p_ is the number of bits in the machine word

With these choices, the modulo operation implies the retention after multiplication of the _d_ rightmost digits of the product (or _p_ rightmost bits) as the new random number. In most machines this operation is performed implicitly and therefore uses no computer time.

When _m_ has been selected, r_0 and _b_ must be chosen. We summarize the properties that these numbers should have, following the discussion given in [D.3]. In all cases r_0 and _m_ should be coprime to avoid having too short a cycle. For decimal machines, r_0 should not be a multiple of 2 or 5, and, for binary machines, r_0 should not be a multiple of 2. Therefore, we always start the sequence with an odd number. This is an obvious choice which can be demonstrated by computing a few examples. If this condition is ignored, the common factor would appear in all numbers generated and would shorten the cycle. Therefore, the initial value is always chosen to be an odd number that is not a multiple of 5 in the decimal case.

Choice of _b_. For binary machines, _b_ should be of the form $8j \pm 3$, where _j_ is any positive integer. A further recommendation is to choose _b_ close to $2^{p/2}$. This ensures low autocorrelation between successively generated numbers.

For decimal machines, _b_ should have the form $200t \pm k$, where _t_ is any positive integer and _k_ is one of the following numbers: 3, 11, 13, 19, 21, 27, 29, 37, 53, 59, 61, 67, 69, 77, 83, or 91. Further, _b_ should be close to $10^{d/2}$. For example, consider a decimal machine with four digits. Then:

$$m = 10^d = 10000$$
$$r_0 = 0123$$
$$b = 200t \pm k \quad \text{(we choose } t = 1 \text{ and } k = 91)$$
$$b = 200 - 91 = 109$$

$r_0 = 0123$	$r_0 b = 0123 \times 109 = 13407$
$r_1 = 3407$	$r_1 b = 3407 \times 109 = 371363$
$r_2 = 1363$	$r_2 b = 1363 \times 109 = 148567$
$r_3 = 8567$	etc.

Our immediate observation is that the low-order digits are far from random. In this example we get 3, 7, 3, 7, ... The periodicity of the digits increases with the order of the digit position. This periodicity shows that the procedure we have applied can never give all possible numbers in the range 0 to 9999. The cycle ends when a value r_i equals the initial value r_0 and cannot contain more than 2000 numbers. Sometimes this will present no problem because of the use we make of the random number sequence. However, if periodicity in the lowest digits must be suppressed, one could reject the rightmost digits and use only the leftmost ones. In any event this strategy is unsatisfactory because the cycle has been effectively shortened and the computations should be conducted with all the digits produced.

Normalizing Random Numbers:

The above procedure gives integer random numbers between 0 and $m - 1$. If we require random numbers between 0 and 1, which is usually the case when generating random variates, we divide the numbers produced by m, that is, 2^p in the binary case and 10^d in the decimal. The division operation can sometimes be avoided. In the decimal case, we just consider that the decimal point is in front of the leftmost digit. The sequence of our example above becomes: 0.0123, 0.3407, 0.1363, 0.8567, . . .

D.2 Generation of Random Variates

Suppose that we need to generate sample values of a random variable X defined by its probability density function $f(x)$. We compute its cumulative distribution:

$$F(x) = \int_{-\infty}^{x} f(t)\, dt,\ \text{which by definition is equal to } \Pr(X \le x).$$

The inverse distribution method selects a random number r, uniformly distributed between 0 and 1, sets $F(x) = r$, and solves for x. For a particular value r_0 of r, the construction shown in Figure D.1 gives a value x_0, which is a particular sample

Figure D.1 Continuous function.

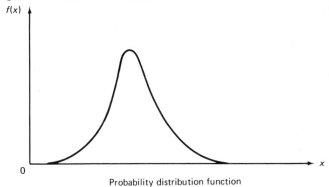

Probability distribution function

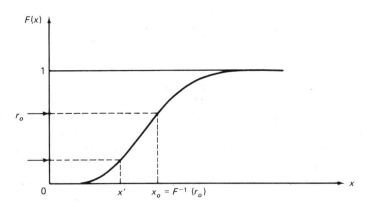

Cumulative distribution function

value of X, and which can be expressed as $x_0 = F^{-1}(r_0)$. This construction is used to generate values x of the random variable X. Before these values can be used in simulation, it is necessary to prove that the values generated by the construction actually have the distribution function $F(x)$.

Let x'_i be the samples of the random variable X' generated and $F'(X')$ the corresponding cumulative distribution function. If we prove that $F'(x') = F(x')$, then X' and X are the same random variable, with the same distribution function:

$$F'(x') = \Pr(X' \leq x')$$

For X' to be smaller than or equal to x' and by virtue of t he geometrical construction, we must have $r \leq r'$, so

$$F'(x') = \Pr(r \leq r')$$

But by construction $r' = F(x')$, so

$$F'(x') = \Pr(r \leq F(x')) = \Pr(r \leq A)$$

where we set $F(x') = A$.

Now, the values of r are uniformly distributed between 0 and 1; thus $\Pr(r \leq A) = A$ and

$$F'(x') = F(x')$$

Therefore, the generated x' are samples of X.

Thus we can generate sample values of a random variable X defined by its cumulative distribution function $F(x)$. We illustrate the method with the following two examples.

EXAMPLES:

(1)   Uniform distribution between two values (Figure D.2).

In any simulation program requiring a random variable uniformly distributed between a and b, we generate a random number r, uniformly distributed between 0 and 1, and transform it by the formula $x = a + r(b - a)$, where it is assumed that r can take the extreme values 0 and 1. A simple check shows that the extreme values of x are a and b. For discrete simulators such as GPSS, the upper limit of r is just under unity and the fractional values obtained are truncated to the nearest integer. In such cases the transformation is modified to $x = a + r(b + 1 - a)$.

(2)   Exponential distribution (Figure D.3).

In queueing systems, random interarrival and service times are described by exponentially distributed random variables. To generate samples x of a random variable X which is exponentially distributed with average interarrival time $E(X)$:

$$f(x) = \lambda e^{-\lambda x} \quad \text{where } \lambda = 1/E(X) \text{ is the arrival rate}$$
$$F(x) = 1 - e^{-\lambda x} = r$$

and, solving for x:

$$x = -\frac{1}{\lambda} \ln(1 - r) = -E(X) \ln(1 - r)$$

Therefore, when we require exponentially distributed values with mean $E(X)$, we generate a random number r and transform it with the above formula.

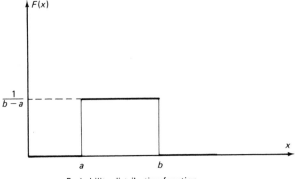

Probability distribution function

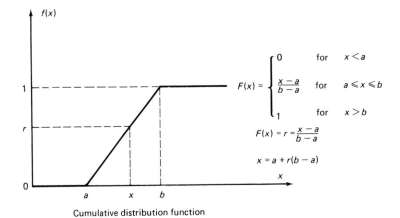

$$F(x) = \begin{cases} 0 & \text{for} \quad x < a \\ \dfrac{x-a}{b-a} & \text{for} \quad a \leqslant x \leqslant b \\ 1 & \text{for} \quad x > b \end{cases}$$

$$F(x) = r = \frac{x-a}{b-a}$$

$$x = a + r(b-a)$$

Cumulative distribution function

Figure D.2 Uniform distribution.

Figure D.3 Exponential distribution.

In particular, when $E(X)$ is unity, the formula becomes:

$$x = -\ln(1-r)$$

which is tabulated in GPSS (see Section 6.3.3). The user who wants to use this distribution with a different mean, multiplies the random variable by the value of the mean.

For discrete functions we use a similar construction. The random variable X is defined by its probability function $f(x)$ for discrete values of x. We construct the

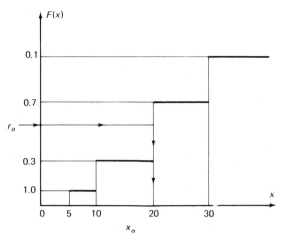

Figure D.4

cumulative probability function $F(x)$. Then we take a random number r_0 and make the random variable equal to the smallest number x_0 such that $F(x_0) \geq r_0$. Graphically we read the value x_0, which corresponds to the interval of $F(x)$ containing r_0. The x values so generated have distribution function $F(x)$. This is shown intuitively in the next example.

Suppose that we require values of a random variable X whose probability function is given by the data shown in Table D.1. We must compute the third column to obtain the cumulative distribution function shown in Figure D.4.

Table D.1

Value of X	Associated Probability (%)	Cumulative Probability
5	10	0.1
10	20	0.3
20	40	0.7
30	30	1.0

To generate a value of the random variable, we obtain a random number r_0 and read out the corresponding value x_0. It is clear from the construction that the probability of getting, for example, $x_0 = 20$ is the same as the probability that the random number r_0 lies between 0.3 and 0.7. This probability is 0.4, because r is uniformly distributed between 0 and 1. The process will therefore generate samples x with the probability distribution given above.

It is usual for the argument of a function to appear on the x-axis. This is shown graphically, for the previous example, in Figure D.5. It is the mirror image of Figure D.4 rotated through 90 degrees.

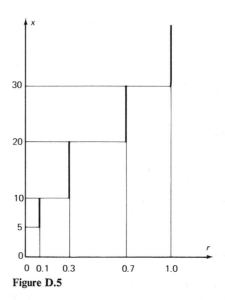

Figure D.5

Random variables are a vital part of all stochastic simulation models, and therefore all simulation languages should provide the analyst with simple techniques to include such variables in simulation programs.

References

D.1. T. H. NAYLOR, *Computer Simulation Experiments with Models of Economic Systems*, Wiley, New York, 1971.

D.2. RAND CORPORATION, *A Million Random Digits with 100,000 Normal Deviates*, Free Press, New York, 1955.

D.3. INTERNATIONAL BUSINESS MACHINES CORPORATION, *Random Number Generation and Testing*, GC20-8011.

E Summary of Current Simulation Languages

The first computer simulation models were coded in general-purpose programming languages. However, the need for simplifying the routine tasks of programming soon led to the development of specialized computer simulation languages during the latter part of the 1950s.

A general simulation language must provide sufficient basic modeling elements to describe many different systems adequately, subject to the limitations of being reasonably simple to implement and use. The block diagramming philosophy of GPSS is just one of many possible simulation language strategies. In this appendix we outline the strategies and instructions of three other current simulation languages and we also list some references to the general literature on simulation languages.

Four of the major simulation languages in current use, listed in order of their introduction, are:

1. The General Purpose Simulation System (GPSS), developed by Geoffrey Gordon (IBM), first released in 1961 (see [E.1] and "Historical Introduction").

2. SIMSCRIPT, developed by H. M. Markowitz, B. Hausner, and H. W. Carr, released by the RAND Corporation in 1962 [E.2]. A completely new version, SIMSCRIPT II, was released by the RAND Corporation in 1968 [E.3].

3. SIMULA, developed by O. J. Dahl and K. Nygaard, released by the Norwegian Computing Center, Oslo in 1965 [E.4] and [E.5]. The latest version is SIMULA 67 [E.6].

4. SIMPL/I, a new simulation language based on PL/I, introduced by IBM in June 1972 [E.7] and [E.17].

Other languages include CSL, a Fortran-based language developed by John Buxton and later extended by Alan Clementson [E.8], and GASP [E.9] and [E.10].

465

To make a detailed comparison of different simulation languages we would describe the languages in terms of characteristics such as:

facilities offered, including monitor routines, sampling, data collection, and report generation

data structures allowed

model structure, which describes the components available in the language and operating rules of the system.

For a detailed description of these characteristics and their relative importance we recommend the article of K. D. Tocher [E.11]. Additional information about the various languages in terms of these and other characteristics is given in [E.12] and [E.13].

The structure of a language provides the user with a framework with which to describe the real world. A knowledge of the general concepts of the structure of existing languages may help the user to judge the suitability of a given language to model a specific system. Simulation languages are often classified as either:

flowchart-oriented languages (GPSS), or

statement-oriented languages (SIMSCRIPT, CSL, SIMULA, SIMPL/I).

The second category is then further subdivided into:

event-oriented (SIMSCRIPT)

activity-oriented (CSL)

process-oriented (SIMULA, SIMPL/I)

A detailed discussion of the event-scheduling approach, the activity-scanning approach, and the process-interactive approach is given in [E.14].

We emphasize that the classification of simulation languages is never absolute. Although GPSS is a flowchart-oriented language, it could also be considered as a process-oriented language or as an event-driven language. GPSS was written in assembler language as a purpose-built simulator for analysts, and later enhancements included interfaces to high-level languages. Most other simulation languages are based on an existing high-level language. This strategy has advantages for skilled programmers because it provides easy access to files and to the computing power of the base language.

E.1 Event-Oriented Approach: SIMSCRIPT II

This language, originally based on Fortran, is sufficiently rich and versatile to be used as a general programming language. In this appendix we comment only on its discrete-event simulation features.

E.1.1 Static structure

The static structure of a Simscript II model is described by entities, attributes, and sets. Entities may be declared as either temporary or permanent in the

PREAMBLE of a SIMSCRIPT II program. Temporary entities are created during program execution by a "CREATE temporary entity name" statement, and the storage allocated to an entity may be released later by a "DESTROY entity name" statement. A group of permanent entities is created by a statement such as:

CREATE EVERY permanent entity name (n)
where n is the number of entities of the group.

In the preamble, entities may be declared to have given attributes by statements of the general form:

EVERY entity name HAS AN attribute name list

as in

EVERY MAN HAS A NAME, AN AGE AND A SOCIAL SECURITY.NUMBER.

Sets are collections of either temporary or permanent entities, whose membership is changed dynamically by FILE and REMOVE statements. The entities of a set may be sequenced in various ways, including FIFO and LIFO, or according to the values of different attributes of the entities to be ordered. At any given time the state of a model is described completely by the current list of the entities, their attributes, and set membership.

E.1.2   The dynamic structure of the model

The time-dependent behavior of the system is modeled by events, which are changes of state taking place instantaneously at discrete points in simulated time, initiated by the execution of an event routine. Simulated time is controlled by the timing routine, which schedules events by means of an events set containing event notices.

An event notice is a temporary entity that has attributes such as the event time. It is created and placed in the events set according to its scheduled time of occurrence. Each activity in SIMSCRIPT II is represented by two events which specify its start and finish.

SIMSCRIPT II requires a model to be specified only in terms of separate events, and scheduling an event means filing an "event notice" in the "events set." This can be done in two ways:

1. "SCHEDULE AN event AT time expression" statement, for internal events caused by another event, for example:

SCHEDULE AN ARRIVAL AT TIME.V + 5.7

This statement schedules an event ARRIVAL to occur at the current simulated time, given by the variable TIME.V, plus 5.7 time units.

2. Event data cards which are read in chronological order. An event data card schedules an external event and contains the name of the event, the time at which it is to occur and other optional data.

Either method causes an event notice with the name of that event to be created.

E.1.3   The timing routine

The timing routine scans the events set for the event notice defining the next scheduled event and uses it to initiate the execution of the event routine associated with that event. The statements of the event routine are executed in the same manner as in FORTRAN, except that if a statement to schedule an event is encountered, an event notice is created and filed in the events set according to its scheduled time of occurrence. An order of priority can be specified for events due to occur at the same simulated time.

When the RETURN statement is executed, control passes back to the timing routine to select the next event. If one of the statements of an event routine is a CALL to a subprogram, control passes from the calling event routine to the subprogram. After execution, the subprogram returns control to the event routine at the statement following the CALL statement.

E.1.4   Miscellaneous features

SIMSCRIPT II provides:

The function RANDOM.F, to generate a stream of pseudo-random numbers between 0 and 1.

Nine functions for generating independent pseudo-random samples from the following statistical distributions: uniform, normal, Poisson, exponential, Erlang, lognormal, binomial, gamma, and Weibull.

Two statements, ACCUMULATE and TALLY, used in the PREAMBLE to instruct the compiler to generate automatic data collection and analysis statements at appropriate places in the program.

E.2   Process-Oriented Approach: SIMPL/I

SIMPL/I is a process-oriented simulation language which is implemented as a superset of PL/I and follows the structure and design philosophy of PL/I. Therefore, it combines the special-purpose features of a simulation system with the flexibility and power of the PL/I high-level language. In particular, the user has access to the standard mathematical and statistical routines of PL/I libraries, a list-processing capability, and specialized facilities necessary for modeling many types of system. Statements are coded in PL/I form, so the user should have some knowledge of PL/I programming.

In this overview we describe the simulation-oriented features and some of the list-processing facilities of SIMPL/I. The components of a system and characteristics of their behavior are represented by SIMPL/I processes, entities, and lists and by PL/I variables, structures, and procedures. Processes and entities are manipulated in sets, called *lists*, with the help of list-processing statements.

E.2.1   The process concept

A key feature of process orientation is that of a single process routine, composed of a number of segments describing a sequence of activities. Each segment behaves as an independently controlled program. On receiving control, only the statements composing the segment are executed, and then control is returned. A timing routine schedules segment activation, as if several programs were controlled independently.

The process routine is a pattern or descriptive unit which is employed repeatedly to simulate individual occurrences, called *processes*. A process is an entity that is alternatively active and passive. An active process executes statements of the descriptive unit to change the state of the system. On encountering a time-delay statement, the process becomes passive and remains at that statement of the descriptive unit until reactivated. This statement, called an *interaction point*, identifies where control may be transferred to another process. Thus a segment of a process routine is composed of the statements which are executed between two time-delay statements.

The *reactivation point* specifies where the process routine will restart execution of the process after execution of the time delay command.

As an example, consider an airport. A model might include the following processes: air-traffic controllers, airport runways, and aircraft. As each aircraft comes under air traffic control, its behavior could be modeled by a process with descriptive unit:

```
            AIRCRAFT: BEHAVIOR;                                  1
            INSERT CURRENT IN (STACK);                           2
            HOLD;                                                3
            TAKE (DESCENT_TIME (HEIGHT,TYPE));                   4
            INSERT CURRENT IN (APPROACH);                        5
            HOLD;                                                6
            TAKE (APPROACH_TIME (TYPE,RUNWAY));                  7
            TAKE (LANDING_TIME (TYPE));                          8
            TERMINATE;                                           9
            END;                                                10
```

Statement 1 indicates that the following statements describe the behavior of the aircraft process. The fact that aircraft orbit in a stack waiting for permission to land is modeled by statement 2, which puts the current aircraft process last in the list called STACK. Statement 3 suspends further execution of statements until told to resume by the air-traffic controller process. On resumption, it descends to lower altitude, and statement 4 suspends execution of the process until the simulated descent time, a function of HEIGHT and aircraft TYPE, has elasped. At statement 5, the aircraft joins the end of the queue of aircraft waiting to make their final approach, and at statement 6 it waits for permission to land. When the controller process gives landing permission at statement 7, the aircraft descends, and lands on the runway specified, statement 8. After landing, the aircraft is removed from the model, statement 9, and the description of aircraft behavior ends with statement 10. Each statement HOLD and TAKE represents an interaction point.

A process may possess attributes specified by a PL/I DECLARE statement to attach descriptive variables to every occurrence of a process. The following declaration could be used to define attributes of height, type, runway, and passengers for each new aircraft entering the model. Statements appearing between the symbols /* and */ are PL/I comments.

```
DECLARE  1  AIRCRAFT PROCESS,
         2  HEIGHT BINARY FLOAT, /*REAL*/
         2  (TYPE, RUNWAY, PASSENGERS) BINARY FIXED;
                                              /*INTEGERS*/
```

It is also possible to introduce new aircraft into the model, with attribute values specified at creation time, by using another process which describes how aircraft arrive:

```
ARRIVALS: BEHAVIOR;
TAKE (NEGEXP(1,2)); /*TIME BETWEEN ARRIVALS*/
  /*SAMPLED FROM NEGATIVE EXPONENTIAL DISTRIBUTION*/
  /*WITH MEAN 2, USING RANDOM NUMBER STREAM 1*/
START AIRCRAFT INITIALLY DO;
  /*VALUES OF PROCESS AIRCRAFT ATTRIBUTES ARE ASSIGNED*/
HEIGHT = RANDFS (2,30000,70000);
  /*UNIFORMLY DISTRIBUTED IN THE*/
  /*INTERVAL 30000-70000*/
  /*USING RANDOM NUMBER STREAM 2*/
TYPE=RANDIS (1,1,10);
  /*RANDOM CHOICE OF TYPE FROM 1-10*/
PASSENGERS=FUNCTION (TYPE);
  /*USER DEFINED FUNCTION*/
END;
END ARRIVALS;
```

Note that:

1. No TERMINATE appears at the end of this behavior. After each creation it will cycle back to its first executable statement (TAKE (NEGEXP (1,2));) and introduce a new aircraft into the system, with the specified interarrival time distribution.

2. The name ARRIVALS is declared as the name of a process in the following statement, placed at the beginning of the model:

DECLARE ARRIVALS PROCESS;

The air-traffic controllers who examine the queues of waiting aircraft (STACK and APPROACH) and decide the landing order and runways for aircraft are also represented by processes. The INSERT statements in the AIRCRAFT process routine above will put the latest aircraft last in the lists STACK and APPROACH. The controllers' behavior will contain such statements as:

NOTIFY FIRST (STACK)

to address the first aircraft in the stack and to remove this aircraft from the queue STACK.

REMOVE FIRST FROM (STACK)

The aircraft, which has been waiting since its behavior said HOLD, can now resume execution at its next statement:

TAKE

for its descent.

Individual processes can also be referenced by ordinary PL/I pointers, in which case the name of the pointer is considered to be the name of the process. An option on the START statement allows the user to set a pointer to the new process. For example:

START AIRCRAFT AFTER TIME(5) SET(P);
P —> HEIGHT = 40000;
P —> TYPE = 1;

By these statements, a new aircraft will be created at current simulation time + 5. The attributes of the aircraft with name P will be given values 40000 and 1, respectively.

Setting a pointer in this way allows processes to refer to the variables of other processes. Individual processes are manipulated, through process-handling statements, by giving the name of the individual process—that is, a pointer that points to it. For example, if the statement:

HOLD P UNTIL NOTIFIED (2);

is executed by another process in the model, the process AIRCRAFT with name P will not be activated until it has received two notifications of the form:

NOTIFY P;

E.2.2 Process-handling

Each process exists for a period of simulated time and its interaction with other processes reflects the way in which the components of the modeled system influence each other. The interaction of processes and their sequencing are controlled by process-handling statements which may:

Start/terminate specific processes (START, TERMINATE).

Resume the execution of an existing process at a specified simulated time (SCHEDULE).

Specify the amount of simulated time required for a process to accomplish the action specified in the next segment of its behavior (TAKE).

Interrupt an existing process and prevent further execution of its behavior until certain specified events have occurred (HOLD).

Notify processes that events have occurred (NOTIFY).

The user may also use advanced process-handling features such as control over certain conditions. For instance, by using an UPON statement one may specify an action to be taken when a certain type of change occurs in the model; for example:

UPON START (AIRCRAFT) PUT LIST ('NEW AIRCRAFT');

This statement says that every time a process of type AIRCRAFT is started anywhere in the model, the PUT LIST statement is executed and NEW AIRCRAFT is written.

E.2.3 The timing routine

The main tasks of the SIMPL/I Timing Routine are to maintain a simulated clock, schedule the execution of segments of the behavior of processes, and decide the actions to be taken when a process is interrupted. Execution of a process segment produces a change of state of the system, called an *event*.

The order in which SIMPL/I statements are executed must represent the events of the system modeled during a period of time; they are therefore not executed in the normal sequence of statements written in an ordinary programming language. For example, in the preceding process routine describing aircraft behavior, statement 5:

INSERT CURRENT IN APPROACH;

will not be executed immediately after statement 4:

TAKE (DESCENT_TIME (HEIGHT, TYPE));

but only after the elapse of the units of simulated time specified in the TAKE statement.

To organize sequencing, the timing routine uses some built-in attributes of the processes, such as:

TIME value, which represents the minimum time that must elapse before the process can execute its next behavior segment.

STATUS, which gives the current state of the process. A process may be in one of the following states: active, ready, scheduled, taking and holding.

BEHAVIOR, which points to the statement at which the process will resume execution when it next becomes active.

Depending upon its state, a process is in one of the timing routine's lists: active, ready, schedule, and hold list. These lists control the sequence in which processes are to be activated. During the course of simulation, processes are moved from one list to another either by the timing routine or as the result of a process-handling statement.

The active list normally contains only the CURRENT process. However, if a START, SCHEDULE, or RESCHEDULE statement without the TIME option forces immediate execution of another process, the new process enters the active list at the top to become the CURRENT process. The old process is pushed down to become the second process in the active list.

The ready list contains processes with TIME value zero which are not in holding state. Such processes are ready for activation at this simulated time. There are two ready lists, READY (0) and READY (1), which contain processes and clock processes, respectively. Clock processes are processes started with the AS CLOCKPROCESS option, and have characteristics which make them suitable for controlling the execution of a model.

The schedule list contains processes which cannot be activated until later.

The hold list contains all the processes interrupted by a HOLD statement, except for those which were held pending future activation as the result of a START, SCHEDULE, or RESCHEDULE with the TIME option, which remain in the schedule list.

To control the logic of the model, the timing routine also uses the system variables:

CLOCK, which represents the absolute simulated time in the model;

CURRENT, which points to the current process;

DT, which is the amount by which the timing routine last incremented CLOCK.

E.2.4 The entity attribute

During a simulation run it is often desirable to manipulate data items representing passive elements of a system which have no behavior. However, we may still wish to create a number of passive elements of a given type, and manipulate them in lists.

A passive element in SIMPL/I is called an ENTITY and is specified by a declaration such as:

$$\text{DECLARE} \quad 1 \quad \text{PASSENGER ENTITY,}$$
$$2 \quad \text{AGE BIN FIXED,}$$
$$2 \quad \text{NAME CHAR (12);}$$

The entity PASSENGER has two attributes: AGE (fixed binary) and NAME (12 characters long).

Entities are entered during a simulation run by the CREATE statement and deleted by the DESTROY statement. It is possible to refer to individual entities by using pointers:

$$\text{CREATE PASSENGER SET (P);}$$
$$P \longrightarrow \text{AGE} = 20;$$

The attribute AGE of the entity PASSENGER with name P is set to the value 20.

E.2.5 List-handling

Collections of elements can be represented in SIMPL/I by list structures, declared with the attribute LIST; for example:

$$\text{DECLARE QUEUE LIST;}$$

Lists may be declared as two-dimensional arrays:

DECLARE LIST1 (10,5) LIST;

A RANKED attribute may be specified, as in:

DECLARE WAIT LIST RANKED (AGE,A);

In a list declared as ranked, the elements are inserted in the specified order by the values of specified variables of the entities concerned. If a variable is followed by "A," ascending order is indicated; "D" denotes descending order. SIMPL/I lists may contain entities, processes, other lists, and classes as elements.

All entities or processes of a given type are grouped together in a special list called the *class list*. Processes and entities are automatically inserted in such lists when created and are automatically removed when destroyed.

List-handling statements are provided for:

Inserting elements anywhere in a list.

Removing first, last, or specific elements from a list.

Scanning a list: sequentially, by steps in specifying the increment and the direction, or as long as a condition is met.

Executing a set of statements for selected elements.

Marking a location in a list for later use.

For example, suppose that in the airport simulation model, aircraft of types 1, 2, and 3 can land on a short runway. Then, if only two short runways are available, the controller may scan the stack for two suitable aircraft:

SCAN PLANE = FIRST TO LAST IN (STACK);
FOR FIRST (2) WITH (PLANE $->$ TYPE $<= 3$);
    REMOVE MEMBER (PLANE) FROM (STACK);
    NOTIFY PLANE;
    END;
END;

Note that SIMPL/I lists have circular organization, so that if a list is scanned item by item, either forward or backward, the scan would wrap around completely to the first selected element and could cycle the list continuously.

E.2.6 Output

Standard output. When simulation terminates, a statistical report giving details of lists and class membership, status of each process in existence, and notifiers is produced automatically. A notifier is a variable which can be used to signal waiting processes whenever its value changes.

Standard output may also be obtained during simulation by using a SIMSNAP statement.

Optional output. By declaring data items PROCESS, ENTITY, NOTIFIER, and LIST with the STATS attribute, it is possible to gather time-dependent statistical information during the run and produce GPSS-like reports.

Histogram feature. The user may also collect observations during execution of the model by means of the HISTOGRAM feature of SIMPL/I. A histogram named WAIT, with fifty classes of width 2, starting at 10—which assumes that observations lie in the range 10 to 110—would be defined by the statement:

DECLARE WAIT (50) HISTOGRAM (2,10);

Values are entered into a histogram by means of the ENTER statement, where an expression (X) specifies the value of an observation:

ENTER OBSERVED (X) IN (WAIT);

A graph of a histogram can be obtained by naming the histogram in a PLOT statement:

PLOT WAIT;

The programmer may also use normal PL/I output statements.

E.2.7   SIMPL/I Library

SIMPL/I provides a wide variety of functions both for simulation and list-processing applications. This library consists of:

List-handling functions, such as

ITEMS: To determine the number of items in a list or a class.

VOID: To determine whether or not a list or class is empty.

Process-handling functions, such as

ACTIVE: To determine whether a process is in active state.

READY: To determine whether a process is in ready state.

Statistical functions.   Statistical functions include uniform, normal, exponential, gamma, Poisson, and Weibull distributions.

Histogram functions, such as

HMAX: To extract the maximum value entered in a histogram.

HSTDV: To determine the standard deviation of the values entered in a histogram.

E.3   Another Process-Oriented Approach: SIMULA 67

SIMULA 67 is a superset of ALGOL 60, so that it is really a general-purpose programming language, despite its name. The instructions have the form of ALGOL statements, and users should have some knowledge of this algorithmic language. The concept of system classes defines a set of characteristics of special interest in certain application areas. The system class SIMULATION provides the process concept and sequencing facilities of a simulation language, without losing the advantages of a powerful general-purpose language. The following summary is based on lectures given by Mr. J. P. Berney, at the Swiss Federal Institute of Technology in Lausanne. The emphasis is mainly on the simulation aspects of the language, with particular reference to the features of the class SIMULATION.

E.3.1   Algorithmic capability, input/output, and string handling

SIMULA 67 extends the block concept, which is the fundamental mechanism for decomposition in ALGOL 60, but, unlike ALGOL 60, SIMULA 67 provides input/output statements as a standard part of the language, and, to allow flexible string handling, character and text type variables are available with different handling procedures.

E.3.2   Manipulation of classes, prototypes, and objects

Class declaration or prototypes of objects.   The new and fundamental concept of SIMULA 67 is that of a class which allows the user to define a prototype of objects that may be created and destroyed during program execution. A class declaration defines (1) the structure, and (2) the operation rule of the objects belonging to that class.

The name of a class, declared within a program, may be used as a prefix to another class declaration, which is then called a *subclass*. This name may itself be used as prefix to another class. This technique defines a concatenation, or chaining, mechanism by which attributes, such as the variables and the procedures declared within a class, and the operation rule of the class named as prefix, are allocated to the newly created subclass. This mechanism increases the structure of a subclass by the static and dynamic structure of the classes to which it is concatenated. The operators *is* and *in* can be used to check whether or not an object belongs to a specified class or subclass.

The name of a class may also be used to prefix a block of a SIMULA 67 program. The characteristics of the named class are then part of the block. The two system-defined classes, SIMULATION and SIMSET, are used in this way.

Creation of an object.   A class declaration defines the prototype of the objects of that class. An expression of the form:

$$new \; \langle \; \text{class identifier} \; \rangle$$

creates an object of the specified class and the partial or complete execution of the statements contained in its operation rule. An object created by *new*. . . exists as long as there is a reference to that object within the program, even though its execution may have been temporarily or permanently suspended.

Ref variables.   A variable of type *ref* is essentially a pointer that denotes or refers to an object. The class of objects that may be referenced by a *ref* variable is contained in its declaration. SIMULA 67 checks the validity of the reference at compilation and execution time. For example, if a *ref* variable is declared to specify an object of class "dog," the compiler will check that this variable does not already point to an object of another, supposedly disjoint, class "rat."

Garbage collection. Every implementation of SIMULA 67 normally has a garbage collector with the routines that supervise the execution of the user's program. The garbage collector recovers the memory released by objects no longer referenced.

EXAMPLES:

Comment Class and subclass declaration;

class	animal (year of birth); *integer*
	year of birth;
begin	*if* year of birth $>$ 1972 *then*
	error;
	.
	.
	.
end	animal;
animal	*class* dog (master); *ref* (man) master;
begin	
	.
	.
	.
end	dog;
class	man;
begin	*ref* (dog) mydog;
	.
	.
	.
end	man;

Comment Declarations of ref variables;

                    ref (dog) FIDO;
                    ref (man) PETER;

Comment Creation;

            PETER: — *new* man;
            FIDO: — *new* dog (1971, PETER);

E.3.3 Behavior of objects and interactions between objects

Quasi-parallel sequencing. With the statement:

            X: — *new* $\langle$ class identifier $\rangle$

the operation rule of the object X just created will be executed until either a final *end* or a first "detach" statement is reached. A detach statement suspends execution of the statements that compose the operation rule of an object and puts this object in a detached state.

The execution of a detached object X will be resumed when another object, say Y, calls the procedure:

$$\text{resume} \langle \text{ detached object } \rangle$$

If in its turn the object X calls a procedure:

$$\text{resume (Y)}$$

the execution of X is suspended and the control is given to object Y.

Control is transferred from one object to another by the above mechanism; this is known as *quasi-parallelism* of the execution of the operation rules of different objects.

Each object possesses a "local sequence counter," which reactivates it from the point at which it was suspended. This process is independent of simulated time; we shall see later that the system class SIMULATION uses this mechanism to organize the time-dependent sequencing of the events of a simulated system.

Remote accessing and connection.   The resume statement gave one possibility for interaction between objects. The concepts of "remote accessing" and "connection" illustrate another type of interaction which can give access to attributes of an object from a point outside the domain of that object.

Remote accessing or dot notation.   The attribute "year of birth" of FIDO given in the declaration example will be obtained from an object other than FIDO by:

$$\text{FIDO.year of birth}$$

It is also possible to declare that FIDO belongs to PETER by writing:

$$\text{PETER.mydog: } - \text{ FIDO}$$

Connection.   The statement:

$$\textit{inspect} \langle \text{ object } \rangle$$

provides the capability of remaining temporarily in the inspected object, and to have access to its attributes, without having to specify that they are the attributes of the inspected object.

For example, within an operation rule of an object, one could have the following segment of program:

```
              inspect FIDO do
                          begin
'connection block'   year of birth
                   = year of birth + 1;
                          .
                          .
                          .
              end connection FIDO;
```

E.3.4 Manipulation of sets of objects

The system class SIMSET. The class SIMSET provides facilities for list processing or manipulation of sets of objects. As objects may belong to a set, two classes, "head" and "link", are defined by SIMSET:

Class head: for objects owning sets.

Class link: for objects which may become members of sets.

Procedures declared as attributes of the class link permit manipulation of members of sets individually: to insert an object into a set in a given position; to remove an object from a set; to determine the predecessor and/or the successor of an object in a set; and so on.

Procedures declared as attributes of the class head permit more global inspection of the sets—for example: to test if a set is empty; to count the number of members of a set; and to remove all members from a set. The elements within a set may be ordered FIFO, LIFO, or according to the value of a given attribute. The list-processing facilities of SIMULA 67 are very general and flexible. Each object may have variables referring to objects belonging to both classes head and link as an attribute, so very complex structures may be represented.

EXAMPLES:

> *ref* (head) doghouse;
> link *class* dog *begin*
>
> .
>
> .
>
> .
>
> *end*;
> *ref* (dog) FIDO, ROVER;

Comment Put FIDO into the doghouse (as last member);

> FIDO.into (doghouse);

Comment Put ROVER into the doghouse before FIDO;

> ROVER.precede (FIDO);

Comment Determine the number of dogs in doghouse, if more than one, remove the first one;

> *if* doghouse.cardinal $>$ 1 *then* doghouse.first.out;

E.3.5 Simulation-oriented features

The system class SIMULATION. The facilities needed to simulate the behavior of a system over a period of time are provided in SIMULA 67 by the class SIMULATION. This is achieved with the following features:

Two types of special objects: *event notice* and *process*. An event notice has two attributes: a reference to the process it represents and the time of its next scheduled event. The event notices are ranked chronologically in a *sequencing set* (SQS), according to the value of their time attribute.

The object MAIN, which is the user's main program of the simulation model, that is, the block prefixed by SIMULATION, and which is used as a permanent component of the quasi-parallel operations of the sequencing procedures.

A set of scheduling procedures that organize the quasi-parallel operation of process objects and that result in manipulations of the SQS.

The class SIMULATION is a subclass of SIMSET, so the manipulation of sets of objects may be made as described in Section E.3.2.

Process objects and scheduling statements. Process objects, which belong to a class prefixed by "process" are used to represent the dynamic structure of a simulated system. A process object may be in one of four possible states: active, suspended, passive, and terminated. The time-dependent behavior of a system is simulated by sequences of "active phases" of process objects. Each active phase represents an event. The scheduling of the next active phase of a process takes place by generating an event notice which is inserted in the sequencing set.

The execution of a sequencing procedure statement by a process object results in the manipulation of an event notice in the SQS.

A process may suspend its execution for a specified time with the statement "hold T."

The statement "passivate" will suspend the active phase of the current active process until it is reactivated by another process.

A process may activate or reactivate another process immediately or after a certain delay, with or without priority, before or after execution of a specified process.

Event notices and sequencing set. The sequencing set of SIMULA 67 represents the simulated time axis. Neither the SQS nor its members, the event notices, are directly accessible to the user, but the scheduling statements of the process objects described above result in event-notice creation, insertion, and extraction from the SQS.

The attribute EVTIME of the event notice, which specifies the time at which the event will take place, is used to rank event notices chronologically in the SQS. When events are scheduled to occur simultaneously, their corresponding event notices appear in arrival order in the SQS, subject to priority.

As in most current simulation languages, simulated time is incremented discretely and remains constant during the execution of an event.

When an event is executed, its event notice is removed; therefore, the SQS contains only the event notice of the current event and event notices of scheduled future events.

EXAMPLES:

(1) Set variable t equal to the value of the current simulated time:

t:= time;

(2) Schedule the next active phase of FIDO just before the next active phase of ROVER:

activate FIDO *before* ROVER;

(3) Schedule the next active phase of the first dog in the doghouse, if any, after the current event:

if ¬ doghouse.empty *then activate* doghouse.first *after* current;

(4) Specify passage of 10 units of simulated time:

hold (10);

(5) Suspend the activity of this process without a predetermined schedule for reactivation:

passivate;

(6) Cancel the next active phase of the master of FIDO:

cancel (FIDO.master);

(7) Reschedule the next active phase of FIDO to occur in 10.5 units of simulated time:

reactivate FIDO *delay* 10.5;

(8) Create a new dog to become active at time 20.6, with priority over all other events which might be scheduled at the same time:

activate new dog *at* 20.6 *prior*;

(9) Put the time interval between the actual time and the next event into variable t:

t: = nextev.evtime − time;

This functional account is limited to a description of concepts. In an actual implementation, the compiler writer would try to optimize the time taken to access the members of the SQS.

E.3.6 Miscellaneous features

Pseudo-random numbers. SIMULA 67 provides 10 random number procedures for drawing samples from probability distributions, including uniform, exponential, normal, Poisson, and Erlang.

Collection of statistics. There is no automatic collection of statistics in SIMULA 67 although the procedure "accum" is provided to accumulate the simulated time integral of a variable. The user will usually define any required statistical algorithms in the base language, ALGOL 60.

References

E.1. G. GORDON, "A General Purpose Simulation Program," pp. 87–104 in *Proceedings of the EJCC, Washington D.C.*, New York: The Macmillan Company, 1961.

E.2. H. M. MARKOWITZ, B. HAUSNER, and H. W. CARR, *SIMSCRIPT—A Simulation Programming Language*. Englewood Cliffs, N.J.: Prentice-Hall, Inc., 1963.

E.3. P. J. KIVIAT, R. VILLANUEVA, and H. M. MARKOWITZ, *The SIMSCRIPT II, Programming Language*. Englewood Cliffs, N.J.: Prentice-Hall, Inc., 1968.

E.4. O. J. DAHL, and K. NYGAARD, "SIMULA—An ALGOL-Based Simulation Language," *Communications of the Association for Computing Machinery*, Vol. 9, Sept. 1966.

E.5. O. J. DAHL, and K. NYGAARD, "*SIMULA—A Language for Programming and Description of Discrete Event Systems: Introduction and User's Manual*," Norwegian Computing Center, Oslo, 5th ed., 1967.

E.6. O. J. DAHL, B. MYHRHAUG, and K. NYGAARD, *SIMULA 67 Common Base Language*, Publication No. S-2, Norwegian Computing Center, Oslo, 1968.

E.7. *SIMPL/I: General Information Manual*, GH19-5035, International Business Machines Corporation.

E.8. IBM United Kingdom Ltd. Data Center, *Control and Simulation Language: User's Manual*, London, 1966.

E.9. P. J. KIVIAT, *GASP—A General Activity Simulation Program*, Project 90.17–019(2), Applied Research Laboratory, United States Steel Corporation, Monroeville, Pa., 1963.

E.10. A. A. B. PRITSKER, and P. J. KIVIAT, *Simulation with GASP II, a FORTRAN-Based Simulation Language*. Englewood Cliffs, N.J.: Prentice-Hall, Inc., 1969.

E.11. K. D. TOCHER, "Simulation Languages," pp. 72–113 in *Progress in Operations Research*, Vol. 3, *Relationship Between Operations Research and the Computer*, J. S. Aronofsky, ed., Wiley, New York, 1969.

E.12. K. D. TOCHER, "Review of Simulation Languages," *Operational Research Quarterly*, Vol. 16, No. 2, pp. 189–218, 1965.

E.13. H. S. KRASNOW, "Simulation Languages," pp. 320–346 in *The Design of Computer Simulation Experiments*, T. H. Naylor, ed., Duke University Press, Durham, N.C., 1969.

E.14. P. J. KIVIAT, *Digital Computer Simulation, Computer Programming Languages*, RM/5883-PR, Rand Corporation, Santa Monica, Calif., 1969.

E.15. F. P. WYMAN, *Simulation Modeling, a Guide to Using SIMSCRIPT*. New York: John Wiley & Sons, Inc., 1970.

E.16. G. P. BLUNDEN, and H. S. KRASNOW, "The Process Concept as a Basis of Simulation Modeling," 28th National Meeting of the ORSA, Houston, Tex., II/65.

E.17. *SIMPL/I: Program Reference Manual*, SH19-5060, International Business Machines Corporation.

Index

A

Absolute clock time, GPSS V attribute, 72, 197
Abstract models, 7
ACM, 401
Accuracy, of simulation, 14
ADVANCE block, 2, 48, 50, 60
  use of, 78
ADVANCE 1 block, avoiding insertion in a
  control loop, 399
Aerospace, uses of GPSS in, 401
ALGOL 60, (*See also* SIMULA 67), 475, 476,
  481
ALL, TRANSFER mode, 86, 157
ALTER block, 47, 51, 157, 174
  use of, 178-79
Alternate exit address, 89
Alternate exit mode, 87, 159
Analysis, of system data, 34-35
Antithetic variates, 408-10
Arguments, tabulation of, 183
Arithmetic variables, 93
Arrival rates:
  in subway problem, 297
  tabulation of, 182
Artificial data, 10
ASSEMBLE block, 49, 51, 61
  use of, 141-42, 143 (*fig.*)

Assembler language, 2
  HELP routines, 236
    ADDCUR routine, purpose, 236
    ADDFUT routine, purpose, 236
    ADDINT routine, purpose, 236
    SUBCUR routine, purpose, 236
    SUBFUT routine, purpose, 236
    SUBINT routine, purpose, 236
Assembly control statements, GPSS language,
  198-200
Assembly line problem, GPSS language, 201–04
Assembly set, definition, 48
ASSIGN block, 50
  use of, 78-79, 174
Attributes:
  access to and handling of, 50, 78-80, 144-45,
    240
  and indirect addressing, 103
  as model feature, 35-36
  definition, 16
  GPSS examples, 45
  GPSS language, 193-97
  GPSS subset, 98-101
Autocorrelation effects, 15
Automatic warehouse simulation, 259-91
  bin assignment, in warehouse problem, 262-63
  bins, in warehouse problem, 259
  conclusions, 290-91

Automatic warehouse simulation *(cont.)*:
  buffers, 261-62, 265
  conclusions, 290-91
  conveyor, 260, 264, 265
    utilization of, 288-89 *(fig.)*
  corridors, 259, 263
  cranes, 261-62, 264, 265
    speed and movement problems with, 288-89
  description of warehouse and operations,
    259-63
  experiments and results, 278, 287-90
  GPSS model, 264-78
  pallets, 259, 263, 265
    movement of, 269 *(fig.)*
  problem, 263-64
  zones, 262-63, 268 *(fig.)*
    allocation choices, 278, 287
AUXILIARY feature, use of, 139
Averages, computation of, 68

B

Banking system design, problem, 32
Barbershop problem:
  arrival-time distributions, 22-24
  coding and operation of, 61-64
  manual simulation, 22-24
  model elements, 21-22
  service-time distributions, 22-24
  simulation concepts used, 24-25
Batching GPSS jobs, 138
Berney, J.P., 476
Blockage at GENERATE, as error, 392
Block attributes, 72, 98-99
Block-definition statements:
  GPSS language, 139-90
  GPSS subset, 75-92
Block-departure time (BDT), 45, 48, 49, 59-60
Block-diagram structure, 1-2
Block diagrams:
  advantages of GPSS, 385
  barbershop, 26 *(fig.)*, 28 *(fig.)*, 29 *(fig.)*
  input pallets, warehouse problem, 271-72
    (fig.)
  inventory control program, 245 *(fig.)*
  machine repair model, 114 *(fig.)*
  as programming aid, 36
  simple factory model, 209-11 *(fig.)*
  simulation study organization, 12 *(fig.)*, 42
    (fig.)
  teleprocessing system, 114 *(fig.)*, 122 *(fig.)*
  traffic lights model, 105 *(fig.)*, 108 *(fig.)*
"Blocking periods," 406

Block-oriented languages, 1-2
Block statement formats, GPSS V, 424-41
Block statistics, debugging checks on, 251-52
Blocks:
  able to refuse entry to transactions, 389-90
  avoid writing useless, 398
  definition, 43
  extended and new in GPSS V, 454
  functional aspects, 388-89
  GPSS, 49-52, 71-72, 424-41
  setting status flag of current-events chain, 391
  specified number of units, 390
  specified time delay, 390
  various ways to look at GPSS, 388-91, 398
Boolean operators, 191
Boolean variable, definition statement, 191-92
Boolean variables, 2, 46, 93, 171
  in job shop problem, 345
BOTH, TRANSFER mode, 157
  use of, 86
Branching control, 50-51
BUFFER block, *(See also* PRIORITY), 157
  use of, 163-65
Byte parameter, 77

C

Catalogue procedure, definition, 419
Central Limit Theorem, 404–05
CHANGE block, 186
Chemical industry, and uses of GPSS, 401
Chi-square test, 403-04
Class list, in SIMPL/I, 474
Classes, manipulation of in SIMULA 67, 476
CLEAR statement, 52
  use of, 74-75
CLEAR/INITIAL statements, improper use of,
  394-95
Clearance of accumulated statistics, as control
  statement, 75
Clearance of model, as control statement, 74-75
Clock mechanism:
  importance of, 58
  as simulation concept, 24
Clock updating, as phase of scanning, 214, 215
  (fig.)
Cold start, definition, 32
Communication, as factor in organizing study,
  41
Compile-time diagnostics, examples, 246
Computational entities, GPSS language, 195
Computer and communication systems, uses of
  GPSS in, 401

Computer programming, as stage in simulation, 16-17

Computer time, definition, 58

Conditional operators, GPSS language, 191

Confidence intervals, 41, 240, 245

Confidence limits, mechanic and McKay method, 242, 245, 406-07, 408

Congruential method, for generating random numbers, 458-60

Connection, in SIMULA 67, 478

Constant (permanent) elements, in model, 21

Continuous function (C type), 94

Control, as characteristic of simulation language, 16

Control of run, *(See also* START), 73-74

Control program:
  rationale, 58-61
  requirements, 58
  response time, 354

Control statements:
  GPSS language, 134-39
  GPSS subset, 70-75
  GPSS V formats, 442-46

Copy transactions in SPLIT block, 139-41

Correlation coefficients, estimation of, 407-08

COUNT block, use of, 153-55

Creation limit of GENERATE, 76

CSL, 465, 466

Current block number, 45, 49

Current-events chain, 48-49, 59

Current-events chain scan, 214-15, 216 *(fig.)*

D

Data collection, 34-35

DD statements, function of, 419-20

Debugging:
  advantages of GPSS, 385
  anticipation of results, 250
  checking generated distributions, 250
  division into modules, 246
  as factor in choice of simulation language, 37
  future developments, 414-15
  glancing at results, 251-52
  and modeling strategy in subway problem, 326-27
  short runs, 250-51
  use of diagnostics, 246-49
  use of PRINT block, 253-54
  use of SAVEVALUE block, 254-56
  use of status printout, 253
  use of TRACE feature, 256-57

Decision rules, 36
  of the model, definition, 30

Delay chain, 216

DEPART block, 47, 49
  use of, 84-85

Deterministic processes, definition, 8-10

Diagnostics, use of in debugging, 246-49

Die throwing for generating random numbers, 456

Direct experimentation, advantages of simulation over, 34

Directly measurable variables, 34

Discrete attribute valued functions (D type), 94

Discrete attribute valued functions (E type), 192

Discrete-event simulation models:
  barbershop, 22-24
  considerations of, 54-58

Discrete functions, 94

Doctor's telephone, introductory model building problem, 18-19

Documentation *(See* Programming)

Dynamic aspect, of modeling, 56-58

Dynamic behavior, of simulation model, 30

Dynamic operations, GPSS, 49-50

E

EJECT statement, 221
  service of, 228

Electronic computing *(See also* Simulation)
  brief historical summary, 416

End of job, as control statement, 74

END statement, 52
  use of, 74

ENDGRAPH statement, 221
  service of, 232

Endogenous variables, 26, 33-34

ENTER block, use of, 82-83

ENTER/LEAVE blocks, 47, 49, 50

Entities:
  avoiding recalculation of same, 398
  clear definition of, 387
  definition, 16
  as model feature, 35-36
  reallocation of, 135
  usual way of specifying, 101

Entity attribute, SIMPL/I, 473

Entity-definition statements:
  GPSS language, 190-93
  GPSS subset, 92-98

Entity function (S type), GPSS language, 193

Entity types, REPORT program, 224, 225, 226, 227 (T), 229

Equipment-oriented blocks:
   GPSS language, 147-56
   GPSS subset, 80-85
Equivalence (EQU) statement:
   use of, 198-99
   in warehouse problem, 270
Error-checking features, of language, 37-38
Errors:
   classical, in GPSS, 391-98
   as model problem, 14
Event notices, SIMULA 67, 480-81
Events:
   ability of simulation language to handle, 16
   GPSS, 48-49
EXAMINE block, 47, 51, 157, 174
   use of, 176-77
EXEC card, 135
EXECUTE block, 186-87
Execution-time diagnostics, examples, 247-49
Exogenous variables, 26, 33-34
Expense, of simulation, 14
EXPON function, for exponential distributions,
   96-97
Exponential distribution, 475
   random variates, 462 *(fig.)*

F

Facilities:
   availability and unavailability, GPSS V,
      187-90
   blocks to modify status of, 80-82
   standard logical attributes, 196
   in teleprocessing system problem, 360, 381 (T)
   X-Mnemonics, 88, 189
Facilities attribute, 100, 101, 194
Facilities blocks, 147-52
FACILITY entity, 44, 46
Facility statistics, 68
   debugging checks on, 252
Facility utilization, computation of, 68
Factor analysis, 410
FAVAIL block, use of, 189-90
FAVAIL/FUNAVAIL blocks, 46, 51
Features, new: GPSS/360 to GPSS V, 453-54
First-in First-out queueing disciplines (FIFO),
      169, 170, 174
   assembly line problem, 201
   barbershop, 22
   job shop problem, 329
   maintenance of, 57
   SIMULA 67, 479
   subway problem, 325

FIFO *(cont.)*:
   teleprocessing system problem, 382
   warehouse problem, 262, 263
Fixed-increment clock, definition, 24
Floating-point parameter, 77
Floating-point variables, 93
Flowcharts:
   barbershop problem, 20 *(fig.)*
   as programming aid, 36
   subway problem, 305 *(fig.)*, 307-08 *(fig.)*, 311
      (fig.), 312 *(fig.)*, 313 *(fig.)*, 314 *(fig.)*, 315
      (fig.)
   warehouse problem, 268, 269 *(fig.)*
FORMAT statement, 221
   service of, 225-27
FORTRAN, 2, 36, 245, 386, 401, 465, 466, 468
   reference information of HELPC routines
      coded in, 241 (T)
FORTRAN subroutines, 220, 232
   access to attributes, 240
   HELP blocks, coding of, 237-40
   use of BATCH1 and CONFID, 242-45
Four-disk system, programming example, 129-33
   rotational delay, 132
   seek time, 129
Free-form coding, 2, 453
Frequency classes, avoiding surplus of, 399
Fullword parameter, 77
FUNAVAIL block, 157
   use of, 188-89
Function-definition statements, 94-97
   GPSS language, 192-93
Function entity, 72, 100
Function modifier, 78, 79
Function number, illegal, as error, 393-94
Function selection mode (FN), TRANSFER
      mode, 158
FUNCTION statement, use of, 94-97
Functions, 46
   in job shop problem, 344
   SIMPL/I, 475
   in subway problem, 302-03
   in teleprocessing system problem, 362-63
   types of, 94, 95 *(fig.)*
   in warehouse problem, 266-67, 270, 276
Future-events chain, 48-49, 59

G

Garbage in-Garbage out (GIGO), 35
GASP, 465
GATE blocks, 46, 47, 50, 51, 156
   use of, 87-90, 159-62

GATHER block, 51, 60
  use of, 147
General purpose language, characteristics of, 36
General Purpose Simulation System, 2
General Purpose System Simulator *(See also GPSS)*, 1
GENERATE block, 44, 45, 48, 49
  blockage at, 392
  use of, 75-77
Generated distributions, check on as debugging device, 250
Gordon, Geoffrey, 1, 465
"Gordon Simulator" *(See* General Purpose System Simulator)
GPSS, 36, 37, 465, 466
  basic concepts:
    blocks, 49-52
    computer simulation, 52-53
    events, 48-49
    implementation level, 45-46
    logical level, 43-45
    model development, 52
    model representation, 44 *(fig.)*
    permanent entities, 46-47
    temporary entities, 48
  case for, 384-86
  classical errors, 391-98
  data sets required to execute, 419-20
  debugging programs, 245-58
  general appraisal, 384-401
  HELP block, 232-45
  practical hints for modeling and programming, 386-91
  procedure to execute, 420-22
  program efficiency, 398-400
  REPORT program, 220-32
  when to use, 400-401
GPSS Control program, re-examination of, 214-19
GPSS V, 16, 43, 46, 47, 51, 401, 416
  additional statements, 138-39
  attributes, 193
  block statement formats, 424-41
  and CLEAR statement, 74-75
  and copy transactions, 140
  design of, 2
  entity types, 225
  extensions to GPSS/360, 453-55
  facilities and storages, 88
    attributes, 197
    availability and unavailability, 187-90
  FORMAT entries, 226
  and GENERATE block, 77

GPSS V *(cont.)*:
  HELP routines—FORTRAN and PL/I, 236-40
  hints for program efficiency, 400
  indirect addressing capabilities, 103
  matrices in, 97, 100
  modes and mnemonics for save locations and matrices, 222
  parameter types, 79
  and PREEMPT statement, 152
  printing of savevalues, 184
  REMOVE, SCAN and ALTER instructions in, 179
  run time feature, 387
  save locations in, 97, 100
  savevalues, 91
  subway transit system simulation, 392–427
  summary of components, 423-52
  system attributes, 197
  use of PRINT block, 184, 253
GPSS language:
  assembly control statements, 198-200
  assembly line program, 201-04
  attributes, 193-98
  block-definition statements, 139-90
  control statements, 134-39
  design of, 1
  entity-definition statements, 190-93
  programming examples, 201-14
  re-examination of control program, 214-19
GPSS programs:
  assembly line, 202 *(fig.)*, 203 *(fig,)*
  debugging, 245-58
  four-disk system, 131 *(fig.)*
  inventory control, 206 *(fig.)*
  machine repair model, 115 *(fig.)*
  simple factory model, 213 *(fig.)*
  subway system model, 316-21 *(fig.)*
  teleprocessing system problem, 369-80 *(fig.)*
  TP program, 121 *(fig.)*, 124-25 *(fig.)*
  traffic lights, 109 *(fig.)*
  warehouse model, 273-76 *(fig.)*
GPSS subset:
  attributes, 98-101
  block-definition statements, 75-92
  control statements, 70-75
  entity-definition statements, 92-98
  and full language, 71-72 (T)
  indirect addressing, 101-03
  programming examples, 103-33
GPSS II, design of, 2
GPSS III, design of, 2

GPSS/360, 36
    design of, 2
    and indirect addressing, 103
GRAPH statement, 221
    service of, 229-30
Group attributes, 195
GROUP entity, 47
    GPSS language, 174-79
    in job shop problem, 332

H

Halfword parameter, 77
    in job shop problem, 343
HELP block, 2, 186, 232-45
    assembler language, 236
    GPSS V routines—FORTRAN and PL/I,
        236-40
    HELPC block and statistical evaluation of
        simulation results, 240-45
Histogram feature, SIMPL/I, 475
Historical data, 10

I

IBM computers, 1
IBM Corporation, 419, 422, 423, 465
IBM European Systems Research Institute, 292
IEEE, 401
Implementation level, GPSS, 45-46
Inactive transaction, 215
INCLUDE statement, 221
    service of, 222-25
INDEX block, 144-45
Indexing constant, 86
Indirect addressing:
    definition, 52
    extensions of, 455
    GPSS subset, 101–03
    teleprocessing system, 118, 121
    traffic lights program, 111, 112 (fig.)
Indirectly measurable variables, 34
Industrial systems, and uses of GPSS, 401
Information, accumulation and printing of in
        GPSS, 179-86
INITIAL statement, use of, 97-98
Initialization interval, 76
Initialization of random-number generators,
        134-35
Input-data analysis, 403-04
Input/output, SIMULA 67, 476
Institute for Transportation Sciences, École
        Polytechnique Fédérale
        de Lausanne (ITEP), 292

Interaction point, in SIMPL/I, 469
Interarrival times, tabulation of, 182
Intergeneration time, mean of, 392-93
Internal number, 45
Inventory control problem, GPSS language,
        204–07

J

Job, definition, 328
Job-creation submodel, 333, 338-40 (fig.), 345
Job due date, job shop problem, 329
Job-processing submodel, 333, 336-37 (fig.), 345
Job-scheduling submodel, 332-33, 345
Job shop, definition, 328
    job slack, 329
    model requirements, 330
    numerical characteristics, 330-32
    priority, 329
    processing time, 329
    scheduling, 328-29
    screening criteria, 333, 334-35 (fig.)
    system characteristics, 329
Job shop simulation, 328–50
    conclusions, 349–50
    experiments and results, 346-9
    GPSS model, 332–46
JOB statement, use of, 138
JOBTAPE block, 44, 45
    use of, 141
Jobtapes, rewinding, 138
JOIN block, 47
    use of, 174-75
JOIN/REMOVE block, 50

K

Katzke, J., 414
Known situations, simulation of, 38-39
Kolmogorov-Smirnov test, 403

L

Label, definition, 43
Language, capability of simulation, 16
Last in-First out (LIFO) order, 148, 170
    SIMULA 67, 479
LEAVE block, use of, 82-83
LINK block, 47, 51, 60
Link indicator, definition, 169
LINK/UNLINK blocks, 157
    use of, 168-73
List attribute valued functions (M type), 94, 193

List functions (L type), 94
List-handling, SIMPL/I, 473-74
LOAD feature, use of, 138-39
Logical attributes, GPSS language, 191
LOGIC block, 47, 50
    use of, 152-53
Logic switch, standard logical attributes, 196-97
Logic switch entity, definition, 47
Logic switch status, 50
LOOP block, 51
    use of, 162-63
Loops, 162-63

M

Machine repair, programming example, 113-16
MACRO facility statement, use of, 199-200
Management game, as simulation model, 11
Managerial and social sciences, uses of GPSS in,
    401
Manpower planning, uses of GPSS in, 401
Manual simulation, barbershop problem, 22-24
Manufacturing and material handling, uses of
    GPSS in, 401
MARK attribute, 45
MARK block, 50
    use of, 144
Mark time, definition, 144
Markowitz, H.M., 465
MATCH block, 51, 60, 145
    use of, 145-46
Matching status, X-Mnemonics for, 160-62
Mathematical analysis:
    and model validation, 39
    as technique, 7
MATRIX statement, 97
    use of, 97
Maximum queue length, computation of, 69
Mean intergeneration time, 76
Mean time, 78
Measurable variables, 34
Mechanic and McKay procedure for confidence
    limits, 242, 245, 406-07, 408
Mid-product technique, for generating random
    numbers, 458
Mid-square technique, for generating random
    numbers, 457-58
Mnemonics, for TITLE statement label field,
    222
Model building:
    barbershop problem, 20-22
        manual simulation, 22-24
        presentation of, 25-30

Model Building (cont.):
    barbershop problem (cont.):
        simulation concepts, 24-25
    doctor's telephone problem, 18-19
Model validation, points to consider, 38-39
Modeling (See also Simulation)
    definition, 4
Modeling concepts:
    dynamic aspect, 56-58
    static aspect, 55
Models:
    abstract, 7
    decision rules of, 30
    defining structure of, 35-36
    definition, 5-6
        as step in simulation study, 35-36
    deterministic and stochastic processes, 8-10
    diagrammatic concept, 5 (fig.)
    physical, 6-7
    presentation of, factors to consider, 25-30
    structure of, 30
    use of, 7-8
    value of, 10-11
Modules, division of programs into, 246
Monte Carlo Method, 8-9, 10
MSAVEVALUE blocks, 50
    use of, 91-92
    use of as debugging device, 254-56
Multidropping, in teleprocessing system
    problem, 357
Multiple comparison techniques, 410
Multiplying function modifier, 76

N

Negative correlation, 408
Next block address (NBA), 45, 49, 60
Normal distribution, 475
Norwegian Computing Center, 465
Numerical data:
    job shop problem, 330-32
    subway problem, 295-98, 303-04
    teleprocessing system problem, 355-56
    warehouse problem, 267-68
Numeric mode, of group operation, 174
Numerics, as error, 393

O

Objects, manipulation of in SIMULA 67, 476,
    479
Offset time, as operand, 141
Operands, in GPSS subset, 75-92

Operation, ease of, as requirement of simulation language, 17
Optimal strategy:
   as aim, 9
   limitation of simulation for finding, 14-15
   problems involved in, 39-41
ORIGIN statement, 221
   service of, 230
Output, in SIMPL/I, 474-75
Output editor, 2, 138
   statements available in, 221
OUTPUT statement, 221
   service of, 222
Output variables, statistical analysis of, 38
Overflow, definition, 180

P

Parameter number:
   illegal, as error, 393
   as operand, 79
Parameter (P), TRANSFER mode, 158
Parameters (See also Variables), 40-41
   importance of specifying numbers and types, 399
   increased number of, 455
   in job shop problem, 340, 343-44
   numbers and types of, 77
   in subway problem, 299-300
   in teleprocessing system problem, 361
   in warehouse problem, 265-66
PARM argument, 135
Permanent entities, 55
   counting and scanning of, 153-56
   GPSS, 46-47
Physical device method, for generating random numbers, 456
Physical models, 6-7
PICK, TRANSFER mode, 158
Planned delays, 50
PL/I, 2, 245, 386, 401, 465, 468, 470
PL/I subroutines, 220, 232
   HELP blocks, modes, 240
Poisson arrivals, 129
Poisson distribution assumption, 35, 96-97, 475
Potentially active transaction, 215
PREEMPT block, priority mode, 81
   use of, 80-81
PREEMPT/RETURN blocks, 46, 49, 50, 51
   use of, 147-52
PRINT block, 51, 52, 179
   use of, 183-84
   use of as debugging device, 253-54
Print-suppression field, 73

PRIORITY block, 50
   and debugging, 258
   use of, 79-80
PRIORITY block with BUFFER option, 80, 157
   and debugging, 258
   use of, 165-67
Priority level, 76
Problem formulation, as step in simulation study, 31-33
Process concept and handling, SIMPL/I, 469-72
Process objects, SIMULA 67, 480
Processing time function, for teleprocessing system, 123 (fig.)
Programming (See also Simulation)
   examples: GPSS language, 201-14
   languages, choice of, 36-38
   as step in simulation study, 36-38
Prototypes, manipulation of in SIMULA 67, 476
Pseudo-random numbers, 9, 405, 457
   SIMULA 67, 481

Q

QTABLE card, 64
Qualitative factors, methods for study of, 410
Qualitative variables, 34
Quantitative factors, methods for study of, 410
Quantitative variables, 34
Quasi-parallel sequencing, in SIMULA 67, 477-78
Queue attributes, 100, 194-95
QUEUE block, 47, 49
   use of, 83-85
QUEUE entity, 47
Queue handling, barbershop, 27, 28 (fig.), 29 (fig.), 30
Queue histograms, tabulation of, 183
Queue length, maximum, computation of, 69
Queue statistics, 68-69
   debugging checks on, 252
Queues:
   blocks used to modify status of, 83-85
   coding and operation of simple, 64-68
   general considerations, 3, 15
   in job shop problem, 332
   in teleprocessing system problem, 361, 381 (T)

R

Random number entity, 72, 100
Random numbers:
   error with, 397
   generation of, 456-60
   generators (RNs), 38, 46

Random numbers *(cont.)*:
  initialization of, 134-35
  seeds, 135
Random variables, 8-9
  ability of simulation language to handle, 16
Random variates:
  generation of, 460-64
  use of in model, 132-33
Ranking procedures, 410
Reactivation point, in SIMPL/I, 469
READ instructions, 136-37
Realism, of simulation, 14
Real time, definition, 58
Real-time data-base/data-communication system
        (*See* Teleprocessing system simulation)
REALLOCATE statement, 48
  use of, 135
Reallocation of entities, 135
Ref variables, in SIMULA 67, 477
Refusal mode, 87, 159
Regression techniques, 410
Reitman, J., 414
Relative transit times, tabulation of, 182-83
RELEASE block, use of, 80
Remote accessing, SIMULA 67, 478
REMOVE block, 47, 51, 157, 174
  use of, 175-76
Replication of run, 405
REPORT program:
  graphic output, 229-32
  statements available, 221
  statements format, 222-29
  in warehouse problem, 278, 279-86 *(fig.)*
REPORT statement, use of, 138
Request for simulation, as control statement, 70,
        73
RESET statement, 52, 75
Response surface methodology, 410
Results:
  accumulation and production of, 51-52
  anticipation of, 250
  constant checks on, 251-52
RETURN block, use of, 81-82
REWIND (jobtapes) statement, 138
Risk aversion, 34
RMULT card, 134-35
Run length feature, 453
Run termination count, 73
Run timer, 2, 73, 251, 453

S

SAVAIL block, use of, 190
SAVAIL/SUNAVAIL blocks, 47, 51

Save locations and matrices, 100
  in subway problem, 300-301
  in warehouse problem, 266
Save-matrix-definition statement, 97-98
SAVE/READ feature:
  data sets associated with, 453-54
  use of, 136-37
Saves, definition, 46
SAVEVALUE block, 46, 50
  use of, 90-92
  use of as debugging device, 254-56
Savevalue number, illegal, as error, 393
SAVEVALUE procedures, 90-92
  in teleprocessing system problem, 362
Saving and reading-in models, 136-37
SCAN block, 47, 51, 157, 174
  use of, 177-78
Scanning operation, main phases, 214-19
Scan-status indicator, 215
Scheduling statements, SIMULA 67, 480
SEIZE block, use of, 80
SEIZE/RELEASE blocks, 46, 49, 50
  use of, 147-52
SELECT block, 51, 157
  use of, 155-56
Self-locking system, 247, 248 *(fig.)*, 249
  avoidance of, 388
  as error, 393
Sensitivity analysis, and model validation, 39
Sequencing mechanism, as simulation concept,
        24-25
Sequencing set (SQS), SIMULA 67, 480-81
SHARE, 401
Short runs, ways to produce for debugging,
        250-51
Simple factory model problems, GPSS language,
        207-14
SIMPL/I, 385, 401, 465, 466
  simulation-oriented features and list-
        processing facilities, 468-75
SIMPL/I Library, 475
SIMSCRIPT, 385, 465, 466
SIMSCRIPT II, 465
  event-oriented simulation features, 466-68
SIMSET class, 479
SIMULA, 385, 465, 466
SIMULA 67, 467, 475-81
SIMULATE statement, use of, 70, 73
Simulated time, definition, 58
Simulation:
  advantages of GPSS, 385-86
  automatic warehouse, 259-91
  basic concepts, 11-13

Simulation *(cont.)*:
  comparisons of system responses, 410
  concepts used in barbershop model, 24-25
  current languages, 465-82
    SIMPL/I, 468-75
    SIMSCRIPT II, 466-68
    SIMULA 67, 475-81
  definitions, 4-6
  difficulties of organizing, 56
  future of, 413-16
  future programming, 414-15
  input-data analysis, 403-04
  job shop, 328-50
  languages, 16-17, 465-84
  limitations and problems of models, 14-15
  model types, 6-10
  planning experiments, 402-12
  statistical reliability, 404-10
  statistical tools, 402-03
  subway system, 292-327
  as technique, 8
  teleprocessing system, 351-83
  value of models, 10-11
SIMULATION class, in SIMULA 67, 479
Simulation Council, 401
Simulation languages (*See also* Programming
    languages)
  functions of, 16-17
Simulation model, improving efficiency by
    reducing costs, 415
Simulation runs, study of, 39-41
Simulation study organization:
  analysis and critique of results, 41
  choice of method, 33
  collection and analysis of system data, 34-35
  defining structure, 35-36
  included variables, 33-34
  problem formulation, 31-33
  programming model, 36-38
  stages in, 12 *(fig.)*
  validation of model, 38-39
Simultaneous conditions, testing for error, 396
Simultaneous events, in traffic lights problem,
    110-11
Simultaneous (SIM), TRANSFER mode, 86
Single server queue models, with and without
    user chain, 168 *(fig.)*
Skill, of practitioner, as factor, 13
SMALL manufacturing and delivery company,
    programming example, 103-07
Snap interval count, 73
SPACE statement, 221
  service of, 228-29

Specialized simulation languages, 36
Spectral analysis, 408
SPLIT block, 44, 51
  and debugging problems, 257-58
  use of, 139-40, 143 *(fig.)*
SPLIT/ASSEMBLE blocks, 48, 49
Spread, 76, 78
Standard logical attributes, 72, 101
  GPSS language, 195-97
Standard Numerical Attributes (SNA), 55, 57,
    72, 98-101
  additional, in GPSS V, 454-55
  GPSS language, 194-95
  GPSS V, 447-52
  and indirect addressing, 101-03
  in job shop problem, 340
Standard output, statistics for tables in, 223,
    224, 225
START instruction, 62
  use of, 73-74
STATEMENT statement, 221
  service of, 231
Statements:
  extensions, in GPSS V, 454
  incorrect replacement of as error, 396-97
Static aspect, of modeling, 55
Static description, of simulation model, 30
Statistical functions, GPSS, 62-64
Statistical reliability, 404-10
Statistical tables:
  GPSS language, 193
  in subway problem, 303
Statistics:
  ability of simulation language to handle, 16
  collection capabilities of model, 25
  collection of in SIMULA 67, 481
  computation of in GPSS, 68
  standard output, 223, 224, 225
Status change flag:
  function of, 66
  setting of, 214, 218
Status printout:
  definition, 45
  use of as debugging device, 253
Status printout signal, 73
Steady-state information, 15
Stochastic processes, 25
  definition, 8-10
Storage:
  availability and unavailability, GPSS V, 187,
    190
  blocks to modify status of, 82-83
  in job shop problem, 340

Storage *(cont.)*:
  standard logical attributes, 196
  in teleprocessing system problem, 360-61, 381 (T)
  wasting of, 399
  X-Mnemonics, 88
Storage allocation and management, teleprocessing problem, 353-54
Storage attributes, 100, 194
Storage-definition statement format, 92
STORAGE definition statement, use of, 92
STORAGE entity, 45, 47
Storage statistics, 68
  debugging checks on, 252
String handling, SIMULA 67, 476
Submodel validation, 39
Subroutine (SBR), TRANSFER mode, 158-59
Subruns, decomposition into, 406
Subsystem, definition, 5
Subway transportation system simulation: 292–327
  alternative modeling strategies, 325-27
  conclusions, 327
  experiments and results, 321-25
  GPSS model, 298-321
  passenger entry and exit, 294
  passenger generation, 312-15
    and modeling strategy, 326
  passenger interarrival times, 303–04
  passenger parameters, 300
  passenger representation, and modeling strategy, 325-26
  passengers, defined, 298
  problem, 294-98
  station operations, 295, 296, 298-99, 306, 307–08 *(fig.)*, 309-10
    and modeling strategy, 326
  system described, 292-94
  train capacity, 298
  train generation at each terminus, 304, 305 *(fig.)*, 306
  train movement pattern, 293-94, 296-97, 299, 310, 311 *(fig.)*
  train parameters, 299-300
  train scheduling, 296, 299
    departure, 315
  train suppression, 310-12
SUNAVAIL block, use of, 190
Swiss Federal Institute of Technology, Lausanne, 476
Switches:
  LOGIC block and, 152-53
  X-Mnemonics for, 160

Symbolic names, as source of error, 393
System, definition, 4-5
System attributes, 50, 98
System design and simulation, 11
Systems analysis, as stage of simulation study, 16

T

Table attributes, 195
TABLE definition statements, 179, 180-83
TABULATE block, 51, 52, 150, 151
  use of, 179-80
Teleprocessing system, 351-383
  programming example, 117-29
  simulation, 351-83
    application programs, 357
    conclusions, 381-83
    experiments and results, 380-81
    file description, 356
    GPSS model, 357-80
    hardware, 352
    measurements of storages, 382 (T)
    multitasking, 352-53
    problem, 354-57
    program management, 354
    response times, 354, 382 (T)
    submodels and outline of, 172–3
    support routines, 365, 367
    system description, 351-54
Temporary (transient) elements, in model, 21
Temporary entities, 55
  GPSS, 48
TERMINATE block, 45, 48, 49
  use of, 77-78
TEST blocks, 50, 51, 87, 156
  avoidance of refusal mode, 398-99
  use of, 87, 88-90
Testing conditions, 87-90, 159-62
TEXT statement, 221
  services of, 227-28
Time:
  as characteristic of simulation language, 16
  as factor in study, 40
Time control, in warehouse program, 278
Time delay, modeling of in GPSS, 78
Time-dependent variables, 36
Time division, considerations of, 56-58
Time-division multiplexing, 54
Time-independent variables, 36
Time units:
  in subway problem, 298
  in teleprocessing system problem, 357, 360
  in warehouse problem, 264
Timing routine:
  SIMPL/I, 472-73

Timing routine *(cont.)*:
    SIMSCRIPT II, 468
TITLE statement, 221
    service of, 222, 223-24
Total utilization, computation of, 68
TRACE/UNTRACE blocks, 52, 179
    use of, 184-85
    use of as debugging device, 256-57
Tracing facility, of simulation language, 37-38
Traffic lights:
    programming example, 107–13
    in subway problem, 299
Traffic systems, 1-3
Transaction assembly set, 139
Transaction attributes, 50, 72, 99, 194
Transaction-flow modification:
    GPSS language, 156-67
    GPSS subset, 85-90
Transaction location undefined, as error, 393
Transaction mode, of group operation, 174
Transaction move, as phase in scanning, 215-16,
    217 *(fig.)*, 218
Transaction-oriented blocks:
    GPSS language, 139-47
    GPSS subset, 75-80
Transaction parameters:
    referencing of, 102
    in subway problem, 299-301
    in teleprocessing system problem, 361
    in warehouse problem, 265-66
Transactions, 1
    avoiding problems with, 399
    in barbershop model, 21-22
    behavior of, 15
    characteristics of, 355-56
    control of movement of, 59-60, 388
    creation and destruction of, 75-78, 139–43
    delays, 50
    estimation of total number, 387
    flow modification, 50-51
    GPSS, 45-46
    possible states of, 60-61
    progress of, 60
    sequencing of, 60
    standard logical attributes, 195
    synchronization of, 51, 145-47
        as error, 395
    in teleprocessing system problem, 354-55
    as temporary entities, GPSS, 48
TRANSFER block, 50
    modes of, 85-87, 157-59
    use of, 85-87, 157-59
Transfer modes, use of, 86-87

Transient phenomenon, as problem, 406
Transit times, tabulation of, 180-81
Transmit time, definition, 144
Transportation, uses of GPSS in, 401

U

Uniform distribution assumption, 35, 475
    random variates, 462 *(fig.)*
Unique blocking condition, definition, 216
United Aircraft Corporation, Norden Division,
    414
UNLINK block, 47, 51, 61
UNTRACE block, (*See also*
        TRACE/UNTRACE), 51, 52
User chain attributes, 72, 195
USER CHAIN entity, 47
User chains, 2
    GPSS language, 168-73
    in job shop problem, 332
User-defined attribute, 45

V

Validation:
    advantages of GPSS, 385-86
    of data, 35
    future developments, 414-15
Variable entity, 72, 100
Variable, definition statement format, 93
Variable, increment clock, definition, 24
VARIABLE statement, use of, 93
Variables, 46
    classification and choice of, 33-34
    evaluation of, 93
    in GPSS, 45-46
    in job shop problem, 344-45
    in subway problem, 301–02
    in teleprocessing problem, 363-64
    in warehouse problem, 267
Variance-reduction technique: antithetic
        variates, 408-10

W

Waiting time statistics, 69
War games, as simulation model, 11
Warehouse (*See also* Automatic warehouse
        simulation)
    description of, 259-63
Worksheets, barbershop problem, 22, 23, 24
WRITE block, 179
    use of, 185-86

X

X-Logical operator, GPSS subset, 89-90
X-Mnemonics:
    facilities and storages, 88-89, 189-190
    logic switches, 160
    matching status, 160-62
X-statement, 221
    service of, 230-31

Y

Y-statement, 221
    service of, 231

Z

Zero entries, 69
Zero-time loops, avoidance of, 388